BIBLIOGRAPHY OF NIGERIA

BIBLIOGRAPHY OF NIGERIA:

A SURVEY OF ANTHROPOLOGICAL AND LINGUISTIC WRITINGS FROM THE EARLIEST TIMES TO 1966

NDUNTUEI O. ITA, LL.B. (London), F.L.A.

FRANK CASS : LONDON

First published in 1971 by
FRANK CASS AND COMPANY LIMITED
67 Great Russell Street, London WC1B 3BT

Distributed in the United States by
International Scholarly Book Services, Inc.
Beaverton, Oregon 97005

Library of Congress Catalog Card Number 79–169811

ISBN 0 7146 2458 6

Printed in Great Britain by
Clarke, Doble & Brendon Limited
Plymouth

TO

MY MOTHER

PREFACE

African studies has in recent years received tremendous impetus in the major centres of learning the world over, and hardly a month passes by without some new contributions to the already vast literature of this field. To the Africanist as well as the Librarian, this development poses a serious problem of bibliographical control which is not receiving the full attention it deserves. The dearth of bibliographies in the field of African history and culture has complicated in no small measure the problems of research and has been a source of frustration to Africana Librarians. This is particularly so in libraries and research centres in Africa most of which are neither adequately stocked, especially as regards the older materials, nor have their staff access to the catalogues of the more adequately stocked centres in Europe and America, except in a few cases where such catalogues have been published.

Some significant attempts have been made to improve this state of affairs, notably by the International African Institute. But the resulting publications almost invariably take in the whole continent or large parts thereof, and therefore cannot do sufficient justice to any one country. There is thus no sizeable bibliography devoted to a country as much studied as Nigeria. In fact the only bibliographies on this country published so far are each so limited in scope that together they can chart but a small proportion of the extensive literature. It is to help remedy this situation in so far as Nigeria is concerned that this work has been produced.

The bibliography contains publications in archaeology, all branches of anthropology, linguistics and relevant historical and sociological studies, and covers the period from the earliest times to 1966. Materials listed include books, pamphlets, government publications and articles in periodicals. Unpublished materials except theses and dissertations are excluded. Also excluded are publications in Arabic. Although the limiting date is 1966, some important publications, including a sizeable number of reprints, published after 1966 have been included.

The bibliography is general rather than selective. It attempts to be comprehensive, but lays no claim to exhaustiveness. As a pioneer, one-man venture, and considering the vast scope comprehended, exhaustiveness, even if practicable, could hardly be a wise priority. The more sober goal aimed at here has been the provision of a general repertory listing anthropological and linguistic writings on the various peoples of Nigeria, and meeting, however partially, the urgent need of scholars and librarians in this field. It is hoped too that a general repertory of this type, because of its special scheme of arrangement, will stimulate interest in the compilation of less extensive but more exhaustive bibliographies each limited to one ethnic division or to some portion of the country. Each of the ethnic divisions of Part Two forms virtually a separate bibliography which can usefully serve as the starting point for such specialized compilations.

Throughout this work, entries have been catalogued as fully as possible, but numbers of maps and illustrations are generally not given. Bibliographical details for articles in periodicals are given in the following sequence: title (abbreviated where necessary), volume, part (in brackets), month and year of publication, inclusive pagination, and lastly mention of illustrations, maps and bibliography, where any. For example:

Africa, 21 (4) Oct. 1951: 261–278, illus. This means that the relevant article appeared in the journal *Africa,* volume 21, no. 4, published in October 1951. The article covered pages 261–278, and was illustrated. Many of the works carry indicative or informative annotations. Works not inspected are indicated with an asterisk. All entries are numbered serially, and this has facilitated the generous use of cross references.

The bibliography is divided into two parts. The first part contains works which deal with Nigeria as a whole or with several ethnic divisions. The second part is concerned with individual ethnic divisions. These are arranged alphabetically for easy consultation. The scheme of sub-arrangement under each part is clearly shown by the table of contents. In part two, because of the multiplicity of ethnic groups or divisions, it has been found impracticable to take each of them separately. Accordingly, many of them are treated in clusters, with the name of one ethnic group or division chosen as the heading of the cluster. The Table of Contents lists only those ethnic groups treated separately or used as headings of clusters. To locate the other ethnic groups, especially the more obscure ones, it is advisable to use the comprehensive ethnic index.

The types of work collected under the heading 'Linguistic Studies' both in Part One and under the various ethnic divisions of Part Two deserve explanatory comment here. Under this heading have been assembled all types of work on each language to limit the number of sub-divisions and simplify reference. These include dictionaries, vocabularies, phrase books, grammars as well as linguistic studies proper. Numerous vernacular publications in the form of school readers, religious texts, adult education pamphlets, story books, etc., are available for most of the better known Nigerian languages. No attempt has been made to list all these here. Rather, for each language, a few readers, one or two religious texts and possibly an adult education pamphlet have been included to serve as specimens of what are available in this class of literature. Translations of the Bible and of one or two other standard works have been similarly treated.

Three indexes are provided, an author index, an ethnic index and an index of Islamic Studies. Attempt has been made in the ethnic index to grapple with the problems posed by the plurality of ethnic names by including as many of the alternative names and variant forms as possible. The need for a subject index has been largely offset by the scheme of arrangement adopted.

The main body of this work had been completed before the constitutional and administrative changes in the form of new states were introduced. References to Regions throughout the text refer to the four old Regions as they existed before these changes.

N.O.I.

Oron,

15th August, 1970

ACKNOWLEDGEMENTS

This work has been generously supported with grants by the University of Nigeria Research Committee, the first in 1964 and the second in 1965. These made possible my travel and research within Nigeria. I am grateful to the Committee for this support, and also to its then secretary Professor Barry Floyd for the personal interest he showed in the work. I am also grateful to the British Council for an equally generous grant which enabled me to spend some time in Britain working in a number of libraries.

My personal indebtedness goes to the following persons: Mr P. C. Hogg of the British Museum, for supplying useful lists of items he compiled in the Museum; Dr F. W. Parsons and Dr D. W. Arnott, both of the School of Oriental and African Studies, for sending lists of their publications; Mr S. C. Nwoye and Professors C. Smith and J. E. Flint, for helpful comments at the initial stages of planning; Professor M. Achufusi, Professor D. D. Hartle and Dr (Mrs) J. A. Hartle, for their interest and encouragement; Miss R. Jones of the International African Institute Library and her staff, for their generosity and readiness to help; Miss R. M. Talmage of Brown University, for xerox copies of her library catalogue cards; Messrs S. Okoro, S. Okwulehie and D. Ugwu, for going through the tedium of typing the manuscript; and lastly my wife Dr (Mrs) J. M. Ita, for giving up part of her summer vacation to help in Hamburg and in the British Museum, for invaluable assistance with most of the foreign language publications, and for checking parts of the manuscript. I have also received assistance, encouragement and advice from many other librarians, anthropologists, sociologists and language experts who cannot all be listed here. I deeply appreciate their help and register here my gratitude.

In a work of this nature, many bibliographies and published library catalogues must necessarily be consulted. I have found the following especially helpful: African abstracts, and West Africa: General, Ethnology/Sociology, Linguistics, both published by the International African Institute; Nigerian publications, issued by the University of Ibadan Library; and the catalogue of the School of Oriental and African Studies, London. I am grateful to their authors and publishers. The relevant numbers of the International African Institute's Ethnographic Survey of Africa and Professor G. P. Murdock's Africa; its Peoples and their Culture History, have been very useful in the isolation and location of ethnic groups.

N.O.I.

CONTENTS

PART ONE: NIGERIA—GENERAL

PART TWO: NIGERIA—ETHNIC DIVISIONS

B

CONTENTS

KEY TO ABBREVIATIONS

Apr.	April
Aug.	August
Bd.	Band
bibliog.	bibliography
c.r.	comptes rendus
co.	companv
conf.	conference
Dec.	December
diss.	dissertation
ed.	edited, edition, editor
f.	für
Feb.	February
front.	frontispiece
H.M.S.O.	Her Majesty's Stationery Office
hrsg.	herausgegeben
illus.	illustrated, illustration(s)
impr.	imprimerie
inc.	incorporated
inst.	institute
int.	international
Jan.	January
Je.	June
Jl.	July
Mar.	March
Mitt.	Mitteilungen
MS	Manuscript
N.F.	Neue Folge
n.s.	new series
no.	number
Nov.	November
Oct.	October
p.	page
port.	portrait
pp.	pages
proc.	proceedings
publ.	published
rev.	revised
ser.	series
Sept.	September
v.	volume, von
Veroff.	veroffentlichungen
vol.	volume
Völkerkde.	völkerkunde

LIST OF PERIODICALS INDEXED

Abh. u. Ber. staatl. Mus. Völkerkde. — Abhandlungen und Berichte des staatlichen Museums für Völkerkunde [Dresden]

Acta psychologica

Acta tropica

Afr. affairs — African affairs

Afr. ecclesiastical rev. — African ecclesiastical review

Afr. en marche — Afrique en marche [Paris]

Afr. hist. — African history

Afr. ital. — Africa italiana [Roma]

Afr. lang. stud. — African language studies

Afr. mail — African mail

Afr. mus. — African music

Afr. mus. soc. newsletter — African music society Newsletter

Afr. news — African news

Afr. q. — African quarterly; a journal of African affairs

Afr. report — Africa report

Afr. stud. — African studies

Afr. u. Übersee — Afrika und Übersee

Afr. women — African women

Afr. world — African world

Afr. world ann. — African world annual

Africa — Africa; journal of the International African institute

Africa [Madrid]

Africa south

Africa—Tervuren

Africa today

Africana — Africana [Newcastle-on-Tyne]

Afrika [The Hague]

Afrika heute

Afrique française — L'Afrique française; bulletin mensuel du Comité de l'Afrique française

Amer. anthrop. — American anthropologist

Amer. Catholic sociol. rev. — American Catholic sociological review

Amer. imago — American imago

Amer. j. phys. anthrop. — American journal of physical anthropology

xxi

Baessler-Archiv

Baileya   Baileya; a journal of horticultural
                                       taxonomy

Belvedere   Belvedere; Monatsschrift für Sammler
                                       und Kunstfreunde [Wien]

Berl. Gesell. f. Anthrop. Verhandl.   Berliner Gesellschaft für Anthropologie.
                                       Verhandlungen

Berliner Mus.   Berliner Museen; Berichte aus den
                                       preussischen Kunstsammlungen

Bibliotheca afr.   Bibliotheca africana

Black Orpheus

Blackfriars

Blackwood's mag.   Blackwood's magazine

Bol. cultural Guiné Portug.   Boletim cultural da Guiné Portuguesa

Books for Afr.   Books for Africa

Boston University papers in African
history

Brit. j. educ. psychology   British journal of educational psycho-
                                       logy

Brit. j. nutrition   British journal of nutrition

Brit. j. psychology   British journal of psychology

Brit. j. sociol.   British journal of sociology

Brit. med. j.   British medical journal

Brit. Mus. q.   British Museum quarterly

Bull. Allen mem. art mus.   Bulletin of the Allen memorial art
                                       museum

Bull. Chicago art inst.   Bulletin of the Chicago art institute

Bull. Com. étud. hist. sci. A. o. f.   Bulletin du Comité d'études historiques
                                       et scientifiques de l'Afrique occidentale
                                       française

Bull. des musées royaux d'art et
d'histoire [Bruxelles]

Bull. IFAN   Bulletin de l'Institut français
                                       d'Afrique noire Section B

Bull. Imp. inst.   Bulletin of the Imperial institute
                                       [London]

Bull. Liverpool libraries, museums and   Bulletin of the Liverpool public
arts committee   libraries, museums and arts committee

Bull. Mus. roy. belges d'art et d'hist.   Bulletin des Musées royaux belges d'art
                                       et d'histoire

Bull. Mus. sci. & art. [Philadelphia]   Bulletin of the Museum of science and
                                       art [Philadelphia]

Bull. news Hist. soc. Nig.   Bulletin of news [of the] Historical
                                       society of Nigeria

Bull. St. Louis mus.   Bulletin of St. Louis museum

Bull. Soc. Afr. Ch. hist.   Bulletin of the Society of African
                                       Church history

Bull. Soc. belge d'étud. géogr.	Bulletin de la Société belge des études géographiques
Bull. Soc. ét. camerounaises	Bulletin de la Société d'études camerounaises
Bull. Soc. géog.	Bulletin de la Société de géographie
Bull. Soc. géog. Alger	Bulletin de la Société de géographie d'Alger
Bull. Soc. géog. de Marseille	Bulletin de la Société de géographie de Marseille
Bull. Soc. neuchâteloise	Bulletin de la Société neuchâteloise des sciences naturelles
Bull. Soc. rech. cong.	Bulletin de la Société des recherches congolaises
Bull. Soc. roy. géog. Anvers	Bulletin de la Société royale de géographie d'Anvers
Bull. W. H. O.	Bulletin of the World Health Organisation
Burl. mag.	Burlington magazine
Cah. d'art.	Cahiers d'art
Cah. étud. afr.	Cahiers d'études africaines
Cah. l'hom.	Cahiers de l'homme; ethnologie-géographie-linguistique
Church miss. intell.	Church missionary intelligencer
Church miss. intell. & record	Church missionary intelligencer and record
Church miss. record	Church missionary record
Church miss. rev.	Church missionary review
Church overseas	Church overseas; a quarterly review of the missionary work of the Church of England
Cicerone	Cicerone [Leipzig]
Civilisations	
Col. j.	Colonial journal [Colonial Office, London]
Col. rev.	Colonial review
Comm. dev. bull.	Community development bulletin
Comp. stud. soc. hist.	Comparative studies in society and history; an international journal
Comptes rendus mens. séances Acad. sci. col.	Comptes rendus mensuels des séances l'Académie des sciences coloniales
Comptes rendus sommaires des séances Inst. français anthrop.	Comptes rendus sommaires des séances de l'Institut français d'anthropologie
Congo, rev. générale de la colonie belge	Congo, revue générale de la colonie belge
Connoisseur	
Corona	
Craft horiz.	Craft horizons

Crisis | Crisis [New York]
Cuadernos de historia primitiva
Décade philosophique. | Décade philosophique, littéraire et politique

Design
Deutsche Kolon. ztg. | Deutsche Kolonialzeitung
Diogenes | Diogenes [New York]
Discovery | Discovery; the magazine of scientific progress [London]

Discovery [Norwich]
Dokita | Dokita [Ibadan]
Documents | Documents [Paris]
Duquesne rev. | Duquesne review
E.A.I.S.R. Conf. proc. | East African Inst. of Social Research. Conference Proceedings

E. Afr. med. j. | East African medical journal
East & West rev. | East & West review
Eastern anthrop. | Eastern anthropologist
Echo missions afr. [Lyon] | Echo des missions africaines [Lyon]
Econ. bull. Afr. | Economic bulletin for Africa [United Nations. Economic Commission for Africa]

Econ. dev. & cultural change | Economic development and cultural change

Econ. geog. | Economic geography
Economic weekly
Edinburgh new phil. j. | Edinburgh new philosophical journal
Edinburgh rev. | Edinburgh review
Empire cotton growing rev. | Empire cotton growing review
Empire forestry rev. | Empire forestry review
Ency. colon. et maritime mens. | Encyclopédie coloniale et maritime mensuelle [Paris]

Eng. illus. mag. | English illustrated magazine
Eng. stud. | English studies
Erdball
Erdkunde | Erdkunde; Archiv für wissenschaftliche Geographie
Ethnol. Anzeiger | Ethnologischer Anzeiger
Ethnol. cran. | Ethnologia Cranmorensis; being extracts from the collections at Cranmor Ethnological Museum

Ethnologica
Ethnology | Ethnology; international journal of cultural and social anthropology

Ethnos [Stockholm]
Étud. cam. | Études camerounaises
Étud. dahom. | Études dahoméennes

Imperial and Asiatic rev. — Imperial and Asiatic review

INCIDI — Institut international des civilisations différentes (International institute of differing civilizations) Brussels. Comptes rendus

Information [Paris]

Int. arch. ethnog. — International archives of ethnography (Internationales Archiv für Ethnographie)

Int. j. Amer. ling. — International journal of American linguistics

Int. rev. educ. — International review of education

Int. rev. missions — International review of missions

Int. soc. sci. bull. — International social science bulletin

Der Islam

J.A.I. see J. Anthrop. inst.

J. Afr. admin. — Journal of African administration

J. Afr. hist. — Journal of African history

J. Afr. law — Journal of African law

J. Afr. soc. — Journal of the African society

J. agric. trop. bot. appl. — Journal d'agriculture tropicale et de botanique appliquée

J. Amer. folkl. — Journal of American folklore

J. Amer. mus. nat. hist. — Journal of the American museum of natural history

J. Amer. orient. soc. — Journal of the American oriental society

J. & proc. Roy. geog. soc. — Journal and proceedings of the Royal geographical society

J. Anthrop. inst. — Journal of the Anthropological institute

J. Canadian psychiatric assoc. — Journal of the Canadian psychiatric association

J. child psychol. psychiat. — Journal of child psychology and psychiatry

J. civilization — Journal of civilization

J. comp. leg. — Journal of comparative legislation

J. econ. hist. — Journal of economic history

J. Egyptian archaeology — Journal of Egyptian archaeology

J. Ethnol. soc. — Journal of the Ethnological society

J. Folk. inst. — Journal of the Folklore institute

J. geog. — Journal of geography

J. Hist. soc. Nig. — Journal of the Historical society of Nigeria

J. hum. rel. — Journal of human relations

J. Iron & steel inst. — Journal of the Iron and Steel institute

J. Liver. geog. soc. — Journal of the Liverpool geographical society

J. local admin. overseas — Journal of local administration overseas

J. Manch. geog. soc.	Journal of the Manchester geographical society
J. mental sci.	Journal of mental science
J. mod. Afr. stud.	Journal of modern African studies
J. negro hist.	Journal of negro history
J. Nig. med. assoc.	Journal of the Nigerian medical association
J. obst. & gynaec. Brit. emp.	Journal of obstetrics and gynaecology of the British empire
J.R.A.I.	Journal of the Royal anthropological institute
J.R.A.S.	Journal of the Royal African society
J.R.S.A. see J. Roy. soc. arts.	
J. Roy. Asiatic soc.	Journal of the Royal Asiatic society
J. Roy. geog. soc.	Journal of the Royal geographical society
J. Roy. soc. arts	Journal of the Royal society of arts
J. Roy. united service institutions	Journal of the Royal united service institutions
J. Soc. afr.	Journal de la Société des africanistes
J. soc. psychology	Journal of social psychology
J. trop. geog.	Journal of tropical geography
J. trop. med. & hyg.	Journal of tropical medicine and hygiene
J. Tyneside geog. soc.	Journal of the Tyneside geographical society
J. voyages, découvertes et navigations modernes	Journal des voyages, découvertes et navigations modernes. (Société de géographie française et étrangère) Paris
Jahresbericht des Württembergischen Vereins für Handelsgeographie	
Jeune afrique [Elizabethville]	
Jewish q. rev.	Jewish quarterly review
Jorden runt.	Jorden runt; magasin for geografi och resor. [Stockholm]
Kano studies	
Kew bull.	Kew bulletin
Kol. runds.	Koloniale Rundschau
Korrespondenzblatt der deutschen Gesellschaft f. Anthrop.	Korrespondenzblatt der deutschen Gesellschaft für Anthropologie
Kr. Soob. I. E.	Kratkie soobscenija. Institut etnografi imeni N.N. Mikluho-Maklaja [Moscow]
Kulturgeografi	Kulturgeografi; tidsskrift for befolknings geografi. [Copenhagen]
Das Kunstwerk	
Lancet	

Language — Language; journal of the Linguistic society of America

Libri — Libri; international library review

Lingua — Lingua; international review of general linguistics

Listener

Litterae orientales [Leipzig] — Litterae orientales; orientalistischer Literaturbericht. [Leipzig]

Liturg. arts — Liturgical arts

Loc. govt. chron. — Local government chronicle (Association of Chief Executive Officers of Local Government Councils) [Calabar]

Lore

M. S. O. S. — Mitteilungen des Seminars für orientalische Sprachen zu Berlin. Dritte Abteilung: Afrikanische Studien

Macmillan's j. — Macmillan's journal

Mademoiselle

Mag. art. — Magazine of art

Malayan j. trop. geog. — Malayan journal of tropical geography

Man — Man; a monthly record of anthropological science

Man in soc. — Man in society; journal of the Sociological association, University of Nigeria [Nsukka]

Mass educ. bull. — Mass education bulletin

Medical world

Mélusine — Mélusine; revue de mythologie

Mém. soc. ethnol. — Mémoires de la Société d'ethnologie [Paris]

Memoirs Manch. lit. & phil. soc. — Memoirs of the Manchester literary and philosophical society

Mensário admin. — Mensário administrativo [Luanda]

Minerva — Minerva; a review of science, learning and policy [London]

Miss. Cathol. — Les Missions Catholiques

Missionary record of the United Presbyterian Church

Mitt. anthrop. Gesell. [Wien] — Mitteilungen der anthropologischen Gesellschaft in Wien

Mitt. der Auslandshochschule an der Universität Berlin — Mitteilungen der Auslandshochschule an der Universität Berlin

Mitt. geog. Gesell. [Wien] — Mitteilungen der geographischen Gesellschaft zu Wien

Mitt. Inst. Orientforsch — Mitteilungen des Instituts für Orientforschung [Berlin]

Mois col. mar. — Le Mois colonial et maritime [Paris]

Le Monde colonial illustré

Mosl. world.   Moslem world

Mus. & youth   Music and youth [London]

Mus. in Nig.   Music in Nigeria

Mus. j.   Music journal; educational music
                               magazine

Musée vivant

Les musées de Genève

Le Museon [Louvain]

Die Musikforschung

Narody Azii i Afriki [Moscow]

Nation [London]

National geog. mag.   National geographic magazine

National rev.   National review [London]

Natural hist.   Natural history (American museum of
                               natural history)

Nature

La Nature [Paris]

Negro hist. bull.   Negro history bulletin

Neues Afr.   Neues Afrika [Munich]

New commonwealth

New Eng. j. med.   New England journal of medicine

New soc.   New society [London]

Nig. & the classics   Nigeria and the classics [Ibadan]

Nig. & Yoruba notes   Niger & Yoruba notes

Nig. chronicle   Nigerian chronicle

Nig. digest   Nigeria digest

Nig. field   Nigerian field

Nig. geog. j.   Nigerian geographical journal

Nig. j. econ. soc. stud.   Nigerian journal of economic and social
                               studies

Nig. mag.   Nigeria magazine

Nig. teacher   Nigerian teacher

Nig. today   Nigeria today

Nig. trade j.   Nigerian trade journal

NISER conf. proc.   Nigerian institute of social and econo-
                               mic research. Conference proceedings

Northern Nigeria gazette

Notes afr.   Notes africaines

Numen   Numen; international review for the
                               history of religions

Numismatist   Numismatist (American numismatic
                               society)

Objets et mondes

Occasional paper on Nigerian affairs   Occasional paper on Nigerian affairs
                                        (Nigeria society) [London, Lagos]

Odù

Odù; a journal of Yoruba studies (a journal of Yoruba, Edo and related studies)

Odu

Odu; University of Ife journal of African studies

Orientalia suecana [Uppsala]

Outre—Mer

Oversea educ.

Oversea education

Paideuma

Paideuma; Mitteilungen zur Kulturkunde

Panorama

Panorama [Washington]

Papers Mich. acad. sci., arts & letters

Papers of the Michigan academy of science, arts and letters

Parnassus

Petermanns geog. Mitt.

Petermanns geographische Mitteilungen

Petermanns Mitt.

Petermanns Mitteilungen

Pharmaceutical j.

Pharmaceutical journal

Phonetica

Phonetica; international journal of phonetics [Basel]

Phylon

Phylon; Atlanta university review of race and culture

Pi Lambda Theta j.

Pi Lambda Theta journal

Pop. stud.

Population studies; a quarterly journal of demography [London]

Pract. anthrop.

Practical anthropology

Présence afr.

Présence africaine

Primitive man

Primitive man [Washington]

Prob. vos.

Problemy vostokovedeniya

Proc. Prehist. soc.

Proceedings of the Prehistoric society

Proc. Roy. col. inst.

Proceedings of the Royal colonial institute

Proc. Roy. geog. soc.

Proceedings of the Royal geographical society

Proc. Sci. assoc. Nig.

Proceedings of the Science association of Nigeria

Progress

Progress; the magazine of Lever Brothers and Unilever, Ltd. [London]

Przeglad orientalistyczny

Race

Raumforsch. u. Raumord.

Raumforschung und Raumordnung

Rech. afr.

Recherches africaines, études guinéennes. [Conakry]

Rech. étud. cam.

Recherches et études camerounaises [Yaounde]

Reliq. illus. arch.

Reliquary and illustrated archaeologist

Rens. col.

Renseignements coloniaux

Res. and progress

Research and progress; a quarterly

	review of German science. [English edition of Forschungen und Fortschritte. . . .]
Res. notes	Research notes (Dept. of Geography, University of Ibadan)
Research bulletin	Research bulletin (Centre of Arabic Documentation, Institute of African Studies, University of Ibadan)
Rev. afr.	Revue africaine [Algiers]
Rev. col.	Revue coloniale [Paris]
Rev. ethnog. sociol.	Revue d'ethnographie et de sociologie [Paris]
Rev. générale des sciences	Revue générale des sciences pures et appliquées
Rev. géog.	Revue de géographie
Rev. géog. humaine et ethnol.	Revue de géographie humaine et d'ethnologie
Rev. hist. col. franc.	Revue de l'histoire des colonies françaises
Rev. Inst. sociol.	Revue de l'Institut de sociologie [Bruxelles]
Rev. ling. et philolog. comp.	Revue de linguistique et de philologie comparée
Rev. of int. co-op.	Review of international co-operation
Rev. troupes col.	Revue des troupes coloniales
Revista di etnografia	
Revue du monde musulman	
Riv. de Antrop. [São Paulo, Brazil]	
Roy. geog. soc. Austr. South Austr. branch	Royal geographical society of Australia South Australia branch. Proceedings
Rural missions	Rural missions [New York]
Rural sociology	
S. Afr. arch. bull.	South African archaeological bulletin
S. Afr. geog. j.	South African geographical journal
S. Afr. j. sci.	South African journal of science
S.-W. j. anthrop.	Southwestern journal of anthropology
SAMAB	South African museum association bulletin
Saturday rev.	Saturday review
Sbornik museya antropologii, arkheologii i etnografii	
Sch. & soc.	School and society
Sci. digest	Science digest
Scot. art rev.	Scottish art review
Scot. geog. mag.	Scottish geographical magazine
Sierra Leone lang. rev.	Sierra Leone language review

Soc. & econ. stud. [Univ. of the West Indies]
Social and economic studies [University of the West Indies]

Social forces

Social order

Social res.
Social research [New York]

Sociol. & soc. res.
Sociology and social research

Sociol. rev.
Sociological review

Sociologus

Southwestern soc. sci. q.
Southwestern social science quarterly.

Sov. et.
Sovetskaya etnografiya

Sov. vost.
Sovetskoye vostokovedeniye

Spectator
Spectator [London]

Staden-Jahrbuch
Staden-Jahrbuch; Beiträge zur Brasilkunde [Sao Pãulo]

Statist. & econ. rev.
Statistical & economic review

Studia islamica

Studio
Studio [London]

Sudan notes and records

Sudan soc.
Sudan society (University of Khartum)

Tarikh [Ibadan]

Teacher educ.
Teacher education (Institute of Education, University of London)

Teachers' monthly

Terre et la vie.
La Terre et la vie; revue d'histoire naturelle [Paris]

Theology today

Tijdschrift van het Koninklijk Nederlandsch aardrijkskundig genootschap.

Times Brit. col. rev. see Times col. rev.

Times col. rev.
Times colonial review

Times rev. col. see Times col. rev.

Tin and its uses

Togo-Cameroun

Trans. Amer. phil. assoc.
Transactions of the American philological association

Tr. & papers Inst. Brit. geog.
Transactions & papers of the Institute of British geographers

Tr. Hist. soc. Ghana.
Transactions of the Historical society of Ghana

Tr. Ill. acad. sci.
Transactions of the Illinois academy of science

Tr. Liv. geog. soc.
Transactions of the Liverpool geographical society

Tr. New York acad. sci.
Transactions of the New York academy of science

c

Tr. Roy soc. trop. med. & hyg.   Transactions of the Royal society of tropical medicine and hygiene

Travel

Tribus

Trop. agric.   Tropical agriculture

Trop. geog. med.   Tropical and geographical medicine

Tropenpflanzer

Tropiques

Übersee-Rundschau

Unesco chronicle

Unesco courier

United empire

United service j   United service journal

United service mag.   United service magazine

Univ. Penn. mus. j.   University of Pennsylvania museum journal

University herald

Universo [Firenze]

Vanity fair

Venture   Venture [London]

Veröff. Mus. Völkerkde. [Leipzig]   Veröffentlichungen des Museums für Völkerkunde zu Leipzig

W. Afr.   West Africa

W. Afr. arch. newsletter   West African archaeological newsletter

W. Afr. j. educ.   West African journal of education

W. Afr. med. j.   West African medical journal

W. Afr. rel.   West African religion

W. Afr. rev.   West African review

W. Eq. Afr. dioc. mag.   Western equatorial Africa diocesan magazine

WAISER conf. proc.   West African institute of social and economic research. Conference proceedings

WALA news

Wasu   Wasu [West African students union, London] Journal

Westermanns Monatshefte [Braunschweig]

Wiener Beiträge zur Kulturgeschichte und zur Linguistik

Wiener völkekdl. Mitt.   Wiener völkerkundliche Mitteilungen

Wiener Z. f. Kunde Morgen.   Wiener Zeitschrift für Kunde des Morgenlandes

Wiss. Z. Karl Marx-Univ.   Wissenschaftliche Zeitschrift der Karl-Marx-Universität, Gesellschafts-und Sprachwissenschaftliche Reihe

Wissenschaftliche Veröffentlichungen des deutschen Museums für Länderkunde zu Leipzig.

PART ONE

NIGERIA—GENERAL

SECTION ONE
REFERENCE AND GENERAL WORKS

1. BIBLIOGRAPHIES

Only bibliographies devoted wholly or substantially to anthropological works on Nigeria are included here. Lists in books and journals, unless extensive, are not included. Bibliographies limited to one aspect of the subject or to one ethnic division will be found at the beginning of the appropriate sub-division.

1 Adedipe, G. A. K.
A special list of records on land and survey, Nigerian secretariat record group. Ibadan, National archives, 1963. [ii] iv, 23p.
Chapter vii (pp. 13–14) includes items relating to traditional land tenure systems.

2 Alagoa, Ebiegberi Joe
A special list of material concerned with tribal and related studies among Kaduna secretariat record groups. Kaduna, National archives, 1962. vi, 84p.

3 —Special list of records related to historical, anthropological and social studies among provincial administration record groups at National archives, Kaduna. Kaduna, National archives, 1962. vi, 71p.

4 Amosu, Margaret
Nigerian theses; a list of theses on Nigerian subjects and of theses by Nigerians. Ibadan, University press, 1965. [vi] 36p.

5 —A preliminary bibliography of creative African writing in the European languages. Ibadan, Institute of African studies, University of Ibadan [1964] v, 35p.
Issued as a special supplement to *African studies*. Lists the works of 251 authors arranged alphabetically by country.

5a Arif, Aida S. and Hakima, Ahmad M. Abu
Descriptive catalogue of Arabic manuscripts in Nigeria: Jos Museum and Lugard Hall Library. London, Luzac & Co., 1961. viii, 216p.
An annotated title list of Arabic MSS. kept in the Jos Museum and the Lugard Hall Library.

6 Ashikodi, L. N.
A special list of annual, half-yearly and quarterly reports among Kaduna secretariat record group. Kaduna, National archives, 1962. iii, 73p.

7 Carson, Patricia
Materials for West African history in the archives of Belgium and Holland. London, Athlone press, 1962. viii, 86p. (Guides to materials for West African history in European archives, no. 1)
A handy volume listing materials on all aspects of West African history in archives, museums, libraries and government ministries in the two countries. See also [13] and [41]

8 Coleman, James S.
Nigeria: background to nationalism. 1958.
Bibliography: pp. 481–496.

8a Conover, H. F.
Nigerian official publications ... See [48]

9 Dipeolu, J. O.
Bibliographical sources for Nigerian studies. Evanston, African studies center, Northwestern University, 1966. 26p.

9a Dubester, H. J.
Population census and other official demographic statistics of British Africa. See [49]

10 Eicher, Joanne B.
Bibliography of African dress (with emphasis on Nigeria) [Enugu, the author, 1966] 13p.
Mimeographed. "Draft only. Not for publication."

11 Enwere, J. C.
A provisional guide to official publications at the National archives, Kaduna. National archives, Kaduna, 1962. iii, 78p.

12 —A special list of records on chieftaincy matters, Nigerian secretariat record group. Ibadan, National archives, 1962. iii, 43p.

12a Forde, Cyril Daryll, *ed.*
Select annotated bibliography of tropical Africa. See [27]

13 Gray, Richard and Chambers, David Sanderson
Materials for West African history in Italian archives. London, Athlone press, 1965. viii, 164p. (Guides to materials for West African history in European archives, no. 3)
See also [7] and [41]

14 Gunton, D. and Martin, D.
An author catalogue of books about Nigeria in the Regional library, Kaduna. [Kaduna, Regional library, 1962] 59p.

15 Gwam, Lloyd Chike

A handlist of Nigerian official publications (provisional) Ibadan, National archives, 1961. 2v. v.1 1961. viii, 84p.

16 —A handlist of Nigerian official publications in the National archives headquarters, Ibadan. Ibadan, National archives, 1964, iv. 188p.

17 —A preliminary index to the intelligence reports in the Nigerian Secretariat record group. Ibadan, National archives, 1961. ii, 39p.

18 Hambly, Wilfrid Dyson
Bibliography of African anthropology, 1937–1949; supplement to Source book for African anthropology, 1937. [Chicago] Natural history museum, 1952. 155–292p. ([Natural history museum] Fieldiana: anthropology, v. 37, no. 2. Publication 688)

19 —Source book for African anthropology. Paul S. Martin, editor. Chicago, Field museum of natural history, 1937. 2v. illus., maps. (Field museum of natural history. Anthropological series, v. 26. Publication 394, 396)
Paged continuously. Bibliography, v. 2. pp.728–866.

20 Harris, William John
Books about Nigeria: a select reading list. 3rd ed. Ibadan, University press, 1962. 46p.
Lists some 350 of the more easily accessible works chosen with the need in mind of those wishing to obtain up-to-date information about modern Nigeria. Helpful annotations. 1st ed., 1959; 2nd ed., 1960.

21 — —4th ed. 1963. 51p.

Historical society of Nigeria.
Bulletin of news. See [65]

22 Howard university. Library. Moorland foundation. A catalogue of the African collection in the Moorland foundation, Howard university library. Compiled by students in the Program of African studies; edited by Dorothy B. Porter. Washington, D.C., published for the Moorland foundation and the Program of African studies by Howard university press, 1958. 398p.
Nigeria specifically, pp. 155–180.

23 Hunwick, J. O.
Arabic manuscript material bearing on the history of the Western Sudan. *Bull. news Hist. Soc. Nig.*, 7 (2) 1962. Supplement.

24 Ibadan. University. Library.
Nigerian periodicals & newspapers, 1950–1955. Ibadan, 1956. 23p.
A list of periodicals and newspapers received in the library from April 1950 to June 1955. Subsequent listing continued in *Nigerian publications* [36]

25 Ibadan university press.
Catalogue of publications. 1963. 23p.
A catalogue of all works published by the Ibadan University press from its establishment in 1949, with a few items which though not published by it, are obtainable through it.

26 — —2nd ed. 1965.

27 International African institute.
Select annotated bibliography of tropical Africa, compiled under the direction of Daryll Forde. London, New York, 1956. 1v. (various pagings)

28 —West Africa: general, ethnography/sociology, linguistics. Compiled by Ruth Jones. London, 1958. v, 116p. (Africa bibliography series: ethnography, sociology, linguistics and related subjects)
A bibliography of West Africa based on the card catalogue at the Institute's library in London. Similar volumes issued also for East Africa, South East Central Africa and Madagascar, and North East Africa.

29 Jahn, Janheinz
A bibliography of neo-African literature from Africa, America and the Caribbean. London, André Deutsch, 1965. xxxv [1] 359p. map.

29a Jones, Ruth
West Africa: general, ethnology/sociology, linguistics. See [28]

30 Kensdale, William Elliott Norwood
The Arabic manuscript collection of the library of the University College, Ibadan, Nigeria. *WALA news,* 2 (2) Je 1955: 21–25.

31 —A catalogue of the Arabic manuscripts preserved in the University library, Ibadan, Nigeria. Ibadan, University library, 1955-1956. 2v.
Paged continuously. Fascicule I 1955. pp. 1–14. Fascicule II 1956. pp. 15–27.

32 — —2nd ed. Ibadan, 1958. 38p.
Manuscripts collected in Northern Nigeria, and now available in the University library.

33 Lewin, Evans
Annotated bibliography of recent publications on Africa South of the Sahara, with special reference to administrative, political, economic and sociological problems. London, Royal empire society, 1943. [v] 104p. (Royal empire soc. bibliographies, no. 9)

34 Mba, V. C. J.
A preliminary index to the intelligence reports in the Enugu Secretariat record group. Enugu, National archives, 1962. v, 15p.

35 Merriam, Alan P.
An annotated bibliography of African and African-derived music since 1936. *Africa,* 21 (4) Oct. 1951: 319–329.

36 Nigerian publications. Ibadan. 1950–52 (1953)–.
Annual. Prepared by Ibadan university library. Serves as current national bibliography for Nigeria. Lists works published in Nigeria, and from 1955, also works about Nigeria published abroad. Items in Nigerian languages as well as government publications in-

cluded. Quarterly mimeographed supplements.

37 Northwestern university, Evanston, Ill. Library.
A bibliography of labor migration in Africa South of the Sahara, compiled by Hans E. Panofsky. Evanston, Ill., Northwestern university, 1961. 28p. Processed.

38 O'Connell, James
A survey of selected social science research on Nigeria since the end of 1957. In *Nigerian political scene . . . by R. O. Tilman, 1962:* 287-327.

39 Ogunsheye, Felicia Adetowun
Maps of Africa—1500-1800: a bibliographic survey. *Nig. geog. j.,* 7 (1) Je 1964: 34-42, maps, bibliog.

40 Royal empire society
Subject catalogue of the Royal empire society, formerly Royal colonial institute . . . v. 1. London, 1930. [vii] x, 139, 582, cxxiii p.
An important bibliographical reference tool. Vol. 1 deals with the British empire generally and with Africa. Nigeria, pp. 139-157. Also relevant is the section on West Africa, pp. 93-111.

41 Ryder, Alvan Frederick Charles
Materials for West African history in Portuguese archives. London, Athlone press, 1965. vi, 92p. (Guides to materials for West African history in European archives, no. 2)
See also [7] and [13]

42 Rydings, H. A.
The bibliographies of West Africa. Ibadan, University press, for West African library association, 1961. 36p.
Includes bibliographies in books.

43 Smith, Henry Frederick Charles
Nineteenth-century Arabic archives of West Africa. *J. Afr. hist.,* 3 (2) 1962: 333-336.

44 —Source material for the history of the Western Sudan. *J. Hist. soc. Nig.,* 1 (3) Dec. 1957: 238-246.
A bibliographical list of Arabic manuscripts bearing on the history of the Western Sudan.

45 *Solomon, Marvin D. and Warren, L. d'Azevedo
A general bibliography of the Republic of Nigeria. Evanston, Ill., Northwestern university press, 1962. 68p.

46 Thieme, D. L.
A selected bibliography of periodical articles on the music of the native peoples of sub-Saharan Africa. *Afr. mus.* 3 (1) 1962: 103-110.

47 U.S. Library of Congress
Africa south of the Sahara: a selected, annotated list of writings, 1951-1956. Washington, Library of Congress, 1957. vii, 269p.
Arranged by regions and countries. Lengthy annotations.

48 —Ref. dept.
Nigerian official publications, 1869-1959: a guide, compiled by Helen F. Conover. Washington, Library of Congress, 1959. xii, 153p.
Lists some 1,204 items arranged in three sections covering respectively: 1947-1959; 1923-1946; and 1861-1922. Last nine items are bibliographical sources. L.C. class marks and location symbols (for American libraries) given for most items. Processed.

49 —Ref. dept.
Population census and other official demographic statistics of British Africa: an annotated bibliography compiled by Henry J. Dubester. Washington, Govt. Printer, 1950. v, 78p.
Nigeria, pp. 14-19. Lists and describes the census reports of 1911, 1921 and 1931, as well as the earlier Lagos censuses.

50 —Ref. dept.
Research and information on Africa: continuing sources. Washington, library of Congress, 1954. vii, 70p.
Records sources, institutions, societies, periodical publications, etc., which are wholly or partly concerned with Africa.

51 Urvoy, Yves François Marie Aimé
Essai de bibliographie des populations du Soudan Central (Niger français, nord de la Nigéria anglaise) *Bull. Com. étud. hist. sci. A.o.f.,* 19, 1936: 243-333.
A very important listing, made less useful by often scanty bibliographic details.

52 Vajda, G.
Contribution à la connaissance de la littérature arabe en Afrique occidentale. *J. Soc. afr.,* 20 (2) 1950: 229-237.

53 Varley, Douglas H.
African native music; an annotated bibliography. London, Royal empire society, 1936. 116p. (Royal empire soc. bibliographies, no. 18)

54 Waniko, Samuel Sidali
A descriptive catalogue of the early papers of the Secretariat, Northern provinces. [Kaduna, National archives, 1961] 57p. (National archives record group, S.N.P. series 10)

55 —A descriptive catalogue of the early Lugard-Sultan of Sokoto correspondence, including a description of 131 Arabic letters found in Sokoto in 1903. [Kaduna, National archives, 1961] iv, 24p.

56 *Whitting, C. E. J.
The unprinted indigenous Arabic literature of Northern Nigeria. *J. Roy. Asiatic soc.,* 1943-44.

57 Wieschoff, H. A.
Anthropological bibliography of negro Africa. New Haven, Conn., American oriental society, 1948. xi, 461p. (Amer. oriental ser., v. 23)

2. PERIODICALS

Anthropological writings on Nigeria are

scattered in numerous journals in different subject fields and in various languages, as a glance
at the list at pages xxi to xxxv will indicate.
Many of these journals are not easily accessible
and in most of them, articles touching on
Nigeria are few and far between. The following
list is limited to the more important journals
which regularly carry relevant studies of a
serious nature.

58 Africa; journal of the International
    African institute. London. v. 1 (Ja.
    1928)– Quarterly.

59 African abstracts. London. v. 1 (1950)–
    Quarterly.

60 African affairs; journal of the Royal
    African society. London. v. 1 (Oct.
    1901)–
        Quarterly. Title varies: v. 1–34 no. 135
    (Oct. 1901–Apr. 1935) as Journal of the
    African Society. v. 34 no. 136–v. 43
    no. 171 (Jl. 1935–Apr. 1944) as Journal
    of the Royal African Society.

61 African notes; bulletin of the Institute
    of African studies, University of Ibadan.
    v. 1 (Oct. 1963)–
        Quarterly. Each issue describes the
    research activities and programmes of
    the Institute, with a list of publications
    by staff members.

61a African society.
    Journal. See [60]

62 Church missionary intelligencer. Lon-
    don. 1859–1927.
        Title varied: In 1876, absorbed
    Church missionary record and became
    Church missionary intelligencer and re-
    cord. From Jan. 1907, known as Church
    missionary review. This and [63] [72] and
    [88] were C.M.S. journals devoted to
    reporting missionary activities in West
    Africa, especially on the Niger and in
    the Yoruba country. They frequently
    carried descriptions of the area and ac-
    count of native life and customs.

63 Church missionary record. London. v.
    1–28 (Ja. 1830–Dec. 1875).
        Absorbed in 1876 by Church mis-
    sionary intelligencer [62] q.v.

63a Church missionary review. See [62]

64 Farm and forest. Ibadan. v. 1–11 (1940–
    1952).
        Irregular. Published under the auspices
    of the Nigerian dept. of forestry.

65 Historical society of Nigeria.
    Bulletin of news. Ibadan. v. 1 (1956)–
        Quarterly. A medium of news of his-
    torical significance to society members.
    Carries a bibliographical section list-
    ing "Some recent publications" in
    history and allied fields.

66 —Journal. Ibadan. v. 1 (Dec. 1956)–

67 Ibadan; a journal published at Univer-
    sity of Ibadan. no. 1 (Oct. 1957)–
        3 times a yr. General, but with em-
    phasis on Nigerian and West African
    themes.

68 Ibadan. University. Dept. of geography.

Research notes. no. 1 (Je. 1952)–
    Irregular. Mimeographed.

69 —Institute of African studies. Centre for
    Arabic documentation. Research bul-
    letin. v. 1. (Jl. 1964)–
        A new publication high-lighting re-
    search activities and publications in the
    field of Arabic and Islamic studies
    bearing on West Africa. Special em-
    phasis on researches towards the docu-
    mentation of unknown or newly dis-
    covered Arabic materials.

70 Kano studies. Kano. v. 1. (Sept. 1965)–
        Published by Abdullahi Bayero Col-
    lege, Ahmadu Bello University.

71 Music in Nigeria. Nsukka. v. 1 (May
    1964)–
        Annual. Proceedings of the African
    music seminar held annually at Univer-
    sity of Nigeria, Nsukka, from 1964.

72 Niger and Yoruba notes. London. v. 1
    no. 1–v. 10 no. 120 (Jl. 1894–Je. 1904).
        10 v. monthly. From v. 11, continued
    as Western equatorial Africa diocesan
    magazine [88] q.v.

73 Nigeria
    Blue book, 1914–[?]. Lagos, Govt.
    printer.
        Annual govt. publication giving a ré-
    sumé of general, administrative, statisti-
    cal and ethnographic information on
    Nigeria. Superseded the Southern
    Nigeria blue book, published 1906–1913,
    and the Northern Nigeria blue book,
    1900–1913. The Southern Nigeria blue
    book itself superseded the Lagos blue
    book, 1863–1905.

74 Nigeria. Dept. of antiquities.
    Annual report. Lagos. 1st (1946)–
        1946–1950/51, as Education dept. An-
    tiquities branch. 1951/52–? as Antiqui-
    ties service.

75 Nigeria digest. Lagos. v.1 no. 1–10 (Dec.
    1944–May 1946).
        Published by the Public relations dept.

76 Nigeria magazine. Lagos. no. 9 (Ja.
    1937)–
        A richly illustrated popular quarterly
    devoted to Nigerian life and culture, and
    to local history. Supersedes Nigerian
    teacher [82] and continues its volume
    numbering. Title varies: 1937–1959, as
    Nigeria; a quarterly magazine of general
    interest.

77 Nigeria review. Lagos. v. 1–8 (1941–Feb.
    1953).
        Published by the Public relations
    dept.

78 Nigerian field; journal of the Nigerian
    field society. London. v. 1 (1931)–
        Quarterly.

79 Nigerian geographical journal. Ibadan.
    v. 1 (1957)–
        Semi-annual. Published by the Niger-
    ian geographical association.

80 Nigerian institute of social and economic
    research. Conference proceedings. Iba-
    dan. 1st (1952)–
        Annual. From 1952–[1957?] the con-

ference was organized by the former West African institute of social and economic research to which the NISER is a part successor.

81 Nigerian journal of economic and social studies. Ibadan. v. 1 (1959)–
3 times a year. Published by the Nigerian economic society.

82 Nigerian teacher. Lagos. no. 1–8 (1933–Sept. 1936).
From no. 9 (1937) continued as Nigeria magazine [76] q.v.

83 Odù; a journal of Yoruba, Edo and related studies. Ibadan. no. 1–? (1955–1964).
Formerly sub-titled a journal of Yoruba studies; then a journal of Yoruba and related studies. Continued as Odu; University of Ife journal of African studies

84 Odu; University of Ife journal of African studies. Ibadan. v. 1 (Jl. 1964)–
Supersedes Odù; a journal of Yoruba, Edo and related studies.

84a Royal African society.
Journal. See [60].

85 Tarikh. Ibadan. v. 1 (Nov. 1965)–
A new journal published by the Historical society of Nigeria and intended to reduce the results of researches in African history to a form suitable for schools, colleges and undergraduates. Semi-annual.

86 West African archaeological newsletter. Ibadan. No. 1 (Dec. 1965)–
A medium of information on current archaeological activities in West Africa.

86a West African institute of social and economic research.
See [80].

87 West African religion, Nsukka. no. 1 (May 1963)–
Irregular. Mimeographed. Described as an occasional review of recent studies. Includes original articles as well as book reviews.

88 Western equatorial African diocesan magazine. London. v. 11 no. 121 (n.s. no. 1)–v. 60 no. 649 (n.s. no. 552) (Jl. 1904–Oct./Dec. 1956)
Title varied: Apr. 1922–Dec. 1956, as Western equatorial African church magzine. Superseded Niger and Yoruba notes [72] q.v.

3. GENERAL WORKS

This section collocates a selection of general, descriptive and historical works considered relevant in that they help in one way or the other to throw light on some aspects of Nigerian anthropology. Works of travel and description predominate, and in selecting them from the great mass of travel literature, emphasis has been placed on items containing worthwhile descriptions of the life and customs of the people.

89 'Abd al-Rahmän ibn 'Abd Allah, al-Sa'dí

Documents arabes rélatifs à l'histoire du Soudan: Tarikh es-Soudan, par Abderrahman ben Abdallah ben 'Imran ben 'Amires Sa'dí. Edité par O. Houdas, avec la collaboration de E. Benoist. Paris, E. Leroux, 1898–1900. 2v. (Publications de l'Ecole des langues orientales vivantes, 4ème sér., vol. 12–13)

90 Achufusi, Modilim
Die Zerstörung des Sokoto-Reiches durch die europäischen Kolonialmächte. 1962. 58p.
Inaug. Diss. (Ph.D) Karl-Marx University, Leipzig. Published as manuscript in Wissenschaftliche Zeitschrift der Karl-Marx Universität. Gesellschafts-und Sprachwissenchaftliche Reihe. Heft 1, 1962: 43–101, map.

91 Adams, John
Remarks on the country extending from Cape Palmas to the River Congo, including observation on the manners and customs of the inhabitants. London, Whittaker, 1823, repr. London, Frank Cass, 1966. ix, 265p. maps.

92 —Sketches taken during ten voyages to Africa between the years 1786–1800. London, Hurst, Robinson, 1822. 119p.

93 Adolf, Friedrich, *Duke of Mecklenburg-Schwerin.*
Ins innerste Afrika,—Bericht über den Verlauf der deutschen wissenschaftlichen Zentral-Afrika-Expedition, 1907–1908. Leipzig, Klinkhardt & Biermann, 1909. xii, 476p. front., illus.
Account of the 1907–1908 German Central-Africa expedition.

94 —Vom Kongo zum Niger und Nil. Berichte der deutschen Zentralafrika-expedition, 1910–1911. Leipzig, F. A. Brockhaus, 1912. 2v. fronts., illus.
Account of the German Central African expedition of 1910–1911 which was a follow-up of the 1907–1908 expedition. Includes descriptions of the Cameroons, Bornu and Lake Chad regions and the Benue.

95 Africa. London, J. Duncan, 1829. 3v. illus. (The modern traveller, a popular description . . . of the various countries of the world.)
Volumes 2 and 3 include useful account of Bornu, Kano, Sokoto and other parts of Nigeria.

96 African association. See Association for promoting the discovery of the interior parts of Africa.

97 *Afzelius, Adam
Remedia Guineensia. Uppsala,1813–17. 10 pts.
Description of plants of the upper Guinea, with notes on their medicinal value.

98 Agboola, S. A.
The Middle Belt of Nigeria—the basis of its unity. *Nig. geog. j.,* 4 (1) Aug. 1961: 41–46, map, bibliog.

99 —Some geographical influences upon the population and economy of the

Middle Belt west of the Niger. 1962.
M.A. thesis, London.

100   Ajayi, Jacob F. Ade
Population census of Nigeria, May 1962:
lists of historical events for determination of individual ages. Foreword by
Ademola A. Igun. Ibadan, Regional census office, 1962. [700]p,.
For each census district, historical
events of local significance are enumera-
ted in chronological order, with dates.
Concentrates on the Western and Mid-
Western Regions of Nigeria. Mimeographed.

101   Alexander, Boyd
From the Niger, by Lake Chad, to the
Nile. *Geog. j.*, 30, Aug. 1907: 119–152; *J.
Manch. geog. soc.*, 24 (4) 1908: 145–162,
illus., map.
Also reprinted in *Smithsonian institu-
tion, Annual report, 1909*. Washington,
1910: 385–400, illus.

102   —From the Niger to the Nile. London,
E. Arnold, 1907. 2v. fronts., illus., maps.
Account of the Alexander-Gosling expedition. Chapters 4–6 of vol. 1 written
by Percy Amaury Talbot.

103   Allen, William
Picturesque views on the River Niger
sketched during Lander's last visit in
1832–33. London, Murray, 1940. 16p. +
10 plates, 1 map.
Sketches, with descriptive notes, of
life and sceneries along the Niger.

104   *—Records of an expedition up the
Quorra with Lander. *United service j.*,
30, 1938: 310–325, ff.

105   Allen, William and Thomson, T. R. H.
A narrative of the expedition sent by
Her Majesty's Government to the River
Niger, in 1841, under the command of
Captain H. D. Trotter, R.N. London,
Richard Bentley, 1848, repr. London,
Frank Cass, 1968. 2v. front., illus. (incl.
ports.) maps, tables.
Volume 2 includes vocabularies of
some African languages.

106   Ames, C. G.
Gazetteer of Bauchi Province, compiled
in 1932. Recently abridged and revised
[by H. Hale Middleton] Jos, Native administration, 1934. 349p. maps., repr.
London, Frank Cass, 1971.

107   Arnett, Edward John
Census of Nigeria, 1931. *J. Afr. soc.*, 32
(129) Oct. 1933: 398–404.
A review of the census data.

108   —Gazetteer of Sokoto Province. London, Waterlow, 1920. 79p., repr. London, Frank Cass, 1971.

109   —Gazetteer of Zaria Province. London,
Waterlow, 1920. 40p., repr. London,
Frank Cass, 1971.

110   Association for promoting the discovery
of the interior parts of Africa.
Proceedings, 1788–1810. London, 1810.
2v. maps.
The Association's proceedings published irregularly from its foundation in
1788 up to 1810 were reprinted in two
octavo volumes in 1810. It includes accounts of Bornu and the Hausa country,
especially in pp. 127–173 of vol. 1.

111   *Avity, Pierre d'
Description générale de l'Afrique avec
tous ses empires, royaumes, états et ré-
publiques. Paris, 1637.

112   Ayandele, Emmanuel Ayankanmi
The missionary impact on modern
Nigeria, 1842–1914: a political analysis.
London, Longmans, Green, 1966. xx,
393p. illus., maps (Ibadan history series)

113   —The political and social implications
of missionary enterprise in the evolution
of modern Nigeria, 1875–1914. 1964.
Ph.D. thesis, London.

114   —The political significance of missionary
activity in nineteenth century West
African history. *Historia*, 11 (1) Apr.
1965: 16–34.

115   Azurara, Gomes Eannes de
The chronicle of the discovery and con-
quest of Guinea. Translated from the
Portuguese by C. Raymond Beazley and
E. Prestage. London, Hakluyt society,
1899. 2v.

116   Baikie, William Balfour
Brief summary of an exploring trip up
the Rivers Kwora and Chadda, or
Benue, in 1854. *J. Roy. geog. soc.*, 25,
1855: 108–121, map.

117   —Narrative of an exploring voyage up
the Rivers Kwóra and Binue (commonly
known as the Niger and Tsádda) in 1854.
London, Murray, 1856, repr. London,
Frank Cass, 1966. xvi, 456p. front., map,
plan.

118   —Notes of a journey from Bida in Nupe
to Kano in Hausa, performed in 1862.
J. Roy. geog. soc., 37, 1867: 92–109, map.
Account of Baikie's journey, extracted
from portions of his journals in the
Foreign office by J. Kirk. Includes des-
cription of market and sale of slaves in
Zaria, and also lists of kings for Kano,
Zaria, Zamfara, Katsina, Gobir, Azbeu,
Ader, Daura and Nupe.

119   Baker, Richard St. Barbe
Africa drums. London, Lindsay Drum-
mond, 1942. 159p. front., illus.
Descriptions of African life and
customs in Kenya and Nigeria by a
former forestry officer who had served
in both countries.

120   —Men of the trees in the mahogany
forests of Kenya and Nigeria. London,
G. Allen & Unwin, 1932. 283p. front.,
illus.

121   Barbot, Jean
A description of the coasts of North and
South Guinea; and of Ethiopia inferior,
vulgarly Angola: being a new and accurate account of the western maritime
countries of Africa . . . with an appendix,
being a general account of the first discoveries of America . . . London, 1732.
716p. illus., maps.

122 — —[Another ed.] *Churchill's voyages*, vol. 5, pp. 1–588.

Accounts based on journeys made between 1678 and 1682 when author was Agent-General of the Royal Company of Africa. Includes a description of Benin, pp. 354–362 (of later edition)

123 Barth, Heinrich
Barth's travels in Nigeria: extracts from the journals of Heinrich Barth's travels in Nigeria, 1850–1855. Selected and edited, with an introduction, by A. H. M. Kirk-Greene. London, O.U.P., 1962. [xii] 300p. front., illus., plates (including facsim.)

Selections from the English translation of author's Reisen und Entdeckungen in Nord-und Central Afrika. The introduction covering 75 pages presents a useful background to the selections.

124 —Reisen und Entdeckungen in Nord-und Central Afrika in den Jahren 1849 bis 1855, Tagebuch seiner im Auftrag der britischen Regierung unternommenen Reise . . . Gotha, J. Perthes, 1857–58. 4v. illus., maps, plans.
German edition of [125]

125 —Travels and discoveries in North and Central Africa; being a journal of an expedition undertaken under the auspices of H. B. M's government, in the years 1849–1855. London. Longman, Brown, Green, Longmans, & Roberts, 1857–58. 5v. fronts., illus., maps, plans.

125a —Travels and discoveries in North and Central Africa; being a journal of an expedition undertaken under the auspices of H. B. M's government, in the years 1849–1855. Centenary Edition with the complete text, maps and illustrations and with a biographical introduction by A. H. M. Kirk-Greene. London, Frank Cass, 1965. 3v. illus., maps.

126 Baumann, H. and Westermann, Diedrich
Les peuples et les civilizations de l'Afrique; suivi de les langues et l'éducation. Traduction française par L. Homburger. Paris, Payot, 1957. 605p. illus., maps, bibliog. (Bibliothèque scientifique)

127 Benezet, Anthony
Some historical account of Guinea, its situation, produce, and the general description of its inhabitants. With an inquiry into the rise and progress of the slave trade, its nature and lamentable effects. New ed. London, J. Phillips, 1788, repr. London, Frank Cass, 1968. xv, 131p.

128 Bernard, Augustin
Les populations indigènes [Afrique occidentale] In his *Géographie universelle, vol. XI. Afrique septentrionale et occidentale, 1939*: 420–447. illus., maps, bibliog.

Notes on the peoples of West Africa including the Fulani, Hausa, Yoruba, and Kanuri.

129 Biobaku, Saburi O.

African studies in an African university. *Minerva*, 1 (3) Spring, 1963: 285–301.

130 Bittinger, Desmond Wright
The Soudan's second sunup. Elgin, Ill., Elgin press, [c. 1938] 254p. illus. (incl. ports.) map.
Reminiscences of Nigeria of the 1930's.

131 Bivar, A. D. H.
Arabic documents of Northern Nigeria. *B.S.O.A.S.*, 22 (2) 1959: 324–349, facsims.

A detailed examination of some correspondence of the rulers of Bornu and Sokoto, as well as of foreign princes. Notes the form and physical appearance of these letters, and provides facsimiles of text pages, transcripts, translations and commentaries.

132 Blake, John William
European beginnings in West Africa, 1454–1578: a survey of the first century of white enterprise in West Africa, with special emphasis upon the rivalry of the great powers. London, Longmans, Green, for the Royal empire society, 1937. xi, 212p. maps, bibliog.

133 —Europeans in West Africa, 1450–1560: documents to illustrate the nature and scope of Portuguese enterprise in West Africa, the abortive attempt of Castilians to create an empire there, and the early English voyages to Barbary and Guinea. London, Hakluyt society, 1942. 2v. front., maps. (Works issued by the Hakluyt society . . . second series, nos. 86–87)

134 Blyden, Edward Wilmot
Islam in Western Soudan. *J. Afr. soc.*, 2 (5) Oct. 1902: 11–37.

135 Boahen, A. Adu
British penetration of the Sahara and and Western Sudan, 1788–1861. 1959. Ph.D. thesis, London.

136 Bosman, Willem
A new and accurate description of the coast of Guinea, divided into the Gold, the Slave, and the Ivory coasts; containing a geographical, political and natural history of the kingdoms and countries. With a particular account of the rise, progress and present condition of all the European settlements upon that coast; and the just measures for improving the several branches of the Guinea trade. Written originally in Dutch by William Bosman, and now faithfully done into English. To which is prefixed an exact map of the whole coast of Guinea, that was not in the original. London, J. Knapton, 1705. 493 [16]p. illus., map.

136a — —1st ed. Amsterdam, 1704. Reprinted, with an introduction by J. R. Willis, and notes by J. D. Fage and R. E. Bradbury. London, Frank Cass, 1967. xxi [8] 577p. illus., maps.

137 —Another edition. In *A general collection of the best and most interesting voyages and travels, by John Pinkerton.*

London, 1803–1814. v. 16, 1814: 337–547.

138   Bourne, H. R. Fox.
Blacks and whites in West Africa: an account of the past treatment and present conditions of West African natives under European influence or control. London, P. S. King, 1901. 88p.

139   Bovill, Edward William
The Bornu mission, 1822–25. Cambridge, C.U.P., 1966. 3v. illus., maps (Hakluyt society. Publication, 2nd ser., no. 128–130. Missions to the Niger, v. 2–4).
    A new edition of Denham, Clapperton and Oudney's "Narrative of travels and discoveries in Northern and Central Africa" [192]

140   Brass, Adolph
Eine neue Quelle zur Geschichte des Fulreiches Sokoto. Berlin. Vereinigung Wissenchaftlicher Verleger (Walter de Gruyter) 1919. [iii] 73p. map.

141   Bretton, Henry
Power and stability in Nigeria: the politics of decolonization. New York, F. A. Praeger, 1962. xii, 208p. bibliog. (Books that matter ser.)
    The patterns of political, social and economic movements in Nigeria during the process of decolonisation are critically examined with a view to determining the effects of their interplay on the development and sustenance of political stability.

142   Brønnum, Niels H.
Mellem Aekvator og Sahara; dansk forenet Sudan missions historie. Copenhagen O. Lohses Forlag, 1955. 354, [4] p. illus. (incl. ports.) maps.

143   Brooke, N. J.
Census of the Northern Provinces. London, Published on behalf of the Govt. of Nigeria by the Crown Agents for the Colonies, 1933. 234p. 1 map (fold.) (Census of Nigeria, 1931, v. 2)
    Detailed report of the 1931 census in Northern Nigeria, excluding the Medical census.

144   —Village directory, Northern Provinces, Nigeria (based on 1931 census material) Lagos, Govt. Printer, 1934. 150p. (Census of Nigeria, 1931, vol. 2A.)
    "This Village directory contains the Districts, Divisions, Emirates, Provinces and populations of all villages in the Northern Provinces, as recorded in the Census of 23rd Apr. 1931"—Foreword.

145   Brounger, S. G.
Nigeria past and present: some reminiscences. *J. Afr. soc.,* 12 (47) Apr. 1913: 249–255, illus.

146   Buchanan, Keith McPherson
Internal colonisation in Nigeria. *Geog. rev.,* 1953: 416–418.

147   —The Northern Region of Nigeria: the geographical background of its political duality. *Geog. rev.,* 43 (4) Oct. 1953: 451–473.

148   Buchanan, Keith McPherson and Pugh, John Charles
Land and people in Nigeria: the human geography of Nigeria and its environmental background; with a contribution by A. Brown. London. University of London press, 1955. xii, 252p. illus., maps, bibliog.

149   Buell, Raymond Leslie
The native problem in Africa. New York, Macmillan, 1928, repr. London, Frank Cass, 1965. 2v. maps, tables, bibliog.

150   Burdo, A.
Ascent of the River Binue in August, 1879; with remarks on the systems of the Shary and Binue. *Proc. Roy. geog. soc., n.s.,* 2, 1880: 289–305.

151   —The Niger and the Benueh; travels in Central Africa. [Translated] from the French by Mrs. George Sturge. London, Richard Bentley, 1880. ix, 277p. front., illus.
    English ed. of [152]

152   —Niger et Bénué; voyage dans l'Afrique Centrale. Paris, E. Plon, 1880. 297p.

153   Burdon John A.
The Fulani emirates of Northern Nigeria. *Geog. j.,* 24, Jl.–Dec. 1904: 636–651, illus.
    A general description, giving physical features, recent history, indigenous governmental structure, and prospects for the success of indirect rule. Based largely on Bida emirate.

154   Burns, Alan Cuthbert Maxwell
History of Nigeria. 6th ed. London, Allen & Unwin, 1963. 362p. maps.
    A general account of the modern history of Nigeria, from the European explorations of the late 18th century down to independence in 1960.

155   Burton, Richard Francis
Two trips to gorilla land and the Cataracts of the Congo. London, S. Low, Marston, Low and Searle, 1876. 2v. illus., maps.
    Travel and description in West Africa and the Congo.

156   —Wanderings in West Africa from Liverpool to Fernando Po. By a F.R.G.S. London, Tinsley, 1863. 2v. illus., map.
    The last chapters of vol. 2 (pp. 186–293) describe his travels in and impressions of Lagos, Benin and the Delta area. Burton was British Consul for the Bight of Benin and was stationed in Fernando Po from 1861–1864. See also [1716]

157   Cardi, Charles Napoleon, comte de
A short description of the natives of the Niger Coast Protectorate, with some account of their customs, religion, trade, etc. In *West African studies, by M. H. Kingsley, 1899:* 443–566, illus.
    Includes account of govt. and religion in Benin, origin of the people of Benin City, account of Brass (Nembe), New Calabar, and Old Calabar.

158 Chapiseau, Félix
Au pays des esclaves; moeurs & coûtumes de l'Afrique centrale. D'Après des notes recueillies par Ferdinand Béhagle. Paris, Maisonneuve, 1900. [vii] 282p. (Les littératures populaires de toutes les nations . . . v. 37)

159 Chevalier, Auguste
L'Afrique centrale française. Récit du voyage de la mission . . . Appendice par Pellegrin, Germain, Courtet, Petit Bouvier, Lesness Du Buysson, Surcouf. Paris, A. Challamel, 1907. xv. 776p. front., illus., maps.
At head of title: Mission Chari-Lac Tchad, 1902–1904.

160 Church missionary society
Nigeria the unknown; a missionary study text-book on Nigeria. London, C.M.S., 1918. 56p. illus., map.

161 Church, Ronald James Harrison
West Africa: a study of the environment and of man's use of it. London, Longmans, Green, 1957. xxvii, 547p. illus. (Geographies for advanced studies)

162 Clapperton, Hugh
Journal of a second expedition into the interior of Africa, from the Bight of Benin to Soccatoo, to which is added the journal of R. Lander from Kano to the sea-coast . . . London, John Murray, 1829, repr. London, Frank Cass, 1966. xxiv, 355p. map.

163 Clarke, John Digby
A visual history of Nigeria. Illus. by Ann and Donald Goring. London, Evans Bros., [1956] 48p. illus.

164 Clarke, John Henrik
Le Nigéria ancien et le Soudan occidental. Prés. afr., (32/33) Je.–Sept. 1960: 187–193.

165 Coleman, James S.
Nigeria: background to nationalism. Berkeley and Los Angeles, University of California press, 1958. xiv, 510p. illus., maps, bibliog. (pp. 481–496)
A penetrating study of the historical and social background and the development and rise of modern nationalism in Nigeria. Particularly relevant here is part 1 (pp. 11–60) which surveys "The cultural and historical setting". Elaborate bibliographical notes, in addition to main bibliography. Based on author's Ph.D. thesis: Nationalism in Nigeria. Harvard University, 1953.

166 Collier, G. R. and Maccarthy, Charles
West African sketches; compiled from the reports of G. R. Collier, Charles Maccarthy and other official sources. London, printed for L. B. Seeley, 1824. ix, 273p.
Notes on the Fulani, pp. 30–38, 42–43; Benin pp. 70–84. "Methods of obtaining slaves" pp. 152–158.

167 Collis, William Robert Fitz-Gerald
A doctor's Nigeria: London, Secker & Warburg, 1960. 265p. illus., map.
American ed. has title: African encounter.

168 The contribution of Islam to national life in West Africa. Oversea educ., 28 (3) Oct. 1956: 99–105.

169 Cook, Arthur Norton
British enterprise in Nigeria. Philadelphia, University of Pennsylvania press, 1943, repr. London, Frank Cass, 1964. xi, 330p. bibliog.
The planting and development of British imperial power in Nigeria traced from its beginnings to the amalgamation of 1914. Two final chapters survey economic and political development since 1914. Originally a thesis for the Ph.D. Degree, University of Pennsylvania, 1927, with the title: "Nigeria: a study in British imperialism."

170 Cooper, Harold
Our towns. Lagos, Public relations dept. [n.d.] 14p. illus. (Crownbird series, no. 13)
Impressions of five towns—Zawan, Kano, Maiduguri, Ife, Oron, and Owo—gathered during a tour in 1947.

171 Cooper, J. A.
Northern Nigeria as I saw it. United empire, 4, 1913: 243–258.

172 Corry, Joseph
Observations upon the windward coast of Africa: the religion, character, customs, etc., of the natives; with a system upon which they may be civilized; and a knowledge attained of the interior of this extraordinary quarter of the globe; and upon the natural and commercial resources of the country; made in the years 1805 and 1806. . . . London, G. and W. Nicol, 1807, repr. London, Frank Cass, 1968. xiv, 163p. front., illus., map.

173 Cowan, Alex. A.
Early trading conditions in the Bight of Biafra. J.R.A.S., 34 (137) Oct. 1935: 391–402; 35 (138) Jan. 1936: 53–64, map.

174 Cox, H. B.
Census of the Southern Provinces. London, published on behalf of the Govt. of Nigeria by the Crown agents for the colonies, 1932. 46p. (Census of Nigeria, 1931, v. 3)
The full report of the 1931 census in the Southern Provinces. Arranged in four parts—The General census—mainly a synthesis of existing records. The Intensive census—giving data on age groups, sex, birth place, occupation, etc., Appendices; and Tables.

175 Crawford, W. E. B. Copeland
Nigeria. J. Manch. geog. soc., 31, 1915: 1–15.

176 Crouch, Archer P.
Glimpses of fever land; or A cruise in West African waters. London, Samson, Low, Marston, Searle & Rivington, 1889. xi, 323p. map.
Account of life and scenes in the West Coast of Africa in the late 19th century, by a member of a cable-laying expedition. Chapters 1–5 (pp. 6–74) describes Southern Nigeria—Lagos, Niger delta and Old Calabar.

177 Crow, Hugh
Memoirs of the late Captain Hugh Crow
of Liverpool; comprising a narrative of
his life together with descriptive sketches
of the Western Coast of Africa; particularly of Bonny; the manners and customs
of the inhabitants, the productions of
the soil, and the trade of the country.
To which are added anecdotes and observations illustrative of the negro character. Compiled chiefly from his own
manuscripts: with authentic additions
from recent voyages and approved authors. London, Longmans, Rees, Orme,
Brown and Green, 1830. xxxiii, 316p.
front., illus., map., repr. London, Frank
Cass, 1970.
Pp. 270–286 carry a description of Old
Calabar, with notes on the people, their
customs and occupations, by Grant, a
Liverpool trader who visited the West
Coast as a slave dealer and later for
legitimate trade. See [2883]

178 Crowder, Michael
Pagans and politicians. London, Hutchinson, 1959. 224p. front., plates, map.
Description of modern West Africa as
seen during a six-month trip.

179 —The story of Nigeria. London, Faber
and Faber, 1962. 307p. illus., bibliog.

180 Crowther, Samuel Adjai
Experiences with heathens and Moham-
medans in West Africa. London,
S.P.C.K., 1892. 60p.

181 —Journal of an expedition up the Niger
and Tshadda Rivers undertaken by
McGregor Laird in connection with the
British Government in 1854. London,
Church missionary house, 1855. xxiii,
234p. map., repr. London, Frank Cass,
1970.

182 —The Niger expedition. J. civilization,
1842: 73–76; 133–136; 155–158.

183 —The River Niger; . . . and a brief account of missionary operations . . . in
the Niger territory. London, Church
missionary house, 1877. 37p.
Geographical features of the Niger,
with comments on the people of the surrounding country with which the Bishop
had become acquainted through his
frequent visits.

184 Crowther, Samuel Adjayi, and Taylor,
John Christopher
The gospel on the banks of the Niger.
Journals and notices of the native missionaries accompanying the Niger expedition of 1857–1859. London, Church
missionary house, 1859. xi, 451p. map.
Crowther's journal covers pp. 1–240,
and 385–423, while Taylor's journal written at Onitsha where he stayed for
twenty months to organize a mission
centre, covers pp. 241–384.

185 Crozier, Frank Percy
Five years' hard; being an account of the
fall of the Fulani empire and a picture of
the daily life of a regimental officer
among the peoples of the Western

Sudan. London, J. Cape, 1932. 221p.
illus., map.

186 Cudjoe, Robert
Some reminiscences of a senior interpreter. Introduction by P. F. Grant. Nig.
field, 18 (4) Oct. 1953: 148–164.
Memoirs of a former govt. carpenter
recruited from Elmina, Gold Coast in
1902. Served for 48 years in many parts
of Eastern Nigeria, rising from a carpenter to a senior interpreter. In his
memoirs, he recalls life in Eastern Nigeria and many important events in the
early administration of the region.

187 Daniel, F. de F. [and others]
Some provinces of Nigeria: Ilorin, Kano,
Plateau, the Emirate of Zazzau, Ijebu,
Nig. mag., (15) Sept. 1938: 179–199.

188 Dapper, Olfert
Nakeurige   Beschrijringe   der   Afri-
kaensche gewesten van Egypten Bar-
baryen, Lybien, Biledulgerid. Negros-
lant, Guinea, Ethiopiën, Abyssinie . . .
Getrokken uyt verscheyde hedendaegse
lantbeschrijvers   en   geschriften   van
bereisde ondersoekers dier landen.
Amsterdam, J. van Meurs, 1676. 4 [2]
428, 349 [17] p. illus., maps.
An early work of description, later
translated into German and French,
and on which many of the later works
were based. Original ed. published in
Amsterdam in 1668.

189 Darwin, Leonard
The Niger territories. National review, 23
(136) Je. 1894: 566–576.
History and the several explorations of
the Royal Niger Coy. under its various
names. Describes the Niger, the surrounding country and its people, and
pleads for the establishment of trade
with the region.

190 Davidson, Basil
Black mother; Africa: the years of trial.
London, Victor Gollancz, 1961. 269p.
plates, bibliog.
Outline history of Africa from the
beginning of the slave trade to the commencement of legitimate trade. Especially relevant is part VI (pp. 179–
232) which deals with the slave trade and
general conditions in West Africa.

191 Davies, J. G.
The Biu book: a collation and reference book on Biu Division (Northern
Nigeria. Zaria, NORLA, 1956. v, 357p.
maps.

192 Denham, Dixon
Narrative of travels and discoveries in
Northern and Central Africa in the years
1822–1823 and 1824, by Major Denham,
Captain Clapperton, and the late Dr.
Oudney; extending across the great
desert to the tenth degree of northern
latitude, and from Kouka in Bornu to
Sackatoo, the capital of the Fellatah
empire. With an appendix. Published . . .
by Major Dixon Denham . . . and Captain Hugh Clapperton . . . London,

John Murray, 1826. xlviii [ie., lxviii] 355 [iv] 269p. front., illus., plates, maps.

193 — —2nd ed. in 2v. published 1826.

194 — —3rd ed. in 2v. published 1828.

195 Desanti, Hyacinthe
Du Dahomé au Bénin-Niger. Paris, Larose, 1945. 268p. illus., maps.

195a Desanti, Jean Hyacinthe See Desanti, Hyacinthe

195b Detzner, Hernann
Im Lande des Dju-dju. See [4249].

196 Dickson, Mora
New Nigerians. London, D. Dobson, 1960. 256p. front., illus.
Life and activities in Man O'War Bay Training Centre and the achievements of some of its students, by the wife of the first Principal of the Centre.

197 Dike, Kenneth Onwuka
History and African nationalism. *W.A.I.S.E.R. conf. proc., 1952:* 31–42.

198 —100 years of British rule in Nigeria, 1851–1951; being the 1956 Lugard lectures. 2nd ed. Lagos, Federal Ministry of Information, 1960. 51p. front., illus.

199 — —1st ed. 1958 49p.

200 —Origins of the Niger Mission, 1841–1891: a paper read at the centenary of the Mission at Christ Church, Onitsha, on 14 Nov. 1957. Ibadan, University press, for C.M.S. Niger Mission, 1957. 21p. bibliog.

201 —Problems of archive administration in Nigeria. *W.A.I.S.E.R. conf. proc. (Sociology section) 1953:* 106-114.
Details the problems facing archive administration and indicates possible lines of action.

202 —Trade and politics in the Niger Delta, 1830–1885: an introduction to the economic and political history of Nigeria. vii, 250p. map, tables, bibliog. (Oxford studies in African affairs.)
A detailed study of the intensive and expanding commercial enterprise in the area and of the processes by which political authority passed from the hands of the native chiefs to the British. Based on his Ph.D. thesis:- Trade and politics in the Niger Delta, 1830–1879. London, 1951.

203 —Trade and the opening up of Nigeria. *Nigeria, 1960:* 49–57, illus.

203a Dittel, Paul
Die Besiedlung Südnigeriens von den Anfängen bis zur britischen Kolonisation. *Wissenschaftliche Veröffentlichungen des deutschen Museums für Länderkunde zu Leipzig, n.s.* (4) 1936: 71–146.

204 Dobinson, Henry Hughes
Letters of Henry Hughes Dobinson, late Archdeacon of the Niger in the Diocese of Western Equatorial Africa. With a prefatory memoir. London, Seeley, 1899. viii, 230p. front., illus., map.

205 Duff, E. Creighton
Gazetteer of Ilorin Province. Revised by W. Hamilton-Browne, with additional notes. London, Waterlow, 1920. 72p., repr. London, Frank Cass, 1971.

206 Duff, E. Creighton and Hamilton-Browne, W.
Gazetteer of Kontagora Province. London, Waterlow, 1920. 72p., repr. London, Frank Cass, 1971.

207 Du Plessis, Johannes
The evangelisation of pagan Africa; a history of Christian missions to the pagan tribes of Central Africa. Cape Town & Johannesburg, J. C. Juta [1930] xii, 408p. map, bibliog.
Survey of European commercial penetration and missionary activity in Africa. A whole chapter (pp. 132–159) devoted to Nigeria.

208 Dyer, Hugh McN.
The West coast of Africa as seen from the deck of a man-of-war. London, Portsmouth, J. Griffin, 1876. viii, 171p. front., illus.
Sketches of life in West Coast of Africa by a British naval captain who had participated in the British attack on Lagos in 1850. Description of Lagos, pp. 54–59; Bonny, with account of the Jaja-Oko Jumbo war and the subsequent peace treaty (pp. 151–160)

209 Eaglesfield, Carrol Frederick
Listen to the drums; Nigeria and its people. Nashville, Tenn., Broadman press, 1950. [ii] 82p. illus.

210 Edrisi
Description de l'Afrique et de l'Espagne. Texte arabe publié pour la première fois d'après les man. de Paris et d'Oxford avec une traduction, de notes et un glossaire, par R. Dozy et M. J. de Goeje. Leyde, E. Brill, 1866. xxiii, 391, 242p.
Arabic text in last 242pp.

211 Eibeshutz, Harold
Some British explorations of the Niger River and Nigeria, 1795–1842. 1936. 160p.
M.A. thesis, Columbia University.

212 Ekwensi, Cyprian Odiatu Duaka
Beautiful feathers. London, Hutchinson, 1963. 160p.
A novel.

213 —Jagua Nana. London, Hutchinson, 1961. 192p.
A novel.

214 —People of the city. London, Andrew Dakers, 1954. 237p.
A novel set in modern Lagos.

215 English, M. C.
An outline of Nigerian history. London, Longmans, Green, 1959. xi, 212p. illus., plates, maps.

216 —What history does the Nigerian pupil need? *J. Hist. soc. Nig.,* 1 (2) Dec. 1957: 111–118.
Believes that history teaching should reflect three historical elements supporting the Nigerian society: exclusively tribal history, common general traditions evolving from cultural interaction of the

tribes, and the body of imported culture permeating the Nigerian society.

216a Epaulard, A., *tr.*
Description de l'Afrique. See [344]

217 Epelle, Kiea
Our land & people, part I—the East. Lagos, Crownbird publications, Public relations dept., [n.d]. 16p. illus. (Crownbird series, no. 31.)
Brief general description introducing the Eastern Region. See also . . . Gana, M. A.; Sowunmi, A.

218 Fage, John D.
An atlas of African history. [London] E. Arnold, 1958. 64p. maps.

219 —An introduction to the history of West Africa. 2nd ed. Cambridge, University press, 1959. xii, 214p. maps, tables, bibliographical notes.
Outline survey of the history of West Africa from the period of European exploration and trade, with brief treatment of the earlier "pre-European" era.

220 Falconer, John Downie
On horseback through Nigeria; or Life and travel in the Central Sudan. London, T. Fisher Unwin, 1911. 312p. front., illus., map.
Description of Northern Nigeria as seen between 1908 and 1911 by the then govt. geologist in charge of mineral survey.

221 Fawckner, James
Narrative of Captain Fawckner's travels on the Coast of Benin, West Africa. Edited by a friend of the Captain. London, A. Schloss, for the proprietor, 1837. viii, 128p.

222 Fax, Elton C.
West Africa vignettes. N.Y., American society of African culture, 1960. 93p. illus.
Sketches of West Africans, with brief comments on each sketch. Nigerians, pp. 12–47.

223 Fiévet, Jeannette M.
L'Enfant blanc de l'Afrique noire. Paris, Flammarion, 1957. 236 [2]p. illus., map.
Life and personal experiences of a French painter's wife in West Africa in 1951.

224 —White piccaninny: adventures of a mother and child in West Africa. Translated from the French by Alan Houghton Brodrick. London, Jarrolds, 1959. 224p. illus., map. English translation of [223].

225 Fiévet, Jeannette M. and Fiévet, Maurice
Beyond the Bight of Benin. *National geog. mag.*, 116 (2) Aug. 1959: 221–253, map.

226 Fiévet, Maurice
Nigeria as seen through the eyes of a French artist. *Nig. mag.*, (34) 1950: 180–206, illus.

227 Fisher, Humphrey J.
Ahmadiyyah: a study in contemporary Islam on the West African coast. London, O.U.P., for N.I.S.E.R., 1963. 206p. bibliog.

A pioneering study of the latest Islamic sect's impact in West Africa. Discusses its doctrine in general, and its history, doctrine and organisation in West Africa. Based on his D.Phil. thesis: Ahmadiyya: a study in contemporary Islam in West Africa. Oxford, 1960. See a critical review in *Ibadan* (19) Je. 1964: 21–23; reprinted in *Research notes,* 1 (2) Jan. 1965: 31–39.

228 —The Ahmadiyya movement in Nigeria. In *African Affairs, number one (St. Anthony's papers, no. 10)* ed. by Kenneth Kirkwood. *1961:* 60–88.
Traces the history of the Ahmadiyya sect in Nigeria from its introduction during the first world war to the present.

229 —The planting of Ahmadiyya in Nigeria, *W. Afr.*, (2234) Mar. 1960: 347.
On the establishment of Ahmadiyya in Lagos in 1916 and its early vissicitudes and strife with other Muslim sects.

230 —Some novelties introduced into West African Islam by Ahmadiyya. *N.I.S.E.R. conf. proc., 1958:* 220–231.

231 Flegel, Eduard R.
Der Benue von Gande bis Djen. *Petermanns geog. Mitt.*, 26, 1880: 220–228.

232 Floyer, R. K.
The Eastern Region of Nigeria. In *Population census of the Eastern Region of Nigeria, 1952:* 51–58. See [406]
A short descriptive account of Eastern Nigeria and its people.

233 Foote, Henry Grant (Mrs.)
Recollections of Central America and the West Coast of Africa. London, T. Cantley Newby, 1869. [6] 221p.
In two parts, with Part II (especially pp. 189–221) devoted to description of life in Lagos in the 1860's. Author's husband was appointed British consul in Lagos in 1860.

234 Forman, Brenda-Lu and Forman, Harrison
The land and people of Nigeria. Philadelphia, Lippincott, 1964. 160p. illus. (Portraits of the nations series).

234a Foureau, Fernand
D'Alger au Congo par le Tchad. See [236].

235 —Documents scientifiques de la Mission saharienne, Mission Foreau-Lamy, d' Alger au Congo par le Tchad. Paris, Masson, 1903–05. 3v. illus., maps, + atlas of 17 folded maps. (Société de géographie. Publication.)

236 —Mission saharienne Foreau-Lamy. D'Alger au Congo par le Tchad. Paris, Masson, 1962. 11, 829p. front., illus., map.
Includes a section on Bornu and the Lake Chad region (pp. 616–674)

237 France. Ministère des colonies.
Documents scientifiques de la mission Tilho (1906–1909) Paris, Imprimerie nationale, 1910–11. 2v. illus., maps.

238 Fraser, Douglas C.
Impressions: Nigeria, 1925. London,

Herbert Jenkins, 1925. 188p. front., illus., map.

239 Fremantle, John Morton, *ed.*
Gazetteer of Muri Province (up to December, 1919.) [London Waterlow, 1920] [1] iii, 77p.

240 —Two African journals & other papers of the late John Morton Fremantle. Edited by A. F. Fremantle. London, 1938. 95p.
"Printed for private circulation"— T-p. Author joined the Northern Nigeria administration in 1904, working at different times in Kano, Kabba and other places. His journals represent a record of people, places, life and events.

241 Gall, F. B.
Gazetteer of Bauchi Province. London, Waterlow, 1920. 32p. repr. London, Frank Cass, 1971.

242 Galloway, A. D.
Missionary impact on Nigeria. *Nigeria, 1960:* 58–65, illus.

242a Gallwey, H. L. See Galway, Henry Lionel.

243 *Galway, Henry Lionel
Pioneering in Nigeria. *Roy. geog. soc. Austr. South Aust. Branch,* 16, 1914: 77–107.

244 Gana, M. Abba
Our land & people, part II—the North. Lagos, Crownbird publications, Public relations dept., 1953. 16p. illus. map. (Crownbird series, no. 32)

245 Gertzel, C.
The early years of an African trader; John Holt: 1862–1874. *Ibadan,* (10) Nov. 1960: 12–16.
Biographical sketch of the pioneering days of John Holt, founder of the trading firm that still goes by his name.

246 Geschichte und Geschichtsbild Afrikas. Berlin, Akademie-Verlag, 1960. [vii] 230p. maps. (Studien zur Kolonialgeschichte und Geschichte der nationalen und kolonialen Befreiungsbewegung, v. 2)
Papers read at a symposium on the modern and contemporary history of Africa. Two papers—*Zur historischen und sozialen Bedeutung der Fulbe-Hegemonie,* by Jean Suret-Canale (pp. 29–59) and *Die jüngste Etappe der Unabhängigkeitsbewegung Nigerias 1957 bis 1958,* by M. Achufusi (pp. 124–144)— are especially relevant.

247 Gilles, Helen Trybulowski
Nigeria: from the Bight of Benin to Africa's desert sands. *National geog. mag.,* 85 (5) May 1944: 537–568, map.

248 Gilmour, T. L.
The two Nigerias. *J. Afr. soc.,* 11 (43) Apr. 1912: 275–284.
A review article on C. W. J. Orr's *The making of Northern Nigeria,* [441] and E. D. Morel's *Nigeria: its peoples and its problems* [392].

249 Gollock, G. A.
Sons of Africa. New York, Friendship press, 1928. 241p.

Includes a brief account [p. 199–203] of Garrick Sokari Braid, known as Elijah II, who founded a Church of his own with a large following in the Niger delta area.

250 Gowers, W. F.
Gazetteer of Kano Province. London, Waterlow, 1921. 56p. map., repr. London, Frank Cass, 1971.

251 Great Britain. Commission to enquire into the fears of minorities and the means of allaying them.
Report. [Henry Willink, Chairman] London, H.M.S.O., 1958. vii, 114p. maps (G.B. Parliament. Papers by Command, cmnd. 505).
Report of the "Minorities commission" appointed to investigate the fears of ethnic minorities in Nigeria and the means of allaying them.

252 —Foreign office.
Report by Major Macdonald of his visit as Her Majesty's commissioner to the Niger and Oil Rivers. London, 1890. 102p.

253 Green, C. Sylvester
New Nigeria: Southern Baptists at work in Africa. Richmond, Va., Foreign Mission Board, Southern Baptist Convention, 1936. 142p. front., illus., bibliog.
"A fresh and original presentation of the story of Southern Baptist missions in Nigeria"—Foreword. Chapter 1 (pp. 13–32) gives a brief historical and descriptive sketch of the Country, and chapter 2 (pp. 33–54) is an ethnographic sketch of the Yoruba.

254 Green, Lawrence G.
White man's grave: the story of the West African coast—the cities, sea-ports and castles, white exiles and black magic. London, Stanley Paul, 1954. 249p. front., illus.

255 Groves, C. P.
The planting of christianity in Africa. London, Lutterworth press, 1948–1958. 4v. maps.
A comprehensive history of Christianity in Africa from its first introduction into pre-Roman Egypt to the present day.

256 Gunther, John
Inside Africa. London, H. Hamilton, 1955. xi, 959p. bibliog.
Nigeria, pp. 731–774.

257 Haig, E. F. G.
Nigerian sketches. London, G. Allen & Unwin, 1931. 251p.
Sketches of life and events in Southeastern Nigeria.

258 Hailey, William Malcolm
An African survey; a study of problems arising in Africa south of the Sahara. Issued by the committee of the African Research Survey under the auspices of the Royal Institute of International Affairs. London, O.U.P., 1938. xxviii, 1837p. map.
A general, comprehensive survey of

political, economic, social, educational and administrative conditions in Africa and the problems they pose.

259 ——Revised ed. London, O.U.P., 1957. xxviii, 1676p. maps.
This ed. brings the survey to 1955.

260 Hall, Herbert C. (Johnny)
Barrack and bush in Northern Nigeria. London, G. Allen & Unwin, 1923. 154p. front., illus.

261 Hallett, Robin
The pattern of Northern Nigerian history. Kaduna, Information division, Ministry of internal affairs, 1959. 28p. illus., map.
Brief account of Northern Nigerian history up to the British administration. First appeared as an article with the title "Light on the past" in the Ministry's Northern Region Self Govt. publication: Advancing in good order (March 1959).

262 ——Records of the African Association, 1788–1831, edited with an introduction by Robin Hallett for the Royal geographical society. London, T. Nelson, 1964. viii, 318p.

263 Hänel, Karl
Nigerien; am Nil der Schwarzen. Leipzig, Wilhelm Goldmann Verlag, 1943 146p. bibliog.

264 Hano, *Carthaginian navigator*
The periplus of Hano; a voyage of discovery down the West African coats, by a Carthaginian admiral of the fifth century B.C. Translated from the Greek by Wilfred H. Schoff, with explanatory passages quoted from numerous authors. Philadelphia, Commercial museum, 1912. [ii] 28p. illus,. map.

265 Harden, D. B.
The Phoenicians on the West Coast of Africa. *Antiquity,* 22 (87) Sept. 1948: 141–150.
Stories of Phoenician exploration of the West African coast from ancient writers.

266 Harford, John
A voyage to the African Oil Rivers twenty-five years ago. In *West African studies, by M. H. Kingsley, 1899:* 567–611, map.
Describes his trading adventures in West Africa which took him to Bonny, Opobo, Qua Iboe and other centres in the Oil rivers.

267 Hartman, Robert
Die Völker Afrikas. Leipzig, F. A. Brockhaus, 1879. xxiii, 341p. illus.

268 Harward, F. H.
Education in Nigeria. *J. Afr. soc.,* 15 (59) Apr. 1916: 216–224.
A brief review of education in Southern Nigeria by the then Inspector of Schools.

269 Hastings, Archibald Charles Gardiner
Nigerian days. With an introduction by R. B. Cunninghame. London, John Lane, 1925. xii, 255p. front., plates, maps.
Reminiscences of author's eighteen

years in Nigeria as an administrative officer from 1906 to 1925.

270 ——The voyage of the *Dayspring*: being the journal of the late Sir John Hawley Glover, together with some account of the exploration up the Niger river in 1857. London, John Lane, 1926. x, 230p. illus.

271 Haywood, Austin Hubert Wightwick
Sport & service in Africa: a record of big game shooting, campaigning & adventure in the hinterland of Nigeria, the Cameroons, Togoland, & c., with an account of the ways of native soldiers & inhabitants & a description of their villages & customs as well as of the fauna and flora. London, Seeley, Service, 1926. 285p. front., illus., map.

272 Hazzledine, George Douglas
The white man in Nigeria. London, E. Arnold, 1904. xv, 228p. illus., map.
General review of conditions—administrative, economic and human—in Northern Nigeria.

273 Heneker, William Charles Gifford
Bush warfare. London, Hugh Ress, 1907. [vii] 196, viiip. illus., maps, plans.
On the organisation and tactics of warfare in West Africa. Includes description of the organisation and tactics of the Bida-Ilorin, Benin, Afikpo, Aro, and other expeditions.

274 Hermon-Hodge, Henry Baldwin
Gazetteer of Ilorin Province. London, G. Allen & Unwin, 1929. 301p. front., illus., map, bibliog.

275 ——Up against it in Nigeria, by Langa Langa [pseud.] New York, Dutton, 1922. 244p. illus., (incl. ports).
Personal narrative of a former administrative officer in Northern Nigeria.

275a Hiskett, M., *tr.*
Tazyin al-Waraqat. See [394].

276 Hodgkin, Thomas
Islam, history and politics. *J. mod. Afr. stud.,* 1, 1963: 91–97.

277 ——Islam in West Africa. *Afr. South,* 2 (3) 1958: 89–99.

278 ——Nigerian perspectives: an historical anthology. London, O.U.P., 1960. xx, 340p. front., plates, maps.

279 Hofland, Barbara
Africa described in its ancient and present state; including accounts from Bruce . . . Park . . . Portuguese missionaries and others . . . New ed. London, A. K. Newman, 1834. viii, 292p.
Includes details taken from Denham, Oudney, Clapperton and the Landers. "Intended for the use of young persons and schools"—t.-p.

280 Hogben, Sidney John
The Muhammadan emirates of Nigeria. London, O.U.P., 1930. xii, 204p. maps, tables, bibliog.
A general history of Northern Nigeria is followed by sketches of the history of

the various emirates, arranged under their respective provinces.

281 Hogben, Sidney John and Kirk-Greene, Anthony Hamilton Millard
The emirates of Northern Nigeria; a preliminary survey of their historical traditions. London, O.U.P., 1966. xxvii, 638p. front., illus., maps, bibliog.
A revised and enlarged edition of the first author's *Muhammadan emirates of Nigeria.*

282 Holland, J. H.
The useful plants of Nigeria. London, 1908–1922. 4v. (963p.) (Kew bull. Additional ser., 9).

283 Holles, Robert O.
The bribe scorners. London, Harrap, 1956. 202p.
A novel.

284 Hope, R. E.
With pen and camera in Nigeria. *J. Manch. geog. soc.,* 23, 1907: 115–151.

285 Hopkins, A. G.
Richard Beale Blaize, 1845–1904: merchant prince of West Africa. *Tarikh,* 1 (2) 1966: 70–79, illus.

286 Horton, James Africanus Beale
West African countries and peoples, British and natives: With the requirements necessary for establishing that self-government recommended by the committee of the House of Commons, 1865; and a vindication of the African race. London, W. J. Johnson, 1868. viii, 287p.
Includes account of "Empire of the Eboes", pp. 171–198.

287 Houdas, Octave Victor, *trans.*
Documents arabes relatifs à l'histoire du Soudan: Tedzkiret en-Nisian fi Akhbar Molouk es Soudan. Traduction française par H. O. Paris, Leroux, 1901. [14] 416p. (Publications de l'Ecole des langues orientales vivantes, 4th ser., vols. 19–20).
French translation of the Arabic text published in 1899 by Houdas and Benoist. Includes Hajji Sa'id's History of Sokoto, 1817–1849, for the English translation of which, see [2489].

288 Houdas, Octave Victor, *trans.*
Tarikh es-Soudan. See [89].

289 Howard, C., *ed.*
West African explorers: selections chosen . . . by C. Howard, with an introduction by J. H. Plumb. London, O.U.P., 1951. ix, 598p.
Anthology of extracts from the writings of explorers of Africa from 1600–1914.

290 Hulbert, Charles
African fragments; comprising William Leo's narrative of two expeditions into the interior of Africa, the travels of a tartar to Timbuctoo; sketch of Whydah, customs of the Gold Coast, and other articles by Captain Pierce. . . . Shrewsbury [Privately printed] 1826. 64p.
Bound with his *Museum Africanum.*

291 Hunwick, J. O.
Islam in West Africa, A.D. 1000–1800. In *A thousand years of West African history, ed. J. F. A. Ajayi and I. Espie, 1965: 113–130.*

292 Hutchinson, Edward
Ascent of the River Binué in August 1879; with remarks on the systems of the Shary and Binue, *J. & proc. Roy. geog. soc.,* (5) May 1880: 289–305, map.

293 Hutchinson, Thomas Joseph
Impressions of Western Africa, with remarks on the diseases of the climate and a report on the peculiarities of trade up the rivers in the Bight of Biafra. London, Longman, Brown, Green, Longmans, & Roberts, 1858. xvi, 313p.
Author, the British consul for the Bight of Biafra (1856?–1865) here gives a detailed account of the West African coast as he saw it in the middle of the 19th century. Chapters V–XI (pp. 71–172) concern the area extending from Whydah to the Cameroons, with Chapters VIII to XI devoted to Old Calabar and the Egbo cult.

294 —Narrative of the Niger, Tshadda and Binue exploration: including a report on the position and prospects of trade up those rivers, with remarks on the malaria and fevers of Western Africa. London, Longman, Brown, Green, and Longmans, 1855, repr. London, Frank Cass, 1966. viii, 267p. map.

295 —Ten years' wanderings among the Ethiopians; with sketches of the manners and customs of the civilized and uncivilized tribes, from Senegal to Gaboon. London, Hurst and Blackett, 1861, repr. London, Frank Cass, 1967. xx, 329p. front.

296 Huxley, Elspeth Josceline
Four guineas: a journey through West Africa. London, Chatto & Windus, 1954. xi, 303p, illus., maps.
A journey through Gambia, Sierra Leone, Gold Coast (Ghana) and Nigeria. Describes these countries and the political and social life of each. Nigeria, pp. 164–295.

297 Ibadan. University and Nsukka. University of Nigeria.
Eastern Nigeria history research scheme. Ibadan, University [1966] 4p. map.
Brief explanation of the proposed scheme, by its director Dr. K. O. Dike, followed by estimate of the cost.

298 Ibadan. University. Institute of African Studies. First year, 1960–63. Ibadan, University press [1965?] 16p.

299 —Institute research programme, 1963–1964. *Afr. Notes,* 1 (1) Oct. 1963: 1–31.

300 Ibn Batuta
Travels in Asia and Africa, 1325–1354, translated and selected by H. A. R. Gibb. With an introduction and notes. London, G. Routledge, 1929. vii, 398p. front., illus., maps. (Broadway travellers.)

301 Igwe, D. C.

The need of enclosure and land resettlement in Nigerian agriculture. *Trop. agric.*, 31 (1) Jan. 1954: 57–68.

301a Jackson, James Grey
An account of Timbuctoo and Housa ...
See [2412].

302 Jacob, S. M.
Nigeria. London, Published on behalf of the Govt. of Nigeria by the Crown agents for the colonies, 1933. viii, 155p. map. (Census of Nigeria, 1931, v. 1.)
This forms the general report on the whole census of 1931, including the medical census. Gives history of the census, procedures followed, detailed results, with data on age, sex, immigration, disease, longevity, stature, etc.

303 Jacolliot, Louis
Voyage aux rives du Niger au Bénin et dans le Borgou. Paris, Flammarion, [1879] 308p.

303a Jean-Léon de l'Africain. See Leo Africanus.

304 Jeekel, C. A.
Onze Bezittingen op de Kust van Guinea. Amsterdam, C. F. Steinler, 1869. [iii] 83p. front. (map).

305 Jeffreys, M. D. W.
Arab knowledge of the Niger's course. *Africa*, 25 (1) 1955: 84–90.

306 Johnson, Henry
A journey up the Niger, in the autumn of 1877. London, C.M.S. house, [1878] 66p. front. (map).
Rev. Johnson, an African missionary associated with the Sierra Leone and Yoruba Missions was later transferred to the Niger Mission and appointed Archdeacon of the Upper Niger. In this account of his first visit to the Mission in company of Bishop Crowther in 1877, he gives his impressions of the country from the coast up to Bida. The coastal stations of Brass, New Calabar and Bonny come in for special treatment.

307 Johnston, Harry Hamilton
A history of the colonization of Africa by alien races. New ed. revised throughout and considerably enlarged. Cambridge, University press, 1913. xvi, 505p. maps.
General summary of the history of Africa from the era of prehistoric race migrations to the European administration of the 20th century. 1st edition published in 1899.

308 —Notes [on Ptolemy's West Africa] *J. Afr. soc.*, 14 (56) Jl. 1915: 423–426.
Comments on Migeod's interpretation of Ptolemy's map of West Africa [380] Notes on p. 426 early commercial links between Northern Nigeria and the Mediterranean and Romanised Egypt.

309 —Pioneers in West Africa. London. Blackie, 1912. 336p. front., plates.
History of early explorations in West Africa. Mostly the explorations of Mungo Park, Denham, Clapperton and the Landers.

310 Johnstone, Keith, *ed.*
Stanford's compendium of geography and travel. Based on Hellwald's "Die Erde und ihre Völker": Africa, edited and extended by Keith Johnstone, with ethnological appendix by A. H. Keane. London, Edward Stanford, 1878. xiv, 611p. front., illus., maps.
Specifically relevant sections are chapters 11 to 13 (especially pp. 151–188) which carry useful geographical and ethnographic information on parts of Nigeria.

311 — —2nd rev. ed. 1907.

311a Jones, B. C.
Medical census, Northern Provinces. See [403].

312 Kāti, Mahmūd
Tarikh el-fettach; ou Chronique du chercheur; pour servir à l'histoire des villes, des armées et des principaux personnages par Mahmoûd Kāti ben el-Hâdj el-Motaouakkel Kāti et l'un de ses petits-fils; traduction française accompagnée de notes par O. Houdas, M. Delafosse. Paris, Ernest Leroux, 1913. 363p. map. (Publication de l'école des langues orientales vivantes).

313 Kemmer, V. A. D.
Katsina Ala as seen by an Ijaw. *Nig. mag.*, (22) 1944: 71–72.

314 Kennedy, J. D.
The Jos Plateau, its people and some aspects of forestry. *Empire forestry rev.*, 28 (2) Je. 1949: 152–161.

315 Kingsley, Mary Henrietta
The story of West Africa. London, H. Marshall [n.d.] viii, 169p. (Story of the empire series.)
History of English exploration, trade and administration in West Africa.

316 —Travels in West Africa: Congo français, Corisco and Cameroons. London, Macmillan, 1897. xvi, 743p. front., illus.
Pages 548–627 on the Cameroons, with brief mention of a visit to Calabar on p. 627. 2nd ed., 1900; 3rd ed., with an introduction, by John E. Flint. London, Frank Cass, 1965. xxxii, 743p. illus. maps.

317 —West African studies. London, Macmillan, 1899. xxiv, 639p. front., illus., map.
There are useful appendices on (1) the inhabitants of the Niger Coast Protectorate, by M. le comte C. N. de Cardi [157] (2) A voyage to the African Oil Rivers twenty-five years ago, by John Harford [266] and (3) Trade goods used in the early trade with Africa [930] 2nd ed., 1901; 3rd ed., with an introduction, by John E. Flint. London, Frank Cass, 1964. lxviii, 507p. illus. map. The revised 2nd edition and the 3rd edition do not contain the appendices of the first edition.

318 Kirk-Greene, Anthony Hamilton Millard

Adamawa past and present: an historical approach to the development of a Northern Cameroons Province. London, O.U.P., for International African institute, 1958. ix, 230p. maps, bibliog.

History of British colonization and administration, followed in pp. 125–179 by separate histories of the three Divisions—Adamawa, Muri and Numan—from the Fulani invasions of the 19th century to the British administration. Chapter II (pp. 15–25) gives a general ethnological account in which are noted the Jukun, Chamba, Bata, Marghi, Highi, Mumuye and Fulani.

319 —The early empires of Northern Nigeria. *W. Afr. annual,* 1958: 42–44, 76, illus., map.

319a —The emirates of Northern Nigeria. See [281].

320 —Expansion on the Benue, 1830–1900: a review of the exploration and commercial history of the River Benue, with special reference to the administration of the Royal Niger company. *J. Hist. soc. Nig.,* 1 (3) Dec. 1958: 215–237.

An extended and well documented review encompassing exploration, and commercial and administrative activities from Lander's journey in 1830 to Lugard and the Northern Nigeria Protectorate of 1900.

321 —Nigerian explorers. *Nigeria, 1960:* 66–74, illus.

Includes extracts from explorers' accounts.

322 —This is Northern Nigeria: background to an invitation. Illustrations by J. F. Hindle. Kaduna, Govt. printer, 1955. 96p. front., illus., maps.

An excellent introduction to Northern Nigeria, giving brief descriptions of the region, its peoples, its history and its present state. Intended to inform oversea officials who might wish to work in the region.

323 Kisch, Martin S.
Letters and sketches from Northern Nigeria. London, Chatto & Windus, 1910. xii, 232p. front., illus., maps, bibliog.

324 Knight, Charles
History of the expansion of evangelical christianity in Nigeria. 1951.
D.Th. Degree, S. Baptist Theological Seminary.

325 Kumm, Hermann Karl Wilhelm
From Hausaland to Egypt through the Sudan. *Geog. j.,* 36, Jl.–Dec. 1910: 148–159, illus., maps.
The illustrations include sketches showing characteristic hair styles and face types of various tribes, among them Hausa, Angas and Fulani. See also [2414].

326 —From Hausaland to Egypt. *Scot. geog. mag.,* 27, 1911: 225–242, illus., map.
See also [2414].

327 Labarthe, P.
Voyage à la Côte de Guinée; ou, Description des côtes d'Afrique, depuis le cap Tagrin jusqu'au cap de Lopez-Gonzalues . . . Paris, Chery Debray, 1803 310p. front. (map).

328 Lair, Vene V.
Implications of governmental, educational and social changes in developing a Baptist college in Nigeria. 1960.
D.R.E. thesis, Southwestern Baptist Theological Seminary.

329 Laird, Mcgregor and Oldfield, R. A. K.
Narrative of an expedition into the interior of Africa, by the river Niger, in the steam-vessels Quorra and Alburkah, in 1832, 1833 and 1834. London, R. Bentley, 1837. 2v. front., repr. London, Frank Cass, 1971.

330 Lander, Richard Lemon
Records of Captain Clapperton's last expedition to Africa: by Richard Lander, his faithful attendant, and the only surviving member of the expedition: with the subsequent adventures of the author. London, H. Colburn and R. Bentley, 1830, repr. London, Frank Cass, 1967. 2v. front. (port.) illus.

331 Lander, Richard Lemon and Lander, John
Extracts from the journal of an expedition to determine the course and termination of the Niger; more properly named Quorra, from Yáoori to the sea. *J.R. geog. soc.,* 1, 1831: 179–191.

332 —Journal of an expedition to explore the course and termination of the Niger: with a narrative of a voyage down that river to its termination. London, J. Murray, 1832. 3v. front., illus., map.

333 —The Niger journal of Richard and John Lander, edited, abridged and introduced by Robin Hallett. London, Routledge & K. Paul, 1965. ix, 317p. illus., maps.

334 Landolphe, Jean François
Mémoires du capitaine Landolphe, contenant l'histoire de ses voyages pendant trente-six ans, aux côtes d'Afrique et aux deux Amériques; rédigés sur son manuscrit, par J. S. Quesne. Paris, A. Bertrand, 1823. 2v. front. (ports) plan.
Memoirs of a French slave dealer who visited Benin, Warri, and other centres in the Guinea Coast in 1778 and 1786.

334a Langa Langa See Hermon-Hodge, Henry Baldwin.

335 Large, W. H.
Over the hills to Yola. *Nig. mag.,* (29) 1948: 180–221, illus., map.

336 Larymore, Constance
A resident's wife in Nigeria. London, G. Routledge, 1908. xiii, 306p. front. (port.) illus.
Record of her five years life, travels and impressions in Nigeria.

337 Lasbrey, B.
The Church in Nigeria. *East & West rev.,* 13 (1) Jan. 1947: 18–22.

338 Latham, Norah
A sketch-map history of West Africa.
London, Hulton educational publica-
tions, 1959. 80p.
Brief sketches of the main events in
West African history, supported with
outline maps.

339 —The use of source material in the
teaching of history. *J. Hist. soc. Nig.,*
1 (2) Dec. 1957: 145–155.
Advocates the use of source materials,
including archaeological remains, by the
teacher in teaching history in Nigerian
schools.

340 Leith-Ross, Sylvia
A glimpse of Nigeria fifty years ago. (A
talk given to the Jos Branch) *Nig. field,*
22 (4) Oct. 1957: 160–164.
Impressions of Northern Nigeria,
especially Zungeru, in 1907–1910.

341 Lembezat, Bertrand
Les populations païennes du nord-
Cameroun et de l'Adamaoua, Paris,
Presses universitaires de France, 1961.
252p. map at end. (Monographies
ethnologiques africaines.)

342 Lenfant, E. A.
De l'Atlantique au Tchad par la voie
Niger-Benoué—Toubouri-Logone.
Afrique française, 14, 1904: 186–199,
illus. map.

343 —From the Atlantic to the Chad by the
Niger and the Benue. *Scot. geog. mag.,*
20, 1900: 306–316, map.
English version of [342].

344 Leo Africanus
Description de l'Afrique. Nouvelle
édition traduite de l'Italien par A.
Épaulard, et annotée par A. Épaulard,
Th. Monod, H. Lhote et R. Mauny.
Paris, Adrien-Maisonneuve, 1956. 2v.
(xvi, 629p.) front., maps, facsims.
A modern translation based on an
early Italian edition (Ramusio's)
published in Venice in 1550. See notes
below [345].

345 —The history and description of Africa
and of the notable things therein contained, written by Al-Hassan Ibn-
Mohammed Al-Wezaz al-Fasi, a moor,
baptised as Giovanni Leone, but better
known as Leo Africanus. Done into
English in the year 1600, by John Pory,
and now edited, with an introduction
and notes by Robert Brown. London,
Hakluyt society, 1896. 3v. illus., maps
(Hakluyt society publication, v. 92–94).
The original English edition by Pory
which appeared in 1600 was translated
from the Italian edition of Ramusio
published 1550. Leo Africanus travelled
extensively in the Western Sudan. The
kingdoms of Kano, Casena, Zegzeg,
Zanfara and Borno which he visited
about 1510 are all described in vol. III
pp. 828–835, with accompanying explanatory notes at pp. 848–851.

346 Lethbridge, Alan Bourchier
West Africa the elusive. London, John
Bale & Danielsson [1921] viii, 321p.
front., plates, map.

347 Lewis, L. J.
Society, schools and progress in Nigeria.
Oxford, Pergamon press, 1965. xv, 160p.
bibliog.

348 Lindsay, Anne
Africa on a shoestring. London, Mills &
Boon, 1960. 190p.

Lugard, Flora Louisa (Shaw) See Shaw,
Flora

349 Lugard, Frederick John Dealtry
The diaries of Lord Lugard. Volume
four: Nigeria, 1894–5 and 1898, edited
by Margery Perham and Mary Bull.
London, Faber, 1963. 444p. front.,
maps, bibliog.

350 —The dual mandate in British tropical
Africa. Edinburgh, London, W.
Blackwood, 1922. 643p.

350a ——Fifth Edition, with an introduction,
by Margery Perham. London, Frank
Cass, 1965. xlix, 643p.

351 —Instructions to political and other
officers, on subjects chiefly political and
administrative. Revised September
1906. London, Waterlow, 1906. 2v.
(319p.)
Series of instructions or "political
memoranda" written by Lugard in 1905
when High Commissioner for Northern
Nigeria, to serve as guides to administrative officers in the correct execution of
their duties.

352 —Journey in West Africa, and some
points of contrast. *Scot. geog. mag.,* 11,
1895: 609–625.

353 —Northern Nigeria. *Geog. j.,* 23 (1)
Jan. 1904: 1–29, illus., map.

354 —Revision of instructions to political
officers on subjects chiefly political &
administrative, 1913–1918. London,
Waterlow, 1919. 3v. (455p.)
Revision of [351], repr. London,
Frank Cass, 1970.

355 Lyon, George Francis.
A narrative of travels in Northern Africa
in the years 1818, 19, and 20; accompanied by geographical notices of
Soudan, and of the course of the Niger.
With a chart of the routes, and a variety
of coloured plates, illustrative of the
costumes of the several natives of
Northern Africa. London, J. Murray,
1821, repr. London, Frank Cass, 1966.
xii, 384p. illus., map.
Author travelled as far South as
Tegerhi in Southern Libya. The "geographical notices" descriptive of parts
of the Western Sudan were gathered
from Arab travellers.

356 Macdonald, Claude M.
Exploration of the Benue and its northern
tributary the Kebbi. *Proc. Roy. geog.
soc.,* 13 (8) Aug. 1891: 449–477, map.
on p. 512.

357 Macintyre, J. L.
Islam in Northern Nigeria. *Mosl. world,*
2, 1912: 144–151.

358 Mackenzie, Donald
The flooding of the Sahara: an account
of the proposed plan for opening central
Africa for commerce and civilization
from the North-west coast, with a description of Soudan and western Sahara,
and notes on ancient manuscripts, etc.
London, Sampson Low, Marston,
Searle & Rivington, 1877. xx, 287p.
front., illus., map.
Descriptions of important centres and
regions of Africa (including "Gando"
and the "Province of Yariba", Sokoto,
Kano, Bornu and the Chad area, pp. 11–
159) followed by a survey of the then
system of trade and a proposal to flood
the plain of El Juf with water from the
Atlantic by clearing the sand around
Sakiet El Hamra or Red Channel.
Presented to the Chamber of Commerce
of Great Britain.

359 Mackenzie, W. J. M. and Robinson,
Kenneth
Five elections in Africa: a group of
electoral studies. Oxford, Clarendon
press, 1960. xi, 496p. plates, maps,
Elections in Africa, as a democratic
institution of foreign origin, examined
through the study of five actual elections
in parts of the continent. Includes the
Western and Eastern Nigeria elections of
1956 and 1957 respectively.

360 Macleod, Olive
Chiefs and cities of central Africa, across
Lake Chad by way of British, French
and German territories. London, W.
Blackwood, 1912. xiv, 300p. front.,
illus., map.
Account of a journey undertaken
along with Mr. & Mrs. P. A. Talbot from
Aug. 1910–May 1911, starting in Forca-
dos and going up the Niger and Benue to
Lake Chad, Kano, the Cameroons and
the Chad Territory.

361 Macmillan, Allister, comp.
The red book of West Africa: historical
and descriptive, commercial and industrial facts, figures & resources.
London, W. H. & L. Collingridge, 1920,
repr. London, Frank Cass, 1968. 312p.
illus.
A profusely illustrated work of commercial and general reference on Gambia,
Sierra Leone, Gold Coast and Nigeria,
with articles on topography, history,
commerce, agriculture, industry, education, transport, etc., on each of these
countries. Directories of major cities
(Lagos, Calabar and Kano for Nigeria)
are also included, as well as biographical
sections. The latter for Nigeria covers
pp. 128–137, with some 67 entries. Considerable space given to commercial
houses and agents.

362 Maiden, R. L. B.
Historical sketches; studies in explora-
tion and history African and Islamic.
Zaria, N.R.L.A., 1955. v. 115p. illus.

363 Mansfeld, Alfred
Westafrika. Aus Urwald und Steppe

zwischen Crossfluss und Benue. München, G. Müller, 1928. viii, 76p.

364 Marees, Pieter de
Beschryvinghe ende historische verhael
van het Gout koninckrijck van Gunea
anders de Gout-Custe de Mina genaemt
liggende in het deel van Africa, uitg.
door S. P. L'Honoré Naber. S'Graven-
hage, M. Nijhoff, 1912. 2 p.l. [vii]–
lxxvi, 11., 314p. illus., map, bibliog.
(Werken uitg. door de Linschoten-
vereeniging, v.)
S. P. L'Honoré Naber's edition of an
early work on travel in West Africa. It
carries a reproduction of the original
title page, and includes a useful description of Benin, apparently by Derick
Ruiters, see [1751]. The original work,
first published in 1602, quickly went
through several editions, including a
translation into French, and was drawn
on by later writers, among them Dapper
and Ogilby.

365 Marquardsen, Hugo
Der Niger-Benuë. Eine historisch-geo-
graphische Beschreibung der natürlichen
Verbindung Nord-Kameruns mit der
Küste. Berlin, 1909. 81p. illus.

366 Mattei, A.
Bas Niger, Bénoué, Dahomey. Grenoble,
Impr. E. Vallier, 1890. xv, 196p. illus.
Mattei, a French consul at Brass and
an agent of Compagnie française de
l'Afrique equatoriale, travelled up the
Niger and Benue several times in the
1880's. In this account he describes the
areas he visited and the life and customs
of the people.

367 *—Rapports sur le Niger et le Bénoué.
Archives des missions scientifiques et
littéraires, 3rd ser. 10, 1883: 417–431.

368 Mauny, Raymond
Nigeria as seen by Leo Africanus, 1526.
Nig. mag., (69) Aug. 1961: 189–190.

369 —Tableau géographique de l'ouest
Africain au moyen age; d'après les
sources écrites, la tradition et l'archéologie. Dakar, IFAN, 1961. 587p. illus.,
maps, bibliog.
Lengthy bibliography, covering pp.
547–575.

370 Maxwell, John Lowry
Half a century of grace: a jubilee history
of the Sudan United Mission. London
S.U.M., [1954?] 330p. maps.

371 —Nigeria: the land, the people and
Christian progress. London, World
dominion, press, 1927. 164p. maps.
(World dominion survey series.)

372 Maxwell, Joseph Renner
Advantages and disadvantages of European intercourse with the West Coast of
Africa: a lecture delivered before the
members of St. Jude's Institute, Mildway
Park, London, Smart & Allen, 1881.
23p.

373 —The negro question; or Hints for the
physical improvement of the negro race

with special reference to West Africa. London, T. Fisher Unwin, 1892. 188p.

374 May, Jacques M.
The ecology of malnutrition in middle Africa (Ghana, Nigeria, Republic of the Congo, Rwanda Burundi and the former French Equatorial Africa) New York, Hafner, 1965. xvi, 255p. maps, bibliog.
Outlines the conditions under which food is produced in West and Equatorial Africa and the problems resulting from the current transition from a subsistence economy and a tribal way of life to a technological society. Nigeria, pp. 39–82.

375 Meek, Charles Kingsley
The Niger and the Classics: the history of a name. *J. Afr. hist.*, 1 (1) 1960: 1–17.

376 Mellor, F. H.
The British protectorate in Northern Nigeria. *Geog. mag.*, 6 (4) Feb. 1938: 225–244.

377 —Sword & spear. London, Selwyn & Blount [1934?] 288p. front., illus., map.
Experiences of a soldier, and later a police officer in India, Anatolia, Constantinople, and Northern Nigeria where he arrived in 1925, and served as Assistant Commissioner of Police.

378 *Migeod, C. O.
Gazetteer of Yola Province. Lagos, Govt. printer, 1927, repr. London, Frank Cass, 1971.

379 Migeod, Frederick William Hugh
British Cameroons, its tribes and natural features. *J. Afr. soc.*, 23 (91) Apr. 1924: 176–187, illus.
The former Northern and Southern Cameroons.

380 —Notes on West Africa according to Ptolemy. *J. Afr. soc.*, 14 (56) Jl. 1915: 414–422, map.
Interpretation of a number of 15th and 16th century maps based on Ptolemy's, with a view to throwing light on the early exploration of West Africa. Shows that the Fulani were already in the Futa Jalon region in the days of Ptolemy. See also comment on this article by H. H. Johnston, ibid., pp. 423–426. [308.]

380a —Through Nigeria to Lake Chad. See [3912].

381 Miller, Ethel P.
Change here for Kano: reminiscences of fifty years in Nigeria. Zaria, Gaskiya corporation, 1959. [2] ii, 27p.

382 Miller, Walter Richard Samuel
For Africans only. London, United society for Christian literature, 1950. 80p.
On varied themes—race prejudice, leadership, friendship, force, bribery and corruption, sex, etc., in Nigeria.

383 —Have we failed in Nigeria? London, United society for Christian literature, 1947. 156p. illus.

384 —Reflections of a pioneer. London, C.M.S., 1936. [iv] 227p. front., illus.
Reminiscences of Dr. Miller's mis-

sionary work in Northern Nigeria, mostly in Zaria, from 1900 to the 1930's.

385 —Yesterday and tomorrow in Northern Nigeria. London, Student Christian movement press, 1938. xvi, 182p. illus.

386 Mockler-Ferryman, A. F.
British Nigeria. *J. Afr. soc.*, 1 (2) Jan. 1902: 160–173.
A summary of his book with the same title [387].

387 —British Nigeria: a geographical and historical description of the British possessions adjacent to the Niger River, West Africa. London, Cassell, 1902. viii, 351p. illus., map.

388 —British West Africa; its rise and progress. 2nd ed. London, Swan Sonnenschein, 1900. xvi, 512p. front., illus., maps.
2nd ed. of his Imperial Africa [389] Gives the history of British activities and possessions in West Africa. pp. 105–313 which deal with Nigeria contain a useful account from Park's explorations down to the consolidation of the Niger Coast Protectorate.

389 —Imperial Africa: the rise, progress and future of the British possessions in Africa. V. 1 British West Africa. London, Imperial press, 1898. xvi, 512p. front., illus., maps. (Imperial library, v. 1.)
2nd ed. published as *British West Africa; its rise and progress*. See notes under this. [388.]

390 —Up the Niger. Narrative of Claude Mcdonald's mission to the Niger and Benue Rivers, West Africa. To which is added a chapter on native musical instruments, by C. R. Day, London, G. Philip, 1892. xx, 326p. front., illus., map.
This mission was sent in 1889 by the British government to investigate the working of the Royal Niger Company against which there were many complaints. The narrative gives detailed account of their journeys in the Niger and Benue regions, with useful ethnographic data.

391 Morel, Edmund D.
Affairs of West Africa. London, W. Heinemann, 1902. xv, 382p. front., illus., maps (fold.).
On "the problems, racial, political and commercial . . . connected with the administration of West Africa by Great Britain"—Preface. Nigeria, pp. 35–173.

391a — —2nd Edition, with an introduction, by Kenneth Dike Nworah. London, Frank Cass, 1968. xxvii, 382p. illus. maps (fold.).

392 —Nigeria: its peoples and its problems. London, Smith, Elder, 1911. xviii, 266p. front., illus., maps (fold.).
Draws attention to both Northern and Southern Nigeria and to the problems facing their administrative officers and the responsibilities of the imperial government. Many of the

sections are revisions of articles published earlier by the author in 'The Times'. See a review—"The two Nigerias" by T. L. Gilmour. [248].

392a —— —3rd Edition, with an introduction, by Kenneth Dike Nworah. London, Frank Cass, 1968. xl, 264p. illus. maps (fold.).

393 Moseley, Lich H.
Regions of the Benue. *J. & proc. Roy. geog. soc.*, 14, 1899: 630–637, map.

394 Muḥammad, 'Abdullāh Ibn
Tazyin al-Waraqāt. Edited, with a translation and introductory study of the author's life and times, by M. Hiskett. Ibadan, University press, 1963. [xi] 144p. illus., map, bibliog.

394a Muhammad ibn 'Abd Allāh, called Batutah. See Ibn Batuta.

395 Murray, Hugh
Narrative of discovery and adventure in Africa, with illustration of the geology, mineralogy and zoology. 6th ed. London, T. Nelson, 1849. 472p. front.
Gives account of the major explorations in Africa, followed by detailed account of life and conditions in specific areas. West Africa, pp. 285–298, with "Adam's account of Benin, Waree and Bonny," pp. 295–296; Bonny and Old Calabar, pp. 296–297.

396 Mveng, Engelbert
Die afrikanische Kunst von gestern und das Afrika von heute. *Neues Afr.,* 3 (12) Dec. 1961: 475–479, illus.

397 *Nachtigal, Gustav
Briefe aus Nord-Central Afrika. *Petermanns Mitt.,* 1871: 130–150; 334–345.

398 Nduka, Otonti Amadi
Western education and the Nigerian cultural background. Ibadan, O.U.P., 1964, viii. 166p. illus., bibliog.
Brief history of the origins and development of Western education in Nigeria from the middle of the 19th century to date.

399 Neisser, Charles S.
Community development and mass education in British Nigeria. *Econ. dev. & cultural change,* 3 (4) Jl. 1955: 352–365.

400 Newland, H. Osman
West Africa: a handbook of practical information for the official, planter, miner, financier & trader. Edited, with an introduction by Evans Lewin. London, Daniel O'Connor, 1922. xi, 441p. front., col. map.
A description of West Africa under four headings: geology and history; ethnology and psychology; commercial exploitation; and administration, trade and transport.

401 Niane, Djibril Tamsir and Suret-Canale, Jean
Histoire de l'Afrique occidentale. Conakry, Ministère de l'éducation, 1960. 167p. maps.

402 Nigeria. Chief secretary's office.
The Nigeria handbook containing statistical and general information respecting the colony and protectorate. Lagos, Govt. printer, 1917–1953. 12v. maps, bibliog.
1st ed., 1917; 2nd ed., 1919; 3rd ed., 1921; 4th ed., 1923; 5th ed., 1924; 6th ed., 1925; 7th ed., 1926; 8th ed., 1927; 9th ed., 1929; 10th ed., 1933; 11th ed., 1936; 12th ed., 1953. A general handbook now o.p. Each edition carries general, statistical, economic, commercial and ethnographic data on Nigeria.

403 Nigeria
Census of Nigeria, 1931. London, published on behalf of the Government of Nigeria by the Crown agents for the colonies, 1932–1934. 6v. in 7.
v. 1. Nigeria, by S. M. Jacob. 1933. viii, 155p. map. [302.]
v. 2. Census of the Northern Provinces, by N. J. Brooke. 1933. 234p. map. [143.]
v. 2A. Village directory, Northern Provinces, by H. B. Cox. 1932. 46p. [144.]
v. 4. Census of Lagos, by H. N. G. Thompson. 1932. 53p.
v. 5. Medical census, Northern Provinces, by B. C. Jones. 1932. 92p.
v. 6. Medical census, Southern Provinces, by J. G. S. Turner, 1932. 101p. [545.]
Vol. 1 is a general report on the census for the whole country; vol. 2 gives details of the census for the North; vol. 2A "contains the Districts, Divisions, Emirates, Provinces and populations of all villages in the Northern Provinces."—Foreword.
Vol. 3 gives details for the South, vol. 4 for Lagos, and vol. 5 and 6 for the medical censuses in the North and South respectively. Vol. 2A. published by Government printer, Lagos.

404 Nigeria. Department of statistics.
Population census of Lagos, 1950. Lagos, Government statistician, 1951. 114p. map.

405 —Population census of Nigeria, 1952–53. Lagos, Census superintendent, 1954? 13p.
Summary of the census figures as published in the three Regional reports and thirty provincial bulletins.

406 —Population census of the Eastern Region of Nigeria, 1952. Bulletins nos. 1–8. Lagos, Census superintendent (Govt. statistician) 1956. 1v.
Various pagings. The bulletins were published separately. No. 1 surveys the Eastern Region as a whole, while nos. 2–8 contain detailed census results for the then provinces, viz:
Bulletin no. 2. Bamenda Province
Bulletin no. 3. Rivers Province
Bulletin no. 4. Ogoja Province
Bulletin no. 5. Cameroons
Bulletin no. 6. Calabar Province

Bulletin no. 7. Onitsha Province
Bulletin no. 8. Owerri Province

407 —Population census of the Northern
Region of Nigeria, 1952. Bulletins nos.
1–13. Lagos, Census superintendent
(Govt. statistician), 1954. 1v.
Various pagings. Bulletins published
separately. No. 1 surveys the Northern
region as a whole, while nos. 2–13 con-
tain detailed census results for the
provinces, viz:
Bulletin no. 2. Benue Province
Bulletin no. 3. Katsina Province
Bulletin no. 4. Zaria Province
Bulletin no. 5. Niger Province
Bulletin no. 6. Plateau Province
Bulletin no. 7. Bornu Province
Bulletin no. 8. Kano Province
Bulletin no. 9. Bauchi Province
Bulletin no. 10. Adamawa Province
Bulletin no. 11. Sokoto Province
Bulletin no. 12. Ilorin Province
Bulletin no. 13. Kabba Province

408 —Population census of the Western
Region of Nigeria, 1952. Bulletins nos.
1–9. Lagos, Census superintendent
(Govt. statistician), 1955. 1v.
Various pagings. Bulletins published
separately. No. 1 surveys the Western
Region as a whole, while nos. 2–9 con-
tain detailed census results for the pro-
vinces, viz:
Bulletin no. 2. Ijebu Province
Bulletin no. 3. Ondo Province
Bulletin no. 4. Oyo Province
Bulletin no. 5. Colony Province
Bulletin no. 6. Benin Province
Bulletin no. 7. Ibadan Province
Bulletin no. 8. Abeokuta Province
Bulletin no. 9. Delta Province

409 Nigeria. Northern. Information services.
Social and economic progress in the
Northern Region of Nigeria. Kaduna,
Govt. printer, 1955. 97p. front., illus.,
map.
Agricultural, economic and social
development in the region from 1946–
1955.

410 Nigeria. Survey department.
Gazetteer of place names in 1/500,000
map of Nigeria. Zaria, Gaskiya corporation, 1945. [v] 167p.

411 —Tribal map of Nigeria. Lagos, Survey
department, 1951. 1:3,000,000.

412 Nigeria, 1960, a special independence
issue of *Nigeria magazine*. Editor:
Michael Crowder. Lagos, "Nigeria
magazine", 1960. xvi, 232, xvii–lvi p.
illus., map.
Articles on Nigerian history and culture, and sumptuous illustrations depicting varied Nigerian scenes.

413 Niven, Cecil Rex
The Kabba Province of the Northern
Provinces of Nigeria. *Geog. j.*, 68 (4) Oct.
1926: 289–302, illus., map.

414 —The lands and peoples of West Africa:
Gambia—Sierra Leone—Ghana—Ni-
geria. 2nd ed. London, Adam & Charles
Black, 1961. vii, 84p. front., illus., map.

415 —Nigeria: outline of a colony. London,
T. Nelson, 1945. vi, 162p. front., illus.,
maps, bibliog.

416 —Nigeria past and present. *Afr. affairs,*
56, Oct. 1957: 225, 265–275.
Brief summary of Nigerian history
from the earliest times to the 19th
century.

417 —The Northern Region of Nigeria. In
*Nigeria. Dept. of Statistics. Population
census of the Northern Region of Nigeria,
1952.* [*1953*]: 43–48.
A brief descriptive and historical
account of the Region and its people.

418 —Our emirates. Lagos, Public relations
department [n.d.] 16p. illus. (Crownbird
series no. 36.)
Notes on the present organisation and
historical background of the emirates in
Northern Nigeria.

419 —A short history of Nigeria. 7th ed.
(revised) London, Longmans, Green,
1958. viii, 286p. maps.
1st ed. 1937; 2nd ed. 1940; 3rd ed.
1948; 4th ed. 1950; 5th ed. 1952; 6th
ed., 1955; 7th ed. 1957.

420 Northern Nigeria. *J. Afr. soc.,* 5 (20)
Jl. 1906: 387–403.
Extracts from F. Lugard's report
(Colonial report no. 476). Gives useful
account of the past history of the region
as well as notes on his own administration.

421 Nwabara, Samuel N.
British foundation of Nigeria: a saga of
hardship, 1788–1914. *Civilisations,* 13
(3) 1963: 308–317.
Brief commentary on British ex-
ploratory, trading and administrative
efforts in Nigeria between 1788 and
1914. French summary on pp. 318–320.

422 —The Fulani conquest and rule of the
Hausa kingdom [sic] of Northern
Nigeria (1804–1900) *J. Soc. afr.,* 33 (2)
1963: 231–241.

423 Ogilby, John
Africa: being an accurate description
of the regions of Aegypt, Barbary,
Lybia and Billedulgerid, the land of
Negroes, Guinee, Aethiopia and the
Abyssines . . . London, Printed by Tho.
Johnson, for the Author, 1670. [xviii]
767 [1] p. maps, illus. (English atlas, v. 1)
Description of 17th century Africa,
based on the works of other writers.
Includes accounts, often rather short, of
many areas of present day Nigeria, e.g.
Kano, Zamfara, Bornu, and the coastal
region.

424 Ogueri, Eze Anyanwu
Indirect rule and the growth of representative government in Nigeria. 1955.
488p.
Ph.D. thesis, Harvard University.
Includes in part I a discussion of
political traditions in Nigeria and the
political and social organisation of the
Hausa, the Yoruba and the Ibo (pp.
73–162).

425 Oji, B. A.
Social and political history of Nigeria for schools and colleges. Aba, International press, 1961. 125p. front. (map).

426 Ojo, G. J. Afolabi
Geographical problems of land use in West Africa. 1958.
M.A. thesis, National University of Ireland.

427 Okonkwo, D. Onuzulike
History of Nigeria in a new setting. Aba, International press, 1962. 378p. maps, bibliog.
A simply written summary of Nigerian history from a Nigerian viewpoint.

428 Okoye, Mokwugo
African cameos: a peep into African history and some leisurely lines in rhymes. Onitsha, the author, [1956] 61p.
Printed by Amacs press, Port Harcourt.

429 —African responses. Devon, A. H· Stockwell; Ilfracombe, 1964. 420p· bibliog.
A review of African history and cultures including the ancient empires and their civilisations, and a general survey of the events and problems of contemporary Africa.

430 —Against tribe. Enugu, Zik enterprises, 1960. 36p.
A sharp and vigorous denunciation of tribalism in Nigeria.

431 —Blackman's destiny: an excursus into the customs and traditions of the Egyptians, Abyssinians, Greeks, Indians, Hebrews, Ibos, Yorubas, Hausas, Ashantis and English, with glimpses on the blackman's adventures, culture & future. Port Harcourt, Amacs printing press, 1956. 122p.

432 —Nigeria today. *Présence afr.*, Eng. ed., 16 (44) 1962: 60–66.
A survey and description of the political, economic and cultural situation and tendencies in post independence Nigeria.

433 —Some men and women; studies in life and conduct, and a portrait gallery of extraordinary people. Part I. Onitsha, the author [n.d.] 69p.

434 —Vistas of life: a survey of views and visions. Enugu, E.N.P.C., 1961. xx, 228p.
Presents a sharply critical survey of orthodox views on age-old social phenomena and philosophical topics ranging from evolution to religion, morality, society and politics. Written while in prison for sedition.

434a Oldfield, R. A. K.
Narration of an expedition into the interior of Africa. See [329.]

435 Oliver, Roland, ed.
The dawn of African history. London, O.U.P., 1961. vii, 103p. plates, maps.
Outline history of Africa. Chapters 6, 9 and 10 dealing with parts of West Africa relevant.

436 Oloko, Tunde

Religion and politics in Nigeria. *W. Afr.*, (2077) 2 Feb. 1957: 103; (2078) 9 Feb. 1957: 131.
On the attitude to politics of the Anglican, Roman Catholic and Muslim religious groups in Nigeria.

437 —A tale of 4 cities. *Nigeria, 1960:* 83–93. illus.
Portrait of Lagos, Ibadan, Kaduna and Enugu.

438 Oluwasanmi, H. A.
The agrarian situation in Nigeria. *J. hum. relations,* 8 (Spring/Summer) 1960: 657–667.

439 Orizu, Akweke Abyssinia Nwafor
British and native administration in Nigeria. 1944. 238p.
M.A. thesis, Columbia University.

440 Ormsby-Gore, William G. A.
Some contrasts in Nigeria. *Geog. j.,* 69 (6) Je. 1927: 497–516, illus., maps.
Contrasts rain forest and savannah, pagans and Muslims, and discusses their civilisations, state structures, etc.

441 Orr, Charles William James
The making of Northern Nigeria. London, Macmillan, 1911. x, 306p. front., maps, bibliog.
History of the occupation and early administration of Northern Nigeria by the British Government. Captain Orr was an active participant in the process. See a review by T. L. Gilmour entitled "The two Nigerias" [248].

442 — —2nd ed., with a new introduction by A. H. M. Kirk-Green. London, F. Cass, 1965. xxxviii, 306p. maps, bibliog.
The "2nd edition" is only a reprint of the 1st., with the new introduction added.

443 —The Northern provinces of Nigeria. J.R.A.S., 36 (142) Jan. 1937: 8–16.

444 Owen, William FitzWilliam
Narrative of voyage to explore the shores of Africa, Arabia and Madagascar performed in H.M. ships Leven and Barracouta, under the direction of Captain W. F. W. Owen. New York, J. & J. Harper, 1833. 2v. illus., maps.

445 Pacheco Pereira, *Duarte*
Esmeraldo de situ orbis. Ediçaõ commemorativa da descoberta da America por Christovao Colombo no seu quarto centenario, sob a direcçao de Raphael Eduardo de Azevedo Basto. Lisboa, Imprensa nacional, 1892. xxxv, 127p. illus.

446 —Esmeraldo de situ orbis; translated and edited by G. H. T. Kimble. London, Hakluyt society, 1937. 193.
English ed. of [445].

447 Palmer, Herbert Richmond
Arriving in Northern Nigeria (about 35 years ago) *J.R.A.S.*, 41 (163) Apr. 1942: 108–110.
Usual way to get to Northern Nigeria was via Forcados. Describes a typical journey and the then prevalent conditions.

448 —Gazetteer of Bornu Province. Revised by J. B. Welman. Lagos, Government printer, 1929. ii, 112p. map, bibliog.

449 Panikkar, K. Madhu
The serpent and the crescent: a history of the negro empires of Western Africa. Bombay, Asia publishing house, 1963. [xi] 386p.
History of the Western Sudan from earliest times to the French and British takeover of the 20th century.

450 Park, Mungo
The journal of a mission to the interior of Africa in the year 1805; together with other documents, official and private, relating to the same mission. To which is prefixed an account of the life of Mr. Park. London, printed for John Murray, by W. Bulmer, 1815. [v] cxxx, 219p. map.
Journal of Mungo Park's last mission to the Niger.

451 —Travels in the interior districts of Africa: performed under the direction and patronage of the African Association in the years 1795, 1796, and 1797. With an appendix containing geographical illustrations of Africa by Major Rennell. London, printed by W. Bulmer for the author, 1799. xxviii, 372, xcii, [v] p. front., illus., maps.
Original edition of the journals of Park's first travels in West Africa.

452 Parrinder, Geoffrey
Islam in West Africa. W. Afr. rev., 31 (397) Dec. 1960: 12–15.
On the spread of Islam in West Africa, especially after British and French colonial rule had been established.

453 —Moslem revival in Nigeria. W. Afr., Jl. 30, 1955: 698.

454 Passarge, Siegfried
Adamawa; Geog. j., 5, 1895: 50–53.
A paper read before the Geographical Soc. (Berlin) in 1894. Summarises his book Adamaua [455] q.v.

455 —Adamaua: Bericht über die Expedition des Deutschen Kamerun-Komitees in den Jahren, 1893–94. Berlin, 1895. xvi, 573p. illus., map.
Travelled as medical officer in Von Uechtritz's expedition to Adamawa in 1893. For a résumé of this work, see [454]. See also A. H. M. Kirk-Greene, J. Hist soc. Nig., 1 (2) 1957: 86–98, for another synopsis with useful introductory notes.

456 Paulitschke, Philipp
Die Sudanländer nach dem gegenwärtigen Stande der Kenntnis. Freiburg im Breisgau, Herdersche Verlagshandlung, 1885. xii, 311p. fronts., illus., map, bibliog.

456a Pereira, Pacheco, duarte. See Pacheco Pereira, duarte

457 Perham, Margery
The census of Nigeria, 1931. Africa, 6 (4) Oct. 1933: 415–430.
A review of the 1931 census, noting its anthropological, economic, religious, educational, demographic and medical aspects.

458 —Native administration in Nigeria. London, O.U.P., 1937. xvi, 404p. maps, bibliog.
An intensive study of the administrative patterns applied in various parts of Nigeria by the British Government in the first decades of its administration.

459 Perham, Margery and Simmons, J.
African discovery; an anthology of exploration. London, Faber and Faber, 1942. 280p. illus., map.
A selection of important extracts from the records and diaries of British African explorers from 1769 to 1873. Includes extracts from Mungo Park, Clapperton, Lander and Baikie.

460 Perry, Ruth
New sources for research in Nigerian history. Africa, 25 (4) Oct. 1955: 430–432.
Notes four categories of local research material and their significance in the study of Nigerian history, viz, Nigerian archival material, locally printed books and pamphlets, local newspapers, and Arabic manuscripts from Northern Nigeria.

461 Petermann, A.
Die Binue- (oder Tschadda-) Expedition in Jahre 1854: nach Dr. W. B. Baikies officiellem Bericht und des Geistlichen Samuel Crowthers Tagebuch. Petermanns Mitt., 1855: 205–230.

462 Pierce-Gervis, Leslie
Of emirs and pagans; a view of Northern Nigeria. London, Cassell, 1963. xvi, 210p. front., map.

463 *Potts, M. I.
A school history of Nigeria. Lagos, C.M.S. bookshop, 1937.

464 Prescott, J. R. V.
The evolution of Nigeria's boundaries, Nig. geog. j., 2 (1) Je. 1958: 80–104, maps, bibliog.

465 —The evolution of the Anglo-French inter-Cameroons boundary. Nig. geog. j., 5 (2) Dec. 1962: 103–120, maps, bibliog.

466 —The geographical basis of Nigerian federation. Nig. geog. j., 2 (1) Je. 1958: 1–13, maps, bibliog.
Distinctive cultural differences, social and religious disharmony and the disparity in educational progress among the three regions of Nigeria are discussed and viewed as constituting a threat to the development of a strong federal government.

467 —Nigeria's regional boundary problems. Geog. rev., 49 (4) 1959: 485–505, maps.
A geographical and historical study of several boundary disputes which have arisen in Nigeria so far. These include the Ilorin-Kabba dispute, the Aboh-Asaba dispute, the Western Ijaw

dispute and several minor ethnic minority problems.

468 Pribytovskiy, Lev Naumovich
Nigeria in the struggle for independence. Washington, Joint publications research service, 1962. 217p. bibliog. (Scholarly books translation series, no. 931)
English translation of [469].

469 —Nigeria v bor'be' za nezavisimost. Moskva, Izdatelstvo vostochnoi litera-tury, 1961. 192p.
At head of title: *Akademiya Nauk SSSR. Institut Afriki.* A political and social history of Nigeria from the time of the 2nd World War. The development and principal stages of the liberation movement are traced, and prominence given to social and class patterns.

470 Problems of girl's education in Nigeria, Northern Region, *Afr. women,* 1 (3) 1955: 68–70.

471 Prothero, R. Mansell
Heinrich Barth and the Western-Sudan. *Geog. J.,* 125 (3) 1958: 326–339.

472 —The population census of Northern Nigeria, 1952: problems and results. *Pop. stud.,* 10 (2) Nov. 1956: 166–183, map.

473 —The population of Eastern Nigeria. *Scottish geog. mag.,* 71 (3) 1955: 165–170, maps.

474 —Problems of population mapping in an under-developed territory (Northern Nigeria). *Nig. geog. j.,* 3 (1) Dec. 1959: 1–7, maps.

475 —Some observation on desiccation in north-western Nigeria. *Erdkunde,* 16 (2) 1962: 112–119.

476 —Tropical studies: the geographical approach and the need for integration. *S. Afr. geog. j.,* 35, Dec. 1953: 46–48.
On the need for coordinated, inte-grated appraisal and interpretation of geographical studies in the tropics.

477 Quinn-Young, C. T. and Herdman, T.
Geography of Nigeria. 5th ed. London, Longmans, Green, 1957. vii, 223p. illus., maps.

478 Raphael, John R.
Through unknown Nigeria. London, T. Werner Lauriè, [1914] xxiii, 361p. front., illus.

479 Reade, Winwood
The African sketch-book. London, Smith, Elder, 1873. 2v. front., illus., maps.
v. 1. xi, 483p. v. II. vii, 529p. Travels in various parts of West Africa. The "Slave coast", Lagos and the bights described in v. 2 pp. 176–217.

480 —Savage Africa; being the narrative of a tour in equatorial, south-western and north-western Africa; with notes on the habits of the gorilla, on the existence of unicorns and tailed men; on the slave trade; on the origin, character, and capabilities of the negro and on the future civilisation of Western Africa.

London, Smith, Elder, 1863. xv, 587p. front., illus., map.
Includes description of the Niger Delta, and an account of, and interview with King Pepple (pp. 54–63)

481 Rennell, James
Elucidations of the African geography from the communications of Houghton and Magra, 1791; compiled in 1793. London, Printed by W. Bulmer & co., 1793. 31p. maps.
Communications from Houghton and Mr. Magra (British Consul at Tunis) relative to the course of the Niger.

482 Reynolds, Alexander Jacob
Down the Niger. *United empire,* May 1930: 247–249.

483 Richardson, James
Narrative of a mission to Central Africa, performed in the years 1850–51, under the orders and at the expense of Her Majesty's government. London, Chap-man and Hall, 1853. 2v. map.

484 Richet, Etienne
Voyage au Cameroun et dans la Nigeria. *Bull. Soc. roy. géog. Anvers,* 47 (1/2) 1927: 1–46; (3/4) 1927; 205–305; 48 (1) 1928: 1–41; (2/3) 1928: 109–176; (4) 1928: 267–333.

485 Robertson, G. A.
Notes on Africa, particularly those parts which are situated between Cape Verd and the River Congo . . . London, Printed for Sherwood, Neely, and Jones, 1819, repr. London, Frank Cass. xvi, 460p. front. (map.)
Badagri, Lagos and environs, pp. 283–299. "Oedo" (i.e. Edo), Benin and environs, pp. 299–311; Qua, Old Cala-bar and environs, pp. 312–320, with vocabulary of Old Calabar (English-Efik) on pp. 318–320.

486 Robinson, Charles Henry
Nigeria; our latest protectorate. London, Horace Marshall, 1900. xii, 223p. illus., map.
General descriptive account of Nigeria, with considerable attention on the Hausa people, especially on pp. 8–59, 138–167, and 179–189.

486a Rohlfs, Gerhard
Quer durch Afrika. See [3926].

486b —Reise durch Nord-Afrika. See [3927].

487 Ross, David A.
The career of Domingo Martinez in the Bight of Benin, 1833–64. *J. Afr. hist.,* 6 (1) 1965: 79–90.

488 Rotberg, Robert I.
A political history of tropical Africa. New York, Harcourt, Brace & World, 1965. 440p. illus., maps, bibliog.
A general survey of African history.

489 Ruxton, G.
Cinq années en Nigéria: souvenirs et impressions. *La géographie,* 28, 1913: 95–112.

490 Ryder, Alvan Frederick Charles
Dutch trade on the Nigerian coast

during the seventeenth century. *J. hist. soc. Nig.*, 3 (2) Dec. 1965: 195–210.

491 —Historians for Nigeria. *Ibadan*, (8) Mar. 1960: 12–14.
On the need for a multi-disciplinary approach to the problem of reconstructing Nigeria's earlier past.

491a Sadi, Abdurrahman Al. *See* 'Abd al-Rahmán ibn 'Abd Allah, al-Sa'di.

492 Sadler, George
Mohammedanism in Nigeria. *Mosl. world,* 35 (2) Apr. 1945: 133–137.

493 *Schacht, J.
Islam in Northern Nigeria. *Studia Islamica* [Paris] 8, 1957:

494 Schön, James Frederick
Journals of the Rev. James Frederick Schön and Mr. Samuel Crowther who . . . accompanied the expedition up the Niger in 1841, on behalf of the Church missionary society. With appendices and map. London, Hatchard, 1842. 4 p.l., xxiv, 393p. front., map., repr. London, Frank Cass, 1970.

495 Schubert, Gustav von
Heinrich Barth, der Bahnbrecher der deutschen Afrikaforschung; ein Lebens- und Charackterbild auf Grund ungedruckter Quellen entworfen. Berlin, D. Reimer, 1897. x, 184p. illus., facsims.

496 Schwarz, Frederick A. O.
Nigeria: the tribes, the nation or the race—the politics of independence. Cambridge, Mass., M.I.T. press, 1965. xiii, 316p. illus., maps, bibliog.

497 *Sciortino, J. C.
Notes on Nassarawa Province, Nigeria. London, Waterlow, 1920. 32p.

498 Shaw, Flora Louisa (Lady Lugard)
Nigeria. *J. Roy. soc. arts,* (52) 1904: 370–384, map.

499 —A tropical dependency: an outline of the ancient history of the Western Soudan, with an account of the modern settlement of Northern Nigeria. London, J. Nisbet, 1905. viii, 508p. maps (fold.)

500 — —2nd impression, 1965. maps (fold.)
A comprehensive history of West Africa from the earliest times to the British occupation of Northern Nigeria.

501 Shorthouse, W. T.
Spade and sport in paganland; being the narrative of a rolling stone in Nigeria. London, H. F. & G. Witherby, 1934. 224p. front., illus., map.
Reminiscences of a mining officer's life in Nigeria from 1927 to 1932.

502 Simpson, William A.
A private journal kept during the Niger expedition, from the commencement in May, 1841, until the recall of the expedition in June, 1842. London, John F. Shaw, 1843. xii, 139p.

503 Sinclair, Gordon
Loose among devils: a voyage from Devil's Island to those jungles of West Africa labelled "The white man's grave."

London, Hurst & Blackett, 1935. 287p. front., illus.

504 Sklar, Richard Lawrence
Nigerian political parties; power in an emergent African nation. Princeton, N.J., Princeton university press, 1963. xii, 578p. maps, bibliog.
"The core of . . . [the] analysis is the social composition and construction of those parties which stood at the forefront of the movement for independence."—Preface. Based on his Ph.D. thesis "Nigerian political parties: the social basis and structure of a party system in emergent Africa. Princeton university, 1961."

505 Smirnov, S. R.
Angliiskaya politika "kossvenogo upravlenia" v yugo-vostochnoi Nigerii. *Sov. et.,* (3) 1950: 137–152.
Reviews the British policy of 'indirect rule' as applied in Eastern Nigeria and the subsequent ethnographic researches necessitated by its failure. Rejects some conclusions of these researches which portrayed the people as having no social or political organisation beyond the family groups, and holds that there were developed systems of administration before the arrival of the Europeans.

506 Smith, Henry Frederick Charles
Arabic manuscript material bearing on the history of the Western Sudan: the archives of Segu. *Bull. news Hist. soc. Nig.,* 4 (2) 1959: supplement.

507 —Islam in West Africa. *Ibadan,* (15) Mar. 1963: 31–33.

508 —Nineteenth century Arabic archives of West Africa. *J. Afr. hist.,* 3 (2) 1962: 333–336.

509 —Writing on the history of West Africa. *WALA News,* 3 (3) Je. 1959: 138–146.
Surveys the pattern and course of historical writing in West Africa from the earliest period to the present century. Relevant section wrongly paged.

510 Smith, William
A new voyage to Guinea: describing the customs, manners, soil, climate, habits, buildings, education . . . habitations, diversions, marriages and whatever else is memorable among the inhabitants . . . London, J. Nourse, 1744, repr. London, Frank Cass, 1967. iv, 276 [8]p. front., illus.

511 —Voyage de William Smith en Guinée.
In *Collection des relations de voyages par mer et par terre, en différentes parties de l'Afrique, par C. A. Walckenaer.* Paris, 1842: vol. 8, pp. 312–372.

512 Smythe, Hugh H.
Nigeria: African paradox. *Crisis,* 65 (1) Jan. 1958: 17–20.

513 Stapleton, George Brian
Adult education in Northern Nigeria. *Venture,* 8 (4) Sept. 1956: 4–5.

514 Snelgrave, William
A new account of some parts of Guinea,

and the slave trade, containing 1. The history of the late conquest of the kingdom of Whidaw by the King of Dahomé . . . 2. The manner how the negroes become slaves. The number of them yearly exported from Guinea to America . . . London, Printed for James, John, and Paul, 1734. [xii] 288p. map., repr. London, Frank Cass, 1971.

515 Sowunmi, Akintunde
Our land and people. Part III—the West. Lagos, Public relations department, 1953. 16p. illus., map. (Crownbird series, 33)

516 Soyinka, Wole
The interpreters. London, André Deutsch, 1965. 254p.
A novel.

517 Spicer, E.
The people of Nigeria. Ikeja, Longmans of Nigeria, 1962. viii, 71p. illus., map.
Simple accounts of the Hausa, Fulani, Kanuri, Idoma, Birom, Yoruba, Ibo, and Kalabari.

518 Stamp, L. Dudley
Land utilization and soil erosion in Nigeria. Geog. rev., 28 (1) Jan. 1938: 32–45, maps.

519 Stanislaus, Joseph
The growth of African literature: a survey of the works published by African writers in English and French. 1952.
Ph.D. thesis, University of Montreal.

520 Stapleton, George Brian
The wealth of Nigeria. London, O.U.P., 1958. ix, 228p. illus., bibliog.

521 Steel, E. A.
Explorations in Southern Nigeria. Geog. j., 32 (1) Jl. 1908: 6–25, map; J. Roy. united service institutions, 54, Apr. 1910: 433–449.
Travel and description of the region between the Niger and Cross Rivers, brought under Government control in 1904–1908.

522 Stuart-Young, John Moray
The coaster at home, being the autobiography of Jack O'Dazi, palm oil ruffian and trader man of the River Niger. London, A. H. Stockwell, 1916–1917. 2v.
v. 1 1916. 404p. v. 2. entitled The iniquitous coaster, being the second volume of The coaster at home, Jack O'Dazi's autobiography. 1917. 389p. Description of conditions in Southern Nigeria, especially in Onitsha, 1905–1917. "A romantically over-written account . . . with some cultural descriptions of meagre quality"—S. Ottenberg.

523 —A cupful of kernels: stories, studies and sketches mainly from the West African coast. London, J. Ouseley, 1909. ix, 196p.

524 Takes, Charles Antoine Peter
Problems of rural development in Southern Nigeria. Tijdschrift van het Koninklijk Nederlandsch aardrijkskundig genootschap, 81 (4) 1964: 438–452, illus., map.
Also offprinted (1964) by N.I.S.E.R., Ibadan.

525 Talbot, Percy Amaury
Anthropology in Nigeria. Nature, 130 (3285) Oct. 15, 1932: 561–562.

526 —From the Gulf of Guinea to the Central Sudan. J. Afr. soc., 11 (44) Jl. 1912: 373–393, illus.
Account of his journey from Calabar to Lake Chad.

527 Tamuno, S. M.
The development of British administrative control of Southern Nigeria, 1900–1912: a study in the administrations of Sir Ralph Moor, Sir William MacGregor and Sir Walter Egerton. 1962.
Ph.D. thesis, University of London.

528 Tamuno, Tekena Nitonye
Some aspects of Nigerian reaction to the imposition of British rule. J. Hist. soc. Nig., 3 (2) Dec. 1965: 271–312.

529 Tardieu, Amédée
Sénégambie et Guinée . . . Paris, Firmin Didot Frères, 1847. 388p. illus. (L'Univers, ou Histoire et description de tous les peuples)
The section on Guinea covers pp. 191–386, with description of Yorubaland 287–313, Benin 313–334, Hausa and tribes of the lower Niger and Benue, 334–365, Bonny to Old Calabar, 365–373.

530 Taylor, Frank William
The word 'Nigeria'. J.R.A.S., 38 (150) Jan. 1939: 154–159.

530a Taylor, John Christopher
The gospel on the banks of the Niger. See [184]

531 Temple, Charles Lindsay
Native races and their rulers; sketches and studies of official life and administrative problems in Nigeria. Cape Town, Argus, 1918. xi, 252p. front., illus.
Reflections on administrative problems and indirect rule by a former Lt. Governor of Northern Nigeria, 1914–1917.

531a ——2nd. edition, with a critical introduction, by Mervyn Hiskett, London, Frank Cass, 1968. xlix, 252p. illus.

532 —Northern Nigeria. Geog. j., 40, 1912: 149–168, map.

533 Tenkorang, S.
British slave trading activities on the Gold and Slave Coasts in the 18th century and their effect on African society. London, 1964.
M.A. thesis, University of London.

534 Thomson, Joseph
Mungo Park and the Niger. George Phillips, 1890. xiii, 338p. front., illus., maps. (The world's great explorers and explorations)
Biographical record of Park and his efforts on the Niger, with account of subsequent explorations and history of

the region down to the Royal Niger Company.

535 —Niger and central Sudan sketches. *Scot. geog. mag.,* 2, 1886: 577–596, illus., map.

536 Thorburn, J. W. A.
Nigerian memories in lighter vein: 1925–1947. *Nig. field,* 28 (1) Jan. 1963: 45–48.
Reminiscences of a former education officer in Nigeria. Includes a recount of early Benin history and glimpses of the social life of British personnel in Benin and other towns.

537 Thorn, G. W. P.
Our inland waterways. Lagos, public relations Dept., [n.d.] 13p. illus. (Crownbird series, no. 19)
Describes towns and sceneries in the Niger Delta area, especially in the area west of the Niger.

538 Thorp, Ellen
Ladder of bones. London, Jonathan Cape, 1956. 320p. illus.
History of British administrative, commercial and evangelical activities in Nigeria in the latter half of the 19th century with brief glimpses at events in the 20th century.

538a Tilho, Jean Auguste Marie
Documents scientifiques de la mission Tilho. See [237]

539 Tonkin, T. J.
Muhammadanism in the Western Sudan *J. Afr., soc.,* 3 (10) Jan. 1904: 123–141.
History, present position and future prospects of Mohammedanism in West Africa, especially in central Hausaland.

540 Tremearne, Arthur John Newman
The Niger and the West Sudan; or The West African's note book. A vade mecum containing hints and suggestions as to what is required by Britons in West Africa, together with historical and anthropological notes, and easy Hausa phrases used in everyday conversation. London, Hodder & Stoughton, 1910. [vii] 151p.

541 —Some Austral-African notes and anecdotes. London, J. Bale, 1913. xii, 215p. front., illus.
Includes notes on parts of N. Nigeria (pp. 71–94)

542 Tremlett, Mrs. Horace
With the tin gods. London, J. Lane, 1915. x, 308p. front., illus.

543 Trimingham, J. Spencer
A history of Islam in West Africa. London, O.U.P., for University of Glasgow, 1962. x, 262p. maps.

544 —Islam in West Africa. Oxford, Clarendon press, 1959. x, 262p. map.
A study of the consequences—religious, social and cultural—of the impact of Islam on West Africa. Shows the effects of the assimilation of Islam on aspects of West African culture and society, as well as on Islam itself. There

is a good review by H. F. C. Smith in *Ibadan,* (13) Mar. 1963: 31–33.

545 Turner, J. G. S.
Medical census, Southern provinces. London, Crown Agents for the Colonies, for Government of Nigeria, 1932. 101p. (Census of Nigeria, 1931, v. 6)
Full report of the medical census of the Southern Provinces undertaken in 1931.

546 Udoma, E. U.
"The lion and the oil palm". (A study of British rule in West Africa) Dublin, 1943. 36p.

[547 Uwemedimo, Rosmary
Mammy-wagon marriage. London, Hurst & Blackett, 1961. 238p.

548 Vagrant [pseud].
Life in Northern Nigeria. *Blackwood's mag.,* Sept. 1908: 310–318.

549 Vandeleur, Seymour
Campaigning on the upper Nile and Niger. With an introduction by George T. Goldie. London, Methuen, 1898. xxvii, 320p. front., plates, maps.
Detailed eye witness account of the military expeditions in East and West Africa in the late 19th century. The West African expeditions were those conducted against the Emirs of Bida and Ilorin by the Royal Niger Company's forces under Sir George Goldie in 1897. Useful description of the country of the lower Niger. Texts of the principal treaties concluded between the company and the local princes up to 1897 are appended.

550 Vanter, W.
The war against ignorance in Northern Nigeria. *Oversea educ.,* 32 (4) Jan. 1961: 174–179.

551 Viard, Edouard
Au Bas-Niger. Paris, L. Guérin, 1885. [5] xvii, 267p. illus., maps.
In two parts. Pt. I describes the geography of the Niger and commerce in the area, and Pt. II includes cultural accounts of the inhabitants. Useful table of location and number of European forts and factories in the region as at the end of 1883 (pp. 206–207)

552 — —3rd ed. 1886. 309p. illus., maps.

552a Village development in the Eastern Provinces. Lagos, Twentieth century press [n.d.] 22p.

553 Villault, Nicolas
Relation des costes d'Afrique, appellées Guinée; avec la description du pays, moeurs & façon de vivre des habitans, des productions de la terre, & des marchandises qu'on en apporte, avec les remarques historiques sur ces costes. Le tout remarqué par le sieur Villault . . . dans le voyage qu'il y a fait en 1666 & 1667. Paris, D. Thierry, 1669. [vi] 456p.

554 Vischer, Hanns

Journeys in Northern Nigeria. *Geog. j.,* 28 (4) Oct. 1906: 368–377, map.

555 Walker, Frank Deaville
A hundred years in Nigeria: the story of the Methodist mission in Western Nigeria District, 1842–1942. London, Cargate press, 1942. 138p. front., illus., map.

556 Ward, W. E. F.
A history of Africa. Book one: the old kingdoms of the Sudan; Nigeria before the British; South Africa. London, G. Allen, 1960. 148p. plates, maps.

557 Watson, G. D.
A human geography of Nigeria. London, Longmans, Green, 1960. [vii] 180p. illus., maps.

558 Watt, James
Southern Nigeria. *Scot. geog. mag.,* 22, 1906: 173–181, illus.

559 West African review (Nigeria jubilee number) 21 (275) Je. 1950: 601–788.

560 White, Arthur Silva
The development of Africa; a study in applied geography. 2nd ed. London, G. Philip, 1892. xiii, 307p. maps.

561 White, Stanhope
Dan Bana; the memoir of a Nigerian official. London, Cassell, 1966. xix, 268p. illus., map.

562 Whitford, John
Trading life in Western and Central Africa. Liverpool, [the author] 1877. viii, 335p. map.
Travels and description in West Africa. Author visited many parts of the area several times between 1853 and 1875. The Niger and Benue and much of the area now Nigeria, pp. 81–314.

562a — —2nd Edition, with an introduction, by A. G. Hopkins. London, Frank Cass, 1967. xviii, 335p. map.

563 Whitlock, G. F. A.
The Yola-Cross River boundary commission, Southern Nigeria. *Geog. j.,* 36, 1910: 426–438.

564 Wilks, I.
A medieval trade-route from the Niger to the Gulf of Guinea. *J. Afr. hist.,* 3 (2) 1962: 337–341, bibliog.

565 Williams, David
Nigeria today. *Afr. affairs,* 55 (219) Apr. 1956: 109–119.
A general survey of Nigeria including the social and cultural aspects.

566 Williams, Harry
Nigeria free. London, R. Hale, 1962. 190p. plates, map.
Description of modern Nigeria, with disconnected historical notes.

567 Williams, Joseph John
Hebrewisms of West Africa: from the Nile to the Niger with the Jews. New York, Dial press, 1930. viii, 443p. illus., map., bibliog.
On the relics of Hebrew customs, traditions, etc., among the Ashanti, Yoruba and other peoples of West Africa.

568 Williamson, Balfour
A vanished age—West Africa in the 1920's. Based on a talk given to the Enugu branch [of the Nigerian Field Society] 2nd December, 1958. *Nig. field.* 25 (3) Jl. 1960: 112–124.

568a Willink, Henry
Report of the commission to enquire into the fears of minorities . . . See [251]

569 Wilson, J. Leighton
Western Africa: its history, conditions and prospects. London, Sampson Low, 1856. 527p. front., illus., map.

570 Wilson-Haffenden, J. R.
The red men of Nigeria: an account of a lengthy residence among the Fulani, or 'red men', & other pagan tribes of central Nigeria, with a description of their headhunting, pastoral & other customs, habits & religion. London, Seeley Service, 1930, repr. London, Frank Cass, 1967. 318p. front., illus., map.

SECTION TWO

PHYSICAL ANTHROPOLOGY; ARCHAEOLOGY

1. PHYSICAL ANTHROPOLOGY

570a Barnicot, N. A. (and others)
Haptoglobin and transferrin inheritance in Northern Nigeria. *Ann. Hum. genet.,* 24, 1960: 171–183.

570b Boyer, Samuel H. and Watson-Williams, E. J.
The y– globulin, Gm^{ab}, in Nigerians. *Nature,* 190, 1961: 456.

571 Boyo, A. E.
Studies in the population biology of abnormal haemoglobins in Nigeria. 1961.
D.Phil. thesis, Oxford University.

572 Charmers, J. N. M. [and others]
The ABO, MNS and Rh blood groups of the Nigerians. *Ann. eugenics,* 17 (3) 1953: 168–176.
The three blood groups among the Hausa, Ibo and Yoruba. See also [575]

573 Edington, G. M. and Lehmann, H.
The distribution of haemoglobin C in West Africa. *Man,* 56, 1956: 34–36.
Concerned mostly with the African population of Accra, including some of the Ibo residents therein, as well as the Yoruba of Nigeria.

574 Garlick, J. P.
Blood groups and sickling in Nigeria. 1961.
Ph.D. thesis, London University.

575 Hardy, Joan
The ABO blood groups of Southern Nigerians and their relation to the history of the area. *J.R.A.I.,* 92 (2) Jl.—Dec. 1962: 223–231, maps.
A comparative study, with the results examined in relation to the history and migration of ethnic groups in the area.

576 Herskovits, Melville J.
Physical types of West African negroes. *Human biology,* 9, 1937: 483–497.

577 Juergens, H. W. [and others]
Über Beziehungen zwischen Sichelzellmerkmal und Körperform in Süd-Nigeria. *Z. Morph. Anthrop.,* 56 (1/2) Sept. 1964: 142–163, illus., bibliog.
A study to determine whether heterozygote and homozygote carriers of the sickle-cell gene have peculiarities of body form, and whether such peculiarities could serve as a basis for morphological characterization of the different haemoglobin carriers.

578 Keith, Arthur
On certain physical characters of the negroes of the Congo Free State and Nigeria. *J.R.A.I.,* 41, 1911: 40–71, illus.
A comparison of physical measurements and crania from the Ekoi and Ogoni areas with similar data from the Congo.

578a Lagercrantz, S.
A contribution to the study of anomalous dentition and its ritual significance in Africa. See [993]

579 Lehmann, H. and Ross, J. G.
Haemoglobin phenotypes in Nigerian cattle. *Man,* 61, 1961: 81–82 (art. 101) illus.

580 Livingstone, Frank B.
Anthropological implications of sickle-cell gene distribution in West Africa. *Amer. anthrop.,* 60 (3) Je. 1958: 533–562, maps, bibliog.

581 Massé, G. and Hunt, E. E.
Skeletal maturations of the hand and wrist in West African children. *Human biology,* 35 (1) 1963: 3–25, illus., bibliog.

582 Mulhall, H.
The application of multivariate statistical analysis to problems of physical anthropology, with special reference to the physical anthropology of certain peoples in Nigeria. 1954.
Ph.D. thesis, Cambridge.

583 Talbot, Percy Amaury
A note on West African anthropometry. *Man,* 28, Mar. 1928: 40 (art. 29)
Gives the cephalic index of the semi-Bantu and other peoples of Southern Nigeria.

584 —Notes on anthropometry of some Central Sudan tribes. *J. Anthrop. inst.,* 46, Jan.–Je. 1916: 173–183.

585 Talbot, Percy Amaury and Mulhall, H.
The physical anthropology of Southern Nigeria: a biometric study in statistical method. Cambridge, University press, 1962. xvi, 127p. map, bibliog.
Data obtained by Talbot from his anthropometric survey of the area are analysed and subjected to statistical treatment by Dr. H. Mulhall. The first published attempt to apply statistical method to physical anthropology in Nigeria.

2. ARCHAEOLOGY

Only general archaeological works and those not readily identified with any ethnic divisions are included here. The bulk of archaeological writings in this bibliography are, for convenience of arrangement, treated from the viewpoint of cultural anthropology, and are therefore subsumed within this class in the appropriate ethnic divisions. There they will be found grouped with other pertinent works in the sections on material culture.

2. (i) Bibliography

586 Council for old world archaeology
COWA bibliography: current publications in old world archaeology. Area 11. Cambridge, Mass., no. 1 (1957). See also [593]

2. (ii) General Studies

587 Alimen, Henriette
The prehistory of Africa; translated [from the French] by Alan Houghton Brodrick. London, Hutchinson, 1957. xviii, 438p. illus., maps, tables, bibliog.
A basic work on African prehistory. Embodies the findings of archaeological investigations in many parts of the continent. Chapter 7 devoted to West Africa.

588 Arkell, A. J.
Archaeological research in West Africa. *Antiquity*, 18 (71) 1944: 147–150.

589 Balfour, Henry
Occurence of "cleavers" of lower palaeolithic type in Northern Nigeria. *Man*, 34, Feb. 1934: 21–25 (art. 25) illus.
Describes 'cleavers' or axe-like stone implements found in the mine fields near Jos.

590 Braunholtz, H. J.
Quartz microliths from Wana, Northern Nigeria. *Man*, 46, 1946: 55–56. (art. 49)

591 —Stone implements of palaeolithic and neolithic types from Nigeria. London, Waterlow, for Nigerian Govt., 1926. 20p. illus., map (Nigeria. Geological survey. Occasional paper, no. 4)

592 Conference on history and archaeology in Africa, 2nd, London, 1957.
History and archaeology in Africa. [Report of the] second conference held in July 1957 at the School of Oriental and African studies. Edited by D. H. Jones. London, S.O.A.S., 1959. 58p.

593 Council for old world archaeology
COWA surveys and bibliographies. Area 11: West Africa. Series I, 1958–59. Cambridge, Mass., Council for old world archaeology.
Formed by the merging of [586] and COWA surveys. One of the 22 area reports sponsored by the Council for Old World Archaeology and covering the world outside of the Americas from palaeolithic to recent, historical times. Each area report surveys archaeological activity in the relevant area for the last two or three years and carries a well annotated bibliography.

594 Davies, O.
The neolithic revolution in tropical Africa. *Tr. Hist. soc. Ghana*, 4 (2) 1960: 14–20.

Surveys the distribution of heavy stone hoes in tropical Africa, and holds that yam was domesticated in the Congo basin about 5,000 B.C., and spread from there to the Upper Nile and Upper Niger valleys, the cultivators in the latter region moving downwards into the rain forests in later times.

595 —The distribution of old stone-age material in Guinea. *Bull. IFAN.*, 21 (1/2) Jan.–Apr. 1959: 102–108, maps.
Maps showing the distribution of pebble tools and the Chellean, Acheulean and Sangoan cultures, with an attempt to date them. "Guinea" here refers to Ivory Coast, Togo, Ghana, Dahomey and Nigeria.

596 —The old stone age between the Volta and the Niger. *Bull. IFAN.*, 19 (3–4) 1957: 592–616, illus.
A summary of the palaeolithic period in parts of Northern Nigeria and the corresponding areas in Dahomey, Ghana and Togo.

597 —The stone age in West Africa. *Ghana j. sci.*, 3 (1) Apr. 1963: 1–7.

597a Desplagnes, Louis
Le plateau central Nigérien. See [652]

598 Discovery of rock paintings in Bauchi. *Africa*, 28 (3) 1958: 278.
Brief note on the paintings at Geji, near Bauchi town.

599 Eyo, Ekpo
1964 excavations at Rop rock shelter. *W. Afr. arch. newsletter*, (3) Oct. 1965: 5–14.
Describes excavations he carried out at the Rop rock shelter near Barakin Ladi on the Jos Plateau, and the finds. French summary, pp. 13–14.

600 Fagg, Bernard E. B.
Archaeological notes from Northern Nigeria. *Man*, 46, May–Je. 1946: 49–55. (art. 48) illus., map.
A historical survey with illustrated descriptions of palaeolithic, neolithic and microlithic implements, pottery, etc., found in the tin deposits of Bauchi Plateau.

601 —The cave paintings and rock gongs of Birnin Kudu. In [*Proc.*] *3rd Pan-African congress on pre-history, Livingstone, 1955*, ed., J. D. Clark and S. Cole, 1957: 306–312, illus., map.
Describes paintings of humpless cattle which are no longer found in the area; excavated iron and stone implements suggesting Neolithic-Metal age transitional culture; and rock gongs and boulders found in the vicinity.

602 —The discovery of multiple rock gongs in Nigeria. *Man*, 56, 1956: 17–18 (art. 23) illus., map.
Rock gongs found in several parts of Northern Nigeria, especially the area around Jos.

603 —An outline of the stone age of the Plateau minesfield. *Int. W. Afr. conf.*

proc., 3rd, 1949. 1956: 203–222, illus., map.

Account of the stone implements and terracottas found around the Jos Plateau. The illustrations include photographs showing five terracotta heads; a stone axe and an iron axe.

604   —Preliminary report on a microlithic industry at Rop rock shelter, Northern Nigeria. In: *Proc. Prehist. soc., n.s.,* 10, 1944: 68–69, illus.

605   —The rock gong complex today and in prehistoric times. *J. Hist. soc. Nig.,* 1 (1) Dec. 1956: 27–42, illus.

Rock paintings and rock gongs in Birnin Kudu, Mbar, Bokkos, Daffa, and rock gongs in Jos, Fobur and other parts of Northern and Western Nigeria, with briefer notes on rock gongs and rock slides in other parts of Africa, Europe and elsewhere.

606   —A stone bowl from West Africa. *Man,* 64, Nov.–Dec. 1964: 187 (art. 226) illus.

A letter reporting the discovery of a stone bowl on the Jos Plateau some 18 miles south of Jos town.

607   Goodwin, A. J. H.
Rock gongs, chutes, paintings and fertility. *South Afr. arch. bull.,* 12 (45) Mar. 1957: 37–40, illus.

Review of rock gongs and other items discovered by Bernard Fagg in Nigeria and elsewhere, with notes from author's own visits to Nigeria in 1955 and 1956.

608   —Walls, paving, water-paths and landmarks. *Odú* (6) Je. 1958: 45–53.

Calls attention to the significance and problems of locating and mapping important historical monuments in Nigeria, noting as examples the walls and paving of ancient Ife and similar landmarks in Benin.

609   Hartle, Donald D.
An archaeological survey in Eastern Nigeria. *W. Afr. arch. newsletter,* (2) May 1965: 4–5.

Brief review of archaeological surveys, and excavations in Eastern Nigeria conducted between October 1963 and Feb. 1965. Summary in French.

610   Heger, Franz
Nigeria-Archaeology. *Ymer,* 1921: 25–46, illus.

610a   Jacobson, Reginald R. E. [and others]
Ring-complexes in the younger granite province of Northern Nigeria. London, 1958. 72p. plates (Geological soc. of London. Memoir no. 1)

611   Jeffreys, M. D. W.
Some notes on the neolithic of West Africa. In *[Proceedings] 3rd pan-African congress on pre-history, Livingstone, 1955, ed. J. Desmond Clark and S. Cole, 1957:* 262–273, illus., bibliog.

Reviews information in available literature bearing on stone implements in West Africa, and describes some of the neolithic materials he collected.

611a   Jones, D. H., *ed.*
History and archaeology in Africa. See [617]

612   Kennedy, Robert A.
West Africa in prehistory. *History today,* 8 (9) Sept. 1958: 646–653, illus., map.

613   Lebeuf, Jean Paul
Archéologie tchadienne; les Sao du Cameroun et du Tchad. Paris, Hermann, 1962. 147p. illus., map. (Actualités scientifiques et industrielles, 1295)

614   Lower Palaeolithic "cleavers", Northern Nigeria. *Nature,* 133, 7 Apr. 1934: 535.

615   Mauny, Raymond
Les contacts préhistoriques entre le monde Méditerranéen et l'Afrique occidentale tropicale. *Int. W. Afr. conf. Proc., 3rd, 1949. 1956:* 68, map.

A brief note, with a detailed map of the Western Sudan and the Guinea Coast.

616   —Pierres sonnantes d'Afrique occidentale. *Notes afr.,* (75) Jl. 1958: 73.

Notes on rock gongs found in Nigeria by Bernard Fagg, and on similar finds in other parts of West Africa.

617   Milton, R. A., *ed.,*
History and archaeology in Africa: Report of a conference held in July 1953 at the School of Oriental and African Studies. London, S.O.A.S., 1955. 99p. maps.

Includes a survey of oral tradition among the Yoruba, pp. 55–57, and among the Nupe, pp. 57–59.

618   Murray, Kenneth Crosthwaite
Archaeology in Nigeria: an official report. *Antiquity,* 22 (86) 1948: 57–60.

A reprint of the "Annual report" of the Antiquity Section of the Dept. of Education, for the year 1946.

618a   Nigeria. Dept. of antiquities
Annual report. See [74]

619   Rock paintings found in Bauchi: discovery after 800 years. *W. Afr. rev.,* 29 (367) 1958: 269–271, illus.

620   Rousseau, Madeleine
Les fouilles archéologiques en Nigeria. *Musée vivant,* 12 (36–37) Nov. 1948: 84–86.

621   Sasson, Hamo
Cave paintings recently discovered near Bauchi, Northern Nigeria. *Man,* 60, Apr. 1960: 50–53 (art. 70) illus.

Paintings at Geji, near Bauchi.

622   —Grinding grooves and pits in Northern Nigeria. *Man,* 62, Oct. 1962: 145. (art. 232) illus.

On pits or grooves formed in rocks in Geji near Bauchi by years of intermittent grinding of clay for potting. Also deeper grooves in rocks in the Plateau formed by the pounding of ore from the furnace in the process of iron smelting.

623   Shaw, C. Thurstan
The approach through archaeology to

early West African history. In *A thousand years of West African history*, ed. J. F. A. Ajayi and I. Espie, 1965: 23–38.

624 —Archaeology and Nigeria; an expanded version of an inaugural lecture delivered at the University of Ibadan on 29 November, 1963. Ibadan, University press, for Institute of African studies. [ii] 33p. front.

The nature and meaning of archaeology and the relevance and importance of archaeological investigations in Nigeria.

625 —Field research in Nigerian archaeology (a brief survey and discussion of policy)

J. Hist. soc. Nig., 2 (4) Dec. 1963: 449–464.

A rapid review of archaeological periods and finds in Nigeria, and proposals for future policy.

626 Soper, R. C.
The stone age in Northern Nigeria. *J. Hist. soc. Nig.*, 3 (2) Dec. 1965: 175–194, illus., map, bibliog.

627 *Wainwright, G. A.
Pharaonic survivals, Lake Chad to West Coast. *J. Egyptian archaeology*, 1949.

628 Willett, Frank
Digging for history in Nigeria. *Corona*, 12 (3) Mar. 1960: 103—105.

SECTION THREE
SOCIAL AND CULTURAL ANTHROPOLOGY;
ETHNOGRAPHY

GENERAL

629 Abiri, John Omoniyi Olayiole
A semantic differential study of some
Nigerian adolescent attitudes. 1965.
M.Ed. thesis, Birmingham University.

630 Adam, L.
De na-oorlogse economische en staat-
kundige opbouw von Nigeria. Leiden,
Afrika Instituut, 1954. 73p.

631 Agbebi, Mojala
The West African problem. In *Papers
on inter-racial problems communicated
to the first Universal races congress
held at the University of London, July
26–29, 1911. Ed. G. Spiller, 1911*: 341–
348.
Discusses West African customs and
institutions—ancestral and hero-wor-
ship, witchcraft, marriage, secret societies, Islam, etc.—and the problems
posed by the disrupting effect on these
of European political and social system.

632 Ainslie, James Robert.
A list of plants used in native medicine
in Nigeria. Oxford, Imperial forestry
institute, 1937. 92, 9, 7p. (Imperial
forestry institute papers, no. 7)

633 Ajayi, Jacob F. Ade
Christian missions in Nigeria, 1841–
1891: the making of a new elite. London,
Longmans, 1965. xvi, 317p. illus., maps,
bibliog. (Ibadan history series)
A study of Christian missionary
enterprise in Nigeria within the period
and of the role and influence of Christian
missions in the evolution of an indigenous Nigerian elite. Based on his
Ph.D. thesis, London, 1958.

634 Akiwowo, Akinsola
The place of Mojola Agbebi in the
African nationalist movements: 1890–
1917. *Phylon*, 26 (2) Summer 1965:
122–139.

635 Awa, Eme O.
Roads to socialism in Nigeria. *NISER
conf. proc., 9th, Ibadan, 1962*: 16–30,
bibliog.
A broad review of the trends and
vicissitudes to date of socialist thought
and socialist movements in Nigeria.

636 Balogun, Kolawole
Interpreting "Nigeria in cartoons",
Lagos, Ijaiye press, 1944, iv. 28p.
The pamphlet "Nigeria in cartoons"
by Akinola Lasekan depicts in pictures
contemporary Nigerian life. Here, Mr.
Balogun expresses in words what is
depicted in Lasekan's cartoons. See [695]

637 Bamata, N.
The Ibadan symposium on African
culture. *Unesco chronicle*, 7 (1) May
1961: 174–180.

638 Bascom, William Russell
African culture and the missionary.
Civilizations, 3 (4) 1953: 491–504.

639 —West Africa and the complexity of
primitive cultures. *Amer. anthrop.*, 50
(1) Jan.–Mar. 1948: 18–23.

640 Bascom, William Russell and Herskovits, Melville J., *eds.*
Continuity and change in African cultures. Chicago Ill., University of Chicago
press, 1959. x, 309p.

641 Bittinger, Desmond Wright
An educational experiment in Northern
Nigeria in its cultural setting. Elgin, Ill.,
Brethren publishing house, 1941. xvi,
343p. bibliog.
In three parts. Parts 1 and 2 give a
historical sketch of Northern Nigeria
from the ancient kingdoms of the
Western Sudan to the British administration of the 20th century. Pt. 3 is a
summary of the development and patterns of education in the region. Based
on author's Ph.D. thesis, Pennsylvania,
1941. Also issued under title "Black and
white in the Sudan".

642 Bohannan, Paul J.
Translation—a problem in anthropology. *Listener*, 51 (1315) May 13th
1954: 815–816.
A general view, with illustrations from
the writings of Amos Tutuola (Yoruba)
and from the Tiv language.

643 Brinkworth, Ian
Nigeria's cultural heritage. *Geog. mag.*,
31 (9) Jan. 1951: 425–438, map.

644 Callaway, Archibald
Nigeria's indigenous education: the
apprentice system. *Odu*, 1 (1) Jl. 1964:
62–79.
A study of the nature, conditions
and economic aspects of the apprentice
system in Nigeria—a system in which
young people wanting to learn a trade
are attached to indigenous proprietors
of private enterprises, the trades learned
ranging from traditional crafts like
wood-carving, bronze casting, cloth,

mat and basket weaving, leather work, and trading to modern skills like dry cleaning, motor vehicle repairs, electrical wiring, etc. The study is based on a survey made in Ibadan in July and August 1961.

644a Chard, L. W. la See La Chard, L. W.

645 Coker, Increase Herbert Ebenezer
Grammar of African names: a guide to the appreciation of the cosmic significance of Nigerian and Ghanaian names. [Lagos, Daily Times of Nigeria, 1964.] 40p. front., illus. (A Daily Times publication)

646 —Grammer of African names: an outline guide to the study and appreciation of the significance of African names selected from the Akan (Gold Coast), Yoruba, Ibo, Ijaw and Efik-Ibibio language groups. [Lagos, the author, 1954.] [4] 32p. illus.
Printed by Techno literary works, Yaba.

647 Conference on the Church and native customs, Ozala, Onitsha, May 12th, 1914.
The Church and native customs. Lagos, C.M.S. press, 1914. 24p.

648 Cooksey, J. J. and Mcleish, Alexander
Religion and civilization in West Africa: a missionary survey of French, British, Spanish and Portuguese West Africa, with Liberia. London, World dominion press, 1931. 277p. front., maps.

648a De Cardi, C. N. See Cardi, Charles Napoléon, comte de.

649 Delafosse, Maurice
Haut-Sénégal-Niger (Soudan français) Le pays, les peuples, les langages, l'histoire, les civilisations. Paris, E. Larose, 1912. 3v. maps, bibliog.
v. 1. Le pays, les peuples, les langages. 428p. v. 2. L'histoire. 428p. v. 3. Les civilisations. 316p.

650 —Les nègres. Paris, Editions Rieder, [1927] 80p. illus., bibliog. (Bibliothèque générale illustrée, 4.)

651 —The negroes of Africa: history and culture. Translated from the French by F. Fligelman. Washington, Associated publishers, [1931] xxxiii, 313p. maps, bibliog.
Three books on the negroes—Les noirs de l'Afrique (1921), Civilisations négro-africaines (1925) and Les nègres (1927)—all by the author, are here combined and translated. Only four chapters were included from the last named book.

652 Desplagnes, Louis
Le plateau central Nigérien, une mission archéologique et ethnographique au Soudan français. Paris, Emile Larose, 1907. 504p. 119 illus., map.
An elaborate treatise on the archaeology, ethnography and traditional history of the peoples of the central plateau, especially the non-Muslim inhabitants.

653 Dodge, Stanley D.
The distribution of population in Northern Nigeria. *Papers Mich. acad.*

of sci., arts & letters, 14, 1931: 297–303, map.

654 Dowd, Jérôme
The negro races; a sociological study, vol. I, West Africans: The Negritos, comprising the Pygmees, Bushmen and Hottentots of Central and South Africa. The Nigritans comprising the Yolofs, Mandingos, Hausas, Ashantis, Dahomeans, etc., of the Sudan and the Fellatahs of Central Sudan. New York, London, Macmillan, 1907. xxiii, 493p.

655 Echeruo, Michael Joseph Chukwudalu
Zik and the beginnings of Nigeria's intellectual history. [Nsukka, the author, 1965] 42p.
Mimeographed.

656 Escayrac de Lauture, Stanilas, comte de.
Mémoire sur le Soudan, géographie naturelle et politique, histoire et ethnographie, moeurs et institutions de l'empire des Fellatas, du Bornou, du Baguermi, du Waday, du Dar-Four, rédigé d'après des renseignements entièrement nouveaux et accompagné d'une esquisse du Soudan oriental. Paris, A. Bertrand, 1855–56. 184p.

657 Esin, E. Ekanem
Cause & effect. C.M.S. bookshop, 1915. 15p.
A powerful assault on what he considers the weaknesses or "the outstanding foibles" of the African.

658 Ferguson, John
Race relations in Nigeria. *Afr. q.,* 2 (4) Jan.–Mar. 1963: 230–239.

659 Forde, Cyril Daryll
The cultural map of West Africa: successive adaptations to tropical forests and grasslands. *Tr. N.Y. acad. sci.,* ser. 2, 15 (6) 1953: 206–219, maps, bibliog.
A broad survey of patterns of cultural contacts and ecological adaptations in the Western Sudan and the Guinea Coast. Later reprinted (with revisions) in *Cultures and societies of Africa,* ed. Simon and Phoebe Ottenberg, 1960: 116–138. [720]

659a Forde, Cyril Daryll, ed.
Ethnographic survey of Africa: Western Africa.
Pt. 3. The Ibo and Ibibio speaking peoples of South-Eastern Nigeria. See [3170]
Pt. 4. The Yoruba-speaking peoples of South-Western Nigeria. See [4535]
Pt. 7. Peoples of the plateau area of Northern Nigeria. See [678]
Pt. 8. The Tiv of Central Nigeria. See [4262]
Pt. 10. Peoples of the Niger-Benue confluence. See [661]
Pt. 12. Pagan peoples of the central area of Northern Nigeria. See [677]
Pt. 13. The Benin Kingdom and the Edo-speaking peoples of South-Western Nigeria, together with a section on the Itsekiri. See [1766]
Pt. 15. Peoples of the Middle Niger region, Northern Nigeria. See [679]

660 —Peoples of Nigeria. *Times Brit. col. rev.*, 38, 1960: 19–20, illus.

661 Forde, Cyril Daryll [and others]
Peoples of the Niger-Benue confluence: The Nupe, by Daryll Forde; The Igbira, by Paula Brown; The Igala, by Robert G. Armstrong; The Idoma-speaking peoples, by Robert G. Armstrong. London, Int. Afr. Inst., 1955. 160p. maps, bibliog. (Ethnographic survey of Africa. Western Africa, pt. 10)

662 Frobenius, Leo
Atlantis; Volksmärchen und Volks-dichtungen Afrikas . . . Muenchen, Veröffentlichungen d. Forschungs-instituts für Kulturmorphologie [1921–28] 12v. illus., maps, plans.
Separate entries made for individual volumes.

663 —Die atlantische Götterlehre. Jena, Eugen Diederichs, 1926 [iii] ix, 320p. illus., maps. (Atlantis; Völksmärchen und Volksdichtungen Afrikas, v. 10)

664 —Aus den Flegeljahren der Menschheit; Bilder des Lebens, Treibens und Denkens der Wilden . . . Hannover, Gebrüder Janecke, 1901. xi, 416p. illus.
A general account of ethnology of primitive peoples. See also English translation, with title "The childhood of man . . ." [666]

665 —Auf dem Wege nach Atlantis. Bericht über den Verlauf der zweiten Reise-periode der D.I.A.F.E. in den Jahren 1908 bis 1910. Berlin-Charlottenburg, Vita, Deutsches Verlagshaus [1911] xv, 412p. front., illus., maps,
Half-title reads: Deutsche Inner-Afrikanische Forschungs-Expedition. Zweiter Reisebericht.

666 —The childhood of man; a popular account of the lives, customs and thoughts of the primitive races. Trans-lated by A. H. Keane. London, Seeley, 1909. 504p. front., illus.

667 —Kulturtypen aus dem Westsudan: Auszüge aus den Ergebnissen der zweiten Deutschen Innerafrikanischen Forschungsexpedition, nebst einem Anhang über Kulturzonen und Kultur-forschung in Afrika. Gotha, J. Perthes, 1910. 126p. illus., map. (Petermanns Mitteilungen. Ergänzungsheft, 166)

668 —Monumenta africana; der Geist eines Erdteils. Frankfurt am Main, Frank-furter Societätsdruckerei g.m.b.h., Abteilung Buchverlag, 1929. 527p. illus.

669 —Vom Schreibtisch zum Äquator: planmässige Durchwanderung Afrikas. Frankfurt am Main, Frankfurter Societätsdruckerei, g.m.b.h., Abteilung Buchverlag, 1925. 472p. maps.

670 —Das sterbende Afrika: die Seele eines Erdteils: I vollständige Ausg. Frankfurt am Main, Frankfurter Societätsdruc-kerei g.m.b.h., Abteilung Buchverlag, 1928. 503p. (His Erlebte Erdteile, Bd. 5)

671 —Das unbekannte Afrika: Aufhellung der Schicksale eines Erdteils. München, Beck, 1923. xi, 185p. plates, maps.
Includes a discussion of Yoruba art (especially sculpture) and religion, pp. 127–175.

672 —The voice of Africa: being an account of the travels of the German inner African exploration expedition in the years 1910–1912. Translated by Rudolf Blind. London, Hutchinson, 1913, repr. London, Frank Cass, 1969. 2v. fronts., illus.
Contains extensive ethnological data on West Africa.

673 Frobenius, Leo and Bieber, F. J.
Zur Herrlichkeit des Sudans, mit einer Widmung von Leo Frobenius. Stuttgart, Union deutscher Verlagsgesellschaften [1923] 314p. illus.

674 Gavrilov, N.
O migratsii rabochey sily v Zapadnoy Afrike. *Prob. vos.*, (3) 1959: 82–90.
Discusses the implications and prob-lems of migrant labour in West Africa.

675 Gill, Dhara Singh
Aspects of rural life in Northern Nigeria with implications for agricultural ex-tension work. 1964. 256p.
Ph.D. thesis, Cornell University. A study of social, economic and edu-cational aspects of rural life in Makarfi District of Zaria Province in terms of their relation to, and implications for agricultural extension activities.

675a Goodwin, A. J. H.
Rock gongs, chutes, paintings and fertility. See [607]

676 Gourou, Pierre
Géographie du peuplement en Nigéria méridionale. *Bull. Soc. belge d'étud. géogr.*, 17 (1–2) 1947: 58–64.
Investigation of the high concentra-tion of population in parts of the Yoruba and Ibo areas of Nigeria.

677 Gunn, Harold D.
Pagan peoples of the central area of Northern Nigeria (The Butawa, War-jawa, etc. of the Bauchi-Kano border-land. The Kurama, etc., the Katab group, the Kadara, etc., of Zaria Province) London, Int. Afr. Inst., 1956. 144p. map, bibliog. (Ethnographic survey of Africa. Western Africa, pt. 12)

678 —Peoples of the plateau area of Northern Nigeria. London, Int. Afr. Inst., 1953. 111p. map. (Ethnographic survey of Africa. Western Africa, pt. 7)

679 Gunn, Harold D. and Conant, Francis P.
The peoples of the Middle Niger region, Northern Nigeria. London, Int. Afr. Inst., 1960. 138p. map, tables, bibliog. (Ethnographic survey of Africa. Western Africa, pt. 15)

680 Hambly, Wilfrid Dyson
Culture areas of Nigeria: Frederick H. Rawson—Field Museum ethnological expedition to West Africa, 1929–1930. Edited by Paul S. Martin. Chicago, Field Museum of Natural History, 1935.

pp. 365–502. plates, map, bibliog. (Field Museum of Natural History. Publication no. 346. Anthropological series, v. 21, no. 3)

681   —Ethnology of Africa. Chicago, Field Museum of Natural history, 1930. 226p. plates, maps, bibliog. (Field museum of natural history. Dept. of anthropology. Guide, pt. 3)

682   *Hartert, Ernst
Über Religion und Lebensweise der Bevölkerung in den von ihm bereisten Gegenden des Nigergebietes, Sowie über Handel und Verkehr daselbst. *Verh. Ges. f. Erdkde.* (13) Jan.–Dec. 1886: 431–440.
Description in general terms of the Hausas, Yoruba, Nupe, and other Nigerian peoples by a member of the German Niger-Benue expedition.

683   Haward, L. R. and Roland, W. A.
Some inter-cultural differences on the draw-a-man test: Goodenough scores. *Man*, 54, Je. 1954 (art. 127): 86–88.

684   Hefel, Annemaire
Der afrikanische Gelbguss und seine Beziehungen zu den Mittelmeerländern. *Wiener Beiträge zur Kulturgeschichte und zur Linguistik*, 5, 1943: 1–87.

685   Herskovits, Melville J.
Some recent development in the study of West African native life. *J. negro hist.*, 24 (1) Jan. 1939: 14–32.
Broad summary and appraisal of anthropological researches conducted in West Africa by scholars of different nationalities.

686   Hovelacque, Abel
Les nègres de l'Afrique sus-équatoriale (Sénégambie, Guinée, Soudan, Haut-Nil) Paris, Lecrosnier et Babé, 1889. xiv, 468p. illus.
In book one (pp. 1–237) dealing with ethnology of specific peoples, account is given of many Nigerian groups, including the Yoruba, Hausa, Kanuri, etc. Book two (pp. 238–459) deals with specific ethnological topics e.g. physical characteristics, marriage, family, agriculture, etc.

687   Institut français d'Afrique noire
Les Afro-Américains. Dakar, IFAN, 1952. 268p. illus., bibliog. (Mémoires IFAN, 27)

688   Ita, Eyo
Heralds of dawn. Calabar, Hope Waddell press, 1962. [x] 41p. illus.
Forceful and inspiring philosophical reflections on religion, ethics and moral rearmament.

689   Kirk-Greene, Anthony Hamilton Millard
The peoples of Nigeria: the cultural background to the crisis. *Afr. affairs*, 66 (262) Jan. 1967: 3–11.

690   Kitson, Albert Ernest
Southern Nigeria: some considerations of its structure, people and natural history. *Geog. j.*, 41, 1913: 16–38, illus., map.

691   La Chard, L. W.
The correlation of finger impressions and racial characteristics. *J. Afr. soc.*, 19 (73) Oct. 1919: 55–63, tables.
Describes his experiments to correlate racial and ethnic characteristics with finger imprints, using the finger prints of Hausa, Kanuri, Nupe, Yoruba and "pagan" convicts.

692   Lambo, T. Adeoye
Characteristic features of the psychology of the Nigerian. In *C.S.A. meeting of specialists on the basic psychology of African and Madagascan populations, Tananarive, 27 Aug.–3 Sept. 1959. Recommendations and reports. Publ. no. 51.* London, C.C.T.A. / C.S.A., 1959. Annex 2.

693   —Characteristic features of the psychology of the Nigerian. *W. Afr. med. j.*, n.s. 9 (3) Je. 1960: 95–104.

694   —Important areas of ignorance and doubts in the psychology of the African. In *Proc. 1st Int. conf. Africanists, 1962, ed. L. Bown and M. Crowder, 1964:* 337–344.
Based on author's work and observations in Nigeria.

695   Lasekan, Akinola
Nigeria in cartoons. [Lagos, 1944?] [3]p. 50 illus., one to a leaf.
Aspects of contemporary Nigerian life presented in cartoons. See also [636]

696   Leitch, J. N.
The native remedies and poisons of West Africa. 1932. 4v.
Ph.D. thesis, London.

696a   Lembezat, Bertrand
Les populations païennes du Nord-Cameroun et de l'Adamoua. Paris, Presses universitaires de France, 1961. 256p. map, bibliog.

697   Leonard, Arthur Glyn
Transmigration among the Southern Nigerian tribes. *Asiatic rev.*, 29, 1910: 338–351.

698   Long, Charles Houston
Myth, culture and history: an inquiry into the cultural history of West Africa. 1963.
Ph.D. thesis Chicago university.

698a   Macgregor, J. K.
Some notes on *Nsibidi. J.R.A.I.*, 39 [n.s. 12] 1909: 209–219, illus.
Historical and descriptive account of *Nsibidi* signs of which the author obtained some from boys from the Abiriba district. See also [2080] and [2084]

699   Martin, E. F.
Notes on some native objects from Northern Nigeria. *Man*, 3, 1903: 150–151 (art. 87); 4, 1904: 19–20 (art. 11) illus.
The objects described include a coat of mail, horse collar, ostrich feather slippers, lamps, beads, cloths, musical instruments, metal weapons and other articles of daily use obtained by the author from parts of Northern Nigeria.

700 —Notes on the ethnology of Nigeria. *Man*, 3, 1903: 82–86. (art. 46)

Author's impressions of Nigeria, forming an outline geographical and ethnographic sketch.

701 Meek, Charles Kingsley
The Northern tribes of Nigeria; an ethnographical account of the Northern Provinces of Nigeria, together with a report on the 1921 decennial census. London, O.U.P., 1925. 2v. front., plates.

702 —Tribal studies in Northern Nigeria. London, K. Paul, Trench and Trubner, 1931. 2v. fronts., plates, map, diagr.

Original ethnographic studies of some 50 non-muslim tribes in Northern Nigeria.

703 Mesle, E.
Inventaire ethnique du Nord-Cameroun. *Int. W. Afr. conf. proc., 5th, 1953 [1954?]:* 137–138.
Abstract only.

704 Meyer, Paul Constantin
Westsudan, mit Berücksichtigung seiner historischen, ethnologischen und wirtschaftlichen Verhältnisse. Gotha, J. Perthes, 1897. 107p. (Petermanns Mitteilungen. Ergänzungsheft, no. 121)

705 Morgan, Gordon Daniel
The adjustment of Nigerian students in American colleges. 1964. 130p.
Ph.D. thesis, Washington State university.

706 Morgan, W. B.
Settlement patterns of the Eastern Region of Nigeria. *Nig. geog. j.*, 1 (2) Dec. 1957: 23–30, maps.

707 The Moslem areas of Nigeria under British rule. *Nig. mag.*, (22) 1944: 30–41.

708 Mundy-Castle, A. C.
Considerations for psychological research in West Africa. *NISER conf. proc., 8th, Ibadan, 1962:* 171–173.

709 Murdock, George Peter
Africa: its peoples and their culture history. New York, McGraw-Hill, 1959. xiii, 456p. illus., maps, bibliog.

A bold ethnographic summary of Africa, sketching its ethnic and linguistic groupings and analysing their traditional economic, social and political systems. Based entirely on a survey of relevant literature. Excellent bibliographies at end of sections.

710 Newland, H. Osman
Ethnology and psychology of West Africa. In his *West Africa; a handbook of practical information . . . 1922:* 73–206.

Notes on customs, laws, languages, religion, secret societies, etc., of the major ethnic groups.

711 Nigeria's population explosion. *W. Africa*, (2439) Feb. 29 1964: 225.

712 Niven, Cecil Rex
Some Nigerian population problems. *Geog. j.*, 85 (1) Jan. 1935: 54–58.

713 Nwokolo, U.

Practice of medicine by laymen in Nigeria. *Dokita*, 1, 1960: 59–62.

714 Nzekwu, Onuora
Kola nut. *Nig. mag.*, (71) Dec. 1961: 298–305, illus.

On the cultural significance of kola nuts among some Nigerian ethnic groups, especially Yoruba and Ibo.

715 *Offodile, E. P. Oyeaka
Growth and influence of tribal unions. *W. Africa*, 18 (239) 1947.

716 Offonry, H. Kanu
Some customs that have ceased. *W. Afr. rev.*, 20 (256) 1949: 23–24.

717 Okonjo, Chukuka
Patterns of population growth. *Nig. j. econ. soc. stud.*, 6 (1) Nov. 1964: 6–22.

718 Oldfield, Genevieve Ambrose
The native railway worker in Nigeria. *Africa*, 9 (3) Jl. 1936: 379–402, tables.

A detailed general and sociological analysis of Nigerian employees of the Railway, noting their salaries, distribution within the various departments, tribal groupings, education, religion, diet, housing, attitudes, efficiency and potential. French summary, pp. 401–402.

719 Onipede, Aladipo F.
Nigerian plural society; political and constitutional development, 1870–1954. 1956. 389p.
Ph.D. thesis, Columbia university.

720 Ottenberg, Simon and Ottenberg, Phoebe V., *eds.*
Cultures and societies of Africa, edited, with a general introduction, commentaries and notes. New York, Random house, 1960. [ix] 614p. illus., maps, bibliog. (pp. 565–598)

Thirty-two studies dealing with the environmental, social, governmental, religious and other aspects of African peoples, previously published in various journals and books, and now aptly selected and collocated to reflect the extent and pattern of anthropological researches conducted on Africa. The general introduction by the editors presents a suitable background to the studies. For specifically relevant papers, see [659] [2190] [2448] [4191] [4286] and [5250]

721 Pilkington, Frederick
Pagan and anti-pagan. *Afr. affairs*, 58 (230) Jan. 1959: 61–64.

Illustrates the different levels of progress in Nigeria by comparing the general and especially social progress of Lagos with the still primitive state of the inhabitants of Plateau Province.

722 Potekhin, I. I.
O samobytnoy Afrikanskoy' demokratii v Nigerii. *Sov. et.*, (4) 1947: 234–247.

723 Prothero, R. Mansell
African ethnographic maps, with a new example from Northern Nigeria. *Africa*, 32 (1) Jan. 1962: 61–64.
On ethnographic mapping of Africa.

Discusses the ethnographic aspects of the 1952 census in Northern Nigeria, illustrating this with the map based on that census and first published in 1958 as an appendix to the Minorities Commission Report.

724 —Labour migration in British West Africa. *Corona,* 9 (5) May 1957: 169–172.
A brief discussion of migration in Nigeria and Ghana.

725 —Migrant labour in West Africa. *J. loc. admin. overseas,* 1 (3) 1962: 149–155, map.
Reviews studies of the problem made by the Human Sciences section of the Congrès International des Africanistes de l'Ouest (C.I.A.O.) and by C.C.T.A.

726 —Migrations and social change in Africa. In *Africa im Wandel seiner Gesellschaftsformen. Herausgegeben von W. Fröhlich, 1964:* 14–34, maps, bibliog.
Population movements as a continuous feature of life in Africa, its causative factors, and the resultant social changes. Treatment is general, but with supporting evidence drawn from the Fulani, among others.

727 —Migratory labour from Northwestern Nigeria. *Africa,* 27 (3) Jl. 1957: 251–261, maps, table.
A study of labour migration, mostly from Sokoto Province, to different parts of West Africa.

728 Roemer, Michael
Cultural influences in African manufacturing organisations. 1962. 146p.
Ph.D. thesis, School of Industrial Management, Massachusetts Institute of Technology. Topics dealt with include acculturation in work organisations, African manufacturing organisation—(a) in Uganda, and (b) in Eastern Nigeria.

729 Rogers, Cyril A.
A study of race attitudes in Nigeria. *Human probl.,* (26) Dec. 1959: 51–64.
Race attitudes of Europeans and educated Nigerians towards each other. Results of a survey among the students of University College, Ibadan.

730 Russell, T. A.
The kola of Nigeria and the Cameroons. *Trop. agric.,* 32 (3) Jl. 1955: 210–240, bibliog.
A botanical study of the kola, with useful notes on its cultural significance and its place in the social and religious customs of the people of Nigeria, especially the Hausa and Yoruba.

731 Seligman, C. G.
Races of Africa. London, T. Butterworth, 1930. 256p. maps, bibliog.
A major attempt at an all-embracing classification of the races of Africa.

732 Skinner, Elliot P.
Strangers in West African societies. *Africa,* 33 (4) Oct. 1963: 307–320.
On "stranger elements" and tribalism in the new West African states. French summary, p. 320.

733 *Smith, Henry Frederick Charles
A note on Muhammed al-Maghili. *Bull. news Hist. soc. Nig.* 7 (3) Dec. 1962: 11–12.

734 *Smith, Michael Garfield
Social and cultural pluralism. *Ann. N.Y. acad. sci.,* 83 (art. 5) Jan. 20, 1960: 763–785.

735 Smyth, M. J. and Obaseki, J. O.
Observations on the influence of cultura. factors on psychiatric nursing in Nigerial In *Pan-African psychiatric conference, 1st, Abeokuta, 1961. [1962?]:* 203–206.

736 Smythe, Hugh H.
Disturbances at University College, Ibadan. *Sch. & soc.,* 86, Apr. 1958: 175–176.

737 —Education in Nigeria. *Sch. & soc.,* 87, Mar. 1959: 149–151.

738 Solarin, Tai
Towards Nigeria's moral self-government. Ikenne, the author, 1959. viii, 95p.
A Nigerian educator challengingly discusses the problems of education, squalor, sloth, corruption and other social issues in Nigeria.

739 Spengler, Joseph J.
Population movements and economic development in Nigeria. In *The Nigerian political scene, ed. Robert O. Tilman and Taylor Cole, 1962:* 147–197.

740 Stephan, Klaus
Nigeria: Reise gegen die Zeit. Munich, Prestel-Verlag, 1961. 149p. illus., map.

741 Stoutemeyer, J. H.
Religion and race education: (including Nigeria, Sierra Leone, South Africa) 1910.
Ph.D. thesis, Clark university.

742 Talbot, Percy Amaury
The peoples of Southern Nigeria: a sketch of their history, ethnology and languages, with an abstract of the 1921 census. London, O.U.P., 1926, repr. Frank Cass, 1969. 4v.
v. 1. Historical notes. xii, 365p. maps.
v. 2. Ethnology, xx, 423p. illus., maps.
v. 3. Ethnology [cont.] x, 425–976. illus., maps. v. 4. Linguistics and statistics. [iii] 234p. maps.

743 —Some foreign influences on Nigeria. *J. Afr. soc.,* 24 (95) Apr. 1925: 178–201, map.
An extended discussion of cultural and religious traits in Nigeria considered to be of possible eastern and Egyptian origin.

744 Temple, Olive
Notes on the tribes, provinces, emirates and states of the Northern Provinces of Nigeria, compiled from official reports by O. Temple. Edited by C. L. Temple. 2nd ed., Lagos, C.M.S. bookshop, 1922: [iv] 577, xiii, p.
1st ed. 1919. Tribes listed alphabetically from Ade to Zyemawa,

followed by provinces (and emirates) likewise arranged. Information on each tribe includes location, occupation, brief history, etc. Many genealogical tables.

744a —Reprint of 2nd ed., with a new bibliographical note. London, Frank Cass, 1965. ix, 595p.

745 Tidjani, A. Serpos
Note sur la migration humaine à la Côte du Bénin. *Bull. IFAN*, 22 (3–4) Juil.–Oct. 1960: 509–513.
Migrations in Nigeria and Dahomey.

746 Tong, Raymond L.
School antiquities society. *Nig. mag.*, (43) 1954: 258–262.
Notes the importance of such societies in schools and gives an account of one founded in Edo College, Benin City.

747 Tremearne, Arthur John Newman
Education and anthropology in West Africa. *United empire*, 1, 1910: 408–413.

748 —Some Nigerian head-hunters. *J. Roy. soc. arts*, 59, 1911: 295–319.

748a —The tailed head-hunters of Nigeria. See [3856]

749 Trimingham, J. Spencer
The Christian church and Islam in West Africa. London, S.C.M. press, 1955. 56p. map. (I.C.M. research pamphlets, no. 3)

750 Udo, R. K.
A geographical analysis of rural settlements in the Eastern Region of Nigeria. 1963.
Ph.D. thesis, London.

751 —The migrant tenant farmer of Eastern Nigeria. *Africa*, 34 (4) Oct. 1964: 326–339, illus., maps.
Reviews the movements of farmers from densely populated and overfarmed districts to sparsely populated areas and notes the causes and socio-economic implications of these migrations. French summary, pp. 338–339.

752 Urvoy, Yves François Marie Aimé
Petit atlas ethno-démographique du Soudan entre Sénégal et Tchad. Paris, Larose, 1942. 46p. illus., maps. (Mémoires IFAN, no. 5)

753 Wallerstein, I.
Ethnicity and national integration in West Africa. *Cah. étud. afr.*, 3, 1960: 129–139.

754 Webster, J. B.
Bible and the plough. *J. hist. soc. of Nig.*, 2 (4) Dec. 1963: 418–434.

755 Werder, Peter von
Herrschaft und Gemeinschaft im West-sudan. *Africa*, 10 (3) Jl. 1937: 293–307, bibliog.
English summary, pp. 306–307.

756 Whitaker, Cleophaus Sylvester
The politics of tradition: a study of continuity and change in Northern Nigeria, 1946–1960. 1964. 629p.
Ph.D. thesis, Princeton university.

2. HISTORY

757 Aderibigbe, A. A. B.
Peoples of Southern Nigeria. In *A thousand years of West African history*, ed. J. F. A. Ajayi and I. Espie, 1965: 187–200, map.

758 Ajayi, Jacob F. Ade
West African states at the beginning of the nineteenth century. In his *A thousand years of West African history, 1965*: 248–261, map.

759 Ajayi, Jacob F. Ade and Espie, Ian, *eds.*
A thousand years of West African history: a handbook for teachers and students. Ibadan, University press, London, Nelson, 1965. xi, 543p. maps, bibliog.

760 Anene, J. C.
Benin, Niger delta, Ibo and Ibibio peoples in the nineteenth century. In *A thousand years of West African history*, ed. J. F. A. Ajayi and I. Espie, 1965: 294–308, map.

761 —Towards a national history. *Ibadan*, (16) Je. 1963: 7–10.
A critical reassessment of the treatment and interpretation of Nigerian history by past writers, especially European, and a plea for a more impartial approach which would give a more faithful picture of Nigeria's history

762 Arikpo, Okoi
Legends and folklore. *W. Afr. rev.*, 30 (383) Oct. 1959: 665–667.
Traces the traditional myths and folklore of the Hausas and Yorubas, to show that both had had early contacts and had migrated into Nigeria about the same time, together with the Kanuris. The Bini, Itsekiri and the Igalla are shown to have a common origin with the Yoruba.

763 —Who are the Nigerians?; a reprint of the 1957 Lugard Lectures. Lagos, Federal information service, 1957. 32p. illus. (Lugard lectures, 1957)
Analyses the legends, folklore and customs of Nigeria's ethnic constituents to show that they belong to one racial stock.

764 Armattoe, R. E. G.
The golden age of West African civilization, with an introduction by E. Schroedinger. Londonderry, N. Ireland, "Londonderry Sentinel" for Lomeshie research centre, 1946. 96p. illus., bibliog.
12 of the illustrations are of Nigerian sculptures.

765 Ashaolu, T. A. [and others]
A history of West Africa: A.D. 1000 to the present day. Ibadan, Onibonoje press, 1966. ix, 191p. maps.

766 Biobaku, Saburi O.
An historical account of the evolution of Nigeria as a political unit. In *Constitutional problems of federalism in Nigeria. 1961*. pp. 221–229.

767 Bovill, Edward William

Caravans of the old Sahara: an introduction to the history of the Western Sudan. London, O.U.P., for Int. Inst. Afr. Languages and Cultures, 1933. [xii] 300p. front., illus., maps, bibliog.

768 —The golden trade of the Moors. London, O.U.P., 1958. ix, 281p. front., maps, bibliog.
Essentially a revision of the author's earlier work.

769 Burdon, John A., *comp.*
Northern Nigeria: historical notes on certain emirates and tribes. (Selected and arranged by J. A. Burdon) London, Waterlow, 1909. 98p.
A collection of historical notes sent in by various authors. Includes the translation of Mischlich's "Contribution to the History of the Hausa States" [2512] and a translation of the "Kano chronicle", by H. R. Palmer.

770 Davidson, Basil
The lost cities of Africa. Boston, Little, Brown, 1959. 209p. illus., maps, bibliog.
American edition of Old Africa rediscovered [771]

771 —Old Africa rediscovered. London, V. Gollancz, 1959. 287p. illus., maps, bibliog.
A survey of the ancient civilisations of Africa south of the Sahara. Chapter 3 (pp. 61–132) deals mostly with West African cultures from the Nok era down to the Ife and Benin periods.

772 De Graft-Johnson, John Coleman
African glory; the story of vanished African civilisations. London, Watts [1954] 209p. illus.

773 Fage, John D
Some thoughts on state-formation in the Western Sudan before the seventeenth century. In *Boston university papers in Afr. hist.*, 1, 1964: 19–34.

774 Frobenius, Leo
Histoire de la civilisation africaine. Traduit par H. Back et D. Ermont. 6 éd. Paris, Gallimard [1936] 370p. front., illus., maps.

775 —Kulturgeschichte Afrikas; Prolegomena zu einer historischen Gestaltlehre. Zurich, Phaidon-Verlag, 1933. 652p. front., illus., plates, maps, bibliog.

776 Greenberg, Joseph Harold
Historical inferences from linguistic research in sub-Saharan Africa. In *Boston university papers in African history*, 1, 1964: 3–15.
Describes methods by which historical inferences can be drawn from linguistic studies, illustrating such methods with examples from Hausa, Kanuri, and other West African languages.

777 Hallam, W. K. R.
The men behind traditions, *Nig. mag.*, (91) Dec. 1966: 271–278, illus.

778 Hunwick, J. O.
The nineteenth century jihads. In *A thousand years of West African history*,

ed. *J. F. A. Ajayi and I. Espie, 1965:* 262–278.

779 Ifemesia, C. Chieka
The peoples of West Africa around A.D. 1000. In *A thousand years of West African history, ed. J. F. A. Ajayi and I. Espie, 1965*: 39–54. map.

780 —Unwritten sources for historical reconstruction in Africa. *Historia,* 2 (1) Apr. 1965: 56–66.
On the importance of archaeology, oral tradition, ethnography, linguistics, etc., in the reconstruction of African history.

781 Jeffreys, M. D. W.
Niger: origins of the word. *Cah. étud. afr.,* 4 (3) 1964: 443–451.

782 —Who were the aborigines of West Africa? *W. Afr. rev.,* 22 (248) May 1951: 466–467, illus.

783 Macadam, Conrad
Lost civilizations of ancient Nigeria. *Travel,* 74 (5) Mar. 1940: 36–38.

784 Mathews, A. B.
The Kisra legend. *Afr. stud.* 9 (3) Sept. 1950: 144–147, illus.
Notes on the Kisra legend in Northern Nigeria and the possibility of its connection with Chosroes of Persia. Relics of Kisra in Karissen, Wukari and Bussa are described.

785 Meek, Charles Kingsley
The Nilotic Sudan and West Africa. *Man,* 33, Feb. 1933: 39–40 (art. 43).
A letter listing several tribes in Northeastern Nigeria which have the same word for chief or god.

786 Migeod, Frederick William Hugh
Migration and distribution of races and tribes [in West Africa] In his *The languages of West Africa, 1911–1913.* v. 1, pp. 15–44. [1491]

787 Olderogge, D. A.
Proiskhozhdeniye narodov Tzentral' nogo Sudana: Iz drevneyshey istorii Yazykov grupy Khausa-Kotoko. *Sov. et.,* (2) 1952: 23–38.
On the history of the Central Sudanese peoples and of the Hausa-Kotoko group of languages.

788 Olderogge, D. A. and Potekhin, I. I., *eds.*
Narody Afriki. Moscow, Izdatelstvo Akademiya Nauk SSSR, 1954. 732p. illus., maps.
A collective work on the history and ethnography of African peoples, published in the series "Peoples of the world", Devoted some 100 pages (259–359) to the peoples of the Western Sudan. See [790]

789 —Die Völker Afrikas. Ihre Vergangenheit und Gegenwart. Unter der Redaktion von D. A. Olderogge und I. I. Potechin. Berlin, Deutscher Verlag der Wissenschaften, 1961. 2v. illus., maps.
German translation of Narody Afriki. See [788]

790 —Zapadny Sudan. In *Narody Afriki, 1954:* 259–359.

An ethnographic study of the Western Sudan.

791 —Zapadny Sudan v XV–XIX vv. Ocherki po istorii kulturi. Moskva-Leningrad, Izdatelstvo Akademiya Nauk SSSR, 1960. 267p. (Akademiya Nauk SSSR. Trudi Instituta etnografii im N. Miklukho-Maklaya, Novaya seriya, t. 53)
Outline history of the Western Sudanese states from the 15th to the 19th centuries. Considerable attention given to the Hausa states, which take the whole of chapter 4, with chapter 5 devoted to the Fulani rising under Usman Dan Fodio. Emphasis is laid throughout on cultural patterns and social changes during the period.

791a Palmer, Herbert Richmond
Sudanese memoirs. See [3994]

792 —Western Sudan history: the Raudthât' ul afkâri. J. Afr. soc., 15 (59) Apr. 1916: 261–273.
Translation of a manuscript on the history of the Western Sudan, written by Muhammad Bello, Emir of Sokoto between 1823 and 1837.

793 Queen's School, Enugu
The history and culture of Eastern Nigeria. [by] Lower, Upper and Senior VIth forms, Queen's school, Enugu. Enugu [the school], 1963. [10] 100p. map.
Mimeographed.

794 Schweeger-Exeli, Annemarie
Probleme mediterraner Kultureinflüsse in Westafrika. Tribus, (9) Sept. 1960: 181–89, illus.
Supports and tries to substantiate the view that West Africa had in prehistoric or early historic times been influenced by extraneous cultures, particularly from the Mediterranean region.

795 Segy, Ladislas
Towards a new historical concept on negro Africa. J. negro hist., 38 (1) Jan. 1953: 27–40

796 Shinnie, Margaret
Ancient African kingdoms. London, E. Arnold, 1965. 126p. illus., bibliog.
Outline history of a number of African states before the arrival of Europeans. Includes Kanem, Bornu, Nok culture, Yoruba, and Benin (pp. 67–83)

797 Smith, Henry Frederick Charles
A neglected theme of West African history: the Islamic revolutions of the 19th century. J. Hist. soc. Nig., 2 (2) 1961: 169–185.

798 Tamuno, Tekena Nitonye
Peoples of the Niger-Benue confluence. In A thousand years of West African history, ed. J. F. A. Ajayi and I. Espie, 1965: 201–211, map.

799 Urvoy, Yves François Marie Aimé
Histoire des populations du Soudan central. (Colonie du Niger) Paris, Larose, 1936. 350p. illus., maps, bibliog. (Publications du Comité d'études historiques et scientifiques occidentale française. Ser. A. no. 5)

800 Vansina, J. [and others] eds.
The historian in tropical Africa: studies presented and discussed at the fourth International African seminar at the University of Dakar, Senegal, 1961. London, O.U.P., for International African Institute, 1964. ix, 248p. map, bibliog.
Four of the papers are specifically relevant and deal respectively with Hausa society [2469] Idoma and Yoruba history [3609], history of the Chad region [3979] and Benin and Yoruba history [1790]

801 Vuillet, Jean
Essai d'interpretation de traditions légendaires sur les origines des vieux empires soudanais. Comptes rendus mens. séances acad. sci. col., (10) 1950: 268–288.

802 Westermann, Diedrich
Geschichte Afrikas—Staatenbildungen südlich der Sahara. Köln, Greven-Verlag, 1952. xi, 492p. illus., maps, bibliog.
Historical account of the rise, decline, rulers (and reigns) of African states south of the Sahara. Includes the Fulani, Hausa, Jukun, Tiv, Kanuri, Nupe, Borgawa, Yoruba, and Bini. Extensive bibliography, pp. 455–470.

802a Williams, Joseph John
Hebrewisms of West Africa; from the Nile to the Niger with the Jews. See [567]

803 Woelfel, Dominik J.
Die Kanerischen Inseln, die westafrikanischen Hochkulturen und das alte Mittelmeer. Paideuma, (4) 1950: 231–253, illus.
A highly critical article stressing points of similarity between the Canary Islands and ancient West African civilizations, and regarding both as originating from the ancient Mediterranean, especially from Crete and the Aegean. Theories suggesting Etruscan, Phoenician, or Coptic-Byzantine origin of West African cultures are rejected.

3. MARRIAGE, FAMILY, LINEAGE STRUCTURE

804 Arikpo, Okoi
The future of bride price. W. Afr., (2018) Oct. 29, 1955: 1017.

805 Broadbent, J. D. S.
The marriage problem in Nigeria. East & West rev., 12 (4) Oct. 1946: 105–111.

806 Childs, Stanley H.
Christian marriage in Nigeria. Africa, 16 (4) Oct. 1946: 238–246.

807 Coleman, R. W. A.
Changing customs in Nigeria. W. Afr. rev., 20 (263) 1949: 897–899.

808 Copeland-Crawford, W. E. B.

A letter re native marriages. *W. Equatorial Afr. diocesan mag.,* 12 (140) Feb. 1906: 117.

A letter from the Divisional Commissioner stationed at Onitsha on govt. aims regarding the abolition of infant marriage.

809 Delano, Isaac O.
An African looks at marriage. London, United society for Christian literature. 1944. 47p. (Africa's own library, no. 3)

810 James, R. W. and Kasunmu, A. B.
Alienation of family property in Southern Nigeria. Ibadan, University press, 1966. xvii, 117p.

811 Jones, F. Melville
Polygamy in West Africa. *Int. rev. missions,* 12, Jl. 1923: 403–411.

812 Leech, William David
Changing attitudes towards sex and marriage among urban Nigerians. See [1309]

813 Little, Kenneth L.
Some urban patterns of marriage and domesticity in West Africa. *Sociol. rev.,* 7 (1) Jl. 1959: 65–82.

Descriptive study of the changing patterns of married life in modern West African towns.

814 Marris, Peter
The approach of sociologists and anthropologists to the study of family relationships. *NISER conf. proc., 1958:* 164–167.

815 Meek, Charles Kingsley
Marriage by exchange in Nigeria: a disappearing institution. *Africa.* 9 (1) Jan. 1936: 64–74.

The system of marriage by exchange, practised by the Afo, Anaguta, Ayu, Basa, Borok, Birom, Gurkawa, and other Nigerian tribes, is examined and the factors militating against its continued existence considered.

815a Nwogugu, E. I.
Legitimacy in Nigerian law. See [860]

816 Okoro, N. A.
The customary laws of succession in Eastern Nigeria and the statutory and judicial rules concerning their application. 1963.
Ph.D. thesis, Cambridge.

817 Omari, T. P.
Changing attitude of students in West African society towards marriage and family relationships. *Brit. j. sociol.,* 11 (3) Sept. 1960: 197–210.

818 Pakenham, E. T.
Polygamy: a problem in Nigeria. *Church miss., rev.,* Mar. 1923: 15–21.

819 The problem of polygamy. Preface by B. Lasbrey, Bishop on the Niger. Lagos, C.M.S. bookshop, London, S.P.C.K., 1926. vii, 85p.

Papers attacking polygamy as wrong in the Christian church. Occasioned by independent African churches' tendency to excuse polygamy.

819a Salacuse, Jeswald

A selective survey of Nigerian family law. See [865]

820 Smythe, Hugh H.
Inter-marriage in West Africa. *Sociol. & soc. res.,* 42 (5) May–Je. 1958: 353–357.

821 —Patterns of kinship structure in West Africa. 1945.
Ph.D. thesis, Northwestern university.

822 Tegnaeus, Harry
Blood-brothers, an ethno-sociological study of the institutions of blood-brotherhood with special reference to Africa. Stockholm, Ethnological museum, 1952. 181p. illus., bibliog. (Ethnological museums of Sweden, Stockholm. Publications. New series, no. 10)

Its practice among the northern tribes of Nigeria and among the Yoruba, pp. 134–141.

822a Usoro, Eno J.
The place of women in Nigerian society. See [896]

4. GOVERNMENT, KINGSHIP, LAW

Works on traditional land law and land tenure systems are considered from the viewpoint of customary law and are therefore included here rather than in the section on Agriculture.

823 Ajayi, Festus Adebisi
The future of customary law in Nigeria. In *The future of customary law in Africa. Symposium, Amsterdam, 1955.* 1956. 42–69.

824 —The interaction of English law with customary law in Western Nigeria. *J. Afr. law,* 4 (1) Spring 1960: 40–50; (2) Summer 1960: 98–114.

825 —The judicial approach to customary law in Southern Nigeria. 1958.
Ph.D. thesis, London.

826 Akpan, Ntieyong U.
Chieftaincy in Eastern Nigeria. *J. Afr. admin.,* 9 (3) Jl. 1957: 120–124.

Sets out the categories and grades of chiefs and people with traditional authority or influence in Eastern Nigeria. Anticipated in part the findings of the Jones Commission

827 —Have traditional authorities a place in modern local government systems? *J. Afr. admin.,* 7 (3) Jl. 1955: 109–116.

828 Anderson, J. N. D.
Law and custom in Muslim areas in Africa: recent developments in Nigeria. *Civilisations,* 7 (1) 1957: 17–31.
French summary, pp. 29–31.

829 Anya, O. U.
Chiefs and government in Eastern Nigeria. 1963.
Diss. for Dip. Pub. Admin., London.

830 Azikiwe, Nnamdi
Land tenure in Northern Nigeria; a study of the treaty rights of the Royal Niger Company, Chartered and Limited. Lagos, African book company [1942?] 44p. bibliog.

831	—Nigerian political institutions. *J. negro hist.*, 14, Jl. 1929: 328–341.

832	Baldwin, Kenneth D. S.
Land-tenure problems in relation to agricultural development in the Northern Region of Nigeria. In *African agrarian systems, edited by D. Biebuyck, 1963:* 65–82, bibliog.

833	—Some problems of government in land settlement. *WAISER conf. proc., 1956:* 36–44.
On the problems of population redistribution and planned land settlement in Nigeria.

834	Biebuyck, Daniel, *ed.*
African agrarian systems: studies presented and discussed at the second international African seminar, Lovanium University, Leopoldville, January 1960. London, O.U.P., for Int. Afr. inst., 1963. xiii, 408p. maps, bibliog.
An introductory survey of the whole field in Pt. I is followed in Pt. II by papers on specific aspects. Two of these: *Land-tenure problems in relation to agricultural development in the Northern region of Nigeria,* by K. D. S. Baldwin [832] and *'Land', 'tenure' and land-tenure,* by Paul Bohannan [4289] relate specifically to Nigeria.

835	Brook, N. T.
Some legal aspects of land tenure in Nigeria. *Afr. stud.*, 5 (4) Dec. 1946: 211–220.
A survey of the conflict between English and traditional or customary systems of land tenure in Nigeria.

836	Brown, Paula
Patterns of authority in West Africa. *Africa,* 21 (4) Oct. 1951: 261–278, bibliog.
Useful analysis of patterns of authority among the Ibo, Yoruba, Nupe, Yakö, Ashanti, Mende and the Tallensi. French summary, p. 278.

837	Buell, Raymond Leslie
Chieftains enthroned; British rule in Nigeria as a significant colonial experiment. *Asia,* 28 (1) Jan. 1928: 56–62.

838	Bulmer-Thomas, Ivor
The political aspects of immigration from country to town—Nigeria. *INCIDI,* 27, 1952: 476–484.

839	Cole, Cedric William
Village and district councils in the Northern Provinces of Nigeria. *J. Afr. admin.,* 3 (2) Apr. 1951: 91–94.
Reviews the patterns of village administration in Northern Nigeria from the days of the Habe kingdoms through the Fulani era to the British administration.

840	Daniel W. C. Ekow
Some principles of the law of trust in West Africa. *J. Afr. law,* 6 (3) Autumn 1962: 164–178.
French summary, p. 178.

841	Derrett, J. Duncan M., *ed.*
Studies in the laws of succession in Nigeria: essays edited, with an introductory chapter, by J. Duncan M. Derrett. London, O.U.P., for NISER, 1965. x, 293p. maps, bibliog.

842	Drake, St. Clair
Traditional authority and social action in former British West Africa. *Human organisation,* 19 (3) fall 1960: 150–158.

843	Elias, Taslim Olawale
Impact of English law on Nigerian customary law. Lagos, Govt. printer, 1960. 32p. front., illus. (Lugard lectures, 1958)

844	—Insult as an offence in African customary law. *Afr. affairs,* 53 (210) Jan. 1954: 66–69.
Includes illustrative instances from Zaria and from among the Ibos of Eastern Nigeria.

845	—The nature of African customary law. Manchester, university press, 1956. xii, 318p. bibliog.

846	—Nigerian land law and custom. 3rd ed. London, Routledge & K. Paul, 1962. xxx, 386p. map, bibliog.
The first attempt to organize into a coherent statement the principles underlying indigenous systems of land tenure in Nigeria. 1st ed. published in 1951. Based on his Ph.D. thesis of the same title (London university, 1950)

847	Garigue, Philip
An anthropological interpretation of changing political leadership in West Africa. 1953.
Ph.D. thesis, London.

848	Geary, William Nevill M.
Land tenure and legislation in British West Africa. *J. Afr. soc.,* 12 (47) Apr. 1913: 236–248, illus.

849	*Gibson, Thomas Ogbe
A handbook on West African native laws and customs (with particular reference to Southern Nigeria) [n.p.,n.d.] 26p.

850	Irons, Alden Hatheway
The changing sources of African local authority in the Colony and Protectorate of Nigeria, 1900–1950. 1961. 65p.
A.B. honours thesis, Harvard University.

851	James, Rudolph W.
The changing role of land in Southern Nigeria. *Odu,* 1 (2) 1965: 3–23.
Examines the changes in the role of land as reflected in customary law and customary case law.

851a	—Alienation of family property in Southern Nigeria. See [810]

852	Jeffreys, M. D. W.
Dual organisation in Africa. *Afr. stud.,* 5 (2) Je. 1946: 82–105; 5 (3) Sept. 1946: 157–176, bibliog.
A survey of the phenomenon of dual organisation in Africa, based on government reports and field work in several parts of Nigeria and on similar studies in other parts of Africa.

852a Jones, G. I.
Report on the position, status and influence of chiefs and natural rulers . . . See [859a]

853 Keith, A. Berriedale
Land tenure in Nigeria. *J. Afr. soc.,* 11 (43) Apr. 1912: 325–331.
A review of the Report of the Northern Nigeria Land Committee and of its Minutes of evidence, both laid before the British Parliament in 1910 as Cd. 5102 and 5103.

854 Luning, H. A.
The impact of socio-economic factors on the land tenure pattern in Northern Nigeria. *J. Local admin. overseas,* 4 (3) Jl. 1965: 173–182.
Reviews "the economic and social forces which are at work and the degree to which the original land tenure system has evolved under these forces."

855 McDowell, C. M.
An introduction to the problems of ownership of land in Northern Nigeria. Zaria, Institute of administration, 1966. iv, 80p. (Research memorandum)

856 Mai-Doya
"Native authority" in Nigeria: chiefs, title-holders and elders. *W. Afr. rev.,* 16 (208) Jan. 1945: 33–38.

856a Meek, Charles Kingsley
Land law and custom in the colonies. London, O.U.P., 1946, repr. London, Frank Cass, 1968. xxvi, 337p.
Each colony is treated separately. Nigeria, pp. 145–168.

857 —Land tenure and land administration in Nigeria and the Cameroons. London, H.M.S.O., 1957. vi, 420p. maps, bibliog. (Colonial research studies, no. 22)
Excludes urban lands.

859 Murdock, George Peter
Traditional socio-political systems of Nigeria: an introductory survey. In *The Nigerian political scene, ed. by Robert O. Tilman and Taylor Cole, 1962:* 3–16.
A brief view of Nigerian ethnographic groupings and a historical survey of their socio-political organisation and structure.

859a Nigeria. Eastern. Commission to enquire into the position, status and influence of chiefs and natural rulers in the Eastern Region. Report, by G. I. Jones [sole commissioner] Enugu, Govt. printer [1957] [iv] vi, 71p.

860 Nwogugu, E. I.
Legitimacy in Nigerian law, *J. Afr. law,* 8 (2) 1964: 90–105.

861 Ogunwa, Vincent O.
Traditional authorities in local government. *Loc. govt. chron.,* Jan. 1964: 17–19.
The role of traditional rulers in local govt. in Nigeria is briefly traced from the days of Lord Lugard and the indirect rule system to the modern set up with elected councils. Emphasis on Eastern Nigeria.

862 Ohonbamu, D. Obarogie
The law of mortgage of land in Southern Nigeria. Oxford, 1960. [21] 144p.
B. Litt. thesis, Oxford. Includes a discussion of the indigenous system of mortgage and the interaction between this and the introduced English system.

862a Olderogge, D. A.
Feodalism v Zapadnom Sudane v 16–19vv. See [880]

863 Park, A. E. W.
A dual system of land tenure: the experience of Southern Nigeria. *J. Afr. law,* 9 (1) Spring 1965: 1–19.
On the problem arising from the disparity between English and customary law regarding land tenure in Eastern Nigeria.

863a Redmayne, A. H.
The concept of feudalism in African ethnology. See [882]

864 Rowling, Cecil William
Report on land tenure: Plateau Province. Kaduna, Govt. printer, 1952. iv, 80p.

865 Salacuse, Jeswald
A selective survey of Nigerian family law. Zaria, Institute of administration, 1965. iv, 113p. (Research memo series).

866 Smythe, Hugh H.
The problem of national leadership in Nigeria. *Social res.,* 25 (2) Jl. 1958: 215–227.

867 Tremearne, Arthur John Newman
Native law and procedure in British West Africa. *J. comp. leg.,* 2nd ser. 15, 1915: 95–103.

868 Udoma, E. U.
Law and British administration in South-Eastern Nigeria.
Ph.D. thesis, Dublin.

5. SOCIAL ORGANISATION AND STRUCTURE, SOCIAL RELATIONSHIPS

869 Butt-Thompson, Frederick William
West African secret societies, their organisation, officials and teaching. London, H. F. & G. Witherby, 1929. 320p. front., illus., map, bibliog.
A useful study of different categories of secret societies—religious, mystic, criminal, patriotic, etc., found on the West African Coast from Morocco to Angola.

870 Callaway, Helen L.
Nigeria's young elite; University College, Ibadan. *Mademoiselle,* 52, Jan. 1961: 76–81.

871 Gibson, A. E. M.
Slavery in Western Africa. *J. Afr. Soc.,* 3 (9) Oct., 1903: 17–52.
A general study of slavery in all its aspects among the peoples of West Africa.

872 Harris, J. H.
Domestic slavery in Nigeria: being a report to the committee of the Anti-

slavery and aborigines protection society, and correspondence. London, the society, 1911. 16p.

873 Leith-Ross, Sylvia
The development of a middle class in the Federation of Nigeria. *INCIDI.*, 29, 1955: 174–183.

874 —The rise of a new élite amongst the women of Nigeria. *Afr. women*, 2 (3) Dec. 1957: 51–56; *Int. soc. sci. bull.*, 8 (3) 1956: 481–488.

875 Little, Kenneth L.
The African elite in British West Africa. In *Frontiers in general hospital psychiatry, ed. Louis Linn, 1961:* 263–288.

876 *—The African elite in British West Africa. In *Race relations in world perspective: papers read at the Conference on race relations in world perspective, Honolulu, 1954, ed. A. W. Lind. 1956.*

877 Mockler-Ferryman, A. F.
Slavery in West Africa. *Macmillan's j.*, Jl. 1897: 190–198.

877a Murdock, George Peter
Traditional socio-political systems of Nigeria. See [859]

878 O'Connor, C. S. J.
Status and roles of West African women: a study in cultural change. 1964. Ph.D. thesis, New York university.

879 Ogunsheye, Felicia Adetowun
Les femmes du Nigeria. *Présence afr.*, (32) Je.–Sept. 1960: 121–138.

880 Olderogge, D. A.
Feodalism v Zapadnom Sudane v 16–19 vv. *Sov. et.*, (4) 1957: 91–103.
Analysis of social structure in the Western Sudanese empires of Songhai and Mali, and in the Hausa states. The Fulani rising is interpreted as a social revolt stemming from class disparity.

881 Ransom-Kuti, F.
The status of women in Nigeria. *J. hum. relations*, 10 (1) autumn 1961: 67–72.

882 Redmayne, A. H.
The concept of feudalism in African ethnology. 1962.
B.Litt. thesis, Oxford university.

883 *Smith, Michael Garfield
Slavery and emancipation in two societies. *Soc. & econ. stud.* [Univ. of the West Indies] 3, 1954:
In Zaria and Jamaica.

884 Smythe, Hugh H.
Human relations in Nigeria: the young elite. *J. hum. relations*, 6 (2) Feb. 1958: 54–73.

885 —Nigerian elite: role of education. *Sociol. & social res.*, 45, Oct. 1960: 71–73.

886 —Nigeria's "marginal men". *Phylon*, 19 (3) Oct. 1958: 268–276.
On the general disappointments and the social and economic problems to which Nigerians trained in foreign countries are exposed on their return home.

887 —Social stratification in Nigeria. *Social forces*, 37 (2) Dec. 1958: 168–171.

887a Smythe, Hugh H. and Smythe, Mabel M
Das Entstehen der neuen afrikanischen Oberschicht in Nigeria. *Afrika Heute*, 1960: 44–56.
On the rise of a new Nigerian elite.

888 —The new Nigerian elite. Stanford, Calif., Stanford university press, 1960. xii, 196p. map.
A study of the expanding "upper class" of Nigerian society.

889 —New Nigerian elite: corporate consciousness. *Social order*, Feb. 1960: 13–23.

890 —The Nigerian elite: some observations. *Sociol. & social res.*, 44 (1) Sept.–Oct. 1959: 42–45.

891 —Occupation and upper class formation in Nigeria. *Southwestern soc. sci. q.*, 41 (3) Dec. 1960: 250–256.

892 —The social identity of the Nigerian elite. *Sociol. & social res.*, 11 (1) Jan. 1960: 29–31.

893 —Subgroups of the new Nigerian elite. *Duquesne rev.* 6 (1) Nov. 1960: 35–42.

894 Tamuno, Tekena Nitonye
Emancipation in Nigeria. *Nig. mag.*, (82) Sept. 1964: 218–227.
"This article, in the main, attempts to analyse problems connected with, and the approach towards emancipation in Nigeria from 1833 . . . to 1916." Includes also notes on traditional approaches to emancipation, especially among the Bini, the Efiks and the Ibibios. Extensive bibliographical footnotes.

895 Temple, Olive
Women in Northern Nigeria. *Blackwood's mag.*, (197) Aug. 1914: 257–267.

896 Usoro, Eno J.
The place of women in Nigerian society. *Afr. women*, 4 (2) Je. 1961: 27–30
On the increasing participation of women, especially married women, in careers outside the home and the resulting social and family problems.

6. ECONOMY, AGRICULTURE, TRADE (INCLUDING CURRENCY)

897 Andree, Richard
Aggriperlen. *Z. f. ethnol.*, 17, 1885: 110–115; 373–374.
On the origin of aggrey beads. The second instalment is a reply to comments by other readers on the first instalment.

898 Balfour, Henry
The origin of West African crossbows. *J. Afr. soc.*, 8 (32) Jl. 1909: 337–356, illus.
Also reprinted in Smithsonian institution's Annual report, 1910. Washington, 1911: 635–650.

899 Bell, A. S.
Manilla token: currency of the West
African slave trade. *Numismatist, 63,*
1950: 518–523, illus.

900 Boahen, A. Adu
The caravan trade in the nineteenth
century. *J. Afr. hist.,* 3 (2) 1962: 349–
359.
A documented account of the trans-
Saharan trade routes that linked the
Western Sudan with North Africa.
Discusses the organisation and character
of the caravans, the various currencies
employed, and the composition of
merchandise.

901 Bridges, A. F. B.
The oil palm industry in Nigeria. *Farm
and forest,* 7 (1) Jan.–Je. 1946: 54–59.

902 Buchanan, Keith McPherson
Recent development in Nigerian peasant
farming. *Malayan j. trop. geog.,* 2, Mar.
1954: 17–34, maps.

903 Dalziel, John M.
The useful plants of West tropical
Africa; being an appendix to "The
flora of West tropical Africa", by J.
Hutchinson and J. M. Dalziel. London,
Crown Agents, 1937. xii, 612p.
Lists plants by their botanic names in
systematic order, and gives for each the
areas found, vernacular names, brief
description, and notes on local uses—
domestic, commercial, medicinal, etc.—
and sometimes popular beliefs connected
with it. Useful vernacular, common
name, and scientific name indexes on
pp. 555–612. "Bibliography (additional
to works cited in F.W.T.A.)", pp. ix-xi.

904 Einzig, Paul
Cowries, slaves, cloth and gin money
in Nigeria. In his *Primitive money in its
ethnological, historical and economic
aspects, 1949:* Bk. 1. pp. 146–153.

905 Fage, John D.
Some remarks on beads and trade in
lower Guinea in the 16th and 17th
centuries. *J. Afr. hist.,* 3 (2) 1962: 343–
347.
On the nature and sources of akori
or aggrey beads used in West Africa
during the period. Useful bibliographical
notes.

906 Feilberg, C. G.
Traek af det traditionelle afrikanske
landburg i Nigeria. *Geografisk tids-
skrift,* 57, 1958: 75–108, maps.
Notes on traditional agriculture in
Nigeria. English summary, p. 106–107.

907 Forde, Cyril Daryll and Scott, Richenda
The native economy of Nigeria; being
the first volume of a study of the economics of a tropical dependency. Edited
by Margery Perham. London, Faber
and Faber, 1946. xxiv, 312p. maps,
tables.
In two parts, with part I by Daryll
Forde concentrating on the rural,
traditional economies of the various
peoples of Nigeria, while part II by

Richenda Scott deals with the cash
crops and the livestock industry.

908 Fyfe, Christopher
West African trade, A.D. 1000–1800.
In *A thousand years of West African
history, ed. J. F. A. Ajayi and I. Espie,
1965:* 232–247, map.

908a Gill, D. S.
Aspects of rural life in Northern Nigeria.
See [675]

909 Grey, R. F. A.
Manillas. (Based on a talk given to the
Lagos Branch [of the Nigerian Field
Society]) *Nig. field,* 16 (2) Apr. 1951:
52–66, illus.
Historical and descriptive account of
manilla which had flourished as a
currency in many parts of Nigeria.
See also [951] where its economic
aspects are more fully considered.

910 Grove, A. T.
Population densities and agriculture in
Northern Nigeria. In *Essays on African
population, ed. by K. M. Barbour and
R. M. Prothero, 1961:* 115–136, sketch
maps.
A study of population movements in
Northern Nigeria and of the relation
between agriculture and population
densities.

911 Hallaire, A.
Koubadje: étude d'un terroir agricole
de l'Adamaoua. *Rech. étud. cam.,* 5,
1961–62: 47–72, illus., maps, bibliog.

913 Hiskett, Mervyn
Materials relating to the cowry currency
of the Western Sudan—I: A late nineteenth-century schedule of inheritance
from Kano. *B.S.O.A.S.,* 29 (1) 1966:
122–142.

914 —Materials relating to the cowry
currency of the Western Sudan—II:
Reflections on the provenance and
diffusion of the cowry in the Sahara and
the Sudan. *B.S.O.A.S.,* 29 (2) 1966:
339–366.

915 Isong, Clement Nyong
Modernisation of the esusu credit
society. *NISER conf. proc., 1958:* 111–
120.
Analytical study of the operation of
the esusu credit system in Nigeria,
with proposals for its modernisation.

916 Jeffreys, M. D. W.
Average size of a native hoe farm in
Nigeria. *Farm and forest,* Jan.–Je. 1947:
32–35.

917 —Aggrey beads. *Afr. stud.,* 20 (2) 1961:
97–113, bibliog.
A detailed and much documented
study intended to settle finally the
long-drawn dispute about aggrey beads:
what they are, their origin, history and
uses, especially in West Africa.

918 —Le associazioni 'osusu' nell' Africa
occidentale. *Revista di etnografia,* 5
(1/2) 1951: 3–12.
On the *osusu* or credit system in West
Africa.

919   —The cowrie shell: a study of its history and use in Nigeria. *Nig. mag.,* (15) 1938: 221–226, 256, illus.

920   —The diffusion of cowries and Egyptian culture in Africa. *Amer. anthrop.,* 50 (1) Jan.–Mar. 1948: 45–53.
Surveys the systems of counting cowries among the Ibo, Yoruba, Urhobo and Hausa and finds that all are based on a duodecimal or sexagesimal notation which was also used among the ancient Egyptians. Infers from this that the cowry and its sexagesimal notation reached Nigeria from Egypt.

921   —The history of maize in Africa. *S. Afr. j. sci.,* 50 (8) Mar. 1954: 197–200, bibliog.

922   —How ancient is West African maize? *Africa,* 33 (2) Apr. 1962: 115–131, bibliog.

923   —Maize impressions on ancient Nigerian pottery. *Man,* 59, Nov. 1959: 200 (art. 313); 60, Apr. 1960: 61 (art. 61).
Two brief letters disagreeing with F. Willett's view on the age of maize in West Africa. See Willett's article [4871] and subsequent correspondence [4870] on the subject. See also author's further correspondence, *Maize in West Africa* [924]

924   —Maize in West Africa. *Man,* 63, Dec. 1963: 194–195 (art. 247)
Further correspondence on the introduction of maize into West Africa.

925   —Pre-Columbian maize in Africa. *Nature,* 172 (4386) Nov. 21, 1953: 965–966, bibliog.
Asserts that recent archaeological finds in Yorubaland suggest much earlier introduction of maize from America to Africa through Arab or negro contacts with the Americas from about A.D. 900—long before Columbus.

926   —Some negro currencies in Nigeria. *SAMAB,* 5 (16) Dec. 1954: 405–416, illus.
Currencies such as beads, cowrie shells, manillas, brass rods, etc., in use in Nigeria before the introduction of modern money in 1900.

927   Jones, G. Howard
The earth goddess; a study of native farming on the West coast. London, Longmans, Green, 1936. xi, 205p. front., illus., bibliog.

928   Jones, Gwilym Iwan
Native and trade currencies in Southern Nigeria during the eighteenth and nineteenth centuries. *Africa,* 28 (1) Jan. 1958: 43–54, bibliog.
A survey of the currency systems operating in the area at the period, especially in the Delta Province and Old Calabar. French summary, pp. 53–54.

929   Jones, William O.
Manioc in Africa. Stanford, Calif., Stanford University press, 1959. (Food research institute. Studies in tropical development, no. 2).
Includes (pp. 72–80) notes on the introduction and spread of manioc or cassava in Nigeria and other parts of West Africa, collocated from the literature of 17th and 18th centuries explorers.

930   Kingsley, Mary Henrietta
Trade goods used in the early trade with Africa as given by Barbot and other writers of the seventeenth century. In her *West African studies, 1899:* 612–633.
Extracts describing the types of goods carried by European traders to Benin, Warri, New Calabar, Old Calabar and other centres along the West African coast and some of the exports from these areas.

931   Kirk-Greene, Anthony Hamilton Millard.
The major currencies in Nigerian history. *J. Hist. soc. Nig.,* 2 (1) Dec. 1960: 132–150.
Description of the various currencies known in Nigeria's commercial history—from copper bracelets used in Bonny in 1810 to coinage introduced by the British Government.

932   Kalous, Milan
A contribution to the problem of akori beads. *J. Afr. hist.,* 7 (1) 1966: 61–66.

933   Krieger, Kurt
Studien über afrikanische Kunstperlen. Besprechungen. *Baessler-Archiv,* 25 (2) 1943: 53–106, bibliog.
On akori beads.

934   Leggent, J.
Strange currency: cowries and manillas. *W. Afr. rev.,* 30 (381) 1959: 633, illus.

935   Lely, Hugh Vandervaes
The useful trees of Northern Nigeria. London, Crown Agents for the colonies, 1925. xiip. 120 numb. 1., 121–128p. incl. port., illus.

936   Mauny, M. R.
Akori beads. *J. Hist. soc. Nig.,* 1 (3) Dec. 1958: 210–214, bibliog.
Traces historical writings bearing on akori beads from about 1506 to the middle of the 18th century to show that the beads were not imported into, but originated in West Africa.

937   Miracle, Marvin P.
Interpretation of evidence on the introduction of maize into West Africa. *Africa,* 33 (2) Apr. 1963: 132–135.
A criticism of Willett's article: *The introduction of maize into West Africa: an assessment of recent evidence* [4870], q.v. See also a fuller criticism, *How ancient is West African maize?* by Jeffreys [922]

938   Morgan, W. B.
The change from shifting to fixed settlement in Southern Nigeria. *Research notes,* (7) Apr. 1955: 15–25, map.

939   —Agriculture in Southern Nigeria (excluding the Cameroons) *Econ. geog.,* 35 (2) Apr. 1959: 138–150, map.

940 Neville, George W.
West African currency. *J. Afr. soc.*, 17
(67) Apr. 1918: 223–226, illus.
Brief historical notes on coins and
other forms of currency in West Africa.

941 Nzeribe, Benjamin Uzoukwu
A socio-economic approach to pro-
moting economic development in
Eastern Nigeria: with special reference
to agriculture. 1958. 430p.
Ph.D. thesis, Cornell university.
Chapters V and VI (pp. 187–288)
discuss the social obstacles to agri-
cultural development and expansion in
Eastern Nigeria.

942 O'Connell, James
Some social and political reflections on
the plan. *Nig. j. econ. & soc. stud.*, 4 (2)
Jl. 1962: 131–146.
Social and political implications of
the 1962–68 Nigerian development plan.

943 Palm wine. *Nig. mag.*, (51) 1956: 366–
379, illus.
Notes on its production and consumption in different parts of Nigeria,
especially in the Yoruba (Igbomina) and
Ibo areas, and on the social and cultural
conventions and observances relevant
thereto.

944 Payne, John Augustus Otonba
Cowries table and value in silver and
gold coins. In *Payne's Lagos and West
African almanack and diary, 1879. 1878:*
69–72.

944a Perham, Margery, *ed.*
The native economy of Nigeria. See [907]

945 Porteres, R.
L'introduction du maïs en Afrique. *J.
agric. trop. bot. appl.*, 2 (5–6) 1955: 221–
231.

946 Smith, Sidney R.
Markets and marketing in Nigeria.
Empire cotton growing rev., 6 (4) Oct.
1929: 315–325.

947 Stanton, W. R.
The analysis of the present distribution
of varietal variation in maize, sorghum,
and cowpea in Nigeria as an aid to the
study of tribal movement. *J. Afr. hist.*,
3 (2) 1962: 251–262, maps, bibliog.

948 —The ethnobotanical basis for the
present distribution of cereals in Nigeria.
Samaru, Zaria, Northern Nigeria
Ministry of Agriculture, Research and
specialist services division, Cereals
section. Technical report, no. 3, 1959.
Mimeographed.

949 Tuley, P.
How to tap a raffia palm. *Nig. field*, 30
(3) Jl. 1965: 120–132, illus.

950 —How to tap an oil palm. *Nig. field*, 30
(1) Jan. 1965: 28–37, illus.
Detailed description of the tapping
procedure and of the materials used.

951 United Africa company
The manilla problem. *Statist. & econ.
rev.*, (3) Mar. 1949: 44–56; (4) Sept.
1949: 59–60.

History of the introduction and use
of manilla as a currency in Nigeria, and
of its eventual withdrawal from circulation in 1948–1949.

7. FOOD PREPARATION AND CONSUMPTION, STANDARD OF LIVING

952 Berry, C. O.
Nutritional anaemia in the Africans of
Lagos, Nigeria. 1956.
M.D. thesis, Birmingham university.

953 Dema, I. S.
An experimental study of the protein
values of Nigerian diets and the relation
of the results to the development of the
native food economy. 1959.
Ph.D. thesis, London.

954 —A review of recent nutritional surveys
in Nigeria as a guide to social action in
the country. *Proc. sci. assoc. Nig.*, 6,
Oct. 1963: 73–86, bibliog.

955 Ekandem, M. J.
Preparation of cassava in the human
diet of Nigeria. Ibadan, Federal Dept.
of Agricultural Research, 1961. 8 [1]p.
illus.
Traditional methods of preparing
cassava food products in Southern
Nigeria.

956 Gray, J. E.
Native methods of preparing palm.
*Nigeria, Dept. of agric. Annual report,
1922:* 29–51.

957 Nicol, Bruce M.
Fertility and food in Northern Nigeria.
W. Afr. med. j., n.s. 8 (1) Feb. 1959:
18–21.
Estimated demographic data obtained
from six rural areas in Northern Nigeria
are found on comparison to be com-
patible with the increase in population
indicated in the 1931 and 1952 censuses.
Also some tendency towards lower
reproduction rates is found in areas
where yams, as opposed to sorghum and
millet, are the staple food.

958 Nigeria. Dept. of statistics
Urban consumer surveys in Nigeria:
report on enquiries into the income and
expenditure patterns of lower and middle
income wage-earner households in
Lagos, 1959–60. Lagos, Ministry of
information, Printing division, 1963.
61p.

959 —Urban consumer surveys in Nigeria:
Reports on enquiries into the income
and expenditure patterns of wage-
earner households in Kaduna and
Zaria, 1955–56. Lagos, Govt. statistician, 1959. 88p.

960 Snuff-making in Nigeria. *Nig. mag.*, (19)
1939: 190–193. illus.

961 Thomson, I. G.
Nutritional deficiency in relation to
health and disease in Northern Nigeria.
1959.
M.D. thesis, Aberdeen.

8. RELIGION (INCLUDING ASSOCIATED FESTIVALS)

Only works on traditional indigenous religious beliefs and practices are included here. Writings on Christianity or Islam are not included except when they discuss the relations of these religions with, or the effects of their impact on the traditional religions.

962 Abdel-Rasoul, Kawthar
Funeral rites in Nigeria. *Wiener Völkekdl. Mitt.*, 4 (2) 1956: 167–179.
Hausa, Ibo, Nupe, Yoruba and Ibibio burial rites described and Egyptian origin or influence suggested.

963 Adande, Alexandre
Functions et signification sociales des masques en Afrique noire. *Présence afr., n.s.,* (1/2) Apr.–Jl. 1955: 24–38, bibliog.
On the social significance and functions of masks in West Africa, mostly in the French-speaking countries, and among the Yoruba (pp. 34–35) with brief mention of Benin masks and bronzes (p. 36)

964 Adiguna, Benjamin Abimbola
Religione e istruzione nella Federazione della Nigeria. *Africa* [Roma] 16 (4) Jl.–Aug. 1961: 163–167.

965 Aina, J. Ade
The present-day prophets and the principles upon which they work. A reproduction, with an introduction by H. N. Turner. Nsukka, Crowther College of Religion, University of Nigeria, 1964. vii, 10p.
Typescript, mimeographed. The original which was printed, was published about 1932.

966 Ajose, Oladele A.
Old and new in Nigeria: custom, religion and disease. *Lancet,* (1) 15 May 1954: 1024–1025.

967 —Preventive medicine and superstition in Nigeria. *Africa,* 27 (3) Jl. 1957: 268–274, bibliog.
A general survey of traditional practices. Summary in French, pp. 273–274.

968 Balarabe, A.
Northern Nigeria festivals. *Kano studies,* (1) 1965: 81–88.

969 Balfour, Henry
Ritual and secular uses of vibrating membranes as voice-disguisers. *J.R.A.I.,* 78, 1948: 49–65, illus., bibliog.
Among the Ibo, Hausa, Tiv, and other Nigerian tribes.

970 Banton, M.
African prophets. *Race,* 5 (2) 1963: 42–55, bibliog.

971 Bascom, William Russell
Folklore research in Africa. *J. Amer. folkl.,* 77 (303) 1964: 12–31, bibliog.

972 Bastian, Adolf
Der Fetisch an der Küste Guineas auf den deutscher Forschung nähergerückten Stationen der Beobachtung. Berlin, Weidmannsche Buchhandlung, 1884. [iv] 134p.

973 —Zur Mythologie und Psychologie der Nigritier in Guinea mit Bezugnahme auf socialistische Elementargedanken. Berlin, D. Reimer (Hoef & Vohsen) 1894. xxxi, 162p., map.

974 Baudin, P.
Fetichism and fetich worshippers, by Rev. P. Baudin. Translated by M. McMahon. New York, Benziger brothers, 1885. 127p. illus.
English edition of [975]

975 —Fétichisme et féticheurs, par Rev. P. Baudin. Lyon, Séminaire des missions africaines, 1884. [iii] 112p., illus.

976 Cherubim and Seraphim. *Nig. mag.,* (53) 1957: 119–134, illus.

977 Dennett, R. E.
At the back of the black man's mind; or Notes on the kingly office in West Africa. London, Macmillan, 1906, repr. London, Frank Cass, 1968. xvi, 288p. front., illus.
A study of African kingship and fetishism and of the relation of the latter to a higher religion. Chapters 17–22 (pp. 172–241) devoted to the Bini. There is an appendix of 29 pages on Yoruba religion.

978 —Notes on West African categories. London, Macmillan, 1911. xi, 68p.
Further efforts to elaborate and prove the existence in the African's subconscious mind of certain basic categories which form the foundation of his religious and social systems.

979 Fishing festival. *Nig. mag.,* (47) 1955: 273–274, illus.
Brief note on fishing festivals held annually in honour of the gods of the sea by each of the several fishing communities around Lagos.

980 Fortes, Meyer
Oedipus and Job in West African religion. Cambridge, University press, 1959. 81p.

981 Friend, Donald
Masks. *Nig. mag.,* (81) 1939: 100–104.

982 Frobenius, Leo
Dämonen des Sudan; Allerhand religiöse Verdichtungen. Jena, Eugen Diederichs, 1924. [iii] 373p. (Atlantis; Volksmärchen und Volksdichtungen Afrikas, v. 7)
Specially relevant are chapters III & IV (pp. 213–369) on Jukun and Hausa magical and religious beliefs.

983 —Die Masken und Geheimbünde Afrikas. Halle, Druck von E. Karras, 1898. 278p. illus., maps. (Leopoldinisch-Carolinische deutsche Akademie der Naturforscher. Nova Acta. Bd. 574, nr. 1)
Illustrations and descriptions of Efik and Yoruba masks included.

984 *Garner, R. O.
Superstitions of the West African

tribes. *Austr. assoc. adv. sci.*, 6, 1895: 589–595.

985 Horton, Robin
Destiny and the unconscious in West Africa. *Africa,* 31 (2) Apr. 1961: 110–116.
A review article on M. Fortes's book, *Oedipus and Job in West African religion* [980] q.v. French summary, p. 116.

986 —The high god: a comment on Father O'Connell's paper. *Man,* 62, Sept. 1962 (art. 219): 137–140.

987 Huber, H.
Death and mourning in the Western Sudan. *Anthropos,* 46 (3/4) May–Aug. 1951: 453–486, bibliog.

988 Idowu, E. Bolaji
God in Nigerian belief. Lagos, Ministry of information, 1963. [iv] 40p. illus. (Nigerian broadcasting corporation. October lectures)

989 Jeffreys, M. D. W.
The cult of twins among some African tribes. *S. Afr. j. sci.,* 59 (4) 1963: 97–107, bibliog.

990 —Notes on twins. *Afr. stud.,* 6 (4) Dec. 1947: 189–195, illus., bibliog.
Notes on customs and beliefs associated with twins in Bamenda and other parts of the Cameroons.

991 —Psychical phenomena among negroes. *J.R.A.S.,* 39, Oct. 1940: 354–360.
Describes instances of hysteria and or religious fervour in West Africa, including the women's riot at Aba, the Prophets' movement led by Garrick Braid from Bonny, and cases of individual hysteria and spirit possession.

992 Lambo, T. Adeoye
African traditional beliefs, concepts of health and medical practice: a lecture given before the Philosophical Society, University College, Ibadan, on 24 October, 1962. Ibadan, University press, 1963. 11p. bibliog.

993 Lagercrantz, S.
A contribution to the study of anomalous dentition and its ritual significance in Africa. Stockholm, Tryckeri Aktiebolaget Thule, 1939. 43p. maps (Statens Ethnografiska Museum. Smärre meddelanden, 16).
Features on pp. 6–11 the Edo, Ijaw, Ibo, Ibibio, Tiv and Ekoi of Nigeria.

994 Le Coeur, Ch.
Le culte de la génération et l'évolution religieuse et sociale en Guinée. Paris, E. Leroux, 1932. [v] 147p.

995 Leonard, Arthur Glyn
The lower Niger and its tribes. London, Macmillan, 1906, repr. London, Frank Cass, 1968. xxii, 564p. map.
An extended study of the religion and philosophy of the peoples of Southern Nigeria—the Ibo, Ibibio, Efik, Ijaw, Itsekiri, Urhobo and Bini.

996 —Southern Nigeria—religion and witchcraft. *Imperial and Asiatic rev., 3rd ser.,* 24, 1907: 279–311.
A good account summarising some of the information in author's book: *The lower Niger and its tribes* [995]

997 Longo, Lawrence D.
Medicine and medical education in Nigeria. *New Eng. j. med.,* 268, May 9th 1963: 1044–1055, illus., maps, bibliog.
Includes a discussion of "traditional Nigerian medicine" as practised by native doctors or medicine men. Also reprinted in *African studies papers,* (5) 1963: 12p.

998 Malcolm, L. W. G.
Short notes on soul-trapping in Southern Nigeria. *J. Amer. folklore,* 35, Jl. 1922: 219–222.

999 Meek, Charles Kingsley
The religions of Nigeria. *Africa,* 14 (3) Jl. 1943: 106–117.
Outline account of the indigenous religions of Nigeria, including the Mohammedan religion. Prefaced with a historical account of the origin of the name "Nigeria".

1000 Mendelsohn, Jack
God, Allah, and juju; religion in Africa today. Edinburgh, Nelson, 1962. 245p.
On religion in modern African life. Much of the discussion refers to Nigeria.

1001 Nzekwu, Onuora
Masquerade. *Nigeria: 1960.* 134–144, illus.
Discusses the traditional significance of masquerade in Eastern Nigeria which is today disappearing, and notes its use in Christmas and similar celebrations.

1002 O'Connell, James
The withdrawal of the high god in West African religion: an essay in interpretation. *Man,* 62, May 1962: 67–69 (art. 109).

1003 Ohiaeri, A. E.
A research in the traditional Nigerian medicine. Nsukka, the author [1965] 15p.

1004 Okoye, Godfrey Mary Paul
Our sacred gods: a survey of some forms of false worship in twentieth century Nigeria. Onitsha, Ude's printing and publishing co., 1965. 54p. illus.

1005 Omoyajowo, J. Akinyele
Witches?—A study of the belief in witchcraft and of its future in modern African society. Ibadan [the author] 1965. 44p.

1006 Palmer, Herbert Richmond
Trident gods in Sahara and Western Sudan. *Man,* 41, May–Je. 1941: 60–62. (art. 40)

1007 Parrinder, Geoffrey
African traditional religion. London, Hutchinson's, 1954. 160p. map, bibliog.

1008 —Indigenous churches in Nigeria. *W. Afr. rev.,* 31 (394) Sept. 1960: 87–93.
A general description of indigenous

Christian sects many of which split from the established mission Churches.

1009 —Islam and West African indigenous religions. *Numen*, 6 (2) 1959: 130–141.
The relations of Islam with the traditional religions of the people of West Africa and the cultural and social consequences of such relations.

1010 —The possibility of Egyptian influence on West African religion. *Int. W. Afr. conf. proc., 3rd, 1949. 1956*: 61–67.
A brief discussion, presented from the viewpoint of comparative religion.

1011 —West African psychology; a comparative study of psychological and religious thought. London, Lutterworth press, 1951. ix, 229p. (Missionary research series, no. 17).

1012 —West African religion; illustrated from the beliefs and practices of the Yoruba, Ewe, Akan and kindred peoples. London, Epworth press, 1949. xiv, 223p.

1013 ——2nd ed. West African religion: a study of the beliefs and practices of Akan, Ewe, Yoruba, Ibo and kindred peoples. Completely rewritten, revised and enlarged. London, 1961. xv, 203p. map, bibliog.
A comprehensive study, embracing the different gods worshipped, ancestral and other cults, charms and magic, totems and taboos, secret societies, etc.

1014 —Witchcraft [a critical study of the belief in witchcraft from the records of witch hunting in Europe yesterday and Africa today] Harmondsworth, Penguin books, 1958. 208p.

1015 Petri, H.
Religion and art in ancient Nigeria. *W. Afr.*, (1774) 1951: 155, illus.

1016 Pettazzoni, Raffaele
Miti e legende: 1. Africa, Australia, Turin, Unione Tipografico-Editrice Torinese, 1948. xxviii, 480p. illus., maps.

1017 Segy, Ladislas
Initiation ceremony and African sculptures. *Amer. imago.*, 10 (1) spring, 1953: 75–82.

1018 Seligman, C. G.
Egypt and negro Africa: a study in divine kingship. London, Routledge, 1934. [iv] 82p. front., illus., map. (Frazer lectures for 1933)
The front. shows the Atah of Idah in full regalia.

1019 Sydow, Eckart von
The Image of Janus in African sculpture. *Africa*, 5 (1) Jan. 1932: 14–27, illus.
On Janus figures carved on masks, statues, and utensils, found in different parts of Africa, including Nigeria (Yoruba, Ijaw, Ibibio and Ekoi). French summary, p. 27.

1020 —Westafrikanische Gebrauchkunst. *Cicerone*, 13, 1921: 614–620.

1021 Talbot, Percy Amaury

*The earth goddess cult in Nigeria. *Edinburgh rev.*, Jl. 1929.

1022 —Some aspects of West African religions. *Edinburgh rev.*, 220, 1914: 96–114.

1023 —Some Nigerian fertility cults. London, O.U.P., 1927, repr. London, Frank Cass, 1967. vi, 140p. front., illus.

1024 Thomas, Northcote Whitridge
The incest tabu. *Man*, 10, 1910: 123–124 (art. 72)

1025 —Totemism in Southern Nigeria. *Anthropos*, 10–11, 1915: 234–248; 14–15, 1916: 543–545.

1025a Turner, H. W.
The present-day prophets and the principles upon which they work. See [965]

1026 Uchendu, Victor Chikezie
Missionary problems in Nigerian society. *Pract. anthrop.*, 11 (3) May/June 1964: 105–117.
On the persistence of non-Christian concepts and practices e.g. polygyny, magic and sacrifice, among Nigerian Christians of today and the keen rivalry between the Roman Catholic and Protestant Churches.

1027 Welch, James W.
Witchcraft in Nigeria. II, The Christian answer. *Church overseas*, 5 (17) 1932: 31–45.

1028 Westermann, Diedrich
Gottesvorstellungen in Oberguinea. *Africa*, 1 (2) Apr. 1928: 189–209, bibliog.
Reviews conceptions of God among West Africans, including the Yoruba, Efik, Ibo, Nupe and Edo. French summary, pp. 279–281; English summary, pp. 281–283.

1029 Williams, Joseph John
Africa's God. III—Nigeria. Boston, Boston College press, Chestnut Hill, Mass., 1936. 183–238p. map, bibliog. (Anthropological series of the Boston College Graduate School, v. 1 no. 3, Oct. 1936)
One of a series of studies on the religious beliefs and practices of African peoples.

1030 Zeven, A. C.
The idolatrica palm. *Baileya*, 12 (1) Mar. 1964: 11–18, illus., bibliog.
Botanical characteristics of the idolatrica palm, a species of the oil palm (elaeis guineensis) in West Africa, with brief notes on its religious and magical significance, especially among the Bini, Yoruba and Ibo.

9. RECREATION, GAMES, MUSIC, DANCE

1031 Armstrong, Robert G.
Talking drums in the Benue-Cross River region of Nigeria. *Phylon*, 15 (4) Dec., 1954: 355–363.
Discusses the philological aspects of talking drums and the advantages of

drums and other 'talking instruments'. Based mostly on observations in Idoma Division of Benue Province.

1032 —Talking instruments in West Africa. *Explorations,* (4) Feb. 1955: 140–153.
"Talking" musical instruments among the Idoma, Igbira, etc.

1033 Buzu wrestlers of Northern Nigeria. *W. Afr. rev.,* 26 (332) 1955: 394–395, illus.

1034 Chauvet, Stephen
Musique nègre. Paris, Société d'éditions géographiques, maritimes et coloniales, 1929. [v] 242p. illus., (incl. mus. scores.)
An important study of African music, including African musical instruments.

1035 Drum as a factor in the social life of Nigeria. *Nig. teacher,* 1 (4) 1935:5.

1036 Echeruo, Michael Joseph Chukwudalu
Concert and theatre in late nineteenth century Lagos. *Nig. mag.,* (74) Sept., 1962: 68–74.

1037 Edet, Edna Marilyn (née Smith)
An African orchestra. *Mus. in Nig.,* 1 (2) May, 1965: 67–71.
On the possibility of employing West African instruments in the making of symphonic music.

1038 —Musical training in tribal West Africa. *Afr. mus.,* 3 (1) 1962: 6–10, illus.

1039 —Music in West Africa. 1961.
Thesis (Ed.D.) Columbia university.

1040 —Popular music in West Africa. *Afr. mus.,* 3 (1) 1962: 11–17, illus.

1041 —Recommendations for music education in West Africa. *Mus. in Nig.,* 1 (1) May 1964: 21–31; *W. Afr. j. educ.,* 6 (3) Oct. 1962: 122–125.
Recommendations for the development of a programme of music education which would rest on a "bi-musical base that reflects the bi-cultural nature of the communities in West Africa." Includes detailed proposals for music teaching at the primary and secondary school and teacher-training college levels.

1042 Euba, Akin
[Nigerian music] an appreciation. *Nigeria, 1960:* 193–210 (incl. adverts.)

1043 —Nigerian music: an appreciation. *Negro hist. bull.,* 24, Mar. 1961: 130–133.

1044 —Preface to a study of Nigerian music: in the light of references which made it what it is. *Ibadan,* (21) Oct. 1965: 53–62, illus., bibliog.
A historical survey of Nigerian music from the pre-colonial era through the colonial era to the present day.

1045 *Goins, William
Music of Nigeria. *Mus. j.,* 19, May 1961: 34.

1046 Gorer, Geoffrey
Africa dances; a book about West African negroes. London, Faber and Faber, 1935. xv, 363p. illus. (incl. ports.), maps.

Description, with many illustrations, of West African traditional dances.

1047 Griffith, W. J.
On the appreciation of African music. *Nig. field.,* 16 (2) April 1951: 88–93, illus.
With notation of Bamenda music.

1048 Hall, Leland
What price harmony? *Atlantic monthly,* 144, Oct. 1929: 511–516.
Discussion of Nigerian music by a European trained musician.

1049 Jones, A. M.
Indonesia and Africa: the xylophone as a culture indicator. *J.R.A.I.,* 89 (2) Jl. Dec. 1959: 155–168, illus., map, bibliog.

1050 Kelly, B.
African music in the school. *Mus. in Nig.,* 1 (1) May 1964: 64–70.
Considers the problems involved in the teaching of African music in schools, noting some of the achievements made. Draws heavily on his experience with music and music education in Eastern Nigeria, especially in Enugu and Onitsha.

1051 Lane, Michael G. M.
The origin of present day musical taste in Nigeria. *Nig. field,* 21 (3) Jl. 1956: 99–105; *Afr. mus.,* 1 (3) 1956: 18–22.
On Nigerian music and its historical background and cultural environment.

1052 Lannert, E.
The card game of *karta* in Northern Nigeria. *Nig. field,* 31 (4) Oct. 1966: 154–158, illus.
Describes a card game played in most parts of Northern Nigeria.

1053 Mackay, Mercedes
African music. *Nig. field,* 16 (3) Jl. 1951: 139–140.
A letter to the editor.

1054 —Nigerian folk musical instruments. *Nig. Mag.,* (30) 1949: 337–339, illus.

1055 —The traditional musical instruments of Nigeria, *Nig. field,* 15 (3) Jl. 1950: 112–133, illus.
Many kinds of musical instruments used among the Ibo, Hausa, Yoruba and other tribes are collected by the author and described under three headings: Percussion instruments, Wind instruments, and Stringed instruments.

1056 Merriam, Alan P.
African music. In *Continuity and change in African cultures,* ed. by W. R. Bascom and M. J. Herskovits. *1958:* 49–86.

1057 Moloney, C. Alfred
On the melodies of the Volof, Mandingo, Ewe, Yoruba and Hausa people of West Africa. *J. Manch. geog. soc.,* 5, 1889: 277–298, illus.

1058 Murray, Kenneth Crosthwaite
Dances and plays. *Nig. mag.,* (19) 1939: 214–218, illus.

1059 —Music and dancing in Nigeria. *Afr.*

mus. soc. newsletter, (5) Je. 1952: 44–45.

1060 Onyido, Udemezuo
Music in West Africa: work of the Nigerian institute of music. *W. Afr. rev.,* 26 (336) 1955: 820.
Letter by the secretary of the Institute to the editor explaining the institute's work.

1061 Phillips, T. K. E.
Nigerian church music. *Music in Nig.,* 1 (1) May 1964: 4–12.
On the suitability of the African type of music for use in churches, and the development of church music in Nigeria.

1062 Reed, E. M. G.
The Nigerian at home. *Mus. & youth,* 5, 1925: 159–163.
On musical instruments, songs and dances in Nigeria.

1063 Rhodes, Steve
Is Nigerian music losing its national character? *Nig. mag.,* (67) Dec. 1960: 297–300, illus.
Smith, Edna Marilyn See Edet, Edna Marilyn (née Smith)

1064 Sowande, Fela
African music. *Africa,* 14, 1944: 340–342.

1065 —African music. *United empire,* 39, 1948: 165–167.

1066 —African music and Nigerian schools. *Ibadan,* (16) Je. 1963: 13–15.
Supports the inclusion of African music in Nigerian school curriculum, and suggests that such music should seek "to retain its artistic integrity" and "to take, to adapt and to use whatever proves congenial and necessary to it for its proper development, from Western forms of the Art."

1067 —Language in African music. *Music in Nigeria,* 1 (2) May 1965: 4–36.

1068 Thompson, R. F.
Highlife in Nigeria. *Saturday rev.,* 44 (34) Aug. 26, 1961: 34–35, illus.
Yoruba highlife.

1069 Tremearne, Arthur John Newman
Bull-fighting in Nigeria and Portugal: a humane sport. *Man,* 10, 1910: 147–150 (art. 87).

1069a Varley, Douglas H.
African native music; an annotated bibliography. London, Royal empire society, 1936.
116p. (Royal empire society bibliographies, no. 8)
Nigeria specifically, pp. 44–47.

10. STORIES, PROVERBS, RIDDLES

1069a African folktales and sculpture. See [1182]

1070 Burton, Richard Francis
Wit and wisdom from West Africa; or, A book of proverbial philosophy, idioms, enigmas and laconisms. London, Tinsley, 1865. xxxi, 455p.
A collection of proverbs, idioms, etc.,

with English translations, from a number of West African languages, including Efik, Yoruba and Kanuri.

1071 Clarke, K. W.
A motif-index of the folk tales of culture area V, West Africa. 1958.
Ph.D. thesis, Indiana university.

1072 Epelle, Kiea
Our folk lore and fables, part II. Lagos, Crownbird publications, Public relations dept. [n.d.] 16p. illus. (Crownbird series, no. 37)
A collection of eight Eastern Nigerian folk tales centred round the tortoise.

1073 Frobenius, Leo
African genesis. New York, Stackpole, 1937. 236p. illus.
Stories from the Western Sudan and other parts of Africa. Those in the first two sections originally appeared in the *Atlantis* series, and those in the third appeared in *Erythräa* also published by Frobenius. At head of title: Leo Frobenius and Douglas C. Fox.

1074 —Dichten und Denken im Sudan. Jena, E. Diederichs, 1925. 385p. illus., map. (Atlantis; Volksmärchen und Volksdichtungen Afrikas, Bd. 5)
Kanuri—pp. 154–172. Nupe legends and traditions—pp. 178–256.

1075 —Erzählungen aus dem Westsudan. Jena, Eugen Diederichs, 1922. [iii] 392p. (Atlantis; Volksmärchen und Volksdichtungen Afrikas, Bd. 8)

1076 —Volksdichtungen aus Oberguinea. 1. Band: Fabuleien dreier Völker. Jena, Eugen Diederichs, 1924. [iii] 356p. (Atlantis; Volksmärchen und Volksdichtungen Afrikas, Bd. 11).

1077 —Volkserzählungen und Volksdichtungen aus dem Zentral-Sudan. Jena, Eugen Diederichs, 1924. [iii] 427p. (Atlantis; Volksmärchen und Volksdichtungen Afrikas, Bd. 9)
Folk tales & folk poetry from the central Sudan. Includes Nupe, 13–277; Hausa, 277–415.

1078 Ramsaran, J. A.
African twilight: folktale and myth in Nigerian literature. *Ibadan,* (15) Mar. 1963: 17–19.
On the problems and potentialities of Nigerian folktales in creative writings, especially creative writing in English; and a review, from this point of view, of the efforts of four Nigerian authors— Tutuola, Fagunwa, Achebe and J. P. Clark.

1079 Shelton, Austin J.
Behaviour and cultural value in West African stories: literary sources for the study of culture contact. *Africa,* 34 (4) Dec. 1964: 353–359.
Seeks to understand "values and attitudes" among modern Africans in relation to "tradition, contact and change", by a close study of four works by West African writers, to wit: Camara Laye's *Le Regard du roi* (1954); Onuora Nzekwu's *Wand of noble wood*

(1961); Chinua Achebe's *No longer at ease* (1960); and Wole Soyinka's *The lion and the jewel* (1963).

11. LITERARY EXPRESSION, LITERATURE

1080 Beier, Horst Ulrich
Nigerian literature. *Nigeria, 1960:* 212–228, illus.

1081 —Public opinion on lovers; popular Nigerian literature sold in Onitsha markets. *Black Orpheus*, (14) Feb. 1964: 4–16.
A critical review of the popular fiction in pamphlet form, mostly on love themes, written by authors with limited knowledge of the English language, and sold in large numbers in Onitsha markets.

1082 Bivar, A. D. H. and Hiskett, Mervyn
The Arabic literature of Nigeria to 1804: a provisional account. *BSOAS*, 25 (1) 1962: 104–148, illus. (facsims.)

1083 Okwu, Edward C.
A language of expression for Nigerian literature. *Nig. mag.*, (91) Dec. 1966: 289–292, 313–315.

1084 Schmidt, Nancy Jeanne
Anthropological analysis of Nigerian fiction. 1966. 398p.
Ph.D. thesis, Northwestern University.

12. COSTUME, DRESS, BEAUTY CULTURE

1085 Danford, John Alexander
Catalogue [of] an exhibition [of] documentary water colour paintings of the ceremonial robes, uniforms, festival costumes and national dress of the people of Nigeria [No imprint] [4]p.
The exhibition was held at the University of Ibadan library from 15 to 18 Nov. 1955.

1086 —[Costumes of Nigeria: water colours] [Ibadan, 1958]
33 5×5 cm. colour slides (transparencies) made at the Ibadan University library.

1086a —Nigeria in costume. See [1092]

1087 De Negri, Eve
Hair styles of Southern Nigeria. *Nig. mag.*, (65) Je. 1960: 191–198, illus.
Notes on hair styles, mostly women's, among the Yoruba, Ibo and other groups in Southern Nigeria.

1088 —Nigerian jewellery. *Nig. mag.*, (74) Sept. 1962: 42–54.

1089 —Tribal marks—decorative scars and painted patterns. *Nig. mag.*, (81), Je. 1964: 106–116, illus.

1089a Eicher, Joanne B.
Bibliography of African dress (with emphasis on Nigeria) See [10]

1090 Goose, D. M.
Tooth mutilation in West Africans. *Man*, 63, 1963: 91–93 (art. 113) illus., bibliog.

1090a Negri, Eve de See De Negri, Eve

1091 Oliver, Bep
Beauty in the bush. *Nigeria mag.*, (67) Dec. 1960: 247–255, illus.
Describes local traditional preparations used as cosmetics in Nigeria.

1092 Shell Company of Nigeria
Nigeria in costume. Amsterdam and London, L. Van Leer, 1960. 102p. plates (coloured)
With descriptive text.

1093 Wilson-Haffendon, J. R.
Some notes on fork guards in Nigeria. *Man*, 29, 1929: 172–174 (art. 132)
On women's dress in Plateau Province.

13. MATERIAL CULTURE

(i) General

1094 Abosede, A.
A Nigerian at the Eisteddfod. Art festivals in Wales and West Africa: some comparisons. *W. Afr. rev.*, 26 (339) 1955: 1066–1069.

1095 Bascom, William Russell
Folklore research in Africa. *J. Amer. folkl.*, 77 (303) 1964: 12–31, bibliog.

1096 Battis, Walter W. [and others]
The art of Africa, by Walter W. Battis [and others] Edited and arranged by J. W. Grossert. Pietermaritzburg, Shutter & Shooter, 1958. 140p. front., illus., bibliog.
A brief account of the history and distribution of African races in chapter one is followed in chapters two to seven by a regional survey of African arts and crafts. West Africa, including Yoruba and Benin, in chapter 2 (pp. 20–47).

1097 Beier, Horst Ulrich
Art in Nigeria, 1960. Cambridge, University press, in collaboration with the Information division, Ministry of home affairs, Ibadan, 1960. 24p. illus.
Reviews critically modern and traditional art in Nigeria.

1098 —Attitude of the educated African to his traditional art. *Phylon*, 18, Apr. 1957: 162–165.
Believes that western educated Africans do not always admire African art, illustrating the view with a reference to the attitude of some Nigerians to Ife art.

1099 —Contemporary Nigerian art. *Nig. mag.*, (68) Mar. 1961: 27–51, illus.
Reviews Nigerian painting and sculpture exhibited in Lagos in 1960 as part of the independence celebration. The exhibition was sponsored by the Lagos branch of the Nigerian Council for the Advancement of Art and Culture.

1100 —Nigerian folk art. *Nig. mag.*, (75) Dec. 1962: 26–32. illus.
A distinction between professional and folk art in Nigeria is drawn, and four types of Nigerian folk art—Yoruba cement sculpture, Kano embroidery, signwriting, and copperwork—samples

of which were shown at the first exhibition of Nigerian folk art in May 1962, are described.

1101 Brook, Donald
Anglicising African art. *W. Afr.,* (2144) May 17th 1958: 465.

1102 —Nigerianising Nigerian art. *W. Afr.,* (2145) May 24th 1958: 491.

1103 Brooks, Dorothy
The influence of African art on contemporary European art. *Afr. affairs,* 55 (218) Jan. 1956: 51–59, illus.
Three of the illustrations are of Nigerian art pieces.

1104 Carline, R.
Dating and provenance of negro art. *Burl. mag.,* 77, 1940: 114–120.

1105 —West African art and its tradition. *Studio,* 109, 1935: 186–193.

1106 Carrol, K.
Christian art in Nigeria. *Liturg. arts.,* 26, May 1958: 91–94.

1107 Danford, John Alexander
Art in Nigeria. *Afr. Affairs,* 48 (190) Jan. 1949: 37–47.
A general survey. Includes brief notes on some living Nigerian artists.

1108 —Nigerian art. *Nig. mag.,* (33) 1950: 153–174, illus.
Deplores uncritical acceptance of European art and advocates development along traditional lines whenever possible.

1109 Dark, Philip John Crossley
Bush negro art; an African art in the Americas. London, A. Tiranti, 1954. vi, 66p. front. (map), illus., bibliog.
A study of the art and culture of the Bush Negro, a tribe in Surinam or Dutch Guiana, descended from negro slaves. The 66 pages of text (with several text figures) are followed by 52 half tone plates, with notes describing them on pp. 57–66.

1110 Duerden, Dennis, G.
African art and its critics, *Ibadan,* (6) 1959: 14–17.

1111 —Low visibility in Nigerian art. *Arts rev.,* 16 (6) 1964: 2, illus.

1112 —Nigeria's art. *Nigeria,* 1960: 20–33, illus.

1113 Edwards, H. S. W.
Primitive culture in Nigeria. *Antiquity,* 15 (59) Sept. 1941: 287–290.
Describes houses, pottery, iron smelting, etc.

1114 Ena, Adams J. U.
African art. *Nigeria mag.,* (9) 1937: 62, illus.

1115 Enwonwu, Ben
Modern Nigerian artists' work. *Illus. London news,* 213, 1948: 12, illus.

1116 —Problems of African art today. *Présence afr.,* 8–10, 1956: 174–178.
Political, social and other problems with which the African artist is confronted.

1117 Fagg, William Buller
The dilemma which faces African art. *Listener,* 46 (1176) Sept. 13th 1951: 413–415, illus.

1117a —Merveilles de l'art nigérién. See [1128]

1118 —Notes on some West African Americana. *Man,* 52 (165) 1952: 119–122, illus.

1119 —On the nature of West African art. *Memoirs Manch. lit. & phil. soc.,* (94) 1952: 93–104, illus.,

1120 —The sibylline books of tribal art. *Black friars,* [Oxford] 33 (382) Jan. 1952: 38–44, illus.

1121 —The study of African art. *Bull. Allen mem. art mus.,* (12) 1955–56: 44–61.

1122 —Tribes and forms in African art. London, Methuen, 1965. 1 v. (various pagings) illus.

1123 Griaule, Marcel
Arts of the African native. Photographs by Emmanuel Sougez. [Translated from the French by Michael Heron.] London, Thames & Hudson, 1950. 126p. illus. (Primitive arts series)

1124 Hardy, Georges
L'art nègre, l'art animiste des noirs d'Afrique. Paris, Henri Laurens, 1927. [iv] 168p. illus., bibliog.
On the influence of religious beliefs, traditional and tribal discipline and natural forces on African art. The illustrations include some from Benin.

1125 Herskovits, Melville J.
Backgrounds of African art: three lectures given on the Cooke-Daniels lecture foundation, in conjunction with an exhibition of African art assembled by the Denver art museum, January and February 1945. Denver, 1945. 64p. illus., map. (Cooke-Daniels lecture series).

1126 Hulbert, Charles, *comp.*
Museum Africanum, or Select antiquities, curiosities, beauties, and varieties of nature and art in Africa, compiled from eminent authorities . . . London, G. & W. B. Whittaker, [1826] 234p. illus., map. (His select museum of the world, v. 2).
With this are bound the author's *African fragments,* 1826, and *Celestial musings* [1826?]

1127 Leuzinger, Elsy
Africa: the art of the negro peoples; translated by Ann E. Keep. London, Methuen, 1960. 247p. front., illus., maps, bibliog. (Art of the world; a series of regional histories of the visual arts.)
A regional survey of African art, giving for each area the main characteristics and stylistic features, and illustrated with 63 coloured plates and numerous text figures. Nigeria (Nok culture, Ife, Benin, Yoruba, Ijaw, Ibo, Ibibio, Ekoi, Hausa, etc., pp. 115–138.

1128 List, Herbert
Merveilles de l'art nigérién. Photographies de Herbert List. Texte de

William Fagg. Paris, Editions du Chêne, 1963. 39p. 144 plates.

1129   Macrow, Donald
Art club. *Nig. mag.*, (43) 1954: 250–257.
On the 'Aghama Youth Club of Fine Arts' in Lagos and the place of such clubs in the country.

1130   Marg; a magazine of the arts. 15 (3) Je. 1962. Bombay, Marg Publications, 1962. 66p. illus., map, bibliog.
A special issue devoted wholly to African art. Has a sub-title—"Homage to Africa" on the front cover. A preface, also with the title "Homage to Africa" and three articles (pp. 2–18) attempt to convey to Indian readers a broad idea of the nature and significance of African art; with the third article (pp. 12–18) giving special prominence to the history of Great Benin and to Benin and Yoruba sculpture. These articles are followed on pages 22–64 by 58 beautiful photographs and many line drawings of African sculptures selected from collections and museums in Europe and America. Of the 58 photographs, 11 are of Nigerian sculptures (Ibibio 1, Ibo 1, Yoruba 2, Benin 6 and Ekoi 1).

1131   Mauny, Raymond
Gravures, peintures et inscriptions rupestres de l'Ouest africain. Dakar, IFAN, 1954. 91p. illus. (Initiations africaines, 11)
A presentation of the prehistoric art of West Africa, covering especially the former French territories and parts of Nigeria.

1132   Murray, Kenneth Crosthwaite
Art courses for Africans. *Oversea educ.*, 21 (2) Jan. 1950: 1020–1021.

1133   —The artist in Nigerian tribal society. In *The artist in tribal society, ed. Marian W. Smith, 1961*: 95–101, illus.

1134   —Arts and crafts of Nigeria: their past and future. *Africa*, 14 (4) Oct. 1943: 155–164.
The problems and prospects of encouraging on governmental basis, the development of Nigerian arts and crafts.

1135   —The chief art styles of Nigeria. In *Conference International des Africanistes de l'Ouest; comptes rendus, v. 2, 1951*: 318–330.

1136   —The condition of arts and crafts in West Africa. *Oversea educ.*, 4 (4) 1932: 173–180; 5 (1) Oct. 1933: 1–8.

1137   —Some Nigerian toys. *Nig. mag.*, (17) 1939: 24–25, illus.

1138   Nigeria; a quarterly magazine. (14) 1938: 90–172, illus., map.
A special number of the magazine devoted to arts and crafts. Copiously illustrated.

1139   Olderogge, D. A.
Iskusstvo narodov zapadnoy Afriki v muzeyakh SSSR. Moskva-Leningrad, "Iskusstvo," 1958. 93p. 48 plates, (full page) notes, bibliog.

A study of West African works of art now in Russian museums, mainly in the Anthropological and Ethnographic Museum, Leningrad, and the Moscow University Anthropological Museum. Includes a review of archaeological diggings in the Nok valley and in Ife, and has a section entitled "Art in Medieval Benin" in which Benin history is briefly surveyed and early Benin and Yoruba culture discussed.

1140   Osula, A. O.
Nigerian art. *Nigeria mag.*, (39) 1952: 244–252, illus.,

1141   Preserving Nigeria's heritage; Antiquities commission begins its work. *W. Afr. rev.*, 26 (332) 1955: 396–397, illus.

1142   Sadler, Michael Ernest, *ed.*
Arts of West Africa (excluding music). London, O.U.P., for Inter. inst. for Afr. languages and culture, 1935. xi, 101p. (excl. illus.) illus., bibliog.
Works of art from different parts of West Africa, including Nigeria (Yoruba, Ijaw, Urhobo, and Ibo) The text comprises introductory material and detailed notes describing the illustrations, as well as three brief essays bearing on the significance and teaching of African art.

1143   Schmalenbach, Werner
African art. Translated from the German by Glyn T. Hughes. New York, Macmillan, Basel Holbein, 1954. 176p. illus.
General treatment. Many of the illustrations are of Nigerian works.

1144   Segy, Ladislas
African art studies. New York, Wittenborn, 1956. 240p. plates.
In two parts: 1. Analysis of art appreciation; 2. The African background.

1145   Smith, Marian W., *ed.*
The artist in tribal society: proceedings of a symposium held at the Royal Anthropological Institute. London, Routledge & K. Paul, 1961. xiii, 150p. illus.
See especially pp. 85–120 for two papers and discussion specifically relevant to Nigeria [4316] and [1133]

1146   Stevens, G. A.
Educational significance of indigenous African art. In *Art of West Africa, ed. M. E. Sadler, 1935*: 13–19.

1147   Stocker, John
Our festival of the arts. Lagos, Public relations department [1952] 19p. illus. (Crownbird series, no. 5)
Brief history of the annual Nigerian festival of the arts, written just before the 1952 festival.

1148   Trowell, Margaret
African design. London, Faber and Faber, 1960. 78p. of text, with front., followed by 76 plates, map.
Types of work represented include wall decoration, patterns on mats, screens and calabash, beadwork, decorations on wood, carved ivory, pottery

and metal work. Nigerian specimens
drawn from Hausa, Fulani, Tiv, Nupe,
Yoruba, Benin, Ibo and Ibibio areas.

1149   Underwood, Leon
       Abstraction in African and European
       art. *Studio*, 136, Jl.–Dec. 1948: 182–185,
       illus.
           Deals generally with West African
       art, including its impact on European
       art. The illustrations include some
       Yoruba pieces.

1150   —Nigerian art. *Nig. mag.*, (24) 1946:
       215–220, illus.

13. (ii) Museums, Collections, Exhibitions
       (Including Catalogues and Guides)

1151   Allison, P. K.
       Collecting for Nigeria's museums. *Nig.
       mag.*, (77) Je. 1963: 125–130, illus.

1152   Bascom, William Russell and
       Gebauer, Paul
       Handbook of West African art. (Part 1.
       West African art [by] William R.
       Bascom. Part 2. Art of the British Came-
       roons [by] Paul Gebauer) Assembled
       and edited by Robert E. Ritzenthaler.
       Milwaukee, Bruce publ. co., 1953. 83p.
       (Popular science handbook series, no. 5)
           Handbook and guide to a special
       exhibition of West African art at the
       Milwaukee Public Museum. 62 of the
       works illustrated were of Nigerian
       origin.

1153   British empire exhibition, Wembley,
       1925.
       Nigeria: its history and products.
       London, 1925. 108p. illus., map.

1154   Fagg, William Buller
       Nigerian tribal art. London, Arts
       council of Great Britain, 1960. [40]p.
       illus., map.
           Catalogue of an exhibition of
       Nigerian art.

1155   —The Webster Plass collection of
       African art: the catalogue of a memorial
       exhibition held in the King Edward VII
       galleries of the British Museum, 1953.
       London, British museum, 1953. 45p.
       illus., map.

1156   Kirk-Greene, Anthony Hamilton Millard
       Nigeria's regimental museum. *W. Afr.
       rev.*, 30 (377) Feb. 1959: 94–96, illus.
           Notes on the museum of the Queen's
       own Nigeria regiment at the Regimental
       training centre in Zaria, with a review of
       some of the exhibits therein.

1157   Millot, J.
       Le Nigérien museum de Lagos. *Objets et
       mondes*, 1 (2) 1961: 3–16.

1158   Murray, Kenneth Crosthwaite
       Art in Nigeria: the need for a museum.
       J.R.A.S., 41 (165) Oct. 1942: 241–249.

1159   —The Colonial art exhibition. *Nig. field*,
       17 (1) Jan. 1952: 41–42.
           Notes on some of the exhibits from
       Nigeria at the exhibition of colonial
       sculpture held at the Imperial Institute,
       London in the summer of 1951. Well

over half of the exhibits came from
Nigeria.

1160   —An exhibition of masks and head-
       dresses of Nigeria at the Zwemmer
       Gallery, London, 21st Je. to 16th Jl.
       1949. *Nig. field*, 15 (1) Jan. 1950: 26–41,
       illus.
           Exhibition of some 110 carvings from
       Nigeria collected at various times by
       the author.

1161   —The exhibition of wood-carvings,
       terracottas and watercolours, the work
       of five Nigerians trained under the
       Nigerian Government, held at the
       Zwemmer Gallery, London, 6th Jl. to
       7th Aug. 1937. Photographs by G. I.
       Jones. *Nig. field.*, 7 (1) Jan. 1938: 12–15,
       illus.
           Extracts of U.K. press appraisal of
       the exhibits given.

1162   —A museum for Nigeria. *Nig. mag.*,
       (20) 1940: 271–274, illus.

1163   —Nigeria's first exhibition of antiqui-
       ties. *Oversea ed.*, 18 (3) Apr. 1947:
       507–510, illus; *Nig. mag.*, (26) 1947:
       401–407, illus.
           Reprinted from "Mutende".

1164   —The provision of a Nigerian museum.
       Nig. field, 8 (4) Oct. 1939: 169–175.
           Detailed proposals for the establish-
       ment, staffing and running a Nigerian
       "national museum".

1165   Museums: an urgent need in Nigeria.
       Nig. mag., (14) 1938: 98–100, illus.

1166   Nigeria. Ministry of information.
       Preserving the past: a short description
       of the Museum of Nigerian antiquities,
       traditional art and ethnography, together
       with a note on the principal art treasures
       and their sources of origin. Lagos, the
       Ministry [1959] 31p. illus.

1167   Nigeria. Western.
       An exhibition of Nigerian art and hand-
       crafts at the Tea centre, 22 Regent
       Street, S.W.1; Monday, 28th May-
       Saturday 19th June, 1956. [Ibadan, the
       Regional Government, 1956] 20p. (incl.
       adverts.)

1168   Preserving Nigeria's heritage: new
       Nigerian museum of antiquities at
       Lagos. *W. Afr. rev.*, 28 (355) Apr. 1957:
       368–371, illus.

1169   Stockholm. National museum
       Negerkonst Utställningen ordnad av
       Nationalmuseum i samarbete med
       statens Etnografiska Museum, Etno-
       grafiska Museet i Goteborg och
       Malnio Museum. Stockholm, National-
       museum, 1953. 128p. illus.

1170   Sweeney, James Johnson, *ed.*
       African negro art. New York, Museum
       of modern art, 1935. 58p. illus., bibliog.
           Catalogue of works exhibited by the
       Museum of modern art. Many of the
       items are of Nigerian origin.

13. (iii) Architecture
1171   Beier, Horst Ulrich

Carvers in modern architecture. *Nig. mag.*, (60) 1959: 60–75, illus.

1172 *—Modern architecture in Nigeria. *Baukunst und Werkform,* 10 (2) 1957: 80–83.

1173 Engestrom, Tor
Origin of pre-Islamic architecture in West Africa. *Ethnos,* 24 (1–2) 1959: 64–69, illus., map.

1174 Feilberg, C. G.
Remarks on some Nigerian house types. *Folk,* 1, 1959: 15–26, illus.
Describes different house types to be found in the Yoruba, Ibo and Hausa areas of Nigeria.

1175 Foyle, Arthur M.
Architecture in West Africa, *Afr. South,* 3 (3) Apr.–Je. 1959: 97–105, illus.

1176 —Nigerian architecture. *Geog. mag.,* 23 (5) Sept. 1950: 173–180, map.

1177 —Some aspects of Nigerian architecture. *Man,* 53, 1953 (art. 1): 1–3, illus.
Survey and description of houses in villages around Vom and in Benin City, from the architect's viewpoint.

1178 Godwin, John
Architecture in Nigeria. *Nig. mag.,* (91) Dec. 1966: 247–254, illus.
A brief general survey of architecture in Nigeria. Covers the traditional and early imported patterns, as well as modern development.

1179 Haselberger, H.
Zur traditionellen Architektur der west-afrikanischen Neger: der Bauvorgang in den westlichen Guinealändern und im Westsudan. *Z. f. Ethnol.,* 88 (2) 1963: 180–215, illus., bibliog.

1180 Jeffries, W. F.
Mud building in Northern Nigeria. *Nig. mag.,* (14) 1938: 110.

13. (iv) Sculpture, Carving

1181 Adande, Alexandre
Masques africaines. *Notes afr.,* (51) Jl. 1951: 78–80.

1182 African folktales and sculpture. [Folktales selected and edited by Paul Radin, with the collaboration of Elinore Marvel. Introduction to the tales by Paul Radin. Sculpture selected, with an introduction, by James Johnson Sweeney. New ed.] London, Secker & Warburg, 1965. xxiii, 357p. illus., bibliog.
Introduction to the tales pp. 1–19. There are 81 stories chosen from different parts of Africa, with the tribe of origin given at the end of each story. Section on sculpture has separate title page—African negro sculpture. The introduction to this section (pp. 232–338) takes up the problem of appreciation of African art. It also notes the early European visits to Benin. Many of the 187 beautifully reproduced photographs are of Nigerian sculptures. "Catalogue of plates"—pp. 343–351.

1st ed. publ. 1952 in Bollingen series, no. 32.

1183 Akeredolu, J. D.
Thorn carvings by native Nigerian artists. *Design,* 47, 1945: 8, illus.

1184 Bascom, William Russell
Modern African figurines: satirical or just stylistic? *Lore,* 7 (4) Fall 1957: 118–126.

1185 Beier, Horst Ulrich
African mud sculpture. Cambridge, University press, 1963. 96p. 77 illus.
Photographs of mud sculptures, mainly from Yoruba, Benin and Ibo areas, with explanatory notes and ethnographic background information.

1186 Brinkworth, Ian
Living art of the dead. *W. Afr. rev.,* 29 (373) 1958: 826–829, illus.
On cement tomb monuments in Eastern Nigeria.

1187 Bunt, Cyril G. E.
Two examples of Nigerian wood-carving. *Burl. mag.,* 82 (483) Je. 1943: 146–149, illus.

1188 Clark, Dora
Negro art: sculpture from West Africa. *J. Afr. soc.,* 34 (135) Apr. 1935: 129–137.
Reviews *Arts of West Africa,* edited by Michael Sadler [1142] and an exhibition held in connection with it at the Adams Gallery, Pall Mall Place.

1189 Clarke, John Digby
These disgusting images: "What of the future?" *Nig. teacher,* 1 (5) 1935: 6–8, illus.

1190 Cordwell, Justine Mayer
The problem of process and form in West African art. *Int. W. Afr. conf. proc. 3rd, 1949, 1956:* 53–60.
Training, organisation, economies, material, technique, approach to work and the social status and role of sculptors in the Yoruba and Benin areas.

1191 Dark, Philip John Crossley
West African bronzes. *Africa South,* 3 (2) 1959: 109–116, illus.

1192 De Salverte-Marmier, P. J. F.
A study of the social background of plastic art in selected West African societies. 1960.
B.Litt. thesis, Oxford.

1193 Einstein, Carl
Afrikanische Plastik. Berlin, E. Wasmuth a.g., [1921] 32p. 48 illus. (Orbis pictus; Weltkunstbücherei . . . Bd. 7)
African sculptures assigned to areas of origin. Many are Bini and Yoruba.

1194 —Negerplastik. München, Kurt Wolff, 1920. xxvii, 107p.
A collection of some 116 illustrations of African carvings, some of the best ones being of Nigerian origin. Useful descriptive notes. The introduction discusses inter alia, the connection between art and religion in Africa.

1195 Elisofon, Eliot.
The sculpture of Africa, by Eliot Elisofon. Text by William Fagg, design by Bernard Quint. London, Thames and Hudson, 1958. 256p. illus., map (on end paper) bibliog.
Beautifully reproduced illustrations of the sculpture of the Western Sudan, the Guinea Coast, and the region extending from the Cameroons to Northern Angola, with introductory texts on the cultural background and art styles of each region. Yoruba, Benin, Ijaw, Ibo, Ibibio and Ekoi are all included, with text at pp. 55–66, and sculpture at pp. 112–147.

1196 Fagg, Bernard E. B.
Figures from Northern Nigeria. *Nigeria digest*, 1 (5) May 1945: 5–6.

1197 Fagg, William Buller
African art: the contrast with western tradition. *Times rev. col.*, 1951: 6–7, illus.
All the illustrations (8 in number) are of Nigerian art objects.

1198 —Afro-Portuguese ivories. Text by W. B. Fagg; photographs by W. and B. Forman. London, Batchworth press [1959] xxiv p. illus. (plates).
The introductory text is a general account of these ivories in museums and other collections. Discusses the problem of their origin and history and affirms that they were executed by negro sculptors. See also Ryder, A. F. C. [1227]

1199 —Art without age. *Corona*, 2 (1) Jan. 1950: 24–26.

1200 —Nigeria: 2000 Jahre Plastik. See [1215]

1200a —Nigerian antiquities in the Oldman collection. *Brit. mus. q.*, 16 (4) 1952: 106–109, illus.

1201 —Tribal sculpture from the British colonies. *J. Roy. soc. arts.*, 99 (4852) 1951: 168–706, illus.
7 of the 9 illustrations are from Nigeria.

1202 Fagg, William Buller and List, Herbert
Nigerian images, by William Fagg. Photographs by Herbert List. London, P. Lund, Humphries, 1963. 124, [68] p. (incl. 144 plates), map, bibliog.
A representative collection of Nigerian sculptures intended to portray the country's cultural spirit and image, beautifully illustrated in full page plates. The text (pp. 19–40, 117–124) presents an interesting historical commentary on Nigerian art, divided into two periods—ancient and recent.

1203 Guillaume, Paul and Munro, Thomas
Primitive negro sculpture, with illustrations from the collection of the Barnes foundation at Merion, Pennsylvania. New York, Harcourt, Brace, 1926. [viii] 134p. front., illus., map.

1204 Hall, Henry Usher
West African masks. *Connoisseur*, 93, 1934: 380–383.

1205 Himmelheber, Hans
Negerkunst und Negerkünstler. Braunschweig, Klinkhardt & Biermann, 1960. vii, 436p. illus., map, bibliog. (Bibliothek für Kunst- und Antiquitätenfreunde, v. 40)
A survey of African art, especially African sculpture, with useful area break-down, including Yoruba, Benin, Ibo, Ijaw and Ibibio areas (pp. 248–285). The bibliography, also broken down by regions, covers pp. 415–427.

1206 Jones, Gwilym Iwan
The distribution of negro culture in Southern Nigeria. *Nig. field*, 7 (3) Jl. 1938: 102–108, illus., map.
A survey of sculpture and sculpture styles among the Yoruba, Bini, Ijaw, Ibo, Ibibio and Ekoi.

1207 —Some Nigerian masks. *Geog. mag.*, 18 (5) Sept. 1945: 200, plates.
Describes Ibo, Ijaw and Ibibio masks.

1208 Kjersmeier, Carl
Centres de style de la sculpture nègre africaine. [Traduit par France Gleizol] Paris, Editions Morancé; Copenhagen. Fischers Forlag, 1935–1938. 4v. illus.
A comprehensive survey of African sculpture, describing, with suitable illustrations, the characteristic style of each area. Volume 2 covers Portuguese Guinea, Sierra Leone, Liberia, Ivory Coast, Togo, Dahomey and Nigeria.

1209 Krieger, Kurt and Kutsher, Gerdt
Westafrikanische Masken. Berlin, Museum für Völkerkunde, 1960. 93p. 80 plates, map.

1210 Lavachery, Henri
Statuaire de l'Afrique noire. Brussels, Office de publicité, 1954. 157p. illus.
Nigerian sculpture, pp. 20–35.

1211 *Lawrence, A. W.
Some problems of the plastic arts in British West Africa. *Int. W. Afr. conf. proc., 5th, 1953 [1954?]*

1212 Lester, Susan
Craft of 'cire-perdue'. *W. Afr. rev.*, 28 (356) 1957: 569–575, illus.
Notes on an exhibition by the Inst. of contemporary arts. Many of the illustrations represent Nigerian works.

1213 Lippman, Martin
Westafrikanische Bronzen. Frankfurt A/M., Breidenstein [1940] 79p. illus., map, bibliog.
Ph.D. thesis, Friedrich Wilhelm University.

1213a List, Herbert
Nigeria: 2000 Jahre Plastik. See [1215]

1214 Meyerowitz, Eva Lewin Richter
Ancient Nigerian bronzes. *Burlington mag.*, 79 (462) Sept. 1941: 89–93: 79 (463) Oct. 1941: 121–126, illus.
Bronzes from Ife, Tada and Jebba are described and their technique as well as the early Jukon, Nupe and Yoruba art is viewed as derived from Nubia and the east. See also comments by J. A. Palmer in same magazine 81 (475) Oct.

1942: 252–254, supporting author's conclusions.

1215 Munich. Städtische Galerie
Nigeria: 2000 Jahre Plastik: Ausstellung vom 19. September 1961 bis 7. Januar 1962. Katalog: William Fagg; Photos: Herbert List. [Munich, 1961] [iv] p. 73 plates, map.
A catalogue of some 2000 items depicting Nigerian sculpture, on exhibition in the city museum in Munich from 19th Sept. 1961 to 7th Jan. 1962.

1216 Murray, Kenneth Crosthwaite
Our art treasures. Lagos, Public relations department [n.d.] 16p. illus. (Crownbird series, no. 28)
Brief general description of Nigeria's wealth of art (sculptures and carvings).

1217 —West African wood-carving. *Afr. South,* 2 (4) 1958: 102–105.

1218 —Wood-carving: its place in the cultural life of the African. *Nig. mag.,* (14) 1938: 139.

1219 —Wood-work for elementary schools. *Nig. mag.,* (20) 1940: 290–292, illus.

1220 Murry, J. M.
Negro sculpture. *Nation* [London] 27, 1920: 69–70, illus.

1221 Museck, J. B.
Group of seven African sculptures in wood. *Bull. St. Louis museum,* (27) 1942: 45–49.

1222 Noske, Margot
Afrikanische Masken; achtundvierzig Aufnahmen von Margot Noske, eingeleitet von Julius F. Glück. Baden-Baden, Klein [1956] 16p. illus.
General description, with examples which include Yoruba and Ibibio masks.

1223 Paulme, Denise
Sculptures de l'Afrique noire. Paris, Presses Universitaires de France, 1956. viii, 129p. illus.
Chapter three is on the sculpture of the Guinea Coast, which includes those of the Yoruba, Bini, Ibo, Ijaw and Ekoi in Nigeria. There is an English translation by Michael Ross. London, Elek books, 1962, 160p.

1224 Plass, Margaret
African tribal sculpture. Philadelphia, Pennsylvania university museum, [1956] 57p. illus., map.
Includes Nigerian sculpture, pp. 26–38.

1225 Portier, André and Poncetton, F.
Les arts sauvages: Afrique. Paris, Albert Morancé, 1930. 15p. illus. (50 plates).
Includes beautiful illustrations of works from Nigeria drawn from French collections.

1225a Radin, Paul
African folktales & sculpture. See [1182]

1226 Robertson, K. A.
Brass work. *Nig. mag.,* (14) 1938: 169–170, illus.

1227 Ryder, Alvan Frederick Charles
A note on the Afro-Portuguese ivories.

J. Afr. hist., 5 (3) 1964: 363–365, illus.
Notes some entries in the extant account book of the *Casa de Guinea* which show payments by sailors on ivory goods they brought to Lisbon from the Guinea Coast, and which may throw light on the problem of the origin of the Afro-Portuguese ivories raised by William Fagg. See [1198]

1228 Schweeger-Hefel, Annemarie
Afrikanische Bronzen. Vienna, Wolfrum [1948] 34p. illus., map, bibliog. (Wolfrumbücher, 17)
The illustrations include some 48 plates, of which 41 are of Nigerian bronzes.

1229 Segy, Ladislas
African sculpture. London, Constable [New York, Dover, 1958] 32p. illus., map.
About 18 of the illustrations represent Nigerian products.

1230 —African sculpture and writing. *J. hum. relations,* 1 (3) Winter, 1953: 13–21, bibliog.

1231 —African sculpture speaks. New York, A. A. Wyn, 1952. 254p. front., illus., bibliog.
A presentation of the historico-cultural backgrounds to African sculpture, followed with a listing, with brief, illustrated descriptions, of West African style regions; and a discussion, in the last chapters, of the influences of African art on modern European art.

1232 Sieber, Roy
African tribal sculpture. 1957.
Ph.D. thesis, Iowa State University.

1233 —Sculpture of Northern Nigeria. New York, Museum of primitive art, distributed by university publishers, 1961. 82p. illus., map.
"Prepared in conjunction with an exhibition held at the Museum of Primitive Art of the Roy Sieber collection".

1233a Sweeney, James Johnson
African folktales & sculpture. See [1182]

1234 Sydow, Eckart von
African sculpture. *Africa,* 1 (2) Apr. 1928: 210–227, illus. (plates).
A general and historical survey of African sculpture including Nigerian sculpture—Yoruba, Bini, Ekoi, Ijaw, Ibibio, Urhobo, Itsekiri, and Ibo.

1235 —Afrikanische Plastik; aus dem Nachlass herausgegeben von G. Kutscher. Berlin, Gebr. Mann, New York, G. Wittenborn, 1954. 176p. 144 plates, bibliog.
A study of the stylistic and psychological aspects of African art, including a systematic survey of the style regions of African sculpture (Nigeria and Dahomey, pp. 124–132). Edited posthumously from author's manuscripts, and planned as vol. 2 of his Handbuch der Afrikanische Plastik. See [1236]

1236 —Handbuch der Westafrikanischen

Plastik. Berlin, D. Reimer, E. Vohsen, 1930. xii, 495p. illus. (plates) (Handbuch der Afrikanischen Plastik, v. 1)

A comprehensive presentation of West African sculpture, taking the regions in order from Senegambia down to Northern Angola. Southern Nigeria, pp. 139–218.

1237 Trowell, Margaret
Classical African sculpture. London, Faber and Faber, 1954. 103 [xlviii]p. 48 plates, maps, bibliog.

A discussion of the problems of appreciating African art is followed by ethnological and historical survey of the Guinea Coast and the Western Sudan, and a descriptive study of the sculptures of these areas.

1238 — —2nd edition. 1964.
Mentions the Nok culture and William Fagg's new chronology of Bini sculpture.

1239 Underwood, Leon
Bronzes of West Africa. London, Tiranti, 1949. vii, 32p. (excl. plates). illus.

There are 64 full page plates as well as text illustrations. Of the full page plates all but 3 illustrate Ife and Bini bronzes.

1240 —Figures in wood of West Africa. London, Tiranti, 1947. xlixp. 48 illus., map, bibliog.

A collection of photographs of West African carvings in 48 plates, 17 of which are from Nigeria. Title and text also in French.

1241 —Masks of West Africa. London, Tiranti, 1948. vi, 49p. (excl. plates), illus.
Title page and text in English and French. Illustrations comprise 48 full page plates, of which 20 are of Nigerian masks.

1242 Williams, Denis
The Nigerian image. Problems in Nigerian art history. Odu, 1 (2) 1965: 83–91.

Review of Nigerian Images by W. Fagg and H. List [1202] q.v.

1243 Wingert, Paul S.
Anatomical interpretation of African masks. Man, 54, 1954: 69–71 (art. 100) illus.

1244 —The sculpture of negro Africa. New York, Columbia University press, 1950. vii, 96p. 118 plates, bibliog.

Pages 31–45 on Nigerian sculpture—Yoruba, Bini, Ibo, Ibibio, Ijaw and Ekoi. The plates illustrate works in American collections.

13. (v) Pottery

1245 Braunholtz, H. J.
Pottery in Nigeria. Congr. int. sci. anthrop. et. ethnol., 3e, Bruxelles, 1948. 1960: 24–25.

1246 Cardew, Michael
Nigerian traditional pottery. Nig. mag., (39) 1952: 180–201, illus.

1247 —West African pottery. Africa south, 3 (1) Oct.–Dec. 1958: 109–113, illus.

1248 Duckworth, E. H.
The art of the potter. Nig. mag., (14) 1938: 114–117, illus.

1248a Jeffreys, M. D. W.
Maize impressions on ancient Nigerian pottery. See [923]

1249 King, John B.
A commentary on contemporary Nigerian pottery. Nig. mag., (74) Sept. 1962: 16–24, illus.

1250 Nigerian pottery. Nig. teacher, 1 (2) 1934: 54–56, illus.

1252 Omoregie, S. O.
Pottery in Nigeria. W. Afr. rev., 25 (325) 1954: 939, illus.

13. (vi) Painting, Drawing

1253 Crownover, David
Pink people! Europeans in the tribal art of Nigeria. Expedition, 2 (3) Spring 1960: 33–35.

1254 Duerden, Dennis G.
Is there a Nigerian style of painting? Nig. mag., (41) 1953: 51–59, illus.

1255 Enwonwu, Ben
Painting and natural history: an artist's eye-view of Nigeria. W. Afr. rev., 23 (293) 1952: 131–132, illus.

Appraisal of paintings of Nigerian people and sceneries by Maurice Fiévet, a French painter.

1256 Murray, Kenneth Crosthwaite
Painting in Nigeria. Nig. mag., (14) 1938: 112–113, illus.

13. (vii) Textile Weaving and Dyeing

1257 Ene, J. Chunwike
Indigenous silk-weaving in Nigeria. Nig. mag., (81) Je. 1964: 127–136, illus.

Describes in detail materials and methods of silk-weaving in different parts of Nigeria and the pattern of use of woven silk material.

1258 Kiewe, Heinz Edgar
Can migration of man be traced by African textile designs? W. Afr., (2000) Je. 25, 1955: 579, illus.

Describes Nigerian designs at an Oxford exhibition.

1259 Maguire, Peter
West African dyeing. J. Afr. soc., 5 (18) Jan. 1906: 151–153.

Describes dyeing in, and dyed cloths from West Africa, including those from Lagos and "Niger".
Reprinted from the Manchester Guardian.

1260 Murray, Kenneth Crosthwaite
Weaving in Nigeria: a general survey. Nig. mag., (14) 1938: 118–120.

1261 Roth, Henry Ling
African looms. J.R.A.I., 47, 1917: 113–150.

1262 Southern, A. E.
Cloth making in Nigeria. Nig. mag., (32) 1949: 35–40, illus.

1263 Worsley, M.
Nigerian weavers. *Handweaver and craftsman,* 12 (2) Spring 1961: 45–47.

13. (viii) Basket and Mat Making, Cane and Raffia Work, Knotting

1264 Ahmed, S. Gimba
Grass weaving. *Nig. mag.,* (74) Sept. 1962: 10–15, illus.
Notes on the grass plaiting and weaving industry in Northern Nigeria.

1265 Haddon, Kathleen *and* Treleaven, Hilda A.
Some Nigerian string figures. *Nig. field,* 5 (1) Jan. 1936: 31–38; 5 (2) Apr. 1936: 86–95, illus., bibliog.
Illustrated description of string figures collected in Nigeria by Mrs. Treleaven.

1266 Hambly, Wilfrid Dyson *and* Hambly, A. E.
Weavers of West Africa: mats and basketry in Nigeria and Angola. *Craft horiz.,* 14, 1954: 29–31, illus.

1267 Lindblom, K. G.
String figures in Africa. Stockholm, Riksmussets etnografiska avdelning, 1930. 12p. (Smärre meddelanden, N. r. 9)
Includes string figures of the Yoruba and Cross River peoples.

1268 Murray, Kenneth Crosthwaite
Basket making. *Nig. mag.,* (14) 1938: 158–159, illus.

1269 —A list of the chief varieties of craft work in the Eastern provinces of Nigeria. *Nig. mag.,* (17) 1939: 33–37.

1270 Obaseki, J. K.
Rope industry (minor forest produce) *Farm & forest,* 10, 1950: 22–24.

1271 Robertson, K. A.
The mat and hat industry. *Nig. mag.,* (14) 1938: 165–168, illus.
On hat and mat making among the Nupe and the Gwari, with two of the illustrations showing Ibibio and Okobo mats.

13. (ix) Calabash Decoration

1272 Murray, Kenneth Crosthwaite
Calabash carving: a beautiful Nigerian art. *Nig. mag.,* (10) 1937: 72, illus.

13. (x) Leatherwork

1273 Jeffries, W. F.
Leather work in Northern Nigeria. *Nig. mag.,* (14) 1938: 160–162, illus.

1274 Nyanbongo, A. K.
Leather industries. *Negro hist. bulletin,* 8, Nov. 1944: 34–35.

1275 Wills, Colin
Nigerian hides and skins. *Progress* [London] 46 (260) autumn 1958: 258–265, illus.

13. (xi) Metal Work, Smithing, Glass and Bead Work

1276 Cline, Walter

Mining and metallurgy in negro Africa. Menesha, Wis., George Banta publishing coy. agent, 1937. 154p. illus., maps, bibliog.
A study of traditional African mining and metallurgical processes.

1277 Justice, J. N.
The ancient metal workings in East Nigeria. *Man,* 22, 1922: 3–4 (art. 3) illus.
In the mining districts of Bauchi Plateau.

1277a Neher, Gerald
Brass casting in North-east Nigeria. See [4125]

1278 Staudinger, Paul
Zinnschmelzen afrikanischer Eingeborener. *Z. f. Ethnol.,* 43, 1911: 147–148, illus.
On tin smelting by natives in Bauchi.

14. ACCULTURATION AND SOCIAL CHANGE, CONTACT SITUATION, URBANIZATION

1279 Akiwowo, Akinsola
Social changes in Nigeria: their effects on the individual, the family and the society. In *Report of the first conference of Eastern Nigeria councils of social service . . . 1965:* 24–27.
Revised version of an address delivered at the conference. For the full report of the proceedings. See [3529]

1280 *Akunneto, I. O.
Tribalism in Nigeria. Lagos [n.d.]

1281 Aldous, Joan
Urbanization, the extended family, and kinship ties in West Africa. *Social forces,* 4 (1) Oct. 1962: 6–12, bibliog.
A survey of the effects of urbanization on extended family and kinship ties in West Africa, based on investigations in the cities of Brazzaville, Dakar, Senegal, Lagos, Leopoldville and Stanleyville.

1282 Aloba, Abiodun
Tribal unions in party politics. *W. Afr. Jl.* 10th 1954: 637.
Contribution of tribal unions to local progress among the Ibo and Ibibio peoples, and of their subsequent involvement in party politics.

1283 Armstrong, Robert G.
The development of complex societies in West Africa. *NISER conf. proc., 7th, Ibadan, 1960:* 20–27.

1284 Azikiwe, Nnamdi
Tribalism; a pragmatic instrument for national unity: lecture delivered under the auspices of the Political Science Association of the University of Nigeria, Nsukka, Friday, 15 May, 1964. Aba, International press, 1964. 37p. illus. (port.)

1285 Baker, Tanya and Bird, Mary E. C.
Urbanization and the position of women. *Sociol. rev.,* n.s. 7 (1) Jl. 1959: 99–122, bibliog.
On the changing position of women

in urban centres in Africa, including Nigeria.

1286   Bloy, P. P.
       Industrial and urban development in Nigeria: some tasks for the Church. London, Church Missionary Society, 1959. 11p.
       Report of a survey of industrialization and urbanization in Nigeria carried out by author in March and April 1959. Gives suggestions as to how the work of the church may be introduced and expanded among industrial workers in urban centres.

1287   Busia, K. A.
       The impact of industrialization on West Africa. *WAISER conf. proc., (Sociology section) 1952:* 31–37.

1288   Church, Ronald James Harrison
       West African urbanization: a geographical view. *Sociol. rev.,* n.s. 7 (1) Jl. 1959: 15–28, bibliog.

1289   Coleman, James S.
       The role of tribal associations in Nigeria. *WAISER conf. proc., 1952:* 61–66.
       Summary only of the original paper read at the conference. Deals with the origins and functions (political, social and economic) of tribal/cultural organizations in Southern Nigeria.

1290   *Comhaire-Sylvain, S.
       Associations on the basis of origin in Lagos, Nigeria. *Amer. Catholic sociol. rev.,* 11, 1950:

1291   Conference on problems of urbanization in Northern Nigeria, Zaria, Nigeria, 1962. Report of the conference [held] 5th to 10th Nov. 1962 . . . Ed. by M. J. Campbell and J. Wilson. Pittsburgh, Graduate school of public and international affairs, 1963. 30p.

1292   Forde, Cyril Daryll
       The conditions of social development in West Africa: retrospect and prospect. *Civilisations,* 3 (4) 1953: 471–489.

1293   Great Britain. Colonial office
       Nigeria: report of the commission appointed to enquire into the fears of minorities and the means of allaying them. London, H.M.S.O., 1958. vii, 144p. maps in end pocket. (Cmnd. 505)
       Popularly known as "The minorities' report", or "The minorities commission report." Chairman—H. Willink.

1294   Gunter, Guy
       The new societies of tropical Africa: a selective study. London, Issued under the auspices of the Institute of race relations [by] O.U.P., 1962. xx, 376p. plates, maps, tables, bibliog.
       Penetrating studies of the social, economic and political problems of the emergent African states, conducted between 1959 and 1961. Wealth of information on Nigeria but scattered throughout the book.

1295   Hanna, M. I.
       Lebanese emigrants in West Africa: their effects on Lebanon and West Africa. 1959.
       D.Phil thesis, Oxford.

1295a Harrison-Church, R. J. See Church, Ronald James Harrison.

1296   Heads, J.
       Urbanization and economic progress. *NAISER conf. proc. 1958:* 65–73.
       Examines the relationship between the progress of urbanism and the rise of real income per head in the Nigerian economy.

1297   Herskovits, Melville J.
       The human factor in changing Africa. London, Routledge and K. Paul, 1962. xiv, 500p.

1298   Hodgkin, Thomas
       Islam and national movements in West Africa. *J. Afr. hist.,* 3 (2) 1962: 323–327.

1299   Igun, Adenola A.
       The demographic consequences of social change in West Africa. *WAISER conf. proc., 4th, Accra, 1955:* 52–67.

1300   Ilogu, Edmund C. O.
       Ethics of a new nation: an examination of Nigeria's present society in the light of the social ethics of Reinhold Niebuhr. 1959.
       Ph.D. thesis, Columbia University.

1301   —The problem of ethics in Nigeria: an organic society undergoing change under the influence of technical culture.
       M.A. thesis, Columbia.

1302   —The problem of indigenization in Nigeria. *Int. rev. missions,* 49 (194) Apr. 1960: 167–182.

1303   —Religion and culture in West Africa. *Theology today,* 20, Apr. 1963: 53–60.

1304   —Social philosophy for the new Nigerian nation. Onitsha, Etudo press, 1962. 42p.
       Attempts to sift and compare Nigeria's problems and advantages in her process of transforming from a mere political unit or state into a closely knit nation-state.

1305   —Some problems of culture change in Nigeria. *Man in soc.,* 1 (1) May 1963: 34–36.
       Mainly limited to Eastern Nigeria.

1306   Imohiosen, A. E.
       Socio-cultural and personality systems under situations of change: theory and measurement exemplified with data from West Africa. 1963.
       Ph.D. thesis, Cornell.

1307   Kilson, Martin L.
       Social forces in West African political development. *J. hum. rel.,* 8, spring/ summer 1960: 576–598.

1308   Kuper, Hilda, *ed.*
       Urbanization and migration in West Africa. Berkeley, University of California press; London, C.U.P., 1965. [x] 227p. map, bibliog.

1309   Leech, William David
       Changing attitudes towards sex and marriage among urban Nigerians as

revealed in two Lagos newspapers, the *West African Pilot* and the *Daily Service*, 1946.

M.A. thesis, University of Pennsylvania, Philadelphia, Topics investigated include courtship, polygamy, sexual obligations, extra-marital sexual relations, divorce, relative position of spouses: dominance and submission, companionship, economics, home management, family and children.

1310   Liell, John [and others]
A research design for a comparative study of urbanisation and fertility: a progress report. *Nig. j. econ. soc. stud.*, 7 (1) Mar. 1965: 63–69.
Urbanisation, fertility and related topics, in two far flung cultures—Nigeria and Greece.

1311   Little, Kenneth L.
From tribalism to modern society. *Yearbook of educ., 1954:* 119–134.
A general discussion of the dynamics of culture contact and social change, with frequent references to West Africa and Nigeria.

1312   —The organisation of voluntary associations in West Africa. *Civilisations,* 9 (3) 1959: 283–297.

1313   —The role of voluntary associations in West African urbanization. *Amer. anthrop.,* 59 (4) 1957: 579–596.

1314   —Some social consequences. *Afr. affairs,* 65   (259) Apr. 1966: 160–169.
On social consequences of urbanization in Africa.

1315   —Some traditionally based forms of mutual aid in West African urbanization. *Ethnology,* 1 (2) Apr. 1962: 197–211.

1316   —The study of 'social change' in British West Africa. *Africa,* 23 (4) Oct. 1953: 274–284.
French summary, p. 284.

1317   —The urban role of tribal associations in West Africa. *Afr. stud.,* 21 (1) 1962: 1–8, bibliog.
The nature, organisation and social functions of tribal unions in West Africa briefly discussed.

1318   —Urbanism in West Africa. *Sociol. rev.,* 7 (1) Jl. 1959: 5–131.
A whole issue carrying several articles devoted to problems of urbanism in the tropics.

1319   —The West African town: its social basis. *Diogenes,* (29) Spring 1960: 16–31.

1320   Lloyd, Peter Cutt
Tribalism in Nigeria. In *The multi-tribal society; proceedings of the 16th conf. of the Rhode-Livingstone Institute, 1962:* 133–147 [sic] i.e. 151–165, bibliog.
A brief survey of the phenomenon of tribalism in Nigeria and its effects on political and social developments in the country.

1321   Mabogunje, Akin L.
Economic implications of the pattern of urbanisation in Nigeria. *Nig. j. econ. soc. stud.,* 7 (1) Mar. 1965: 9–30, illus.
Two aspects of urbanism—functional specialisation and spatial location of cities—are briefly reviewed, and in relation to these, the Nigerian pattern of urbanisation and some of its possible economic implications are discussed.

1322   Maccall, Daniel F.
Urban problems in West Africa. *WAISER conf. proc., 1952:* 77–81.
Summary only of the original paper read at the conference.

1323   Mair, L. P.
Some social implications of economic change in Nigeria. *Nig. j. econ. & soc. stud.,* 1 (1) May 1959: 8–16.

1324   Manshard, W.
Verstädterungserscheinungen in West-afrika. *Raumforschung und Raumordnung,* 19, 1961: 27–41.
On the problems of urbanization in West Africa.

1325   Melvin, Ernest E.
Native urbanism in West Africa. *J. geog.,* 60 (1) Jan. 1961: 9–16.

1326   Mitchel, N. C.
The Nigerian town: distribution and definition. *Res. notes.,* (7) 1955: 1–13, map.

1327   Moore, W. Robert
Progress and pageantry in changing Nigeria. *National geog. mag.,* 110 (3) Sept. 1956: 325–365, illus, map.
"Bulldozers and penicillin, science and democracy come to grips with colorful age-old customs in Britain's largest colony"—sub-title.

1328   Morgan, W. B.
The influence of European contacts on the landscape of Southern Nigeria. *Geog. j.,* 125 (1) Mar. 1959: 48–64, maps.

1329   Morton-Williams, Peter
Cinema in rural Nigeria; a field study of the impact of fundamental education films on rural audiences in Nigeria. [Lagos] Federal information service [1957] [207]p. map.

1330   Nigerias bevolkingsgroci en economische ontwikkeling. *Afrika* [The Hague] 18 (5) May 1964: 160–161.

1331   Odutola, S. O.
Islam as it affects life in Nigeria. In *The church in changing Africa; report of the all-Africa church conference. 1958:* 65–67.

1332   Okediji, Francis Olu
Some correlates of ethnic cohesiveness: a further analysis of African students' adjustment in two United States communities. *Nig. j. econ. soc. stud.,* 7 (3) Nov. 1965: 347–362.

1333   Okigbo, Pius
Social consequences of economic development in West Africa. *Ann. Amer. acad. pol. soc. sci.,* 305, May 1956: 125–133.

1334 Oloko, Olatunde
Some socio-cultural factors affecting
response to innovation. *Nig. j. econ. &
soc. stud.*, 4, 1962: 147–154.
    Comment by Raymond Apthorpe,
pp. 154–155.

1335 —The impact of advanced technology
on the social structure of traditional
societies. *Nig. j. econ. soc. stud.*, 6 (1)
Mar. 1964: 23–36.

1336 Omololu, Z. Oluyemi
Report of the Commission appointed to
enquire into the fears of the minorities
and the means of allaying them—a
review. *Nig. j. econ. & soc. stud.*, 1 (1)
May 1959: 60–61.

1337 Oyolola, Akin
The influence of the cinema in Nigeria.
Nig. mag., (39) 1952: 211.

1338 Ozou, M. U.
The social aspects of urbanization:
being a short survey of the trends in
Eastern Nigeria and proposals for the
solution of some of the problems. *C.S.A.
meeting of specialists on urbanization and
its social aspects, Abidjan, 1961. London,
CCTA, 1961.*

1339 Patterson, Charles J.
Pressures on the church in Nigeria.
Afr. report, 8, Mar. 1963: 17–19.

1340 Phills, G. H.
Social perception and anxiety in
Nigerian and British students. 1963.
Ph.D. thesis, London.

1341 Pilkington, Frederick
In the Nigerian background. *Afr. affairs,*
57 (227) Apr. 1958: 138–140.
    Discusses Nigerian traditional customs
and religious beliefs which are receding
from or merging into the spreading
western civilisation and Christian beliefs.

1342 —Money and morals in a changing
Nigeria. *W. Afr. rev.*, 21, 1950: 924–925.

1343 Rosman, Abraham
Africa: background to change. *Antioch
rev.*, 21 (3) fall 1961: 261–269.
    Discusses the religious, political and
socio-cultural problems besetting
Nigeria in her evolution to nationhood.

1344 Smythe, Hugh H.
Urbanization in Nigeria. *Anthrop. q.*,
33 (3) Jl. 1960: 143–148.

1345 U.N. Economic commission for Africa.
Leopoldville and Lagos: comparative
study of urban conditions in 1960.
Econ. bull. Afr., 1 (2) 1961: 50–55.

1346 —Report of the workshop on urban
problems: the role of women in urban
development. New York, 1963. 45p.
(U. N. [document] E/CN. 14/241)
    Women in Lagos.

1347 Urbanization in African social change;
proceedings of the Inaugural seminar
held in the Centre of African studies,
University of Edinburgh, 5th–7th Jan.
1963. [Edinburgh, University, Centre
of Afr. stud., 1963] vi, 206p. maps.

1348 Verger, Pierre
Influence du Brésil au Golfe du Bénin.
In: *Les Afro-Américains* [Mémoires
IFAN, no. 27] 1953: 11–101, illus.
(plates), bibliog.

1349 West, Ralph Lee
A study of indigeneity among Nigerian
Baptists. 1953.
    Ph.D. thesis, New Orleans Baptist
Theological Seminary.

15. SOCIAL PROBLEMS, APPLIED ANTHROPOLOGY

Numerous works which bear on applied
anthropology will be found in many of the
preceding sub-divisions of Section III, especially
sub-division 14: 'Acculturation and Social
Change'. For fuller coverage, reference should
be made to these sub-divisions.

1350 Achonu, Thomas A.
Study of some housing programs and
how they apply to Nigeria. 1955. viii,
75p. maps,.
    M.A. thesis, Howard University,
Washington, D.C.

1351 Agbim, G. Nwabeze
A survey of social welfare services in
selected rural communities in Nigeria
from 1900–1955, as reflected in published
and unpublished material. 1956. 65p.
maps.
    M.A. thesis, Howard University,
Washington, D.C.

1352 Akak, Eyo O.
Bribery & corruption in Nigeria.
[Ibadan, the author, 1953] 120p.
    Printed by Kajola press, Ibadan.

1353 Aluko, Timothy Mofolorunso
Problems of housing and town planning
in Nigeria. *J. Nig. med. assoc.*, 1 (3) Jl.
1964: 86–90.
    Financial, land and man-power prob-
lems of housing and town planning, and
the slum clearance and sanitary problems
of rehousing in Nigeria, especially in
Lagos and Ibadan.

1354 Arnett, Edward John
Native administration in West Africa;
a comparison of French and British
policy. *J. Afr. soc.*, 32 (128) Jl. 1933:
240–251.

1355 Asuni, T.
Community development and public
health: by-product of social psychiatry
in Nigeria. *W. Afr. med. j.*, *n.s.*, 13,
1964: 151–154.

1356 Azikiwe, Nnamdi
How shall we educate the African? *J.
Afr. soc.*, 33 (131) Apr. 1934: 143–150.
    Attacks the over-stressing of voca-
tional and agricultural aspects of African
education to the detriment of academic
and literary pursuits. Advocates a more
progressive and comprehensive curriculum for African education, embracing
"both literary and technical, and moral
subjects" so that "not all Africans
should become artisans and farmers".

Followed by a brief review by Rev. E. W. Smith, pp. 150–151.

1357 Batley, S. K.
The privately owned maternity home in Nigeria. *Afr. women*, 3 (2) Je. 1959: 39–41.
Describes the system of private maternity homes in Nigeria, operated mostly by married women, and notes some of its disadvantages.

1358 Bertelsen, P. H.
The relationship between adult education and economic and social development in West Africa. *NISER conf. proc., 7th, Ibadan, 1960*: 39–46.

1359 Boroffka, A. and Marinho, A. A.
A preliminary survey of the in-patient population of the mental hospital in Lagos-Yaba. In *Pan-African psychiatric conference, 1st, Abeokuta, 1961. [1962?]*: 195–197.

1360 Brokensha, David
Applied anthropology in English-speaking Africa. Lexington, Ky., Society for applied anthropology, 1966. 31p. bibliog.
A general survey describing recent examples of applied anthropology and evaluating their significance. Extensive bibliography, pp. 18–31.

1361 Brosnahan, L. F.
Bilingualism and society in Nigeria. *WAISER conf. proc., 1954*: 82–89.

1362 Callaway, C.
School leavers and the developing economy in Nigeria. *NISER conf. proc., Dec. 1960*: 60–72.
A study of the unemployment problem in Nigeria with particular reference to its social and economic aspects. First published in *West Afr.*, (2286–2289) Mar.–Apr. 1961: 325, 353, 371–2 and 409.

1363 Cameron, Donald
Native administration in Nigeria and Tanganyika. *J.R.A.S.*, 36, Extra supplement, 30 Nov. 1937. 29p.

1364 Collis, William Robert Fitz-Gerald
The paediatric problem in environmental hygiene and urban development in Nigeria. *J. Nig. med. assoc.*, 1 (3) Jl. 1964: 91–93.

1365 —Prevention of Kwashiorkor in Nigeria. In *Progress in meeting protein needs of infants and preschool children* (National academy of sciences-National research council, Washington) 1961: 169–176. (NAS–NRC. publication no. 843).

1366 Conference of provincial representatives, Zaria, 1950. Report on a conference to discuss the adult literacy campaign, Northern Region. Zaria, Gaskiya corporation [1950]

1367 Coomassie, A.
Unesco associated projects XIII: adult education campaign in the Northern Region of Nigeria. *Fundamental & adult educ.*, 9 (1) Jan. 1957: 39–45.

1368 Court, John W.
The adult literacy campaign in Northern Nigeria. *Oversea educ.*, 30 (2) Jl. 1958: 64–68.
Describes the organisation and operation of adult education scheme in Northern Nigeria.

1369 —Reading in Nigeria. *Oversea educ.*, 32 (2) Jl. 1960: 51–53.
Problems of adult education in Northern Nigeria.

1370 Crowder, Michael
Gaskiya corporation of Nigeria: a powerful agency for education in the North. *Afr. world*, Dec. 1954: 15.

1371 Davy, T. H.
Disease and population pressure in the tropics. Ibadan, University press, 1958. 22p.

1372 Duggan, A. J.
Survey of sleeping sickness in Northern Nigeria from earliest times to present day. *Tr. Roy. soc. trop. med. & hyg.*, 56, 1962: 439–486.

1373 Egbuonu, Ndukwe Ndim
Indirect rule and its application in Southeastern Nigeria: a study in the techniques of British colonial administration. 1964. [vi] 402 p. bibliog.
Ph.D. thesis, Columbia University.

1374 Enemo, Eliazar Obiakonwa
The social problems of Nigeria. *Africa*, 18 (3) Jl. 1948: 190–198.
On linguistic multiplicity, religious diversity, uninformed public opinion, bribery, and other factors producing or complicating social problems in Nigeria.

1375 Faulkner, Donald E.
Boy's welfare work in Nigeria. *Oversea educ.*, 18 (2) Jan. 1947: 447–451.

1376 —A juvenile court. *Nig. mag.*, (29) 1948: 257–261.
Describes the composition and functioning of a juvenile court in Lagos.

1377 —Social welfare and juvenile delinquency in Lagos, Nigeria. London, Howard league for penal reform [n.d.] 7p.

1378 Firth, Raymond
Social problems and research in British West Africa. *Africa*, 17 (2) Apr. 1947: 77–92, illus; 17 (3) Jl. 1947: 170–180.
In the first instalment, the socio-economic problems existing or likely to arise in the then British territories of Gambia, Sierra Leone, Ghana and Nigeria are examined first generally, and then territory by territory (with Nigeria on pp. 87–89.) The second instalment lists and discusses types of research projects that could be profitably undertaken. French summary of first instalment—pp. 91–92.

1379 Gans, B.
Some socio-economic and cultural factors in West African paediatrics. *Archiv. dis. childhood*, 38, 1963: 1–12.

1380 Gardiner, R. K. A.
Adult education in Nigeria. *Adult educ.*, 23 (1) Je. 1950: 56–62.

1381 Gibb, J. P. P.
Some problems of resettlement of the displaced population. *Proc. sci. assoc. Nig.*, 5, 1962: 42–53, map.
On the problem of resettling people affected by the reservoir formed by the Kainji dam. The areas affected include parts of Borgu, Gwandu, Kontagora and Yauri emirates of Northern Nigeria.

1382 Grove, A. T.
Land use and soil conservation on the Jos Plateau. Lagos, Govt. printer, 1952. 63p. map. (Nigeria. Geological survey. Bull. no. 22)

1383 Hodgkin, Thomas
Adult and workers' education in the Gold Coast and Nigeria. *Fund. and adult educ.*, 5 (1) Jan. 1953: 28–32.

1384 Howard, A. C.
Notes on nervous and mental diseases encountered in Nigeria. *Tr. Roy. soc. trop. med. and hyg.*, 41 (6) May 1948: 823–828.

1385 Igboko, Pius Mbonu
Adult education in Nigeria. 1964. xii, 247p. maps, bibliog.
Ph.D. thesis, Birmingham.

1386 Jeffries, W. F.
The literacy campaign in Northern Nigeria. *Fund. & adult educ.*, 10 (1) Jan. 1958: 2–6.

1387 Lambo, T. Adeoyo
The concept and practice of mental health in African cultures. *E. Afr. med. j.*, 37, Je. 1960: 464–471.

1388 —A form of social psychiatry in Africa (with special reference to general features of psychotherapy with Africans) Leopoldville, C.C.T.A. Permanent Inter-African bureau for tsetse and trypanosomiasis, 1959.
(Publication no. 2/0) Mimeographed. Also *World mental health*, 13, Nov. 1961: 190–203.

1389 —Further neuropsychiatric observations in Nigeria, with comments on the need for epidemiological study in Africa. *Brit. med. j.*, 2, 10 Dec. 1960: 1696–1704.

1390 —The influence of cultural factors on epidemiological surveys in Africa. *W. Afr. med. j.*, 10, Apr. 1961: 87–92.

1391 —Medical and social problems of drug addiction in West Africa (with special emphasis on psychiatric aspects). *W. Afr. med. j., n.s.*, 14 (6) Dec. 1965: 236–254, illus., maps, tables, bibliog.

1392 —Mental health in Africa. *Medical world*, 95, Sept. 1961: 198–202.

1393 —Mental health in Nigeria. *Nig. trade j.*, 12 (3) Jl./Sept. 1964: 95–99, illus.
A review, in general terms, of the problems of mental health in Nigeria, and a description of the method of treatment adopted in the Neuro-psychiatric centre in Aro village, near Abeokuta.

1394 —Mental health in Nigeria: research and its technical problems. *World mental health*, 13, Aug. 1961: 135–141.

1395 —Neuropsychiatric observations in the Western Region of Nigeria. *Brit. med. j.*, 2, 15 Dec. 1956: 1388–1394.

1395a —Pan-African psychiatric conference. See [1407]

1396 —A plan for the treatment of the mentally ill in Nigeria: the village system in Aro. In *Frontiers in general hospital psychiatry, ed. L. Linn, 1961*: 215–231.

1397 *Lambo, T. Adeoyo [and others]
A report on the study of social and health problems of Nigerian students in Britain and Ireland. Ibadan, Govt. printer, 1959.

1398 Lloyd, Peter Cutt and Post, Kenneth William John
Where should we vote? *J. Afr. admin.*, 12 (2) Apr. 1960: 95–106.
A study of the 1953, 1955 and 1959 electoral regulations used in Western Nigeria, to illustrate the problem raised in tribal societies, of whether a person's constituency should be determined by descent or by residence.

1399 Mcqueen, A. J.
Aspirations and problems of Nigerian school leavers. *E.A.I.S.R. conf. proc., Je. 1963*: [243–252]

1400 Marris, Peter
Slum clearance and family life in Lagos. *Human organisation*, 19 (3) fall 1960: 123–128.

1401 Mayer, T. F. G.
Distribution of leprosy in Nigeria with special reference to the aetiological factors on which it depends. Lagos, Govt. printer, 1930. 13p. maps.

1402 Morley, D.
Fighting Nigerian child mortality. *New soc.*, 72, Feb. 13, 1964: 14–15, illus.

1403 Nigeria. Eastern. Ministry of internal affairs.
Problems and needs of youth in Eastern Nigeria: being report of a seminar on youth welfare work held at the University of Nigeria, Nsukka: September 1–4, 1964. Enugu, Ministry of internal affairs, 1964. [78]p.

1404 *Ogunlesi, J. S.
Mass education and the citizen. Ibadan, Social development office, 1959.

1405 Okala, Julius B. C. Etuka
Bilingualism in Eastern Region of Nigeria: a psychological and socio-psychological study. Enugu, E.N.P.C. [n.d.] 16p.

1406 Otolorin, T. R.
A proposed national health scheme for Nigeria. *Occasional paper on Nigerian affairs*, (1) Oct. 1954: 33–47.
A brief survey of existing medical service and recommendations in broad terms for radical improvements via a co-ordinated scheme.

1407 Pan-African psychiatric conference, 1st, Abeokuta. 1961.
Conference report, edited by T. Adeoyo Lambo. Ibadan, printed by

Govt. printer [1962] [ii] vii, 320p. illus., bibliog. (pp.303–320).

1408 Prince, Raymond H.
The 'brain fag' syndrome in Nigerian students. *J. mental sci.*, 106, April 1960: 559–570.

1409 —The use of rauwolfia for the treatment of psychoses by Nigerian native doctors. *Amer. j. psychiatry*, 117 (2) Aug. 1960: 147–149.

1410 Pullen, Grenville
Some problems of rapid urbanization in Lagos. *J. trop. geog.*, 23, Dec. 1966: 55–61, illus., map,

1411 Raybould, S. G.
Adult education in Nigeria. *Int. rev. educ.*, 2, Je. 1956: 250–253.

1412 Read, Margaret
Education and social control. *WAISER conf. proc., 1956:* 1–17.
Examination of the theoretical aspects of the topic, followed by a discussion of aspects and problems of education in Nigeria to which the anthropologist could profitably attend.

1413 Schram, R.
Development of rural health centres in Nigeria. 1960.
Ph.D. thesis, London.

1414 Sonubi, O.
A note on Nigeria's youth employment problems. *Nig. j. econ. & soc. stud.*, 4 (3) Nov. 1962: 228–232.
See also [1362] on which some comments are made here.

1415 A survey of mass education in British African colonies. *Mass educ. bull.*, 1 (1) Dec. 1949: 4–15.
Description of resettlement and mass education schemes in Nigeria and other territories.

1416 Takes, Charles Antoine Peter
Problems of rural development in Southern Nigeria. *Tijdschrift van het Koninklijk Nederlandsch aardrijkskundig genootschap,* 81 (4) 1964: 438–452, illus., map.
Also reprinted as no. 9 in NISER reprint series.

1417 Ude, A. O.
The social problems of Nigerian girls. Onitsha, Ude's publishing co., [n.d.] 58p.
Problems of education, employment, and marriage.

1418 Uka, Ngwobia
Growing up in Nigerian culture; a pioneer study of physical and behavioural growth and development of Nigerian children. Ibadan, Institute of education, University of Ibadan, 1966. xi, 111p. illus., bibliog.

1419 Wells, F. A. and Warmington, W. A.
Studies in industrialisation: Nigeria and the Cameroons. London, O.U.P., for NISER, 1962. vii 266p. maps.
Detailed study of three industrial enterprises—the Sapele timber industry, the Kano groundnut crushing industry, and the Cameroons plantations industry.

1420 Wraith, R. W.
Community development in Nigeria. *J. local admin. overseas.*, 3 (2) 1964: 92–102.

1421 Young African delinquents. The standard VI boy in Nigeria. *Colon, rev.,* 7 (7) Sept. 1952: 212:
On the social and economic problems posed by boys with Standard VI certificate who drift into towns for employment. Indicates possible steps for improving the situation.

SECTION FOUR
LINGUISTICS

1. BIBLIOGRAPHIES

1422 East, Rupert Moultrie
A vernacular bibliography for the languages of Nigeria. Zaria, Literature Bureau, 1941. [iv] 85p.
A bibliography of works published in Nigerian languages including bilingual dictionaries and vocabularies, and translations of Christian religious works and hymns. Arranged alphabetically by tribes.

1422a Hair, P. E. H.
The early study of Nigerian languages: essays and bibliographies. See [1462a]

1423 Hintze, Ursula
Bibliographie der Kwa-Sprachen und der Sprachen der Togo-Restvölker. Berlin, Akademie-Verlag, 1959. vi, 102p. 10 maps (fold. in end pocket) (Deutsche Akademie der Wissenschaften zu Berlin. Institut für Orientforschung. Veröffentlichung, no. 42)
A useful bibliography of ten West African languages regarded as belonging to the Kwa group. Includes Yoruba (pp. 66–76), Nupe (pp. 77–80), Edo (pp. 81–84) and Ibo (pp. 85–90).

1423a *Latham, R. G.
Upon the philological ethnography of the countries around the Bight of Biafra. *Edinburgh new phil. j.*, 40, 1845–6: 327–329; *J. Ethnol. soc.*, 1, 1848: 224–227.

1424 Struck, Bernhard
Linguistic bibliography of Northern Nigeria, including Hausa and Fula, with notes on the Yoruba dialects. *J. Afr. soc.*, 11 (41) Oct. 1911: 47–61; (42) Jan. 1912: 213–230, maps.
A useful list of some 345 references. The notes (pp. 47–58) discuss dialect and linguistic groups within the area.

2. PERIODICALS

1425 African language studies. London. no. 1 (1960)—
Annual.

1426 Journal of African languages. London. v. 1 (1962)—
Quarterly.

1427 The Journal of West African languages. London, v. 1 (Jan. 1964)—

3. LINGUISTIC STUDIES

1427a Ainslie, J. R.

Vocabulary of Nigerian names of trees, shrubs and herbs. See [1504]

1428 Allen, William and Thomson, T. R. H.
A narrative of the expedition sent by Her Majesty's Government to the River Niger, in 1841, under the command of Captain H. D. Trotter, R.N. London, Richard Bentley, 1848, repr. London, Frank Cass, 1968. 2v. front., illus. (incl. ports.) maps, tables.
Volume 2 contains vocabularies of a number of West African languages.

1429 Armstrong, Robert G.
Roy Clive Abraham, 1890–1963. *J. W. Afr. lang.*, 1 (1) Jan. 1964: 49–53.
A biographical sketch of the great linguist R. C. Abraham.

1430 —The study of West African languages: an expanded version of an inaugural lecture delivered at the University of Ibadan on 20 Feb., 1964 [Ibadan] University press, for Inst. of African Studies, 1964. [iv] 74p.
Bibliographical notes—pp. 24–31, 73.

1431 Barth, Heinrich
Collection of vocabularies of central African languages in English and German . . . London, K. Paul, Trench, Trubner, 1862–1866. cccxxxiv, 295p., repr. London, Frank Cass, 1971.
In three parts. The first part gives the vocabularies of Kanuri, Hausa, Fulani, Teda and other languages, as well as aspects of their grammar, especially pronouns, particles and numerals. The second and third parts continue with further treatment of the grammar.

1432 —Sammlung und Bearbeitung central-afrikanischer Vocabularien . . . Collection of vocabularies of Central Africa compiled and analysed by Heinrich Barth. Gotha, J. Perthes, 1862–1866. cccxxxiv, 295p.
German edition of [1431] q.v.

1433 ——Another ed. 1862–66. cccxxxiv, 206p.

1434 Baumann, H.
Les peuples et les civilisations de l'Afrique; suivi des langues et l'éducation. Paris, 1957.
See full entry at [126]

1435 Benton, P. Askell
Notes on some languages of the Western Sudan, including 24 unpublished vocabularies of Barth, extracts from correspondence regarding Richardson's and Barth's expeditions, and a few

Hausa riddles and proverbs. London, Henry Frowde, O.U.P., 1912. viii, 304p.

Reprinted as vol. I of *The languages and peoples of Bornu, being a collection of the writings of P. A. Benton*. With an introduction by A. H. M. Kirk-Greene. London, Frank Cass, 1968. 2v.

1436 Bertho, Jacques
Aperçu d'ensemble sur les dialectes de l'ouest de la Nigeria. *Bull. IFAN*, 14 (1) Jan. 1952: 259–271, illus.

A general survey of the Yoruba, Nupe, Gwari, Kamberi, Bini, Ijaw and other languages and language groups in Nigeria.

1437 Brosnahan, L. F. and Spencer, J. W.
Language and society: four talks given for the Nigerian broadcasting corporation. Ibadan, University press, 1962. 16p.

1438 Bryan, M. A.
The distribution of the Semitic and Cushitic languages of Africa; an outline of available information. London, O.U.P., for Int. Afr. inst., 1947. 36p. bibliog.

1439 Bryan, M. A. and Tucker, A. N.
Distribution of the Nilotic and Nilo-Hamitic languages of Africa, by M. A. Bryan. Linguistic analysis, by A. N. Tucker. London, O.U.P., for Int. Afr. inst., 1948. 60p. map (fold in end pocket)

1440 Büchner, H.
Vokabulare der Sprachen in und um Gava (Nordnigerien) *Afr. u. Übersee*, 48 (1) Dec. 1964: 36–45.

Comparative study of the vocabularies of the languages in and around Gava in Sardauna Province, Northern Nigeria.

1440a Burton, R. F.
Wit and wisdom from West Africa. See [1070]

1441 Christophersen, Paul
The problem of spoken English. *Oversea educ.*, 26 (1) Apr. 1954: 20–25.

On the problem involved in teaching English to young Nigerians.

1442 —Some special West African English words. *Eng. stud.*, 34, Dec. 1953: 1–9, bibliog.

1443 Clarke, John
Specimens of dialects; short vocabularies of languages, and notes of countries and customs in Africa. Berwick-upon-Tweed, Printed by D. Cameron, 1848. v, 104p.

1443a Crabb, David W.
Ekoid Bantu languages of Ogoja, Eastern Nigeria.
See [2123]

1444 Cust, R. N.
A sketch of the modern languages of Africa, accompanied by a language map, by E. E. Ravenstein. London, K. Paul, Trench, Trubner, 1883. 2v. 31 illus. (ports.) map (fold.) (Trubner's oriental series)

1445 Dakar. Université. West African language survey.

Actes du second colloque international de linguistique négro-Africaine. Dakar, 12–16 avril, 1962. Dakar, Université, 1963. xx, 302p. illus.

1446 Delafosse, Maurice
Haut-Sénégal-Niger (Soudan français) Paris, E. Larose, 1912. 3v. maps, bibliog.

v. 1 Le pays, les peuples, les langages. 428p.

See [649] for full entry.

1447 *Dennett, R. E.
The language map of Nigeria. *United empire*, n.s. 2, 1911: 618.

1448 Drexel, Albert
Gliederung der afrikanischen Sprachen ... *Anthropos*, 20, 1925: 210–231.
Die Fulah-Sprachen, 210–220.
Die Bornu-Sprachen, 220–228.
Das Hausa, 228–231.

1449 Greenberg, Joseph Harold
The Afro-Asiatic (Hamito-Semitic) present. *J. Amer. orient. soc.*, 72 (1) 1952: 1–8.

1450 —An application of new world evidence to an African linguistic problem (Hausa) In: *Les Afro-Américains* [Mémoires IFAN, no. 27] 1953: 129–131.

1450a —Historical inferences from linguistic research in sub-Saharan Africa. See [776]

1451 —The languages of Africa. Bloomington Indiana University, 1963. vi, 171p. maps. (Indiana university. Research center in anthropology, folklore and linguistics. Publication 25. International journal of American linguistics, suppl. v. 29 no. 1 pt. 2)

Extended and extensively revised version of author's "Studies in African linguistic classification." [1453]

1452 —The relation of a West African linguistic survey to the teaching of African languages. In *National conference on the teaching of African languages and area studies, 1960*: 20–23.

1453 —Studies in African linguistic classification. *S.–W. j. anthrop.*, 5, 1949: 79–100, 190–198, 309–317; 6, 1950: 47–63, 143–160, 223–237, 388–398; 10, 1954: 405–415. Subsequently off-printed, with minor corrections. New Haven, Conn., Compass Publishing Co., 1955. [v] 116p.

For individual instalments, see below.

1454 —Studies in African linguistic classification. I. The Niger-Congo family. *S.–W. j. anthrop.*, 5 (2) Summer 1949: 79–100.

1454a —Studies in African linguistic classification. II. The classification of Fulani.
See [2302]

1455 —Studies in African linguistic classification. III. The position of Bantu. *S.–W. j. anthrop.*, 5 (4) Winter, 1949: 309–317.

1456 —Studies in African linguistic classification. IV. Hamito-Semitic. *S.-W. j. anthrop.*, 6 (1) Spring, 1950: 47-63.

1457 —Studies in African linguistic classification. V. The eastern Sudanic family. *S.-W. j. anthrop.*, 6 (2) Summer, 1950: 143-160.

1458 —Studies in African linguistic classification. VI. The click languages. *S.-W. j. anthrop.*, 6 (3) Autumn, 1950: 223-237.

1459 —Studies in African linguistic classification. VII. Smaller families. Index of languages, *S.-W. j. anthrop.*, 6 (4) Winter' 1950: 388-398.

1460 —Studies in African linguistic classification. VIII. Further remarks on method: revisions and corrections. *S.-W. j. anthrop.*, 10 (4) Winter, 1954: 405-415.

1461 —The tonal system of Proto-Bantu. *Word*, 4 (3) 1948: 198-208.

1462 —Urbanism, migration and language. In *Urbanization and migration in West Africa, ed. Hilda Kuper, 1965:* 50-59.
On the effects of migration and urbanisation on the language realm in Africa. Several illustrations from Hausa, Yoruba, Kanuri and other Nigerian languages.

1462a Hair, P. E. H.
The early study of Nigerian languages: essays and bibliographies. Cambridge, C.U.P., in association with the West African languages survey and the Institute of African studies, Ibadan, 1967. xiv, 110p. fronts., map.
History of the study of Yoruba, Hausa, Kanuri, Nupe, Ijaw, Ibo, Idoma, Igala, Igbira, Tiv and Jukun, with an accompanying bibliography for each except Idoma, Jukun and Tiv.

1463 Hause, Helen E.
Terms for musical instruments in the Sudanic languages; a lexicographical inquiry. Supplement 7, *J. Amer. orient. soc.*, 68, Jan.-Mar. 1948. 70pp.

1464 Homburger, Lilias
Études de linguistique négro-Africaine. No. 1. Les formes verbales. Chartres, Durand, 1939. vi, 95p.

1465 —Les Langues négro-Africaines et les peuples qui les parlent. Nouvelle ed., revue et augmentée d'un chapitre sur le Sindo-Africain. Paris, Payot, 1957. 343p. bibliog.
First ed. publ. 1941.

1466 —The negro-African languages, London Routledge and K. Paul, 1949. vii, 275p. bibliog.
English trans. of [1465]

1467 —Les préfixes nominaux dans les parlers peul, haoussa et bantous. Paris, Institut d'Ethnologie, 1929. xi, 167p. map. (Trav. et mém. Inst. d'ethnol., 6)

1468 Houis, M.
Schèmes et functions tonologiques. *Bull. IFAN*, 18 (3/4) Jl.-Dec. 1956: 335-368.

1469 International African institute
Practical orthography of African languages [London] O.U.P., for Int. Afr. inst., 1930. 24p. bibliog. (pp. 7-8) (Int. Afr. inst. Memorandum, no. 1)

1470 International institute of African languages and cultures. See International African institute.

1471 Jeffreys, M. D. W.
Some historical notes on African tone languages. *Afr. studies*, 4 (3) Sept. 1945: 135-145, bibliog.
Historical discussion of the gradual appreciation by European scholars of the tonal basis of West African languages. Frequent references to Yoruba, Hausa, Ibibio and other Nigerian languages.

1472 Johnson, Henry and Christaller, Johann G.
Vocabularies of the Niger and Gold Coast, West Africa. London, S.P.C.K., 1886. iv, 34p.
Six short vocabularies—English-Yoruba, English-Nupe, English-Kankanda, English-Ibira, English-Igara, English-Ibo,—by Archdeacon Henry Johnson; and two equally short ones—English-Ga (Akrä) and English-Obutu—by Rev. J. Christaller.

1473 Johnston, Harry Hamilton
A comparative study of the Bantu and semi-Bantu languages. Oxford, Clarendon Press, 1919-1922. 2v. maps, bibliog.

1474 —The Semi-Bantu languages of Eastern Nigeria [sic] *J. Afr. soc.*, 20 (79) Apr. 1921: 186-194.
Linguistic notes on Jarawa, Birom, Tiv and 6 other languages in Northern Nigeria, east of the Niger. Birom and Jarawa vocabularies, pp. 189-194.

1475 Kirk-Greene, Anthony Hamilton Millard
The vocabulary and determinants of schoolboy slang in Northern Nigeria. *J. Afr. lang.*, 5 (1) 1966: 7-33.

1476 Koelle, Sigismund Wilhelm
Polyglotta Africana; or Comparative vocabulary of nearly three hundred words and phrases in more than one hundred distinct African languages. London, K. Paul, Trench, Trubner, 1854. 24, 188p.

1477 Ladefoged, Peter
A phonetic study of West African languages; an auditory instrumental survey. Cambridge, C.U.P., in association with West African languages survey, 1964. xviii, 74p. illus., map. bibliog. (West African language monographs, 1)
An analysis of the phonetic structure and elements of West African languages, based on data from sixty-one of those languages, including many Nigerian languages.

1478 Larochette, J.
La racine du type consonne-voyelle dans les langues soudanaises. *Zaïre*, 4 (6) Je. 1950: 583-612.

1479 Leonard, Arthur Glyn
A glimpse into the grammatical con-

struction of the various tongues. In his *The Lower Niger and its tribes*, 1906, repr. 1968: 505–519.

Brief comparative view of some grammatical elements of Efik, Ibo, Ijaw and other languages and dialects of South-eastern Nigeria.

1480 Lukas, Johannes
Are there class languages in the Central Sudan? *Res. and progress*, 4 (4) 1938: 175–178.

1481 —Der gegenwärtige Stand der Gliederung der westsudanischen Sprachen. *Tribus*, Neue Folge, 4/5, 1954–1955: 87–93.

Present state of the West Sudan languages classification.

1482 —Der Hamitische Gehalt der Tschado-hamitischen Sprachen. *Z.f.E.S.*, 28, 1937/1938: 286–299.

1483 —Linguistic research between the Nile and Lake Chad. *Africa*, 12 (3) Jl. 1939: 335–349.

French summary, p. 349.

1484 —Linguistic situation in the Lake Chad area in central Africa. *Africa*, 9 (3) Jl. 1936: 332–349.

A general linguistic survey of the main language groups of this area, namely, Kanuri, Maba, Chado-Hamitic, Bagirmi, and Mandara groups. French summary, pp. 348–349.

1485 Meek, Charles Kingsley
The semi-Bantu languages of the Benue valley. *J. Afr. soc.*, 21 (83) Apr. 1922: 222–223.

A letter written to H. H. Johnston to report the location of the Afudu, Boritsu, and Mbarike languages, first mentioned in Koelle's *Polyglotta Africana*.

1486 —Tribal studies in Northern Nigeria. London, K. Paul, Trench, Trubner, 1931. 2v.

Contains short vocabularies of the languages and dialects of most of the tribes studied.

1487 Meinhof, Carl
An introduction to the study of African languages. Translated by A. Warner. London, J. M. Dent, N.Y., Dutton, 1915. vii, 169p. map.

"Note to the 'Sketch map of African language-families' by Bernhard Struck", pp. 159–169.

1488 —Die Sprachen der Hamiten; nebst einer Beigabe: Hamitische Typen, von T. V. Luschan. Hamburg, 1912. 256p. illus., map, bibliog. (Hamb. Kol. Inst., vol. 9)

Hausa—pp. 58–86.
Fulani—Chap. 2.

1489 Merrick, G.
Languages in Northern Nigeria. *J. Afr. soc.*, 5 (17) Oct. 1905: 43–47.

A listing of some of the tribes of Northern Nigeria with brief notes fixing their geographical location and mentioning their language.

1490 *Merrick, Joseph
Kurzgefasste Neger-Englische Grammatik. Bautzen, 1854. 67p.

1491 Migeod, Frederick William Hugh
The languages of West Africa. London, K. Paul, Trench, Trubner, 1911–1913. 2v.

v. 1. 1911. viii, 373p. 1 map (fold.)
v. 2. 1913. ix, 436p. bibliog.

1492 Nigeria. Education board
Alphabets for the Efik, Ibo and Yoruba languages. London, International institute of African languages and culture, 1949.

1493 Norris, Edwin
Outline of a vocabulary of a few of the principal languages of West and Central Africa. London, 1940. vii, 213p.

1493a Olderogge, D. A.
Proiskhozhdeniye narodov Tzentral nago Sudana. See [789]

1494 —Sledy sushchestvovaniya pis'mennosti u narodov Verkhnei Gvinei do Yevropeyskoy kolonizatsii. In: *Kr. Soob. I. E.*, (28) 1957: 68–73.

An investigation into the languages of the west coast of Africa to determine if there were any written script before the arrival of the Europeans. Hieroglyphs, numerical notations, notched symbols on carved ivory tusks, etc., are taken as traces of existence of written script.

1494a Pil'shchikova, N, See Pilszczikowa, Nina

1495 *Pilszczikowa, Nina
Mestoimeniya yazykov Nigero-Chadsky gruppy. In *Afrikanskiy etnograficheskiy Sbornik, 3. ed. D. A. Olderogge. Moskva, 1959*.

1496 Rowlands, E. C.
Notes on some class languages of Northern Nigeria. *Afr. lang. stud.*, 3, 1962: 71–83.

Comparative vocabularies of Dakarkari, Duka, Kambari, Kamuku (Ngwoi) and other languages and dialects in the area.

1497 Strevens, Peter
Pronunciation of English in West Africa. *WAISER confr. proc. 4th, Accra, 1955*: 12–20.

1497a Struck, Bernhard
Linguistic bibliography of Northern Nigeria . . . with notes on the Yoruba dialects. See [1424]

1498 Strümpell-Garua, Hauptmann
Vergleichendes Wörterverzeichnis der Heidensprachen Adamauas. *Z. f. Ethnol.*, (3–4) 1910: 444–488.

Comparative vocabularies of Adamawa pagan languages.

1499 Talbot, Percy Amaury
The peoples of Southern Nigeria: a sketch of their history, ethnology and languages . . . London, 1926, repr. 1969. 4v.

Vol. 4, linguistics and statistics.
See main entry at [742]

1500 Thomas, Northcote Whitridge

The Bantu languages of Nigeria. In *Festchrift. Karl Meinhof. Sprachwissenchaftliche und andere Studien, 1927:* 65–72. map.

Discusses the enclave of Bantu-speaking peoples N.E. of Calabar, and the Jarawa group in Adamawa.

1501 —Specimens of languages from Southern Nigeria. London, Harrison, 1914. 143p. 2 maps (fold.)

1502 Tressan, de Lavergne de
Inventaire linguistique de l'Afrique occidentale française et du Togo. Dakar, IFAN, 1953. 241p. maps (in end pockets) (Mémoire IFAN. no. 30)

1503 Tucker, A. N.
Systems of tone-marking in African languages. *B.S.O.A.S.,* 27 (3) 1964: 594–611, illus.

1504 Vocabulary of Nigerian names of trees, shrubs and herbs. Lagos, Govt. printer, 1936. 64p.
In three parts:
pt. 1. Vernacular-Scientific
pt. 2. Scientific-Vernacular
pt. 3. Certain English and trade names in common use.

1504a Ward, Ida Caroline
Practical phonetics for students of African languages.
See [1517]

1505 —Practical suggestion for the learning of African languages in the field. [London] O.U.P., for International African institute, 1937. 39p. bibliog. (Int. Afr. inst. Memorandum, no. 14)

1506 —Tonal analysis of West African languages. *Z. Phonetik u. Sprachwiss.,* 3 (1–2) Jan.–Apr. 1949: 54–67.

1507 —Verbal tone patterns in West African languages. *B.S.O.A.S.,* 12 (3–4) 1948: 831–837.

1508 Welch, James W.
The linguistic situation in the western parts of the Niger delta. *Africa,* 6, 1933: 220–222.
Summary of the linguistic situation with regard to the Ijaw, Itsekiri, Urhobo and Isoko languages and dialects.

1509 Welmers, William E.
Associative *a* and *ka* in Niger-Congo. *Language,* 39 (3) 1963: 432–447.

1510 Westermann, Diedrich
Charakter und Einteilung der Sudan-sprachen. *Africa,* 8 (2) Apr. 1935: 129–148.

1511 —Form und Funktion der Reduplika-

tion in einigen westafrikanischen Sprachen. *Afrika* [Berlin] 3 (2) 1944: 83–104.
Illustrated with examples from Fulani, Yoruba, and other West African languages.

1512 —The linguistic situation and vernacular literature in British West Africa: a report. *Africa,* 2 (4) Oct. 1929: 337–351.
A report on the use of the vernacular as literary languages in West Africa and the production of vernacular literature. Considerable attention given to Nigerian languages—Efik, Ibo, Yoruba, Edo, etc.,—especially on pp. 338–344.

1513 —Nominalklassen in westafrikanischen Klassensprachen und in Bantusprachen. *M.S.O.S.,* 38, 1935: 1–53.

1514 —Die Sudansprachen: eine sprachvergleichende Studie. Hamburg, L. Friederichsen, 1911. viii, 222p. map. (Abhandlungen des Hamburgischen Kolonialinstituts, Band 3. Reihe B. Völkerkunde, Kulturgeschichte und Sprachen. Band 3)

1515 —Die Westlichen Sudansprachen und ihre Beziehungen zum Bantu. Berlin, Walter de Gruyter, 1927. 313p. map (col.) (*M.S.O.S.* Beiheft. Jahrg. 30)

1516 Westermann, Diedrich and Bryan, M. A.
The languages of West Africa. London, O.U.P., for Int. Afr. inst., 1952. 215p. col. map. (in end-pocket) bibliog. (Handbook of African languages, pt. 2)
A classification of West African languages, delineating for each the area spoken and differentiating its various dialects. Based substantially on the first author's *Westlichen Sudansprachen.* See [1515]

1517 Westermann, Diedrich and Ward, Ida Caroline
Practical phonetics for students of African languages. London, O.U.P., for Int. Afr. Inst., 1933. xvi, 169p. illus., bibliog.

1518 Wolff, Hans
Nigerian orthography. Zaria, North Region Adult Education Office, 1954. 6lp.
Brief suggestions for establishing orthographies of Nigerian languages are followed by a list of recommended orthographies for twenty-two languages in Northern Nigeria.

1519 —Subsystem typologies and area linguistics. *Anthrop. linguistics,* 1 (7) Oct. 1959: 1–88.

PART TWO

NIGERIA—ETHNIC DIVISIONS

PART TWO
NIGERIA—ETHNIC DIVISIONS

In part two, to effect economy in space, it has been found necessary not to take every ethnic division separately. Only those ethnic divisions with a good range of literature and those which for some other reasons have not been grouped with others, are taken separately. All others are treated in groups or clusters, each cluster containing two or more related ethnic divisions. This grouping is all the more necessary because many of the works listed often deal not with one but with several of the ethnic divisions within a cluster. The choice of one ethnic group for the heading of a cluster is often arbitrary and does not suggest any greater importance or pre-eminence of the one over the others.

The extent and range of literature on each ethnic division or cluster determine its number of sub-divisions.

In view of the system of grouping adopted and the difficulties posed by the multiplicity of ethnic names, the use of the comprehensive ethnic index in locating the more obscure ethnic divisions is strongly recommended.

AFU
(Afao, Afo, Eloi, Eloyi)

1. GENERAL AND ETHNOGRAPHIC STUDIES

1520 Afao or Afu. In *Notes on the tribes ... by O. Temple, 2nd ed., 1922, repr. 1965:* 1–2.

1521 Armstrong, Robert G.
The Afu. In *Peoples of the Niger-Benue confluence, by Daryll Ford [and others] 1955:* 136–139.
Brief notes on the Afo or Afu, or Eloi in Nasarawa and Loko Districts of Northern Nigeria.

1522 Fagg, Bernard E. B.
A fertility figure of unrecorded style from Northern Nigeria. *Man,* 48 (140) Nov. 1948: 125, illus.
Describes the figure said to be a fertility idol from Onda in Benue Province, but which has some characteristics of the images representing the Yoruba Earth Mother.

1522a Meek, Charles Kingsley
Marriage by exchange in Nigeria: a disappearing institution. See [815]

1523 Rohlfs, Gerhard
Die Art der Begrüssung bei verschiedenen

Negerstämmen. *Petermanns Geographische Mitteilungen* [Gotha] 1867: 333–336.

1524 Tschudi, Jolantha
Aus dem sozialen Leben Afos, Hügelland von Nasarawa, Nigeria. *Baessler-Archiv,* N.F. 4 (2) 1956: 147–172, illus,.
On marriage system, pregnancy, birth rites and other social customs of the Afo in the hill district of Nasarawa.

2. LINGUISTIC STUDIES

1525 Armstrong, Robert G.
A few more words of Eloyi. *J. W. Afr. lang.,* 1 (2) 1964: 60.

1526 Mackay, Hugh D.
A word list of Eloyi. *J. W. Afr. lang.,* 1 (1) Jan. 1964: 5–12; (2) 1964: 60.
A tentative word-list of Eloyi.

1527 The Songs of God
Amu iyukpo ikenzu ngeloyi. Ika, Stewards company press, 1962 [18]p.
"The Songs of God" translated into the Eloyi language by Hugh D. Mackay. Mimeographed.

ANGAS

(Angassawa)

Including:

Ankwe	Lardang
Burrum *(Boghorom, Borrom, Burmawa)*	Larr
	Mikiet
Bwol	Miriam *(Merniang, Mirriam)*
Chip	Montol *(Montoil)*
Dimuk	Ron *(Baram, Baron, Boram)*
Goram *(Gworam)*	Schalla *(Scha)*
Gurka *(Gerkawa, Gurkawa)*	Sura
Kunnum	Yergum *(Yergam)*
Kwolla	

1. GENERAL AND ETHNOGRAPHIC STUDIES

1528 Angas. In *Notes on the tribes . . . by O. Temple, 2nd ed., 1922, repr. 1965:* 8–17.

1529 Ankwe. In *Notes on the tribes . . . by O. Temple, 2nd ed., 1922, repr. 1965:* 17–22.

1530 Dimuk. In *Notes on the tribes . . . by O. Temple, 2nd ed., 1922, repr. 1965:* 95–96.

1531 Fitzpatrick, Joseph F. J.
Some notes on the Kwolla district and its tribes. *J. Afr. soc.,* 10 (37) Oct. 1910: 16–52; (38) Jan. 1911: 213–221; 490.
Ethnographic and linguistic notes. The latter takes up the whole of the second instalment and is a comparative vocabulary of Yergum, Montol, Gurkawa and Ankwe languages.

1532 Findlay, R. L.
The Dimmuk and their neighbours. *Farm and Forest,* 6 (3) Jl.–Dec. 1945: 137–145.
The Dimmuk in Shendam Division, Plateau Province, Northern Nigeria.

1533 Gurkawa. In *Notes on the tribes . . . by O. Temple, 2nd ed., 1922, repr. 1965:* 118.

1533a Meek, Charles Kingsley
Marriage by exchange in Nigeria. See [815]

1534 Mirriam, Mikiet, Lardang, Larr. In *Notes on the tribes . . . by O. Temple, 2nd ed., 1922, repr. 1965:* 276–278.

1535 Mohr, Richard
Ein Besuch bei den Schalla des Plateau von Nordnigerien. *Tribus,* (9) Sept. 1960: 107–120, illus.
Account of a visit to the Schalla, in the Pankshin district. Describes the people and some of their customs.

1536 —Religiöse Grundvorstellungen und Kulte der Angas von Nord-Nigeria. *Int. arch. ethnog.,* 48 (2) 1958: 199–226.
On the religious concepts and cults of the Angas.

1537 —Zur sozialen Organisation der Angas

in Nord-Nigeria. *Anthropos,* 53 (3–4) 1958: 457–472, illus.

1538 Montol. In *Notes on the tribes . . . by O. Temple, 2nd ed., 1922, repr. 1965:* 278–279.

1539 Pfeffer, Gulla
Die Stämme des Shendam-Distriktes (Nigeria). *Erdball,* 3 (5) 1929: 161–164, illus.

1540 Ron or Boram. In *Notes on the tribes . . . by O. Temple, 2nd ed., 1922, repr. 1965:* 339–341.

1540a Ruxton, U. F. H.
Notes on the tribes of the Muri Province. See [2183]

1541 Salacuse, Jeswald
Angas family law. In his *A selective survey of Nigerian family law, 1965:* 9–28.

1542 Sura. In *Notes on the tribes . . . by O. Temple, 2nd ed., 1922, repr. 1965:* 343–346.

1543 Vernon-Jackson, H. O. H.
A leprosy transmission belief amongst the Angas in Northern Nigeria. *Man,* 61 Mar. 1961 (art. 52): 55–56.
On Angas belief in the power of magically afflicting another with leprosy.

1544 Yergum. In *Notes on the tribes . . . by O. Temple, 2nd ed., 1922, repr. 1965:* 369–374.

1544a Dangel, R.
Grammatische Skizze der Yergum-Sprache. *Bibliotheca afr.,* 3 (2/3) 1929: 135–136.
See note under (4331)

2. LINGUISTIC STUDIES

1545 Fitzpatrick, Joseph F. J.
Notes on the Yergum, Montol, Gurkawa and Ankwe languages. *J. Afr. soc.,* 10, 1910–1911: 213–221; 490.
Brief general notes, followed by comparative vocabularies of the four languages.

1546 Foulkes, H. D.
Angas manual; grammar and vocabulary. London, K. Paul, Trench, Trubner, 1915. xviii, 313p.

1547 Jungraithmayr, Hermann
Internal a in Ron plurals. *J. Afr. lang.*, 4 (2) 1965: 102–107.

1548 —Die Laryngale ḫ und 'im Scha (Süd-Plateau, Nordnigerien) *Afr. u. Übersee*, 49 (3) 1966: 169–173.

1549 —Materialien zur Kenntnis des Chip, Montol, Gerka und Burrum (Südplateau Nordnigerien) *Afrika u. Übersee*, 48 (3) Oct. 1965: 161–182.

1550 —On the ambiguous position of the Angas. *J. Afr. lang.*, 2 (3) 1963: 272–278.

1551 —Die Sprache der Sura (Maghavul) in Nordnigerien. *Afr. u. Übersee*, 47 (1–2) Jan. 1964: 8–89; 47 (3–4) Je. 1964: 204–220.

On the structure of the language, with Sura-German and German-Sura vocabularies. The Sura live in Plateau Province about 55 miles south of Jos, with Panyam as their centre.

1552 —Texte und Sprichwörter im Angas von Kabwir (Nordnigerien) mit einer grammatischen Skizze. *Afrika u. Übersee*, 48 (1) Dec. 1964: 17–35; 48 (2) Mar. 1965: 114–127.
A collection of Angas texts and phrases from the Kabwir area, with German translation. Prefaced with brief grammatical note on the language.

1553 Ormsby, George
Some notes on the Angas language. *J. Afr. soc.*, 12 (48) Jl. 1913: 421–424; 13 (49) Oct. 1913: 54–61; (50) Jan. 1914: 204–210; (51) Apr. 1914: 313–315.
Grammatical notes, followed by sample sentences with English translation, and an English-Angas vocabulary.

ARAGO
(Alago)

1. GENERAL AND ETHNOGRAPHIC STUDIES

1554 Armstrong, Robert G.
The Arago (Alago). In *Peoples of the Niger-Benue confluence*, by Daryll Forde [and others] 1955: 125–127.

1555 Arago. In *Notes on the tribes . . . by O. Temple*, 2nd ed., 1922, repr. 1965: 26–28.

1556 Nzekwu, Onuora
Keana salt camp. *Nig. mag.*, (83) Dec. 1964: 262–278, illus.

Brief historical note on Keana town, with illustrated account of salt production by the townswomen.

2. LINGUISTIC STUDIES

1557 Judd, A. S.
Notes on the language of the Arago or Alago tribe of Nigeria. *J. Afr. soc.*, 23 (89) Oct. 1923: 30–38.
Grammatical notes.

BACHAMA
(Bashama, Bashamma)
Including:
Mbula (Bula, Bulla)

1. GENERAL AND ETHNOGRAPHIC STUDIES

Batta and kindred tribes of Bashamma. See [1578]

1558 *Bronnum, Niels H.
Folkeliv i Sudan. Copenhagen, Loshe, 1923.

1559 *—Under daemoners aag. Copenhagen, Loshe, 1926.
This and the above book are said to give detailed aspects of Bachama life and customs. Author was a member of the branch of the S.U.M. established in Numan, Bachama chief town, and spoke the language fluently. See *J. Afr. soc.*, 29 (115) Apr. 1930: 269.

1560 Fegan, Ethel S.
Some notes on the Bachama tribe, Adamawa Province, Northern Provinces, Nigeria. *J. Afr. soc.*, 29 (115) Apr. 1930: 269–279; (116) Jl. 1930: 376–400.
General ethnographic notes on Bachama women. Include marriage, childbirth, infantile mortality, religion, death, and inheritance.

1561 Kirk-Greene, Anthony Hamilton Millard
Festival at Farei. *Nigeria mag.*, (45) 1954: 60–74, illus.
Relates the mythology of Nzeanzo, a cult shared by the Bachama, Bata and Mbula tribes of Adamawa Province, and describes the festival held annually at Farei. Also reprinted in his *Adamawa past and present, 1958*: 208–213.

1562 M'bula. In *Notes on the tribes . . . by O. Temple*, 2nd ed., 1922, repr. 1965: 274–276.

1563 Meek, Charles Kingsley

The Bachama and Mbula. In his *Tribal studies in Northern Nigeria, v.1, 1931:* 1–68, illus.
Ethnographic reports. The Bachama specifically, pp. 1–57; Mbula, pp. 57–68.

1564 —A religious festival in Northern Nigeria. *Africa,* 3 (3) Jl. 1930: 323–345.
Account of the magico-religious beliefs of the Bachama with a description of their annual religious festival at Farei some seven miles East of Numan, their chief centre. French summary, pp. 345–346.

2. LINGUISTIC STUDIES

1565 Meek, Charles Kingsley
Mbula vocabulary. In his *Tribal studies in Northern Nigeria, 1931.* v. 1, pp. 62–68.

1566 —Schedule of [Bachama] words and phrases. In his *Tribal studies in Northern Nigeria, v. 1. 1931:* 49–57.
Bachama, vocabulary, with a short grammatical note by Dr. Bronnum, pp. 55–57.

BASSA
(Basa)
Including:

Bassa Kaduna *(Basa Kaduna)*

1. GENERAL AND ETHNOGRAPHIC STUDIES

1567 Bassa. In *Notes on the tribes . . . by O. Temple, 2nd ed., 1922, repr. 1965:* 40–48.

1568 Byng-Hall, F. F. W.
Notes on the Bassa Komo tribe. *J. Afr. soc.,* 8 (29) Oct. 1908: 13–20.
History and customs of a small tribe on the Benue.

1569 Clifford, Miles
Notes on the Bassa Komo tribe in the Igala Division. *Man,* 44, Sept.–Oct. 1944: 107–116 (art. 95).

1570 Gunn, Harold D.
Basa (Bassa) including Basa Komo and Basa Kaduna. In his *Peoples of the middle Niger region, Northern Nigeria, 1960:* 71–85.
Ethnographic notes.

1571 Kennett, Daphne K.
Dance of the Bassas at Abaji. *Geog. j.,* 88, 1936: 457–458.

1572 Macfie, John W. Scott
A Bassa-Komo burial. *Man,* 11, 1911: 185–186 (art. 103).

Bassa Komo *(Basa Komo)*

1572a Meek, Charles Kingsley
Marriage by exchange in Nigeria. See [815]

1573 Wilson, E. F.
An itineration in the Basa country. *Niger and Yoruba notes,* 3 (35) May 1897: 86–87.

2. LINGUISTIC STUDIES

1574 Azunga atua uw'agwatana. Ika, Stewards company press, 1963. 55 1.

1575 Bible. N. T. Bassa Komo. James Itekride Jemes. Ayangba, Benue Gospel mission, 1962. 1p. 1., 15p.
Printed by Stewards company press, Ika.

1576 Dibble, S. J.
Beyebiyizo keni ibiri. [Ika, Stewards co. press, 1961] 7 p.
Mimeographed.

1577 Schürle, Georg
Die Sprache der Basa in Kamerun: Grammatik und Wörterbuch. Hamburg, L. Friederichsen, 1912. 292p.

BATA
(Batta)
Including:

Bolki
Bulai
Gudu *(Gudo)*
Holma
Kofa *(Kofo)*

Malabu
Njei *(Jenge, Kobochi, Njai, Nzangi, Zani)*
Zumu *(Jimo)*

1. GENERAL AND ETHNOGRAPHIC STUDIES

1578 Batta and kindred tribes of Bashamma. In *Notes on the tribes . . . by O. Temple, 2nd ed., 1922, repr. 1965:* 48–55.
Ethnographic notes on Bata and Bachama tribes.

1579 Kirk-Greene, Anthony Hamilton Millard, Bata. In his *Adamawa past and present, 1958:* 17–18.
Short historical note.

1579a —Festival at Farei. See [1561]

1580 Malabu. In *Notes on the tribes . . . by*

O. Temple, 2nd ed., 1922, repr. 1965: 264–267.

1581   Meek, Charles Kingsley
The Bata-speaking peoples of the Adamawa Emirate. In his *Tribal studies in Northern Nigeria, vol. 1, 1931:* 69–136, illus.
   Ethnographic notes on the Zumu or Jimo, Bulai, Malabu, Kofa, Muleng, Bolki, Holma, Gudu, and Njai or Nzangi.

1582   —The Njai or Nzangi. In his *Tribal studies in Northern Nigeria, 1931.* V. 1, pp. 282–293.

1583   Schaeffner, André
Sur deux instruments de musique des Bata (Nord-Cameroun) *J. Soc. afr.,* (13) 1943: 123–151.

2. LINGUISTIC STUDIES

1584   Meek, Charles Kingsley

The Gudu vocabulary. In his *Tribal studies in Northern Nigeria, v. 1, 1931:* 126–136.
   Includes vocabulary of the Kumbi dialect.

1585   —Holma vocabulary. In his *Tribal studies in Northern Nigeria, v. 1, 1931:* 121–123.

1586   —Malabu vocabulary. In his *Tribal studies in Northern Nigeria, v. 1, 1931:* 110–113.

1587   —Nzangi vocabulary. In his *Tribal studies in Northern Nigeria, v. 1, 1931:* pp. 290–293.

1588   —Zumu (Jimo) [vocabulary] In his *Tribal studies in Northern Nigeria, v. 1, 1931:* 80–86.
   Zumu (Jimo or Zomo) are a section of the Bata group.

BIROM

(Berom, Burum, Burumawa, Kibbo, Kibyen)

Including:

Aike

Aten *(Ganawuri, Ganawarri,*
   Jal, Ngell, Njell)

Ayu *(Ayob, Ayub)*

Pyem *(Fem, Fyem, Paiema,*
   Pem, Pyemawa)

Ninzam *(Sanga, Sangawa)*

Numana

Nungu *(Lungu)*

Sigidawa *(Segiddawa)*

1. GENERAL AND ETHNOGRAPHIC STUDIES

1589   Aike. In *Notes on the tribes . . . by O. Temple, 2nd ed., 1922, repr. 1965:* 6.

1590   Ayu or Ayub. In *Notes on the tribes . . . by O. Temple, 2nd ed., 1922, repr. 1965:* 36–37.

1591   Ames, C. G.
The Birom tribe. In his *Gazetteer of Bauchi Province. Recently abridged and revised, 1934:* 61–76.
   Historical and ethnographic sketch.

1592   —The Ganawuri tribe. In his *Gazetteer of Bauchi Province, Recently abridged and revised, 1934:* 76–80.
   Brief historical and descriptive notes.

1593   Baker, T. M.
Political control among the Birom. *WAISER conf. proc., 1956:* 111–119.
   Ethnographic sketch of the Birom and the patterns of modern local government administration among them.

1594   —Social organisation of the Birom tribe. 1963.
   Ph.D. thesis, London university.

1595   Baker, Tanya
[Women's role in] Nigeria. *INCIDI,* 31, 1959: 73–83.
   Brief view of the legal status and the political, economic and social roles and responsibilities of Yoruba and Birom women in Nigeria.

1596   Bouquiaux, Luc
Les instruments de musique Birom (Nigeria septentrional) *Africa-Tervuren,* 8 (4) 1962: 105–111, illus.

1597   Clarke, A. Fielding
An experimental school in Nigeria. *JRAS,* 39 (154) Jan. 1940: 36–53.
   Reviews the aims and progress of a "post elementary" school at Riyom, a Birom town. Useful information on the Birom people.

1598   Gannawarri. In *Notes on the tribes . . . by O. Temple, 2nd ed., 1922, repr. 1965:* 115.

1599   Gardiner, R. F. R. and Gardiner, E. S.
Infant mortality in Northern Nigeria, with special reference to Birom tribe. *J. obst. & gynaec. Brit. emp.,* 65, 1958: 749–758.

1600   Gunn, Harold D.
The Birom, Aten and Irigwe. In his *Peoples of the Plateau area of Northern Nigeria, 1953:* 75–100, bibliog.

1601   —The Pyem. In his *Peoples of the Plateau area of Northern Nigeria, 1953:* 101–106.
   Brief notes on the Pyem: a community in Gindiri District, Plateau Province,

variously referred to as Paiem, Pem, Fem, Fyem or Pyemawa, etc.

1602 —Sigidi village: The Sigidawa. In his *Peoples of the Plateau area of Northern Nigeria, 1958*: 106–107.
Short note on the people inhabiting the single village of Sigidi in the Lere Village-Area, Lere District, Bauchi emirate.

1603 Kibyen or Burumawa. In *Notes on the tribes . . . by O. Temple, 2nd ed., 1922, repr. 1965*: 228–230.

1604 Matthews, H. F.
Notes on the Nungu tribe, Nassarawa Province, Northern Nigeria, and the neighbouring tribes which use the duo-decimal system of numeration. In *Harvard Afr. studies, 1, Varia Africana* (1) 1957: 83–94, illus.

1604a Meek, Charles Kingsley
Marriage by exchange in Nigeria. See [815]

1605 Miles, David
Plight of the Biroms. *W. Afr. rev.*, 29 (37) Aug. 1958: 653–655, 671.
A discussion of the economic problems of the Birom arising from lack of employment and the poor condition of agricultural land, a condition worsened by the mining activity going on in the area.

1606 Ngell or Njell. In *Notes on the tribes . . . by O. Temple, 2nd ed., 1922, repr. 1965*: 309–310.

1607 Ninzam. In *Notes on the tribes . . . by O. Temple, 2nd ed., 1922, repr. 1965*: 314–315.

1608 Numana. In *Notes on the tribes . . . by O. Temple, 2nd ed., 1922, repr. 1965*: 316.

1609 Nungu. In *Notes on the tribes . . . by O. Temple, 2nd ed., 1922, repr. 1965*: 316–319.

1610 Pitcairn, G. D.
First attempts at rural development in the Plateau. *Farm and forest*, 7, Oct. 1941: 55–61.

1611 Pyemawa. In *Notes on the tribes . . . by O. Temple, 2nd ed., 1922, repr. 1965*: 338.

1612 Salacuse, Jeswald
Birom family law. In his *A selective survey of Nigerian family law, 1965*: 29–46.

1613 Sangawa. In *Notes on the tribes . . . by O. Temple, 2nd ed., 1922, repr. 1965*: 342.

1614 Sasson, Hamo
Birom blacksmithing. *Nig. mag.*, (74) Sept. 1962: 25–31, illus.

1615 —A burial among the Birom. *Man*, 64, Jan.–Feb. 1964: 8–11.

1616 Segiddawa. In *Notes on the tribes . . . by O. Temple, 2nd ed., 1922, repr. 1965*: 342.

1617 Suffill, T. I.
The Birom—a pagan tribe on the Plateau, Nigeria. *Farm and forest*, 4 (4) Dec. 1943: 179–182.
Notes on the history, political organisation and economy of the Biroms.

2. LINGUISTIC STUDIES

1618 Bouquiaux, Luc
A word list of Aten (Ganawuri). *J. W. Afr. lang.*, 1 (2) 1964: 5–25.
Aten spoken near Jos in Northern Nigeria.

1619 Bristow, W. M.
Birom texts. *Afr. u. Übersee*, 31 (4) Nov. 1953: 145–150.
A collection of five Birom folk stories in Burum (Birom language) with literal translations.

1620 Susu Karatu. [Zaria, NORLA, 1955] 22p. illus.
Adult education pamphlet in Birom.

1621 Wolff, Hans
Noun classes and concord in Birom. In *Actes 2e colloque int. ling. négro—afr., Dakar, 1962. 1963*: 86–95.

BOLEWA

(Bole, Borlawa, Fika)

Including:

Auyukawa *(Ayokawa)*
Bede *(Bedde)*
Beri-Beri *(Beriberi)*
Keri-Keri *(Karekare, Kerekere)*

Ngamo *(Gamawa)*
Shirawa
Teshenewa

1. GENERAL AND ETHNOGRAPHIC STUDIES

1622 Auyokawa, Shirawa and Teshenewa, In *Notes on the tribes . . . by O. Temple, 2nd ed., 1922, repr. 1965*: 32–33.

1623 Bolewa. In *Notes on the tribes . . . by O. Temple, 2nd ed., 1922, repr. 1965*: 62–68.

1624 The Bolewa of Fika. *Nigeria mag.*, (51) 1956: 337–365, illus.
Historical and descriptive notes on the Bolewa.

1625 Fremantle, John Morton
A history of the region comprising the Katagum Division of Kano Province.

J. Afr. soc., 10 (39) Apr. 1911: 298–319; (40) Jl. 1911: 398–421; 11 (41) Oct. 1911: 62–74; (42) Jan. 1912: 187–200, map.

The inhabitants mentioned include the Shirawa, Teshenawa, Auyukawa, Lerewa, Nguzumawa, Keri-Keri, Mangawa, Gumelewa, Bedde, Beri-Beri, etc.

1626 Gamawa. In *Notes on the tribes . . . by O. Temple, 2nd ed., 1922, repr. 1965:* 110–112.

1627 Gau, Maina
Bolewa history. Tasihin Bolewa. Edited and translated into English by J. G. Davis. Potiskum, 1956, 15p.
Mimeographed.

1628 Keri-Keri. In *Notes on the tribes . . . by O. Temple, 2nd ed., 1922, repr. 1965:* 224–227.

1629 Meek, Charles Kingsley
The Bolewa of Fika. In his *Tribal studies in Northern Nigeria, v. 2, 1931:* 288–310, illus.

1630 —The Gamawa of Ngamo. In his *Tribal studies in Northern Nigeria, v. 2, 1931:* 269–289, illus.
Ethnographic account of the Gamawa (Ngamaya) or Ngamo in Bornu Province.

1631 —The Kare-Kare. In his *Tribal studies*

in Northern Nigeria, v. 2, 1931: 220–247, illus.

1632 Merrick, G.
The Bolewa tribe. *J. Afr. soc.,* 4 (16) Jl. 1905: 417–426.
Ethnographic sketch.

1633 Reynolds, F. G. B.
The drum of succession of the emirs of Fika. *Man,* 30, Sept. 1930: 155–156 (art. 123)
Brief account of the installation procedure of the Mai, with notes on the drum and its role as part of the regalia.

1634 Reynolds, F. G. B.
The rock-hewn wells in Fika emirate. *Man,* 30, Dec. 1930: 221–224. (art. 156) illus., map.

2. LINGUISTIC STUDIES

1635 Meek, Charles Kingsley
Bolewa [vocabulary] In his *Tribal studies in Northern Nigeria, v. 2, 1931:* 304–310.

1636 —Kare-Kare [vocabulary] In his *Tribal studies in Northern Nigeria, v. 2, 1931:* 239–247.

1637 —Ngamo vocabulary. In his *Tribal studies in Northern Nigeria, v. 2, 1931:* 282–288.

BORGAWA

(Bargu, Borgu, Burgu)

Including:

Bariba *(Barba, Barbar)*

Busa *(Boussa, Bussa, Bussawa)*

1. GENERAL AND ETHNOGRAPHIC STUDIES

1638 Anene, J. C.
The eclipse of the Borgawa. *J. Hist. soc. Nig.,* 3 (2) Dec. 1965: 211–230.

1639 Bussawa. In *Notes on the tribes . . . by O. Temple, 2nd ed., 1922, repr. 1965:* 74–76.

1640 Duff, E. Creighton
Bussa history. In his *Gazetteer of the Kontagora Province, 1920:* 23–27.

1641 Campbell, M. J.
Borgu journey. *Nigeria mag.,* (48) 1955: 60–83, illus.

1642 Heath, D. F.
Bussa regalia. *Man,* 37, May, 1937: (art. 91): 77–80, illus.
Describes the Kisra regalia of Bussa, which include among other items, the Big Drum (Gangan Kisra) Kettledrums, spears, and Brass bowls.

1643 Hermon-Hodge, Henry Baldwin
[The Borgawa and Bussawa] In his *Gazetteer of Ilorin Province, 1929:* 39–51.
Ethnographic notes on the two peoples.

Kyengawa *(Kengawa, Kiengawa, Kyenga, Shangawa, Tienga, Tiengawa)*

1644 Jacolliot, Louis
Voyage aux pays mystérieux: Yébou, Borgou, Niger. Paris, C. Marpon, 1880. 290p. illus.

1645 Kengawa. In *Notes on the tribes . . . by O. Temple, 2nd ed., 1922, repr. 1965:* 223–224.

1646 *Le Garrénes, R.
Dahomey: cercle du Borgou. Le secteur de Parakou. *Rev. col., n.s.,* 8, 1908: 513–530, 592–599; 703– ?

1647 Lugard, Frederick John Dealtry
Expedition to Borgu. *Geog. j.,* 6 (3) Sept. 1895: 205–227, illus., map.

1648 Lupton, K.
The death of Mungo Park at Bussa. *Nig. mag.,* (72) Mar. 1962: 58–70, illus., maps.

1649 Nicholson, W. E.
Notes on some of the customs of the Busa and Kyenga tribes at Illo. *J. Afr. soc.,* 26 (102) Jan. 1927: 92–100, illus.
Illo, near the Niger where it enters Nigerian territory.

1650 Rouch, J.
Les rapides de Boussa et la mort de

Mungo Park. *Notes afr.*, (43) juil. 1949: 89–98.

1651 Native races of the Niger territories: the Barbars; and the kingdom of Borgu. *Niger & Yoruba notes*, 2 (14) Aug. 1895: 12–13.

1652 Wallace, W.
Hausa territories: notes on a journey through the Sokoto empire and Borgu. *Geog. j.*, 8, 1896: 211–221.

1653 Yauri. In *Notes on the tribes . . . by O. Temple, 2nd ed., 1922, repr. 1965:* 368.

2. LINGUISTIC STUDIES

1654 Funke, E.
Die Sprache von Busa am Niger. *M.S.O.S.*, 18, 1915: 52–84.

1655 Welmers, William E.
Notes on the structure of Bariba. *Language*, 28 (1) Jan.-Mar. 1952: 82–103.
An extended study of the phonological and morphological structure of Bariba; a language spoken in Northern Dahomey and adjacent area of Nigeria.

BUDUMA

(Boudouma, Jedina, Yedina)

See also Kanuri

1. GENERAL AND ETHNOGRAPHIC STUDIES

1656 Alexander, Boyd
Our first voyage on Lake Chad. In his *From the Niger to the Nile, v. 1, 1907:* 316–334, illus.,
Includes useful account of the Buduma See also v. 2 pp. 43–110 for further occasional descriptions.

1657 Buduma. In *Notes on the tribes . . . by O. Temple, 2nd ed., 1922, repr. 1965:* 69–70.

1658 Talbot, Percy Amaury
The Buduma of Lake Chad. *J.R.A.S.I.*, 41, 1911: 245–259, illus.

Ethnographic sketch, with a Guria-Buduma vocabulary, pp. 251–253.

2. LINGUISTIC STUDIES

1659 *Barth, Heinrich
Vocabulary of Buduma, spoken by the inhabitants of the islands in Lake Chad. *J. Roy. geog. soc.*, 21, 1851: 214; ff.

1660 Gaudiche
La langue Boudouma. *J. Soc. afr.*, 13, 1938: 11–32.

1661 Talbot, Percy Amaury
A Guria-Buduma vocabulary. *J.R.A.I.*, 41, 1911: 251–253.

BURA

(Burra)

Including:

Gabin

Hona

Pabir *(Babir, Babira, Babur Baburr)*

1. GENERAL AND ETHNOGRAPHIC STUDIES

1662 Babur. In *Notes on the tribes . . . by O. Temple, 2nd ed., 1922, repr. 1965:* 38–39.

1663 Barth, Heinrich
The Ba'bir tribe. In his *Travels and discoveries in North and Central Africa, v. 2, 1857:* 403–409.

1664 Burra. In *Notes on the tribes . . . by O. Temple, 2nd ed., 1922, repr. 1965:* 72–74.

1665 Davies, J. G.
Biu. *Nigeria mag.*, (45) 1954: 75–92, illus., map.
Describes the 400th anniversary of the founding of the dynasty which once reigned over Biu.

1666 —The Biu book; a collation and

reference book on Biu Division (Northern Nigeria). Zaria, N.O.R.L.A., 1954–1956. v, 357p.
A useful work of general information about Biu. Includes history, tribes, languages, administrative divisions, religion and witchcraft, chieftainship, social life, judicial organisation, etc.
Typescript. Mimeographed.

1667 Helser, Albert David
African stories. Foreword by Fremz Boas. New York, Chicago [etc.] Fleming H. Revell [1930] 233p. front., illus.
A collection of stories illustrative of the folklore of the Bura.

1668 —Education of primitive people; a presentation of the folklore of the Bura animists, with a meaningful experience curriculum. New York [etc.] Fleming

H. Revell [1934] 316p. front., illus., bibliog.

Educational activity of the Church of the Brethren Mission at Garkidda, Northern Nigeria, as well as the folklore of the people. Also issued as thesis for the Ph.D. Degree of Columbia University. Bibliography pp. 306-316.

1669 —In sunny Nigeria: experiences among a primitive people in the interior of North Central Africa. Introduction by Otho Winger. New York, Chicago [etc.] Fleming H. Revell [1926] 188p. front., illus., map.

Experiences of a Church of the Brethren Mission worker in Northern Nigeria.

1670 Hona. In *Notes on the tribes . . . by O. Temple, 2nd ed., 1922, repr. 1965:* 139-141.

1671 Meek, Charles Kingsley
The Bura and Pabir (Babur) tribes. In his *Tribal studies in Northern Nigeria, v. 1, 1931:* 137-180, illus.

1672 —The Gabin. In his *Tribal studies in Northern Nigeria, v. 2, 1931:* 369-395, illus.

Ethnographic notes on the Gabin, Ganda and Boga in Adamawa Province.

1673 —The Hona. In his *Tribal studies in Northern Nigeria, v. 2, 1931:* 395-416, illus.

1673a Neher, Gerald

Brass casting in North-east Nigeria. See [4125]

2. LINGUISTIC STUDIES

1674 Church of brethren mission, Jos.
Bura first reader. Jos, The mission, 1951. 99p. illus.

Printed by Niger press, Jos.

1675 —Bura second reader. Jos, The mission, 1952. 83p.

1676 —Bura grammar notes. [Jos, The mission, 1952] 96p.

Mimeographed. Bura & English.

1677 —Mdukur na pwa . . . [Garkida, Jos, the mission] 1954. 132p.

1678 Hoffmann, Carl F.
Untersuchungen zur Struktur und sprachlichen Stellung des Bura. 1955.

Phil. F. thesis, Hamburg University. Discusses the structure and linguistic affinity of Bura language.

1679 Meek, Charles Kingsley
Gabin language. In his *Tribal studies in Northern Nigeria, v. 2, 1931:* 389-395.

Gabin vocabulary, with an appendix of a short vocabulary of the Boga dialect.

1680 —Hona language. In his *Tribal studies in Northern Nigeria, v. 2, 1931:* 410-416. Hona vocabulary.

1681 —Schedule of words and phrases: Bura. In his *Tribal studies in Northern Nigeria, v. 1, 1931:* 174-180.

BUTAWA

(Mbotuwa, Mbutawa)

Including:

Kudawa

Ningawa *(Ningi)*

1. GENERAL AND ETHNOGRAPHIC STUDIES

1682 Butawa. In *Notes on the tribes . . . by O. Temple, 2nd ed., 1922, repr. 1965:* 76-78.

1683 Gunn, Harold D.
The Butawa, Kudawa and Ningawa. In his *Peoples of the central area of Northern Nigeria, 1956:* 17-21.
See also ibid., pp. 11-16.

1684 Kudawa. In *Notes on the tribes . . . by O. Temple, 2nd ed., 1922, repr. 1965:* 243.

1685 Ningawa. In *Notes on the tribes . . . by O. Temple, 2nd ed., 1922, repr. 1965:* 312-314.

1686 Ningi. In *Notes on the tribes . . . by O. Temple, 2nd ed., 1922, repr. 1965:* 422.

CHAMBA

(Chamba, Dschamba, Tsamba)

Including:

Daka

Donka

Kungana

Lekon *(Laego, Leco)*

Mumbake

Suntai

Takum

Tsugu

Wom

1. GENERAL AND ETHNOGRAPHIC STUDIES

1687 Chamba. In *Notes on the tribes . . . by*

O. Temple, 2nd ed., 1922, repr. 1965: 79-84.

1688 Kirk-Greene, Anthony Hamilton Millard

Chamba. In his *Adamawa past and present, 1958:* 16–17.
Short historical note.

1689 Meek, Charles Kingsley
The Chamba. *In his Tribal studies in Northern Nigeria, 1931.* v. 1, pp. 328–412, illus.
Ethnographic notes on various Chamba groups in Benue and Adamawa Provinces, to wit Daka, Donka, Kungana, Lekon, Mumbake, Suntai, Takum, Tsugu and Wom.

1690 Mumbake. In *Notes on the tribes . . . by*

O. *Temple, 2nd ed., 1922, repr. 1965:* 281–286.

2. LINGUISTIC STUDIES

1691 Meek, Charles Kingsley
[Chamba vocabularies] In his *Tribal studies in Northern Nigeria, 1931.* v. 1, pp. 372–377, 382–384, 385–387, 392–394, 403–412.
Vocabularies of Donka, Lekon, Wom, Mumbake, Gandole, Taram and Dirrim dialects.

CHAWAI

(Atsam)

Including:

Irigwe *(Aregwa, Irrigwe, Rigwe)*

Kwoll

1. GENERAL AND ETHNOGRAPHIC STUDIES

1692 Ames, C. G.
The Irigwe tribe. In his *Gazetteer of Bauchi Province. Recently abridged and revised, 1934:* 80–88.
Origin, history and ethnography.

1692a Chawai, Jengre, Rukuba group. See [3797]

1693 Gunn, Harold D.
The Chawai of Zaria Province. In his *Peoples of the Plateau area of Northern Nigeria, 1953:* 53–59, bibliog.

1694 —Irigwe. In his *Peoples of the Plateau area of Northern Nigeria. 1953:* 98–100.

1695 Kwoll. In *Notes on the tribes . . . by O. Temple, 2nd ed., 1922, repr. 1965:* 253–254.

1696 Madaki, Peter Rawa and Kirk-Greene, Anthony Hamilton Millard
Nkashe Ta: the story of the leg; a Miango folktale. *Nig. field,* 27 (4) Oct. 1962: 161–169, illus.
Miango is an Irigwe village.

1697 Meek, Charles Kingsley
The Chawai. In his *Tribal studies in Northern Nigeria, v. 2, 1931:* 145–164, illus.

2. LINGUISTIC STUDIES

1698 Meek, Charles Kingsley
Chawai [vocabulary] In his *Tribal studies in Northern Nigeria, v. 2, 1931:* 158–164.

DAKAKARI

(Dakarawa, Dakarkari, Dakkakerri)

Including:

Bangawa
Fakawa

Kalewa
Lilawa

1. GENERAL AND ETHNOGRAPHIC STUDIES

1699 Boyd, C. E.
Dakkakerris. In *Gazetteer of the Kontagora Province, by E. C. Duff, 1920:* 55–61.
Ethnographic notes.

1700 Conant, Francis P.
Dakakari (Bangawa, Fakawa, Kalewa and Lilawa). In *Peoples of the middle Niger region, Northern Nigeria, by H. D. Gunn and F. P. Conant, 1960:* 29–49.
Ethnographic notes.

1701 Dakkakarri. In *Notes on the tribes . . . by*

O. *Temple, 2nd ed., 1922, repr. 1965:* 88–94.

1702 Fitzgerald, R. T. D.
Dakakari grave pottery. *Nig. field,* 23 (2) Apr. 1958: 76–84, illus.

1703 —Dakakari grave pottery. *J.R.A.I.,* 74 (1–2) 1944: 43–55, illus., maps.
Description of pots of various shapes found on graves among the Dakakari. See also [1705] and [1706]

1704 —The Dakakari peoples of Sokoto Province, Nigeria: Notes on their material culture. *Man,* 42, Mar.–Apr. 1942: 25–36 (art. 19) illus.
Includes information on tribal marks, games, house decorations, etc.,

1705 Harris, Percy Graham
Notes on the Dakakari peoples of
Sokoto Province, Nigeria. *J.R.A.I.*, 68,
Jan.–Je. 1938: 113–152, illus.
Education, economy, religion, death,
inheritance, marriage.

1706 Hollis, Rosemary
Dakakari grave pottery. *Nig. field.*, 23
(1) Jan. 1958: 23–26, illus.
Reference is made to a more im-
portant paper on the subject by R. T. D.
Fitzgerald. [1703] See also [1705]

EDO

Including:

Bini
Etsako
Ineme
Ishan *(Esa, Esan, Isa)*

Ivbiosakon
Kukuruku

See also Urbobo

1. BIBLIOGRAPHY

1707 Bradbury, R. E.
Bibliography [of the Edo-Speaking
peoples] In his *The Benin kingdom, 1957*:
165–171.

2. GENERAL

1708 Adams, John
[Description of Benin] In his *Sketches
taken during ten voyages to Africa . . .
1822*: 28–43.

1709 Bacon, Reginald Hugh Spencer
Benin; the city of blood. London, New
York, Edward Arnold, 1897. 151p.
front., illus., map.
Record of the 1897 British military
expedition to Benin, written by the
expedition's intelligence officer.

1709a Barbot, Jean
A description of the coasts of North and
South Guinea. See [121]

1710 Beauvois, Baron A. Palisot de
Notice sur le peuple du Bénin. *La
décade philosophique*, 9 (12) 1801: 141–
151.

1711 Benin: city of memories. *W. Afr. rev.*,
31 (397) Dec. 1960: 82–83.

1712 Boisragon, Alan
The Benin massacre. London, Methuen,
1897. vii, 190p. front., map.
Eye-witness account of the Benin
massacre by one of the two survivors
and of the subsequent British expedition.
Includes notes on Benin history and a
description of the area then known as
the "Niger Coast Protectorate". 2nd
ed. 1898.

1713 Bouchaud, J. R. P.
Les Portugais dans la Baie de Biafra
au XVIème siècle. *Africa*, 16, 1946:
217–227, illus., map, bibliog.
The illus. show four Bini plaques.

1714 Brinkworth, Ian
Benin: "city of blood" and bronze.
Geog. mag., 27 (5) 1954: 248–255, illus.,
map.

1715 Büchner, M.
Benin und die Portugiesen. *Z. f. Ethnol.*,
40 (6) 1908: 981–992, illus.

1716 Burton, Richard Francis
My wanderings in West Africa; a visit
to the renowned cities of Warri and
Benin. By an F.R.G.S.: *Fraser's mag.*,
67 (398) Feb. 1863: 135–157; (399)
Mar. 1863: 273–289; (400) Apr. 1863:
407–422.
In two parts. Pt. 1 (no. 398) deals with
wars; and pt. II (nos. 399 and 400)
deals with the kingdom of Benin. See
also his main account [156]

1717 Caturla, Eduardo del val
Benin, la ciuidad cruenta. *Africa*
[Madrid] 49–50 Jan.–Feb. 1946: 28–30,
illus.

1718 Corbeau, J.
L'empire du Bénin. *Echo Missions afr.*
[Lyon] 49 (3) May–Je. 1950: 10–12; 51
(6) Sept.–Oct. 1952: 90–94, illus.

1719 Crahmer, Wilhelm
Über den indo-portugiesischen Ursprung
der Beninkunst. *Globus*, 95, 1909: 345–
349; 360–365.

1720 —Über den Ursprung der 'Beninkultur'.
Globus, 94, 1908: 301–303.

1721 Da Mota, Avelino Teixena
Novos elementos sobre a acçâo dos
portugueses e franceses em Benin na
primeira metade do seculo XVI. *Bol.
cultural Guiné Portug.*, 7 (27) 1952:
525–531.

1722 Desanti, Hyacinthe
Du Dahomé au Bénin-Niger. Paris,
Larose, 1945. 268p. illus., maps.

1723 Du Pouget, Jean Francois Albert,
Marquis de Nadaillac.
Le royaume de Bénin; massacre d'une
mission anglaise, extrait du correspon-
dant. Paris, De Soye, 1898. 32p.

1724 Fawckner, James
Narrative of Captain Fawckner's travels
on the coast of Benin, West Africa.
Edited by a friend of the Captain.
London, A. Schloss, for the Proprietor,
1837. viii, 128p.
Description of Benin especially at
pp. 67–92; 101–106.

1725 The First voyage [of M. Thomas
Windham] to Guinea and Benin. In
*The principal navigations, voyages,
traffiques & discoveries of the English
nation . . . by Richard Hakluyt. Glasgow,
J. Maclehose, 1904:* v. 6, pp. 145–154.
Describes their visit to the king of
Benin, his gentleness to them and their
trade in pepper.

1726 Gaffarel, Paul
Le Capitaine Landolphe et le premier
établissement des Français au Bénin.
Ann. l'Institut col. de Marseille, 8 (1)
1901: 45–74.

1727 Galway, Henry Lionel
Journeys in the Benin country, West
Africa. *J. & proc. Roy. geog. soc.,* 1893:
122–130.

1728 —Nigeria in the nineties. *j. Afr. soc.,*
29 (115) Apr. 1930: 221–247.
Gives his reminiscences while serving
in the Oil Rivers Protectorate, and recounts his mission to Benin to conclude
a peace treaty in 1892. Describes the
Benin massacre and subsequent British
expedition.

1729 Hide, R. H.
The Bini as a botanist. *Nig. field,* 11,
Dec. 1943: 169–179.

1731 King, John, *lieutenant.*
Extrait d'une relation inédite d'un
voyage fait en 1820 aux royaumes de
Benin et de Waree. *J. voyages, décou-
vertes et navigations modernes,* 13, 1822:
313–318.

1732 The Kingdom of Benin. *Times rev. col.,*
1956: 181–182.

1733 Kukuruku. In *Notes on the tribes . . . by
O. Temple. 2nd ed., 1922, repr. 1965:*
247–252.

1734 Legum, Colin
Great Benin, the elusive city. *Nigeria,
1960:* 103–112, illus.

1734a Lloyd, P. C.
The development of political parties in
Western Nigeria. See [4792].

1735 Mclaren, Jack
Gentlemen of the empire: the colourful
and remarkable experiences of district
commissioners, patrol officers and other
officials in some of the British empires
tropical outposts. London, Hutchinson,
1940. 256p.
Two of the twelve accounts related to
Nigeria: *In pursuit of murders* (in a
Kukuruku village) pp. 48–68, and *The
City of blood* (the Benin massacre and
the punitive expedition) pp. 69–82.

1736 Nadaillac, de. See Du Pouget, Jean
François Albert, Marquis de Nadaillac.

1737 Nee-Ankrah, S. W.
Whither Benin? Ibadan, [the author]
1951. 48p.
Printed by Union press, Ibadan.

1738 Nigeria. Midwestern. Commission appointed to enquire into the Owegbe cult.
Report of the Commission, including
statement by the Government of the

Midwestern Group of Provinces.
[D.A.R. Alexander, sole commissioner]
Benin City, Government printer, 1966.
x, 159p.
Statement by Government, p. 159.

1739 Nyendael, David van
A description of Rio Formosa, or The
River of Benin; being the first supple-
mental, or the one and twentieth letter.
In *A new and accurate description of the
Coast of Guinea, by W. Bosman.
London, Printed for A. Roper, 1703:*
423–468.

1740 Obano, G. A.
Path to national unity of Benin. [Benin
City, the author, 1953] xii, 47p.
Printed by Ife-Olu printing works,
Lagos.

1741 Ogieriakhi, Emwinma
My wife or my wives? and, The marriage
couldn't continue. Benin City, Language
press, 1965. xix, 101p.
Two plays.

1742 Ogilby, John
The monarchy of Benyn. In his *Africa. . .
1670:* 470–478, illus.

1743 Ososo. *Nig. mag.,* (45) 1954: 30–47.
Ososo is a town in the rocky northern
edge of Afenmai Division.

1744 Palisot de Beauvois, Ambroise Marie
Francois Joseph
Flore d'Oware et de Bénin en Afrique.
See [3787].

1744a —Insectes recueillis en Afrique et en
Amerique dans les royaumes d'Oware
et de Benin . . . See [3788].

1745 Pinnock, James
Benin: the surrounding country, inhabitants, customs and trade. Liverpool,
"Journal of commerce" printing works,
1897. 55p. illus., map.

1746 Pinnock, James and Auchterlone, T. B.
City of Benin: the country, customs and
inhabitants. *J. Liver. geog. soc.,* 16,
1898: 5–16.

1747 —Personal experiences in Benin. *J.
Tyneside geog. soc.,* 3, 1897: 392–403,
illus., map.

1748 Résumé des premiers voyageurs sur la
géog. du Bénin. In *Histoire générale des
voyages; ou Nouvelle collection des
relations de voyages . . . par C. A.
Walckenaer, v. 11, 1842:* 7–61.

1749 Roth, Felix N.
Diary of a surgeon with the Benin
punitive expedition. *J. Manch. geog. soc.,*
14, 1898: 208–221.
Also reprinted in *Great Benin; its
customs, art and horrors, by N. Roth,
1903:* ii–xii [at end of book].

1750 Royaume de Bénin. In *Anecdotes
Africaines, depuis l'origine ou la
découverte des differents royaumes qui
composent l'Afrique, jusqua nos jours.
Paris, Chez Vincent, 1775:* 38–47.

1751 *R[uiters], D[ierick]
Beschryvinghe vande ghelegentheydt
end maniere van de groote Staadt

Bennin, gelegen inden eersten Bocht ofte Inwijck. In *Beschryvinghe ende historische verhael van het Gout Koninckrijck van Gunea . . . by Pieter de Marees. Amsterdam, 1602:*

An important description of Benin included in Pieter de Marees' work and attributed to Dierick Ruiters. It is signed with the initials D. R.

1752 —Beschryvinghe vande ghelegentheydt . . . vande groote Stadt Bennin . . . In *Hakluytus posthumus; or Purchas his Pilgrimes: containing a history of the world in sea voyages and lande travells by Englishmen and others. Glasgow, J. MacLehose, 1905–07.* 20v. vol. 6, pp. 354–359.

An abridgement of above.

1753 Thorburn, J. W. A.
The city of Benin. *Nig. mag.*, (10) Apr. 1937: 65–69, illus.

1754 Tong, Raymond L.
The ancient city of Benin. *Corona*, 3 (1) 1951: 30–32.

1755 —Fabled city. *Afr. affairs*, 53 (211) Apr. 1954: 130–132.

A poem describing the journey to, and arrival at Benin in 1485 of the Portuguese, John Affonso d'Aveiro.

1756 —Fabled city: West African poems. [London] William Maclellan, 1960. 40p.

An anthology of twenty-five poems by author on West African (especially Nigerian) topics and scenes. Includes "Fabled city" q.v. [1755]

1757 —Figures in ebony: past and present in a West African city. London, Cassell, 1958. ix, 131p. illus.

Impressions of modern Benin, with notes on the historical background.

1758 Voyages and travel to Benin, containing a description of that country, and the coast as far as Kongo. In *Astley's voyages, vol. 3, 1746, repr. London, Frank Cass, 1968:* 87–131.

1759 Wallace, W.
Through the swamps to Benin. *Macmillan's mag.*, Mar. 1897: 336–342.

1760 Welsh, James
Two voyages to Benin beyond Guinea in 1588 and 1590. In *Astley's voyages, vol. 1, 1745, repr. London, Frank Cass, 1968:* 199–205.

1761 —A voyage to Benin beyond the country of Guinea. In *The principal navigations, voyages . . . of the English nations, by R. Hakluyt, 1598:* vol. 6, pp. 450–467.

3. ARCHAEOLOGY

1762 Connah, Graham
Archaeological research in Benin City, 1961–64. *J. Hist. soc. Nig.*, 2 (4) Dec. 1963: 465–477, map, illus.

A report (interim) of the extensive archaeological excavations in Benin City carried out by the author from December 1961 to 1964.

1762a Goodwin, A. J. H.

Walls, paving, water paths and landmarks. See [608].

4. SOCIAL AND CULTURAL ANTHROPOLOGY, ETHNOGRAPHY.

(i) General

1763 Benin's ceremonious art. *W. Afr. rev.*, 29 (374) Nov. 1958: 914–915, illus.

1764 Benin's own antiquarian. *W. Afr.*, (1725) 1950: 221.
On Chief J. U. Egharevba.

1765 Benson, E. M.
Benin: a dead people and a living art. *Amer. mag. art.*, 29, 1936: 36–38, illus.

1766 Bradbury, R. E.
The Benin kingdom and the Edo-speaking peoples of South-Western Nigeria: the Benin kingdom; the Ishan; the Northern Edo; the Urhobo and Isoko of the Niger Delta; together with a section on the Itsekiri by P. C. Lloyd. London, Int. Afr. Inst., 1957. 164p. maps, bibliog. (Ethnographic survey of Africa, edited by Daryll Forde. Western Africa, pt. 13).

1767 —The Etsako tribes. In his *The Benin kingdom . . . 1957:* 100–109.

1768 —The Ineme. In his *The Benin Kingdom . . . 1957:* 123–126.

1769 —The Ivbiosakon tribes. In his *The Benin kingdom . . . 1957:* 84–100.

1769a Cordwell, Justine M.
Some aesthetic aspects of Yoruba and Benin cultures. See [4521].

1770 De Negri, Eve
'. . . the King's beads'. *Nig. mag.*, (82) Sept. 1964: 210–216, illus.

Historical and descriptive notes on the beads forming part of the regalia of the Oba of Benin.

1771 Egharevba, Jacob Uwadiae
Concise lives of the famous Iyases of Benin. Lagos, Temi Asunwon press, 1946. 48p.

"2nd ed. February 1947"—Verso of t.-p.

1772 Enahoro, Anthony E.
Fugitive offender; the story of a political prisoner. London, Cassell, 1965. xii, 436p. illus., map.

The first two chapters (pp. 1–50) give useful account of village life and customs in the early thirties, especially in Arewa, Uromi, the author's home town.

1773 Hau, Kathleen
Evidence of the use of pre-Portuguese written characters by the Bini? *Bull. IFAN*, 21 (1–2) Jan.-Apr. 1959: 109–154, illus.

Suggests some of the figures carved on Benin ivories may be ideographic or hieroglyphic characters, supporting this with local Bini tradition that they wrote with chalk on wooden and ivory slabs. Reviews routes via which writing might have spread to Benin in pre-

Portuguese times from classical and Arabic worlds.

1774 Macrow, Donald W. and Stanfield, D. Change in the hills. *Nig. mag.*, (45) 1954: 21–47, illus.
A study of communities in Kabba, Afenmai and Benin regions.

1775 Mercier, Paul
Civilisations du Bénin. Paris, Société continentale d'éditions modernes illustrées, 1962. 365p. illus. maps. (Connaissance de l'Afrique)
Ethnographic study of the Yoruba-Benin culture complex.

1776 Roth, Henry, Ling.
Great Benin; its customs, art and horrors. Halifax, England, F. King, 1903. xii, 234, xxxiip. front. (port.) illus.
A general account of Benin, its people and their culture as seen by European travellers before its collapse in the late 19th century. Has appendices containing the diary of Flex M. Roth, surgeon with the Benin punitive expedition, pp. ii–xii; account of the surrender and trial of the king, pp. xii–xviii; notes on land tenure and inheritance in Yoruba, by Cyril Punch, pp. xxi–xxiv; etc.

1777 —Benin customs. *Int. arch. ethnog.*, 11, 1898: 235–242.

1779 Sydow, Eckart von
D. Panther-Ornament auf d. Panzern von Benin. Zur Stilgeschichte d. Benin-Platten. *Ethnol. Anzeiger*, 3 (5) 1934: 231-238, illus.

1780 Thomas, Northcote Whitridge
Anthropological report on the Edo-speaking peoples of Nigeria. London, Harrison, 1910. 2v.
Part 1. Law and custom. 163p. maps (some fold.)
Part II. Linguistics. ix, 251p.

1781 —The Edo-speaking peoples of Nigeria. *J. Afr. soc.*, 10 (37) Oct. 1910: 1–15.
Lecture given at a meeting of the Society on 15th July 1910. Notes language, population, marriage law and custom and religion. The lecture was accompanied by lantern slides and phonographic records of native music and songs.

1782 —The Edo week. *Man.* 20, 1920: 152–153, (art. 73).

1783 Tong, Raymond L.
Christianity in early Benin. *W. Afr.*, May 21, 1955: 468.

1784 Westermann, Diedrich
Das Leben des Igbinokpogie Amadasu aus Benin, Südnigerien. In *Afrikaner erzählen ihr Leben, Elf Selbstdarstellungen afrikanischer Eingeborener aller Bildungsgrade und Berufe und aus allen Teilen Afrikas, 1938*: 189–227, illus.
Autobiography of Amadasu, a Bini, written partly in Bini and partly in English and now translated into German.

Gives account of his journey to Cape Coast, education there, and employment in Nigeria. Assisted Dr. Melzian in his investigations in Siluks and visited Warri with him to record the Urhobo language. Includes account of bewitchings, marriage customs and funeral rites.

4. (ii) History

1785 Aderibigbe, A. A. B.
Benin. In *A thousand years of West African history, ed. J. F. A. Ajayi and I. Espie, 1965*: 193–196.

1786 Akenzua, Edun
Benin, 1897: a Beni's view. *Nig. mag.* (65) Je. 1960: 177–190, illus.
Account of events leading to the Benin massacre of Jan. 1897, the subsequent British military expedition against the town, and the exile of the Oba. Written by his great-grandson.

1787 *Amu, J. W. A.
The Ora history book. Lagos, Asaoku press [n.d.]
Edo (Bini)

1788 Arriens, C.
Die Epigonen von Benin. *Kol. runds.*, 12, Dec., 1929: 377–381.

1789 Bradbury, R. E.
Chronological problems in the study of Benin history. *J. Hist. soc. Nig.*, 1 (4) Dec. 1959: 263–287.
Critical review of Benin history, in particular, the lists of her kings so far compiled, with a view to establishing a more accurate chronology.

1790 —The historical uses of comparative ethnography with special reference to Benin and the Yoruba. In *The historian in tropical Africa, edited by J. Vansina [and others] 1964*: 145–160, bibliog. [800].
Benin and Yoruba history approached from a comparative study of their respective political structures, especially the contrasting features of these structures. Author engaged for several years in the Benin research scheme. Summary given in French.

1791 Dike, Kenneth Onwuka
Benin: a great forest kingdom of medieval Nigeria.
Unesco courier, 12 (10) Oct. 1959: 12–14; *Pract. anthrop.*, 8 (1) Jan.–Feb. 1961: 31–35.

1792 —The Benin scheme. *Ibadan*, (1) Oct. 1957: 8–10.

1793 —The Benin scheme begins. *Corona*, 9 (9) Sept. 1957: 325–328.

1794 —The medieval kingdom of Benin. *Panorama*, 1 (Winter) 1960: 21–23.

1795 Edyang, E.
Emotan of Benin (a play in three acts). *Nig. mag.*, (76) Mar. 1963: 58–70.

1796 Egharevba, Jacob Uwadiae
The city of Benin. [Benin, the author, 1952] 27p. illus.
Printed by Aguebor printers, Benin.

1797 —Erkherhe vbe ebe itan Edo. [Benin City, the author] 1933. 42p.
History of Benin.

1798 —The murder of Imaguero and tragedy of Idah war. Sapele, Central press, 1948. 35p.

1799 —Okha Edo. New ed. Lagos, C.M.S., 1937. 111p.

1800 —The origin of Benin. Benin, [the author] 1953. [2] 24p.
Printed by Ribway printers, Lagos.

1801 — —2nd ed. 1964. 31p. Printed by African industrial press, Benin.

1802 —A short history of Benin. 3rd ed. Ibadan, University press, 1960. xiii, 101p.

1803 — —2nd ed. (revised and enlarged). Benin, the author, 1953. xii, 118p. front. (port.). Printed at Ibadan University press.

1804 Emokpae, D. U.
The murder of Adesua. Lagos, Ribway printers [n.d.]

1805 Graham, James D.
The slave trade, depopulation and human sacrifice in Benin history. *Cah. étud. afr.*, 5 (2) 1965: 317–334, bibliog.

1806 Olderogge, D. A.
Drevnosti Benina (po kollektsiyam muzeya antropologii i etnografii) *Sbornik muzeya antropologii, arkheologii i etnografii*, 15, 1953: 357–410; 16, 1955: 283–307; 17, 1957: 345–361, bibliog.
Social and cultural history of Benin reconstructed largely from evidence furnished by bronze monuments from Benin.

1807 Omo-Ananigie, Peter Inahoureme
A brief history of Etsakor; being a critique of the history of Etsakor (in three parts) Lagos, Ope-Ifa press, 1946. [x] 170p. illus., map.

1808 Omorogie, S. O.
Binis own Lagos. [Benin, the author, 1954] 5p.
Printed by Olowonilara press, Benin-City.

1809 Ryder, Alvan Frederick Charles
The Benin missions. *J. Hist. soc. Nig.*, 2 (2) Dec. 1961: 231–259.
Account of Portugese missionary activity in the kingdom of Benin from 1515 to 1713.

1810 —A reconsideration of the Ife-Benin relationship. *J. Afr. hist.*, 6 (1) 1965: 25–37.

1811 Sharevskaya, B. I.
Nachalo proniknoveniya portugaliev v Gvineyu i popuitki khristianizakyi Benina. (*Dokladui i soobslicheniya na istoricheskom fakultete M.G.U.*) Moskva, 1948.
On the early attempts by the Portuguese to penetrate the Benin country and to Christianize the people.

1812 Smith, Henry Frederick Charles

The Benin study. *J. Hist. soc. Nig.*, 1 (1) Dec. 1956: 60–61.
Brief note describing the Benin historical research scheme.

1813 Struck, Bernhard
Chronologie der Benin-Altertümer. *Z. f. Ethnol.*, 55 (5–6) 1923: 113–167.

1814 Ughulu, Emmanuel Obehioye
The short history of (Esan) Ishan-Benin. Lagos, Ribway printers, 1950. [iv] 120p., illus.

1815 Ukeje, L. O.
Urhore. *Nig. mag.*, (76) Mar. 1963: 29–44, illus.
History and customs of Urhore, a town in Afenmai Division, Benin Province.

1816 Uwaifo, Hawdon Omoregbe
Benin community intelligence report on Benin Division (being the political history of Benin from 1936 to 1948). [Benin, the author, 1949?] [ii] 37p.
Printed by F.M.S. press, Box 97 Oshogbo.

1817 Wyndham, John
The curse of Obo: a tragedy of Benin. London, Duckworth, 1926. 71p. illus.
Drama.

4. (iii) Marriage, Family, Lineage Structure

1818 Egharevba, Jacob Uwadiae
Marriage of the princesses of Benin. [Benin City, author, 1962] 24p. front. (port.)
Describes the customs and traditions observed in the marriage of the princesses of Benin.

1819 Legogie, C. K.
Marriage custom in Ekperi-land, Benin Province, Western Nigeria. Kano, [the author, 1951] 12p.
Printed by Ife-Olu printing works, Kano. Ekperi in Etsakor group, Afenmai Division.

1820 Thomas, Northcote Whitridge
Marriage and legal customs of the Edo-speaking peoples of Nigeria. *J. comp. legis.*, 1910: 94–101.

4. (iv) Government, Kingship, Law; Social Organization and Structure

1821 Ajisafe, Ajayi Kolawole
Laws and customs of the Benin people. Lagos, Kash & Klare bookshop, 1945. 101p.

1822 Bradbury, R. E.
Divine kingship in Benin. *Nig. mag.*, (62) 1959: 186–207, illus.
Describes the institution of divine kingship and the ritual ceremonies associated with it.

1823 —The social structure of Benin, with special reference to the politico-ritual organisation (the village community). 1957.
Ph.D. thesis, London.

1824 —Some aspects of the political organisation of the Benin kingdom. *WAISER conf. proc.*, 1952: 50–60.

I

Summary of paper read at the WAISER 1952 conference. Deals with status and authority structure at the ward, village, village-group and state levels among the Benin section of the Edo-speaking peoples.

1825 Butcher, H. L. M.
Some aspects of the *Otu* system of the Isa sub-tribes of the Edo people of Southern Nigeria. *Africa*, 8 (2) Apr. 1935: 149–162.
On the *Otu* or "rank" system among the Ishan. French summary, p. 161–162.

1826 *Edo National Union
Constitution and rules. Benin City, 1943.

1827 Egharevba, Jacob Uwadiae
Benin law and custom. 3rd ed. Port Harcourt, C.M.S. press, 1949. 120p. front.
A simply written description dealing with all aspects of Benin life and customs. 1st ed. published in 1946.

1828 —Bini titles. [Benin, the author] 1956. 42p.
Printed by Kopin-Dogha press, Benin.

1829 Evbiamen and Ovbiowun family unions
Facts about the dispute on Emai chieftaincy system. (Being an accurate summary of the streams of thought and the declaration of all Emai people on the customary law relating to the exercise of traditional authority in Emai clan, Afemai Division, Benin Province, Nigeria) [Ibadan, the unions, 1957]15p.
Printed by Adeyemi printing works, Ibadan.

1830 Hau, Kathleen
A royal title on a palace tusk from Benin. *Bull. IFAN*, 26 (1–2) Jan.–Apr. 1964: 21–39, illus.

Marti, Montserat Palau. See Palau-Marti, Montserat.

1831 Notes on the form of the Bini government. *Man*, 4, 1904: 50–54 (art. 3)
Descriptive notes on the governmental structure and administrative and religious hierachy in Benin before the British occupation. Extracted from a report to the Colonial office.

1832 Okojie, Christopher B.
Ishan native laws and customs. Irrua, the author (Yaba, printed by John Okwesa & co., and bound by the Nigerian national press) 1960. 338p. illus,. maps.
A useful record and interpretation of Ishan laws and customs by an Ishan author.

1833 Omoregie, S. O.
A glance at Benin politics. Sapele, [the author] 1952. 14p.
Printed by Central press, Sapele.

1834 Palau-Marti, Montserat
Le roi-dieu au Bénin, sud-Togo, Dahomey, Nigeria occidentale. Paris, Berger-Levrault, 1964. 259p. illus., maps, bibliog.
A study of divine kingship in Benin,

Ife, Oyo, Ketu, Dahomey and Porto Novo.

1835 *Rowling, Cecil William
Notes on land tenure in the Benin, Kukuruku, Ishan and Asaba Divisions of Benin Province. Lagos, Government printer, 1948.

1836 Sklar, Richard Lawrence
The contribution of tribalism to nationalism in Western Nigeria. *J. human rel.*, 8 (3–4) 1960: 407–418.
See also [4792]

1836a Thomas, Northcote Whitridge
Marriage and legal customs of the Edo-speaking peoples. See [1820]

1837 Uwaifo, Hawdon Omoregbe
Benin custom and law regarding land, burial rites and inheritance. Benin City [the author] 1965. [ii] 20p.
Printed by O.U.E. & brothers printing press, Benin City.

1838 —Eguae societies of Benin. [Benin, the author, 1952] 14p.
Printed by the Union press, Ibadan.

4. (v) Birth and Death Rituals; Miscellaneous Beliefs and Rites

1839 Bradbury, R. E.
Father and senior son in Edo mortuary ritual. In *African systems of thought; studies presented and discussed at the third international African seminar in Salisbury, Dec. 1960. 1965*: 96–115.
Summary in French pp. 115–121.

1840 Cambron, L.
La circoncision dan la région des Bini et des environs. *Congo, revue générale de la colonie belge*, 5 (2) 1924: 364–371.

1841 Elakhe, Peter
Ekue rites. *Nig. mag.*, (76) Mar. 1963: 45–56, illus.
Traditional rites associated with the circumcision of girls in Ikhin, a village in Afenmai Division, Benin Province.

1842 Rumann, W. B.
Funeral ceremonies for the late ex-oba of Benin. *J. Afr. soc.*, 14 (53) Oct. 1914: 35–39, illus.
i.e. Oba Overami who died in exile in Calabar on 14th January 1914.

1843 Thomas, Northcote Whitridge
Birth customs of the Edo-speaking peoples. *J.R.A.I.*, 52, 1922: 250–258.

1844 —Notes on Edo burial customs. *J.R.A.I.* 50, 1920: 377–411.

1845 —Twins. *Man*, 19, 1919: 173–174 (art. 87).

1845a Uwaifo, Hawdon Omoregbe
Benin custom and law regarding land, burial rite and inheritance. See [1837]

4. (vi) Economy, Agriculture, Trade

1846 Adams, John
[Trade at Benin and Warre] In his *Sketches taken during ten voyages to Africa . . . 1822*: 109–111.

1847 Hide, R. H.

Bini snares. *Nig. field*, 18 (3) Jl. 1953: 130–134, illus.
Describes several kinds of Bini traps for game birds and animals.

1848 Strieder, Jakob
Negerkunst von Benin und deutsches Metallexportgewerbe im XV und XVI Jahrhundert. *Z. f. Ethnol.*, 64, 1932: 249–259.

1849 Thomas, Northcote Whitridge
Agricultural rites. *Man*, 18, 1918: 138–142 (art. 75).

4. (vii) Religion

1850 *The Address of the Oba of Benin in connection with Aruosa (Edo national Church of God) re-established 11. 12. 45. Benin City, Olowu press, 1946.

1851 Akpata, A.
Notes on altars and bronze heads of Benin. *Ethnol. Cran.*, (1), 1937: 5–10, illus.

1852 Balfour, Henry
"Thunderbolt" celts from Benin. *Man*, 3, 1903: 182–183. (art. no. 102) illus.
Description of a small stone celt purchased by the author in Benin and believed to have been regarded as a thunderbolt, symbolising the local god of thunder.

1853 Beasley, Harry G.
'Thunder-bolt celts' from Benin. *Man*, 37 Sept. 1937: 137 (art. 175) illus.
Further notes on stone celts in Benin. See [1852]

1854 The book of the holy Aruosa. Benin City, Olowu press, 1946–1948. 2v.
v. 1. 1946.
v. 2. 1948.

1855 Bradbury, R. E.
Ehi: three stories from Benin. *Odù*, (8) Oct. 1960: 40–48.
Three traditional stories are used to illustrate the religious and philosophic significance of the *ehi* (the spiritual counterpart of the individual).

1856 —Ezomo's *ikegobo* and the Benin cult of the hand. *Man*, 61 (165) Aug. 1961: 129–138, illus.
Ikegobo, the 'shrine of the hand' owned by the Ezomo, one of the two traditional military leaders in Benin, is carefully described, and the significance of this and of similar Benin bronzes as historical records is discussed.

1857 The Catechism of Aruosa (Edo and English). Benin City, Olowu press, 1946.

1858 *Correia, Miguel Pupo
Por terras de Benin . . . Dahomé—O reino da serpenta. *Mensário admin.*, 61–62, 1952: 5–12, illus.

1859 Egharevba, Jacob Uwadiae
Some tribal gods of Southern Nigeria. [Benin City, the author] 1951. 59p.

1859a Gallwey, Henry Lionel. See Galway, Henry Lionel.

1860 Galway, Henry Lionel

Benin: altars and compounds. *Ethnol. Cran.*, (3) 1938: 3–8, illus.
Includes additional notes by G. P. L Miles.

1861 Hall, Henry Usher
Great Benin royal altar. *Univ. Penn. mus. j.*, 13 (2) Je. 1922: 105–168, illus.
Describes Benin religion and the Benin altar set up at the University of Pennsylvania museum.

1862 Hardie, A. D. K.
Okoubaka—a rare juju. *Nig. field*, 28 (2) Apr. 1936: 70–72.
Notes on a West African tree believed to kill its neighbours, and used by the Bini for protection and for inflicting a curse on an enemy.

1863 Melzian, Hans J.
Zum Festkalendar von Benin. *M.S.O.S.*, 1955: 87–107.
Gives order of various ceremonies and rituals in Benin.

1864 Miles, G. P. L.
Additional notes on Benin altars and compounds. *Ethnol. cran.*, (3) 1938: 5–8.

1865 Sharevskaya, B. I.
Pamyatmik zhertvenogo kul'ta drevnego Benina. *Sov. et*, (3) 1947: 128–140.
On the relic of the sacrificial cult in ancient Benin.

1866 *—Religiya drevnego Benina. In *Ezhegodnik Muzeya istorii religii i ateizma, Leningrad, 1957.*

1866a Thomas, Northcote Whitridge
Agricultural rites. See [1849]

1867 —Astronomy. *Man*, 19, 1919: 179–183 (art. 92).

4. (viii) Recreation, Games

1868 Egharevba, Jacob Uwadiae
Benin games and sports. Benin City [the author] 1949. 27p.

1869 — —2nd ed. 1951. 27p.
Brief account of many traditional games and sports in Benin.

1870 —Ihun—an Edo vbobo. Benin, D.C.C. press, 1950. [i] 26p.
Edo songs.

4. (ix) Stories, Proverbs, Riddles

1871 Aigbe, Emmanuel Ikponmwosa
Iyeva yan ariasen vbe itan Edo na zedu ere ye ebo. 1040 Edo proverbs, with their English translations. [Lagos, the author, 1960] 57p.
Printed by Ribway printers, Lagos. Parallel text in Edo and English.

1872 Akenzua, Edun
The Oba's palace in Benin. *Nig. mag.*, (87) Dec. 1965: 244–251, illus.

1873 Butcher, H. L. M. and Gbinigie, E. O.
Four Edo fables. *Africa*, 10 (3) Jl. 1937: 342–352.
Four Bini fables, reproduced in Bini, with English translation.

1874 Egharevba, Jacob Uwadiae

Some stories of ancient Benin. [Lagos, the author, 1951] 55p.
Printed by Ribway printers, Lagos.

1875 Sidahome, Joseph E.
Stories of the Benin empire. London, Ibadan, Oxford University press, 1964. ix, 196p. illus.
Twelve traditional Bini stories narrated to author by Ishan story-tellers.

4. (x) Material Culture: Sculpture, Carving, Miscellaneous Arts and Crafts

1876 *African art—the relics of royal Benin. *Vanity fair*, (45) Dec. 1935: 18–19.

1877 Art of ancient Benin. *Illus. Lond. news*, (211) 1947: 666–667, illus.

1878 Baumann, H.
Bénin. *Cah. d'art.*, 7 (3–5) 1932: 197–203, illus.

1879 Beier, Horst Ulrich
Idah, an original Bini artist. *Nig. mag.*, (80) Mar. 1964: 5–16, illus.

1880 Benin art and artists. *Nig. today*, 9 (7–8) 1966: 2–7, illus.
Illustrated commentary on Benin art and artists, both ancient and modern.

1881 Benin art seen in Paris show. *Art news*, 30, 1932: 6.

1882 Benin boom continues. *W. Afr.*, (2084) 1957: 278, illus.

1883 Benin bronze panthers from the Ratton collection. *Afr. news*, 34, 1935: 11.

1884 Benin carvings; specimens of Mr. Erhabor's work. *Nig. mag.*, (14) 1938: 146–148, illus.

1885 Benin—City of memories. *W. Afr. rev.*, 31 (397) 1960: 49–53.

1886 Benin crafts. *Teachers' monthly*, 6 (6) Je. 1960:
Summarised in *Oversea quart.*, 2 (4) Dec. 1960: 118.

1887 Benin ebony carvers. *Nig. field*, 12 (2) 1947: 83, illus.
An illustrated note on a modern Benin school of carvers.

1888 Benin ivory. *Connoisseur* [Amer. ed.] 128, 1951: 143.

1889 Benin: letters to the editor. *Ethnol. Cran.*, 2, 1938: 23–26.

1890 Benin's past glories. *Times rev. col.*, 21, 1956: 23, illus.

1891 Blauensteiner, Kurt
Bildwerke aus Benin im Wiener Museum für Völkerkunde. *Belvedere*, 10, 1931: 63–67, illus.

1892 Boston, D.
An early Benin bronze. *Bull. Liverpool libraries, museums and arts committee*, 7 (1) 1958: 3, illus. (on front cover).

1893 Boulton, Laura C.
Bronze artists of West Africa: the natives of Benin and Ife, their beliefs, customs and art forms. *Natural hist.*, 36 (1) Je. 1935: 17–28.

1894 Brass masks of a man in Benin. *Bull*

Chicago art inst., 30, 1936: 35, illus. at p. 29.

1895 The Brassmakers of Benin. *Times rev col.*, (28) 1957: 20, illus.

1896 Braunholtz, H. J.
Two bronze plaques from Benin. *Man*, 22, 1922: 161–162 (art. 91) illus.

1897 Brinkmann, J.
Die Bronzen von Benin. München, 1898. 62p. (Correspondenzblatt der deutschen Gesellschaft für Anthropologie, 29).

1898 Brinkworth, Ian
Benin ancient craft. *W. Afr. rev.*, 30 (382) 1959: 546–547, illus.

1899 —Mud sculpture of Benin. *W. Afr. rev.*, 31 (390) May 1960: 30–31, illus.
British museum
Antiquities from the City of Benin. See [1997].

1900 Bunt, Cyril G. E.
Two examples of Nigerian wood-carving. *Burl. mag.*, 82 (483) Je. 1943: 146–149, illus.
On two carved woods from Benin and on the nature and origin of Nigerian art.

1901 Burland, C. A.
Art of old Benin. *W. Afr. rev.*, 25 (318) 1954: 208–209, illus.

1902 Burland, C. M.
Lost wax: metal casting on the Guinea Coast. *Studio*, 154, Dec. 1957: 18–21, illus.
On Bronze casting in Ife and Benin as well as in Ashanti.

1903 Carré, Louis
Benin, city of bronzes. *Parnassus*, 8, 1953: 13–15.

1904 Carved ivory fly-whisk handle from Benin. *Br. mus. q.*, 4, 1929: 3, illus.

1904a Carver from Benin (F.O. Idubor). *W. Afr.*, 2 Feb, 1957: 102, illus.

1905 Caturla, Eduardo del val
Busto de bronce de Benin. *Cuadernos de historia primitiva* [Madrid] 1 (2) 1946: 102–103, illus.

1906 *Chaves, L.
Bronzes de Benin—a escultura Afro-Portuguesa de Benin. *Sociedad de Geografia de Lisboa. Congresso, vol. centenario, 1946.* pp. 251–370.

1907 Chicago. Natural history museum
The art of Benin: a catalogue of an exhibition of the A. W. F. Fuller and Chicago natural history museum collections of antiquities from Benin, Nigeria, by Philip J. C. Dark. [Chicago, 1962] 74p. plates.

1907a Cordwell, J. M.
The problem of process and form in W. African art. See [1190].

1908 Crowder, Michael
The Chase Manhattan sculpture. *Nig. mag.*, (70) 1961: 285–289, illus.
On the sculpture in concrete at the head office of the Chase Manhattan bank in Lagos, commissioned by the bank and executed by Festus Idehen and Paul Mount.

1909 Dalton, Ormonde Maddock
Booty from Benin. *Eng. illus. mag.*, 18, Jan. 1897: 419–429, illus.

1910 —Note on an unusually fine bronze figure from Benin. *Man*, 3, 1903: 185 (art. 105) illus.
Brief description of a bronze figure of a man brought from Benin and presented to the British Museum.

1911 —Works of art from Benin-City. *J. Anthrop inst.*, 27, 1898: 362–382, illus.
Dark, Philip John Crossley
The art of Benin. See [1907].

1912 —Benin, a West African kingdom. *Discovery*, 18 (5) May 1957: 199–207, illus., map.
The origin of Benin art and especially of bronze casting is discussed. The technique is traced to Ife from where it was introduced into Benin in the 13th century A.D., it having reached Ife itself from Egypt about 600 A.D. through the Kisra migration.

1913 —A preliminary catalogue of Benin art and technology: some problems of material culture analysis. *J.R.A.I.*, 87 (2) Jl.–Dec. 1957: 175–189, illus.

1914 —Two bronze heads from Benin. *Scot. art. rev.*, 8 (1) 1961: 5–11.

1915 Della Santa, E.
Deux remarquables ivoires nigériens de la collection . . . le Prince et Princesse de Ligne au Château de Beloeil. *Bull. Mus. roy. belge d'art et de hist.*, 4e serie, 30, 1958: 111–132, illus.

1916 Dresler, A.
Die Siegener Taufschüssel, ein Zeugnis der sogenannten "Benin-Kultur". *Deutsche kolon. Ztg.*, 52 (9) 1940: 341–342, illus.

1917 Ehenua's bronze: shrine of the hand. *W. Afr. rev.*, 29 (372) Sept. 1958: 750–751, illus.
Illustrations with descriptive notes of a complex bronze work belonging to the Ezomo of Benin, and known as the "Shrine of the hand".

1918 Fagg, William Buller
The Allman collection of Benin antiquities. *Man*, 53, Nov. 1953: 165–169 (art. 261) illus.
Notes on a collection made during the 1897 Benin expedition.

1919 —Un art sans âge. *Jeune afrique* [Elisabethville] Jl.–Sept. 1950: 4–11, illus.

1920 —A bronze figure in Ife style at Benin. *Man*, 50 (98) 1950: 69–70, illus.
Notes close resemblance between a Benin bronze figure and the characteristic Ife head, and sees this as a corroboration of the local belief in Ife origin of Benin sculpture.
—Ife and Benin; two pinnacles of African art. See [5094].

1921 —A Nigerian bronze figure from the Benin expedition. *Man*, 52, 1952: 145 (art. 210) illus.
A bronze figure representing a kneeling hunter with an antelope across its shoulder. Suggests it is of Igbirra or Igala origin.

1922 —On a Benin bronze plaque representing a girl. *Man*, 58, 1958: 105 (art. 154) illus.
Describes one of the many rectangular bronze plaques collected from Benin during the 1897 British expedition.

1923 —The Seligman ivory mask from Benin: the Royal Anthropological Institute Christmas card for 1957. *Man*, 57 (144) Aug. 1957: 113, illus.
On an ivory mask from Benin, owned by Mrs. B. Z. Seligman, and chosen by the R.A.I. for its 1957 Christmas card.

1924 Foote, H. S.
Two bronzes from Benin acquired by Cleveland museum. *Cleveland museum bull.*, 25, 1938: 48–50, illus.

1925 Forbes, H. O.
On a collection of cast metalwork from Benin. *Bull. Liverpool museum*, 1, 1897: 49; 2, 1899: 13.

1926 Forman, W. [and others]
Benin art. London, Batchworth press, for Artia, 1960. 59p. plates, map, bibliog.
Photographs of the leading Benin art objects in the British Museum by W. and B. Forman, with an introduction and descriptive notes by Philip Dark. The introduction gives the pre-history, history and ethnographic significance of Benin art. Useful review by K. C. Murray in *Nig. mag.*, (71) Dec. 1961: 370–378.

1927 —Von der Kunst von Benin, von W. und B. Forman und Philip Dark. [Prague] Artia, 1960. 64p. plates, map.
German ed. of above.

1928 Fox-Pitt-Rivers, Augustus Henry Lane
Antique works of art from Benin; collected by Lieutenant-General Pitt-Rivers. [London] privately printed, 1900. iv, 100p. plates.

1929 Foyle, Arthur M.
Houses in Benin. *Nig. mag.*, (42) 1953: 132–139, illus.

1930 Froehlich, Willy
Das westafrikanische Elfenbeinhorn aus dem 16. Jahrhundert im Reut im Reutenstrauch-Joest-Museum. *Ethnologica*, N. F., (2) 1960: 426–432.
Describes a 16th century ivory horn wind instrument in the Cologne museum and suggests it was carved in Benin or in a place under Benin influence.

1931 *Gaskell, W.
The influence of Europe on early Benin art. *Connoisseur*, Je. 1902.

1932 Goodwin, A. J. H.
Archaeology and Benin architecture. *J. Hist. soc. Nig.*, 1 (2) Dec. 1957: 65–85.
Reports on excavations carried out on several sites in Benin in 1954 and 1956.

1933 —A bronze snake head and other recent

finds in the old palace at Benin. *Man*, 63, 1963: 142–145, (art. 174) illus., bibliog.

1934 Hagen, Karl
Altertümer von Benin in Hamburgischen Museum für Völkerkunde. Hamburg, Lütcke u. Wulff, 1900–1918. 2v. illus., bibliog. (Mitt. Mus. Völkerk., Hamburg, 6).
v. 1. 1900. 26p. illus.
v. 2. 1918. 90p. illus., bibliog.

1935 —Bericht über einen Vortrag von K. Hagen: das Negerreich Benin und seine alte Kunst. *Geog. Gesell. Hamburg. Mitt.*, 16, 250–252.

1936 Hall, Henry Usher
African cups embodying human forms. *Univ. Penn. mus. j.*, 15, 1924: 190–227.

1937 —Congo and West African wood carvings. *Univ. Penn. mus. j.*, 14, 1923: 47–84.

1938 —Fetish figures of equatorial Africa: *Univ. Penn. mus. j.*, 11, 1920: 27–55, illus.

1939 —An ivory standing cup from Benin. *Univ. Penn. mus. j.*, 17 (4) Dec. 1926: 416–432, illus.
Describes the cup and identifies the chief personage carved on it as Olokun.

1940 —A large drum from Benin. *Univ. Penn. mus. j.*, 19 (2) Je. 1928: 130–143, illus.

1941 Hardy, Georges
Un embryon d'art libre: le Bénin et ses abords. In his *L'art nègre; l'art animiste des noirs d'Afrique.* 1927: 145–152. [1124].

1942 Heger, Franz
Die Altertümer von Benin. *Mitt. geog. Gesell.*, [Wien] 44 (1–2) 1901: 9–28, illus.

1943 —Benin und seine Altertümer. *Mitt. anthrop. Gesell.*, [Wien] 29, 1899, Sitzungsb. 2–6.

1944 —Drei merkwürdige Bronze-Figuren von Benin; mit einem Anhange—Die Benin-Sammlung des Naturhistorischen Hofmuseums in Wien. *Mitt. anthrop. Gesell.* [Wien] 46 (4–5) 1916: 132–182, illus.
Describes three metal figures in the Benin collection of the Natural history museum in Vienna. Speculates on significance of decorations on these pieces.

1945 —Merkwürdige Altertümer aus Benin in West-Afrika. Anlässlich der Herausgabe des Werkes F. v. Luschan, 'Die Altertümer von Benin'. *Mitt. geog. Gesell.* [Wien] 64 (4–9) 1921: 104–119.

1946 High sums for Benin bronzes. *Art news*, 28, 1930: 3.

1947 Hooton, E. A.
Benin antiquities in the Peabody Museum. In *Harvard Afr. stud.*, 1, *Varia Africana* (1) 1917: 130–146, illus.

1948 Jeffreys, M. D. W.
Origins of the Benin bronzes. *Afr. stud.*, 10 (2) Je. 1951: 87–92, bibliog.

Discounts the theory that the technique of bronze casting reached Benin through the Portuguese, and holds instead that the Bini acquired the art from the Yoruba. Draws on cultural and traditional evidence to show further, that the art reached Nigeria from the East, via Lake Chad and Bornu, with the Kisra migrations.

1949 —Those Benin bronzes: an explanation of the puzzle offered. *W. Afr. rev.*, 23 (292) Jan. 1952: 5–8, 13, illus., bibliog.

1950 Joyce, T. A.
An ivory ewer from Benin in the British museum. *Man*, 31, 1931: 1–2 (art. 1) illus.

1951 —Note on the relation of the bronze heads to the carved tusks, Benin City. *Man*, 8, 1908: 2–4 (art. 2) illus.
See [1991] for further notes.

1952 Knoedler, M. & co., inc.
Bronzes and ivories from the old kingdom of Benin: exhibition from November 25 to December 14, 1935, at the galleries of M. Knoedler & co., 14 East 57 Street, New York. [Paris, Printed by Dehon, 1935] 36p. illus., maps, bibliog.
Includes an account of "The royal art of Benin" by Louis Carré, pp. 4–9.

1953 Krieger, Kurt
Das Schicksal der Benin-Sammlung des Berliner Museums für Völkerkunde. *Baessler-Archiv*, N.F. 5 (2) 1957: 225–232, illus.

1954 Kus-Nikolajev, Mirko
Beninska plastika i problem migracije (crtezi zdenke sertic) Zagreb, 1931. 32p. illus. (Etnolaska biblioteka, 13).

1955 Kusters, M.
Die figürlichen Darstellungen auf den Beninzähnen des Linden-Museums, Stuttgart. *Jahresbericht des Württembergischen Vereins für Handelsgeographie*, (50) 1932: 116–120.

1956 Labouret, Henri
Les arts du Bénin. *Le Monde colonial illustré.*, 10 (108) Aug. 1932: 150–152.

1957 —Les bronzes à cire-perdue du Benin. *Cah. d'art*, 7, 1932: 204–208, illus.
Also reprinted in its *numéro special*, 1932: 8–12.

1958 Lallemand, Jacqueline
Ivoires et bronzes du Bénin. *Art et décoration*, 61, 1932: 257–264, illus.

Lane-Fox, Augustus Henry. See Fox-Pitt-Rivers, Augustus Henry Lane.

1959 Lang, H.
Famous ivory treasures of a negro king. *J. Amer. mus. nat. hist.*, 18, 1918: 527–552.

Leiden. Rijksmuseum voor Volkerkunde
Die Benin-Sammlung des Reichsmuseums für Völkerkunde in Leiden. See [1971].

1960 Lindblom, Gerhard
Bronsskatterna fren det gamla negerkungariket Benin. *Jorden runt.*, 10 (3) Mar. 1938: 139–144.

1961 —Einige Benin-Bronzen im Staatlichen Ethnographischen Museum in Stockholm. *Z. f. Ethnol.*, 70 (3–5) 1938: 193–198.
Describes the collection and how the bronzes were acquired.

Ling Roth, Henry. See Roth, Henry Ling.

1962 Linné, S.
Masterpiece of primitive art. *Ethnos* [Stockholm] 23 (3–4) 1958: 172–174, illus.
Description of the Seligman ivory mask from Benin. See also Fagg, W. [1923].

1963 Luquet, G. H.
L'art du Bénin au Musée du Trocadéro. *La Nature* [Paris] (2886) Aug. 1st 1932: 97–101.

1964 Luschan, Felix von
Die Altertümer von Benin; mit 889 Abbildungen nach Zeichnungen von B. Ankermann, G. Kilz, L. Sütterlin u.a. Sowie nach Photographien usw., herausgegeben mit Unterstützung des Reichs-Kolonialministeriums, der Rudolf Virchow und der Arthur Baessler-Stiftung. Berlin und Leipzig, Vereinigung Wissenschaftlicher Verleger, 1919. 3v. illus.
v. 1. xii, 522 [26]p.—Text.
v. 2 and 3.—Illustrations consisting of 129 plates. The last 26 pages numbered A–Z. At head of title: Staatliche Museen zu Berlin. Imprint on cover: Berlin, G. Reimer, 1919.

1965 —Benin-platte. *Berl. Gesell. f. anthrop. Verhandl.*, 1899: 633–634.

1966 —Bruchstück einer Benin-platte. *Globus*, 78, 1900: 306–307.

1967 —Die Karl Knorrsche Sammlung von Benin-Altertümer im Museum für Länder—und Völkerkunde in Stuttgart. Stuttgart, Druck von W. Kohlhammer, 1901. [4] 95p. illus.

1968 —Uber Benin-Altertümer. *Z. f. Ethnol.*, 48, 1916: 307–327.
Describes bronze casting from Benin, and attempts to interpret various features on specific castings. Believes the technique reached Benin from Egypt.

1969 Mackenzie, H. F.
Bronze plaque from Benin. *Bull. Chicago art. inst.*, 28, 1934: 19–20, illus.

1970 Malsten, K.
A Benin bench. *Ethnos.*, 2 (4) 1937/38: 199–207.

1971 Marquart, Josef
Die Benin-Sammlung des Reichsmuseums für Völkerkunde in Leiden, beschrieben und mit ausführlichen. Prolegomena zur Geschichte der Handelswege und Völkerbewegungen in Nordafrika. Leiden, Buchhandlung und Druckerei, E. J. Brill, 1913. 16, ccclxvii, 132p. illus., maps. (Veröffentlichungen des Reichsmuseums für Völkerkunde in Leiden, ser. 2, no. 7).

1972 Meyer, H.
Die Altertümer von Benin. *Kol. Runds.*, 1920: 60–68.

1973 Meyerowitz, Eva Levwin Richter
Ancient bronzes in the royal palace at Benin. *Burl. mag.*, 83 (487) Oct. 1934: 248–253, illus.
On the bronzes collected from Benin during the punitive expedition, and on the origin and history of Benin sculpture.

1974 —Four pre-Portuguese bronze castings from Benin. *Man*, 40, Sept. 1940: 129–132 (art. 155) illus.

1975 Miles, G. P. L.
Benin: ring and bronze head: a suggestion. *Ethnol. crans.*, 1, 1937: 11.

1976 Milliken, W. M.
Treasure of ivories and bronzes from the ancient kingdom of Benin. *Bull. Cleveland mus.*, 24, 1937: 34–36, illus.

1977 Monod, Th.
Autour de l'exposition du Bénin. *La terre et la vie*, 2 (9) Sept. 1932: 542–555.

1978 Mud shrines of Olokun. *Nig. mag.*, (50) 1956: 280–295, illus.
Mud shrines erected in honour of the goddess Olokun in Benin and environs.

1979 Murray, Kenneth Crosthwaite
Benin art. *Nig. mag.*, (71) 1961: 370–378, illus.

1980 —Nigerian bronzes: work from Ife. *Antiquity*, 15 (57) Mar. 1941: 71–80, illus.
Contends that the techniques of Benin and Ife bronzes neither evolved in West Africa nor were derived from the Portuguese, but might have come with the Kisra migrations.

1981 A new carver. *Nig. mag.*, (41) 1953: 22–27, illus.
On Felix Idubor.

1982 Olbrechts, Frans M.
Notre ivoire sculpté du Bénin. *Bull. des Musées royaux d'art et d'histoire* [Bruxelles] 3e série, 3e année, (2) Mar. 1931: 51–55.

1983 Page, P. R.
Benin arts and crafts today. *Farm & forest*, 5 (4) Dec. 1944: 161–169, illus.

1984 Paris. Musée de l'homme
. . . Exposition, bronzes et ivoires du Bénin au Musée d'ethnographie, palais du Trocadéro. Paris, "Cahiers d'Art" [1932] 17p. illus. (Cahiers d'art . . . numéro spécial, 7e année, 1932).
Contents: Bénin, par Hermann Baumann, pp. 1–2; Les bronzes à cire-perdu du Bénin, par Henry Labouret, pp. 8–12; Les bronzes du Bénin, par Charles Ratton, pp. 13–17.

1985 *Paulme, Denise
Un problème d'histoire de l'art en Afrique: les bronzes du Bénin. *Comptes rendus sommaires des séances Inst. française anthrop.*, Jan. 1944–Dec. 1946: 4–6.

1986 Pennsylvania. University. Museum

The art of great Benin. *Univ. Penn. mus.*
j., 3 (4) 1912: 76–81.

1987   Pettazzoni, Raffaele
        Avori scolpiti Africani in collezioni
        Italiane; contributo allo studio dell' arte
        'di Benin'. Rome, E. Calzone, 1912. iv,
        44p. illus.

        Pitt-Rivers, Augustus Henry. See Fox-
        Pitt-Rivers, Augustus Henry Lane.

1988   Pittard, Eugène
        L'art du Bénin. *Les Musées de Genève,*
        7 (10) 1950: 3, illus.

1989   Plass, Margaret
        Art of Benin. *Expedition* [Penn. Univ.
        Museum] 1 (4) summer, 1959: 2–6, illus.,
        map.
        Distinguishes two styles of Benin art,
        the court style which developed within
        the city and is symbolised by the bronze
        castings; and the village style which
        flourished outside the capital. Believes
        the former style has been imported into
        Benin and being alien to Benin culture,
        had gradually degenerated.

1990   Powell-Cotton, P. H. C.
        Benin brass-casting and handicrafts in
        the Cameroons. *Man,* 32, 1932: 284 (art.
        329).

1991   Punch, Cyril
        Further notes on the relations of the
        bronze heads to the carved tusks, Benin
        City. *Man,* 8, 1908: 84 (art. 44) illus.
        See also [1951].

1992   Quick, Richard
        Notes on Benin carvings. *Reliq. illus.
        arch.,* 5, 1899: 248.

1993   Rachewiltz, Boris de
        Incontro con l'arte africana, Milano,
        Aldo Martello, 1959. 7 p.l., 246p. illus.
        African art generally, but with Benin
        and Ife featuring prominently.

1994   Ratton, Charles
        Les bronzes du Bénin. *Cah. d'art,* 7,
        1932: 209–216, illus.

1995   Read, Charles Hercules
        Notes on certain ivory carvings from
        Benin. *Man,* 10, 1910: 49–51. (art. 29)
        illus.

1996   —On a carved object from Benin in the
        British Museum. *Man,* 18, 1918: 129–
        130 (art. 72) illus.

1997   Read, Charles Hercules and Dalton,
        Ormonde Maddock
        Antiquities from the city of Benin and
        from other parts of West Africa in the
        British museum. London, British
        museum, sold by Longmans, 1899 [vi]
        61p. illus. (incl. 32 plates).

1998   —Works of art from Benin city. *J.A.I.,*
        27, 1898: 362–378.

1999   The Recovery of Benin antiquities. *Nig.
        mag.,* (32) 1949: 63–71, illus.

2000   Rivière, Georges-Henri
        L'art du Bénin au Musée d'ethnographie
        du Trocadéro. *L'Afrique française,* Jl.
        1932: 394–397.

2001   Rogers, M. R.
        Bronze head of a youth, Benin, Nigeria,
        1360–1500 A.D. *Bull. St., Louis mus.,*
        (22) 1937: 9–11, illus.

2002   Roth, Henry Ling
        Examples of metal work from Benin.
        Halifax naturalist, Je. 1898: 32–38, illus.

2003   —Notes on Benin art. *Reliq., illus. arch.,*
        4, 1898: 161, illus.

2004   *—Personal ornaments from Benin.
        Bull. Mus. sci. and art, [Philadelphia]
        2 (1) 1899: illus.

2005   —Primitive art from Benin. *Studio,* 15:
        1898: 174–183, illus.

2006   —Stray articles from Benin. *Int. arch.
        ethnog.,* 13, 1900: 194–197, illus.

2007   Rousseau, Madeleine
        Benin—Königreich der klassischen
        afrikanischen Kunst. *Afrika,* 2 (10) Oct.
        1960: 399–402, illus.

2008   Sachs, H. F. inc., New York. Art gallery
        African bronzes from Ife and Benin;
        exhibition from Nov. 11 to Dec. 6, 1941,
        at the gallery of H. F. Sachs, inc., 63
        East 52nd Street, New York [New York,
        H. F. Sachs, 1941] [16]p. illus.
        Descriptive illustrated catalogue of
        fifteen bronzes, with introduction by
        James Sweeney.

2009   Schweeger-Exeli, Annemarie
        Ein Elfenbeinblashorn aus Benin. *Arch.
        f. Völkerkde.,* 13, 1958: 227–235, illus.
        Describes a Benin ivory blowing-horn
        received at the "Museum für Völker-
        kunde" in Vienna.

2010   —Zur Thematik und Ikonographie der
        geschnitzten Elfenbeinzähne aus Benin
        im Museum für Völkerkunde in Wien.
        Arch. f. Völkerkde. 12, 1957: 182–229,
        illus.
        An extended study and interpretation
        of the thematics and iconography of
        four carved ivory tusks from Benin now
        in the Ethnographic museum in Vienna.

2011   Segy, Ladislas
        African snake symbolism. *Archiv. f.
        Völkerkde.,* 9, 1954: 103–114, illus.
        Notes examples of snake symbolism
        in Benin wood-carving and assigns
        Benin origin to similar phenomenon
        in Dahomey, Togo, Ghana, and
        Cameroons.

2012   Sölken, Heinz
        Innerafrikanische Wege nach Benin.
        Anthropos, 49 (5–6) 1954: 809–933, map.

2013   Stoll, Otto
        Zur Frage der Benin Altertümer. *Int.
        Arch. f. Ethnog.,* 15 (5) 1902: 161–166.

        Sweeney, James Johnson
        African bronzes from Ife and Benin. See
        [2008].

2014   Sydow, Eckart von.
        Ancient and modern art in Benin City.
        Africa, 11 (1) Jan. 1938: 55–62, illus.,
        bibliog.

2015   *—Bronzen aus Benin. *Kunst.* 65, 1932:
        378–380.

2016   —Zur Chronologie der Benin-Platten.
        Jahresbericht des Württembergischen

Vereins für Handelsgeographie, 1932: 121–128.

2017 —Zur Chronologie von Benin-Ornamenten. *Ethnol. Anzeiger*, 4, 1935: 31–38.

2018 —Kunst und Kulte von Benin. *Atlantis*, 10, 1938: 46–56, illus.

2019 Thomas, Northcote Whitridge
Decorative art among the Edo-speaking peoples of Nigeria. 1. Decoration of buildings. *Man*, 10, 1910: 65–66 (art. 37) illus.

2020 —Metal work. *Man*, 18, 1918: 184–186 (art. 100).

2021 —Note on an object from Benin. *Man*, 20, 1920: 109–110 (art. 53).

2022 —Pottery making of the Edo-speaking people. *Man*, 10, 1910: 97–98 (art. 53).

2022a Val Caturla, Eduardo del. See Caturla, Eduardo del val.

2023 Vaughan, M.
Exceptional Benin ivory at Brooklyn Museum. *Connoisseur* [Amer. ed.] 144, Sept. 1959: 67–68.

2024 Webster, W. D.
Catalogues of ethnographic specimens from Australia, New Zealand . . . Benin City, and other parts of Africa . . . Leicester, 1911. 3v. illus.

2025 Wenger, Susanne
Drawings of pagan ceremonies by a Christian boy from Ora. *Odù*, (2) 1955: 3–13, illus.
Six drawings, with explanatory notes. Ora is in Benin Province.

2025a Willett, Frank
On the funeral effigies of Owo and Benin. See [5200].

2026 Wolf, Siegfried
Bemerkungen zu drei Benin-Gelbgussköpfen des Museums für Völkerkunde, Leipzig. *Abh. u. Ber. staatl. Mus. Völkerkde.* [Dresden] 22, 1963: 109–134, illus., bibliog.
Three cast brass heads from Benin in the Ethnographic museum at Leipzig are described, with an attempt at dating and interpreting them.

2027 —Die Gelbguss-Köpfe der Dresdener Benin-Sammlung. Beschreibung und Vergleich. *Abh. u. Ber. staatl. Mus. Völkerkde.* [Dresden] 21, 1962: 91–121, illus., bibliog.
Describes and compares brass heads in the Benin collection at Dresden.

2028 —Vogelgestaltiges Benin-Zeremonialgerät aus Elfenbein. *Abh. u. Ber. staatl. Mus. Völkerkde.*, 22, 1963: 135–142, illus., bibliog.
Describes bird-shaped ivory implements from Benin and relates the ceremonial associated with them to the absolute power of the Oba.

2029 —Zwei Benin-Arbeiten im Staatlichen Museum für Völkerkunde Dresden: Vogelgestaltiges Zeremonialgerät und Relief-platte mit Vogel. *Veröff. Mus. Völkerkde.* [Leipzig] (1) 1961: 719–738.

Description of two Benin castings in the State Museum of Ethnography in Dresden.

2030 Zwernemann, Jürgen
Die Benin-Maske des Linden-Museums. *Tribus*, (14) Aug. 1965: 149–159, illus.
An ivory mask from Benin now in the Linden Museum is carefully described and compared with masks in the British Museum and other collections.

5. LINGUISTIC STUDIES

2031 Addeh, B. I.
Okha Esan isinlin. Ibadan, Ministry of education, Adult education branch, 1956. 17p.
Adult education pamphlet, Ishan.

2031a Aigbe, E. I.
Iyeva yan ariasen vbe itan Edo . . . See [1871]

2032 Aihe, Jos. Osam.
Ruẹ Ẹdo kevbe ebo nazẹ. Learn to speak Edo and English. Pt. II. Benin City, W.P.P., 1964. 36p. illus., maps.

2033 *Butcher, H. L. M.
Elementary dictionary of the Bini language. [Lagos?] C.M.S., 1936.

2033a Butcher, H. L. M. and Gbinigie, E. B.
Four Edo fables. See [1873].

2034 Dennett, R. E.
Notes on the language of the Efa (people) or the Bini commonly called Uze Ado. *J. Afr. soc.*, 3 (10) Jan. 1904: 142–153.
Brief grammatical notes.

2035 Ebe ene ewanlẹn. Ibadan, Ministry of education, Adult education branch 1956. 28p. illus.
Adult education, pamphlet, Ishan.

2036 Edegbe, Joshua E.
Benin-English grammar. Lagos, C.M.S. bookshop, 1936. 62p.

2037 *—Emwe Ebo kevbe Edo (English and Edo syntax) Lagos, C.M.S. bookshop, 1935.

2038 Egharevba, Jacob Uwadiae
Ama z'evbo omwan tawiri. Who does not speak his native language is lost. [Benin, the author] 1956. 44p. front.
Printed by Olowonilara printing press, Benin. Alternate chapters in Bini and English.

2039 —Ọzedu—interpreter. 2nd ed. enlarged. [Benin, the author] 1953. 24p. Printed by Ribway printers, Lagos.
Mostly a collection of 236 short sentences in Bini, with English translation.

2040 Eguavon, Samuel Igbinoghenen
Ebe Edo [books] 1–IV. Benin City, Mrs. G. O. and Imalele Eguavon, 1950–56. 4v. illus.
Printed by C.M.S. (Nigeria) press, Port Harcourt.

2041 —Ebe Edo V. Illustrated by O. I. Osula. Benin City, Imalele Eguavon, 1959. 95p. illus.

Printed by C.M.S. press, Port Harcourt.

2042 —Itan Edo. Benin City, Mrs G. O. Eguavon, 1956. 40p. (incl. front cover).
Printed by Alebiosu press, Odogbolu.

2043 Igodan, E. O.
Egui nei fo vbe okha I. [Ibadan, Ministry of health and social welfare, 1958] 23p. illus.

2044 Ishan divisional education committee
R ebe esan I: compiled by a sub-committee of the Ishan divisional education committee, May 1950. Aba, Assemblies of God press [1950] 40p. illus.

2045 Iyawe, J. I. O.
Oseikpo. [Ibadan, Ministry of health and social welfare, 1958] 27p. illus.

2046 Melzian, Hans J.
A concise dictionary of Bini-language of Southern Nigeria. London, K. Paul, Trench, Trubner, 1937. xviii, 233p.

Based on research by author in Benin, with three Bini men, including J. U. Egharevba, author of *A short history of Benin* [1802] as chief informants, and on the works of H. L. M. Butcher, *Bini dictionary* [2033] and N. W. Thomas's *Anthropological report on the Edo-speaking peoples* [1780] Intonation of words and sentences indicated in five levels represented with dots in descending order as in I. C. Ward's *The phonetic and tonal structure of Efik* [3084].

2047 —Zum Konsonantismus in den Dialekten der Beningruppe. *Archiv für vergleichende Phonetik. (Archiv für die gesamte Phonetik)* 6 (2), 1942: 49–58.

2048 —Vergleichende Charakteristik des Verbums im Bini (Südnigerien) Berlin, Institut für Lautforschung an der Universität Berlin, 1942. 131p. (Arbeiten aus dem Institut für Lautforschung an der Universität Berlin, no. 12).
Phil. F. thesis, Univ. of Berlin, 1940.

Compares and contrasts Bini verb with that of other neighbouring languages, especially those of the Kwa group.

2049 Oghe Edo (Benin reader, book I). Lagos, C.M.S. bookshop, 1934. 24p.

2050 —(Benin reader, book II). Lagos, C.M.S. bookshop, 1934. 32p.

2051 Strub, P. E.
Essai d'une grammaire de la langue Kukuruku (Nigéria, Afrique Occidentale) *Anthropos*, 10–11, 1915–16: 450–465, 888–907.

2052 Thomas, Northcote Whitridge
Anthropological report on the Edo-speaking peoples of Nigeria. London, Harrison, 1910. 2v.
Part II. Linguistics, ix, 251p.

2053 —Notes on Kukuruku. *Man*, 17, 1917: 43–45 (art. 32).
Linguistic notes on the Wano dialect of Afenmai, with text of a story.

2054 Uwaifo, Hawdon Omoregbe
A guide to the writing of the Bini language. Part I. [Benin, the author, 1954] 15p.
Printed by Union printing press, Ibadan. Text in English and Bini.

2055 Wescott, Roger W.
A Bini grammar. 1. Phonology. 2. Morphology. 3. Lexemics. New Haven, Conn., Bartlett Hofman, 1962–1963. 119, 34, 168p.

2056 —The metalinguistics of Bini: a West African language. *Anthrop. ling.*, 2 (6) Je. 1960: 19–21.

—Speech-tempo and the phonemics of Bini. *J. Afr. lang.*, 4 (3) 1965: 182–190.

2057 Westermann, Diedrich
Das Edo in Süd-Nigerien. Seine Stellung innerhalb der Kwa-Sprachen. *MSOS*, 29, 1926: 32–60 (Westsudanische Studien, 3).

EGEDE

Including :

Akweya
Etulo *(Turu, Turumawa, Utur)*

Yachi *(Iyace, Iyashi)*

1. GENERAL AND ETHNOGRAPHIC STUDIES

2058 Armstrong, Robert G.
The Akweya-Yachi (Iyace) In *Peoples of the Niger-Benue confluence by Daryll Forde [and others] 1955*: 148–150.

2059 —The Egede. In *Peoples of the Niger-Benue confluence, by Daryll Forde [and others] 1955*: 140–147, map.
Ethnographic sketch.

2060 —The Etulo. In *Peoples of the Niger-Benue confluence, by Daryll Forde [and others] 1955*: 134–135.
Brief notes on the Etulo or Utur (also called Turu, Turumawa).

2061 Iyashi. In *Notes on the tribes . . . by O. Temple. 2nd ed. 1922, repr. 1965*: 161.

Watson, C. G. B.
Death and burial among the Yakoro and Yache. See [2120]

2. LINGUISTIC STUDIES

2062 Armstrong, Robert G.
Notes on Etulo. *J. West Afr. lang.*, 1 (2) Jl. 1964: 57–60.
Notes on the language.

2063 Ugbei ka ononyi ka je upu. [Zaria, Norla, 1958] 19p.

Adult literature pamphlet in Egede.

EKOI

Including:

Abayong *(Abaiyonga)*
Abine *(Abani)*
Adun *(Aran)*
Agoi
Akaju *(Ahaju)*
Anyang *(Anjang, Bascho)*
Asiga *(Essiga)*
Atam
Banyang *(Banjang, Konguan,*
    Manyang)
Bete
Boki *(Nki)*
Effium
Ejagham
Ekparabong
Ekumuru *(Ikumuru)*
Ekuri
Enna
Etung
Keaka

Korop *(Korawp)*
Manta
Mbe *(Mbube)*
Mbembe
Nde *(Ndei)*
Nkokolle
Obang
Ododop *(Erorup)*
Ogoja
Okoiyang
Okpoto-Mteze *(Okpoto-Mtezi)*
Olulumaw
Orri
Oshopong *(Eshupum)*
Ufia *(Utoblo, Utobono)*
Uge
Ukelle
Utonkon
Yakoro *(Yakori)*
Yakurr *(Yako)*

Many of the ethnic names listed here are not specifically mentioned in the literature. But because of the profusion of ethnic and clan divisions in the area, it is thought useful to list these divisions so as to bring into focus the total extension of the heading chosen. The general works on the area of course treat many of these groups.

1. GENERAL WORKS

2064 Arden-Close, C.
The Cross River Country in 1895. *Geog. j.*, 98, 1941: 189–197.

2065 Mansfeld, Alfred
Urwalddokumente. Vier Jahre unter den Crossflussnegern Kameruns. Berlin, D, Reimer (E. Vohsen), 1908. xvi, 310p. illus., maps.

2066 Ogoja project. *Africa*, 35 (1) Jan. 1965: 102.
Brief notice in the "Notes and news" section.

2067 Parkinson, John
A note on the Efik and Ekoi tribes of the Eastern Provinces of Southern Nigeria. *J.R.A.I.*, 37 [n.s. 10] 1907: 261–267, illus.

2068 Talbot, Percy Amaury
Land of the Ekoi, Southern Nigeria. *Geog. j.*, 36, 1910: 637–656.

2069 Udo, R. K.
Problems of developing the Cross River district of Eastern Nigeria. *J. trop. geog.*, 20, Je. 1965: 65–72, maps, bibliog.

2070 Walker, J. B.

Notes on the visit, in May 1875, to the Old Calabar and Qua Rivers, the Ekoi country, and the Qua rapids. *Proc. Roy. geog. soc.*, 20, 1875–76: 224–230.

2. PHYSICAL ANTHROPOLOGY

Keith, Arthur
On certain physical characters of the negroes of the Congo Free State and Nigeria.
See [578].

2071 Talbot, Percy Amaury
Measurements of Nkokolle, Cross River, Southern Nigeria, *Man*, 13, 1913: 201–202, (art. 108).

3. SOCIAL AND CULTURAL ANTHROPOLOGY, ETHNOGRAPHY

2072 Allison, Philip A.
Carved stone figures in the Ekoi country of the middle Cross River, Eastern Nigeria. *Man*, 62, Feb. 1962 (art. 15); 17–19, illus.
Detailed description of carved stones found in the mid-Cross River region. See also [2107] and [2111].

2073 Anene, J. C.
The Nigeria-Southern Cameroon boundary: an ethno-political analysis. *J. Hist. soc. Nig.*, 2 (2) Dec. 1961: 186–195.
Historical view of the ethno-political structure of the area sketched to indicate whether local historical and ethnic factors had any influence in the delimitation of the boundary, and the

subsequent effect of the boundary on the indigenous ethnic groupings in the area.

2074   Armstrong, Robert G.
       The Utonkon-Effium. In *Peoples of the Niger-Benue confluence, by D. Forde [and others] 1955*: 151–152.

2075   'Bushman'
       Placating the ancestor. *Nig. field,* 1 (1) 1931: 24–25.
       Ancestor worship among the Boki of Ogoja Province.

2076   —Symbolic chiefs on the Cross River. *Nig. field,* (5), Oct. 1932: 15–17.
       Notes on "priestly" chiefs and on the rites and ceremonies associated with their offices.

2077   Byström, U.
       Notes on the Ekparabong clan, Cross River district, Ogoja Province in S.E. Nigeria. *Orientalia suecana,* [Uppsala] 3, 1954: 3–26.

2078   Charles, Enid and Forde, Cyril Daryll
       Notes on some population data from a southern Nigerian village. *Sociol. rev.,* 30 (2) Apr. 1938: 145–160.
       On fertility and reproduction rate in Ugep (Umor) in Obubra Division.

2079   Dayrell, Elphinstone
       Folk stories from Southern Nigeria, West Africa. With an introduction by Andrew Lang. London, New York, Longmans, Green, 1910. xv, 159p. front.

2080   —Further notes on Nsibidi signs with their meanings, from the Ikom district, Southern Nigeria. *J.R.A.I.,* 41, 1911: 521–540, illus.

2081   —Ikom folk stories from Southern Nigeria. London, R.A.I.G.B.I., 1913. viii, 102p. illus. (R.A.I. Occasional paper no. 3).

2082   —The incest tabu. *Man,* 11, 1911: 153–154 (art. 94).

2083   —Notes on "Nyam Tunerra" or cats' cradle. *Man,* 12, 1912: 156–158 (art. 87) illus.
       On various knots tied in Ikom area and their meaning.

2084   —Some "Nsibidi" signs. *Man,* 10, 1910: 113–114 (art. 67) illus.

2085   Einstein, Carl
       Masque de danse rituelle Ekoi. *Documents,* (7) 1927: 396.

2086   Forde, Cyril Daryll
       The context of belief: a consideration of fetishism among the Yakö. [Liverpool] University Press, 1958. 30p. (The Frazer lectures, 1958).
       Later reprinted in author's *Yako studies,* pp. 254–283 [2103].

2087   —Death and succession: an analysis of Yakö mortuary ceremonial. In *Essays on the ritual of social relations, ed. M. Gluckman, 1962*: 89–123.

2088   —Double descent among the Yakö. In *African systems of kinship and marriage,*

ed. A. R. Radcliffe-Brown and Daryll Forde, 1950*: 285–332.
       Also reprinted (with slight omissions) in author's *Yakö studies,* pp. 85–134.

2089   —Fission and accretion in the patrilineal clans of a semi-Bantu community in Southern Nigeria. *J.R.A.I.,* 68, Jl.–Dec. 1938: 311–338.

2090   —Government in Umor: a study of social change and problems of indirect rule in a Nigerian village community. *Africa,* 12 (2) Apr. 1939: 129–162.
       Analysis of indigenous social and administrative structure in Ugep in Obubra Division of Eastern Nigeria, and of the effect on it of new elements and innovations introduced by the British in the process of indirect rule. Summary in French, p. 162.

2091   —The governmental roles of associations among the Yakör. *Africa,* 31 (4) Oct. 1961: 309–323.
       Reviews governmental and administrative systems among the Yakö and shows that political authority is considerably influenced by the role of self-perpetuating associations with acknowledged ritual and/or secular authority.

2092   —Integrative aspects of the Yakö first fruits rituals. *J.R.A.I.,* 79 (1–2) 1945: 1–10, illus.
       Also reissued in author's *Yakö studies,* pp. 234–253. [2103].

2093   —Kinship in Umor—double unilateral organisation in a semi-Bantu society. *Amer. anthrop. n.s.,* 41 (4) Oct.–Dec. 1939: 523–553.

2094   —Land and labour in a Cross River village, Southern Nigeria. *Geog. j.,* 90, 1937: 24–51.
       Reprinted in his *Yakor studies,* pp. 1–30.

2095   —Marriage and family among the Yakö in South Eastern Nigeria. 2nd ed. London, published for the Int. African Inst. by P. L. Humphries, 1951. [vii] 121p. front., illus., tables.
       1st ed. "published in 1941 as no. 5 in the London School of Economics and Political Science series of monographs on social anthropology."

2096   —On some further unconsidered aspects of descent. *Man,* 63, Jan. 1963 (art. 9): 12–13.
       A critical comment on the meaning and usage of the term descent as advocated in Dr. E. Leach's article "On certain unconsidered aspects of double descent system" (*Man,* 1962, 214). Frequent illustrations from the Yakö.

2097   —Rôle des sociétés dans le cérémonial funéraire des Yakö. *Cah. étud. afr.,* 3 (3) 1963: 307–317.

2098   —Social change in a West African village community. *Man,* 37, Jan. 1937 (art. 5) 10–12.
       On the problems affecting traditional governmental system in Ugep, Obubra

Division, South-Eastern Nigeria, following rapid social and economic changes.

2099 —Spirits, witches and sorcerers in the supernatural economy of the Yakö. *J.R.A.I.*, 88 (2) Jl.–Dec. 1958: 165–178.
Also reprinted in author's *Yakö studies*, pp. 210–233.

2100 —Une analyse sociologique des formalités matrimoniales chez les Yakö. *Cah. étud. afr.*, 3 (4) 1963: 447–457.

2101 —Unilineal fact or fiction: an analysis of the composition of kin-groups among the Yakö. In *Studies in kinship and marriage, ed. I. Schapera. 1963:* 38–57.

2102 —Ward organization among the Yakö *Africa*, 20 (4) Oct. 1950: 267–289, illus., map.
A study of the social and administrative organisation in Yakö villages. French summary, p. 289. Also reissued in author's *Yakö studies*, pp. 135–164.

2103 —Yakö studies. London, Ibadan, O. U. P., for Int. Afr. Inst., 1964. xv, 288p. front., illus., maps.
A collection of author's studies of the Yakö published in various journals and books over the past 25 years and based on field work undertaken in 1935 and 1939. The studies are presented as they were originally written and deal with various aspects of Yakö culture.

2104 Harris, Rosemary L.
The influence of ecological factors and external relations on the Mbembe tribes of South-East Nigeria. *Africa*, 32 (1) Jan. 1962: 38–51, map.
Analytical study of environmental factors which can throw light on the history of the Mbembe people in the late 19th century.

2105 —Intestate succession among the Mbembe of South-Eastern Nigeria. In *Studies in the laws of succession in Nigeria, edited by J. D. M. Duncan, 1965:* 91–138.

2106 —Mbembe chiefs: a study of chiefship among the Mbembe of the middle Cross River, S.E. Nigeria, with special reference to the role of chiefs in the Adun, Okum and Osopong Mbembe groups. 1961.
Ph.D. thesis, London.

2107 —A note on sculptured stones in the mid-Cross River area of South-east Nigeria. *Man*, 59, Jl. 1959: 113–114 (art. 177) illus., map.
Describes carved stones found in a region where they are uncommon, and which according to local tradition were erected as funeral monuments. See also [2072] and [2111].

2108 —The political organisation of Mbembe, Nigeria. London, H.M.S.O., 1965. viii, 224p. front., illus., maps, bibliog. (Ministry of overseas development. Overseas research publication, no. 10).
In two parts. Part 1 surveys the political and social features characteristic of all Mbembe communities, while part 2 presents a detailed study of each of the, three Mbembe sub-groups—Osopong Okum and Adun—noting in particular the main variations in their political and social structures.

2109 —The political significance of double unilineal descent. *J.R.A.I.*, 92 (1) Jan.-Je. 1962: 86–101, bibliog.
An exhaustive study, based largely on the Mbembe and Yakö.

2110 Jeffreys, M. D. W.
Some notes on the Ekoi *J.R.A.I.*, 69 (1) 1939: 95–108.
Ethnographic notes.

2110a N'Idu, Ado
Ekpe: Cross River cult. See [2945].

2111 Partridge, Charles
Cross River natives; being some notes on the primitive pagans of Obubra hill district, Southern Nigeria; including a description of the circles of upright sculptured stones of the left bank of the Aweyong River. London, Hutchinson, 1905. xvi, 332p. illus,. maps.

2112 Rosevear, D. R.
A method of ornamenting the skin. *Nig. field.*, 5 (2) Apr. 1936: 69–72, illus.
The process followed and the herb preparation used in skin ornamentation in the Cross River area.

2113 Staschewski, F.
Die Banyangi. *Baessler Archiv*, 7, 1917: (Beihefte 8): 66, illus.

2114 Sydow, Eckart von
Masques-Janus du Cross-river. *Documents*, (6) 1930: 321–328, illus.

2115 Talbot, Percy Amaury
In the shadow of the bush. London, William Heinemann, 1912. xiv, 500p. front., plates.
A general ethnographic description of the Ekoi of Oban district.

2116 —Notes on the Ekoi. *Nat. geog., mag.*, 23, 1912: 33–38.

2117 —Nsibidi signs. In his *In the shadow of of the bush, 1912*: 447–461.

2118 —Two Ekoi stories. *Man*, 13, 1913: 6–8 (art. 4).
Ekoi and English texts.

2119 Watson, C. B. G.
Burial among the Akaju of Ogoja Division, Southern Nigeria. *Man*, 30, Nov. 1930: 202–203 (art. 144).

2120 —Death and burial among the Yakoro and Yache peoples of Ogoja Division, Southern Nigeria. *Man*, 30, May 1930: 81–84 (art. 66) illus.

4. LINGUISTIC STUDIES

2121 Bamgbose, Ayo
Nominal classes in Mbe. *Afr. u. Übersee*, 49 (1) 1966: 32–53.
Mbe is spoken in parts of Mbube Local Council area in Ogoja Division.

2122 Crabb, David W.
The dia-phonemic principle in field

work. *Sierra Leone lang. rev.*, (44, 1965: 91–94.

2123   —Ekoid Bantu languages of Ogoja, Eastern Nigeria. Part 1: Introduction, phonology and comparative vocabulary. Cambridge, C.U.P., in association with West African Languages Survey and Institute of African Studies, Ibadan, 1965. xii, 108p. maps, bibliog. (West African language monographs, no. 4).

2124   Edmondson, T. and Bendor-Samuel, J. T. Tone patterns of Etung. *J. Afr. lang.*, 5 (1) 1966: 1–6.

2125   Jeffreys, M. D. W. A note on the Ekoi language. *Z.f.E.S.*, 35 (3–4) Je. 1950: 260–263.

2126   Johnston, Harry Hamilton Vocabularies of the six tribes in the Oban district. In *In the shadow of the bush, by P. A. Talbot, 1912*: 424–445. Comparative vocabularies of Ekoi, Kwa, Efik, Ekuri, Ododop and Uyanga.

2127   Kaehler-Meyer, E. Linguistic specimens from Mbembe country in Bamenda District, Cameroon. *Afr. u. Übersee*, 37 (3) Aug. 1953: 108–118; (4) Nov. 1953: 151–182.

2128   Mansfeld, Alfred Urwald-Dokumente. Berlin, D. Reimer, 1908. xvi, 310p. Includes (pp. 269–309) grammatical notes on Ekoi, and vocabularies with phrases, of Ekoi, Boki, Keaka, Obang, Anyang and Banyang and a text in Ekoi. See full entry, at [2065].

2129   Talbot, Percy Amaury A short grammar of the Ekoi language. In his *In the shadow of the bush, 1912*: 416–423.

2130   Winston, F. D. D. The nominal class system of Lokö. *Afr. lang. stud.*, (3), 1962: 49–70. Lokö is the language spoken by the Yakö (in Ugep) Obubra Division, Ogoja Province.

FULANI

(Felata, Fellan, Fellani, Fellata, Filani, Foula, Foulah, Foulbe, Ful, Fula, Fulata, Fulbe, Fulde, Fulfulde, Peul, Poular, Pular, Pullo, Toucouleur, Tukulor)

Works listed here in the General and Ethnographic sections are in the main limited to those dealing with the Fulani in Nigeria. But in the Linguistic section, there is no such limitation.

1. GENERAL

2131   Arnett, Edward John Gazetteer of Sokoto Province. London, Waterlow, 1920. 72p.

2132   *Ba, Amadow Hampaté and Dieterlen, Germaine Koumen: texte initiatique des pasteurs peul. *Cah. l'hom.*, *n.s.*, (1) 1961: Clive, P. A. Notes on a journey to Pali and Mamaidi in the Kingdom of Bauchi, See [2401].

2133   Crowther, Samuel Adjai Trois états foulbés du Soudan occidental et central: le Fouta, le Macina, l'Adamaoua, *Annales de l'Université de Grenoble*, 8, 1896: 257–309.

2134   Daggash, Musa Adamawa Province. *Farm and forest*, 8 (1) 1947: 19–23, map.

2135   Ekwensi, Cyprian Odiatu Duaka Burning grass: a story of the Fulani of Northern Nigeria. Illustrations by A. Folarin. Ibadan, Heinemann, 1962. 150p.

2136   —Three weeks among the Fulani. *Nigeria, 1960*: 124–133, illus.

2137   Hollis, Rosemary Sketching Fulani. *Nig. field*, 30 (1) Jan. 1965: 41–45, illus.

Brief notes on the nomadic Fulani, with five illustrative sketches.

2138   Homburger, Lilian Les peuls. *J. Soc. afr.*, 32 (2) 1962: 331–332.

2139   Lhote, H. Les Peuls. *Ency. colon. et maritime mens.*, 1, Mar. 1951: 66–69.

2140   *Mizon, L. Les royaumes Foulbes du Soudan central. Paris, 1895.

2140a Notes on the Filane. In *Notes on the tribes . . . by O. Temple, 2nd ed., 1922, repr. 1965*: 396–404.

2141   S., W. J. S. and K., M. W. The city of Sokoto. *Corona*, 2 (3) Mar. 1950: 107–109; (4) Apr. 1950: 135–137; May 1950: 187–189. First two instalments by W. J. S. S., and the last instalment by M. W. K.

2142   Williams, Henry Fulani boy. London, Routledge & K. Paul, 1963. viii, 150p. illus., map. A novel.

2. PHYSICAL ANTHROPOLOGY

2143   Blumberg, B. S. [and others] The blood groups of the pastoral Fulani of Northern Nigeria and the Yoruba of Western Nigeria. *Amer. j. phys. anthrop.*, 19, 1961: 195–201.

2143a Blumberg, B. S. and Gentile, Zora Haptoglobins and transferrins of two tropical populations. *Nature*, 189, 1961: 897–9.

Micronesian inhabitants of Rongelap Atoll, Marshall Islands, and the Fulani of Nigeria.

2144 Girard, H.
Notes anthropométriques sur quelques Soudanais occidentaux: Malinkés, Bambaras, Foulahs, Soninkés, etc. *Anthropologie*, 13, 1902: 41–56, 167–181, 329–347.

2144a Lawler, Sylvia D. (and others)
The Lewis and secretor characters in the Fulani and Habe. *Ann. hum. genet.*, 24, 1960: 271–82.

3. SOCIAL AND CULTURAL ANTHROPOLOGY

(i) General

2145 Arnott, D. W.
The far-flung Fulani. *Nig. mag.*, (75) Dec. 1962: 15–25, illus.
Description of the Fulani in West Africa, from Gambia and Senegal in the West Atlantic to the Lake Chad area and Cameroon. Notes, among other things, some distinctions between the nomadic and the settled Fulani, their distribution over this broad area, their ways of life, especially fashions in hair styles and dress, their houses, and types of cattle.

2146 Bã, Amadou Hampaté
Culture peule. *Pres. afr.*, (8–9–10) juin–nov., 1956: 85–97.

2147 Bello, Ahmadu
My life. Cambridge, C. U. P., 1962. x, 245p. illus., maps.

2148 Buisson, E. M.
Caractères descriptifs de quelques Foulbé nobles de Maroua (Haut Cameroun) *J. Soc. afr.*, 3 (2) 1933: 283–288.

2149 Brackenbury, E. A.
Notes on the 'Bororo Fulbe' or nomad 'Cattle Fulani'. *J. Afr. soc.*, 23 (91) Apr. 1924: 208–217; (92) Jl.: 271–277.
In Yola Province of Northern Nigeria.

2150 Chapman, P. R.
Cow Fulani: an impression. *Nig. field*, 24 (3) Jl. 1959: 120–121.
Account of the "Cow" Fulani of the Bamenda Highlands.

2151 Crowder, Michael
Cattle Fulani. *W. Afr. rev.*, 26 (329) Feb. 1955: 133–139, illus.

2152 Crozals, Jacques M. F. J. de
Les peuls, étude d'ethnologie africaine. Paris, Maisonneuve, 1883. 269p.

2153 Dainville, Jacques de
Habitations et types de peuplement sur la rive occidentale du lac Tchad. *Rev. géog. humaine et ethnol.*, 1 (2) avr.–juin 1948: 59–69, illus.
On the Fulani, Duduma and Tubu.

2154 Daniel, F.
Shehu dan Fodio. *J. Afr. soc.*, 25 (99) Apr. 1926: 278–283.
Brief biographical sketch of his career.

2155 De St. Croix, F. W.
The cattle Fulani's modest requirements entail no housing problem. *Farm & forest*, 11, 1952: 15–17.

2156 —The Fulani of Northern Nigeria; some general notes. Lagos, Govt. printer, 1944. 74p.
Descriptive account covering among other topics, legends of origin, discipline and leadership, marriage customs and inheritance, games and festivals, diet, beliefs and sundry rites.

2157 Dupire, Marguerite
Peuls nomades: études descriptives des Wodaabe du Sahel Nigérien. Paris, Institut d'ethnologie, 1964. viii, 336p. illus., maps. (Trav. et mémoires, 64).

2158 —Pharmacopée peule du Niger et du Cameroun. *Bull. IFAN*, 19 (3–4) Jl.–Oct. 1957: 382–417, illus.

2159 El Masri, F. H.
The life of Shehu Usuman dan Fodio before the jihād. *J. Hist. soc. Nig.* 2, (4) 1963: 435–448.

2160 Fliegelman, Frieda
Moral vocabulary of an unwritten language (Fulani) *Anthropos*, 27, 1932: 214–248.

2161 Géo-Fourrier, G.
Les Borroro, pasteurs nomades du Tchad. *La Nature*, (2922) Feb. 1934: 106–110, illus.

2162 Gray, W. T.
Fulani life and customs: hunters and cattle raisers of Northern Nigeria. *Afr. world*, Sept. 1958: 7–8, illus.

2163 Guy, M. C.
Les populations peules (Fulani) *Rev. ethnog. sociol.*, 4, 1913: 252–260.

2164 Hallam, W. K. R.
In the footsteps of the Shehu. *Nig. mag.*, (78) Sept. 1963: 196–206, illus., map.

Hiskett, M.
An Islamic tradition of reform in the Western Sudan from the sixteenth to the eighteenth century.
See [2498].

2165 Hodgkin, Thomas
Uthmān dan Fodio. *Nigeria, 1960*: 75–82, illus.

2166 *Hodgson, W. B.
Notice sur les Foulah. *Bull. Soc. geog.*, 9, 1838:

2167 Homburger, Lilian
Le sérere-peul. *J. Soc. afr.*, 9 (1) 1939: 85–102.

2168 Ibrahim, Mustafa B.
The Fulani—a nomadic tribe in Northern Nigeria. *Afr. affairs*, 65 (259) Apr. 1966: 170–176.

2169 Kirk-Green, Anthony Hamilton Millard
Fulani. In his *Adamawa past and present, 1958*: 21–25, map.

2170 Kirk-Greene, Anthony Hamilton Millard and Sasson, Caroline
The cattle people of Nigeria. London, O.U.P., 1959. 31p. illus., map. (People of the world).

A simple reader on the Fulani cattle rearers of Nigeria, intended for children.

2171 Lacroix, Pierre-François
Matériaux pour servir à l'histoire des peuls de l'Adamawa. *Étud. cam.*, 5 (37–38) Sept.–Dec. 1952: 3–61; 6 (39–40) Mar.–Jl. 1953: 5–40, illus., maps.

2172 Last, D. M.
An aspect of the caliph Muhammad Bello's social policy. *Kano stud.*, 1 (2) Jl. 1966: 56–59.

2173 Last, D. M. and Al-Hajj, Muhammad A.
Attempts at defining a moslim in 19th century Hausaland and Bornu. *J. Hist. soc. Nig.*, 3 (2) Dec. 1965: 231–240.

2174 Lebeuf, Jean-Paul and Masson-Detourbet, Annie
Un campement mbororo dans le Nord-Cameroun. *Notes afr.*, (31) Jl. 1946: 24–26, illus., map.

2174a McCulloch, W. E.
An inquiry into the dietaries of the Hausas and town Fulani. See [2577].

2175 Ma'Feesh
Preserve the nomads. *W. Afr. rev.*, 20 (260) May 1949: 515–517.
Describes the pastoral Fulani of Northern Nigeria and draws attention to the need for official action to improve their lot.

2176 Malcolm, L. W. G.
Notes on the ethno-botany of the cattle Fulbe, Adamawa, West Africa. *Bibliotheca afr.*, (1) 1925: 126–148.

2177 Marunicci, C.
I Fulbe pepulo pastore (Nigeria). *Africa* [Roma] 1959: 66–72.

2178 Mettenden, K.
Cattle trail. *Nig. mag.*, (70) Sept. 1961: 253–265, illus.
Description of the pastoral Fulani of Northern Nigeria.

2179 Moume Etia, Abel
Le Foulbé du Nord-Cameroun. Bergarac, Imprimerie générale du sud-ouest (H. Trillaud), 1948. 32p.

2180 Murdock, George Peter
Fulani. In his *Africa: its peoples and their culture history. 1959*: 413–421, bibliog.

2181 Perrin, J.
Notice sur l'alimentation et l'habitation indigène en pays foulah. *Rens. col.*, 1938: 302–304; 328–329.

2182 Reed, L. N.
Notes on some Fulani tribes and customs. *Africa*, 5 (4) Oct. 1932: 422–454.
Refers to the Fulani of Bornu emirate.

2183 Ruxton, Upton Fitz H.
Notes on the tribes of the Muri Province. *J. Afr. soc.*, 7 (28) Jl. 1908: 374–386.
"The following notes are an attempt to give some ethnographic and historical details concerning the principal tribes found in the Muri Province: the Fulani, Jukun, Wurubọ and Ankwe."

2184 Sainte-Croix, F. W. de See De St. Croix, F. W.

2185 Stapledon, J. H. D.
In their end is their beginning: a Fulani crisis. *Nig. field*, 13 (2) Oct. 1948: 53–59.
Traces the migration of the Bamenda Fulani from Kano to Bamenda, from where further migration is now impossible and considers this check a useful aid to the Administration in breaking their nomadic life.

2186 Stenning, Derrick J.
Field studies of nomadic Fulani in Northern Nigeria: interim report. London, International Afr. inst., 1953. 16p.

2187 —The pastoral Fulani of Northern Nigeria. In *Peoples of Africa, ed. J. L. Gibbs, 1965*: 361–401, illus., bibliog.
A compendious ethnographic summary.

2188 —Problems of sociological field work in a pastoral society. *Discovery* [Norwich] Dec. 1956: 514–518, illus., map.
Problems encountered during research among the pastoral Fulani of Northern Nigeria.

2189 —Savannah nomads: a study of the Wodaabe pastoral Fulani of Western Bornu Province, Northern Region, Nigeria. With a foreword by Daryll Forde. London, published for the International African institute by Oxford university press, 1959. xv, 266p. front., illus., maps, bibliog.
A scholarly study embracing their history, ethnography and administration.

2190 —Transhumance, migratory drift, migration: patterns of pastoral Fulani nomadism. *J. R. A. I.*, 87, 1957: 57–73, illus., maps, bibliog.
A study of population movements among the pastoral Fulani of Northern Nigeria, and the role of climatic and socio-political changes as determinants for such movements.
Later reprinted in *Cultures and societies of Africa, ed. Simon and Phoebe Ottenberg, 1960*: 139–159. [720].

2191 Tremearne, Arthur John Newman
The Fulani. In his *The Niger and the West Sudan, 1910*: 31–51 [540].

2192 Vieillard, Gilbert
Note sur deux institutions propres aux populations peules d'entre Niger et Tchad: le soro et le gerewol. *J. soc. afr.*, 2, 1932: 85–93.

2193 —Notes sur le caractère des Peuls. *Outre-Mer*, 4 (1) Mar. 1932: 8–18.

2194 —Les Peules dans notre Afrique. *Monde colonial illustré*, (174), 1937: 288–289.

2195 —Récits peules du Macina et du Kounari. *Bull. Com. étud. hist. sci. A.o.f.*, 14, 1931: 137–156.

2196 Webster, G. W.
Customs and beliefs of the Fulani; notes collected during 24 years' residence

in Northern Nigeria. *Man*, 31, Nov. 1931: 238–244 (art. 242).

2197 Wilson-Haffenden, J. R.
Ethnological notes on the Shuwalbe group of Bororo Fulani, in the Kurafi District of Keffi Emirate, Northern Nigeria. *J.R.A.I.*, 57, 1927: 275–293.

3. (ii) History

2198 Arnett, Edward John
The rise of the Sokoto Fulani; being a paraphrase and in some parts a translation of the Infaku'l Maisuri of Sultan Mohammed Bello. Kano, Emirate printing dept., 1922. 140, 43p. maps.
Appended at the end and covering the additional 43pp. is "History of Sokoto" in which the events described in Muhammed Bello's book are briefly summarised.

2199 Blue, A. D.
Invaders of the north: the Fulani of West Africa. *W. Afr. rev.*, 19 (251) 1948: 913–917.

2200 Boyle, C. Vicars
Historical notes on Yola Fulanis. *J. Afr. soc.*, 10 (37) Oct. 1910: 73–92, genealogical tables.

2201 Brass, Adolf
Eine neue Quelle zur Geschichte des Fulreiches Sokoto. *Der Islam*, 10, 1920: 1–73.

2202 Burdon, John A.
Sokoto history: tables of dates and genealogy. *J. Afr. soc.*, 6 (24) Jl. 1907: 367–374.
Significant events and reigns in Sokoto from 1804 to 1903.

2203 Delafosse, Maurice
Traditions musulmanes relatives à l'origine des Peuls. *Revue du monde musulman*, 20, 1912: 242–267.

2204 Eichtal, G. d'
Histoire et origine des Foulas ou Fellans. Paris, Dondey-Dupré, 1841. xii, 296p. 1 map (Mémoires de la Societé ethnologique, vol. 1, pt. 2).
Discusses the history and migrations of the Fulani and traces their origin to the Polynesians. Useful appendices on Polynesian migrations and vocabulary. "Vocabulaire comparatif de la langue Foulah", pp. 234–245. Influence of Islam in Africa, pp. 268–289.

2205 Engestrom, Tor
Apport à la théorie des origines du peuple et de la langue peuhle. Stockholm, Staatens etnografiska museum, 1954. 23p. illus. (Staatens etnografiska museum, Stockholm. Smarre meddelanden, 24).
Hajji, Sa'id
History of Sokoto.
See [2489] and [2490].

2206 Ifemesia, C. Chieka
The Fulani. In *A thousand years of West African history*, ed. J. F. A. Ajayi and I. Espie, 1965: 52–54.

2207 Jeffreys, M. D. W.
Banyo; a local history note. *Nig. field*, 18 (2) 1953: 87–91, bibliog.
Review of two accounts—African and German—of the clash of Ardo Umoru, ruler of Banyo in Adamawa Province, with a German team in his tour in 1902, resulting in the ruler's death. Prefaced with brief historical sketch of Banyo.

2208 —L'origine du nom 'Fulani'. *Bull. soc. et. cam.*, 5, 1944: 5–24.

2209 —Two Arabic documents: *Diyyá s-Sultan* and *Tazyîn l-Waraqat*. *Afr. stud.*, 9 (2) Je. 1950: 77–85.
Two Arabic manuscripts obtained from two Fulani in Bamenda about 1944, and said to have been written by Abdullahi, Usuman Dan Fodio's younger brother. The first is a vade mecum for administrators and the second, a history of the Fulani. English translations and specimen pages provided.

2210 Junaidu, *Waziri of Sokoto*
Tarihin Fulani. Zaria, North Regional Literature Agency, 1957. 86p. illus.
History of the Fulani.

2211 Labouret, Henri
Les Sultans peuls de l'Adamaoua. *Togo-Cameroun*, Apr.–Jl. 1935: 88–109, illus., map.

2212 Last, D. M.
Arabic source material and historiography in Sokoto to 1864: an outline. *Research bull.*, 1 (2) Jan. 1965: 3–19.
Outline notes on writings, largely religious and historical, of the leaders of the Fulani jihad and of some of their successors and followers. Includes biographical notes on some of the later writers, useful bibliographical footnotes, and a four page bibliography of relevant manuscripts.

2212a —Arabic source material and historiography in Sokoto since 1864: an outline. *Research bull.*, 1 (3) Jl. 1965: 1–7.
Continues above survey for the period 1864 to the present and notes the historical significance of the wealth of correspondence recovered from Sokoto and Gombe and now housed in the National Archives.

2213 —Sokoto in the 19th century, with special reference to the Vizierate. 1964.
Ph.D. thesis, University of Ibadan.

2214 Lhote, H.
L'extraordinaire aventure des Peuls. *Présence afr.*, 22, Oct.–Nov. 1958: 48–57.

2215 Meek, Charles Kingsley
The Fulani. *Man*, 59, Oct. 1959: 182 (art. 287).
A letter discussing the similarity between the name Filani (Fulani) and the Carthaginian legendary name *Philaeni* found in classical writings and on the possible Assyrian and Babylonian origin of the Fulani.

2216 Mischlich, Adam

E

Über die Herkunft der Fulbe. *M.S.O.S.*, 34, 1931: 183–196.

Text of a Hausa manuscript, with German translation, obtained from a Kano man in Togo. Deals with Fulani history and gives a genealogical tree of Othman Dan Fodio.

2217   Monteil, Charles
Notice sur l'origine des Peuls. *Rev. Afr.*, 55, 1911: 249–254.

2218   —Réflexions sur le problèmè des peuls. *J. Soc. afr.*, 20 (22) 1950: 153–192.
See also [2230].

2218a Muhammad, Abdullah Ibn
Tazyin al-Waraqāt. See [394].

2219   Palmer, Herbert Richmond
Two Sudanese manuscripts of the seventeenth century. *B.S.O.S.*, 5 (3) 1929: 541–560.

2220   —The Fulani in history and legend. *Afr. mail*, 5, 1911–1912: 123–124, 173–174, 303, 323, 343, 363–364, 383–384, 403–404, 433, 493, 513–514; 6, 1912–1913: 3, 43, 53, 77, 97, 107, 127, 421–422, 431–432, 441–442, 451–452.
A series of twenty-two articles presenting an expatiatory and discursive account of Fulani origin, history and language.

2221   —M. Delafosse's account of the Fulani. *J. Afr. soc.*, 13 (50) Jan. 1914: 195–203.
A critical review of Delafosse's *Haut-Sénégal et Niger* [649].

2221a —Sudanese memoirs. See [3994].

2222   Robin, J.
A verser au dossier de l'histoire des Peuls. *Notes afr.*, (109) Jan. 1966: 29–30.

2223   Rousseau, J. A.
Les migrations Foulbé et la linguistique botanique. Courte note suivie d'un vocabulaire botanique peul-française. *Étud. cam*, 1935: 55–62.
Discusses Fulani names of plants in N. Cameroun, showing that plants not known to the Fulani in their area of origin bear indigenous (non-Fulani) names. Believes that a comparative study of these names in the different Fulani dialects would help to throw light on the course of Fulani migration.

2224   Savery, Gorden
Two kings of Katsina. *W. Afr. rev.*, 37 (397) Dec. 1960: 70–72, illus.

2225   Smith, Henry Frederick Charles
The dynastic chronology of Fulani Zaria. *J. Hist. soc. Nig.*, 2 (2) Dec. 1961: 277–285.

2226   Spuler, B.
Fulbe. In *Encyclopaèdia of Islam. New ed.*, 7 (37) 1964: 939–943, bibliog.
Reviews studies to date of the origin, history and spread of the Fulani.

2227   Suret-Canale, Jean
Zur historischen und sozialen Bedeutung der Fulbe-Hegemonie. In *Geschichte und Geschichtsbild Afrikas, 1960*: 29–59, maps, bibliog.

2228   Tauxier, Louis

Moeurs et histoire des Peuls. Paris, Payot, 1937. 420p. illus.

2229   Tremearne, Arthur John Newman
Notes on the origin of the Filani. *J.R. soc. arts*, 58, 1910: 715–725.

2230   Tressan, de Lavergne de
Au sujet des Peuls. *Bull. IFAN*, 14 (4) Oct. 1952: 1512–1559, map.
See also [2218].

2231   Wane, Y.
État actuel de la documentation au sujet des Toucouleurs. *Bull. IFAN*, 25 (3–4) 1963: 457–477, bibliog.

2231a Whitting, C. E. J. *tr.*
History of Sokoto. See [2489] and [2490].

2232   Wolff, Kurt
Das Sesshaftwerden der Ful. Brunswick, Vieweg, 1939. 64p. illus.
Ph.D. thesis, Univ. of Berlin.

3. (iii)   Family; Social Organization and Structure

2232a Blumberg, B. S.
The blood groups of the pastoral Fulani of N. Nigeria . . .
See [2143].

2233   Buttner, Thea
Zu Problemen der Staatenbildung der Fulbe in Adamaua. *Wiss. Z. Karl Marx-Univ.*, 13 (2) 1964: 223–237.

2234   Crowder, Michael
A new emir turbanned. *Nig. mag.*, (63) 1959: 320–339, illus.
Eye witness account of the installation of Malam Sulu Gambari as the emir of Ilorin on 10th July 1959.

2235   Dupire, Marguerite
The position of women in a pastoral society (The Fulani Wo Daabe, nomads of the Niger) In *Women of tropical Africa, ed. by Denise Paulme, 1963*: 47–92, illus.

2236   Elias, Taslim Olawale
Fulani inheritance. *Nig. mag.*, (54) 1957: 198–207, illus.

2237   Froelich, Jean-C.
Le commandement et l'organisation sociale chez les Foulbé de l'Adamaoua. *Étud. cam.*, (45–46) Sept.–Dec. 1954: 3–91, map.
Social organization, rules of succession, coronation ceremonies, and administration of justice.

2238   Hopen, C. Edward
A note on *Alkali Fulfulde*: a reformation movement among the nomadic Fulbe (Fulani) of Sokoto Province. *Africa*, 34 (1) Jan. 1964: 21–27, bibliog.
On the development of a system of "courts" among young Sokoto Fulani to reform and uphold Fulani ways and moral standards by punishing those who misbehave. The sociological significance of the institution is discussed. French summary, pp. 26–27.

2239   —The pastoral Fulbe family in Gwandu. London, O.U.P. for Int. Afr. inst., 1958. xiii, 165p. plates, maps.

A close study of aspects of the family of Gwandu pastoral Fulani and of the relation of the herd to the family.

2239a Jeffreys, M. D. W.
Two Arabic documents. See [2209].

2239b Stenning, Derrick J.
Economic aspects of family organization among the pastoral Fulani. See [2255].

2240 —Household viability among the pastoral Fulani. In *Developmental cycle in domestic groups, ed. J. R. Goody, 1958*: 92–119.

2241 Traore, Dominique
La condition de l'esclavage bawagemdou dans l'ancien royaume peul de Sokoto. *Notes afr.*, (4) Oct. 1948: 13.

Yeld, E. R.
Islam and social stratification in Northern Nigeria.
See [2559].

3. (iv) Religion; Miscellaneous Beliefs and Rituals

2242 Al-Hajj, Muhammad A.
The Fulani concept of Jihād; Shehu Uthmān dān Fodio. *Odu,* 1 (1) Jl. 1964: 45–58.
A study of the writings of Uthmān dan Fodio, his brother Abdullahi and his son Muhammad Bello, to demonstrate that the Fulani jihad headed by the first named was essentially a religious upheaval provoked by the Fulanis who had a deeper, long-standing contact with Islam against the 'half-islamized' half-pagan Hausa rulers. Includes Arabic texts.

2243 Bivar, A. D. H.
The *Wathīqat ahl al-Sudān:* a manifesto of the Fulani jihad. *J. Afr. hist.,* 2 (2) 1961: 235–243.

2244 Dieterlen, Germaine
L'initiation chez les pasteurs peul (Afrique occidentale) In *African systems of thought . . . prefaced by M. Fortes and G. Dieterlen. 1965*: 314–327.

2245 Dodds, Alex M.
Soro: the Fulani flogging custom. *Nig. teacher,* 1 (3) 1934: 9–10.

2246 East, Rupert Moultrie
Initiation of Fulani boys in Adamawa. *Africa,* 11 (2) Apr. 1938: 226–228.
Description of rites and ceremonies connected with the circumcision of boys among Adamawa Fulani.

2247 —Sharo: cruelty or discipline? *W. Afr. ann.,* 1950: 90, illus.

2248 Palmer, Herbert Richmond
An early Fulani conception of Islam: *J. Afr. soc.,* 13 (52) Jl. 1914: 407–414; 14 (53) Oct. 1914: 53–59; (54) Jan. 1915: 185–192.
A translation of "Tanbihu'l Ikhwan" (The admonition to Brethren) which sought to justify on religious grounds the Fulani conquest of the Hausa states. Authorship attributed to Uthmān Dan Fodio.

2249 Sharo: a Fulani test of endurance. *Nig. mag.,* (82) Sept. 1964: 200–209, illus.

2250 Waldman, Marilyn Robinson
The Fulani Jihād: a reassessment. *J. Afr. hist.,* 6 (3) 1965: 333–355.

2251 —A note on the ethnic interpretation of the Fulani jihād. *Africa,* 36 (3) Jl. 1966: 286–291.
French summary, p. 291.

2252 Whitting, C. E. J.
Fulani floggings. *W. Afr. rev.,* 26 (328) Jan. 1955: 10–12.
Describes the Sharo ceremony as staged in Binnin Kuka village.

3. (v) Economy, Husbandry, Trade

2253 De St. Croix, F. W.
Some aspects of the cattle husbandry of the nomadic Fulani. *Farm & forest,* 5 (1) Apr. 1944: 29–33.

2254 Dupire, Marguerite
Trade and markets in the economy of the nomadic Fulani of Niger (Bororo). In *Markets in Africa, ed. P. Bohannan and G. Dalton, 1962*: 335–361, map.
The Bororo in the Niger Republic.

2255 Stenning, Derrick J.
Economic aspects of family organisation among the pastoral Fulani of Northern Nigeria. 1955.
Ph.D. thesis, Cambridge.

3. (vi) Arts and Crafts

2256 Delange, Jacqueline
L'art peul. *Cah. étud. afr.,* 4 (1) 1963: 5–13, illus.

2257 Jest, C.
Décoration des calebasses foulbées. *Notes afr.,* (72) Oct. 1956: 113–116, illus.

3. (vii) Recreation, Music, Dance

2258 Estreicher, Z.
Chants et rythmes de la danse d'hommes bororo. *Bull. Soc. neuchâteloise,* 51 (5) 1954–55: 57–93.

2259 King, A. V.
Music tradition in a changing society. *Mus. in Nig.* 1 (2) May 1965: 37–63, maps, bibliog.
A brief sketch of the social and political history of Katsina, followed by a discussion of music tradition and continuity in the emirate as exemplified by the position and functions of the official or state musicians.

2260 Mellor, F. H.
The Fulani dance. *Saturday rev.,* Oct. 31, 1936: 571.
On Fulani New Year celebration dance, with brief notes on the musical instruments used.

3. (viii) Literary Expression, Literature (Including Stories, Proverbs, Riddles)

2261 Adam, Abdallah
Erzählungen in Fulfulde: niedergeschrieben von Abdallah Adam, transkribiert, übersetzt und mit einem

Nachtrag: Erzählungen im Dialekt von Sokoto von D. Westermann. Berlin, G. Reimer, 1913. lv. (various pagings) (Lehrbücher des S.O.S., Band 30)
Stories in Fulani written by Abdallah Adam, with additional stories in the Sokoto dialect by D. Westermann.

2261a Arnott, D. W.
Proverbial lore and word-play of the Fulani. *Africa*, 27 (4) Oct. 1957: 379–396.
On riddles, proverbs, epigrams, etc., among the Fulani. Numerous examples. French summary, pp. 395–396.

2262 Dupire, Marguerite and Tressan, *Marquis de*
Devinettes Peules et Bororo. *Africa*, 25 (4) Oct. 1955: 375–392.

2262a East, Rupert Moultrie
Stories of old Adamawa. See [2293].

2263 Eberhardt, Jaqueline
The mythical python among the Venda and Fulani: a comparative note. *Archiv f. Völkerkde.*, 13, 1958: 15–24.

2264 Gaden, Henri
Proverbes et maximes peuls et toucouleurs, traduits, expliqués et annotés. Paris, Institut d'ethnologie, 1931. xxxiii, 368p. (Université de Paris. Institut d'ethnologie. Travaux et mémoires, 16).

2265 Hiskett, Mervyn
Material relating to the state of learning among the Fulani before their Jihãd. *B.S.O.A.S.*, 19 (3) 1957: 550–578.

2266 Kensdale, William Elliott Norwood
Field notes on the Arabic literature of the Western Sudan: Usumanu dan Fodio. *J. Roy. Asiatic soc.*, (34) Oct. 1955: 162–168.
List of the writings of Usman dan Fodio.

2267 —Field notes on the Arabic literature of the Western Sudan. *J. Roy. Asiatic soc.*, (1–2) Apr. 1956: 78–80.
List of the writings of Waziri Abdullahi dan Fodio, brother of Usman dan Fodio.

2268 —Field notes on the Arabic literature of the Western Sudan: Muhammadu Bello. *J. Roy. Asiatic soc.*, (1–2) Apr. 1958: 53–57.
List of the writings of Muhammadu Bello, son of Usman dan Fodio.

2269 Pfeffer, Gulla
Prose and poetry of the Ful'be. *Africa*, 12 (3) Jl. 1939: 285–307.
A useful discussion of Fulani folklore and literature, followed by English translation of five Fulani stories and some riddles, obtained from Yola. French summary, pp. 306–307.

2270 Stephani, Frans von
Legende über den Ursprung der Fulbe und der Bororo nach der Erzählung des Malam Ali Babali. *Islam*, 3, 1912: 351–357.

2270a Westermann, Diedrich

Erzählungen in Fulfulde. See Adam, Abdallah [2261].

2270b Whitting, C. E. J.
Hausa and Fulani proverbs. See [2612].

4. LINGUISTIC STUDIES

Adam, Abdallah
Erzählungen in Fulfulde. See [2261].

2271 Arensdorff, L.
Manuel pratique de langue peuhl. Paris, P. Geuthner, 1913. xxii, 424p. map.

2272 *Arnaud, R.
Contribution à l'étude de la langue peuhle ou foullanniyya. *Bull. Soc. géogr. Algér*, (5–6) 1901:

2273 Arnott, D.W.
The middle voice in Fula. *B.S.O.A.S.*, 18 (1) 1956: 130–144.
Analysis of the three series of verbal affixes or "voices" occuring in Fulani, with special attention to the middle or reflexive voice. Based on the speech of two informants from Gombe in Northern Nigeria.

2274 —Morphological features in the verbal system of Fula. *J. W. Afr. lang.*, 2 (1) 1965: 5–14.

2276 —Sentence intonation in the Gombe dialect of Fula: a tentative analysis. *Afr. lang. stud.*, (6) 1965: 73–100.

2277 —Some features of the nominal class system of Fula in Nigeria, Dahomey and Niger. *Afr. u. Übersee*, 43 (4) Mar. 1960: 241–278.

2278 —The subjunctive in Fula: a study of the relation between syntax and meaning. *Afr. lang. stud.*, (2) 1961: 125–138.

2279 —The tense system in Gombe Fula. 1961.
Ph.D. thesis, London. (SOAS) Subsequently published in *Afrika und Übersee*, vol. 49, 1966: 1–31, 105–135, 173–195, 270–299.

2280 Bible. N. T. Fulani. John
Bisharawol Yohanna. [Tentative ed.] London, 1919.
St. John's Gospel in Fulani.

2281 *Bonifaci, A.
Dictionnaire de langue Peul. Tome I: Français-Peul. Yaoundé, Imprimerie nationale, 1949.

2282 Brackenbury, E. A.
Notes on the Fulfulde. *J. Afr. soc.*, 15 (57) Oct. 1915: 70–82.
Grammatical notes on the language as spoken in Yola area.

2283 —A short vocabulary of the Fulani language. Zungeru, E. D. A. Macaulay, acting Govt. printer, 1907. 30p.
Interleaved.

2284 Brun, R. P. F.
Recueil de fables en dialecte Hal poular. *Anthropos*, 14–15, 1919–1920: 180–214.
Collection of Fulani stories, with French translations.

2285 Cremer, Jean
Dictionnaire français-peul (Dialectes de la Haute-Volta) Paris, P. Geuthner, 1923 [i] xxix, 109p. (Matériaux d'ethnographie et de linguistique Soudanaises' tome 1).

2286 Dauzats, André
Éléments de la langue peule du Nord-Cameroun. Yaoundé, Imprimerie du gouvernement, 1934. 100p.

2287 — —2e éd. Albi, Imprimerie Albigeoise, 1952. 128p.

2288 —Petit lexique Peul-Français. Yaoundé, Imprimerie nationale, 1939. 120p.

2289 — —2e éd. Lexique Français-Peul et Peul-Français. Albi, Imprimerie Albigeoise, 1952. 444p.

2290 Drexel, Albert
Gliederung der afrikanischen Sprachen . . . Die Fulah-Sprachen. Anthropos, 20, 1925: 210–220.

2291 —Kann das Ful als hamitische Sprache gelten? In Festschrift P. W. Schmidt, ed. W. Koppers, Wien, 1928: 45–60.
On whether Fulani can rightly be classified as Hamitic.

2292 —Psychologische Erwägungen zum fulschen Anlautwechsel, nebst einem historisch-kritischen Nachtrag. Bibliotheca Afr., 3 (4) 1929: 299–316.

2293 East, Rupert Moultrie
Stories of old Adamawa; a collection of historical texts in the Adamawa dialect of Fulani, with a translation and notes. Lagos, London, West Africa publicity, for Translation bureau, Zaria, [1935] 143p. maps.
Original texts and English translations on opposite pages.

2294 Eichtal, G. d'
Vocabulaire comparatif de la langue Foulah. In his Histoire et origine des Foulas ou Fellans, 1841: 234–245.

2295 Faidherbe, L. L. C.
Essai sur la langue poul et comparaison de cette langue avec le Wolof, les idiomes sérères et les autres langues du Soudan occidental. Rev. ling. et philolog. comp., 7, 1875: 195–242; 291–321.

2296 —Grammaire et vocabulaire de la langue poul à l'usage de voyageurs dans le Soudan. 2nd ed. Paris, Maisonneur, 1882. 165p. map.
2nd edition of his Essai sur la langue poul. See above [2295].

Fliegelman, Frieda
Moral vocabulary of an unwritten language. See [2160].

2297 —The richness of African negro languages (Fulani as a type) In Comptes rendus Congrès de l'Institut international des langues et civilisations africaines, Paris, 16–19 Octobre, 1931. 1933: 51–75.

2298 Gaden, Henri
Note sur le dialecte foul parlé par les foulbé du Baguirmi . . . Paris, Imprimerie nationale, 1908. 70p.

Reprinted from Journal Asiatique, Jan.–Feb. 1908.

2299 —Le Poular, dialecte Peul du Fouta Sénégalais. Paris, Leroux, 1913–1914. 2v.
v. 1. Étude morphologique, textes, 366p.
v. 2. Lexique Poular-Français. xii, 263p.

2300 Gausson, L.
Un texte Foulah. Rev. ling. et philolog. comp., 39, 1906: 221–235.

2301 *Gibert, E.
Étude de la langue des Pouls. Rev. ling. et philolog. comp., (32), (33) & (34), 1893:

2302 Greenberg, Joseph Harold
Studies in African linguistic classification. II. The classification of Fulani. S.-W. j. anthrop., 5 (3) Autumn 1949: 190–198.
Part of his comprehensive survey of African linguistic classification, for which see [1453] and other entries following it.

2303 Grimal de Guiraudon, T.
Bolle Fulbe; manuel de la langue foule parlée dans la Sénégambia et le Soudan. Grammaire, texte, vocabulaire. Paris, Leipzig, H. Weltern, 1894. viii, 144p.
Grammar, Fulani texts and French-Fulani vocabulary.

2304 —Notes de linguistique africaine. Les Puls. Paris, Leroux, 1887, Vienne, 1888. 55p.
Printed by Brezezowsky & son, Vienna.

2305 Homburger, Lilian
Éléments dravidiens en Peul. J. Soc. afr., 18 (2) 1950: 135–143.

2306 *—Morphèmes africaines en peul et dans les parlers bantous. M.S.L.P., 18 (3) 1913:

2307 —Le peul et les langues nilotiques. B.S.L.P., 37, 1936: 58–72.

2308 —Les préfixes nominaux dans les parlers peul, haoussa et bantou. Paris, Institut d'ethnologie, 1929. xi, 166p. (Trav. et mém. Inst. d'ethnol., 6).

2309 —Les réprésentants de quelques hiéroglyphes égyptiens en peul. B.S.L.P., 23 (5) 1930: 277–312.

2310 —Le verbe en peul et en massai. B.S.L.P., 1936: 555–568.

2311 Houis, M.
Du rapport entre les classes et le conditionnement de l'initiale radicale en peul. Bull. IFAN, 21 (1–2) 1959: 167–178.

2312 Jeffreys, M. D. W.
Speculative origins of the Fulani language. Africa, 17 (1) Jan. 1947: 47–54.
French summary p. 54.

2313 Johnston, Harry Hamilton
The Fulas and their language. J. Afr. soc., 20 (79) Apr. 1921: 212–216.
A review of F. W. Taylor's A first

grammar of Adamawa dialect of the
Fulani language (Fulfulde) [2356].

2314 Kirk-Greene, Anthony Hamilton Millard
A note on the Fulani language. In his
Adamawa past and present, 1958: 206–
207.

2315 Klingenheben, August
Die Diminutiv und Augmentativ-
Klassen des Westful. M.S.O.S., 1955:
76–86.

2316 —Eine neue Nominalklasse des Ful.
Z. deutschen morgen. Ges., 105, 1955:
338–345.

2317 —Die Inversion im Ful. Afr. u. Übersee,
45 (3) Feb. 1962: 161–169.

2318 —Die Klassenelemente der Zahlwörter
des Ful. Z. deutschen morgen. Ges., 99
(1) 1949: 67–92.

2319 —Die Laute des Ful. Berlin, Dietrich
Reimer; Hamburg, C. Boysen, 1927.
155p. (Zeitschrift für Eingeborenen-
Sprachen. Neuntes Beiheft.)
A study of Fulani phonology.

2320 *—Die nominalen Klassensysteme des
Ful. Donum Natalicium Schrijnen
[Utrecht] 1929: 175–181.

2321 —Die Permutationen des Biafada und
des Ful. Z.f.E.S. 15 (3) 1924: 180–213;
(4) 1925: 266–272.
Compares Fulani with Biafada, a
language the only known source of
which is Koelle's Polyglotta Africana
[1476].

2322 —Die Präfixklassen des Ful. Z.f.E.S.,
14, 1923–24: 189–222; 290–315.
A study of prefix morphology in
Fulani.

2323 —Zum problem der Silben in
afrikanischen Sprachen (u.a. der
Nasalverbingdungen in Ful von
Adamaua) Afr. u. Übersee, 37, 1952:
7–20.

2324 —Die Pronomina "o" und "i" des Ful.
Folia Ethnographica, 3 (2–4) Apr.–Dec.
1927: 47–52.
Discusses the views on the use of
these pronouns held by Westermann in
Handbuch der Ful-Sprache [2370] and
Taylor in A first grammar of the
Adamawa dialect of the Fulani language
[2356] Maintains that "i" is not strictly
a pronoun but was originally a
progressive particle.

2325 —Die Sprache der Ful (Dialekt von
Adamaua) Grammatik, Texte und
Wörterverzeichnis. Hamburg, J. J.
Augustin, 1963. xxii, 461p.
(Afrikanistische Forschungen, Bd. 1).

2326 —Die Suffixklassen des Ful. Berlin,
D. Reimer, Hamburg, Friederichsen,
de Gruyter, 1941. 107p. (Beihefte zur
Zeitschrift für Eingeborenen-Sprachen,
23).

2327 Krause, Gottlob Adolf
Ein Beitrag zur Kenntniss der fulischen
Sprache in Afrika. Leipzig, F. A.
Brockhaus,   1884.   [4]   108p.

2328 Labouret, Henri
La langue des peuls ou Foulbé. Dakar,
IFAN, 1952. xii, 286p. bibliog.
(Mémoires de l'Institut français
d'Afrique noire, no. 16).

2329 —La langue des peuls ou Foulbé:
lexique français-peul. Dakar, IFAN,
1955. 160p. illus., maps, bibliog,
(Mémoires de l'IFAN, no. 41).
A 97 page French-Fulani vocabulary.
Preceded by brief bibliographies of
Fulani language and history, observations, illustrated with maps, on the
origins and migrations of the Fulani,
and ethnographic notes on the Fulani
family system.

2330 Lacroix, J.
Observations sur les formes verbales
d'habitude dans les parlers peuls de
l'Adamawa. In Actes du second colloque
international de linguistique négro-
Africaine, 1962. 1963: 39–51.

2331 Laird, Mcgregor and Oldfield, R. A. K.
English-Eboe-Felatah [vocabulary] In
their Narrative of an expedition into the
interior of Africa, v. 2, 1837: 441–442;
443–444.
The second section (pp. 443–444) is
only English-Fulani.

2332 Leith-Ross, Sylvia
Fulani grammar. London, printed by
Waterlow, [1921] 210p. bibliog.

2333 MacBrair, Robert Maxwell
Grammar of the Fulah language, from
a manuscript by the Rev. R. M.
MacBrair in the British Museum.
Edited, with additions, by E. Norris.
1854. 7, 95p.

2334 Meinhof, Carl
Ful. In his Die Sprachen der Hamiten.
Hamburg, 1912. Chapter 2.

2335 —Das Ful in seiner Bedeutung für die
Sprachen der Hamiten, Semiten und
Bantu. Z. deutschen morgen. Ges., 65,
1911: 177–220.

2335a —Die Sprachen der Hamiten . . . See
[1488].

2336 Mukarovsky, Hans G.
Die Grundlagen des Ful und das
Mauretanische. Wien, Afro-Asiatisches
Institut, 1963. 201p. (Wissenschaftiche
Schriftenreihe, Bd. 1).

2337 —Das 'Sonnenrind' der Ful'be.
Linguistische Hinweise der ful-
sprechenden Völkerschaften im westlichen Sudan. Wiener Z. f. Kunde des
Morgen., 54, 1957: 130–140.

2338 —Die Suffixkonjugation im Ful.
Wiener Z. f. Kunde Morgen., 53 (3–4)
1957: 161–180.
Suffix conjugation in Fulani.

2339 Palmer, Herbert Richmond
The Fulani language. Afr. mail, 6 (265,
266, 268) Nov. 1912: 43, 53, 77.
Part of his extended historical study
of the Fulani. See [2220].

2340 —The "Fulas" and their language. *J. Afr. soc.*, 22 (85) Oct. 1922: 121–128
A criticism of H. H. Johnston's article of the same title [2313] Remarks by H. H. Johnson, pp. 128–130.

Pfeffer, G.
Prose and poetry of the Ful'be. See [2269].

2341 Poreko, Diallo O.
À propos des phonèmes spéciaux de la langue peule. *Rech. afr.*, 4, Oct.–Dec. 1960: 37–39.

2342 Prestat, G.
Cours élémentaire de fulfulde. Paris, Université de Paris, Centre de hautes études d'administration musulmane, 1950. 125p. (Langues et dialectes d'outre-mer, no. 2).
Cover title.

2343 Reichardt, Charles Augustus Ludwig
Grammar of the Fulde language. With an appendix of original traditions and portions of Scripture translated into Fulde; together with eight chapters of the book of Genesis, translated by the late Dr. Baikie. London, C.M. House, 1876. xxiii, 339p.

2344 —Primer in the Fulah language. Berlin, C. & F. Unger, printers, 1859. [ii] 29p.

2345 —Three original Fulah pieces in Arabic letters, in Latin transcription and English translation. Berlin, C. & F. Unger, printers, 1859. [iv] 62p.

2346 —Vocabulary of the Fulde language; Fulde-English and English-Fulde. 1878. 357p.

Rousseau, J. A.
Les migrations Foulbé, et la linguistique botanique . . . See [2223].

2347 Schultze, Arnold
Fulbe-Notizen. *M.S.O.S.*, 12, 1909: 123–126.
Lists common Fulani expressions with German translation.

2348 Steane, Karl
Kleine Fullah-Grammatik. Berlin, Georg Reimer, 1909. vii, 15p. (Archiv für das Studium deutscher Kolonialsprachen, B. 7).

2349 Stephani, Frans von
Materialien für das Studium der Fulbe-Sprache. *M.S.O.S.*, 12, 1909: 114–122.
Fulani phrases, etc., with German translation.

2350 - -Taschenbuch der Sprache der Fulbe in Adamaua. Berlin, G. Reimer, 1911. 78p.

2351 Stopa, Roman
The origin of the classification of nouns in Ful. *Folia orientalia*, 2 (1–2) 1960: 89–102.

2352 Storbeck, F.
Fulsprichwörter aus Adamaua. *Z.f.E.S.*, 10, 1919–1920: 106–122.
A collection of Fulani proverbs, from Adamawa, with explanatory notes.

2353 —Fultexte aus Adamaua. *Z.f.E.S.*, 11, 1920–1921: 24–34.

Fulani texts written by Zubeiru Adamu, a lecturer in Fulani at the Seminar für Orientalische Sprachen, Berlin. Describes his journey from Adamawa to Berlin, and tells a story.

2354 Tautain, L.
Contribution à l'étude de la langue foule (Poular). *Rev. ling. et philolog. comp.*, 22, 1889: 347–366; 23, 1890: 28–50; 118–147; 212–221.

2355 Taylor, Frank William
A first Fulani reading book. Deftere arandere jangirtende Fulfulde. London, Crown agents for the colonies, on behalf of the Govt. of Nigeria, 1921. 24p.

2356 —A first grammar of the Adamawa dialect of the Fulani language (Fulfulde) Oxford, Clarendon press, 1921. 135p. (Taylor's Fulani-Hausa series, no. 1).
2nd ed. See [2362].

2357 —A Fulani-English dictionary. Oxford, Clarendon press, 1932. vii, 242p. (Taylor's Fulani-Hausa series, 6).
". . . Only those [words] which are in common use in Adamawa have been inserted"—Preface.

2358 —A Fulani-Hausa phrase book. Oxford, Clarendon press, 1926. 158p. (Taylor's Fulani-Hausa series, no. 3).

2359 —Fulani-Hausa readings in the native scripts. Oxford, Clarendon press, 1929. 259p. (Taylor's Fulani-Hausa series, no. 5).

2360 —A Fulani-Hausa vocabulary. Oxford, Clarendon press, 1927. 136p. (Taylor's Fulani-Hausa series, no. 4).

2361 *—Genesis in Fulani. London, O.U.P., 1927.

2362 —A grammar of the Adamawa dialect of the Fulani language (Fulfulde) 2nd ed. Oxford, Clarendon press, 1953. xiv, 124p.
Not recommended for use without extra assistance in pronounciation. First published 1921. See [2356].

—The orthography of African languages with special reference to Hausa and Fulani. See [2846].

2363 —A second Fulani reading book. Deftere didaure jangirtende Fulfulde. London, Crown agents, for Govt. of Nigeria, 1921. 71p.

2364 —Some English words in Fulani and Hausa. *J. Afr. soc.*, 20 (77) Oct. 1920: 25–32.

2365 —A third Fulani reading book. Deftere tatabre jangirtende Fulfulde. Prepared by the staff of Yola School and edited by F. W. Taylor. London, Crown agents. for Adamawa native administration, 1930. 67p.

2366 Tressan, de Lavergne de
Du langage descriptive en Peul. *Bull. IFAN.*, 14 (2) Apr. 1952: 636–659.

2367 —Pour une transcription phonétique peule unifiée. *Bull. IFAN.*, 13, 1951: 916–923.

2368 Vohsen, Ernst

Proben der Fulah-Sprache. *Z. f. Afr. S.*, 1887–8: 217–237; 1889–90: 295–314.

2369 Westermann, Diedrich
Fullah-Übungen. Berlin, 1910. 30p.

2370 —Handbuch der Ful-Sprache: Wörterbuch, Grammatik, Übungen und Texte.

Berlin, Dietrich Reimer, 1909. viii, 274p.

2371 Whitting, C. E. J.
Hausa and Fulani proverbs. Lagos, Govt. printer, 1940. [v] 192p.

GBARI

(*Goale, Gwali, Gwari, Gwarri*)

Including:

Gade
Gwandera

Kinkera
Koro *(Korro)*

1. GENERAL AND ETHNOGRAPHIC STUDIES

2372 Cardew, Michael
Firing the big pot at Kwali: *Nig. mag.* (70) Sept. 1961: 199–205, illus.
    The firing of a special kind of waterpot (a large spherical cistern) called *Runda* in Hausa, by women potters in Kwali, a Gwari town in Abuja emirate.

2373 —Pioneer pottery at Abuja. *Nig. Mag.*, (52) 1956: 38–59, illus.

2374 Gade. In *Notes on the tribes . . . by O. Temple. 2nd ed. 1922, repr. 1965*: 108–109.

2375 Gunn, Harold D.
Gbari (Gwari) In his *Peoples of the middle Niger region Northern Nigeria, 1960*: 85–109.

2376 —Koro. In his *Peoples of the middle Niger region, Northern Nigeria, 1960*: 109–127.
    Ethnographic notes on a number of far-flung and divergent peoples in Zaria, Niger and Benue Provinces, to whom the name Koro has been applied.

2377 Gwandara. In *Notes on the tribes . . . by O. Temple, 2nd ed., 1922, repr. 1965*: 118–120.

2378 Gwari. In *Notes on the tribes . . . by O. Temple, 2nd ed., 1922, repr. 1965*: 120–137.
    General and ethnographic notes.

2379 Kinkere. In *Notes on the tribes . . . by O. Temple, 2nd ed., 1922, repr. 1965*: 234–235.

2380 Koro. In *Notes on the tribes . . . by O. Temple, 2nd ed., 1922, repr. 1965*: 238–242.

2381 La Chard, L. W.
Ancient funeral rites of the pagan Gwari of Northern Nigeria. *Man*, 11, 1911: 83–84 (art. 53).

Nadel, Siegfried Ferdinand
Witchcraft in four African societies. See [4191].

2382 Na'Ibi, Shuaibu
The Gade people of Abuja Emirate. *Nig. mag.*, (59) 1958: 288–307, illus.

2383 Na'Ibi, Shuaibu and Hassan, *Makaman Abuja*
The Gwari tribe in Abuja Emirate; translated by P.M.C. Scott. Photographs by Noa Onwuka. Lagos, 'Nigerian Magazine' [1960] 35p. front., illus. (Nigeria magazine special publication).
    Brief history and description of two groups of Gwari: Gwarin-Yama and Gwarin-Genge (the Gwari of the West) living in Abuja Emirate.

2384 Pagan festivals. In *A chronicle of Abuja, by Hassan and S. Na'Ibi. 1962*: 83–87.
    Brief notes on the customs and religious festivals of the Gwari and Koro of Abuja emirate.

2385 Slye, Jonathan
Gwari people and their art: traditional skills and affinity with nature. *Afr. world*, Nov. 1964: 6–8, illus.

2. LINGUISTIC STUDIES

2386 Edgar, Francis
A grammar of the Gbari language, with Gbari-English and English-Gbari dictionaries. Belfast, printed by W. & G. Baird, 1909. 373p.
    Grammar covers the first 100 pages, with the two vocabularies taking pp. 101–373.

2387 Low, W. P.
Gbari grammar notes and vocabulary, compiled at Kuta, Northern Nigeria. Zungeru, Govt. printing office, 1908. [iii] 17p.

GUDE

(Cheke)

Including:

Fali

1. GENERAL AND ETHNOGRAPHIC STUDIES

2388 Meek, Charles Kingsley
The Cheke (Mubi District) In his *Tribal studies in Northern Nigeria, v. 1, 1931*: 293–300.

2389 —The Fali. In his *Tribal studies in Northern Nigeria, v. 1, 1931*: 300–312.
Neher, Gerald
Brass casting in Northeast Nigeria. See [4125].

2. LINGUISTIC STUDIES

2390 Meek, Charles Kingsley
Cheke of Muvi (Mubi) vocabulary. In his *Tribal studies in Northern Nigeria, v. 1, 1931*: 297–300.

2391 —[Fali vocabularies] *In his Tribal studies in Northern Nigeria, v. 1, 1931*: 305–312.
Vocabularies of three Fali dialects.

HAUSA

(Haoussa)

Including:

Daurawa
Gobirawa
Kanawa
Katsenawa

Kebbawa
Maguzawa
Zamfarawa
Zazzagawa

1. GENERAL

2392 Adamson, P. B.
The city wall of Kano. *Antiquity*, 24 (96) Dec. 1950: 205–206.

2393 Allen, E. W.
The travels of Abdul Karim in Hausaland and Bornu. Illustrated by Caroline Sassoon. Zaria, NORLA, 1958. 80p. illus. maps.
The journal of Dr. Heinrich Barth abridged and adapted.

2394 Arnett, Edward John.
Gazetteer of Sokoto Province. London, Waterlow, 1920. 72p.

2395 —Gazetteer of Zaria Province. London, Waterlow, 1920. 40p.

2396 Atwood, A. W.
Kano, mud-made city. *Nat. geog. mag.*, 85, 1944: 554–558.

2396a Backwell, H. F. ed.
The occupation of Hausaland 1900–1904. Being a translation of Arabic letters found in the House of the Wazir of Sokoto, Bohari, in 1903. Lagos, Government printer, 1927. iii, 80p.

2396b — —New impression, with an introductory note, by Mervyn Hiskett. London, Frank Cass, 1969. ix, 80p.

2397 Bryant, K. J.
This is Zaria. [Zaria, NORLA, 1958] 34p. illus.

2398 Buchanan, Angus

Exploration of Air; out of the world north of Nigeria. London, J. Murray, 1921. xxiii, 258p. front., illus.

2399 —Kano, die grosse Handelsstadt Zentralafrikas. *Mitt. geog. Gesell.* [Wien] 71 (4–6) 1928: 147–151.
"Kano, the great trading city of central Africa".

2400 Buchanan, Keith McPherson
The Northern region of Nigeria: the geographical background of its political duality. *Geog. rev.*, 43 (4) Oct. 1953: 451–473.

2401 Clive, Percy A.
Notes on a journey to Pali and Mamaidi in the kingdom of Bauchi. *Geog. j.*, 14 (2) Aug. 1899: 177–183, map.

2402 Daumas, Eugène and De Chancel, Ausone
Le grand désert ou itineraire d'une caravane du Sahara au pays des nègres (royaume de Houssa) Paris, N. Chaix, 1848. 443p. map.

2403 Dennis, P. W. C.
The district around Zaria, Northern Nigeria. *Scot. geog. mag.*, 60 (1) Je. 1944: 15–19, illus., map.
Physical features, climate, vegetation, settlement, occupations, communication and trade.

2404 Ekwensi, Cyprian Odiatu Duaka
An African night's entertainment: a tale of vengeance. Illustrated by Bruce

Onabiakpeya. Lagos, A. U. P., 1962. 86p.

2405 —The passport of Mallam Ilia. Cambridge, C. U. P., 1960. 80p. illus.

2406 Flegel, Eduard R.
Lose Blätter aus dem Tagebuche meiner Haussafreunde und Reisege-fährten, übersetzt, eingeleitet, mit allge-meinen Schilderungen des Volks-charakters und der sozialen Verhält-nisse der Haussa's sowie mit kurzer Lebensgeschichte des Maigasinbaki versehen. Hamburg, Friederichsen, 1885. 47p.
Extracts from the diary of a German explorer who travelled widely in the Hausa country, reaching Adamawa and Yola in 1879. These extracts give a general description of the people.

2407 Gowers, W. F.
Gazetteer of Kano Province. London, Waterlow, 1921. 56p. map.

2408 Greenberg, Joseph Harold
The negro kingdoms of the Sudan. Trans. N.Y. acad. sci., ser. 2, 11 (4) Feb. 1949: 126–135, map.

Grey-Jackson, James See Jackson, James Grey

2409 Hallam, W. K. R.
The great emporium. Nig. mag., (81) Je. 1964: 84–97, illus., map.
A brief historical commentary on Kano city and Kano emirate.

2410 Hartert, Ernst
Reiseskizzen aus dem Haussalande. Globus, (52) 1887: 346–352; (53) 1888: 97–101.

2411 Hoppe, E. O.
Kano in Hausaland. Canadian geog. j., 38 (1) Jan. 1949: 39–47.

2412 Jackson, James Grey
An account of Timbuctoo and Housa, territories in the interior of Africa, by El Hage Abd Salam Shabeeny: with notes critical and explanatory. To which is added letters descriptive of travels through west and south Barbary and across the mountains of Atlas; also, fragments, notes, and anecdotes; specimens of the Arabic epistolary style . . . London, Longman, Hurst, Rees, Orme and Brown, 1820, repr. London, Frank Cass, 1967. xxx, 547p. maps.
Travel and description in Morocco and the Western Sudan. Shabeeny's account (about 54 pages) is followed by miscellaneous items, including letters to and from Jackson.

2413 Kano survey, 1950, covering stage two in the Kano Province development pro-gramme. Zaria, Gaskiya corporation, 1950.
A general survey giving brief histori-cal, cultural, economic and political account of Kano Province.

2414 Kumm, Hermann Karl Wilhelm
From Hausaland to Egypt through the Sudan. London, Constable, 1910. xiv 324p.
See also [325] and [326].

Leo Africanus
The history and description of Africa. See [344] and [345].

2415 Lezzi, Giuseppe A.
Cano. Afr. ital., (34) 1915: 91–95, illus.

2416 Maguzawa. In Notes on the tribes . . . by O. Temple, 2nd ed., 1922, repr. 1965: 263–264.

2417 Mani, M. Abdulmalik
Birnin Kano. Lagos, 1946. 37p.

2418 Miller, Ethel P.
Kano: a guide to the city and its en-virons. Zaria, Gaskiya [1951] [ii] 28p. illus., map.

2419 Miller, R.
Katsina, a city of the desert border. Geography, 22, pt. 4 (118) Dec. 1937: 282–292, illus., map.

2420 —Katsina, a region of Hausaland. Scot. geog. mag., 54 (4) Jl. 1938: 203–219, maps.

2421 Miller, Walter Richard Samuel
Fatima; a Hausa novel. Lagos, C. M. S. bookshop, 1933. 92p.
Text in Hausa.

2421a —Reflections of a pioneer. See [384].

2421b —Yesterday and tomorrow in Northern Nigeria. See [385].

2421c Muhammad, Abdullah Ibn Tazayinwal-Waraqät. See [394].

2422 Nagogo, Usman, Emir of Katsina
The Gobarau minaret, Katsina. Nig. mag., (29) 1948: 246.
On the great height of the Gobarau mosque minaret (built about 1400), and the consequent dangers to which muezzins were exposed during prayers.

2423 Niven, Cecil Rex
Kano in 1933. Geog. j., 82 (4) Oct. 1933: 336–343.

2424 Note on the Haussawa. In Notes on the tribes . . . by O. Temple, 2nd ed., 1922, repr. 1965: 405–408.

2425 Pasteyns, Fr.
Nigérie. Kano. Bull. Soc. roy. belge de géog., 52, 1928: 137–140.

2426 Petermann, A.
Dr. H. Barth's Rückreise von Timbuctu nach Kano, vom 8 Juli bis 17 October, 1854. Petermanns Mitt., 1855: 85–89.

2427 Prothero, R. Mansell
Informants and statistics—population changes in Gwadabawa District, Sokoto Province, Northern Nigeria, 1953–54. Nig. geog. j., 3 (2) Nov. 1960: 26–32, maps.

2428 —Sokoto Province, past and future. W. Africa, (2315) Oct. 1961: 1131–1132.

2329 Robinson, Charles Henry
Hausa territories. Geog. j., 8, 1896: 201–211.

2430 —Hausaland. Scot. geog. mag., 12, 1896: 21–24, map.

2431 —Hausaland, or Fifteen hundred miles

through the Central Soudan. London, Sampson, Low, Marston, 1896. xv, 304p. illus.

2431a —Nigeria; our latest protectorate. See [486].

2431b S., W.J.S'. and K., M.W.
The city of Sokoto. See [2141].

2432 Sharwood-Smith, B. E.
Sokoto survey. Zaria, Gaskiya, 1948.

2433 Staudinger, Paul
Im Herzen der Haussaländer. Reise im westlichen Sudan nebst Bericht über den Verlauf der Deutschen Niger-Benuë-Expedition, sowie Abhandlungen über klimatische, naturwissenschaftliche und ethnographische Beobachtungen in den eigentlichen Haussaländern. Berlin, Adolf Landsberger, 1889. [2] x, 758p. map.
An English translation by J. E. Moody, to be published by Frank Cass, is expected to be out shortly.

2434 Thomson, Joseph
Sketch of a trip to Sokoto by the River Niger. *J. Manchester geog. soc.*, 2, 1886: 1–18, map.

2435 Wallace, W.
Hausa territories: notes on a journey through the Sokoto empire and Borgu. *Geog. j.*, 8, 1896: 211–221.

2436 Wellesley-Cole, R. S.
Kano, city of romance. *Africana*, 1 (2) Apr. 1949: 15–18, illus.

2437 Whittlesey, Derwent
Kano: a Sudanese metropolis. *Geog. rev.*, 27 (2) Apr. 1937: 177–199, illus., map.
A compendious geographical essay on Kano city.

2. PHYSICAL ANTHROPOLOGY

2437a Charmers, J. N. M.
The ABO, MNS and Rh blood groups of the Nigerians. See [572].

2438 Roberts, D. F.
The incidence of red-green colour-blindness in Hausa. *Man*, 62, Feb. 1962: 19–2 (art. 16) illus., bibliog.
Describes a test (the Ishihara test) he had conducted on 609 people—Hausa, Fulani, Muzuwa and Maguzawa—in the northern part of Katsina.

2438a Lawler, Sylvia D. (and others)
The Lewis and secretor characters in the Fulani and Habe. See (2144a)

3. SOCIAL AND CULTURAL ANTHROPOLOGY ETHNOGRAPHY

(i) General

2439 Allen, A. R.
The Katsina 'airborn division'. *Oversea educ.*, 26 (4) Jan. 1955: 134–136.

2440 Bartel-Noirot,
Une province haoussa au Niger: le Tessaoua. Essai sur les coûtumes. *Rens. col.*, Feb. 1937: 20–24; May, 1937: 41–45.

2441 Beddoes, H. R.
Hausa notes. *J. Afr. soc.*, 2 (8) Jl. 1903: 451–453.
Twenty-five questions and answers on Hausa life and customs. The answers were supplied by one Adamu, born at Lokoja of Hausa parents, and who had been to Kano.

2442 Bohannan, Paul J.
An alternate residence classification. *Amer. anthrop.*, 59 (1) 1957: 126–131.
General discussion of the problem of residence classification in anthropology, with illustrations from Hausa (pp. 127–128) and Tiv (p. 128).

2443 Dry, D. P. L.
The place of Islam in Hausa society. 1953.
D. Phil. thesis, Oxford.

2444 —The social development of the Hausa child. *Int. W. Afr. conf. proc. 3rd, 1949. 1956*: 164–170.
On the upbringing and training for citizenship of children among the Hausa today. Based on observations in a large village in Zaria emirate, with some cross-checking in other areas.

2445 Dry, Elsie
A comparative study of the play of British and Hausa children to compare the significant differences with special reference to their use in the diagnosis of maladjustment. 1951.
M.A. thesis, Leeds university.

2446 Durand, O.
De l'influence du groupement Haussa dans le brassage des idées en Afrique occidentale. *INCIDI*, 30, 1957: 173–180.

2447 Graham, C.
The Hausa in Hausa country. *Nig. mag.*, (13) Mar. 1938: 19–23, illus.

2448 Greenberg, Joseph Harold
Some aspects of Negro-Mohammedan culture contact among the Hausa. *Amer. anthrop.*, 43 (1) Jan-Mar. 1941: 51–61, bibliog.
Also reprinted in *Cultures and societies of Africa*, ed. Simon and Phoebe Ottenberg, 1960: 477–488 [720].

2449 Harris, Percy Graham
The Kebbi fishermen (Sokoto Province, Nigeria). *J.R.A.I.*, 72 (1–2) 1942: 23–31.
Description of Kebbi fishing methods, and the rituals and ceremonies connected therewith.

2450 —Notes on Yauri (Sokoto Province) Nigeria. *J.R.A.I.*, 60, Jl.–Dec. 1930: 283–334p.

2451 —Some conventional Hausa names. *Man*, 31, 1931: 272–274 (art. 265).
Lists 41 conventional Hausa names, giving the signification of each.

2452 Jeffreys, M. D. W.
West African night commodes. *Man*, 57, 1957 (art. 121): 103, illus.
Brief note on night toilet facilities among the Hausa and other tribes.

2453 Kano's great festival. *W. Afr. rev.*, 30 (379) Apr. 1959: 254–255, illus.

Short note on the festival held just before Northern Nigeria's internal self-government.

2454 Krause, Gottlob Adolf, *tr.*
Merkwürdige Sitten der Haussa. Aus der Haussa-Sprache übersetzt. *Globus*, 69 (23) Je. 1896: 373–375.
German translation of a Hausa text descriptive of various aspects of Hausa life and customs.

2455 Krieger, Kurt
Die Bedeutung statistischer Erhebungen für die Völkerkunde am Beispiel der Stadt Anka in Nord-Nigeria. *Sociologus, N.F.*, 4 (1) 1954: 67–81.
Discusses the importance of population statistics for anthropological investigation, illustrating this with figures for the town of Anka in Northern Nigeria.

2456 La Chard, L. W.
The arrow-poisons of Northern Nigeria. *J. Afr. soc.*, 5 (17) Oct. 1905: 22–27.
Poisons used by the Hausas in tipping their arrows, including the Hausa names of the plants used.

2457 Meek, Charles Kingsley
Fighting-wristlets. *Man*, 27, Mar. 1927: 47–50 (art. 29) illus.
Describes fighting wristlets dug up in the ancient site of Shira town, Bauchi Province and in Zurmi district, Sokoto Province, with brief account of the use of fighting wristlets by the modern Maguzawa, Kyanga and Shanga.

2458 Mischlisch, Adam
Die Hausa. *Archiv. f. Anthrop., n.F.*, 28 (3–4) 1943: 126–133.

2459 —History of Islam in the Hausa states. *M.S.O.S.*, 6, 1904: 86.

2460 —Über Sitten und Gebrauche in Hausa. *M.S.O.S.*, 10, 1907: 155–181; 11, 1908: 1–81; 12, 1909: 215–274.
Hausa texts, with interlinear German translation. The first instalment deals with the Hausas, their history and their states, the second with their customs, and the third with their law and religion (Islam).

2461 Palmer, Herbert Richmond
Notes on traces of totemism and other customs in Hausaland. *Man*, 10, 1910: 72–76 (art. 40).

2462 Pilkington, Frederick
The Hausa trader of Nigeria. *Afr. world*, Feb. 1951: 11–12, illus.

2463 Prietze, Rudolf
Arzneipflanzen der Hausa. *Z. f. Ethnol.*, 4, 1913–14: 81–90.
A list of plants in Hausa, with notes on their uses.

2464 Prothero, R. Mansell
Migrant labour from Sokoto Province, Northern Nigeria. [Kaduna, Govt. printer, 1959] [8] 46p. maps.

2465 —Population patterns and migrations in Sokoto Province, Northern Nigeria. In *Natural resources, food and population in inter-tropical Africa, ed. L. Dudley Stamp, 1956*: 49–54, maps.

2466 Shiloh, Ailon
A case study of disease and culture in action: leprosy among the Hausa of Northern Nigeria. *Human organisation*, 24 (2) summer 1965: 140–147.

2467 Smith, Mary F.
Baba of Karo, a woman of the Muslim Hausa: with an introduction and notes by M. G. Smith. London, Faber, 1954. 299p., illus., map.
Autobiography of Baba recorded by Mrs. Smith between November 1949 and January 1950. Baba, a Hausa woman of Kanuri origin was born in the late 19th century, and lived in Kano and Zaria "between approximately 1890 and 1951". Her story gives a vivid account of life and events in these parts of Nigeria during the period. The Introduction (pp. 11-34) gives as background to the story, a brief ethnological sketch of the Hausas.

2469 Smith, Michael Garfield
The beginnings of Hausa society, A.D. 1000–1500. In *The historian in tropical Africa, ed. by J. Vansina [and others] 1964*: 339–354, bibliog.
Summary in French, pp. 354–357.

2470 *—Le coopératisme en société haoussa. Information* [Paris] (11) Jan. 1957: 1–21.

2471 —The Hausa of Northern Nigeria. In *Peoples of Africa, ed. J. L. Gibbs, 1965*: 119–155, illus., bibliog.
Ethnographic summary.

2472 Staudinger, Paul.
Die Bevölkerung der Haussa-Länder. *Z. f. Ethnol.*, 23, 1891: 228–237.

2473 —Totengebräuche bei den Haussah. *Z. f. Ethnol.*, 28, 1896: 402–405.

2474 Tremearne, Arthur John Newman
Hausa superstitions and customs; an introduction to the folk-lore and the folk. London, John Bale & Danielson, 1913. xv, 548p. illus., map.

2475 —The Hausas . . . In his *The Niger and the West Sudan . . .* 1910: 51–64.

2476 —Notes on some Nigerian tribal marks. *J.R.A.I.*, 41, 1911: 162–178. illus. (2 plates).

2477 Ubiquitous Hausa traders. *Times Brit. colonies rev.*, (24) 1956: 12.

2478 Westermann, Diedrich
Some notes on the Hausa people and their language. In *A Hausa-English dictionary and English-Hausa vocabulary, by G. P. Bargery, 1934*: ix–xix.
Origin, history, religion and language of the Hausa people. The section on language (pp. xiii–xix) includes a bibliographical note (pp. xiv–xvi) on previous publications on the language.

3. (ii) History

2479 Abubakar, Imam
Daura sword is the symbol of the seven states of Hausaland. *W. Afr. ann.*, 1950: 114–115.

Tells the legend surrounding the sword then kept in the palace at Daura in Katsina Province.

2480　—Hausa bakwai. Zaria, NORLA, 1954. 16p.
　　　Origin of the seven Hausa states and other historical topics.

2481　Arikpo, Okoi
　　　Legends and folklore. *W. Afr. rev.*, 30 (383) Oct. 1959: 665–667.
　　　Hausa and Yoruba legends of origin.

2482　Arnett, Edward John *tr.*
　　　A Hausa-chronicle. *J. Afr. soc.*, 9 (34) Jan. 1910: 161–167.
　　　Translation of a Hausa manuscript entitled *"Daura Makas Sariki"* which "records the current Hausa belief as to the origin of their race." It includes a list of Habe and Fulani rulers of Zaria.

2483　—The history of Sokoto. In his *The rise of the Sokoto Fulani . . . 1922.* 43p.
　　　Paged separately and appended at the end of the main work which it briefly summarises. [2198].

2484　Bature [pseud.]
　　　Within a city wall; story of Zaria. *W. Afr. rev.*, 26 (333) Je. 1955: 539–545, illus.
　　　Historical notes on the city.

2485　Campbell, M. J.
　　　The walls of a city. *Nig. mag.*, (60), 1959: 39–59, illus., plan.
　　　History and description of the walls of the city of Zaria.

2486　Charles, P.
　　　Kano chronicle: report from Northern Nigeria. *New Afr.*, 7 (11) Dec. 1965: 7–8.

2487　Daura. *Nig. mag.*, (50) 1956: 224–237, illus.
　　　History of Daura, a town in the northeast of Katsina Province.

2488　Dike, Kenneth Onwuka
　　　Sokoto. In *Ency. Brit.*, 1959, v. 20 pp. 935–936, bibliog.
　　　Description of Sokoto Province, followed by brief account of the Hausa states, the Fulani empire, and the British conquest.

2489　Hajji, Sa'id
　　　History of Sokoto; translated by C. E. J. Whitting. Kano, Ife-Olu printing works, 1949. 38p.

2490　*—Ta'rikh i Sukut. In *Documents arabes relatifs à l'histoire du Soudan: Tedzkiret en-Nisian fi Akhbar Molouk es Soudan. Trad. par O. Houdas, 1901*:
　　　History of Sokoto translated into French from the Arabic original.

2491　Hallam, W. K. R.
　　　An introduction to the history of Hausaland. *Nig. field*, 31 (4) Oct. 1966: 164–177, maps.

2492　Hassan, *Makaman Abuja* and Na'Ibi, Shuaibu
　　　Chronicle of Abuja, translated and arranged [by Frank Heath] from Hausa. Ibadan, University press, for Abuja native administration, 1952. vii, [4] 92p. illus., map.

2493　——Revised and enlarged ed. with new illustrations. Lagos, African universities press, 1962. x, 91p. illus.

2494　—Extracts from 'A chronicle of Abuja'. Translated by F. Heath. *Nig. mag.*, (33) 1950: 135–152, illus.

2495　—Makau: sarkin Zazzau na ha'be laborin Abuja. Babi na I. Zaria, Gaskiya corporation [1952] [4] 43p. (Littattafan hira, 5).

2496　—Tarihi da al'adun ha'be na Abuja. Kashi na II. Zaria, Gaskiya corporation, [1952] 46p. (Littattafan hira, 6).

2497　Hiskett, Mervyn
　　　City of history: the story of Kano. *W. Afr. rev.*, 28 (360) Sept. 1957: 849–856, illus.

2498　—An Islamic tradition of reform in the Western Sudan from the sixteenth to the eighteenth century, *B.S.O.A.S.*, 25 (3) 1962: 577–596.

2499　—The Kano chronicle. *J. Roy. Asiatic soc.*, (1–2) Apr. 1957: 79–81.

2500　—*Kitab al-farq.*: a work on the Habe kingdoms attributed to 'Uthmān dan Fodio. *B.S.O.A.S.*, 23 (3) 1960: 558–579.
　　　Arabic text with English translation of one of the minor works attributed to Shehu dan Fodio, and listed neither by Sultan Bello in the *Infaq al-maysūr*, nor by C. E. J. Whitting in his *The unprinted indigenous arabic literature of Northern Nig.* [56], nor by Vadja in his *Contribution à la connaissance de la littérature arabe en Afrique occidentale.* [52] The English translation is followed by an interesting commentary in which this account of the Habe states is compared with that in the Kano chronicle and those of Clapperton and Barth.

2501　—The 'Song of Bagauda': a Hausa king list and homily in verse. I. *B.S.O.A.S.*, 27 (3) 1964: 540–567; II. 28 (1) 1965: 112–135; III. 28 (2) 1965: 363–385.
　　　Part I gives the Hausa text of the song, with an introduction in English; part II gives an English translation; and Part III deals with its date and authenticity, its account of history, its form and prosody, and its relation to the Islamic tradition in Hausa literature.

2502　Hunwick, J. O.
　　　A collection of MSS belonging to the Kano Native Authority. *Hist. soc. Nig. Bull. news.*, 7 (2) 1962. Supplement.

2503　Ifemesia, C. Chieka
　　　States of the Central Sudan: II. The Hausa states. In *A thousand years of West African history*, ed. J. F. A. Ajayi and I. Espie, 1965: 90–112.

2504　Katsina. *Nig. mag.*, (51) 1956: 298–317, illus.
　　　History of Katsina, with photographs illustrating scenes in the present day town.

2505　Katsina: Northern Nigeria's city of learning. *W. Afr. rev.*, 23 (301) Oct. 1952: 1000–1005, illus.

A profusely illustrated description of the town.

2506 Krieger, Kurt
Zur Geschichte von Zamfara. *M.S.O.S.*, 1955: 51–56.

2507 —Geschichte von Zamfara, Sokoto-Provinz, Nordnigeria. Berlin, Dietrich Reimer Verlag, 1959. 147p. illus., map, bibliog.
A collection of extracts from various sources illustrating the history of Zamfara. Arranged chronologically under the rulers of Zamfara from about 1300 to 1946.

2508 —Weitere Bemerkungen zur Geschichte von Zamfara, Sokoto Provinz, Nord-nigeria. *Baessler-Arch., N.F.*, 12 (1) 1964: 89–139, illus., bibliog.
Continuation of author's earlier studies published as *Geschichte von Zamfara*. Here additional sources are given and a further attempt made at chronological sequence.

2509 —Die Zamfarawa. Ein Stamm der Hausa in Nord-Nigeria. *Geog. Rdsch.*, 6 (10) Oct. 1954: 387–393, map.
Sketches the history of the Zamfarawa, with brief notes on their political and economic structure and religious beliefs.

2510 Mani, M. Abdulmalik
Zuwan Turawa Nijeriya lá arewa. Zaria, NORLA, London, Longmans, Green, 1957. xi, 218p.
History of the British occupation of Northern Nigeria. Text in Hausa.

2511 Mischlich, Adam
Beiträge zur Geschichte der Haussa-staaten. *M.S.O.S.*, 6, 1903: 137–242, map.
Historical notes on Kano, Katsina, Gobir, Kebi, Zaria, Bauchi and other states in Northern Nigeria.

2512 —Contributions to the history of the Hausa states. *J. Afr. soc.*, 4 (16) Jl. 1905: 455–479.
English version of [2511] with useful introduction by J. Lippert, pp. 455–460.

2513 Orr, Charles William James
The Hausa race. *J. Afr. soc.*, 7 (27) Apr. 1908: 278–283; 8 (31) Apr. 1909: 274–278.
Origin and history of the Hausa race.

2514 Palmer, Herbert Richmond
Hausa legend and earth pyramids in the Western and Central Sudan. *B.S.O.A.S.*, 2 (2) 1921–23: 225–233.

2515 —History of Daura. In his *Sudanese memoirs, v. 3, 1928*: 132-146.

2516 —History of Katsina. *J. Afr. soc.*, 26 (103) Apr. 1927: 216–236.

2517 —History of Katsina. In his *Sudanese memoirs, v. 3, 1928*: 74–91.

2518 —The Kano chronicle; translated, with an introduction. *J. R. A. I.*, 38, 1908: 58–98, illus.
See also his *Sudanese memoirs*, vol. 3, pp. 92–132.

—Sudanese memoirs. See [3994].

2519 Sharwood-Smith, Joan
Kano. *Corona*, 4 (12) Dec. 1952: 461–465.
Summary of the city's history.

2520 Smith, Henry Frederick Charles
A forgotten Hausa historian of Timbuktu? *Hist. soc. Nig. bull. news*, 4 (4) Je. 1959:

2521 —A fragment of 18th century Katsina. *Hist. soc. Nig. bull. news*, 5 (4) Mar. 1961.

2522 —A further adventure in the chronology of Katsina. *Hist. soc. Nig. bull. news*, 6 (1) Je. 1961.

2523 —A seventeenth century writer of Katsina. *Hist. soc. Nig. bull. news*, 6 (1) 1961. Suppl.

2524 Smith, Michael Garfield
Field histories among the Hausa. *J. Afr. hist.*, 7 (1) 1961: 87–101.
Detailed description of field work undertaken to establish the pattern of the history of Zaria from 1804–1950.

2525 Sokoto city. *Nig. mag.*, (57) 1958: 110–131, illus.

2526 Sölken, Heinz
Afrikanische Dokumente zur Frage der Entstehung der hausanischen Diaspora in Oberguinea. 1940. 127p.

2527 —Die Geschichte von Kabi nach Imam Umaru (1. Teil) *Mitt. Inst. f. Orient-forsch.*, 7 (1) 1959: 123–162. bibliog.; (2 Teil) 9 (1) 1963: 30–99.
Reproduction, transliteration and a German translation of a MS written in Ajami script between 1855 and 1882 by Umaru, a learned Hausa from Kano. Contains useful chronicles recounting the relations between the Hausa state of Kebi and the Fulani of Sokoto and Gwandu.

2528 Tremearne, Arthur John Newmann
Notes on the origin of the Hausas. *J. Roy. soc. arts.*, 58, 1910: 767–775.

2529 Westermann, Diedrich
Die Volkwerdung der Hausa. Berlin, Deutsche Akademie der Wissenschaften zu Berlin, 1949. 44p. (Sitz.-ber. dtsch. Akad. d. Wiss. Berlin: Philosophisch-historische Klasse, Nr. 2).
Outline account of the social, cultural and political history of the Hausa people.

2530 Whitting, C. E. J.
Extracts from an Arabic history of Sokoto. *Afr. affairs*, 47 (188) Jl. 1948: 160–169.
Extracts from a new translation of Hajji Sa'id's history of Sokoto published 1889 [2489] Gives account of life in Hausaland and of sporadic revolts by the Hausa states against the Fulani rulers.

—History of Sokoto, by Hajji Sa'id. See [2489].

3. (iii) Marriage, Family, Lineage Structure

2531 Dry, D. P. L.

The family organisation of the Hausa of Northern Nigeria, 1950.
B.Sc. thesis, Oxford University.

2532 —Some aspects of Hausa family structure. *Int. W. Afr. conf. proc. 3rd, 1949. 1956*: 158–163.

Hausa lineage and family structure in modern times. Based on data collected largely in the smaller market towns in Zaria emirate.

2533 Elias, Taslim Olawale
Hausa marriage. *Nig. mag.*, (53) 1957: 135–149, illus.

Summary account of Hausa and Fulani marriage law and customs.

2534 Greenberg, Joseph Harold
Islam and clan organisation among the Hausa. *S. –W. j. anthrop.*, 3 (3) Autumn 1947: 193–211.

Analysis of the conflict and interplay between Muslim and traditional kinship systems and marriage customs among the Hausa.

2534a Krusius, P.
Die Maguzawa. See [2583].

2535 Temietan, S. O.
Marriage amongst the Jekri tribes as contrasted with that amongst the Hausa tribes. *Nig. mag.*, (13) Mar. 1938: 75–78.

2536 Tremearne, Arthur John Newmann
Marital relations of the Hausas as shown in their folklore. *Man*, 14, 1914: 23–26 (art. 13); 137–139 (art. 69); 148–156 (art. 76)

3. (iv) Government, Kingship, Law

2537 Anderson, J. N. D.
The Maliki law of homicide. Zaria, Gaskiya, 1953. 14p.

2538 Bala Abuja, J.
Koranic and Moslem Law teaching in Hausaland. *Nig. mag.*, (37) 1951: 25–28.

2539 Cole, Cedric William
Report on land tenure: Niger province. Kaduna, Govt. printer, 1952. [iv] 85p.

2540 —Report on land tenure: Zaria Province. Kaduna, Govt. printer, 1952. [iv] 84p.

2541 Daniel F. de F.
The regalia of Katsina, Northern Provinces, Nigeria. *J. Afr. soc.*, 31 (122) Jan. 1932: 80–83, illus.

Notes on the Sword of Korau, the Bebe sword, the Brazen Pot of Korau, the Bachelor Drum of Katsina, and other drums.

2542 Dry, D. P. L.
The Hausa attitude to authority. *WAISER conf. proc.*, 1952: 15–21.

An examination of the Hausa concept of, and attitude towards, authority.

2543 Geismer, L.
L'administration d'un sultanat haoussa. *Outre-Mer*, (3) Sept. 1929: 307–313.

On the state structure and administration of Gobir.

2544 Gowers, W. F. *tr.*
Notes on Mohammedan law in Northern Nigeria; being extracts mainly from the Risalah of Abu Muhammadu ibn Abu Zayd, translated into Hausa. Lagos, Govt. printer, 1919. 32p.

Includes rules on slavery, land tenure and taxation, contracts, marriage, homicide, etc.

2545 McDowell, C. M.
An introduction to the problems of ownership of land in Northern Nigeria. Zaria, Institute of administration, 1966. iv, 80p. (Research memorandum).

Prothero, R. Mansell
Land use, land holdings and land tenure at Soba, Zaria Province. See [2573].

2546 Rowling, Cecil William
Report on land tenure: Kano Province. Kaduna, Govt. printer, 1952. iv, 80p.

2547 Shekh Mohammed Al-Maghili of Tlemsen
The obligations of princes; an essay on Moslem kingship. Translated from the Arabic by T. H. Baldwin. Beyrouth, Liban, Imprimerie Catholique, 1932. 22p.

The author, a Moroccan who spent a long time as a scholar in N. Africa is said to have visited Kano and Katsina, the former possibly during Mohammed Rumfa's reign, and to have written the "treatise on government" on the invitation of Rumfa.

2548 Smith, Michael Garfield
Government in Zazzau, 1800–1950. London, O.U.P., for Int. Afr. Inst., 1960. xii, 371p. maps, bibliog.

A study, comparative and analytical, of the political organisation of Zaria, under Habe (or Hausa). Fulani, and British administrations, from 1800–1950.

2549 —Hausa inheritance and succession. In *Studies in the laws of succession in Nigeria, edited by J. D. M. Derrett*, 1965: 230–281.

2550 —Historical and cultural conditions of political corruption among the Hausa. *Comp. stud. soc. hist.*, 6 (2) Jan. 1964: 164–194.

With comment by J. J. Van Klaveren, pp. 195–198.

2551 Upward, Allen
In the provincial court: notes of cases tried in the provincial court of Kabba, Northern Nigeria. *J. Afr. soc.*, 3 (12) Jl. 1904: 405–409.

3. (v) Social Organization and Structure, Social Relationships

2552 Burness, H. M.
The position of women in Gwandu and Yauri. *Oversea educ.*, 26 (4) Jan. 1955: 143–152.

2553 —Women in Katsina Province, Northern Nigeria. *Oversea educ.*, 29 (3) Oct. 1957: 116–122.

2554 Sellnow, Irmgard
Die Stellung der Sklaven in der Hausa-Gesellschaft. *Mitt. Inst. Orientforsch.*, 10 (1) 1964: 85–102.

On the status and conditions of slaves in Hausa society.

2555   Smith, Michael Garfield
The Hausa system of social status. *N.I.S.E.R. conf. proc., 1958*: 180–194; *Africa*, 29 (3) Jl. 1959: 239–252.
On status determinants and status structure among the Hausa people.

2556   —Kebbi and Hausa stratification. *Brit. j. sociol.*, 12 (1) Mar. 1961: 52–61.
A rejoinder to E. R. Yeld's article on Islam and social stratification in Northern Nigeria. See [2559].

2557   *—Slavery and emancipation in two societies. *Soc. & econ. stud.*, [Univ. of the West Indies] 3, 1954:
In Zaria and Jamaica.

2558   Traoré, Dominique
La condition de l'esclavage bawa-gandou dans l'ancien royaume peul de Sokoto. *Notes afr.*, (40) Oct. 1948: 13.

2559   Yeld, E. R.
Islam and social stratification in Northern Nigeria. *Brit. j. sociol.*, 11 (2) Je. 1960: 112–128.
Investigation of social stratification and the effects of religious, political, economic, kinship, and occupational factors on social status in the Fulani emirates and in Kebbi. See also [2556].

2560   —A study of the social position of women in Kebbi (Northern Nigeria) 1961.
M.A. thesis, London.

3. (vi) Economy, Agriculture, Trade.

2561   Bovill, Edward William
Jega market. *J. Afr. soc.*, 22 (85) Oct. 1922: 50–60, map.
Notes on the history of the town, with an account of its commerce.

2562   Cardew, Michael
Gobir granaries. *Nig. mag.*, (67) Dec. 1960: 216–223, illus.
Construction, appearance and use of granaries in Gobir village.

2563   Cohen, Abner
Politics of the Kola trade: some process of tribal community formation among migrants in West African towns. *Africa*, 36 (1) Jan. 1966: 18–36, bibliog.
French summary, pp. 35–36.

2564   Daniel, F.
Agricultural implement from Sokoto, Nigeria. *Man*, 31, 1931: 48. (art. 47) illus.

2565   Fiévet, Maurice
Salt caravan. *Nig. mag.*, (41) 1953: 4–20, illus.
Describes the age-old salt trade between Bilma and the Hausa country and explains the people's preference for this desert salt as being due to their belief that it gives men and women strength to have children.

2566   Harris, Percy Graham
Agricultural and pastoral implements of the people of Argungun Emirate. *Man*, 31, 1931: 43–48 (art. 46) illus.

2567   Holden, M. J.
Fishing methods in Sokoto Province. *Nig. field.*, 26 (4) Oct. 1961: 147–158.

2568   Krieger, Kurt
Kola-Karawanen. Ein Beitrag zur Geschichte des Hausahandels. *Mitt. Inst. Orientforsch.*, 2 (2) 1954: 289–324, illus., maps.

2569   Lamb, P. H.
Agriculture in Hausaland. *Bull. Imp. inst.*, 11, 1913: 626–634.

2570   Mischlich, Adam
Über die Kulturen im Mittel-Sudan: Landwirtschaft, Gewerbe, Handel. Berlin, Reimer, 1942. xi, 199p.

2571   Pedler, F. J.
A study of income and expenditure in Northern Zaria. *Africa*, 18 (4) Oct. 1948: 259–271, bibliog.
A detailed analysis of the economy of the indigenous population of the Northern part of Zaria Province. Emphasis is on sources of income and main expenditure.

2572   Prothero, R. Mansell
Land use at Soba, Zaria Province, Northern Nigeria. *Econ. geogr.*, 33 (1) Jan. 1957: 72–86, maps (sketch).

2573   —Land use, land holdings, and land tenure at Soba, Zaria Province, Northern Nigeria. *Bull. IFAN.*, 19 (3–4) Jl.–Oct. 1957: 558–563.

2574   Smith, Michael Garfield
The economy of Hausa communities of Zaria: a report to the Colonial research council. London, H.M.S.O., for Colonial office, 1955. vii, 264p. illus., maps, bibliog. (Colonial research studies, no. 16).
A detailed socio-economic investigation of the Hausa population. Considers indigenous economic activities in relation to their social context.

2575   —Exchange and marketing among the Hausa. In *Markets in Africa, ed. P. Bohannan and G. Dalton, 1962*: 298–334.
Trade and commerce among the Hausa of Northern Nigeria, with detailed study of market operations. Preceded by a historical sketch.

2576   —A study of Hausa domestic economy in Northern Zaria. *Africa*, 22 (4) Oct. 1952: 333–347.
French summary, p. 347.

3. (vii) Food Preparation and Consumption, Standard of Living

2577   McCulloch, W. E.
An enquiry into the dietaries of the Hausa and town Fulani. *W. Afr. med. j.*, 3, 1929–30: 8–22; 62–73.

3. (viii) Religion

2578   Alexander, D.
Notes on "Bori". *Northern Nigeria Gazette*, 11, 1910: 197–199.
On the possession cult known in Hausa as bori.

2579   Brice-Bennett, F. O.

Festival of Kano, 1959. Photographs by F. Uher. London, Brown Knight & Truscott, 1959. viii, 20, ix-xvip. illus. (some col.).

2580 Campbell, M. J.
Incident at Satiru. *W. Afr. rev.*, 29 (371) Aug. 1958: 679–681.
Account of a Mahdist incited anti-British revolt in 1906 in Satiru, a village about twenty-eight miles south of Sokoto.

2581 Ciroma, Mallam A. L.
The dying god of Zagun. *Nig. field*, 19 (4) Oct. 1954: 185.
Account of a religious ceremony celebrated alternately at Zagun and Rishini once every seven years, and in which a chief of one of the villages was made a god to be killed at the end of the 7 years.

2582 Greenberg, Joseph Harold
The influence of Islam on a Sudanese religion. New York, J. J. Augustin, 1946. ix, 73p. map, bibliog. (Amer. ethnol. soc. Monograph no. 10).
Effect of Islam upon the religious beliefs and practices of the pagan Hausa (Maguzawa) of Kano.

2583 Krusius, P.
Die Maguzawa. *Archiv. f. Anthrop.*, N.F., 14, 1915: 288–315, illus.
Describes religious beliefs, ideas about the soul, witches, spirits, and marriage customs of the Maguzawa, pagan Hausas living in Katsina, Zaria and Kano areas. Includes some songs with German translations.

2584 Meinhof, Carl
Ein magisches Quadrat auf einem Hausa-Amulett. *Z.f. E.S.*, 14, 1923–24: 224–226.
Interprets the signification of figures on the facsimile of a Hausa amulet reproduced in C. H. Robinson's "Specimens of Hausa literature." [2824].

2585 Palmer, Herbert Richmond
Bori among the Hausas. *Man*, 14, Jl. 1914: 113–117 (art. 52).

2586 Raulin, H.
Un aspect historique des rapports de l'Islam et de l'animisme au Niger. *J. Soc. afr.*, 32 (2) 1962: 249–274.

2587 Su; Argungu fishing festival. *Nig. mag.*, (55) 1957: 294–316, illus.

2588 Tremearne, Arthur John Newman
The ban of the bori; demons and demon-dancing in West and North Africa. London, Heath, Cranton & Ousley [1914], repr. London, Frank Cass, 1968. 504p. illus.
Pp. 499–504 devoted to extracts from reviews.

2589 —Bori beliefs and ceremonies. *J.R.A.I.*, 45, 1915: 23–69.
—Hausa superstitions and customs. See [2474].

2590 *Zwernemann, Jürgen
Nana Buruku. Ein Beitrag zum Kult eines Gottes in Oberguinea. *Acta tropica*, 17 (4) 1960: 343–364, map, bibliog.

3. (ix) Recreation, Music, Dance

2591 Ames, D. W.
Hausa drums of Zaria. *Ibadan*, (21) Oct. 1965: 62–80, illus.
Detailed description of different kinds of drum found among the Hausa in Zaria Province. Notes their construction and the occasions when each type is used.

2592 East, Rupert Moultrie
Six Hausa plays. Zaria, West Africa publicity ltd., 1936. 80p.
Printed in England.

2593 Funke, E.
Einige Tanz-und Liebeslieder der Hausa. *Z.f.E.S.*, 11 (4) Oct. 1921: 259–278.
Hausa songs, with German translation. Includes incidental references in text to drums and drumming.

2594 Harris, Percy Graham
Notes on drums and musical instruments seen in Sokoto Province, Nigeria. *J.R.A.I.*, 62, 1932: 105–125, illus.

2595 Jeffreys, M. D. W.
Cha-cha. *Nig. field.*, 11, Dec. 1943: 197–200.
On the Egyptian origin of a game of chance called cha-cha widely played in Northern Nigeria. Written in the form of a dialogue.

2596 Kirk-Greene, Anthony Hamilton Millard and Uher, Francis
Makidi—the Hausa drummer. Text by Anthony Kirk-Greene, photographs by Francis Uher. *Nig. mag.*, (71) Dec. 1961: 338–355, illus.

2597 Krieger, Kurt
Knabenspiele der Hausa. *Baessler-Archiv, n.F.*, 3, 1955: 225–232, illus.
Description of some 46 games played by Hausa boys.

2598 Mackay, Mercedes
Shantu music of the harims of Nigeria. *Afr. mus.*, 1 (2) 1955: 56–57, illus.
Notes on the shantu, a gourd musical instrument used within the courtyards by Hausa women.

2599 Smith, Michael Garfield
The social functions and meanings of Hausa praise-singing. *Africa*, 27 (1) Jan. 1957: 26–45; *Ibadan*, (21) Oct. 1965: 81–92.
Summary in French, pp. 44–45, of the first journal.

3. (x) Stories, Proverbs, Riddles

2600 *Basset, René
Contes Haoussa et folk-lore Wolof. *Mélusine*, 3 and 4, 1886–1887:
Benton, P. Askell
Notes on some languages of the Western Sudan . . . and a few Hausa riddles and proverbs. See [1435].

2601 Edgar, Frank
Litafi na tatsuniyoyi na Hausa. Belfast, W. Erskine Mayne, 1911–1913. 3v.

L

A collection of Hausa tales. v.1, 463p.; v. 2, 435p.; v. 3, 464p.

2601a Fletcher, R. S.
Hausa sayings and folklore . . . See [2705].

2602 Hallam, W. K. R.
The Bayajida legend in Hausa folklore. *J. Afr. hist.*, 7 (1) 1966: 47–60.

2603 Lippert, Julius, ed.
Haussa-Märchen. Herausgegeben und übersetzt von J. Lippert. *M.S.O.S.*, 8, 1905: 223–250.

2604 Paddon, E. M.
Hausa proverbs and Hausa character. *Muslim world*, 5, 1915: 409–412.

2605 Rattray, Robert Sutherland
Hausa folk-lore, customs, proverbs, etc., collected and transliterated, with English translation and notes. Oxford, Clarendon press, 1913. 2v. fronts.
A collection of some 46 stories illustrating Hausa customs, reproduced in Arabic, with Hausa and English translations on opposite pages. Explanatory notes are given at the end of v. 2.

2605a Schon, James Frederick
Magana Hausa: native literature; or Proverbs, tales, fables, historical fragments in the Hausa language . . . London, 1885–6.
See full entry at [2834]

2605b Taylor, F. W. and Webb, A. G. G.
Labarun al'adun Hausawa da Zantatukanzu . . . See [2849].

2606 Tremearne, Arthur John Newman
Fifty Hausa folk-tales. *Folk-lore*, 21, 1910: 199–215; 351–365; 487–503; 22, 1911: 60–73; 218–228; 341–348; 457–473.

2607 —Hausa folklore. *Man*, 11, 1911: 20–23 (art. 11); 52–58 (art. 37).
Eight stories.

2608 —Hausa folklore. In His *Tailed head-hunters of Nigeria, 1912*: 320–335.
Seven Hausa folk tales.

2609 —Hausa folk-tales: the Hausa text of the stories in Hausa superstitions and customs, in Folklore, and in other publications. London, J. Bale, 1914. xii, 240p. (West African night's entertainment series, vol. 2).

2610 —Some specimens of Hausa folklore. *J. Roy. soc. arts.*, 58, 1910: 1061–1068.

2611 Tremearne, Mary and Tremearne, Arthur John Newman
Fables and fairy tales for little folk; or Uncle Remus in Hausaland (First series) Cambridge, W. Heffer, 1910. [viii] 135p. front., illus.
Twelve folk stories from Hausaland.

2612 Whitting, C. E. J.
Hausa and Fulani proverbs. Lagos, Govt. printer, 1940. [v] 192p.

3. (xi) Literary Expression, Literature

2613 East, Rupert Moultrie

A first essay in imaginative literature. *Africa*, 9 (3) Jl. 1936: 350–358.
On the problem of encouraging the Hausas of Northern Nigeria to produce in the 1930's imaginative literature in the vernacular for local readers. French summary, pp. 357–358.

2614 Muhammad, Liman
Comments on John N. Paden's A survey of Kano Hausa poetry. *Kano stud.*, 1 (2) Jl. 1966: 44–52.
Reply by J. N. Paden, ibid. pp. 53–55.

2615 Paden, John
A survey of Kano Hausa poetry. *Kano stud.*, 1 (1) 1965: 33–39.

2616 Rattray, Robert Sutherland
Hausa poetry. In *Essays presented to C. G. Seligman, ed. E. E. Evans-Pritchard [and others] 1934*: 255–265.

3. (xii) Architecture

2617 Crowder, Michael
The decorative architecture of Northern Nigeria: indigenous culture expressed in Hausa craftmanship. *Afr. world*, Feb. 1956: 9–10, illus.

2618 Dodge, J. S.
The rudu; a note on local form of sleeping quarters. *Nig. field*, 31 (4) Oct. 1966: 188–191, illus.
Description of raised sleeping huts for unmarried boys in parts of Northern Nigeria.

2619 Elliot, H. P.
Mud building in Kano. *Nig. mag.*, (20) 1940: 275–278, illus.

2620 Essing, D.
Blick auf die Kultur der Hausa. *Neues Afr.*, 6 (8) Aug. 1964: 278–279.
Brief notes on aspects of Hausa architecture, weaving, leather-work, and iron smelting.

2621 Foyle, Arthur M.
The house of a merchant in Kofarmata street, Kano. *Nig. mag.*, (37) 1951: 29–35.

2622 Jeffries, W. F.
Mud building in Northern Nigeria. *Nig. mag.*, (14) 1938: 110–111, illus.

2623 Kirk-Greene, Anthony Hamilton Millard
Decorated houses in Zaria. *Nig. mag.*, (68) Mar. 1961: 53–78, illus.
Discusses the modern trends in the decoration of external walls of houses in Zaria town (including the city) Holds that the practice is associated more with the successful merchant class than with any other group.

2624 —Walls of Zaria. *Craft horizons*, 22, Jan. 1962: 20–27.

2625 Peel, Cyril
Thermal conditions in traditional mud dwellings in Northern Nigeria. *J. trop. med. & hyg.*, 61. (8) Aug 1958: 189–203.
In Hausa houses in Kano.

2626 Tremearne, Arthur John Newman
Hausa houses. *Man*, 10, 1910: 177–180 (art. 99) illus.

3. (xiii) Arts and Crafts

2627 Antiquities of Sokoto. *W. Afr. rev.*, 30 (385) 1959: 843, illus.

2628 Balfour, Henry
Modern brass casting in West Africa. *J.R.A.I.*, 40–41 (n.s. 13–14) 1910: 525–528, illus.
Method of modern brass casting dictated to a Hausa man by a Yoruba man living in Togoland, and now translated from Hausa into English.

2629 —The *tandu* industry in Northern Nigeria and its affinities elsewhere. In *Essays presented to C. G. Seligman, ed. E. E. Evans-Pritchard [and others] 1934*: 15–18, illus.

2630 Beaton, W. G.
Tanning and dyeing of goat skins: native method, Kano, Northern Nigeria. *Bull. Imp. inst.*, 31 (1) 1933: 56–59.

2631 Braunholtz, H. J.
Wooden roulettes for impressing patterns on pottery. *Man*, 34, Je. 1934: 81 (art. 107) illus.
Illustrations, with descriptive notes, of wooden roulettes that should accompany W. E. Nicholson's "Brief notes on pottery at Abuja and Kuta, Niger Province" [2642] q.v.

2632 Cardew, Michael
Firing the big pot at Kwali. *Nig. mag.*, (70) Sept. 1961: 199–205, illus.

2632a —Gobir granaries. See [2562].

2633 —Pioneer pottery at Abuja. *Nig. mag.*, (52) 1956: 38–59, illus.

2634 Daniel, F.
Note on a gong of bronze from Katsina, Nigeria. *Man*, 29, 1929: 157–158 (art. 113) illus.

2635 Harris, Percy Graham
Notes on dyeing in Argungun emirate, Nigeria. *Farm and forest*, 10, 1950: 33–35, illus.
On the making of indigo dye and its use in textile dyeing.

2636 —Notes on tanning in Argungun emirate (Jima) Nigeria. *Farm and forest*, 10, 1950: 32–33.

2637 Indigo dyeing in Nigeria. *Progress*, 41 (230) 1951: 26–29.
Techniques of textile dyeing among Hausa and Yoruba dyers.

2638 Jeffries, W. F.
Leatherwork in Northern Nigeria. *Nig. mag.*, (14) 1938: 160–164, illus.

2639 Kangiwa, Mallam Shehu M. and Mattaden, A. K.
Leatherwork in Northern Nigeria. *Nig. mag.*, (74) Sept. 1962: 2–9, illus.
Mostly in Kano, with brief mention of Bornu and Sokoto.

2640 Krieger, Kurt.
Notizen zur Eisengewinnung der Hausa. *Z. f. Ethnol.*, 88 (2) 1963: 318–331, illus., bibliog.
On iron smelting in Hausaland.

2641 —Töpferei der Hausa (Anka-Distrikt, Sokoto-Provinz, Nordnigeria) In *Beiträge zur Völkerforschung. (Veröff. Mus. Völkerkde. Leipzig, no. 11) 1961*: 362–368, illus.
Describes the pottery industry in the town of Anka in Sokoto Province.

2642 Nicholson, W. E.
Brief notes on pottery at Abuja and Kuta, Niger Province. *Man*, 34, May 1934: 70–71 (art. 88) illus.
Describes the potters' art in the two towns and their use of wooden dies or roulettes in imprinting patterns. Plates illustrating these roulettes appeared later, ibid, 34, Je. 1934: 81 (art. 107).

2643 —Potters of Sokoto, Northern Nigeria. *Man*, 29, 1929: 45–50 (art. 34) illus.

2644 —The potters of Sokoto: B. Zorumawa; C. Rumbukawa. *Man*, 31, 1931: 187–189 (art. 186) Illus.

2645 Pottery work from Kaduna. *Nig. mag.*, (22) 1944: 55–56, illus.

2646 Saulawa, Iro
Thread-making and weaving in Katsina province. *Nig. mag.*, (23) 1946: 115–117, illus.

2647 Slye, Jonathan
Ceramics in Northern Nigeria; fame of traditional Abuja stoneware pottery. *Afr. world*, Apr. 1964: 6–7, illus.

2648 Tremearne, Arthur John Newman
Pottery in Northern Nigeria. *Man*, 10, 1910: 102–103 (art. 57) illus.

3. (xiv) Acculturation and Social Change, Contact Situation, Urbanization

2649 Blair, T. L. V.
Giant of the North. *W. Afr.*, (2401–2404) Je. 1963: 627, 661, 701, 729.
Notes on the changing social, economic and cultural patterns in the city of Kano, by an American professor of sociology and African studies on a research visit to the town.

2650 Carpenter, A. J.
Adult literacy: a survey. *Comm. dev. bull.*, (2) 1951: 69–73.
In Abuja, Northern Nigeria.

2651 Miner, Horace M.
Culture change under pressure: a Hausa case. *Human organisation*, 19 (3) Fall 1960: 164–167.

2652 —Urban influences on the rural Hausa. In *Urbanization and migration in West Africa, ed. Hilda Kuper, 1965*: 110–130.
With special reference to Zaria Province, particularly the Kuban District.

2653 Smith, Michael Garfield
Social and economic change among selected native communities in Northern Nigeria. 1952.
Ph.D. thesis, London university.

2654 Yeld, E. R.
Educational problems among women and girls in Sokoto Province of Northern Nigeria. *Sociologus*, 11 (2) 1961: 160–173.
Discusses sociological problems of

women's education engendered by the conflict between traditional islamic concepts regarding women's role in society and the modern requirements and attitudes following political and economic changes.

3. (xv) Social Problems; Applied Anthropology

2655   An African ruler undertakes community development. *Mass educ. bull.*, 1 (4) Sept. 1950: 62–65.
        Describes modernisation and community development schemes initiated by the Emir of Abuja.

2656   Goodban, J. W. D.
        Land settlement—the requirements and lay-out of a scheme. *Farm and forest*, 7 (1) Jan.–Je. 1946: 60–65.
        A review of the progress of the Daudawa settlement scheme in southern Katsina Province, from its inception in 1924 by the Empire Cotton Growing Corporation to 1946.

2657   Grove, A. T.
        Land and population in Katsina Province, with special reference to Bindawa village in Dan Yusufu District, 1952. Kaduna, Govt. printer, 1957. [vi] 57 [19]p. illus., maps, tables.

2658   Taylor, C. B.
        An experiment in land settlement. *Trop. agric.*, 20 (4) Apr. 1943: 71–73.
        On the Daura farm scheme.

2659   Taylor, P. J. O.
        Community schools: Zaria Province, Northern Nigeria. *Comm. dev. bull.*, 5, Sept. 1954: 79–81.

2660   Wilson, Jennifer
        Social studies, with special reference to housing [in Kano city] Kano, Greater Kano planning authority [n.d.] 83p. plans.
        Mimeographed.

4. LINGUISTIC STUDIES

2661   Abraham, Roy Clive
        Dictionary of the Hausa language, by R. C. Abraham and Malam Mai Kano, London, Crown agents for the colonies, 1949. xxvii, 992p.

2662   — —2nd ed. London, University of London press, 1962. xxvii, 992p.
        Hausa-English only, with tones indicated. Best used with two of his other works to which references are made throughout—*Introduction to spoken Hausa* and *Modern grammar of spoken Hausa,* now renamed respectively, *The language of the Hausa people, Pt. I* and *Pt. II.*

2663   —Hausa literature and the Hausa sound system. London, University of London press, 1959. v, 186p.
        Graded texts with literal translations on facing pages. Constant reference to author's *The language of the Hausa people.*

2664   —An introduction to spoken Hausa and Hausa reader for European students. London, Crown agents, 1940. 213p.
        Two separate works. Introd. to spoken Hausa. pp. 1–86 Hausa reader . . . pp. 90–213.

2665   —The language of the Hausa people. London, University of London press, 1959. x, 236p.
        The author's two earlier books—*Introduction to spoken Hausa* published in 1940, and *A modern grammar of spoken Hausa* published in 1941 are here combined in a new edition.

2666   —A modern grammar of spoken Hausa. London, Crown agents for the colonies, for the Government of Nigeria, 1941. vii, 172p.

2667   —The principles of Hausa. Kaduna, Govt. printer, 1934. vol. 1. [iii] xvii, 230p.

2668   Adedokun, Belo Oyejobi
        Hausa-Yoruba guide. [Kaduna, author, 1950] [5] 43p. Printed by Service press, Lagos.

2669   Almasihu macecin duniya. Jos, S.I.M., 1960. 138p. illus.
        Hausa text.

2670   Baikie, William Balfour
        Observations on the Hausa and Fulfulde languages, with examples. London, printed for private circulation, 1861. 29p.
        Only clue to the author is the preface signed: Wm. Balfour Baikie.

2671   Bargery, George Percy
        A Hausa-English dictionary and English-Hausa vocabulary, compiled for the government of Nigeria. With some notes on the Hausa people and their language, by D. Westermann. London, O.U.P., 1934. liv, 1226p.
        The notes by Westermann includes a list of previous publications on Hausa language and literature (pp. xiv–xvi) See [2478].

2672   Bargery's Bible. *West Africa,* (2191) Apr. 1959: 343. illus. (port.)
        Portrait of Dr. George Percy Bargery, recounting his work in compiling his Hausa dictionary [2671] and translating the Bible into Hausa.

2673   *Barth, Heinrich
        Vocabularies of the Hausa and Emghedesia languages. *J. Roy. geog. soc.*, 21, 1851.

2674   Batten, T. R.
        Koyarwar Labarin K'asa da Tarihi. Zaria, Translation bureau, 1934. ix, 337p.
        Hausa text.

2675   Bible. N.T. Hausa. Acts.
        The Acts of the Apostles. Translated into Hausa by the Rev. James Frederick Schön. London, British and foreign Bible society, 1857. 1p.l., 98p.

2676   Bible. N.T. Hausa. Luke
        Labărí năgărí kămăda an-rŭbŭtasi dagá Lukas. The Gospel according to

St. Luke. Translated from the original into Hausa by the Rev. James Frederick Schön. London, British and foreign Bible society, 1858. 1p.l., 104p.

2677 Bible. O.T. Hausa. Genesis
Letāfin Musa nāfāri. The first book of Moses. Translated from the original into Hausa, by Rev. James Frederick Schön. London, British and foreign Bible society, 1858. 1p.l., 149p.

2678 Brauner, Siegmund
Bemerkungen zum entlehnten Wortschatz des Hausa. *Mitt. Inst. Orientforsch.*, 10 (1) 1964: 103–107.

2679 Brierly, T. G.
Neologism in Hausa. *Africa*, 33 (3) Jl. 1963: 269; 34 (2) Apr. 1964: 170.
The second instalment is a brief explanatory note referring to the first article. See also [2739].

2680 Brooks, W. H. and Nott, Lewis H.
Bátū na Abūbuan Hausa; with translation, vocabulary, and notes. London, Frowde, 1903. 56p.
A collection of Hausa texts, with English translations and explanatory notes.

2681 Bunyan, John
Al hajin almasihu (Pilgrim's progress in Hausa) Abridged and adapted. 2nd ed. Lagos, 1925. [i] 54p. illus.

2682 —Larabin yakin ranmutum. (The Holy War, abridged in the Hausa language.) London, Religious tract society, 1920. 94p.

2683 Campbell, M. J.
A word list of government and local government terms: English-Hausa, for use in Northern Nigeria. [Zaria, Dept. of local govt., Inst. of administration, n.d.] 23p.
Printed by Baraka press, Kaduna.

2684 Carnochan, J.
Gemination in Hausa. In *Studies in linguistic analysis (Philological Society, London) 1957*: 149–181.

2686 —A study of quantity in Hausa. *B.S.O.A.S.*, 13 (4) 1951: 1032–1044.
An examination of the final open syllable of the nominal in Hausa.

2687 Charlton, Lionel Evelyn Oswald
A Hausa reading book containing a collection of texts reproduced in facsimile from native manuscripts . . . with transliteration into Roman characters, translations, notes, etc. London, O.U.P., 1908. 83, 45p.
The texts in facsimile are printed on the last 45 pages numbered separately, beginning from the end of the book.

2688 Clark, E. A.
One hundred birds of the Niger Province. Wushishi, 1931. 78p.
Includes Hausa names for many of the birds described.

2689 Crabtree, William Arthur
The Ntu element in Hausa. *Bibliotheca afr.*, 2 (1) 1926: 208–228.

2690 Dalby, David
The noun gàrii in Hausa: a semantic study. *J. Afr. lang.*, 3 (3) 1964: 273–305.
A detailed analysis to demonstrate the complex, extensive but coherent semantic range covered by the noun gàrii.

2691 Dalziel, John M.
A Hausa botanical vocabulary. London, T. Fisher Unwin, 1916. 119p.
The Hausa plant names are followed in many cases by botanical names, with brief descriptions in English. Includes "Index to general and popular names"—pp. 109–119.

2692 Delafosse, Maurice
Manuel de langue haoussa, ou Chrestomathie haoussa; précédé d'un abrégé de grammaire et suivi d'un vocabulaire. Paris, J. Maisonneuve, 1901. xiv, 134p.

2693 Dim, Julius Patrick
"Language is money". Part I: Hausa-Ibo-English, with Yoruba numerations. Kano [the author, 1954] [i] 16p.
Printed by Adebola printing press, Kano.
List of words in Hausa, with equivalents in Ibo and English.

2694 Dirr, Adolf
Manuel pratique de langue Haoussa: langue commerciale du Soudan. Avec exercices gràdués, suivi, d'une chrestomatie analysée, d'une collection de phrases usuelles, d'un vocabulaire Haoussa-français et d'un vocabulaire systématique. Paris, Ernest Leroux, 1895. 140p.

2695 Drexel, Albert
Gliederung der afrikanischen Sprachen . . . Das Haussa. *Anthropos.*, 20, 1925: 228–231.

2696 —Haussa-Probleme. *Bibliothèca afr.*, 1 (2) 1925: 149–172; 2 (1) 1926: 245–257.

2697 East, Rupert Moultrie
Hausa spelling. Zaria, Gaskiya corporation, 1953. 8p.

2698 —Ikon Allah, labarin halitta iri iri ta cikin duniya, Rupert East da Abubakar Imam suka rubuta J. de Naeyer, ta Zana hotunan. Zaria, NORLA, 1957. 392p. illus.

2699 —Language examinations in the Northern Provinces of Nigeria. Jos, S.I.M. bookshop, 1938. 136p.

2700 —Modern tendencies in the languages of Northern Nigeria. *Africa*, 10 (1) Jan. 1937: 97–105.
On the increasing reception of English words by the Hausa language and the undesirability of inventing vernacular terms to describe objects for which there are no Hausa words.

2701 —Recent activities of the Literature bureau, Zaria, Northern Nigeria. *Africa*, 14 (2) Apr. 1943: 71–77.
On the work of producing the *Gaskiya ta fi kwabo*, pamphlets, news bulletins, etc., all in the Hausa language. French summary, p. 77.

2702 Edgar, Frank
Litafi na tatsuniyoyi na Hausa. Belfast,
W. Erskine Mayne, 1911–1913. 3v.
See full entry at [2601].

2703 English-Hausa dictionary. *Nig. &
Yoruba notes*, 7 (77) Nov. 1900: 37–38.
A review of C. H. Robinson's
Dictionary of the Hausa language.
vol. 2 [2817].

2704 Essen, O. von
Implosive Verschlusslaute im Hausa.
Afr. u. Übersee, 45 (4) 1962: 285–291.

2705 Fletcher, Roland S.
Hausa sayings & folk-lore, with a
vocabulary of new words. London,
O.U.P., 1912. 173p. illus.

2705a Funke, E.
Einige Tanz-und Liebeslieder der Hausa.
See [2593].

2706 —Die Stellung der Hausasprache unter
den Sprachen Togos. *M.S.O.S.*, 19,
1916: 116–128.

2707 Gill, J. Withers
Hausa speech, its wit and wisdom.
B.S.O.S., 1 (2) 1918: 30–46.

2708 Goerner, Margaret [and others].
Two essays on Arabic loan words in
Hausa. Zaria, Dept. of languages,
Ahmadu Bello University, 1966. ii, 32p.
(Its occasional paper, no. 7).
Arabic loan words in Hausa, by
Margaret Goerner and Yousef Salman,
pp. 1–13; and Some common Arabic
loan words in Hausa and Swahili, by
P. B. Armitage, pp. 14–32.

2709 Gouffé, Claude
La lexicographie du Haoussa et le
préalable phonologique. *J. Afr. lang.*, 4
(3) 1965: 191–210.

2710 —Observations sur le degré causatif
dans un parler haoussa du Niger. *J. Afr.
lang.*, 1 (2) 1962: 182–200.

2711 Greenberg, Joseph Harold
An application of new world evidence to
an African linguistic problem (Hausa).
In: *Les Afro-Americains* [*Mémoires
IFAN, no. 27*] *1953*: 129–131.

2712 —Arabic loan words in Hausa. *Word*, 3
(1–2) Aug. 1947: 85–97.

2713 —Hausa verse prosody. *J. Amer. orient.
soc.*, 69 (3) 1949: 125–135.

2714 —Some problems in Hausa phonology.
Language, 17 (4) 1961: 316–323.
On syllabic structure, tone, vowel,
etc.

2715 Hanyar tadi turanci. A dictionary of
English conversation for Hausa students.
Zaria, NORLA, London, Longmans,
Green, 1957. v, 338p.
Text in English and Hausa.

2716 Harris, Herman G.
A concise Hausa dictionary containing
over twelve hundred common words
and many idioms. Weston-super-Mare.
Mendip Press, 1908. 33p.
Also issued bound with author's
"Hausa stories and riddles". [2717].

2717 —Hausa stories and riddles, with notes

on the language, etc. and a concise
Hausa dictionary. Weston-super-Mare,
Mendip press, [1908] 111, 33p.
The "Concise Hausa dictionary".
which takes the additional 33 pages is
also available separately. [2716].

2718 —A pocket dictionary of the Hausa
language: Hausa-English. Weston-
super-Mare, Mendip press, 1908. 33p.

2718a Hassan, C. Inuwa. See Inuwa Hassan,
Charles.

2719 Hiskett, Mervyn
The historical background to the
naturalization of Arabic loan-words in
Hausa. *Afr. lang. stud.*, (6) 1965: 18–26

2720 Haywood, Austin Hubert Wightwick
English-Hausa vocabulary: 1000 words
in everyday use. London, K. Paul,
Trench, Trubner, 1914. 30p.
1st ed. of [2721].

2721 —English-Hausa vocabulary of words
in every-day use. 2nd and enlarged ed.
London, K. Paul, Trench, Trubner,
1914. 31p.

2722 — —3rd enlarged ed. (containing nearly,
1,400 words) London, 1920. 31p.

2723 — —4th [3rd on cover] and enlarged
ed. 1925. 31p.

2723a Heepe, M. *ed.*
Gottlob Adolf Krauses Haussa-
Handschriften in der Preussichen Staats-
bibliothek, Hamburg. See [2750].

2724 Hodge, Carleton Taylor
Morpheme alternants and the noun
phrase in Hausa. *Language*, 21 (2) 1945:
87–91.

2725 —Phonology and morphology of the
noun and verb in Hausa. 1943.
Ph.D. thesis, University of Pennsylvania. Published under title: An outline
of Hausa grammar, Philadelphia, 1947.
61p. Issued as supplement to *Language*,
vol. 47 no. 4, 1947. (Language dissertation, no. 41).

2726 —A sample format for a teaching unit in
Hausa. In *National conference on the
teaching of African languages and area
studies, 1960*: 28–31.

2727 Hodge, Carleton Taylor and Hause,
Helen E.
Hausa tone. *J. Amer. orient. soc.*, 64
(2) Apr.–Je. 1944: 51–52.

2728 Hofmann, Inge
Das Verhältnis der Langvokale zu den
Kurzvokalen im Hausa. *Afr. u. Übersee*,
48 (3) 1965: 202–211.

2729 Howeidy, A.
Concise Hausa grammar. Oxford, G.
Ronald, 1953. xii, 232p. front. (port.)
A modern textbook by a Hausa
author.

2730 Hugot, P.
Cours élémentaire de Hausa. 2eme éd.
entièrement revisée. Paris, Centre de
hautes études d'administration
Musulmane, 1957. 77p. (Langues et
dialectes d'outremer, 1).

2731 Inuwa Hassan, Charles

Turanci a saukake. Zaria, Gaskiya corporation, 1952. 64p.
English made easy.

2732 —Turanci a saukake. Litafi na uku. Zaria, Gaskiya corporation, 1959. 148p.

2733 —Turanci a saukake, Na biyu. [Zaria] NORLA, 1954. [2] 86p.

2734 James, A. Lloyd and Bargery, George Percy
A note on the pronunciation of Hausa. *B.S.O.S.*, 3, 1923–25: 721–728.

2735 King, Philip V.
Some Hausa idioms. *J. Afr. soc.*, 8 (30) Jan. 1909: 193–201.

2736 Kirk-Greene, Anthony Hamilton Millard
Examen préliminaire des néologismes du Hausa (sommaire) *Actes 2e colloque int. négro-africaine, Dakar, 1962*: 204–209.

2737 —The Hausa Language Board. *Afr. u. Übersee*, 47 (3–4) Je. 1964: 187–203.
Describes the Hausa Language Board, its origin, composition, and functions, including its decisions and publications.

2738 —Maiduguri da manyan Bairanen da na Bornu. Zaria, NORLA, 1958. [2] 24p.
English and Hausa texts on Maiduguri and the capitals of Bornu [3973] q.v.

2739 —Neologisms in Hausa: a sociological approach. *Africa*, 33 (1) Jan. 1963: 25–44.
Also offprinted. O.U.P., 1963. See also [2679].

2740 —A preliminary inquiry into Hausa onomatology: three studies in the origins of personal, title and place names. Zaria, Institute of administration, 1964. v, 56p. bibliog.
Includes a section (Appendix C) on the origin of the name "Nigeria", culled from author's article: *Who coined the name Nigeria?* published in *West Afr.*, Dec. 22, 1956.

2741 Klingenheben, August
Die Silbenauslautgesetze des Hausa. *Z. f. E.S.*, 18 (4) 1928: 272–297.

2742 —Die Tempora Westafrikas und die semitischen Tempora. *Z. f. E. S.*, 19, 1928–9: 241–268.
A comparative analysis of Hausa and the Kushitic Semitic languages with a view to throwing light on the tense formation of the latter languages.

2743 —Zwei geschichtliche Hausatexte. *Z. f. E. S.*, 31, 1940–41: 114–129.
Two Hausa texts (with German translation) bearing on the war between King of Bauchi and the King of Bornu and the subjugation of the Fulani emir of Kano by the British.

2744 Kraft, Charles H.
The morpheme *na* in relation to a broader classification of Hausa verbals. *J. Afr. lang.*, 3 (3) 1964: 231–240.

2745 —A new study of Hausa syntax. *J. Afr. lang.*, 3 (1) 1964: 66–74.

2746 —A study of Hausa syntax. 1963.
Ph.D. thesis, Hartford.

2747 —A study of Hausa syntax. Hartford, Conn., Dept. of linguistics, Hartford seminary foundation, 1963. 3v. (Hartford studies in linguistics, nos. 8–10).
". . . A tentative, first attempt at the syntactic analysis of a large body of Hausa material."—Preface to vol. 1.
v. 1. Structure. ix, 261p.
v. 2. Function of words. xi, 209p.
v. 3. Texts. v, 222p.

2748 Kraft, Charles H. and Abubakar, Salisu
An introduction to spoken Hausa. (preliminary edition) East Lansing, African studies center, Michigan State university, 1965. x, 408p. (African language monograph, no. 5).

2749 Kraft, Charles H. [and others].
Workbook in introductory Hausa (Preliminary edition) East Lansing, African studies center, Michigan State university press, 1966. xi, 106p. illus.
Contains mostly illustrations. Supplied with 35 5 inch reels of tape on which is recorded Hausa conversational material.

2750 Krause, Gottlob Adolf
Gottlob Adolf Krause's Haussa-Handschriften in der Preussichen Staats-bibliothek, Hamburg. Herausgegeben von M. Heepe. *M.S.O.S.*, 31, 1928: 105–107, xxviii, lxxx.
Introductory notes on Krause's MS now in the state library at Hamburg, followed by text of the MS.

2750a —Merkwürdige Sitten der Haussa. Aus der Haussa-Sprache übersetzt. See [2454].

2751 —Proben der Sprache von Ghāt in der Sahārā, mit haussanischer und deutscher Uebersetzung . . . Leipzig, F. A. Brockhaus, 1884. iv, 82p. illus., map. (Mitt. der Riebeck'schen Niger-Expedition, 2).

2752 Labarum Hasawa da Makwabtansu. Littafi na biyu. Zaria, Translation bureau, Lagos, C.M.S. bookshop, 1933. 192p.
Historical traditions of the Hausa people and their neighbours.

2753 Laird, Mcgregor and Oldfield, R. A. K.
Hausa vocabulary. In their *Narative of an expedition into the interior of Africa, v. 2, 1837*: 421–441.
English-Hausa vocabulary.

2754 Landeroin, Moïse Augustin and Tilho, Jean Auguste M.
Dictionnaire haoussa. Paris, Imprimerie nationale, 1909. xv, 172, 163p.
Pt. 1. Haoussa-français
Pt. 2. Français-haoussa.

2755 —Grammaire et contes haoussas. Paris, Imprimerie nationale, 1909. xi, 292p.
Hausa grammar, followed by Hausa fables and proverbs.

2756 Le Roux, J. M.
Essai de dictionnaire français-haoussa et

haoussa-français, precédé d'un essai de grammaire de la langue haoussa. Alger. A. Jordan, 1886. xlv, 330p.

2757 Leslau, Wolf
A prefix ḥ in Egyptian, modern South Arabian, and Hausa. *Africa*, 32 (1) Jan. 1962: 65–68.

2758 Linguaphone institute, London
Hausa: a series of conversations and readings in Hausa. With texts, English translation and explanatory notes on the pronounciation of Hausa . . . compiled by G. P. Bargery and B. Honikman. London [1934] 39p. (Linguaphone miniature language series).
Accompanied by two 10–inch phonograph records (4 sides, 78 rpm) for use along with the text.

2759 Malami, Shehu
The claims of Hausa. *W. Afr.*, (2292) May 1961: 483.
On Hausa as a widely spoken language, its rapid spread and the need to widen its vocabulary to accommodate modern developments.

2760 Marre, Ernst von
Die Sprache der Hausa. Grammatik, Uebungen u Chrestomathie, sowie hausanisch-deutsches u deutsch-hausanisches Wörterverzeichnis. Wien & Leipzig, Hartlebeu [1901] xii, 176p. (Die Kunst der Polyglottie . . . 70th).

2761 Maxwell, John Lowry
Yau da gobe; a hausa grammar for beginners. Yau da gobe, ka iya. Revised by Eleanor M. Forshey. Lagos, printed by Niger challenge press, for Sudan interior mission [195?] 192p.
A practical manual for non-Hausa students. Pp. 174–184 left blank for notes.

2762 Meinhof, Carl
Hausa. In his *Die Sprachen der Hamiten, 1912*: 58–86.

2763 Merrick, G.
Hausa proverbs. London, K. Paul, Trench, Trubner, 1905. viii, 113p.
A collection of proverbs, riddles and common expressions in Hausa, with English translations.

2764 —Notes on Hausa and pidgin English. *J. Afr. soc.*, 8 (31) Apr. 1909: 303–307.

2765 Migeod, Frederick William Hugh
A grammar of the Hausa language. London, K. Paul, Trench, Trubner, 1914. xii, 229p.

2766 Miller, Ethel P.
Tafiyar mai ibada. Da ana ce da littafin na Kirista, jure matukar jurewa. [Rev. ed.] Jos, S.I.M. 1960. 2v. illus.

2767 —Wata biyu; a simple study in Hausa for two months. Jos, S.I.M. bookshop, 1931. 93p.

2768 Miller, Walter Richard Samuel
Hausa and English vocabulary. I. Hausa-English. II. English-Hausa. Lagos, C.M.S. bookshop, 1930, 39p.

2769 —Hausa notes. London, O.U.P., H. Frowde, 1901. xii, 127p.

2770 — —2nd ed. Lagos, C.M.S. bookshop, 1922. xii, 167p.
Hausa grammar and vocabulary.

2771 Mischlich, Adam
Hausa. Berlin, Schöneberg Langenscheidt, 1914. 112p. (Methode Toussaint Langenscheidt Sprachführer).

2772 —Lehrbuch der Hausa-Sprache. Berlin, Georg Reimer, 1911. vii, 250p. (Lehrbücher des Seminars für Orientalische Sprachen zu Berlin, v. 27).

2773 —Lehrbuch der hausanischen Sprache (Hausa-Sprache) Berlin, Georg Reimer, 1902. x, 184p. (Archiv für des Studium deutscher Kolonialsprachen, v. 1).

2774 —Neue Märchen aus Afrika gesammelt und aus der Hausasprache übersetzt. Leipzig, 1929. 312p. (Veröffentlichungen des Staat.-Sächs. Forschungsinstituts f. Völkerkde. in Leipzig, 1 Reihe, Bd. 9).

2774a —Über Sitten und Gebräuche in Hausa. See [2460].

2775 —Wörterbuch der Hausasprache. 1 Teil: Hausa-Deutsch. Berlin, Druck G. Reimer, 1906. xxxii, 692p. (Lehrbücher des Seminars für Orientalische Sprachen zu Berlin, v. 20).
An extended Hausa-German vocabulary based largely on the Kano and Zamfara dialects, with alternate forms in each dialect given and the dialect indicated within brackets.

2775a *Müller, Friedrich
Die Hausa-Sprache. In his *Grundriss der Sprachwissenschaft*, 1–2, 1877: 215–237.

2776 Nigeria. Northern. Laws, statute, etc.
Dokar hanyar tafiyad da hukuncin laifi, 1960. [Translated from the English edition by F. W. Parsons] Kaduna, Govt. printer [1963] 2p.l., xiii, 159p.
Hausa version of the Northern Nigeria Criminal Procedure Code, 1960. The translator's preface. (pp.i–x) discusses several points of linguistic interest encountered in the course of translation.

2777 —Tsarin laifuffuka da hukuncinsu. Translated from the English edition by F. W. Parsons. Kaduna, Govt. printer, 1959. [4] C 1–151p.
Hausa translation of the Northern Nigeria Penal Code. The preface like that to the Criminal Procedure Code above, touches on a number of linguistic topics.

2778 *Norris, Edwin, *ed.*
Dialogues and a small portion of the New-Testament (St. Matthew, chap. 2, 3, and part of 4) in the English, Arabic, Sudanese (Haussa) and Bornu languages. London, 1853.
Translated by James Richardson.

2779 Nuttal, Christine E.
Phonological interference of Hausa with English. Zaria, Dept. of languages, Ahmadu Bello university, 1965. iv, 23p.

(Ahmadu Bello university. Dept. of English. Occasional paper, no. 5).

2780 —Phonological interferance of Hausa with English: a study in English as a second language. 1962.
M.A. thesis, Manchester.

2781 Ogilvie, Harold L.
Helps to the study of Hausa. 4th ed. Jos, S.I.M. bookshop, 1951. 80p.

2782 Olderogge, D. A. ed.
Kamus na Hausa-Rushanci: an shirya shi a karkashin shugabancin masanin harsuna da tarihin Afrika D. A. Olderogge. Moscow, Ma'aikatar Shirin na Kasashem Waje ta Kasar Rasha, 1963. 459p.

2783 —The origin of the Hausa language. In Men and cultures: selected papers of the fifth international congress of anthropological and ethnological sciences, Philadelphia, Sept. 1-9, 1956, ed. Anthony F. C. Wallace, 1960: 795–802, bibliog.

2784 —Proiskhozhdenie iazyka Khausa. The origin of the Hausa language. Moskva, Izd-vo Akademii nauk SSSR, 1956. 27p.
Title and text in Russian and English.

2785 —Sledy imennogo klassa lyudey v yazyke Hausa. Sov. vost., (5) 1956: 130–132.

2786 —Yazyk Hausa: kratkiy ocherk, grammatika, khrestomatiya, i slova. Leningrad, Izd. L.G.U., 1954. 170p.
An introductory book on Hausa for Russian readers. Brief outline of Hausa grammar followed by a reader and a vocabulary.

2787 *Osnitskaya, I. A.
K voprosu o slovo-obrazovanii v Yazyke Khausa. In Afrikanskiy etnograficheskiy sbornik, III, ed. D. A. Olderoggee, 1959:
Notes on word-formation in Hausa.

2788 Parsons, Allan Chilcott
Hausa phrase book, with medical and scientific vocabulary. London, Humphrey Milford, 1915. iv, 164p.
Phrases and idioms with English translation arranged under broad headings, e.g. household management, hunting, commercial customs, etc.

2789 — —2nd ed. Revised by G. P. Bargery. London, H. Milford, 1924. vii, 117p.

2790 *Parsons, F. W.
Abstract nouns of sensory quality and their derivatives in Hausa. Veröff. Inst, Orientforsch., (26) 1955: 373–404.

2791 —Further observations on the 'causative' grade of the verb in Hausa. J. Afr. lang., 1 (3) 1962: 253–272.

2792 —An introduction to gender in Hausa. Afr. lang. stud., (1) 1960: 117–136.

2793 —The operation of gender in Hausa: the personal pronouns and genitive copula. Afr. lang. stud., (2) 1961: 100–124.

2794 —The operation of gender in Hausa: stabilizer, dependent nominals and

qualifiers. Afr. lang. stud., (4) 1963: 166–207.

—[Prefaces to the Northern Nigeria Penal Code and Criminal Procedure Code] See [2776] and [2777].

2795 —The verbal system in Hausa: forms, function and grades. Afr. u. Übersee. 44 (1) Sept. 1960: 1–36.

2796 *Pilszczikowa, Nina
[Fables haoussa] Przegląd orientalistyczny, [Warszawa] (3) 1956:365– ?
Hausa texts, with Polish translation.

2797 —System czasownikowy jezyka Hausa. Stosunki miedzy kategoriani aspektu i czasu. Warzawa, Polska Akademia Nauk, 1957. 104p.
On the verbal structure of Hausa. Main text in Polish, with English summary.

2798 Power, Gerald
English grammar for use in Hausa-speaking schools. Kaduna, Education dept. [1921] 105p.

2799 —Hausa-English grammar. Kaduna, Education dept., 1921. 108p.

2800 Prietze, Rudolf
Der Besuch des deutschen Kaisers 1898 in Jerusalem. Nach dem von einem Augenzeugen, dem Haussa-Pilger Achmed, aufgeschriebenen und erläuterten Bericht mitgeteilt von R. Prietze. M.S.O.S., 29, 1926: 99–134, 100a–100t.

2801 —Dichtung der Haussa. Africa, 4 (1) Jan. 1931: 86–95.

2802 —Die Geschichte von Gizo und Koki Nach einem von dem Haussa-Pilger Achmed geschriebenen und erläuterten Text mitgeteilt von R. Prietze. M.S.O.S., 29, 1926: 61–89.

2803 —Gesungene Predigten eines fahrenden Haussalehrers. M.S.O.S., 20, 1917: 1–60.

2804 —Haussa des täglichen Lebens. (Nach einem von dem Haussa-Pilger Achmed geschriebenen und erläuterten Text mitgeteilt von R. Prietze.) M.S.O.S., 29, 1926: 91–98.

2805 —Haussa-Sänger. Göttingen, Dieterische Universitäts-Druckerei, 1916. 69p.
Doct. Diss. Gött. 1915.

2806 —Haussa-Preislieder auf Parias. Gesammelt und erklärt . . . M.S.O.S., 21, 1918: 1–53.

2807 —Haussa-Sprichwörter und Haussa-Lieder. Kirchhain N.-L. Max Schmersow vorm. Zahn & Baendel, 1904. [i] 85p.

2808 —Lieder des Haussavolks. M.S.O.S., 30, 1927: 5–172, i–cxi.

2809 —Lieder fahrender Haussa-Schüler. M.S.O.S., 19, 1916: 1–115.

2810 —Die Mädchen von Gaia. Ein mittelafrikanisches Sittenbild aus den Mitteilungen Ḥāž Ahmed wiedergeben von R. Prietze. M.S.O.S., 29, 1926: 135–190.

2811 —Die spezifischen Verstärkungs-
Adverbien im Hausa und Kanuri.
M.S.O.S., 11, 1908: 307–317; 1909:
215–274.

2812 —Tiermärchen der Haussa. *Z. f. Ethnol.*,
39 (6) 1907: 916–939.
Hausa stories told to author in Tunis
by Ḥāž (i.e. Alhaji) Ahmed from Kano.
Hausa and German texts.

2813 —Wüstenreise des Haussa-Hândlers
Mohammed Agigi. In Gesprächen
geschildert von Ḥāžž Ahmed aus Kano.
Mit seinen Erläuterungen aufgenommen
und herausgegeben von Rudolf Prietze.
M.S.O.S., 26, 1924: 1–36; 28, 1926:
175–246.

2814 —Zwei Haussa-Texte. *Z.A.O.S.*, 3,
1897: 140–156.

2815 Rankin, W. S. de G.
Dabarun talifi. Zaria, NORLA, 1955.
[4] 96p.
Notes on the teaching of the reading
and writing of Hausa.

2816 Rat, Joseph Numa
Elements of the Hausa language; or a
short introductory grammar of the
language, for the use of the Gold
Coast constabulary. London, 1889.
vi, 60p.
Interleaved.

2816a Rattray, R. S.
Hausa folklore, customs, proverbs,
etc. . . . See [2605].

2817 Robinson, Charles Henry
Dictionary of the Hausa language, by
Charles Henry Robinson, assisted by
W. H. Brooks. Cambridge, university
press, 1899–1900. 2v.
v. 1. Hausa-English. 1899. xxxiii,
270p.
v. 2. English-Hausa. 1900. viii, 217p.

2818 —Dictionary of the Hausa language,
(compiled with the assistance of other
students of the Hausa language) Hausa-
English. 2nd ed. revised and enlarged.
Cambridge, university press, 1906.
xxxi, (270–270a) 8p.

2819 —Dictionary of the Hausa language.
3rd ed. revised and enlarged. Cambridge,
university press, 1913–14. 2v.
v. 1. Hausa-English. xiv, 426p.
v. 2. English-Hausa. viii, 289p.

2820 — —4th ed. 1925.

2821 —Hausa grammar, with exercises,
readings and vocabularies. London, K.
Paul, Trench, Trubner, 1897. x, 123p.
(Trubner's collection of simplified
grammars)

2822 — —5th ed. rev. Hausa grammar . . .
and specimens of Hausa script. 1930.
x, 218 [15]p.
Bound with the 1st edition is a 20
page publisher's catalogue of works on
African languages published in the
19th century.

2823 —The Hausa language. In his *Hausaland; or Fifteen hundred miles through
the central Soudan, 1896*: 171–183.

2824 —Specimens of Hausa literature, with
facsimiles. Cambridge, C. U. P., 1896.
xix, 112p. illus. (facsims.) bibliog.

2825 Ross, Alan S. C.
Note on a Hausa problem. *J. Afr.
lang.*, 3 (2) 1964: 201.

2826 Schachter, Paul
A generative account of Hausa ne/ce.
J. Afr. lang., 5 (1) 1966: 34–53.

2827 Schön, James Frederick
Appendix to the Dictionary of the
Hausa language. Hausa-English part,
with additions of Hausa literature.
London, Church missionary house,
1888. iv, 206p.

2828 —Dictionary of the Hausa language.
Part I. Hausa-English; part II. English-
Hausa. With appendices of Hausa
literature. London, Church missionary
house, 1876. 281, 142, xxxiv, [9]p.
facsim.

2828a *[Schön, J. F.]
Fárawá letáfin mágána Haúsa ko
mākóyi māgánan gáskia da hainya ga
rai hal ábbabá wónda góni mállámi
Yakúbu ya rūbutu ya aiké ga Haúsawa
dúka táre da gaisuánsa. Berlin, 1857.
53, 46p.

2829 —Grammar of the Hausa language.
London, Church missionary house,
1862. xiv, viii, 234p.

2830 *—A grammatical sketch of the Hausa
language. *J. Roy. Asiatic soc.*, 14 (2)
1882: 176–217.

2831 —Hausa reading book: with the
rudiments of grammar and vocabularies,
and traveller's vade-mecum. London,
Church missionary house, 1877. viii,
103, xxxivp.
There is an appendix pp. 1–xxxiv,
containing ten Hausa texts.

2832 —Hausa tales told by Dorgu and others.
London, Sheldon press, 1932. 24p.
(Little books for Africa, no. 37).
Selections from the English transla-
tion of "Magana Hausa", entitled
"African proverbs, tales and historical
fragments" [2834].

2833 —Magana Hausa. Hausa stories and
fables. Re-edited by C. H. Robinson.
London, S.P.C.K., 1906.
See notes under the 1st ed. [2834].

2834 —Magana Hausa: native literature;
or Proverbs, tales, fables, historical
fragments in the Hausa language; to
which is added a translation in English.
London, S.P.C.K., 1885–6. xx, 288p.
The English translation has special
title page: African proverbs, tales and
historical fragments.

2835 —Primer of the Hausa language.
London, William Watts, [1850?] 36p.

2836 —Vocabulary of the Hausa language.
Pt. I. English and Hausa. Pt. II. Hausa
and English. And phrases and specimens
of translation. To which are prefixed
the grammatical elements of the Hausa
language. London, Printed for the

Church missionary society, 1843. 3p.1., v, 190p.

2837 Seidel, August
Die Haussasprache. La langue Haoussa. The Hausa language. Grammatik (deutsch) und systematisch geordnetes Wörterbuch: haussa-deutsch-französisch-englisch. Grammaire (en français) et vocabulaire systematique: haoussa-allemand-français-anglais. Grammar (in English) and systematic vocabulary: Hausa-German-French-English. Heidelberg, J. Gross, 1906. xvi, 292p. (Methode Gaspey-Otto-Sauer).

2838 Sellnow, Irmgard
Der Handel in der Hausa-Literatur des ausgehenden 19. und beginnenden 20. Jahrhunderts. *Mitt. Inst. Orientforsch.* 9 (2–3) 1962: 410–432.

2839 Shcheglov, Y. K.
Iz morfologii yazyka Khausa (obrazovaniye mnozhestvennogo chisla imen) *Narody Azii i Afriki*, (3) 1965: 122–132.
A morphological analysis of plural formation in Hausa nominals.

2840 Skinner, A. N.
Hausa for beginners. London, university of London press, 1958. 70p. bibliog.
Elementary introductory course in spoken Hausa, with a short bibliography on the language and the Hausa people.

2841 —Hausa-English pocket dictionary— Kamus na Hausa da Turanci. Zaria, NORLA, London, Longmans, Green, 1959. x, 69p.

2842 Smirnova, M. S.
Hausa yazyk. Moskva, Izdatelstvo vostochnoi literatury, 1960. 82p.
A brief grammatical outline of Hausa intended for the general reader.

2843 Sölken, Heinz, *tr.*
Die Geschichte von Ada. *Mitt. der Auslandshochschule an der Universität Berlin*, 40 (3) 1937: 144–169. + 28 pp. of facsimiles.
Hausa texts transliterated and translated into German, with facsimiles of the Hausa texts appended.

2844 Stewart, A.
A Hausa-English guide. Minna, Sudan, interior mission bookshop, 1943. 32p.

2844a Taylor, Frank William
Fulani-Hausa phrase-book. See [2358],.

2844b —Fulani-Hausa readings in the native scripts. See [2359].

2844c —Fulani-Hausa vocabulary. See [2360].

2845 —Hausa and the late Canon C. H. Robinson. *J. Afr. soc.*, 26 (102) Jan. 1927: 145–159.
A critical review of Canon Robinson's contributions to the study of Hausa, to wit, Specimens of Hausa literature; Hausa grammar; and Dictionary of the Hausa language.

2846 —The orthography of African languages, with special reference to Hausa and Fulani. *J. Afr. soc.*, 28 (111) Apr. 1929: 241–252.
A criticism of the recommendations of the International institute of African languages and cultures on the subject as contained in its first memorandum— *Practical orthography of African languages.* [1469].

2847 —Practical Hausa grammar, with exercises, vocabulary and specimen examination papers. Oxford, Clarendon press, 1923. 141p. (Taylor's Fulani-Hausa series, 2).

2848 — —2nd ed. Oxford, 1959. xix, 157p.

2849 Taylor, Frank William and Webb, Arthur Geoffrey Gascoyne.
Labarun al'adun Hausawa da zantatukansu. Accounts and conversations describing certain customs of the Hausas. . . . With a foreword by Henry Balfour. London, O.U.P., H. Milford, 1932. xii, 225p. (Taylor's Fulani-Hausa series, 7).
English and Hausa on opposite pages. Hausa based on the "Standard Kano dialect."

2850 Vischer, Hanns
Rules for Hausa spelling. Zungeru, Govt. printing office, [1911] 11p.
Also reprinted in *J. Afr. soc.*, 11 (43) Apr. 1912: 339–347.

2851 *Vycichl, W.
Ein passives Partizip im Agyptischen und im Hausa (Britisch Nigeria): die passive Konjugation *sgmm–f. Le Muséon* [Louvain] 70 (3–4) 1957:

2852 *—Haussa und Aegyptisch, eine afrikanische Sprache. *Litterae orientales* [Leipzig] (48) Oct. 1931:

2853 —Haussa und Aegyptisch. Ein Beitrag zur historischen Hamitistik. *M.S.O.S.*, 37, 1934: 36–115.
Compares and discusses the Hamitic character of Hausa and Egyptian languages, and suggests both are related.

2854 Wängler, Hans-Heinrich
Singen und Sprechen in einer Tonsprache (Hausa). *Z, f. Phonetik*, 11 (1) 1958: 23–35.
Examines melody of Hausa songs to discover phonological relevance of tone in Hausa. Suggests Hausa is a tonal language.

2855 —Zur Tonologie des Hausa. Berlin, Akademie-Verlag, 1963. 187p. bibliog. (Schriften zur Phonetik, Sprachwissenschaft und Kommunikationsforschung, Nr. 6).

2856 —Über die Funktion der Töne im Hausa. *Z.f. Phonetik*, 16 (1–3) 1963: 231–240, bibliog.

2856a Westermann, Diedrich
Some notes on the Hausa people and their language. See [2478].

2857 —Die Sprache der Haussa in Zentralafrika. Berlin, D. Reimer, 1911. viii, 88p. (Deutsche Kolonialsprachen, Band 3).

2858   —A standard Hausa dictionary. *Africa*,
       7 (3) 1934: 371–374.
          Review of G. P. Bargery's "Hausa-
       English dictionary . . ." [2671] q.v.

2859   —Die Volkwerdung der Hausa. Berlin,
       Akademie-Verlag, 1950. 44p. (Sitzungs-
       berichte der deutschen Akademie der
       Wissenschaften zu Berlin. Klasse
       Philosophisch-historische, no. 2).

2860   Weydling, Georg

Einführung ins Hausa, Leipzig, Otto
Harrassowitz, 1942. xx, 131p.

2861   Yushmanov, N. V.
       Stroi yazika Hausa. Leningrad, 1937.
       38p.
          On the structure of Hausa.

2862   Zima, P.
       Some remarks on loanwords in modern
       Hausa. *Arch. orient.*, 32 (4) 1964: 522–
       528.

HIGI

(Hiji, Hill Margi)

Including:

Baza *(Bazza)*

1. GENERAL AND ETHNOGRAPHIC STUDIES

2863   Baker, Roger L. and Yola, M. Zubeiro
       The Higis of Bazza clan. *Nig. mag.*, (47)
       1955: 213–222, illus.

2864   Kirk-Greene, Anthony Hamilton Millard
       Higi. In his *Adamawa past and present,
       1958*: 19.
          A short historical note.

2865   —On swearing; an account of some
       judicial oaths in Northern Nigeria.
       Africa, 25 (1) Jan. 1955: 43–53.
          Describes the major forms of
       traditional oaths used in tribal courts
       among the Marghi, Higi, Verre, Kilba,
       Gude, Bachama, Hona, Bura, Mambila
       and other tribes all in Adamawa
       Province.

2866   —Some judicial oaths in Adamawa. In
       his *Adamawa past and present, 1958*:
       218–225.
          Extract from his article *On swearing*.
       See [2865].

2867   —Tax and travel among the hill-tribes
       of Northern Adamawa. *Africa*, 26 (4)
       Oct. 1956: 369–378, map.
          Economic aspects of *cin rani*, a
       seasonal emigration of labour among
       the Higi, Kilba, Marghi and Tur of the
       hill districts of Northern Adamawa,
       and its extended variation, *tafiyar dandi*,
       are here discussed; and in particular,
       the role they play in tax payments and
       bride-price is closely examined.

2868   Meek, Charles Kingsley
       The Higi. In his *Tribal studies in
       Northern Nigeria, vol. 1, 1931*: 252–282.
          Ethnographic notes, pp. 252–269.
       Vocabularies and phrases (various
       dialects) pp. 269–282.

2868a Neher, Gerald
       Brass casting in North-east Nigeria.
       See [4125].

2869   Vaughan, James H. Jr.
       Culture, history and grass-roots politics
       in a Northern Cameroons Kingdom.
       Amer. anthrop., 66 (5) Oct. 1964: 1078–
       1095, map, bibliog.
          A survey of Sardauna Province (the
       Northern Cameroons) embracing a
       study of the traditional political
       structure, the history of Fulani incur-
       sions of the 19th century and the
       political developments of the 20th
       century, including the two United
       Nations plebiscites.

2. LINGUISTIC STUDIES

2870   Laver, J. D. M.
       Some observations on alveolar and
       dental consonant-articulations in Higi.
       J. W. Afr. lang., 2 (1) 1965: 59–61, illus.

2871   Meek, Charles Kingsley
       The Higi language. In his *Tribal
       studies in Northern Nigeria, 1931*.
       v. 1, pp. 269–282.
          Vocabularies of several Higi dialects

IBIBIO

(Agbisherea)

Including:

Abuan	Eket
Anang	Enyong
Andoni	Ibeno
Efiat	Kwa
Efik *(Ebrutu, Eburutu*	Oron
Iboku)	
Efut	

1. BIBLIOGRAPHY

2872 Forde, Cyril Daryll and Jones, Gwilym Iwan
Bibliography [of the] Ibibio. In their *The Ibo and Ibibio-speaking peoples of South-eastern Nigeria, 1950*: 93–94.
Linguistics, p. 94.

2. GENERAL

2873 Bates, D.
"Chopping" on the old Calabar River. *Longman's mag.*, Jl. 1904: 211–228.

2874 Beecroft, * * * and King, J. B.
Details of exploration of the Old Calabar River in 1841 and 1842. *J. Roy. geog. soc.*, 14, 1844: 260–283.

2875 Butterworth, William
Three years' adventures of a minor, in England, Africa, the West Indies, South Carolina and Georgia. Leeds, Thomas Inchbold, 1831. x, vi, 492p.
In chapters II–V (especially pp. 27–98) author describes a voyage to Old Calabar in quest of slaves for the West Indies.

2876 "Calabar" (said to be first capital of Nigeria) A project by 1960 Form IA students (The secondary school, Methodist college, Uzuakoli) [Uzuakoli, Methodist college, 1960] [ii] 53p.
Account of an eleven day study tour of Calabar township by first year students of the School. Contents: Calabar a century ago; Calabar today; Government; Religion; Education; Cultural life; Industrial life; Communications, Commerce, Prominent citizens; Architecture; The people in general; Future. Typescript (Mimeographed).

2878 The Diary of a medical missionary. v. 1. Dublin, Browne and Nolan, 1957. 128p.
Diary illustrating the missionary's day to day life and work in Annua, near Uyo, in Eastern Nigeria, in 1953–54.

2879 Gammie, Alexander
Cruickshank of Calabar. London, Pickering & Inglis [n.d.] 110p. front., illus. (incl. ports.)
Biography of Dr. Alexander Cruickshank, who was a Church of Scotland missionary in Ikot Ofiong, near Calabar, for some 54 years, from 1887–1936. Includes notes on "The country—its people and customs"—pp. 37–45.

2880 Goldie, Hugh
Calabar and its mission. Edinburgh, 1890. 328p. illus., maps.

2881 — —New ed. Edinburgh and London, 1901. 399p.

2882 —Notes of a voyage up the Calabar or Cross River in Nov. 1884. *Scot. geog. mag.*, 1, 1885: 273–283, map.

2883 Grant,
Sketch of Calabar; edited, with notes by Donald C. Simmons. Calabar, Hope Waddell press, 1958. [5] 16p. map. (American association for African research. Publication no. 1).
Excerpt from *Memoirs of the late Captain Hugh Crow . . . 1830*: 270–286. See [177].

2884 Harding, H. J. M.
A short history of the Bamenda Cross River Calabar scheme up to May 1949. *Farm and forest*, 11, 1952: 44–48.

2885 Henshaw, James Ene
Children of the Goddess, and other plays. London, University of London press, 1964. 128p.
Three plays:
1. Children of the Goddess; a play in three acts. pp. 13–78.
2. Companion for a chief; a play in one act. pp. 79–96.
3. Magic in the blood; a play in one act. 97–128.

2886 —Medicine for love: a comedy in three acts. London, University of London press, 1964. 108p.
A useful introduction to the play takes up the problems of monogamy, polygamy, traditional marriage, and the position of the 'medicine man', in contemporary African society.

2887 —This is our chance: plays from West Africa. London, university press, 1956. 95p.

2888 Hogg, Jessie F.
The story of the Calabar mission written

for young people. Edinburgh, Oliphant, Anderson & Ferrier, 1962. 40p. illus.

2889 Holman, James
Holman's voyage to Old Calabar; ed., with notes, by Donald C. Simmons. Calabar, [Presbyterian bookshop] 1959. [3] 28p. (American association for African research. Publication no. 2).
Printed by Hope Waddell press, Calabar.

2890 —A voyage round the world, including travels in Africa, Asia, Australasia, etc. from 1827–1832. London, Smith, Elder, 1834–1835. 4v.
James Holman, the "Blind traveller", in circumnavigating the world, visited the Oil Rivers in 1828. In vol. 1, pp. 356–410 of the 4 volume account of his voyage, he gives his impressions of Old Calabar. Also published in pamphlet form. [2889].

2890a Hutchinson, Thomas Joseph
Impressions of Western Africa. See [293].

2891 Jeffreys, M. D. W.
Black Roberts and Old Calabar. W. Afr. rev., 24 (307) Apr. 1953: 359, illus.

2892 —Fort Stuart: a lost site. Nig. field, 20 (2) Apr. 1955: 89–90.
On the problem of identifying the site of Fort Stuart (in Calabar) mentioned in a report by Kenneth Campbell. A useful digression discusses the origins of the names Calabar and New Calabar.

2893 Johnston, Harry Hamilton
Journey up the Cross River. Proc. Roy. geog. soc., 10, 1888: 435–438.

2894 Livingstone, W. P.
Mary Slessor of Calabar: pioneer missionary. 5th ed. London, Hodder & Stoughton, 1916. xi, 347p. front. illus.

2895 —The white queen of Okoyong, Mary Slessor; a true story of adventure, heroism and faith. London, Hodder and Stoughton, 1917. xii, 208p. front. (col.) illus.

2896 Macdonald, A. B.
Can ghosts arise? The answer of Itu. [Edinburgh] Church of Scotland mission, 1946. 68p. 45 illus., maps.
History and description of Itu leper colony founded by the author in 1928.

2897 McEvoy, Cuthbert
Mary Slessor. 6th ed. London, Carey press [n.d.] 62p. front. (port.) map.

2898 McFarlan, Donald M.
Calabar: the Church of Scotland mission founded 1846. Rev. ed. London, T. Nelson, 1957. viii, 184p.
History of the establishment and growth of the Scottish mission at Calabar, and of missionary work in the region.

2899 M'Cann, Robert
In the land of the Oil Rivers: the story of the Qua Iboe mission. London, Marshall brothers, 1902. 164p. illus., map.
Description of the country, and an

account of the work of the Qua Iboe mission in the area. 1st ed. published in 1891.

2900 M'Keown, Robert
Twenty-five years in Qua Iboe; the story of a missionary effort in Nigeria. London, Morgan & Scott, Belfast, Wm. Strain, 1912. xii, 170p. front. illus. (some col.) map.

2901 Mary Slessor. Nig. mag., (58) 1958: 194–211, illus.

2902 Milligan, Robert H.
The jungle folk of Africa. New York, F. H. Revel, 1908. 380p. front., illus.
Brief note on Calabar, [pp. 45–46].

2903 Nicholls, Henry
Voyage de Henri Nicholls au Calabar, en 1805. In: Histoire genérale des voyages; ou Nouvelle collection des relations de voyages . . . par C. A. Walckenaer, v. 11, 1842: 361–372.

2904 O'Brien, Brian
She had a magic; the story of Mary Slessor. London, J. Cape, 1958. 256p. map.

2905 Oldfield, R. A. K.
Brief account of an ascent of the Old Calabar river in 1836. J. R. geog. soc., 7, 1837: 195–198.

2906 Robb, Alexander
The gospel to the Africans: a narrative of the life and labours of William Jameson in Jamaica and Old Calabar. Edinburgh; London, 1861. x, 299p. front.

2907 *Stewart, R.
Old Calabar. London, Paisely, 1884.

2908 Waddell, Hope Masterton
Twenty-nine years in the West Indies and Central Africa: a review of missionary work and adventure, 1829–1858. London, T. Nelson, 1863. 681p. front., illus., maps, repr. London, Frank Cass, 1970.

2909 Walker, J. B.
Notes on the visit, in May 1875, to the Old Calabar and Qua Rivers, the Ekoi country, and the Qua rapids. Proc. Roy. geog. soc., 20, 1875–76: 224–230.

2910 Ward, William James
In and around the Oron country; or The story of primitive Methodism in S. Nigeria. London, W. A. Hammond [1912?] 95p. illus., map.

2911 Watt, Eva Stuart
The quest of souls in Qua Iboe. London, Marshall, Morgan & Scott, 1951. 158p. front., illus. (incl. ports) map.

2912 Watt, James
Notes on the Old Calabar district of Southern Nigeria. Man, 3, 1903: 103–105. (art. 57).

3. PHYSICAL ANTHROPOLOGY

2913 Jeffreys, M. D. W.
Heights and weights of Ibibios. S. Afr. j. sci., 53 (12) Jl. 1957: 305–307.

2913a Jones, Gwilym Iwan
An examination of the physical types of

certain peoples of South-Eastern Nigeria. See [3147].

4. ARCHAEOLOGY

2914 Kennedy, Robert A.
Necked and lugged axes in Nigeria. *Antiquity*, 34 (133) Mar. 1960: 54–58, illus.; *Bull. IFAN*, 27 (1–2) 1960: 202–210.
Describes a necked and a lugged axe found at Ikpe Ikot Nkun in South-eastern Nigeria.

5. SOCIAL AND CULTURAL ANTHROPOLOGY, ETHNOGRAPHY

(i) General

2915 Akpabio, Udo
The story of Udo Akpabio of the Anang tribe, Southern Nigeria; recorded by W. Groves. In *Ten Africans, ed. by M. Perham, 1936*: 41–61.
Autobiography of Udo Akpabio a "warrant chief" from Ukana area in Anang Province, with a foreword by the recorder explaining the historical and ethnic background.

2916 Calabar. *Nig. mag.*, (52) 1956: 70–98, illus.
Historical and ethnographic sketch.

2917 Calabar-Ogoja-Rivers state movement Memorandum submitted to the Minorities commission by the central executive committee. [Uyo, the movement, 1958] [iii] 47p. map.
Includes a chapter on the cultural and historical relations between the peoples of the C.O.R. area (pp. 21–23).

2918 Christison, Robert
On the properties of the ordeal-bean of Old Calabar, Western Africa. *Pharmaceutical j.*, 14, 1855: 470–476.

2919 Christoffels, H.
Pater Johannes Kirchners Aufzeichnungen im Lande der Ibibios. *Anthropos.*, 56 (1–2) 1961: 267–269. (Micro-Bibliotheca Anthropos, 33).
A review of Johann Kirchner's MS—"Im Lande der Ibibios" [2931]. Gives detailed table of content of the manuscript.

2920 Clinton, J. V.
King Eyo Honesty II of Creek Town. *Nig. mag.*, (69) Aug. 1961: 182–188, illus.
Brief biographical sketch of Eyo Honesty and some humanitarian reforms introduced by him.

2921 Cotton, J. C.
The people of Old Calabar. *J. Afr. soc.*, 4 (15) Apr. 1905: 302–305.
Short notes on the people of Calabar—their origin, feasts, worship, slavery, inheritance, amusements, and the ekpe society.

2922 *Daniel, F. W.
On the natives of Old Calabar. *J. Ethnol. soc.*, 1–2, 1844–50:

2922a Forde, Cyril Daryll and Jones, G. I.

The Ibo and Ibibio-speaking peoples of South-Eastern Nigeria. See [3170].

2923 [Goldie, Hugh]
Memoir of King Eyo VII of Old Calabar, a Christian King in Africa. Old Calabar, United Presbyterian mission press, 1894. vii, 52p.

2924 Ibesikpo convention
The constitution of the Ibesikpo convention. Obot Idim, Uyo, Lutheran press, 1949. 16p.

2925 Ibibio state union
The constitution of the Ibibio state union, 1948. Uyo, National secretariat, 1948. 36p.

2926 Ituen, Bassey P.
The Ibibios and the Efiks. Kano, Ife-Olu printing works, 1950. 18p.

2927 Jeffreys, M. D. W.
Alt-Kalabar und der Sklavenhandel. *Paideuma*, 6 (1) Nov. 1954: 14–24.
"Old Calabar and the slave trade".

2928 —A note on Onoyom Iya Nya Ita. *Nig. field.*, 21 (1) Jan. 1956: 41–47.
Biographical account of Chief Onoyom Iya Nya of Obio Usiere in Enyong Division.

2929 —The oil palm, by Gore More [pseud.] *Nig. field*, 1 (2) 1931: 21–27.

2929a —Old Calabar and notes on the Ibibio language. See [3070].

2930 —Snake stones. *J.R.A.S.*, 41 (165) Oct. 1942: 250–253.
Discusses and tries to explain the belief among the Ibibio and other peoples in Africa that some snakes, notably the python, have jewels in their heads which they can bring out at will.

2931 Kirchner, Johann
Im Lande der Ibibios. Posieux/Freiburg (Schweiz) 1961. viii, 150p. (Micro-Bibliotheca Anthropos, B. 33).

2932 Messenger, John C.
Anang acculturation: a study of shifting cultural focus. 1957.
Ph.D. thesis, Northwestern University.

2932a —Anang art, drama and social control. See [2993].

2933 —The Christian concept of forgiveness and Anang morality. *Pract. anthr.*, 6 (3) May–Je. 1959: 97–103.

2934 *—Reflections on esthetic talent among the Anang. *Mich. State Univ. coll., q.*, Fall 1958.

2935 Parkinson, John
A note on the Efik and Ekoi tribes of Eastern Provinces of Southern Nigeria. *J.R.A.I.*, 37 [n.s. 10] 1907: 261–267, illus.

2936 Simmons, Donald C.
Efik iron gongs and gong signals. *Man*, 55 (117) Je. 1955: 107–108, illus., bibliog.
Describes various types of Efik gong and their use in sending messages.

2937 —An ethnographic sketch of the Efik people. In *Efik traders of Old Calabar, ed. Daryll Forde, 1956*: 1–26.

2938 Talbot, D. Amaury
Among the Ibibios of Southern Nigeria.
Harp. mag., 130, 1915: 600–608.

2939 —Women's mysteries of a primitive
people: the Ibibios of Southern Nigeria.
London, Cassell, 1915, repr. London,
Frank Cass, 1968. viii, 252p. front,
illus.
Account of Ibibio women, their
customs, rites and ceremonies.

2940 Talbot, Percy Amaury
Land of the Ibibios, Southern Nigeria.
Geog. j., 44, 1914: 286–305, illus., map.

2941 —Life in Southern Nigeria: the magic
beliefs and customs of the Ibibio tribe.
London, Macmillan, 1923, repr.
London, Frank Cass, 1967. xvi, 356p.
Mostly on the people of Eket area,
Oron and Calabar.

2942 Udo, Bassey Ukpong
A profile on the Ibibios. *Afr. hist.*, 1 (3)
Mar. 1965: 20–24.
A useful, compendious portrait.

2943 Udo, R. K.
Land and population in Otoro District.
Nig. geog. j., 4 (1) Aug. 1961: 3–19,
illus., maps, bibliog.

2944 Ukpabang youth association
Oron re-awakening. Oron, Central
bureau of information, Ukpabang youth
association, 1960. [i] 24p.

2945 Walker, J. B.
Notes on the politics, religion and
commerce of Old Calabar. *J. Anthrop.
inst.*, 6, 1877: 119–124.

5. (ii) History,

2946 Afigbo, A. E.
Efik origin and migrations reconsidered.
Nig. mag., (87) Dec. 1965: 267–280,
illus.
Questions the view that the Efik are
ethnically Ibibio and suggests that on
the contrary, Efik traditions of origin
tend to point to an Ibo ancestry. See
[2949] for a rejection of this opinion.

2947 Akanu, Jonathan Okorie
The history of Edda. Ekoli Edda, the
author, [1956.] 44p.
Printed by Lutheran press, Obot
Idim, Uyo.

2948 Hart, A. K.
Background of [Calabar] history and
tradition. In *Report of the enquiry into
the obongship of Calabar* [*Sole Commissioner, A. K. Hart*] *1964*: 24–76.
Accounts of Efik migrations to their
present home as given in evidence at
the enquiry by the three contestants and
by representatives of certain Efik
families. Includes a critical commentary
by the sole commissioner. For main
report see [2964].

2949 Jeffreys, M. D. W.
Efik origins. *Nig. mag.*, (91) Dec. 1966:
297–299.
A rejoinder to Dr. Afigbo's article
"Efik origin and migrations re-
considered" [2946] Briefly reviews

available evidence on the subject and
holds that no facts have been established
to demolish the tradition that the Efik
are of Ibibio origin.

2949a Jones, G. I.
Time and oral tradition . . . See [3724].

2950 Obio-Offiong, Udo-Ekong Etuk
An introduction to Nsit history: a
history of Afagha Obio Offiong and a
first step to the study of Ibibio history.
Aba, Aman press, 1958. 68p. tables.

2951 Orok, O. I.
The great trek of Uyanga. 2nd ed.
Calabar, the author, 1965. [iii] 16p.
Printed by Hope Waddell press,
Calabar.

5. (iii) Marriage, Family, Lineage Structure

2952 Cotton, J. C.
The Calabar marriage law and custom.
J. Afr. soc., 4 (16) Jl. 1905: 427–432.

2953 Malcolm, L. W. G.
Note on the seclusion of girls among
the Efik of Old Calabar. *Man*, 25, 1925:
113–114 (art. 69), illus.

2954 Simmons, Donald C.
Sexual life, marriage and childhood
among the Efik. *Africa*, 30 (2) Apr.
1960: 153–165.
Summary in French, p. 165.

2955 Udo Ema, A. J.
Fattening girls in Oron. *Nig. mag.*, (21)
1940: 386, 388–389, illus.
The girl fattening practice and its
cultural significance.

5. (iv) Government, Kingship, Law

Cotton, J. C.
The Calabar marriage law and custom.
See [2952].

2956 Ekere, C. A.
Ibibio indigenous judicial system
(W.A.S.U. study group lecture) *West
Africa*, 28 (1409) 5 Feb. 1944: 103.

2957 Elias, Taslim Olawale
The Calabar rules of inheritance. In his
*Nigerian land law and customs, 2nd ed.,
1962*: 246–247.

2958 Hart, A. K.
Modern institutions and problems [in
Calabar] In *Report of the enquiry into
the dispute over the obongship of Calabar
[Sole Commissioner, A. K. Hart] 1964*:
77–121.
Examines factors relating to kingship
and royalty in Calabar and the problem
of selection and deposition of an Etubom.

2959 Ibibio state union
A memorandum submitted by Ibibio
state union to G. I. Jones' commission
of enquiry into the position, status and
influence of chiefs and natural rulers in
the Eastern Region of Nigeria [Calabar,
the union, 1957]. 5p.
Printed by Ikemesit co., Aba.
States the system of chieftainship and
the position and functions of chiefs in
Ibibioland.

2960 Jeffreys, M. D. W.
Mary Slessor—magistrate. *W. Afr. rev.*, Je. 1950: 628–629; Jl. 1950: 802–805, illus. (incl. facsims.).
On the role of Mary Slessor as magistrate and coroner in Ikot Obong, with extracts from some of her court records.

2961 Jones, Gwilym Iwan
The political organisation of Old Calabar. In *Efik traders of Old Calabar, ed. by Daryll Forde, 1956*: 116–160. [2973].

2962 Messenger, John C.
The role of proverbs in a Nigerian judicial system. *S.–W. j. anthr.*, 15 (1) Spring 1959: 64–73.
Describes traditional court systems among the Anang people and cites some examples in which justice has been affected by the use of appropriate (or inappropriate) adages,

2963 N'Idu, Ado,
Ekpe: Cross River cult. *W. Afr. rev.*, 30 (384) Nov. 1959: 746–749.
Brief account of the origin, operations and significance of the Ekpe society in the Cross River area.

2964 Nigeria. Eastern. Commission of inquiry into the dispute over the obongship of Calabar.
Report . . . [A. K. Hart, sole commissioner] Enugu. Govt. printer, 1964. [vi] 225p. illus., map. (official document, no. 17 of 1964).
Includes in parts 2 and 3 (pp. 24–121) some accounts of early Efik migrations, settlements and family and state organisation. See [2948] [2958].

2965 Payne, E. G. Stumpenhuson
Local government in the county of Eket, Eastern Nigeria. *J. Afr. admin.*, 5 (4) Oct. 1953: 177–182.

2966 Payne, Philippa
Calabar coronation, being the programme of the coronation of his highness Archibong the fifth, Obong of Calabar. With an informal commentary and photographs. *Nig. field*, 19 (2) Apr. 1954: 85–96, illus.
The programme of coronation held from 18th to 28th January 1950, followed by account of the main events.

2967 Udo-Ema, A. J.
The ekpe society. *Nig. mag.*, (16) 1938: 314–316.

5. (v) Social Organization and Structure, Social Relationships

2968 Goldie, Hugh
The nature of Calabar slavery, the laws relating to it and the conduct of the missionaries. *Missionary record of the United Presbyterian Church*, 1855: 17–26.

2969 Jeffreys, M. D. W.
Age-groups among the Ika and kindred people. *Afr. stud.*, 9 (4) Dec. 1950: 157–166, bibliog.

Two types of age groups found in Africa are described and an account of such groups among the Ika, an Ibibio clan, is given in some detail.

2970 Ukot, A. M.
Ñka tradition of Ubenekang, Ibeno, prepared by A. U. Ukot with the co-operation of the chiefs and elders of Ubenekang. Ibeno, Ñka Esinedi of Ubenekang [1964] 20p. Printed by Ideal printing press, Aba.
A concise account of the Ñka or age group system in Ubenekang village. Describes its nature, history, organisation, and ceremonies. Ubenekang is an Ibeno village.

5. (vi) Economy, Agriculture, Trade

2971 Ekandem, M. J.
Ibibio farmers and some of their customs. *Nig. field*, 22 (4) Oct. 1959: 169–175, illus.
Description of traditional farming among the Ibibio.

2972 Essang, Sunday Matthew
The marketing of palm oil in a rural community. 1967.
M.Sc. thesis, London. Marketing of palm oil in Okobo-Oron community.

2973 Forde, Cyril Daryll, *ed.*
Efik traders of Old Calabar, containing the diary of Antera Duke, an Efik slave trading chief of the eighteenth century, together with an ethnographic sketch and notes by D. Simmons, and an essay on the political organisation of Old Calabar by G. I. Jones. Oxford University press, 1956. xiii, 166p. illus., bibliog.
The diary written in 1785–1788 in pidgin English is a highly entertaining personal record, throwing much light on the day to day life in eighteenth century Calabar.

2974 Jeffreys, M. D. W.
Palm wine among the Ibibio. *Nig. field*, 22 (1) Jan. 1957: 40–45.
Notes on palm wine and palm wine-tapping by the Ibibio people, including speculations on the origin of the industry.

2975 Martin, Anne
The oil palm economy of the Ibibio farmer. Ibadan, University press, 1956. v, 53p. map., tables.

2976 Oloko, Olatunde
A study of socio-economic factors affecting agricultural productivity in Annang Province, Eastern Nigeria. Ibadan, NISER, 1963. 96p.
A preliminary report. Mimeographed.

5. (vii) Religion

2976a Cardi, Charles Napoleon, comte de
Ju-ju laws and customs in the Niger delta. See [3732].

2977 Cobham, Henry
The Idem society. *J. Afr. soc.*, 5 (17) Oct. 1905: 41–42.

M

Brief note on a governmental institution, apparently in Calabar.

2978   Ekandem, M. J.
The use of plants as symbols in Ibibio and Ibo country. *Nig. field*, 20 (2) Apr. 1955: 53–64, illus.
Describes the symbolism of various plants in religion, magic and crime prevention.

2979   Haitz, Linn
Juju gods of W. Africa. St. Louis, Missouri, Concordia publishing house, 1961. 113p. illus.
Account of an American missionary's work in Uyo, Ogoja and the Cameroons.

2980   Jeffreys, M. D. W.
Witchcraft in the Calabar Province. *Afr. studies*, 25 (2) 1966: 95–100, bibliog.

2981   Messenger, John C.
Reinterpretations of Christian and indigenous belief in a Nigerian nativist church. *Amer. anthrop.*, 62 (2) Apr. 1960: 268–278.
Describes reactions of the Annang people to Christian religion and the development and spread of indigenous Christian churches which blend traditional Annang beliefs with reinterpreted orthodox Christian doctrines.

2982   —Religious acculturation among the Anang Ibibio. In *Continuity and change in African culture, ed. by W. Bascom and M. J. Herskovits, 1959*: 279–299.

2983   Parkinson, J.
Notes on the Efik belief in "Bush Soul". *Man*, 1906: 121–122 (art. 80).

2984   Schidlowski, Manfred
Ein lokaler Meteoritenkult aus der Calabar-Region von Ost-Nigeria. *Z. f. Ethnol.*, 91 (1) 1966: 141–143, bibliog.
On a local meteorite cult in Uwet.

2985   Simmons, Donald C.
Efik divination, ordeals and omens. *S.–W. j. anthrop.*, 12 (2) 1956: 223–228.

2986   Talbot, Percy Amaury
Some Ibibio customs and beliefs. *J. Afr. soc.*, 13 (51) Apr. 1914: 241–258, illus.
Describes Ibibio burial rites, and their magico-religious beliefs and practices, including the *ekpo* and *idiong* cults.

2987   Udo Ema, A. J.
I consult a witch-doctor. *Nig. mag.*, (20) 1940: 321–322.

2988   Whitehouse, A. A.
An African fetish. *J. Afr. soc.*, 4 (16) Jl. 1905: 410–416, illus.
Describes the "Oyobulo" juju at Allabia in Andoni and the customs associated with its worship.

5. (viii) Recreation, Games, Music, Dance

2989   Brewster, Paul G.
Some Nigerian games, with their parallels and analogues. *J. Soc. afr.*, 24 (1) 1954: 25–43, illus., bibliog.
Mostly Ibibio and Yoruba games.

2990   Efik dancers. *Nig. mag.*, (53) 1957: 150–169, illus.

2991   Efik dances. *Nig. mag.*, (56) 1958: 52–64, illus.

2992   Jeffreys, M. D. W.
The Ekong players. *Eastern anthrop.*, 5 (1) Sept.–Nov. 1951: 41–47.
Account of an Ekong play by Ibibio players in Nung Ita, Uyo district, Eastern Nigeria.

2993   Messenger, John C.
Anang art, drama and social control. *Afr. stud. bull.*, 5 (2) May 1962: 29–35.

2994   Simmons, Donald C.
Efik games. *Folklore*, 69, Mar. 1958: 26–33.

2995   —An Efik Judas play: the metamorphorsis of an ancient Efik ceremony into a new year's eve celebration and a Judas play. *Nig. field.*, 26 (3) Jl. 1961: 101–110, illus.

5. (ix) Stories, Proverbs, Riddles

2996   Akpan, A. Akpakpan
Proverbs-riddles with detailed comments. Ikot Ekpene, author, 1958. 26p.

2997   Cobham, Henry
Animal stories from Calabar. *J. Afr. soc.*, 4 (15) Apr. 1905: 307–309.
Three short stories featuring the tortoise.

2998   Cotton, J. C.
Calabar stories. *J. Afr. soc.*, 5 (18) Jan. 1906: 191–196.
Nine short folk stories from Calabar "written out by a native".

2999   Jeffreys, M. D. W.
Some folklore stories among the Ibibio. *Folklore*, 65, 1954: 168–170.

3000   —The story of the pig and the tortoise; or Why the pig roots in the ground. *Folklore*, 66, 1955: 295–296.
An Ibibio story.

3001   —Why the elephant has small eyes and the worm none. *Folklore*, 64, Dec. 1953: 488–489.
Ibibio folk-tale.

3002   Messenger, John C.
Anang proverb-riddles. *J. Amer. folkl.*, 73 (289) 1960: 225–235.

3003   —Anang proverb-riddles and Efik tone riddles. *J. Amer. folkl.*, 74 (293) 1961: 246.

3004   Simmons, Donald C.
Analysis of cultural reflections in Efik folk tales. *J. Amer. folkl.*, 74 (292) Apr.–Je. 1961: 126–141.
Correlation of folk tales with aspects of Efik culture and the significance of folk tales as sources of ethnographic data.

3005   —Cultural functions of the Efik tone riddle. *J. Amer. folkl.*, 71 (280) Apr.–Je. 1958: 123–138.
Explanation of the cultural significance and uses of tone riddles among the Efik, Oron and Ibibio.

3006   —Eating and its correlatives in Uyo

Ibibio proverbs. *Nig. field*, 31 (4) Oct. 1966: 180–184.

Lists 31 proverbs dealing with aspects of food and eating, with word by word English renderings and explanatory notes.

3007 —Efik riddles. *Nig. field*, 21 (4) Oct. 1956: 168–171.

Two types of Efik riddle described, with examples and English translations.

3008 —Erotic Ibibio tone riddles. *Man*, 56, Je. 1956: 79–82 (art. 78).

Discusses the nature and functions of Ibibio tone-riddles and lists 30 erotic riddles with interlinear English translation.

3009 —Ibibio tone riddles. *Nig. field*, 25 (3) Jl. 1960: 132–134.

Brief explanation of the nature and functions of tone riddles among the Ibibio.

3010 —Ibibio topical ballads. *Man*, 60, Apr. 1960 (art. 70): 58–59.

3011 —Reflections of culture in Efik folktales. 1959.

Ph.D. thesis, Yale University.

3012 —Specimens of Efik folklore. *Folklore*, (66) Dec. 1955: 417–424.

3013 Udoh, G. N.
Ibibio folklore and traditions (a simple guide to their collection). Uyo, Modern business press, 1958. 30p.

Tabulation and explanation of steps to be followed by individuals intending to record Ibibio culture and traditions.

5. (x) Birth and Death Rituals; Miscellaneous Beliefs and Rites

3014 Jeffreys, M. D. W.
The burial bird for an *okuku*. *Afr. stud.*, 14 (3) Sept. 1955: 134–137, illus.

Description of the funeral equipment and burial ceremony of an *okuku*—a priest or spiritual head of a lineage in Okanafun area of Anang Province. Notes several points of similarity in similar Egyptian ceremonies. Based on information by Udo Idiong Ntukidem of Iköt Oku village, himself an *okuku*.

3015 —The Nyama society of the Ibibio women. *Afr. stud.*, 15 (1) 1956: 15–28, illus., bibliog.

On the significance of clitoridectomy among Ibibio people, with a description of the organisation, regalia, etc., of the Nyama society—a guild of women in charge of this operation and its associated ceremonies in each village.

3015a Talbot, Percy Amaury
Some Ibibio customs and beliefs. See [2986].

5. (xi) Sculpture

3016 Aldred, Cyril
A bronze cult object from Southern Nigeria. *Man*, 49 (47) Apr. 1949: 38–39, illus.

Describes a leopard skull cast by the *cire perdue* process and now in the

Royal Scottish Museum. It is of unknown origin, but its similarity to three other objects from Andoni suggests that it might have come from this area.

3017 Beier, Horst Ulrich
Ibibio monuments. *Nig. mag.*, (51) 1956: 318–336, illus.

Notes on Ibibio burial monuments.

3018 Butler, Vincent F.
Cement funeral sculpture in Eastern Nigeria. *Nig. mag.*, (77) Je. 1963: 117–124, illus.

On funeral monuments constructed with cement and common in Ibibio area of Eastern Nigeria.

3019 Kiewe, Heinz Edgar
Nigerian sculpture of a Jewish trader. *Jewish q. rev.*, 44 (2) Oct. 1953: 162–168, illus.

Sees the physical characteristics of a Sephardic or Yemenite Jewish trader in a carved, wooden ancestral figure from Ibibio area in south-eastern Nigeria, and suggests the possibility of ancient Jewish contact with West Africa.

3020 Murray, Kenneth Crosthwaite
Ekpu; the ancestor figures of Oron, Southern Nigeria. *Burl. mag.*, 89 (536) Nov. 1947: 310–314.

Description of carved ancestral figures from Oron. Many of the carvings are now housed in the Oron museum.

3021 —Wood-carvings of Oron. *Nig. mag.*, (23) 1946: 113–114, illus.

3022 —Wood-carving: the carving of masks. *Nig. mag.*, (11) 1937: 79–82, illus.

Techniques of mask carving. Based on observation of an Ibibio carver at work.

3023 Nsugbe, P. O.
Oron ekpu figures. *Nig. mag.*, (71) Dec. 1961: 356–365, illus.

Describes the carved ancestral figures from Oron villages now in the Oron museum and indicates their historical or genealogical significance.

3024 Simmons, Donald C.
The depiction of gangosa on Efik-Ibibio masks. *Man*, 57 (18–19) 1957: 17–20, illus., plate.

Nine masks depicting what is considered to be gangosa, the noseless condition called "Onok" in Efik, are described, with speculation as to the diagnosis of the disease responsible for it.

3024a —Efik iron gongs and gong signals. See [2936].

3025 Udo-Ema, A. J.
Art and handicraft in the Methodist boys' high school, Oron. *Nig. mag.*, (18) 1939: 120–121, illus.

3026 —Teaching claywork in schools. Zaria, Gaskiya [1952] [4] 75p. illus.

3027 Umana, A. P.
Soft wood-carving: a native spoon. Ibibio: Ikpan ibom. Anang: Okomo. *Nig. mag.*, (19) 1939: 224–245, illus.

5. (xii) Weaving, Basket Making, Knotting

3028 Nsugbe, P. O.
Cane and rafia work. *Nig. mag.*, (74) Sept. 1962: 61–66, illus.
Account of an indigenous Ibibio industry based on the cane and rafia crafts and centred around Ikot Ekpene.

3029 Simmons, Donald C.
Efik knots. *Nig. field*, 21 (3) Jl. 1953: 127–134, illus.
Various knots used by the Efiks are illustrated and described. Vernacular names supplied.

3030 Stevens, R. A.
Ikot Ekpene raffia. *Farm and forest*, 6 (1) Jan.–Mar. 1945: 43–46, illus.
Describes the expansion during the war, of raffiawork, a traditional occupation in Ikot Ekpene, the development of a raffia guild, and the making of raffia bags, toys, mats, etc.

3031 Udo-Ema, A. J.
The making of akpan ọfọrọ. *Nig. mag.*, (13) 1938: 82–84, illus.
Describes the tools, materials and method of making 'akpan', a kind of basket used by the Ibibios.

5. (xiii) Urbanization

3032 Morrill, Warren T.
Immigrants and associations: the Ibos in twentieth century Calabar. *Comp. stud. soc. hist.*, 5 (4) Jl. 1963: 424–448.

3033 —Two urban cultures of Calabar, Nigeria. 1960.
Ph.D. thesis, Chicago University. Ibo and Efik inhabitants of Calabar. See also [3032].

5. (xiv) Applied Anthropology

3034 Arnot, A. S. [and others]
Literacy among Calabar women. *Books for Africa*, 8, Oct. 1938: 49–52.

3035 Carpenter, A. J.
A mass literacy campaign in southeastern Nigeria in the autumn of 1949. *Mass educ. bull.*, 1 (4) Sept. 1950. 73–79.
Organization and operation of a four-month literacy campaign in Abak.

3036 Oke, W. O.
Co-operation in a Nigerian province. *Rev. of int. co-op.*, 47 (8–9) Aug.–Sept. 1954: 215–217.
Description of organization of co-operative societies in the former Calabar Province.

3037 Spence, A.
Adult education for women (Calabar Province). *Community dev. bull.*, 6 (1) Dec. 1954: 10–12.
Operation of adult education scheme for women at Calabar.

3038 Ukpabang youth association
Education in Oron. Oron, Central bureau of information, Ukpabang youth association, 1962. [i] 21p.

6. LINGUISTIC STUDIES

3039 Adams, Robert Frederick George
Combined English-Efik and Efik-English vocabulary. 2nd ed. revised. Liverpool, Philip, 1943. [vi] v, 258p.

3040 —Efik vocabulary of living things. *Nig. field*, 11, Dec. 1943: 156–169; 12 (1) Jan. 1947: 23–34; 13 (2) Oct. 1948: 61–67.
List of living things in Efik, with English translation, and remarks as to use, literal meaning, etc.

3041 —English-Efik and Efik-English vocabulary. 2nd ed. revised. Liverpool, Philip, 1943. 2v.
Part 1. English-Efik. [vi] v, 160p.
Part 2. Efik-English. [1] 161–258p.

3042 —English-Efik and Efik-English vocabulary. 3rd ed. (revised). Liverpool, Philip, 1952–1953. 2v.
Pt. 1. English-Efik. 1952. [vi] v, 161p.
Pt. 2. Efik-English. 1953. 162–279.

3043 —Oberi Okaime: a new African language and script. *Africa*, 17 (1) Jan. 1947: 24–34.
Description of a new language and script invented by adherents of a spiritualist Church movement in Itu District, Uyo Province in the 1920's. Gives texts of this language, with transliteration in roman characters, and English and Efik–Ibibio renderings.

3044 —Some Efik plant names. *Nig. field*, 3 (4) Oct. 1934: 166–167.
Explanatory notes on some Efik plant names, with botanical names supplied.

3045 Akpa nwed ukpep nkpọ ikpọ owo. First book of lessons for adults. Calabar, H.W.T.I. press [n.d.] 13p.
Adult education pamphlet.

3046 Akpanyung, Okon Akpan
Guide to the writing of Ibibio. Ikot Ekpene [the author, 1951] 11p.
Printed by Hope press, Ikot Ekpene.

3047 —A study of Efik for schools and colleges. London, T. Nelson, 1962. vii, 127p. maps.

3047a Anderson, W. *tr.*
The proverbs of Solomon . . . See [3052].

3048 Bible. Efik
Edisana Nwed Abasi ibom. Edinburgh, London, 1909. iv, 1314p.

3049 —Edisana Nwed Abasi Ibom. Akani ye Obufa Testament. Edinburgh, National Bible society for Scotland, 1952. 1272p.

3050 Bible. Efik. Selections
Passages from the Bible. Iko uto ke ñwed Abasi. Edinburgh, 1878. 111p.
Text in English and Efik.

3051 Bible. N.T. Efik
Obufa Testament Obong ye Andinyaña nyin Jisus Kraist, ke ikö Efik. Edinburgh, 1899.

3052 Bible. O.T. Efik. Proverbs.
The proverbs of Solomon, translated into Efik, by W. Anderson. Edinburgh, 1866. 47p.

3053 Bible. O.T. Efik. Psalms
The psalms of David, translated into

Efik by the Rev. Hugh Goldie. Edinburgh, 1866.

3054 *Bunyan, John
Mbuk asaña usuñ hevn . . . Edinburgh, 1868.
Bunyan's Pilgrim's progress, translated into Efik by Alexander Robin.

3055 Ebito, Emmanuel Etim
"Edikop nke ye udon iko Efik". The proverbs and idioms and their meanings in English [Uyo, the author, 1958] 47p.

3056 Evangelical Lutheran Church of Nigeria
Nwed iquo Lutheran. Obot Idim, Uyo, Evangelical Lutheran Church, 1947. 1 p.l., 140p.
Lutheran hymn book in Efik.

3057 —Nwed akam eke Ufok Abasi Lutheran. Obot Idim, Uyo, Lutheran press, 1964. [x] 134p.
Lutheran prayer book in Efik.

3058 [Gaskin, E. A. L.]
Akpa nwed ke iko Efik. 19th ed. London, Philip, 1957. 36p. illus.
An elementary Efik primer.

3059 —Twelve proverbs and one folk-story from the Efik country. Africa, 5 (1) Jan. 1932: 68–70.
Efik texts, with English translation and explanatory notes.

3060 Goldie, Hugh
Dictionary of the Efik language. In two parts: Efik and English; English and Efik. Glasgow, Dunn & Wright, 1874. 643p.

3061 — —Addenda. London, S.P.C.K., 1911, 28p.

3062 *—Dictionary of the Efik language, abridged. Glasgow, 1862. 187p.

3063 *—Efik grammar in Efik. Edinburgh, United Presbyterian college, 1874.

3064 *—Efik grammar in English. Edinburgh, United Presbyterian college, 1874.

3065 —Principles of Efik grammar, with specimen of the language. Edinburgh, Muir and Patterson, 1868. 105p.

3066 Green, Margaret Mackson
The classification of West African tone languages: Igbo and Efik. Africa, 19 (3) Jl. 1949: 213–219.
Shows, by examination of their semantic and grammatical structure, some resemblance between Igbo and Efik and questions the placement of Igbo in the Kwa group of the Western Sudanic languages.

3067 Hau, Kathleen
Oberi Okaime script, text and counting system. Bull. IFAN, 23 (1–2) Jan.-Apr. 1961: 291–308.

3067a International African institute
Alphabets for the Efik, Ibo and Yoruba languages. See [1492]

3068 Inyang, Paul E. B.
Language groups of Eastern Nigeria. [Nsukka, the author, 1964] 38p. bibliog.
Descriptive and historical notes on the origins and language of the Ibibio and their neighbours.
Mimeographed.

3069 —"Ukatenañ" (Ikwo ikot utom ke Efik ye Ibibio). Liverpool, Philip [n.d.] 15p.
A collection of six folk songs and one folk tale in Efik, the former often sung by groups of farm workers.

3070 Jeffreys, M. D. W.
Old Calabar, and notes on the Ibibio language. Calabar, H.W.T.I. press, 1935. (v) 120p. bibliog.
In the first 22 pages, the author attempts a historical sketch of the Efik and Ibibio people. The rest of the book deals with their language.

3071 *Kirchner, Johann
Allerlei Lebensweisheit in den Sprichwörten der Ibibios, Nigeria. Echo aus den Missionen, Aug. 1939: 228–230.

3072 Linguaphone institute, London
Efik: a series of words and sentences giving examples of the tones and tone patterns of Efik (Southern Nigeria) with phonetic transcriptions and English translations. Selected from the "Phonetic and tonal structure of Efik," by Ida C. Ward. London [n.d.] 12p. (Linguaphone miniature language series).

3073 Oyoyoh, O. I.
A summary of studies in Efik-Ibibio language; with particular reference to orthography. Calabar, Henshaw press, 1943. 20p.

3074 Samuel's spiritual mission
Obufa nwed iquö emi enöde ke ererimbot ke Samuel's spiritual mission [by] E. A. Ukang [Ete-Ibekwe, Samuel's spiritual mission, 1955] [4] 156p.
Printed by the Eastern states express, Aba. Hymn book for a spiritualist church.

3075 Simmons, Donald C.
Tonal rhyme in Efik poetry. Anthrop. ling., 2 (6) Je. 1960: 1–10.

3076 —Ibibio verb morphology. Afr. stud., 16 (1) 1957: 1–19, bibliog.
"This article describes the affixes and tone changes involved in the construction of Ibibio tenses".—Synopsis.

3077 —Oron noun morphology. J. W. Afr. lang., 2 (2) 1965: 33–37.

3078 —Oron proverbs. Afr. stud., 19 (3) 1960: 126–137.
A collection of 114 Oron proverbs, with English translations and explanatory notes.

3079 —Oron verb morphology. Africa, 26 (3) Jl. 1956: 250–263.
Analytical study of verb morphology in Oron language. Based on the speech of an Oron man.

3080 —Tonality in Efik signal communication and folklore. In Men and cultures: selected papers of the 5th International congress of anthropological and ethnological sciences, Philadelphia, Sept. 1–9, 1956, ed. A. F. C. Wallace [and others] 1960: 803–808.

3081 Ukpaukure, Harry Jehoiada Patrick, *comp*.
Pogident Giophinens Arien pogident Gireh Seccuna. [Uyo, compiler, 1953] 20p. illus.
"A collection of few [sic] biblical chapters and portions printed in Oberi Okaimey [now called Messifident, i.e. Faith-in-the-Messiah] language and script for use in the Messifident holy spiritual churches".

3082 Waddell, Hope Masterton
Notes on the Efik language. In his *Twenty-nine years in the West Indies and Central Africa, 1863*: 673–681.

3083 —A vocabulary of the Efik or Old Calabar language, with prayers and lessons . . . 2nd ed. revised and enlarged. Edinburgh, Grant & Taylor, 1849. 88p.

3084 Ward, Ida Caroline
The phonetic and tonal structure of Efik. London, Heffer [1933] xiv, 186p.
The first detailed analysis of the tonal system and speech sound in Efik language. Tonal system indicated with dots at five levels, representing high, mid, low, falling and rising tones.

3085 Winston, F. D. D.
The 'mid-tone' in Efik. *Afr. lang. stud.*, (1) 1960: 185–192.

IBO

(Igbo)

Including:

Ika
Ikwerri

Onitsha

1. BIBLIOGRAPHY

3086 Forde, Cyril Daryll and Jones, Gwilym Iwan
Bibliography of the Ibo. In their *The Ibo and Ibibio-speaking peoples of south-eastern Nigeria, 1950*: 61–65.
Linguistics, pp. 64–65.

3087 Ottenberg, Simon
The present state of Ibo studies. *J. Hist. soc. Nig.*, 2 (2) Dec. 1961: 211–230, bibliog.
A survey of published literature bearing on the Ibo people. Pleads for more studies to be undertaken, especially in four subject fields—Theoretical problems, Ethnographic and sociological, Historical and archaeological, and Present-day social problems.

3088 —Supplementary bibliography on the Ibo-speaking people of South-eastern Nigeria. *Afr. stud.*, 14 (2) 1955: 63–85.
A very useful, annotated list intended to supplement Forde and Jones' bibliography [3086].

3089 Willis, John Ralph
Bibliographical note to the 1966 edition [of Niger Ibos] In *Niger Ibos, by G. T. Basden. New impression. 1966*: 439–445.
Some seventy-six items annotated and organized into sections—History, literature, and arts and crafts; social organization and political structure; education and community development; religion; etc.

2. GENERAL STUDIES

3090 Achebe, Chinua
Arrow of God. London, Heinemann, 1964. [v] 287p.
A novel.

3091 —No longer at ease. London, Heinemann, 1960. [vi] 170p.
A novel.

3092 —Things fall apart. London, Heinemann, 1958. vi, 185p. illus.
A novel.

3093 Ajayi, W. O.
The Niger mission to 1914. 1963.
Ph.D. thesis, London.

3094 Amugbanite, Tony
Enugu—city of coal: a portrait of Eastern Nigeria's capital. *W. Afr. rev.*, 30 (376) Jan. 1959: 22–24, illus.

3095 Basden, George Thomas
Edith Warner of the Niger: the story of thirty-three years of zealous and courageous work amongst Ibo girls and women. London, Seeley, Service, 1927. 92p.
A biographical account of a C.M.S. missionary who worked mainly at Asaba, Awka and Onitsha.

3096 Bowen, R. L.
Obi Oputa of Aboh. *Nig. mag.*, (22) 1944: 64–65, illus.

3097 Cole, William
Life on the Niger; or The journal of an African trader. London, Saunders, Otley, 1862. [4] 208p.
Reminiscences of the author, a Liverpool trader who ran a factory in Aboh for about a year and visited Onitsha and other towns along the Niger.

3098 Crowther, Samuel Adjai
Description of a visit to Obotshi. *Church miss. intell. & record., n. s.*, 8, 1883: 695–696.
Obotshi is a town to the east of Onitsha. Here, the Bishop describes his visit and gives an account of the town.

3099 —Letters to the *Church miss. record*, 39 (n.s. 13) 1868: 81–82; 40 (n.s. 14) 1869:

82–84, 87–88; 42 (2nd n.s.1) 1871: 51–52, 130–133.

Series of letters describing the work of the C.M.S. mission at Onitsha.

3100 —Report on a visit to the stations on the Niger in the year 1870. *Church miss. intell., n.s.,* 7, 1871: 88–94, 124–128.

3101 Dennis, D.
The rising of the Ekwumekwu. *Niger & Yoruba notes,* 10 (119) 1904: 83–87.

3102 Dennis, Thomas John
A week's itineration in the Ibo country. *Church miss. intell., n.s.,* 24 (285) Sept. 1899: 778–781.

Account of a journey by a missionary party from Onitsha to Awka and back in 1899. Describes the area traversed and the people met.

3103 Dobinson, Henry Hughes
New openings on the Niger: notes of a short journey into Ibo land. *Church miss. intell., n.s.,* 16, Aug. 1891: 572–583.

Journey from Onitsha to Isele, to the west of the Niger, and back. Notes on the area and the people.

3104 —Notes of a second journey into Ibo land. *Church miss. intell., n.s.,* 17, Apr. 1892: 276–281.

Reached Isele and Ubolu.

3105 Egbuna, Obi Benue
Wind versus polygamy, where "wind" is the "wind of change" and polygamy the "change of Eves". London, Faber and Faber, 1964. 128p.

3106 From Iboland to the Sonkwala mountains. *Nig. mag.,* (28) 1948: 87–157, illus.

Account of a journey by some members of the staff of *Nigeria Magazine* to see modern developments in the area.

3107 George, J. T.
[Letters] *Church miss. record,* 38 (n.s. 12) 1867: 81; 39 (n.s. 13) 1868: 82–85; 40 (n.s. 14) 1869: 85–87; 88–89.

A series of letters written by a member of the C.M.S. mission at Onitsha describing the area and the work of the mission there.

3108 Hair, P. E. H.
Enugu: an industrial and urban community in East Nigeria, 1914–1953. *WAISER conf. proc. (Sociology section) 1953:* 143–169, map.

A concise political and social history of Enugu.

3109 —Enugu: an industrial community in Nigeria.
WAISER conf. proc., 1952: 67–70.

Summary of paper read at the 1952 conference of WAISER at Ibadan. Concerned with the social background of the coal miners and mining industry.

3110 Hensley, Frances M.
A fight for life: the story of a West African convert and his friends. London, Church missionary society, 1913. 207p.

Account of Eze, an Ibo convert who became a missionary at Ebu in Owerri Province. See also [3125].

3111 —Niger dawn. London, A. H. Stockwell [1954?] 192p. front.

Reminiscences of a C.M.S. missionary's twelve years of life and work among the Ibos of Eastern Nigeria.

3112 Hives, Frank
Juju and justice in Nigeria; told by Frank Hives and written down by Gascoigne Lumley. London, John Lane, 1930. xi, 254p. front. (port.) illus., map.

Life in South-Eastern Nigeria in the 1900's sketched by a former administrative officer in Bende Division.

3113 —Justice in the jungle. London, John Lane, 1932. x, [1] 239p.

A further account of life and scenes in parts of Eastern Nigeria in the 1900's vividly sketched in popular style.

3114 Horton, James Africanus Beale
Empire of the Eboes. In his *West African countries and peoples, 1868:* 171–198.

3115 Ije, M. C.
Towards lasting peace in Asaba. Enugu, printed by ENIS works, for the author, 1963. 42p. illus. (port.) map.

Instability in Asaba is here attributed to a long-standing land dispute sparked off in 1929 by a civil suit for the ownership of the "Cable Point."

3116 An Irish missionary in Central Africa (Southern Nigeria), by a Maynooth priest. Dublin, Talbot press, 1923. 128p.

3117 Jeffreys, M. D. W.
Settling the Eastern Provinces: *West Afr. rev.,* 25 (321) Je. 1954:
Describes military excursions against unruly areas.

3118 Jennings, J. H.
Enugu: a geographical outline. *Nig. geog. j.,* 3 (1) Dec. 1959: 28–38, maps.

3119 Jordan, John P.
Bishop Shanahan of Southern Nigeria. Dublin, Clonmore & Reynolds, 1949. xiv, 264p. front., illus., maps.

3120 Leith-Ross, Sylvia
African conversation piece. London, Hutchinson [1943?] 132p. front.

Author's life among the Ibo of Onitsha from Jan. to June, 1937, given in diary form.

3121 —Beyond the Niger. London, Lutterworth press, 1951. 124p. illus.

Children's book giving author's experiences in Ibo country.

3122 Leonard, Arthur Glyn
Notes of a journey to Bende. *J. Manch. geog. soc.,* 14, 1898: 190–207.

Journey from Opobo to Bende and back, with account of the area and its people.

3123 Le Poirer, R. P.
Niger (Afrique Occidentale). *Miss. Cathol.,* 23, 1891: 49–52.

Includes an account of Asaba and its chiefs and elders and of missionary activities from 1888.

3124 Livingstone, W. P.
Dr. Hitchcock of Uburu. Edinburgh,
Foreign mission committee of the
United Free Church of Scotland, 1920.
88p.
Life and work of a Church of
Scotland missionary in Iboland. Built
a hospital in Uburu.

3125 Lovell, Kenneth H.
A young pioneer, Eze of the Ibo
country. In *Heroes of the bad bush, 1931*:
25–41.
Biography of Eze an Ibo C.M.S.
missionary at Ebu in Owerri Province.
See also [3110].

3126 Nwankwo, Nkem
Danda. London, André Deutsch, 1964.
205p.
A novel.

3127 Nzekwu, Onuora
Blade among the boys. London,
Hutchinson, 1962. 192p.
A novel.

3128 —Highlife   for   lizards.   London,
Hutchinson, 1965.
A novel.

3129 —Wand of noble wood. London,
Hutchinson, 1961. 208p.
A novel.

3130 Offonry, H. Kanu
Tributes to the builder of Uzuakoli
college. *W. Afr. rev.*, 18 (234) Mar.
1947: 286–288, illus.
The builder was the late Rev. H. L. O.
Williams.

3131 Ogbuagu, Bob
Enugu—coal town. *Nig. mag.*, (70)
Sept. 1961: 241–251, illus.

3132 *Rudkin, W. C. E.
In British West Africa: The operations
in the Agbor district, S. Nigeria, June
to August 1906, consequent upon the
murder of Mr. O. S. Crewe-Read,
District Commissioner. *United service
mag.*, Jl. 1907: 433–448.

3133 Ryan, Isobel
Black man's country. London, J. Cape,
1950. 276p. illus.
Popular account, by the wife of a
British official, of their lives in Agulu
and of their relationship with the
people, including their domestic ser-
vants.

3134 —Black man's palaver. London, J.
Cape, 1958. 252p. illus.

3135 Smith, Sidney R.
The Aro expedition. *Niger and Yoruba
notes*, 8 (95) May 1902: 82–83.
Brief note on the Aro long juju and
on the 1902 Aro expedition.

3136 —Christmas week itineration in the
Ibo-speaking   country.   *Niger and
Yoruba notes*, 4 (46) 1898: 82–83.

3137 Spencer, Julius
Narrative of a trip to Ubulu. *Church
miss. intell. and record, n.s.*, 4, 1879:
239–242.

3138 Taylor, John Christopher

[Letters] *Church miss. record*, 29 (n.s. 3)
1858: 287–288; 30 (n.s. 4) 1859: 31–32;
34 (n.s. 8) 1863: 175–177; 35 (n.s. 9)
1864: 137–147; 36 (n.s. 10) 1865: 133–
149; 37 (n.s. 11) 1866: 201–207; 38
(n.s.12) 1867: 73–76; 40 (n.s. 14) 1869:
81–82.
A series of letters by an Ibo
missionary, giving account of the C.M.S.
mission at Onitsha, and of the people,
their ceremonies, warfare, slavery,
human sacrifices, etc.

3139 Ugwu, Daniel Chukwuma
This is Nsukka. Yaba, John Okwesa
[n.d.] 39p. map.
Description and general notes on
Nsukka by an Nsukka legislator.

3140 Venour, W. J.
Aro country in Southern Nigeria.
Geog. j., 20 (1) Jl. 1902: 88–89.
Geographical account of Aro with
some scanty ethnographic data, by a
member of the Aro field force expedition.

3141 Vickery, C. E.
A West African expedition. *United
service mag.*, 154, 1906: 552–562.
Account of the military exploration
of the Bende-Onitsha hinterland in
1904–1908.

3142 Walker, Frank Deaville
The romance of the black river; the
story of the C.M.S. Niger mission.
London, C.M.S., 1930. xvi, 267p. front.,
illus., maps.

3143 —Rev. ed. 1938. 246p.
A full account of the origins and
development of the C.M.S. mission in
Nigeria, down to 1930.

3144 Zahra, Albert
Yaws eradication campaign in Nsukka
Division, Eastern Nigeria: preliminary
review. *Bull. W.H.O.*, 15 (6) 1956:
911–935.

3145 Zappa, R. P. L.
A travers les pays du Niger. Voyages
d'Asaba à Issele, à Ibou et à Ogbou.
Miss. Cathol., 25, 1893: 586–588, map.
Notes on a journey from Asaba to
three towns in the Western Ibo country.

3. PHYSICAL ANTHROPOLOGY

3145a Charmers, J. N. M.
The ABO, MNS and Rh blood groups
of the Nigerians. See [572].

3145b Edington, G. M.
The distribution of haemoglobin C in
West Africa. See [573].

3146 Hauck, Hazel M. and Tabrah, Frank L.
Heights and weights of Ibo of various
ages. *W. Afr. med. j.*, 12 (2) Apr. 1963:
64–74, bibliog.
Report of investigation carried out
among the Ibo of Awo Omamma in
1959–1960.

3147 Jones, Gwilym Iwan and Mulhall, H.
An examination of the physical type of
certain   peoples   of   South-Eastern

Nigeria. *J.R.A.I.*, 79 (1–2) 1949: 11–19, tables.

A statistical analysis of the head measurements of some 1,718 male Ibos, and a few Abua and Ibibio.

4. SOCIAL AND CULTURAL ANTHROPOLOGY, ETHNOGRAPHY

(i) General

3148 Aligwekwe, E.
Lagging emulation in Southern Nigeria. *Amer. anthrop.*, 67 (6) Dec. 1965: 1518–1521.

3149 Amugbanite, Tony
Iboland's sleeping customs. *W. Afr. rev.*, 30 (383) Oct. 1959: 649–651, illus.
Ibo customs as exemplified by rules and rites associated with the Ozo society.

3150 Ardener, Edwin W.
Life among the Bende Ibos of Nigeria. *W. Afr.*, 5, 1921: 212.

3151 —Some Ibo attitudes to skin pigmentation. *Man*, 54, May 1954 (art. 101): 71–73.
A survey in Mba-Ise area in 1949–51 which showed that people of lighter complexion were considered more beautiful than those of darker, "blacker" complexion.

3152 Asaba. *Nig. Mag.*, (54) 1957: 226–242, illus.
Ethnographic and historical sketch of Asaba.

3153 Ayamelum student union.
Ayamelum in brief. (Compiled through the united efforts of Ayamelum students' union) Enugu, Eastern Nigeria printing corporation, 1962. 68p. illus., map.

3154 Basden, George Thomas
Among the Ibos of Nigeria; an account of the curious and interesting habits, customs and beliefs of a little known African people by one who has for many years lived amongst them on close and intimate terms. London, Seeley, Service, 1921, repr. London, Frank Cass, 1966. 316p. front., illus., map.

3155 —Iboland und seine Bewohner. *Mitt. geog. Gesell.* [Wien] 55, 1912: 476–479.
A German summary of his *Notes on the Ibo country and the Ibo people, Southern Nigeria*.

3156 —Niger Ibos; description of the primitive life, customs and animistic beliefs, &c; of the Ibo people of Nigeria, by one who, for thirty-five years, enjoyed the privilege of their intimate confidence and friendship. London, Seeley, Service, 1938. 448p. front., illus., map, bibliog.
An elaborate account, more detailed and better organized than his earlier work, *Among the Ibos of Nigeria*. [3154].

3156a ——New impression, with a bibliographical note, by John Ralph Willis. London, Frank Cass, 1966. 456p.

3156b —Notes on the Ibo country and the Ibo people, Southern Nigeria. *Geog. j.*, 39, 1912: 241–247, map.
Mainly Onitsha Ibo.

3156c —Notes on the Ibo country, Southern Nigeria. *Geog. j.*, 65 (1) Jan. 1925: 32–41.

3157 Bolinder, Gustaf W.
Svarta folk i Västafrika. Stockholm, 1927. 219p.

3158 Cockin, George
The land and education in the Ibo country of South-Eastern Nigeria. *Int. rev. missions*, 33, 1944: 274–279.

3159 Correia, J. Alves
Les sens moral chez les Ibos de la Nigéria. *Anthropos*, 18–19, 1923–1924: 880–889.

3160 —Un totem Nigérien. *Anthropos*, 16–17, 1921–22: 960–965.
On taboos and totems in Iboland, especially in the Awka area.

3161 Cousens, J. E.
Some notes on Iroko in Onitsha and Owerri Provinces. *Farm and forest*, 7 (1) Jan.–Je. 1946: 28–32.

3162 E., M.
Ibo customs. *W. Eq. Afr. dioc. mag.*, 18 (226) [i.e. n.s. 106] Apr. 1913: 443–449.
Account of various Ibo customs: the new yam festival; coming of age: ju-ju offerings for defilement, cannibalism; second burial, etc.

3163 Ejindu, I. U.
A short story of Enugwu Ngwo. *W. Eq. Afr. dioc. mag.*, 26 (326) [i.e. n.s. no. 200] Aug. 1921: 218–220.
Notes on some Enugwu Ngwo customs which the author disapproved.

3164 Ekejiuba, Felicia
Omu Okwei: the merchant queen of Ossomari. *Nig. mag.*, (90) Sept. 1966: 113–220.
Biographical sketch of Queen Okwei of Ossomari, 1872–1943.

3165 Equiano, Olaudah
The interesting narrative of the life of Olaudah Equiano, or Gustavus Vassa, the African, written by himself. London, 1789. 2v.
Autobiography of an Ibo (believed to have come from Western Ibo country) sold as a slave in 1756. First two chapters give useful account of life in Iboland around 1750.

3166 Ewo, Dixon Ogaranya
The history and customs of Ogbaland. [Port Harcourt, the author, 1952.] [v] 37p.
Printed by C.M.S. Niger press, Port Harcourt.

3167 Eze, J. O. N.
Population and settlement [in Nsukka Division] In *Nsukka Division: a geographic appraisal.* Ed. P. K. Sircar, 1965: 72–88, maps, bibliog.
For main work, see [3192].

3168 Ezeabasili, A. N.
The Ibo in town and village: traditions

and beliefs of Nigeria's second largest tribe. *Afr. world*, Apr. 1960: 8–10, 12.

3169 Ezeanya, Stephen Nweke
The use of Igbo names. *W. Afr. religion*, (3) Oct. 1964: 2–8.
An explanation of the cultural and religious significance of Ibo personal names. Appends a list of such names, giving the meaning of each.

3170 Forde, Cyril Daryll and Jones, G. I.
The Ibo and Ibibio-speaking peoples of South-Eastern Nigeria. London, O.U.P. for Int. Afr. Inst., 1950. 94p. map (fold) bibliog. (Int. Afr. Inst. Ethnographic survey of Africa, edited by Daryll Forde. Western Africa, part 3).
Ibo-speaking peoples, pp. 9–65, incl. bibliog. pp. 61–65. Ibibio-speaking peoples, pp. 67–94, including bibliog. pp. 93–94.

3171 Grove, A. T.
Land use and soil conservation in parts of Onitsha and Owerri Provinces. Zaria, Geological survey of Nigeria, 1951. 79p. (Geog. survey Nig. Bulletin no. 21).
A multi-dimensional investigation including the geology, physiography, soil conditions, population and land economics of these areas.

3172 —Soil erosion and population problems in South-East Nigeria. *Geog. j.*, 117 (3) Sept. 1951: 291–306, illus., maps.
In Onitsha and northern Owerri Provinces, with particular emphasis on Oko village.

3173 Haig, E. F. G.
Restless Ibo. *Spectator*, (183) Dec. 1949: 799.
Relates the 1949 Enugu miners' riots to the cultural and socio-psychological make up of the Ibo.

3174 Hartland, E. Sidney
Ibo-speaking peoples of Southern Nigeria. *J. Afr. soc.*, 14 (55) Apr. 1915: 271–277.
A critique of N. W. Thomas' Anthropological report on the Ibo-speaking peoples of Nigeria [3227].

3175 Ibo state union.
Ibo state union constitution. Port Harcourt, Amac's press [1951?] 77p.

3176 —Memorandum to the Willink's minority commission, including addresses of Ibo counsels at Calabar & Port Harcourt, and the important events in the making of history of Iboland, 1841-1958, including Ibo land distance mileage charts. Port Harcourt, Nigerian popular printing press & bookshops [1958] [iii] 34p.

3177 Ijere, Martin O., *ed.*
Nsu—past and present: an account of its economic, social, educational and political development. Nsukka, the author, 1965. 114p. illus. Printed by Etudo, Onitsha.

3178 —Progress in Nsu. [Nsu] Nsu youth association, 1963. 42p. Printed by International press, Aba.

Short notes by various authors on aspects of Nsu.

3179 Ike, Akwaelumo
Great men of Ibo land. Aba, [the author, 1952] [6] 38p. illus. (ports.)
Printed by Clergyman printing press, Aba.

3180 Inside Arochuku. *Nig. mag.*, (53) 1957: 100–118, illus.

3181 Jeffreys, M. D. W.
The bullroarer among the Ibo. *Afr. stud.*, 8 (1) Mar. 1949: 23–34.
The use of the bullroarer by members of a secret society—"Mmo"—among the Umundri Ibo in Awka and environs,

3182 Kalu, Eke
An Ibo autobiography: the autobiography of Mr. Eke Kalu, Ohafia well-honoured son. *Nig. field*, 7 (4) Oct. 1938: 158–170.
Born about 1875.

3183 Kurunwane, G. M.
The Ibo as I see him. Kano, Federated press, 1963. [iv] 28p.

3184 Leith-Ross, Sylvia
African women: a study of the Ibo of Nigeria. London, Faber and Faber, 1939. 367p. maps.

3185 Lutz, R. R.
Bas-Niger (Afrique occidentale): la mission de Saint-Joseph d'Agouleri. *Miss. Cathol.*, 27, 1895: 433–437.

3186 MacAllister, Donald A.
Southern Nigeria. *Geog. j.*, 32 (2) Aug. 1908: 195.
A short letter noting the Aro expedition. Occasioned by E. A. Steel's Explorations in Southern Nigeria [521] q.v.

3186a Macgregor, J. K.
Some notes on Nsibidi. See [698a].

3187 Meek, Charles Kingsley
Report on social and political organisation in the Owerri Division. Lagos, Government printer, 1937. 87p.
Includes much on family and kinship. marriage, burial customs, etc. Part of the data included in author's *Law and authority in a Nigerian tribe* [3294].

3188 Morgan, W. B.
The 'grassland towns' of the Eastern Region of Nigeria. *Trans. & papers Inst. Brit. geographers*, (23) Nov. 1957: 213–224, maps.

3189 Nigerian union of teachers
A primer of Igbo etiquette. London. Longmans, Green, 1949. 32p.
In Ibo and English, and intended for use in primary schools.

3190 Nkume, E. I. E.
Revolution—the spirit of Ase. Lagos [the author, n.d.] 8p.
Printed by Lucky-way printing works, Lagos.

3191 Nri traditions. *Nig. mag.*, (54) 1957: 273–288.

3192 Nsukka. University of Nigeria. Department of geography.

Nsukka division: a geographic appraisal. Edited by P. K.Sircar. Nsukka, 1965. vi, 111p. maps.

Brief essays on the geography, economy, agriculture and social conditions in Nsukka Division prepared for the use of delegates to the Nigerian geographical association conference held at Nsukka, Dec. 17–22, 1965.

3193 *Nuno, Iweka
Akuko-ala Obosi. 1924.
History and customs of Obosi, a town near Onitsha.

3194 Nwafor, John O.
Survey into the Ibo names: an enlightening and encouraging handbook for the up-to-date "child-naming" by "Okwu-Igbo" John Nwafor. Aba, Nwafor & sons, [1960] 40p. illus. (port.). Printed by Treasure press, Aba.

3195 *Nwangoro, S. O.
Aro land. Calabar, Hope Waddel press, 1922.

3196 *—The clan system and prejudice in Arochuku. Calabar, Hope Waddel press [n.d.].

3197 Nzekwu, Onuora
The Edda. *Nig. mag.*, (76) Mar. 1963: 16–28, illus.
A clan today located a few miles southwest of Afikpo. Gives notes on its history and customs.

3198 —Gloria Ibo. *Nig. mag.*, (64) Mar. 1960: 72–88, illus.
Aguleri Ibo.

3199 —Onitsha. *Nig. mag.*, (50) 1956: 200–223, illus.

3200 Nzimiro, Francis Ikenna
Oguta. *Nig. mag.*, (80) Mar. 1964: 30–34, illus.

3201 Oberdoerffer, M. J.
Heilpflanzen aus d. Volksmedizin Nigerianns *Tropenpflanzen*, 41, 1938: 20–27.
Account of Ibo medical practices, including external and internal medicine, blood letting, etc. Supplies botanical terms for the medical plants discussed. Author who spent some time in Uzuakoli, served with the Empire Leprosy Relief Association.

3202 Obi, Gabriel W. E.
How the primitive Ibo man lives his life. *Nig. mag.*, (15) 1938: 200–202, illus.

3203 Oduche, Okwudinka Nwoye
Life history of Ogbuefi Oduche Akunwata Akamelu. [Enugu, the author, 1951] 47p.
Printed by Ezeana press, Enugu. Biographee lived from 1884–1946.

3204 Offonry, H. Kanu
The Ibo people. *W. Afr. rev.*, 18 (233) Feb. 1947: 167–168.

3205 —The strength of Ibo clan feeling. *W. Afr.*, (1787) May 26, 1951: 467; (1788) Je. 2, 1951: 489–490.
Ibo tribal cohesion discussed in terms of cultural, social and religious factors such as improvement unions, secret societies, ceremonies, festivals, age groups, marriage, etc.

3206 Ogbalu, Frederick Chidozie, *ed.*
Omenala Igbo (The book of Igbo custom). 3rd ed. Onitsha, Varsity bookshop [n.d.] 64p.
"2nd ed., 1960"—verso of t.–p.

3207 Ojike, Mbonu
Life with father in Nigeria. *Sci. digest*, 19 May 1946: 12–16.
Abridgement of the material in the first part of his book, *My Africa*.

3208 —My Africa. New York, John Day, 1946. xiii, 350p. illus., map., bibliog.
Mostly on political, economic and social conditions and problems in Nigeria. The earlier pages (pp. 3–38) give a good account of his childhood, family and life in his village in Aro Ndizuogu.

3209 —Portrait of a boy in Africa. New York, East and West association, 1945. 36p.
Another abridgement of the material in the first section of *My Africa*.

3210 Okala, Julius B. C. Etuka
Educational and cultural dynamics with particular reference to an African kingdom, 1857–1936. 1953.
D.Ed. thesis, Columbia university. The African kingdom here refers to Onitsha.

3211 —The problem of primitive education with particular reference to the Ibo of Nigeria. *Trans. Ill. acad. sci.*, 35 (2) Dec. 1942: 51–53.
Brief description of child upbringing and education in the Ibo home.

3212 Okoli, Joe
People of the Anambra. *Afr. hist.*, 1 Mar. 1963: 19–22.

3213 Oluwasanmi, H. A. [and others]
Uboma: a socio-economic and nutritional survey of a rural community in Eastern Nigeria. Ebbingford, Cornwall, Geographical publications, 1966. xi, 116p. illus., maps, bibliog. (World land use survey. Occasional paper, no. 6).

3214 Onitsha. *Nig. mag.*, (50) 1956: 200–223 illus,.

3215 Onyenacho, B. N.
Education amongst the Mbaise-Ibo. *Afr. hist.*, 1 (3) Mar. 1965: 34–37.
Describes informal training of youths in the traditional skills and methods prior to the introduction of modern education by the British.

3216 Onye-Ocha [pseud.]
Down with everything Ibo. *Nig. mag.*, (23) 1946: 97–99.

3217 Ottenberg, Phoebe V.
The Afikpo Ibo of Eastern Nigeria. In *Peoples of Africa, ed. J. L. Gibbs, 1965*: 1–39, illus., bibliog.
Ethnographic summary of the Afikpo people.

3218 Ottenberg, Simon
Ibo receptivity to change. In *Continuity*

and change in African cultures, ed. W. Bascom and M. J. Herskovits, 1959: 130–143.

3219   —Improvement associations among the Afikpo Ibo. *Africa*, 25 (1) Jan. 1955: 1–28.
    Describes the structure, membership and functions of improvement unions organised by Afikpo people.

3219a —The present state of Igbo studies. See [3087].

3220   Parkinson, John
    Note on the Asaba people (Ibos) of the Niger. *J.R.A.I.*, 36, 1906: 312–324, illus.
    Ethnographic and linguistic notes.

3221   Shields, Nwanganga
    Ogui urban area; a social survey. Enugu, Economic development institute, University of Nigeria, 1965. v, 99p. (E.D.I. working paper, no. 2).
    Mimeographed. Survey of a district within Enugu township.

3222   Simmons, Donald C.
    Notes on the Aro. *Nig. field*, 23 (1) Jan. 1958: 27–33.
    Traditional history of the Aro, followed by account of their kinship system, a list of kinship terminology, and a selected lexikon of an Aro speaker.

3223   Smith, Sidney R.
    The Ibo people: a study of the religion and customs of a tribe in the Southern Provinces of Nigeria. 1929.
    Ph.D. thesis, Cambridge.

3224   —Oka. *W. Equatorial Afr. diocesan mag.*, 12 (133) 1905: 3–5.

3225   Smock, David Robert
    An appraisal of village integration in Abakaliki Division. Enugu, Ministry of rural development, 1966. 31p.
    Mimeographed.

3226   —From village to trade union in Africa: a study of power and decision-making in the Nigerian coal miners' union and the villages from which the coal miners migrated. 1964. 461p.
    Ph.D. thesis, Cornell university.

3226a Talbot, Percy Amaury
    Tribes of the Niger delta . . . See [3745].

3227   Thomas, Northcote Whitridge
    Anthropological report on the Ibo-speaking peoples of Nigeria. London, Harrison, 1913–1914. 6v. fronts. (maps) illus.
        Part I. Law and custom of the Ibo of the Awka neighbourhood, Southern Nigeria, 1913. 161p. front. (map) illus.
        Part II. English-Ibo and Ibo-English dictionary. 1913. vii, 391p.
        Part III. Proverbs, narratives, vocabulary and grammar. 1913. vi, 199p.
        Part IV. Law and custom of the Ibo of the Asaba District, Southern Nigeria. 1913. vi, 208p. front. (map) illus.

        Part V. Addenda to Ibo-English dictionary. 1914. xv, 184p.
        Part VI. Proverbs, stories, tones in Ibo. 1914. ix, 114p.

3228   Uburu and its salt lake. *Nig. mag.*, (56) 1958: 84–96, illus.
    Describes Uburu, an Ibo village on the shore of a salt lake in Eastern Nigeria, and the method used by women in extracting salt from the water.

3229   Uche, Anaga Kalu
    Custom and practices in Ohafia. [the author] 1960. Printed by Research institute of African religion press, Aba. 55p.
    Brief description of traditional law and customs in Ohafia. Includes religious beliefs, wrongs, marriage, family and succession.

3230   Uchendu, Victor Chikezie
    The Igbo of Southeast Nigeria. New York, Holt, Rinehart and Winston, 1965. xiii, 111p. illus., map, bibliog. (Case studies in cultural anthropology)
    Based on his Ph.D. thesis, Northwestern University.

3231   Ucheya, Eke
    Profiles of Bende chiefs. Onitsha, Varsity printing press, 1963. 33p. illus.
    Biographical sketches.

3232   Udeagu, Onyenaekeya
    Ibos as they are. In *An African treasury, ed. L. Hughes, 1961*: 16–19.

3233   Uzoma, R. I.
    Universal schooling in Ngwa clan of Aba Division, Nigeria *Oversea educ.*, 23 (2) Jan. 1952: 234–246.
    Explains a system of universal education in the area supported with money from communal collection of palm produce.

3234   Wieschhoff, H. A.
    Concepts of abnormality among the Ibo of Nigeria. *J. Amer. orient. soc.*, 63, 1943: 262–272.
    Ibo conceptions of mental abnormality discussed and illustrated with description of three types of abnormal mental conditions among them. Based on information by an Onitsha man.

3235   —Social significance of names among the Ibo of Nigeria. *Amer. anthrop.*, 43 Apr. 1941: 212–222.

3236   Wilson, A. L.
    Among Ibo villages. *Church miss. intell.*, n.s., 29 (346) 1904: 751–753.
    Architectural and physical aspects of houses; religious beliefs, betrothal customs and funeral rites in Obosi, Nnewi and Onitsha areas.

4. (ii)   History

3237   Aderibigbe, A. A. B.
    The Ibo. In *A thousand years of West African history, ed. J. F. A. Ajayi and I. Espie, 1965*: 196–199.

3238   Agwuna, Osita
    Umunri in the earliest times. *The light: magazine of the Students/teachers union*

and the Youth association of Enugwu-Ukwu, (1) 1962: 5–6, illus.

History and migrations of Umunri people. A brief and sketchy account, by a former parliamentarian now a chief (*Eze* of Enugwu-Ukwu and *Igwe* of Umunri.)

3239   Alutu, John O.
A groundwork of Nnewi history. Nnewi, Homeland information service, 1963. 315p.

3240   Amasiobi, C.
Ibo government and the rise of the Aros. *Historia*, 3, Apr. 1966: 75–83.

3241   Anene, J. C.
Protectorate government of Southern Nigeria and the Aros. *J. Hist. soc. Nig.*, 1 (1) Dec. 1956: 20–26.
Account of events leading to the Aro expedition of 1901–2, and the course of the expedition.

3242   Azikiwe, Nnamdi
Fragments of Onitsha history. *J. negro hist.*, 15, 1930: 474–497.

3242a   Boston, J. S.
Notes on contacts between the Igala and the Ibo. See [3632].

3243   Ekeghe, Ogbonna O.
A short history of Abiriba. Aba, International press [n.d.] 64p.
Includes "Seasonal and religious festivals" pp. 45–46; "Customary marriage at Abiriba", pp. 46–50; "Signs and Symbolism" pp. 50–51.

3244   Fox, A. J.
The history of Uzuakoli. Uzuakoli, Local history society, Secondary school, Methodist college, 1960. 58p.

3245   Ibeziako, M. Ogo
The founder and some celebrities of Onitsha: some aspects of ancient civilization. [n.p.] 1937. 20p. illus.

3246   Idigo, M. C. M.
The history of Aguleri. [Yaba, the author, 1955] viii [5] 118p. illus. (ports.)
Printed by Nicholas printing, and publishing co.

3247   Igwegbe, Richard Ohizu
The original history of Arondizuogu, from 1635–1960. Aba [the author, 1962] viii, 136p. illus., map.
Printed by International press, Aba.

3248   Igwi, A. O.
The outline history of Nnochiri Oriaku. *Nig. field*, 16 (4) Oct. 1951: 168–179.
A biographical account of Oriaku who hailed from Uzuakoli, became a successful trader, and visited England.

3249   Ike, Akwaelumo
The origin of the Ibos. 2nd ed. Aba, Silent prayer home press, 1951. 44p.
Suggests Hebrew origin of the Ibo, including biblical, as well as Ibo cultural data as evidence. The last chapter attempts a division of the Ibo tribe into culture areas.

3250   Jeffreys, M. D. W.
A note on Abagana town. *Nig. field*, 22 (4) Oct. 1957: 184–185.

Verbatim account by Abagana people of the arrival of the British in their town and of the newcomers' hesitancy in recognizing their chief, Okeke Ezenkwo.

3251   —The Umundri tradition of origin. *Afr. stud.*, 15 (3) Sept. 1956: 119–131.
Legend of origin of Umundri people as narrated to author at Aguku, near Awka.

3252   Jones, Gwilym Iwan
Who are the Aro? *Nig. field*, 8 (3) Jl. 1939: 100–103.
A brief account of the various theories and legends concerning the origin of the Aros.

3253   Kaine, Esama
Ossomari: a historical sketch. Onitsha, the author, 1959. xi, 116p. map.

3254   Ogali, A. Ogali
History of Item past and present. [Enugu, the author] 1960. 40p.
Printed by Etudo press, Onitsha.

3255   Ojiyi, Okwudili
Outline history of Umuezeh ancestry. [sic] [Amawbia, the author, 1964] [i] 40p.
Printed by Mbidokwu's printing press, Onitsha.

3256   Okoro, Patrick D.
A short history of Uratta. 2nd ed. revised and enlarged. Owerri [printed by] Express printing press, 1963. [3] 54p. illus. (ports.)
First ed. pub. 1954 by author and printed by Benson press, Ijebu-Ode. 19p.

3257   Onwuka, James G. Dike
Pioneer and laconic Azuigbo graphic history. [Ibadan, the author, 1950] 26p.
Printed by Laniba press, Ibadan.

3257a   Pratt, J. A.
A brief historical sketch of Opobo . . . See [3729].

3258   Spencer, Julius
The history of Asaba and its kings. *Niger and Yoruba notes*, 8 (87) Sept. 1901: 20–21.

3259   Ukpabi, S. C.
Nsukka before the establishment of British administration. In *Nsukka Division: a geographic appraisal*, ed. P. K. Sircar, 1965: 26–36, map.
A brief survey of the history of the Division from the 16th century to the British administration. For main work, see [3192].

3260   Umo, R. Kanu
History of Aro settlements. Lagos [the author] [n.d.].
Printed by Ife-Olu printing works, Lagos.

4. (iii) Marriage, Family, Lineage Structure

3261   Ardener, Edwin W.
The kinship terminology of a group of southern Ibo. *Africa*, 24 (2) Apr. 1954: 85–99, illus. (diagrs.).
Mba-ise Ibo. French summary, pp. 98–99.

3262 —Lineage and locality among the Mbaise Ibo. *Africa*, 29 (2) Apr. 1959: 113–133, map.
French summary, p. 133.

3263 Curryer, W. H. S.
Mothercraft in Southern Nigeria. *United empire*, 18, 1927: 78–81.

3264 Dodds, F. W.
African marriage laws and customs as found among the Ibos and the influence on them of modern civilisation. *Congrès int. des sciences anthropologiques et ethnologiques, London, 1934*: 217–219.

3265 Esenwa, F. E.
Marriage customs in Asaba Division, *Nig. field*, 13 (2) Oct. 1948: 71–81.
Traditional marriage customs and some aspects of matrimony in Asaba Division. Effects of western culture on some of these customs noted.

3266 Nzimiro, Francis Ikenna
Family and kinship in Ibo land: a study in acculturation process. 1962. [ii] 374p. illus., bibliog.
D.Phil. thesis, University of Cologne, West Germany. Concentrates on two urban communities—Onitsha and Oguta, and one rural area, Nsukka.

3267 Obi, S. N. Chinwuba
Modern family law in southern Nigeria. 1963.
Ph.D. thesis, London.

3268 Offonry, H. Kanu
Dowry (Bride-price) *W. Afr. rev.*, 20 (264) 1949: 1011–1013.

3269 Ottenberg, Phoebe, V.
Marriage relationships in the double descent system of the Afikpo Ibo of Southeastern Nigeria. 1958.
Ph.D. thesis, Northwestern University.

3270 Ottenberg, Simon
Double descent in an Ibo village group. In *Men and cultures: selected papers of the 5th International congress of anthropological and ethnological sciences, Philadelphia, Sept. 1–9, 1956, ed. A. F. C. Wallace [and others] 1960*: 473–481.
Analysis of Afikpo double descent system.

3271 Salacuse, Jeswald
Ibo family law. In his *A selective survey of Nigerian family law, 1965*: 47–64.

3272 Spörndli, J. I.
Marriage customs among the Ibos. *Anthropos*, 37–40 (1–3) 1942–45: 113–121.
Ibo marriage customs from the "engagement" stage to the bridegroom's final taking home of his bride.

3273 Uchendu, Victor Chikezie
Concubinage among Ngwa Igbo of Southern Nigeria. *Africa*, 35 (2) Apr. 1965: 187–197, bibliog.
"In this study, attention is focused on (i) the role of concubinage in the disposal of certain rights in women among the Ngwa Igbo, (ii) the folk evaluation of the status of the partners in this institution, and (iii) the strength of concubinage under the impact of acculturation." French summary, pp. 196–197.

3274 —'Kola hospitality': a clarification. *Man*, 65, Sept.–Oct. 1965: 156 (art. 152).
Clarification of a point in his earlier article on the topic. [3275].

3275 —'Kola hospitality' and Igbo lineage structure. *Man*, 64, Mar.–Apr. 1964: 47–50. (art. 53) bibliog.

3276 Wieschhoff, H. A.
Divorce laws and practices in modern Ibo culture. *J. negro hist.*, 26 (3) Jl. 1941: 299–324.
A study of the simultaneous operation of the traditional, statutory, and missionary modes of marriage in Onitsha Province. Illustrated with specific cases.

4. (iv) Government, Kingship, Law

3277 Awa, Eme O.
The voting behaviour and attitudes of Eastern Nigerians: a study of how and why Ibos vote in elections and their attitudes towards public authorities. Aba, Ofomata's press, 1961. 24p.
The study was conducted in 1958.

3278 Chubb, Llewellyn Travers
Ibo land tenure. 2nd ed. Ibadan, University press, 1961. vii, 115p.
1st ed. published by Gaskiya corporation, Zaria, 1947. 117p.

3279 Epelle, E. M. T.
Chieftaincy titles in Igbo land and church membership. *West Afr. rel.*, (5) Feb. 1966: 3–6.

3280 Elias, Taslim Olawale
The Ibo rules of inheritance. In his *Nigerian land law and customs, 3rd ed., 1962*: 241–247.

3281 Esike, S. O.
The Aba riots of 1929. *Afr. hist.*, 1 (3) Mar. 1965: 7–13.
Includes a description of social and governmental structure in Iboland.

3282 Field, J. O.
Sale of land in an Ibo community, Nigeria. *Man*, 45, May–Je. 1945: 70 (art. 47).

3283 Forde, Cyril Daryll
Justice and judgement among the southern Ibo under colonial rule. In *African law: adaptation and development, ed. H. Kupper and L. Kupper, 1965*: 79–96.

3284 Green, Margaret Mackson
Ibo village affairs, chiefly with reference to the village of Umueke Agbaja. London, Sidgwick and Jackson, 1947. maps, table.

3285 ——2nd ed. London, Frank Cass, 1964. xvii, 262p.
A study of Ibo social structure and political organisation at the village

level. The village chosen is Umueke-Agbaja in Okigwi Division. See also a useful review and commentary on the subject by G. I. Jones in *Africa*, 19 (2) Apr. 1949: 150–156.

3286 —Land tenure in an Ibo village in southeastern Nigeria. London, P. Lund, Humphries, for London school of economics and political science, 1941. ix, 44p. illus., map, plans. (L.S.E. Monographs on social anthropology, no. 6).

System of land tenure in Umueke Agbaja village in Okigwi Division.

3286a Harding, R. W.
The dispute over the Obiship of Onitsha. See [3296].

3287 Jeffreys, M. D. W.
Additional steps in the Umundri coronation ceremony. *Africa*, 9 (3) Jl. 1936: 403–406.

Describes two additional steps—the prostration or humiliation, and the scourging or buffeting—both not mentioned in his earlier account of the ceremony.

3288 —The divine Umundri kings. *Congrès international des sciences anthropologiques, et ethnologiques, 1re, Londres, 1934, Comptes rendus 1934*: 305–306.

3289 —The divine Umundri king. *Africa*, 8 (3) Jl. 1935: 346–354.

Coronation-ceremony of two Umundri kings described and rituals associated with it compared with similar rituals among the Bini, Igala, Yoruba, and the Jukun. The result is seen as illustrating an "essential uniformity of culture among the Bini, the Yoruba, the Igala, the Igbo and the Jukun, with the inevitable conclusion that it has a common source." French summary, p. 354.

3290 —The divine Umundri king of Iboland. 1934.
Ph.D. thesis, London University.

3291 —Sales of land among the Igbo of Nnewi. *Man*, 46, Jl.-Aug. 1946: 103 (art. 96).

3292 Jones, Gwilym Iwan
Ibo land tenure. *Africa*, 19 (4) Oct. 1949: 309–323.
French summary, p. 323.

3292a —Report on the position, status and influence of chiefs . . . See [859a].

3293 Meek, Charles Kingsley
Ibo law. In *Essays presented to C. G. Seligman, ed. E. E. Evans-Pritchard [and others] 1934*: 209–226; *Readings in anthropology, ed. E. Adamson Hoebel [and others] 1955*: 234–249.

3294 —Law and authority in a Nigerian tribe; a study in indirect rule. London, O.U.P., 1937. xvi, 372p. maps.
Extended ethnological study of the Ibo people, with special emphasis on their judicial and governmental institutions.

3295 Nigeria. Eastern. Commission of inquiry into Oguta chieftaincy dispute.
Report of the inquiry into Oguta chieftaincy dispute, 3–14 August, 1959. [H. N. Harcourt, sole commissioner] Enugu, Government printer, 1961. [iii] 80p. (Official document, no. 19 of 1961).

3296 —Commission of Inquiry into the dispute over the Obiship of Onitsha.
Report, by R. W. Harding. Enugu, Government printer, 1963. vii, 213p. (Official document no. 6 of 1963).
Popularly known as the "Harding Commission Report".

3297 —Commission of inquiry into the Ihiala chieftaincy dispute. Report . . . [M. G. Smith, sole commissioner] Enugu, Government printer, 1963. [v] 35p. (Official document, no. 18 of 1963).

3297a —Commission to enquire into the position, status and influence of chiefs and natural rulers . . . See [859a].

3298 —Ministry of customary courts and chieftaincy affairs.
Policy paper. Enugu, Government printer, 1963. 3p. (Official document, no. 12 of 1963).
Sets out the proposed organisation of chieftaincy and customary courts affairs under the newly created Ministry.

3299 Obi, S. N. Chinwuba
The Ibo law of property. London, Butterworths, 1963. xix, 239p. illus., bibliog.
The first detailed and critical examination and explanation of the traditional law relating to property among the Ibo Based on author's LL.M. thesis of the same title (London, 1962).

3300 —Women's property and succession thereto in modern Ibo law. (Eastern Nigeria) *J. Afr. law*, 6 (1) Spring 1962: 6–18.
Extracted from author's *Ibo law of property* [3299] q.v.

3301 Ofoegbu, Raymond
An introductory treatise on the kingship systems of the Ibo peoples. Nsukka [the author] 1966. 6p.
Mimeographed.

3301a Okoro, N. A.
The customary laws of succession in Eastern Nigeria. See [816].

3302 Ottenberg, Simon
Comments on local government in Afikpo Division, South Eastern Nigeria. *J. Afr. admin.*, 8 (1) 1956: 3–10.

3303 —The development of local government in a Nigerian township. *Anthropologica, n.s.*, 4 (1) 1962: 121–161, bibliog.
Surveys the beginnings and development of local government in Abakaliki and makes a detailed study of the structure and functions of the Abakaliki Urban County Council. Prefaced with account of the origin of Abakaliki town itself.

3304 —The development of village

"meetings" among the Afikpo people. *WAISER conf. proc. (sociology section) 1953*: 186–205.

The traditional organization and structure of Afikpo is discussed, and the development of a new type of village organisation or union (mitiri) is studied.

3305 —Inheritance and succession in Afikpo. In *Studies in the laws of succession in Nigeria, ed. J. D. M. Derrett, 1965*: 33–90.

3306 —The system of authority of the Afikpo Ibo of South-eastern Nigeria. 1957.
Ph.D. thesis, Northwestern university.

3307 Sanders, A. D.
A comparative study of leadership in selected communities of the Ibo of South Eastern Nigeria. 1964.
M.Sc. thesis, London University.

3308 Wood, A. H. St. John
Nigeria: fifty years of political development among the Ibos. In *From tribal rule to modern government: Proceedings of the 13th conference of the Rhodes-Livingstone inst., 1960*: 121–136.
Discusses the changes in the Ibo tribe from the traditional system of authority to the modern system of elected local government councils.

4. (v) Social organization and Structure, Social Relationships

3309 Arikpo, Okoi
The end of osu? *W. Afr.*, (2036) Apr. 21, 1956: 201.

3310 Duffy, F. R.
An analysis of the title system of Onitsha village in Nigeria, British West Africa. Washington, 1944.
Ph.D. thesis, School of social science, Catholic University of America.

3311 Edwards, P.
Embrenché and ndiche. *J. Hist. soc., Nig.*, 2 (3) Dec. 1962: 401–402.

3312 Harris, Jack S.
The position of women in a Nigerian society. *Trans. N.Y., acad. sci., ser. 2.*, 2 (5) 1940: 1–8.
On the powers and importance of women in Ibo communities, with illustrations from Ozuitem where the author conducted research.

3313 —Some aspects of slavery in South-Eastern Nigeria. *J. negro hist.*, 27 (1) Jan. 1942: 37–54.
Slave trade and slavery in the Ibo areas of South-Eastern Nigeria, especially Bende. Notes the position and functions of slaves in Ibo society both before and after contact with Europeans.

3314 Horton, W. R. G.
The Ohu system of slavery in a northern Ibo village-group. *Africa*, 24 (4) Oct. 1954: 311–336, illus., maps.
A detailed study of the ohu institution in Nike village-group to the north-east of the Regional capital, Enugu. Includes origin of the institution in the area, legal status, rights and responsi-bilities of ohu slaves, their marriage rules, and ritual functions, and an examination of the structure and judicial institutions of the separate ohu communities, and their link with the corresponding Amadi or free villages.

3315 Jones, Gwilym Iwan
Dual organisation in Ibo social structure. *Africa*, 19 (2) Apr. 1949: 150–156, table.
A critical review of M. M. Green's study of social organisation in Umueke-Agbaja village, published under the title: Ibo village affairs.

3316 —Ecology and social structure among the north-eastern Ibo. *Africa*, 31 (2) Apr. 1961: 117–134, map, bibliog.
A survey of the social, cultural and economic structures of the Ezza, Ikwo, Izi, and Ngbo Ibo shows considerable deviation from those of the main Ibo stock. This deviation is attributed to their response to the completely new environmental conditions to which they are exposed.

3317 —Ibo age organization, with special reference to the Cross River and north-eastern Ibo. *J. Roy. anthr. inst.*, 92 (2) Jl.–Dec. 1962: 191–211, bibliog.
Brief view of Ibo age-grades and age-sets in general, followed by a more exhaustive study of their organization in the north-eastern and Cross River area.

3318 Jordan, John P.
The problem of the Ibo women. In his *Bishop Shanahan of Southern Nigeria, 1949*: 219–227.

3319 Kanu-Umo, R.
Slave markets in East Nigeria. Umuahia-Ibeku, Language academy, 1954. 16p. (Information ser. no. 2).
Printed at National printing works, Umuahia.

3320 Leith-Ross, Sylvia
Notes on the osu system among the Ibo of Owerri Province, Nigeria. *Africa*, 10 (2) Apr. 1937: 206–220.

3321 Madubuotu welfare society, Aba.
The osu system; what do you know about it? [Aba, the society, 1955] 9p.
Printed at Times printing press, Owerri.

3322 Nzekwu, Onuora
Initiation into the Agbalanze society. *Nig. mag.*, (82) Sept. 1964: 173–187, illus.
Describes the processes and ceremonies involved in taking an ozo title in Ibo land, a title which carries with it the priesthood of the ancestral cult, and which promotes the recipient to the Agbalanze hierarchy.

3323 Offodile, E. P. Oyeaka
Title-taking in Awka. *W. Afr. rev.*, 18 (232) Jan. 1947: 16.

3324 Offonry, H. Kanu
Age-grades: their power and influence in village life. *W. Afr. rev.*, 19 (255) Dec. 1948: 1378–1379.
Among the Ibo.

3325 —Ibo untouchables. *W. Afr. rev.*, 22
(286) Jl. 1951: 807.
On the past and modern position of
osu slaves in Ibo land.

3326 Orakwe, Jerry I.
Onitsha custom of title-taking. Onitsha,
the author, 1953. 82p. illus. (ports.).
Printed by Renascent Africa press,
Onitsha. Rites and ceremonies as-
sociated with different titles in Onitsha.

3327 Ottenberg, Phoebe V.
The changing economic position of
women among the Afikpo Ibo. In
Continuity and change in African cultures,
ed. by W. R. Bascom and M. J.
Herskovits, 1959: 205–223.

3328 Tepowa, Adebiyi
The titles of ozor and ndiche in Onitsha.
J. Afr. soc., 9 (34) Jan. 1910: 189–192.
Describes procedures followed by
candidates for these two titles.

3329 Uchendu, Victor Chikezie
Status and hierarchy among the south-
eastern Igbo. 1963.
M.A. Dissertation, Northwestern
University.

3330 —The status implications of Igbo
religious beliefs. *Nig. field*, 29 (1) Jan.
1964: 27–37, bibliog.

3331 Watson, Linvill Fielding
Northern Ibo social stratification and
acculturation. 1952.
Ph.D. thesis, University of Pennsylvania, Philadelphia. Examines the
traditional factors in the social hierarchy
and the changing system of social
stratification and authority among the
northern Ibo, with special reference to
Nnewi; and in conclusion, reviews
"Achieved status and the issue of Ibo
democracy". (pp. 217 ff.). Based on
sources and informants in the United
States.

4. (vi) Birth and Death Rituals; Miscellaneous Beliefs and Rites

3332 Friedrich, M.
Description de l'enterrement d'un chef
à Ibuozo (Niger). *Anthropos*, 2, 1907:
100–106.
Describes the burial ceremony of a
chief of the Ibusa clan in Western Ibo.

3333 Romaine, W. C.
[Letters] *Church miss. record*, 38 (n.s. 12)
1867: 78–81; 41 (n.s. 15) 1870: 113–119;
2nd n.s. 3, 1873: 230–231.
Letters written by an African catechist
from the C.M.S. mission at Onitsha.
Gives account of burial ceremony of a
chief, use of *aratsi* to test a suspected
witch, and notes on his visit to Osomari
to the south of Onitsha.

3334 Thomas, Northcote Whitridge
Some Ibo burial customs. *J.R.A.I.*, 47,
1917: 160–213.

4. (vii) Economy, Agriculture, Trade

3335 Amogu, O. O.
The introduction into and withdrawal
of manillas from the "Oil Rivers" as
seen in Ndoki district. *Nig. mag.*, (38)
1952: 135–139, illus.

3336 Ardener, Edwin W.
"A rural oil-palm industry". *West Afr.*,
(1909) Sept. 26, 1953: 900; (1910) Oct.
3, 1953: 921–923.
On the processing of palm produce
and the organisation of the oil palm
economy of the Mbaise Ibo.

3337 Ardener, Shirley G.
The social and economic significance
of the contribution club among a section
of the southern Ibo. *WAISER conf.*
proc. (Sociology section) 1953: 128–142.
The organisation and working of
contribution clubs *(susu system)* in
Mbaise and its economic value.

3338 Feilberg, C. G.
Some features concerning the agriculture
of the Ibo in East Nigeria. *Folk*
[Copenhagen] 5, 1963: 65–70, illus.
Ibo farming and farm implements.

3339 Floyd, Barry N.
Rural land use in Nsukka Division. In
Nsukka Division: a geographic appraisal,
ed. P. K. Sircar, 1965: 51–71, maps.
bibliog.
Describes the traditional patterns of
agriculture and land use in the
Division and the innovations which are
being introduced.

3340 Harris, Jack S.
Human relationships to the land in
Southern Nigeria. *Rural sociology*, 7
(1) Mar. 1942: 89–92.
Discusses the factors which foster
attachment to the land among the Ibo.

3341 —Papers on the economic aspect of
life among the Ozuitem Ibo. *Africa*,
14 (1) Jan. 1943: 12–23.
On economic activities of Ozuitem
children, sexual division of labour, and
the soil types in relation to farming.

3342 —Some aspects of the economics of 16
Ibo individuals. *Africa*, 14 (6) Apr.
1944: 302–335, tables.
A study of the annual monetary
incomes and expenditures of 16 Ibo
individuals in Ozuitem.

3343 Jeffreys, M. D. W.
Primitive hoes. *Nig. field*, 20 (1) Jan.
1955: 39–41, illus.
On the origin of the hoe, and notes
on wooden hoe used by the Awka Ibo
and stone hoes found by the author in
Bamenda Division in the Cameroons.

3344 Jones, Gwilym Iwan
Agriculture and Ibo village planning.
Farm and forest, 6 (1) Jan.–Mar. 1945:
9–15.

3345 —The human factor in land planning.
Farm and forest, 4 (4) 1943: 161–166.
A study of five types of farmland in
Owerri Province from the view point of
population and land economics.

3346 Leith-Ross, Sylvia
Women of affairs. *JRAS*, 37 (149) Oct.
1938: 477–482.

Notes on Onitsha women cloth traders who get their wares from an agent in Onitsha market.

3347 Morgan, W. B.
Farming practice, settlement pattern and population density in South-Eastern Nigeria. *Geog. j.*, 121 (3) Sept. 1955: 320–333, maps, bibliog.
A study with special reference to Aba Ngwa county and Diobu District near Port Harcourt.

3348 Nzekwu, Onuora
Banda: the secret of Ibo concentration in Maiduguri. *Nig. mag.*, (79) Dec. 1963: 248–253, illus.

3349 Ottenberg, Simon and Ottenberg, Phoebe V.
Afikpo markets: 1900–1960. In *Markets in Africa, ed. P. Bohannan and G. Dalton, 1962:* 118–169, map.
Afikpo market system, its history, development and changes.

3350 Takes, Charles A. P.
Socio-economic factors affecting the productivity of agriculture in Okigwi Division (Eastern Region). Ibadan, NISER, 1963. 91p.
A preliminary report. Mimeographed.

3351 Uchendu, Victor Chikezie
Livestock tenancy among Igbo of Southern Nigeria. *Afr. stud.*, 23 (2) 1964: 89–94, bibliog.
"The aim of this paper is (i) to present data on what students of law call *contract of agisment* [sic] as it operates in a non-literate society, and (ii) to relate this data to the principles of contract developed in the West."— opening paragraph.

3352 Ukwu, Ukwu Igwilo
Markets in Iboland, Eastern Nigeria. 1965. xvi, 349p.
Ph.D. thesis, Cambridge.

3353 West Africa's largest market. *Nig. mag.*, (65) Je. 1960: 131–147, illus.
Descriptive and historical account of Onitsha market.

4. (viii) Food Preparation and Consumption, Standard of living

3354 Oberdoerffer, M. J.
Ernährungsstudien unter den Ibostämmen Südost-Nigeriens. *Arch. f. Schiffs-u. Tropen-Hygiene,* 42, 1938: 245–252.
On food and nutrition in Iboland.

3355 Plummer, Gladys
The Ibo cookery book. Lagos, C.M.S. bookshop, 1947. 87p.
A useful guide which includes some non-Ibo recipes as well as numerous Ibo recipes with European influences.

3356 —Nri ndi Ibo. [Zaria, Gaskiya corporation, 1951] [2] 30p.
Main Ibo dishes and their methods of preparation.

4. (ix) Religion

3357 Azikiwe, Nnamdi

Mythology in Onitsha society. 1933.
M.Sc. thesis, University of Pennsylvania.

3358 Basden, George Thomas
Mbafaw-Ezira, priestes of Awnyilli Awra. *W. Afr.*, (410) Dec. 6, 1924: 1370, 1372.
Account of this oracle in Awka area. Also described in author's Niger Ibos, p. 92, f. [3156].

3359 —The religious beliefs of the Ibo people: chapter iv. Human sacrifices. *W. Eq. Afr. dioc. mag.*, 11 (127) Jan. 1905: 109–111.
One of several instalments describing the religious life of the Ibo.

3360 Beier, Horst Ulrich
Osezi festival in Agbor. *Nig. mag.*, (78) Sept. 1963: 184–195, illus.
Osezi festival which should normally be celebrated annually is an occasion in which the Obi of Agbor remembers his ancestors and in which his subjects demonstrate their homage to him. Its celebration in 1962 is here described in some detail.

3361 Boston, John Shipway
Alosi shrines in Udi Division. *Nig. mag.*, (61) 1959: 157–165, illus.

3362 —Some northern Ibo masquerades. *J.R.A.I.*, 90 (1) Jan.-Je. 1960: 54–65, illus., bibliog.
Religious and social significance of different kinds of masquerade among the north-west Ibos in Nri Awka clan.

3363 Chadwick, E. R.
Bebege. *Nig. field*, 6 (4) Oct. 1937: 165–168, illus.
Details of the making and use of *bebege*, a fetish with magical powers employed as an oracle.

3364 Chukuegge, Aggu
History of the Kemalu juju. *Nig. mag.*, (39) 1952: 252–253.
On the thunder god "Amadioha" said to have originated from Umuaturu in Etchie area.

3365 Cliford, Hugh C.
Murder and magic. *Blackwood's mag.*, 213, 1923: 820–838; 214, 1923: 48–67.
Describes an Awka shrine, "Abera". as seen in 1920.

3366 Correia, J. Alves
L'animisme Ibo et les divinités de la Nigeria. *Anthropos*, 16–17, 1921–1922: 360–366.

3367 Daniel, K.
The pagan religion among the Ibos of Owerri. *Nig. teacher*, Sept. 1936: 16–17.
Account of four local gods and two societies.

3368 Doob, Leonard W.
Eidetic images among the Ibo. *Ethnology*, 3 (4) Oct. 1964: 357–363, illus., bibliog.

3369 Ejiogo, N. O.
The Owerri Mbari houses. *Nig. teacher*, 1 (4) 1935: 9–11.
Description of these houses and their use.

3370 Ekwensi, Cyprian Odiatu Duaka
Ezunaka: the legend of Nkwelle. *Nig. mag.*, (78) Sep. 1963: 176–183, illus.
On the ceremony associated with Ezunaka, legendary founder of Nkwelle town in Anambara District, Onitsha Province, and the annual festival of Iyi–Oji—a famous oracle worshipped by the people of Nkwelle.

3371 Eneli, Goddy I. C.
The place of ancestral worship in the religious beliefs of the Ibos. *University herald*, 4 (2) Je. 1951: 16.

3372 Ezeanya, Stephen Nweke
The method of adaptation in the evangelization of the Igbo-speaking people of Southern Nigeria. Rome, 1956. xx, 278p. map.
D.D. thesis, Pontifical Urban University, Rome.

3373 —The place of the supreme God in the traditional religion of the Igbo. *West Afr. religion*, (1) May 1963: 1–4.
Gives the attributes of the supreme being as conceived in Igbo religion, and its place in Igbo traditional religious worship.

3374 —The "sacred place" in the traditional religion of the Igbo people of the Eastern Group of Provinces of Nigeria. *W. Afr. rel.*, (6) Aug. 1966: 1–9.

3375 Festival at Onitsha. *W. Afr. rev.*, 29 (375) Dec. 1958: 1002–1005, illus.

3376 *Hansen, Peter Wilhelm
Die Religion der heidnischen Igbos in der Owerri-Provinz (Südnigeria, West-afrika.) *Echo aus den Mission. Monatschrift der Missionare vom Heiligen Geist*, 50 (5–6) May–Je. 1950: 87–89.
Ibo religious shrines, and notes on *oha* the society of elders. Based on information from an Ibo school teacher.

3377 Hives, Frank
A side show. *Blackwood's magazine*, 230 1931: 727–745.
Account of the destruction of N'Falu shrine by the Bende-Onitsha hinterland expedition of 1905–1906.

3378 Horton, W. R. G.
God, man, and the land in a northern Ibo village-group. *Africa*, 26 (1) Jan. 1956: 17–28.
Religious beliefs of Nike Ibo to the north-east of Enugu.

3379 Ijere, Martin O.
The economic significance of shrines. *W. Afr. rel.*, (3) Oct. 1964: 9–11.
A study of the economic significance of three shrines—Igwekala of Umunoba, the Long juju of Aro-Chukwu and the Nri of Agukwu in Awka Division.

3380 Ilogu, Edmund C. O.
Christianity and Ibo traditional religion. *Nig. mag.*, (83) Dec. 1964: 304–308.

3381 —Ofo; a religious and political symbol in Iboland. *Nig. mag.*, (82) Sept. 1964: 234–235.

3382 Imegwu, Chidi
The Aros and the oracle. *Afr. hist.*, 1 (3) Mar. 1965: 43–46.

3383 Jahn, Janheinz
Die Götter wechseln nur ihre Gewänder. Vom Christentum in Ostnigerien. *Frankfurter Hefte*, (15) 1960: 563–571.
On concurrent adherence to pagan rites and Christian worship among the Ibo in Eastern Nigeria.

3384 Jeffreys, M. D. W.
Altars or sacred stools: the Ibo 'Tazza' or 'Ada'. *Man*, 55, 1955 (art. 46): 42–44, illus.
Clay stools he found in Ekwulobia, Isuofia and other towns in Awka area and their use in the rituals of title taking. Regards the stools as altars and compares them to Egyptian and Jewish altars of similar description.

3385 —The Anam ofo: a cult object among the Ibo. *S. Afr. j. sci.*, 52 (10) 1956: 227–233.

3386 —The degeneration of the ofo Anam. *Nig. field*, 21 (4) Oct. 1956: 173–177, illus.
Ofo sticks collected by the author in parts of Iboland show differences suggesting degeneration in the ofo cult.

3387 —Holy grails of Africa. *West Afr. rev.*, 7 (109) Oct. 1936: 16; 21, illus.
On "grails" or sacred twin-vessels and their religious significance among the Umundri Ibo.

3388 —Igbo ideas of immortality. *Awka college magazine*, (2) Dec. 1931: 16–17.

3389 —Ikenga: the Ibo ram-headed god. *Afr. stud.*, 13 (1) 1954: 25–40, illus., bibliog.
A full description of the Ibo god *Ikenga* and the religious conceptions and ceremonies associated with it. Prefaced with a summary of the observations of previous writers, and concluded with instances of similar worship in other parts of Africa, including Egypt from which they are said to be derived.

3390 —Sacred twinned vessels. *Man*, 39 (129) 1939: 137–138, illus.
Carved wooden vessels and pottery used among the Ibos for sacrificial offerings.

3391 Johnson, James
Elijah II. *Church missionary rev.*, 67, Aug. 1916: 455–462.
Account of the Church of Garrick Sokari Braid or "Elijah II", said to have been an Ibo from Port Harcourt, who founded a prophetic church of his own with a large following in Southern Iboland and the Delta area.

3392 Jones, Gwilym Iwan
Mbari houses. *Nig. field*, 6 (2) 1937: 77–81.

3393 —Ogbukere Ihuaba. *Nig. field*, 8 (2) Apr. 1939: 81–82, illus.
Account of Ogbukere society—a cult organization found among the Ekpeya Ibo. Gives a description of its annual

ceremony as he saw it in Ihuaba village.

3394 —Ohaffia Obu houses. *Nig. field*, 6 (4) Oct. 1937: 169–171, illus.

3395 —[Treatment of remains of offending ghosts] *Man*, 34, Dec. 1934: 200 (art. 228) illus.

On the exhumation and destruction or burning of remains of dead people whose ghosts are believed to trouble the living. Notes refer to the Okporo, a sub-clan of the Orsu clan.

3396 Lannert, E.
Ekwechi-Anokechi festival. *Nig. mag.*, (80) 1964: 44–56, illus.

3397 MacAllister, Donald A.
Aro county, Southern Nigeria. *Scot. geog. mag.*, 18, 1902: 631–637, illus.

Notes on the region, its shrines and juju houses seen during the Aro expedition by a member of the Aro Field Force.

3397a Messinger, Susan F.
Witchcraft in two West African Societies. See [4954].

3398 Moore, Gerald
The Ila Oso festival at Ozuakoli [sic] *Nig. Mag.*, (52) 1956: 60–69, illus.

3399 Moore, Gerald and Beier, Horst Ulrich Mbari houses. *Nig. mag.*, (49) 1956: 184–198, illus.

Mbari houses inspected by authors near Aba on the road to Owerri in Eastern Nigeria.

3400 Murray, Kenneth Crosthwaite
Ogbom. *Nig. field*, 10, Oct. 1941: 127–131, illus.

Description of carved figures in Okwu Olokoro and other villages, used in a dance called Ogbom, usually performed in honour of the earth deity *Ala*.

3401 Noon, John A.
A preliminary examination of the death concepts of the Ibo. *Amer. anthrop.*, 44 (4 pt. 1). Oct–Dec. 1942: 638–654.

3402 Nzekwu, Onuora
Oche. *Nig. mag.*, (68) Mar. 1961: 4–11, illus.

Account of *Oche*, a local god of fertility inhabiting one of a series of caves near Uwani Uboji in Ngwo Uno in Udi Division. Describes the caves, the approaches to the *Oche* shrine, and the shrine itself.

3403 —Ofala festival. *Nig. mag.*, (61) 1959: 104–122, illus.

Celebrated annually in Onitsha as a culmination of the new yam festival.

3404 —Omo ukwu temple. *Nig. mag.*, (81) Je. 1964: 117–126, illus.

Omo ukwu is an *obu* or shrine in Asaga village of Ndi Ezera clan in Ohafia. Gives useful notes on the origins of this class of shrines.

3405 O'Donnell, William E.
Religion and morality among the Ibo of Southern Nigeria. *Primitive man*, 4 (4) 1931: 54–60.

3406 Ottenberg, Simon
Ibo oracles and intergroup relations. *S.-w. j. anthrop.*, 14 (3) Autumn 1958: 295–317, map, bibliog.

On the role of the Aro Long Juju and other Ibo oracles in facilitating intercourse among the various independent Ibo units before the British occupation.

3407 Pilter, M. T.
More about Elijah II. *Church missionary rev.*, 68, Mar. 1917: 142–145.

Further notes on Garrick Sokari Braid. See [3391].

3408 Schlosser, K.
Prohepeten in Afrika. Braunschweig, (Germany) 1949. 426p.

Includes account of Garrick Sokari Braid, called Elijah II (pp. 266–271).

3409 Shelton, Austin J.
The meaning and method of afa divination among the Northern Nsukka Ibo. *Amer. anthrop.*, 67 (6) Dec. 1965: 1441–1455, illus.

3410 —The presence of the "withdrawn" high god in north Ibo religious belief and worship. *Man*, 65, Jan.–Feb. 1965: 15–18 (art 4) illus.

Describes worship of the high god among the Ibo of Nsukka Division, especially in Aror-Uno, Ohebe-Oba, Owerri-Ezeoba, Umugoje and Umunne-Gwa villages.

3411 Spörndli, J. I.
The Mbari question. *Anthropos*, 37–40 (4–6) 1942–45: 891–893.

Comments on P. A. Talbot's view on the significance of Mbari houses in his *The Peoples of Southern Nigeria*. Thinks rather of Mbari houses as places for moral instruction.

3412 Talbot, Percy Amaury
A priest-king in Nigeria. *Folklore*, 26, 1915: 79–81

Account of the position of head priest in Elele, and of the method of succession thereto.

3413 Ume-Ezeoke, P.
Asala: a ten yearly festival. *Nig. mag.*, (79) Dec. 1963: 267–278, illus.

Celebrated in Amidi, a group of five villages in Onitsha Southern District. Describes, with explanatory historical notes, the celebration as seen in 1953, and mentions the innovations and changes introduced.

3414 Umuna, V. N.
Nigerian paganism as a preparation for the Gospel. *East & west rev.*, 5, 1939: 139–145.

Ibo traditional religious beliefs and practices and Ibo marriage system are discussed within the framework of Christian doctrines, by an Ibo C.M.S. pastor. They are held not to be entirely in opposition to Christian beliefs.

3415 Whitehouse, A. A.
An Ibo festival. *J. Afr. soc.*, 4 (13) Oct. 1904: 134–135, illus.

On an Mbari festival in Owerri.

3416 —Note on the 'Mbari' festival of the natives of the Ibo country, S. Nigeria. *Man*, 4, 1904: 162–163 (art 106), illus.

4. (x) Recreation, Games, Music, Dance

3417 Basden, George Thomas
Pitch and toss. *West Afr.*, (1002) Apr. 11 1936.
An Ibo game of gambling *(Igba-ita)* played with cowries. Also described in author's *Niger Ibos*, pp. 352–354, with illus. at p. 355.

3418 Beier, Horst Ulrich
Dances of Agbor, *Odu*, (7) 1959: 41, illus. (plates between pp. 24 and 25.

3419 Carrol, K.
African music. *Afr. ecclesiastical rev.*, 3 (4) Oct. 1961: 301–307.
Discusses Ibo and Yoruba music.

3420 Daji
Okorosia. *Nig. field*, 3 (4) Oct. 1934: 175–177, illus.
Notes on *Okorosia*, a play performed in several towns in Orlu District and said to have been borrowed from the South.

3421 Echezona, William Wilberforce Chukudinka
Ibo musical instruments in Ibo culture. East Lansing, 1963. x, 200p. illus.
Ph.D. thesis, Michigan State university.

3422 Egbukere Dance. *Nig. mag.*, (56) 1958: 52–64, illus.
Describes Abua dancers.

3423 Erokwu, Edward
The musical instruments of my district. *Nig. field*, (5) Oct. 1932: 18–20, illus.
The instruments described are Ubọ Akwala, Ubó Igo Drum, Ekwe, Ọja Okwe, and Ọgene. The district is not named.

3424 Jeffreys, M. D. W.
A musical pot from Southern Nigeria. *Man*, 40 (215) Dec. 1940: 186–187, illus.
An earthen pot used as musical instrument among the Ibo and Ibibio.

3425 Jones, Gwilym Iwan
Ifogu Nkporo. *Nig. field*, 8 (3) Jl. 1939: 119–121, illus.
A traditional play of the Nkporo clan in the north of Bende Division, said to have been borrowed from the Uwana on the Cross River.

3426 —Masked plays of South-Eastern Nigeria. *Geog. mag.*, 18 (5) Sept. 1945: 190–199, illus., map.
Ibo, Ijaw and Ibibio masked plays and the changes they are undergoing in modern times.

3427 Mackay, Mercedes and Ene, Augustus
The Atilogwu dance. *Afr. mus.*, 1 (4) 1957: 20–22, illus.

3428 Madumere, Adele
Ibo village music. *Afr. affairs*, 52 (206) Jan. 1953: 63–67.
Discusses Ibo songs, especially those sung on particular occasions. Includes Ibo texts of the songs, with English translation. The author comes from Umuahia.

3429 Murray, Kenneth Crosthwaite
Ayolugbe. *Nig. field*, 12 (2) Oct. 1947: 73–75, illus.
Description of one of the Mmọ plays once popular in Umuigwedo and Aguleri in the North-West of Awka. The two illus. show one mask from Nando and one from Aguleri.

3430 Nnachy, D. L. K.
Ite Odo-Ohafia war dance. *Nig. mag.*, (19) 1940: 281, illus.

3431 Nzekwu, Onuora
Ibo dancing. *Nig. mag.*, (73) Je. 1962: 35–43, illus.

3432 Okeke, L. E.
The ogwulugwu dance of Awka. *Nig. teacher*, 2 (6) 1936: 39–41, illus.
Brief account of the dance, held by author to have originated in Nsukka Division. Notes the masks and other instruments used.

3433 Okosa, A. N. G.
Ibo musical instruments. *Nig. mag.*, (75) Dec. 1962: 4–14, illus.
Three categories of Ibo musical instruments are distinguished—string instruments, wind instruments and percussion instruments. Examples of each are briefly described and their use indicated.

3434 Pepper, Herbert
Sur un xylophone Ibo. *African mus. soc. newsletter*, 1 (5) Je. 1952: 35–38, illus.
Description of *abigolo*, a xylophone of 12 slats from Owerri area, with notes on its tones and on *abigolo* dances and songs.

3435 Thomas, Northcote Whitridge
Music: tones in Ibo. *Man*, 15, 1915: 36–38. (art. 21).
Phonograph recordings of Ibo speakers used to study tones in Ibo music with a view to plotting them in musical notation.

3436 Whyte, Harcourt
Types of Ibo music: *Nig. field*, 18 (4) Oct. 1953: 182–186.
Notes on some varieties of Ibo music common to the whole tribe or having only slight variations in different areas. Includes *Ogbutu* or *Ekwe-mgba* (wrestling music) *Okonko* or *Akam* music, and *Ikperelepe* or Egwu-agha (war music).

3437 *Yeatman, W. B.
Ibo musical instruments. Udu and nkwọ-nkwọ. *Nig. teacher*, 1 (3) 1934: illus.

4. (xi) Stories, Proverbs, Riddles

3438 Achebe, Chinua
The sacrificial egg and other short stories. Onitsha, Etudo, 1962. 32p. illus.
Adams, R. F. G.
Ibo texts. See [3541].

3439   Anekwe, P.
Une fable des Ibos de la Nigéria. *Anthropos*, 31, 1936: 241–242.
Short Ibo story about the tortoise, by a catechist from Ozubulu.

3440   Ekwensi, Cyprian Odiatu Duaka
Ikolo the wrestler and other Ibo tales. London, T. Nelson [n.d.] viii, 77p. illus.
A collection of twenty-four short stories.

3441   Green, Margaret Mackson
Sayings of the Ǫkǫnkǫ society of the Igbo-speaking people. *B.S.O.A.S.*, 21 (1) 1958: 157–173.
Describes an Ǫkǫnkǫ dance performed in Ohuhu, near Umuahia in 1947, and lists some 109 sayings of the dancers, with English translations and explanatory notes.

3442   —The unwritten literature of the Igbo-speaking people of South-Eastern Nigeria. *B.S.O.A.S.*, 12 (3–4) 1948: 838–846.

3443   Green, Margaret Mackson and Onwuamaegbu, M. O.
Akuko Ife nke ndi Igbo. London, O.U.P., 1962. 16p.

3444   Ilu-Igbo banyere ṃadu. (Igbo proverbs concerning man). Nkwerre, St. Augustine's college, Society for promoting Igbo language and culture [1951?] 23p.
A collection of some 700 Ibo proverbs, arranged in subject groups.

3445   Jeffreys, M. D. W.
The origin of the Ikelebeji festival. *Nig. field*, 26 (4) 1961: 188–191.
Traditional story or *akuku iru* describing the origin of the festival among the Ibo narrated to author in 1930 by an Ibo informant, from Umundri in Awka area.

3446   —The origin of the names of the Ibo week. *Folklore*, 67 (3) Sept. 1956: 162–167.

3447   —Some Ibo proverbs. *Folklore*, 67 (3) Sept. 1956: 168–169.

3448   Nwafor, John O.
Ibo idioms and proverbs (inu Igbo). Aba [the author, 1955] 32p. illus.
Printed by Education mission press, Aba.

3449   —Tortoise & terrapin in Ibo mythology. Aba [the author, 1962?] 61p. illus.

3450   Nwanodi, G. Okogbule
Ibo proverbs. *Nig. mag.*, (80) Mar. 1964: 61–62.
Lists and discusses eight proverbs to illustrate the significance of proverbs in Ibo culture.

3451   Ogbalu, Frederick Chidozie
The book of Ibo proverbs. Onitsha, Varsity bookshop [n.d.] 27p. illus. on front cover.

3452   —Ilu Igbo (the book of Igbo proverbs) containing over 5,000 Igbo proverbs [Onitsha] University publishing company [1961] 162p.
Printed by Gaskiya corporation, Zaria. Text in Igbo with some English translations.

3453   —Western Igbo rhymes: Nda. Onitsha, Varsity publishing co. [n.d.]
Printed by Mbidokwu's printing press, Onitsha.

3454   Opara, E. O.
Ilu okwu Igbo. Aba, Silent prayer home press, 1950. 12p.
A collection of some 104 Ibo proverbs, with explanations given for the first 34 listed.

3455   Thomas, Northcote Whitridge
Stories (abstract) from the Awka neighbourhood. *Man*, 18, 1918: 23–25; 45–47 (art. 25); 56–57 (art. 32); 73–75 (art. 43); 84–87 (art. 51).
Nineteen stories.

4. (xii)   Costume, Dress, Beauty Culture

3456   Arnot, A. S.
Uri body painting and Aro embroidery. *Nig. field*, 15 (3) Jl. 1950: 133–137, illus.
Women's body painting with fruit juice preparation called *uri*; and the subsequent adoption of the body designs in fine embroidery work by the Aro women.

3457   Ibo body painting design from Arochuku. *Nig. mag.*, (25) 1946: 321.

3458   Jeffreys, M. D. W.
Ibo warfare. *Man*, 56, 1956: 77–79 (art. 77) illus.
Descriptive notes on ancient Ibo weapons and fighting accoutrements.

3459   —Ichi scarification among the Ibo. *Man*, 48, Je. 1948: 72 (art. 89).
A letter disagreeing with a statement by C. K. Meek on Ibo ichi scarification. See [3461].

3460   —Negro abstract art or Ibo body patterns. *SAMAB*, 6 (9) Mar. 1957: 218–229, illus.

3461   —The winged solar disk or Ibo *ichi* facial scarification. *Africa*, 21 (2) Apr. 1951: 93–111, illus., bibliog.
Describes a pattern of facial scarification among the Umundri in Awka Division—the *ichi* scarification—and examines its cultural significance. Traces this practice, as well as other cultural traits and technical skills of the Ibos to Egyptian origin. French summary, p. 111.

3462   Murray, Kenneth Crosthwaite
Body paintings from Umuahia. *Nig. teacher*, 1 (4) 1935: 2–4, illus.

3463   —Ibo headdress, combining human and animal features. *Man*, 48, Jan. 1948: 1–2 (art. 1) illus.

3464   Nzekwu, Onuora
Ibo people's costumes. *Nig. mag.*, (78) Sept. 1963: 164–175, illus.

3465   —Ivory ornaments. *Nig. mag.*, (77) Je. 1963: 105–116, illus.
Significance of ivory ornaments among women in Onitsha.

4. (xiii) Material Culture—General

3466 Arnot, A. S.
Art and industry in Arochuku. *Nig. mag.*, (12) 1937: 10–14, illus.

3467 Chadwick, E. R.
A divisional museum. *Nig. field*, 17 (2) Apr. 1952: 84–89, illus.
Origin of the Divisional museum at Udi which was built at the author's instance. Includes a list of some of the items housed in the museum.

3468 Ezekwe, P. V. N.
Native art and industry in Awka. *Nig. teacher*, 1 (2) 1934: 28–33, illus.
On smithing, wood carving, body painting and wall painting, with comments on their decline in Awka.

3469 Ibo village crafts. *Nig. mag.*, (28) 1948: 118–135, illus.

3470 Nicholson, W. E.
Stone implements of neolithic type. *Nig. field*, 3 (1) Jan. 1934: 34–36, illus.
Five specimens of "neolithic" celts found at Awka.

3471 Saville, A. G.
The Okigwi local craft and industries exhibition. *Nig. mag.*, (36) 1951: 443–468, illus.

3472 Shaw, C. Thurstan
Excavations at Igbo-Ukwu, Eastern Nigeria: an interim report. *Man*, 60 Nov. 1960: 161–164, (art. 210) illus.

3473 —Excavations at Igbo-Ukwu, 1964. *W. Afr. arch. newsletter*, (1) Dec. 1964: 14–15:
New excavations near the site of his earlier (1959–60) excavations. French summary, p. 15.

3474 —Excavations at Iwo Eleru, 1965. *W. Afr. arch. newsletter*, (3) Oct. 1965: 15–17.
French summary, p. 77.

3475 —Nigeria's past unearthed: finds at Igbo-Ukwu. *W. Afr. rev.*, 31 (397) Dec. 1960: 30–37.

3476 —The regalia and ritual instruments of a Nigerian priest-king: the treasure-house of Igbo. *Illus. Lond. news*, 241 (6424) Sept. 15 1962: 404–407, illus.
A continuation of [3477] Here the author who undertook the excavation, describes the discovery of treasure-house buried some two feet in the ground, and which seemed to have housed the sacred vessels and regalia of a priest-king. Objects discovered included beautifully worked bronze bowls of various shapes and designs, a bronze pot-stand with two human figures—male and female, ingeniously decorated mace heads in bronze, calabashes, beads, and numerous decorative bronze objects are shown in the 27 beautiful illustrations, the first of which shows a reconstruction of the royal treasure house.

3477 —Royal tomb at Igbo, Eastern Nigeria. *Illus. Lond. news.*, 241 (6423) Sept. 8 1962: 358–359, illus.

Account of excavation at Igbo and the discovery of what looked like a burial chamber of a priest-king. Describes many of the objects found in this tomb, including skulls, coloured beads, ceremonial bronze fan, bronze (or brass) crown, and other bronze and brass objects. The illustrations include a reconstruction by C. Sassoon, of the burial chamber with the priest-king in sitting position on a bronze-decorated stool.

4. (xiv) Architecture

3478 Mbanefo, Frank
The Iba house in Onitsha. *Nig. mag.*, (72) Mar. 1962: 18–26, illus.
Physical and architectural aspects and religious significance of Iba houses in Onitsha.

3479 Talbot, Percy Amuary
Notes on Ibo houses. *Man*, 16, 1916: 129 (art. 77) illus.

4. (xv) Sculpture, Metal work, Glass and Bead work.

3480 The "Awka" stool. *Nigerian field* (4) Jl. 1932: 23–25, illus.
Further account of the "title" or "Awka" stools, giving notes on the technique of a particular carver. See [3483].

3481 Boston, John Shipway
Ceremonial iron gongs among the Ibo and the Igala. *Man*, 64, Mar.–Apr. 1964: 44–47 (art. 52) illus.

3482 Field, J. M. O.
Bronze castings found at Igbo, Southern Nigeria. *Man*, 40, 1940: 1–6 (art. 1) illus.

3482a Jeffreys, M. D. W.
Altars or sacred stools. See [3384].

3483 —Awka wood carvers, by 'Ntokon' [pseud.] *Nig. field*, (2) Dec. 1931: 35–39, illus.
Account of carved stools and doors, the possession of which indicates owners' grade or rank in some Ibo communities. The stools are popularly known as "Title stools" or "Awka stools". See also [3480].

3484 —Carved bottle corks. *Nig. field*, 18 (1) 1953: 41–43, illus.
Illustrations of several carved wooden bottle stoppers from the Ibo area of Eastern Nigeria compared with a similar object in the Egyptian collection of the British museum.

3485 —Ibo club heads. *Man*, 57, 1957: 57–58 (art. 63) illus.
Describes staff-like objects with rounded heads called *Utali akpukpo*, and their uses among the Ibo of Awka area.

3486 —Letter on the Awka bronzes. *Nig. field*, 10, 1941: 140–142.
On the probable origin of bronze bowls, wire chain, bells, pendants, etc., found at Awka.

3487 —Multiple-stem pipe bowls. *Man*, 55, Jan. 1955: 8–9 (art. 6) illus.

3488 —Notes on the Igbo hoard. *Man*, 40 (138) Jl. 1940: 138.

3489 —The Oreri mask. *Nig. field*, 10, Oct. 1941: 140–142, illus.
       Letter to editor. Describes a mask and other items forming the regalia of the Eze Ndri of Oreri in Awka Division.

3489a —Sacred twinned vessels. See [3390].

3490 —Some beads from Awka. *Nig. field*, 19 (1) Jan. 1954: 37–44, illus.
       Describes beads he purchased from Umundri during an ethnological investigation in the area.

3491 —Unusual designs on Ibo wooden vessels. *Man*, 54, Nov. 1954 (art. 265); 265–266, illus.
       Brief notes on wooden bowls used by Ibo men of title in Awka area.

3492 Jones, Gwilym Iwan
       Ibo bronzes from the Awka Division. *Nig. field*, 8 (4) Oct. 1939: 164–167, illus.
       Bronze objects found at Igbo village in Isuofia area of Awka Division.

3493 —On the identity of two masks from South-Eastern Nigeria in the British Museum. *Man*, 39, 1939: 33–34 (art. 35) illus.
       Suggests Ada, an Ibo clan in Afikpo Division as the place of origin of the two masks. Four additional types of mask from this area are also illustrated and described by way of comparison.

3494 Nwokwu, M. E.
       Awka wood carving. *Nig. field*, 4 (2) Apr. 1935: 86–89, illus.
       Notes explaining the basis of some of the designs used in Awka carving.

3495 Nzekwu, Onuora
       Awka, town of smiths. *Nig. mag.*, (61) 1959: 136–151, illus.

3496 Robinson, Eric
       Enwonwu encore: "Africa dances" in London. *W. Afr. rev.*, 27 (340) 1956: 17–19, illus.

3497 Shaw, C. Thurstan
       Bronzes from Eastern Nigeria: excavations at Igbo-Ukwu. *J. Hist. soc., Nig.*, 2 (1) Dec. 1960: 162–165.
       Bronzes and other finds from excavations in and around Igbo Ukwu, near Awka, are described, and some of the finds assigned provisionally to the 16th or 17th century.

3498 Tovey, D. C.
       Umuome Inyi pots. *Nig. field*, (7) Apr. 1933: 29–38, illus.
       Account of pot making by women potters in Inyi, near Achi in Udi Division.

3499 Wood carvers of Awka. *W. Afr. rev.*, 24 (308) 1953: 449, illus.

4. (xvi) Pottery
3500 Jeffreys, M. D. W.
       An annular pottery vessel in Southern Nigeria. *Man*, 53, 1953: 41 (art. 57) illus.
       Rare annular pottery found at Oreri near Awka.

3501 Pottery training centre at Okigwi. *Nig. trade j.*, 2 (4) Oct.–Dec. 1954: 19–21, illus.
       Notes on the establishment of the centre and on the training policy followed.

4. (xvii) Painting, Drawing
3502 Chadwick, E. R.
       An Ibo village art gallery. *Nig. field*, 4 (4) Oct. 1935: 175–183, illus.
       Mbaja or wall painting in Okwu village, Olokoro clan, Bende Division.

3503 —Wall decorations of Ibo houses. *Nig. field*, 6 (3) Jl. 1937: 134–135, illus.
       Patterns of painting and decoration on walls in Ikwerri, Umuahia and other places.

3504 Murray, Kenneth Crosthwaite
       The okwu wall near Umuahia. *Nig. mag.*, (27) 1947: 19–24, illus.
       Comparison of Ibo and Ibibio art, with the verdict that the former "is primarily abstract" and the latter "representational".

4. (xviii) Textile Weaving and Dyeing; Embroidery
       Arnot A. S.
       Uri body painting and Aro embroidery. See [3456].

3505 Nnadozie, M. A.
       Floor rug making in Umulogho school, Nsu parish, Okigwi District. *Nig. mag.*, (30) 1949: 330–331, illus.
       Describes a new technique of rug making using fibre from the bark of a local tree.

3506 Ukeje, L. O.
       Weaving in Akwete. *Nig. mag.*, (74) Sept. 1962: 32–41, illus.

4. (xix) Basket and Mat Making; Cane and Raffia Work
3507 Ankerman, Bernhard
       Gemusterte Raphiagewebe vom unteren Niger. *Baessler-Archiv.*, 6, 1922: 204–206.
       Describes two rafia cloths from Southern Nigeria, probably from the Ibo or Benin area, now in the Berlin Museum.

3508 Jeffreys, M. D. W.
       Cordage among the Ibo. *Nig. field*, 25 (1) 1960: 42–44.
       On the varieties of cordage or "tie-tie" among the Ibo in Awka area, how they are made, and their various uses.

4. (xx) Acculturation and Social Change, Contact Situation, Urbanization
3509 Attah, Effiong B.
       Nsukka: an emergent urban community. In *Nsukka Division: a geographic*

appraisal. Ed. P. K. Sircar, 1965: 101–111.
For main work, see [3192].

3510 Fuches, Estelle S.
The compatability of western education with Ibo culture: an examination of the complex dynamics involved in the successful diffusion of literacy and schooling to the Ibo of Eastern Nigeria. 1964.
Ph.D. thesis, Columbia University.

3510a Hair, P. E. H.
The first Christian in the village . . . See [3513].

3511 Köbben, A. J. F.
Social change and political structure (a comparative study of two West African societies). In *Afrika im Wandel seiner Gesellschaftsformen. Herausgegeben von W. Fröhlich, 1964*: 71–83, bibliog.
A comparative study of the Agni and the Bote, both in Ivory Coast, but with frequent references to the Ibo of Nigeria.

3511a Morrill, Warren T.
Immigrants and associations. See [3032].

3511b —Two urban cultures of Calabar. See [3033].

3512 Ndem, Eyo Bassey Eyo
Ibos in contemporary Nigerian politics: a study in group conflict. Onitsha, Etudo, 1961. 44p.
Tribal disharmony in Eastern Nigeria seen as arising from sociological and psychological reactions of the minorities to the effervescence, drive and all-pervasiveness of the Ibos in the economic and political spheres as well as to their apparently unaccommodating attitude towards traditional institutions of those minorities among whom they settle.

3513 Okafor-Omali, Sigismund Dilim
The first Christian in the village: a case-history from Eastern Nigeria. *Bull. Soc. Afr. Ch. hist.*, 1 (2) Dec. 1963: 49–61.
Extracts by P. E. H. Hair, with commentary, from author's unpublished MS. which is a biography of his father, Christopher Nweke Okafor, 1898–1944, the first Christian convert in his village, Enuagu in Enugu-Ukwu, Awka District. His record presents a useful picture of the changing life and attitudes of the Ibo people at this period.

3514 Okoye, T. O.
Nsukka as an urban centre. In *Nsukka Division: a geographic appraisal. Ed. P. K. Sircar, 1965*: 89–100.
For main work, see [3192].

4. (xxi) Social Problems; Applied Anthropology.

3515 Chadwick, E. R.
Communal development in Udi Division *Oversea educ.*, 19 (2) Jan. 1948: 627–644.

3516 —Community development. London,

Bureau of current affairs [n.d.] 16p. illus. (West African affairs, no. 6).
An imaginary account of a successful community development effort, typical of what was taking place in Eastern Nigeria.

3517 —Community development in South-Eastern Nigeria. *Nig. field*, 16 (3) Jl. 1951: 113–123, illus.
Copiously illustrated description of communal development projects observed by the author, with statistical summary of achievements so far.

3518 —Community development in Udi. *Corona*, 1 (2) Mar. 1949: 10–13; 1 (3) Apr. 1949: 11–14.
Account of community development efforts in Udi.

3519 —Fundamental education in Udi Division. *Fundamental educ.*, 1 (4) Oct. 1949: 9–21.
A general account of the organisation of adult education in Udi.

3520 —Mass education in Udi Division. *Afr. affairs*, 47 (186) Jan. 1948: 31–41.
Process and progress of adult education and communal labour in Udi villages.

3521 —Mbabu village. *Spectator*, 182, May 27 1949: 713–714.
Describes community development in the village in Udi Division.

3522 —Nigeria: community development in the Eastern Provinces. *Corona*, 3 (11) Nov. 1951: 421–425.
General account of the progress of community development in Eastern Nigeria, with mention of some particular instances.

3523 —Our community effort in the East. Lagos, Public relations department [n.d.] 32p. illus. (Crownbird series no. 30 (special))
Illustrative photographs and brief text describe the progress and prospects of development through community efforts in Eastern Nigeria.

3524 Jackson, I. C.
Advance in Africa: a study of community development in Eastern Nigeria. London, O.U.P., 1956. viii, 110p. illus.

3525 —The community development training centre, Awgu. *Community dev. bull.*, 5 (4) Sept. 1954: 81–85.
Objectives of the Awgu centre opened in 1952 and the methods followed there in training activities.

3526 Mann, M. A.
Community development in Okigwi. *Community dev. bull.*, 2 (4) Sept. 1951: 73–75.
Account of community efforts and communal development projects in the area.

3527 —Village and community development. *Oversea educ.*, 25 (3) Oct. 1953: 89–91.
Account of cottage industries and improved farming developed by community efforts in Okigwi and employing

the services of semi-educated youngsters who might otherwise have had no suitable jobs.

3528 Mass education in Okigwi Division, Eastern Provinces of Nigeria. *Oversea educ.*, 22 (4) Jl. 1951: 159–160.
Account of two village schools—at Atcha and Ibeme villages—built through communal efforts.

3529 Nigeria. Eastern. Ministry of internal affairs. Social welfare division.
Report of the first conference of Eastern Nigeria councils of social service held at Nsukka from 19–21 February 1965. Enugu, Government printer, 1965. [xi]. 88p. (Official document no. 25 of 1965.
Includes reports on social work in Aba, Abakaliki, Calabar, Enugu, Onitsha and Port Harcourt; and a lecture on the effects of social changes on the individual, the family and the society in Nigeria. See [1279].

3530 Prior, Kenneth H.
An African diocese adapts a rural programme. *Int. rev. missions*, 36 (43) Jl. 1947: 370–378.
Describes the part played by the C.M.S. Church (the CMS Niger Mission) in introducing better methods of farming into the rural areas of Eastern Nigeria.

3531 —Rural activities in the Diocese of the Niger. In *The Science of relationships: report of a conference on rural life at home and overseas, 1947*: 11–20.
Account of training and development in agriculture and rural science by the C.M.S. mission at Asaba. The Report of the conference was published by the Church missionary house, 1947.

3532 —Rural development activities in South-Eastern Nigeria. *Books for Africa*, 17 (4) Oct. 1947: 49–54.

3533 —Rural science in Nigeria. *Oversea educ.*, Oct. 1947: 585–589.
General notes on the concept of rural science and an account of its teaching at the C.M.S. training centre at Asaba.

3534 —Rural science in Nigeria. *Rural missions*, 69, Winter 1949: 4, 6.
Describes work at the Asaba C.M.S. Rural training centre.

3535 —Rural training at Asaba. *Nig. mag.*, (47) 1955: 184–212, illus.

3536 —Training for a full life. *W. Afr. rev.*, 20 (265) Oct. 1949: 1167–1169, 1171.
On the work of the Rural science training centre, Asaba.

3537 Riggs, Stanley
Community development in the Eastern Region. *Nig. mag.*, (52) 1956: 2–9, illus.

3538 Rural development in Nigeria. (A C.M.S. experiment in rural self-help). *West Afr. rev.* 19 (254) Nov. 1948: 1283.

3539 The story of village development in Abaja-Udi. Port Harcourt, C.M.S. Nigeria press [n.d.] 12p.

3540 "Udi today" *Corona*, (3) 1951: 454–457.
Reprint of the 1950 Progress report on Udi to Unesco. The report reviews progress in community and general development in Udi.

5. LINGUISTIC STUDIES

3540a *Abraham, Roy Clive
The principles of Ibo. Ibadan, Institute of African Studies, University of Ibadan, 1967. xvi, 127p. (Institute of African studies. Occasional publications, no. 4).

3541 Adams, Robert Frederick George
Ibo texts. *Africa*, 7 (4) Oct. 1934: 452–463, illus.
A selection of four Ibo texts concerning the *Oru* festival in Owerri, marriage, birth celebrations and divorce in Ibo traditional society. English translation offered.

3542 —A modern Ibo grammar. London, O.U.P., 1932. vii, 200p.

3542a Adams, Robert Frederick George and Ward, Ida Caroline
The Arochuku dialect of Ibo: phonetic analysis and suggested orthography. *Africa*, 2 (1) Jan. 1929: 57–70, map.
Includes two short stories, with translations, written in the suggested orthography.

3543 Anisiobi, G. N.
Ibo numeration. [Kano, the author, 1952] 18p.
Printed by Oluseyi printing press, Kano. Lists numbers and West African currency in Ibo with English translation, followed by an Ibo-English vocabulary.

3544 Basden, George Thomas
Glossary of Ibo words and terms . . . In his *Niger Ibos, 1938*: xxxi–xxxii.

3545 Bible. Ibo.
Biblé nso, nke nãnagide Testament Ochiè na Testament Qhu. London, British and foreign Bible society, 1956. 820, 255p.
The Bible in Union Ibo.

3546 Bible. N.T. Ibo. Gospels
Okuomma nke Marki ma Luki. The Gospels according to St. Mark and St. Luke. Translated into the Ibo language by John Christopher Taylor. London, British and foreign Bible society, 1864. 164p.

3547 Bible. N.T. Ibo. John
Qku ómma nke owu Yohanu. The Gospel according to St. John. Translated into the Ibo language by Rev. J. Christopher Taylor. London, British and foreign Bible society, 1865. 78p.

3548 Bible. N.T. Ibo. Matthew
Okwu omma nke Matia. The Gospel according to St. Matthew. Translated into the Ibo language by John Christopher Taylor. London, British and foreign Bible society, 1860. 88p.

3549 Canot, A.
English, Ibo and French dictionary.

Salzburg, Austria, Missionary printing office of the Sodality of St. Peter Claver, 1904. 306p.

3550 *—Grammaire Ibo. [With French-Ibo and Ibo-French vocabularies] Onitsha, Niger Catholic mission; Mezières, Imprimerie Saint-Joseph, 1899. 209p.

3551 Carnochan, J.
The category of number in Igbo grammar. *Afr. lang. stud.*, (3) 1962: 110–115.

3552 —A study in the phonology of an Igbo speaker. *B.S.O.A.S.*, 12 (2) 1948: 417–426.

3553 —Towards a syntax for Igbo. *J. Afr. lang.*, 2 (3) 1963: 222–226.

3554 —Vowel harmony in Igbo. *Afr. lang. stud.*, (1) 1960: 155–163.

3555 Carnochan, J. and Iwuchuka, Balonwu
An Igbo revision course, using the official orthography. London, O.U.P., 1963. 167p.

3556 Central Ibo primer by a Sister of the Holy Rosary Congregation. London, Macmillan, 1952–1953. 2v.
v. 1, 1952. 63p. v. 2, 1953. 80p.

3557 Correia, J. Alves
Vocables religieux et philosophiques des peuples Ibos. *Bibliotheca afr.*, 1, 1925: 104–113.

3558 Crowther, Samuel Adjai
Isoama-Ibo primer. Revised and enlarged by J. C. Taylor. London, C.M.S., 1860. 22p.
First published 1859.

3559 —Vocabulary of the Ibo language. London, S.P.C.K., 1882–1883. 2v.
v. 1, 1882. 109p. v. 2, 1883. 90p. v. 2 prepared, by J. F. Schon.

3560 Dennis, Thomas John [and others]
Dictionary of the Ibo language, English-Ibo. Lagos, C.M.S. bookshop [1923] [7] 189p.
Printed by James Townsend, Exeter.

3561 Dunstan, Elizabeth and Igwe, G. E.
Two views of the phonology of the Ọhụhụ dialect of Igbo. *J. W. Afr. lang.*, 3 (2) 1966: 71–74.
Phonemic and prosodic accounts of the phonology of the Ohuhu dialect.

3562 Esere, John Kalu
Self guide to Ibo-Efik languages for sellers and buyers of goods, scholars and friends. Uyo [the author, 1956] 32p.
Printed by Proficient printing press, Uyo.

3562a Green, Margaret Mackson
The classification of West African tone languages: Igbo and Efik. See [3066].

3563 —Igbo spelling, an explanatory statement. London, C.U.P., 1949. 7p.
Explains the revised Ibo orthography.

3564 —The present linguistic situation in Ibo country. *Africa*, 9 (4) Oct. 1936: 508–523, maps.
A discussion of the problems inherent in the multiplicity of dialects of the Ibo language and of fresh problems raised by the creation of "Union Ibo". French summary, p. 523.

3565 —Suffixes in Igbo. *Afr. lang. stud.*, (5) 1960: 92–114.

3566 Green, Margaret Mackson and Igwe, Georgewill Ezemba
A descriptive grammar of Igbo. Berlin, Akademie-Verlag, 1963. xiv, 236p. (Veröff. Inst. Orientforsch., 3).

3567 Igwe, Georgewill Ezemba and Green, Margaret Mackson
A short Igbo grammar. London, O.U.P., 1964. viii, 60p.

3567a Jeffreys, M. D. W.
Some Ibo proverbs. See [3447].

3568 Kelly, Bernard J.
An introduction to Onitsha Igbo. London, Macmillan, 1954. vii, 63p.
"A practical elementary introduction to Onitsha Igbo" written by the then Supervisor of Catholic Schools in Enugu area.

3569 Laird, McGregor and Oldfield, R. A. K.
English-Eboe [vocabulary] In their *Narrative of an expedition into the interior of Africa, v. 2, 1837*: 444–446.
See also [2331].

3570 Maduekwe, Joseph Chuks
Igbo speech training (Being a collection of Igbo tongue-twisters; nursery rhymes, lullabys [sic] riddles, jingles, stories for dramatization, together with useful hints for the teacher on how to use them) Onitsha, Etudo [1965] 72p.

3570a *Müller, Friedrich
Die Ibo-Sprache. In his *Grundriss der Sprachwissenschaft*, 1–2, 1877: 115–125.

3571 N., C. J.
A glimpse at the Ibo language. *W. Afr.*, (393) Aug. 1924: 824.
Discusses common Ibo words and phrases from Onitsha area.

3572 Nwana, Pita
Omenukọ. London, Longmans, 1958. [ii] 90p., illus.
Short story in Ibo on the life of Omenukọ an Ibo trader.

3573 Ogbalu, Frederick Chidozie
Igbo-English dictionary. Port Harcourt, C.M.S. press, 1959. xiii, 541p.
The dictionary is preceded by ten pages of brief notes on Igbo orthography and sounds. pp. 51–54—advertisements.

3574 —Model answers in Igbo examinations containing past questions and answers in General certificate of education, West African school certificate, Higher elementary certificate, etc., etc. 3rd ed. Onitsha, African literature bureau [n.d.] 97p.
Includes advertisements on pp. 88–91.

3575 —New Igbo grammar: the noun. [Onitsha] Varsity publishing co., 1953. 17p. (Igbo grammatical exposition ser., 1).
Printed by International press, Aba

3576 —Ọsua–Ọkọwa. English-Ibo. Onitsha, African literature bureau [n.d.] Printed

by Gaskiya corporation, Zaria. 55p.
illus. (Bilingual series (adult and mass
education, no. 2)).
An Ibo-Pidgin English-English phrase
book.

3577   —School certificate Igbo: for West
African school certificate, General
certificate of education, Higher elementary, etc. Revised and enlarged. Aba
Printed by Assemblies of God press
[n.d.] 140p. (incl. adverts)
"African literature bureau"—at
bottom of title.

3578   —Teach yourself the all-accepted Igbo
orthography. Onitsha, Varsity publishing
co., [1955?] 14p.

3579   Ogbalu Frederick Chidozie and Erinne,
Daniel Chukudike
An investigation into the Ibo orthography. Nkwerre, Society for promoting Ibo language and culture, 1952.
78p. (S.P.I.L. series) Printed by
Goodwill press, Port Harcourt.

3580   Okonkwo, Matthew Nweke
Complete course in Igbo grammar for
school certificate and allied examina-
tions. (New orthography) Onitsha,
Ikeagu bookshop, 1959. 72p.
Printed by Zik enterprises, Enugu.

3581   Okonyia, Chike
Igbo grammar & composition: a text-
book for secondary schools and teacher
training colleges. Onitsha, Etudo, 1962.
113p.

3582   Okoreaffia, C. O.
Elements of Igbo language studies.
Nsukka [the author, 1966] 56p.

3583   Onuchukwu, Wilfred Igbokwe
English-Ibo phrase book and vocabulary.
[Port Harcourt, Zion bookshop;
Fellowship bookshop, 1951]. 44p.

3584   Oruchalu, S. U.
Rules for Igbo spelling in the latest
approved orthography. Onitsha, author
[n.d.] 12p. Printed by Varsity press,
Onitsha.

3585   Schön, James Frederick
Oku Ibo. Grammatical elements of the
Ibo language. London, W. M. Watts,
1861. [ii] 4, 8, 86p.

3585a —Vocabulary of the Ibo language.
See [3559].

3585b *Smart, Frederick Weeks
An Ibo primer. London, C.M.S. [1870]
19p.

3586   Spencer, Julius
An elementary grammar of the Ibo
language. 3rd ed. Revised by T. J.
Dennis. London, S.P.C.K., 1924. x,
116p.
1st ed. 1892; 2nd ed. 1901. 52p.

3587   Swift, L. B. [and others]
Igbo basic course [by] L. B. Swift, A.
Ahaghotu [and] E. Ugorji. Washington,
Foreign service institute, 1962. xiv,
498p. (Foreign service institute. Basic
course series).
Course based on the speech of two

Ibos from Ezinehite area in Central
Owerri Province.

3588   Thomas, Northcote Whitridge
Anthropological report on the Ibo-
speaking peoples of Nigeria. 1913–14.
6v.
   Part II. English-Ibo and Ibo-English
      dictionary.
   Part III. Proverbs, narratives, vocabu-
      lary and grammar.
   Part V. Addenda to Ibo-English
      dictionary.
   Part VI. Proverbs, stories, tones in
      Ibo.
See main entry at [3227].

3589   —Slang in Southern Nigeria. Man, 14,
1914: 3–4 (art. 3).
On slang expressions in Onitsha and
Asaba Ibo.

3590   Utchay, Thomas Kanu
Improved Igbo orthography accented
with intonation letters "H" and "R"
instead of diacritic marks. [Aba, Education mission press, 1952] 16p.
Recommendation for the improvement of Igbo orthography by using H.
and R for high and low intonations
respectively.

3591   —The problems of the Igbo orthography,
being the solution to the Igbo orthography question. Aba, the author,
1952. 28p.

3592   Ward, Ida Caroline
Ibo dialects and the development of a
common language. Cambridge, W.
Heffer, 1941. vi, 67p. map.

3593   —An introduction to the Ibo language.
Cambridge, W. Heffer, 1936. xiii, 215p.

3594   —A linguistic tour in Southern Nigeria:
certain problems restated. Africa, 8 (1)
Jan. 1935: 90–97.
On the problems of Ibo and Efik as
possible literary languages, including
the question of orthography, attitude of
educated Africans, and future research
needs. French summary: p. 97. An
earlier report on this tour by the author,
entitled "A linguistic tour in South-east
Nigeria" appeared in Africa, 7 (2) Apr.
1934: 228–230.

3595   Wescott, Roger W.
Ibo phasis. Anthrop. ling., 5 (2) Feb.
1963: 6–8, bibliog.

3596   —Two Ibo songs. Anthrop. ling., 4 (3)
Mar. 1962: 10–15.

3597   Westermann, Diedrich
Das Ibo in Süd-Nigerien. Seine Stellung
innerhalb der Kwa-Sprachen. M.S.O.S.,
29, 1926: 1–31. (Westsudanische
Studien, 2).

3598   Williamson, Kay R. M.
The status of /e/ in Onitsha Igbo. J. W.
Afr., lang., 3 (2) 1966: 67–69.

3599   Wilson J. Carven
The extent of the Ibo language. W. Eq.
Afr. dioc. mag., 18 (223) [i.e. n.s. 103]
Jan. 1913: 294–279.
Notes on a tour of the Western Ibo
country to determine the extent of the

area over which the Ibo language was spoken or understood.

3600 Zappa, C.
Essai de dictionnaire français-Ibo, ou français-Iku. Lyon, Imprimerie M. Paquet, 1907. 274p.

IDOMA

Including:

Agala *(Agalawa)*
Agatu
Igumale
Iyala *(Ingkum, Yala)*
Nkim

Nkum
Ogwaka
Okpoto *(Akpoto, Opoto)*
Oturkpo

1. GENERAL AND ETHNOGRAPHIC STUDIES

3601 Agalawa. In *Notes on the tribes . . . by O. Temple, 2nd ed., 1922*: 4.

3601a Agatu. In *Notes on the tribes . . . by O. Temple, 2nd ed., 1922*: 4–6.

3602 Armstrong, Robert G.
The Idoma court-of-lineage in law and political structure. In *Men and cultures: selected papers of the 5th international congress of anthropological and ethnological sciences, Philadelphia, Sept. 1–9, 1956, ed. Anthony F. C. Wallace, 1960*: 390–395.

3603 —The Idoma-speaking peoples. In *Peoples of the Niger-Benue confluence, by Daryll Forde [and others] 1965*: 91–155, bibliog.

3604 —Intestate succession among the Idoma. In *Studies in the laws of succession in Nigeria, edited by J. D. M. Derrett, 1965*: 212–229.

3605 —The Iyala. In *Peoples of the Niger-Benue confluence, by D. Forde [and others] 1955*: 128–132.

3606 —The Nkim. In *Peoples of the Niger-Benue confluence, by Daryll Forde [and others,] 1955*: 134.

3607 —The Nkum. In *Peoples of the Niger-Benue confluence, by Daryll Ford [and others] 1955*: 133–134.

3608 —The religions of the Idoma. *Ibadan*, (13) Nov. 1961: 5–9.
Idoma religion seen as a system of unconnected cults, each with its own beliefs, outlook, form of worship, etc. Among them all, the ancestral cult is considered fundamental.

3608a —Talking drums in the Benue-Cross River region. See [1031].

3608b —Talking instruments in West Africa. See [1032].

3609 —The use of linguistic and ethnographic data in the study of Idoma and Yoruba history. In *The historian in tropical Africa, ed. J. Vansina [and others] 1964*: 127–139.
Summary in French, pp. 140–144.

3610 —A West African inquest. *Amer. anthrop.*, 56 (6 pt. 1) Dec. 1954: 1056–1075, illus., map.

Account of a traditional inquest into the death of a village head in Oturkpo, which developed into a witchcraft trial of a senior elder. The proceedings helped to throw light on Idoma lineage structure, social organisation and attitude to witchcraft.

3611 Ball, A. E.
Itineration in the Okpoto country. *Niger & Yoruba notes*, 9 (101) Nov. 1902: 38–39; 9 (102) Dec. 1902: 43–45.

3612 Bennett, P. A.
A visit to Opoto. *Niger and Yoruba notes*, 1 (2) 1894: 24.

3612a Byng-Hall, F. F. W.
Notes on the Okopoto and Igara tribes. See [3634].

3613 Idoma. In *Notes on the tribes . . . by O. Temple. 2nd ed. 1922, repr. 1965*: 142–147.

3613a Igara and Okpoto. See [3636].

3614 Kay, A. S.
The Idoma tribe of Nigeria. *Col. j.*, 7, 1914: 297–308.

2. LINGUISTIC STUDIES

3615 Abraham, Roy Clive
The Idoma language, Idoma wordlists, Idoma chresthomathy, Idoma proverbs. Oturkpo, published by the author on behalf of Idoma Native administration 1951. [272]p.
Printed by Lowe and Brydone, London. Virtually separate works bound in one volume.

3616 —The principles of Idoma. London, Crown agents, 1938. 429p.

3617 Armstrong, Robert G.
The Idoma verb. In *Actes du second colloque international de linguistique négro-africaine, 1962. 1963*: 127–157.
A study of the structure and morphology of the verb in Idoma language as spoken in Oturkpo area.

3618 —The subjunctive in Idoma. *J. Afr. lang.*, 2 (2) 1963: 155–159.

3619 Bible. N.T. Idoma. Mark
Eho ohoi le babo ni 'Maki' ta. London. British and foreign Bible society, 1962, 63, vii [i]p. map.
St. Mark Gospel in Agatu dialect of

Idoma. Printed at Steward co. press, Ika.

3620   Byng-Hall, F. F. W.
English-Okpoto vocabulary. Zungeru, Govt. printing office, 1908. [1] 21p.

3621   Macleod, T. M.
Report on the Idoma language. Lagos, Govt. printer [1924] 24p.
A brief description of Idoma language. with grammatical notes and Idoma-English, and English-Idoma vocabulary.

3622   Methodist Church, Nigeria.
Ije ku ace oye ogwu Kraist. Idoma, Methodist Church, 1962. 31p.
Printed by Bakara press, Kaduna. A religious pamphlet in Idoma.

3623   Okpa afleyi k'Idoma. Idoma N.A., 1951. 18p. Printed by Gaskiya corporation, Zaria.
First book of Idoma.

3624   Okpa okloce aflei, oko Idoma. Ika, Stewards co. press [1962] iv, 28p. illus.

IGALA

(Agatara, Igara, Igula)

Including:

Ibaji

1. GENERAL AND ETHNOGRAPHIC STUDIES

3625   Allison, Philip A.
The collection of export produce in an agricultural economy: the palm produce and rubber trades in Igala. Farm and forest, 7 (1) Jan-Je. 1946: 11–18, map.
Organisation and conditions of the palm oil economy in Igala.

3626   Armstrong, Robert G.
The Igala. In Peoples of the Niger-Benue confluence, by Daryll Forde [and others] 1955: 77–90.

3627   —A note on the Ibaji. In Peoples of the Niger-Benue confluence, by D. Forde [and others] 1955: 89–90.

3628   Boston, John Shipway
Ceremonial iron gongs among the Ibo and the Igala. Man, 64, 1964: 44–47 (art. 52) illus.

3629   —The hunter in Igala legends of origin. Africa, 34 (2) Apr. 1964: 116–126.
Examines Igala legends in which the hunter is prominent and considers such legends significant more in the context of Igala political and social structure rather than in the realm of their history. French summary, pp. 125–126.

3630   —Igala inheritance and succession. In Studies in the laws of succession in Nigeria, edited by J. D. M. Derrett, 1965: 174–211.

3631   —The Igala oil-palm industry. NISER conf. proc., 1962: 100–110.
A study of the organisation and working of the oil palm industry in Igala, including the social and family arrangements relevant thereto.

3632   —Notes on contacts between the Igala and the Ibo. J. hist. soc. Nig., 2 (1) Dec. 1960: 52–58, map.
Summary of available evidence, both oral and recorded, suggesting contacts and cultural interaction between the Igala and some northern Ibo clans.

3633   —Notes on the origin of Igala kingship.

J. Hist. soc. Nig., 2 (3) Dec. 1962: 373–383.
Examines the various traditions of origin of Igala kingship and draws attention to the need for recognizing the role of different cultural influences in their formation.

3634   Byng-Hall, F. F. W.
Notes on the Okpoto and Igara tribes. J. Afr. soc., 7 (26) Jan. 1908: 165–174.

3635   Clifford, Miles
A Nigerian chiefdom: some notes on the Igala tribes in Nigeria and their "Divine King". J.R.A.I., 66, 1936: 393–436.

3636   Igara and Okpoto. In Notes on the tribes . . . by O. Temple. 2nd ed., 1922. repr. 1965: 147–154.

3637   Moncton, J. C.
Burial ceremonies of the Attah of Idah. J. Afr. soc., 27 (105) Oct. 1927: 16–23; (106) Jan. 1928: 155–166, illus.
Includes an appendix on the "ekwoifia ceremony"—a mock resurrection rite—performed in Oturkpo area, Idoma Division.

3638   Murray, Kenneth Crosthwaite
Ida masks. Nig. field, 14 (3) Jl. 1949: 85–92, illus.
Describes some Igala masks from Idah.

3639   Palmer, Herbert Richmond
The Atagara of Idah on the Niger. Man, 37, 1937: 183 (art. 213).
A commentary on an article on the Ata of Idah by M. Clifford [3635]. Gives additional illuminating notes on the origin of some of the customs of the Igala and neighbouring tribes, especially customs associated with kingship.

3640   *Partridge, Charles
The burial of the Ata of Igaraland, and the 'coronation' of his successor. Blackwood's mag., 1904: 329–337.

3641   —A note on the Igara tribe. J. Afr. Soc., 8, Oct. 1908: 1–2, illus.
A brief note referring to Byng-Hall's

article [3634] and to author's article [3640] both on the Igala to whom the name Igara was originally applied.

3642 The Rise and fall of the Igala state. *Nig. mag.*, (80) Mar. 1964: 17–29, illus.

3643 Seton, Ralph Sydney
Installation of an Attah of Ida (Nigeria) *J.R.A.I.*, 58, 1928: 255–278.

3644 —Notes on the Igala tribe, Northern Nigeria. *J. Afr. soc.*, 29 (113) Oct. 1929: 42–52; (114) Jan. 1930: 149–163.
Religion, medicine, courtship and marriage, burial, dances, inheritance, laws, oaths, and festivals.

3645 Sieber, Roy
The insignia of the Igala chief of Eteh, Eastern Nigeria. *Man*, 65, May–Je. 1965 (art. 65): 80–82, illus.
Describes and illustrates spearheads, a bell and boxstools—all insignia of Azike, chief of Ete village in Eastern Nigeria who owes allegiance to the Ata of Idah.

2. LINGUISTIC STUDIES

Armstrong, Robert G.
Comparative word lists of two dialects of Yoruba with Igala. See [5301]

3646 Bible. N.T. Igala. Gospels and Act. Otakada ola ei ojo. London, Trinitarian Bible society, 1918. 2 p.l., 3–564p.

3647 Bible. N.T. Igala. John
Jọn ejodudu. [Translated, with notes, by R. T. Dibble] Ika, Stewards co., 1960. 16p.

3648 Bible. O.T. Igala. II Kings.
Amonu ekeji. [Translated by R. T. Dibble] Ika, Stewards co., 1959. 1 p;1., 68p.

3649 Bible. O. T. Igala, I Samuel
Samuel ejodudu. [Translated by R. T. Dibble] Ika, Stewards co., 1960. 112p.

3650 Bible. O. T. Igala. 2 Samuel
Samuel ekeji. [Translated by R. T. Dibble] Ika Stewards co., 1959. 1 p.l., 93p.

3651 Bunyan, John
Amilowa ile—The Pilgrim's progress. Idah, Stewards co., 1958. [167]p. illus.

3652 Coomber, A. G.
Igara primer. London, C.M.S., 1867. [ii] 26p.

3653 Eli abolojo. Idah, Stewards co., 1958. [189]p.

3654 Eli Abọlọjọ. [Ika, Stewards co. press, 1962] [218]p.

3655 Ika Bible school
An'onẹ ọla ki def alo etitọ. Tentative edition N. T. concordance in Igala. Ika, Bible school, 1963. 3 1., 320p.
Mimeographed.

3656 Otakada giji goco. [Idah, Stewards co., 1956) 171p.

3657 Philpot, W. T. A.
Notes on the Igala language. *B.S.O.S.*, 7 (4) 1935: 897–912.

IGBIRA

(Egbiri, Igbirra Kotogori)

Including:

Kwotto *(Panda, Wushishi)*

1. GENERAL AND ETHNOGRAPHIC STUDIES

3658 Brown, Paula
The Igbira. In *Peoples of the Niger-Benue confluence, by Daryll Forde [and others] 1955*: 55–74, bibliog.

3659 Groom, A. Holdsworth
The main characteristics of the "Inland" Igbirras in Kabba Province, Northern Nigeria. *J. Afr. soc.*, 9 (34) Jan. 1910: 176–183.
"Inland" as distinct from "Riverside" Igbira. Includes a brief note on their origin and migration.

3660 Igbira. In *Notes on the tribes . . . by O. Temple. 2nd ed. 1922, repr. 1965*: 154–161.

3661 Igbirra progressive union.
A call for unity—Igbirra progressive union, Mokola, Ibadan branch. Ibadan, 1950. 8p.
Printed by Adeyemi printing works, Ibadan.

3662 Lannert, E.
Ekwechi-Anokechi festival. *Nig. mag.*, (80) Mar. 1964: 44–56, illus.
Describes a festival celebrated annually in December by the Igbirra and gives an account of its origin.

3663 Salacuse, Jeswald
Igbira family law. In his *A selective survey of Nigerian family law, 1965*: 65–78.

3664 Wilson-Haffenden, J. R.
Ethnological notes on the Kwottos of Toto (Panda) District, Keffi Division, Benue Province, Northern Nigeria. *J. Afr. soc.*, 26 (104) Jl. 1927: 368–379; (105) Oct. 1927: 24–46; 27 (106) Jan. 1928: 142–154; (107) Apr. 1928: 281–286; (108) Jl. 1928: 380–393.
Traditional account of the origin and early history of the Kwottos as given by members of the royal house at Umaisha.

3665 —Initiation ceremonies in Northern Nigeria. *J. Afr. soc.*, 29 (116) Jl. 1930: 370–375.
On a boys' initiation ceremony called

"Ohikwami ori" or "Grandfather ori" performed by the Kwottos.

3666 —The Kwottos, Igaras & Jukuns. In *The red men of Nigeria . . . by J. R. Wilson-Haffenden, 1930*: 140–308, illus.
Ethnographic study of the Kwottos of Southern and Western Nassarawa Province.

2. LINGUISTIC STUDIES

3667 [Coomber, A. G.]
Igbira otakerida; or Igbira primer. London, C.M.S., 1866. [ii] 35p.

3668 *Coomber, A. G.
Primer and vocabulary of the Igbira language.

3669 Kose iwa Ebira. Zaria, NORLA, 1958. 26p.

3670 Ladefoged, Peter
Igbirra notes and word-list. *J. W. Afr. lang.*, 1 (1) 1964: 27–37.

3671 Uhi anebirra. Zaria, NORLA, 1956. 20p., illus.

3672 Williams, P. J.
Igbira otakida, agubo odan keke kero almadari Kristu yi onurala Igbira. A reading book in the Igbira language for use in the day and sunday schools. London, S.P.C.K., 1883. 30p.

IJAW

(Ijo)

Including:

Bonny
Brass
Kalabari

Ogoni
Opobo

1. GENERAL

3673 Alagoa, Ebiegberi Joe
Akassa raid, 1895. Ibadan, University press, 1960. 20p.

3674 Alex Miller, brother & co.
An account of the disputes at Opobo between King Jaja and consular authority, with correspondence relating thereto. Together with an account of the enquiry at Accra, and remarks thereon. London, H. V. Clements, 1888. 73 [7]p.

3675 Barbot, Jacques
An abstract of a voyage to New Calabar River, or Rio Real in the year 1699. In *A collection of voyages and travels . . . compiled by Awnsham and John Churchill, 1732*, Vol. 5, pp. 455–466

3676 Barbot, Jacques and Grazilhier, Jean
Voyage au nouveau Calabar, à Bandy, et à Dodo. In *Histoire générale des voyages; ou Nouvelle collection des relations de voyages . . . par C. A. Walckenaer, 1842*, vol. 11, pp. 61–112.

3677 Bindloss, Harold
In the Niger country. Edinburgh, Blackwood, 1898. x, 388p. map.
Description of the Niger Delta area he visited in 1897–1898. Reprinted, (London, Frank Cass,) 1968, also contains James Pinnock, *Benin: the surrounding country, inhabitants, customs and trade*. [See 1745].

3678 Clark, John Pepper
Poems. Illustrations by Susanne Wenger. Ibadan, Mbari publications, 1962. 51 [4]p. illus.

3679 —Song of a goat. Ibadan, Mbari publications, 1961. [4] 43p.
A play.

3680 —Three plays: Song of a goat; The masquerade; [and] The raft. London, Ibadan, O.U.P., 1964. [ii] 134p.

3680a Colvile, Zélie
Ten days on an oil-river. *Blackwood's mag.*, Mar. 1893: 372–382.

3681 Galway, Henry L.
West Africa fifty years ago. *J.R.A.S.*, 41 (163) Apr. 1942: 90–100.
Recounts his experiences in the Oil Rivers Protectorate, (especially Bonny and Benin) where he arrived as Deputy Commissioner and Vice Consul, with Major Claude MacDonald in 1891.

3682 Garrard, A. O.
A visit to an Ijaw village. *W. Eq. Afr. dioc. mag.*, 26 (330) [i.e. n.s. 204] Dec. 1921: 328–332.

3683 Girard, Charles
Exploration au Nouveau-Calabar. Extrait du Journal de voyage. *Bull. Soc. geog.*, 5th ser., 3, Jan.–Je. 1867: 548–567, map. Also published separately. Paris, E. Martinot, 1867. 24p.
Account of journey to Bonny, reception by King Pepple who granted him permission to go upstream, description of the hinterland.

3683a Granville, R. and Roth, F. N.
Notes on the Jekris, Sobos and Ijos . . . See [3777].

3684 Jackson, Richard Mather
Journal of a voyage to Bonny River on the west coast of Africa in the ship Kingston, from Liverpool; Peter Jackson, Commander; in 1826. Edited by Roland Jackson. Letchworth, Herts., Garden City press, 1934. 159p. front. (port.)
Author's impressions of Bonny and the Cameroon where he spent seven

months (Jan.–July 1826) Includes a table of slave ships and number of slaves shipped from the port of Bonny between 1825 and 1826 (pp. 155–156).

3685 Johnston, Harry Hamilton
Niger delta. *Proc. Roy. geog. soc.*, 10, 1888: 749–763.

3686 Okara, Gabriel
The voice; a novel. London, André Deutsch, 1964. 157p.

3687 Osika, Isaac Warrior
Clarion call: Grand Bonny! Great Kalabari! Noble Okrika! Daring Nembe! All-ye adventurous people of the Brass Division and the Western Ijaws! Laudable Ogbeya area! Ancient Odual! Proud Opobo! Something is wrong! [Okrika, the author, 1955] [3] 11p. (Pamphlet for national awakening, no. 3).

3688 —Rivers peoples' handbook. What you should know about the rivers: towns, clans, districts, councils, etc. Port Harcourt, J. Thom. Manuel, 1957. 32p. (Information series booklet) Printed by Island press, Port Harcourt.

3689 Scotland, J. Allen
Holiday reminiscences; being a tour from Sierra Leone to Bonny and back. [Freetown, the author] 1907. 53p.

3690 Smith, J.
Trade and travels in the Gulf of Guinea, Western Africa, with an account of the manners, habits, customs and religion of the inhabitants. London, Simpkin, Marshall, 1851. 223p.
Except for brief account of Fernando Po and Kron in Liberia, the bulk of the book deals with the country and people of Bonny and the Oil Rivers.

3691 Warmate, G. James
The Niger Delta people's hand book on the Niger Delta Development Board, the areas concerned, the Shell–B.P. Oil exploration in the Niger Delta area. Port Harcourt [the author] 1963. 2 p.l. 60p. (Historical, geographical and econ. survey series) Printed by Continental press, Port Harcourt.
Part 2 (pp. 15–30) gives brief descriptive and historical sketches of Kalabari, Bonny, Okrika, Ogoni, Brass, Akassa and other towns in the area.

3691a Warrior-Osika, Isaac. *See* Osika, Isaac Warrior.

2. PHYSICAL ANTHROPOLOGY

3692 Harris, R.
Some medical and biological factors determining the genetic structure of the population in the Niger Delta. 1961.
M.D. thesis, Liverpool University.

3693 Harris, R. and Gilles, H. M.
Glucose-6-phosphate dehydrogenase deficiency in the peoples of the Niger delta. *Ann. hum. genet.*, 25 (3) 1961: 199–206.

3693a Keith, Arthur

On certain physical characters of the negroes of the Congo Free state and Nigeria. See [578].

3. SOCIAL AND CULTURAL ANTHROPOLOGY, ETHNOGRAPHY

(i) General

3694 Darker, G. F.
Niger delta natives, with special reference to maintaining and increasing the population of Southern Nigeria. *J. Afr. soc.*, 4 (14) Jan. 1905: 206–220, illus., maps.

3694a Granville, R. and Roth, F. N.
Notes on the Jekris . . . See [3777].

3695 Homfray, J. M. B.
Fishing in the Niger delta. *Discovery*, Dec. 1929: 397–399.

3696 Horton, Robin
An outline of Kalabari culture. In his *Kalabari sculpture, 1965*: 1–8.

3697 Jeffreys, M. D. W.
Some notes on the folklore of the tribes of the Niger delta. *Folk-lore*, 63, 1952: 173–176.
Discusses the traditions of origin held by the Ogoni and Itsekiri as well as by the Ibos of Umundri, matching these with theories of emigration from the Middle East.

3698 Köhler, Hermann
Einige Notizen über Bonny an der Küste von Guinea, seine Sprache und seine Bewohner, mit einem Glossarium. Göttingen, 1848. iv, 183p.
Account of Bonny and its people, including Ibo and other non-Bonny elements of the population, with a vocabulary and grammatical outline of the language. The author, a German doctor, visited the town in 1840.

3699 Leis, Nancy Boric
Economic independence and Ijaw women: a comparative study of two communities in the Niger delta. 1964. 291p.
Ph.D. thesis, Northwestern university. Investigates effects of successful trading and consequent economic independence of Ijaw women of Patani on their marital relationship and contrasts this with the position of Korokorosei women who not being traders, are economically dependent on their husbands.

3700 Leis, Philip E.
Enculturation and cultural change in an Ijaw community. 1962. 245p.
Ph.D. thesis, Northwestern University. A study of social and cultural patterns in the Ijaw town of Korokorosei, between 1958 and 1959, with special emphasis on cultural development during the period between birth and the age of seventeen.

3701 —Ijaw enculturation: a re-examination of the early learning hypothesis. *S.W.j. anthrop.*, 20 (1) Spring 1964: 32–42, bibliog.

o

3702 —Palm oil, illicit gin and the moral order of the Ijaw. *Amer. anthrop.*, 66 (4 pt. 1) Aug. 1964: 828–833, bibliog.

A survey of two economic activities—oil palm processing and illicit gin distilling—in the Ijaw village of Ebiama in the Niger Delta. Notes the almost complete shift from the former to the latter activity in recent years and attributes this to the Ijaw ideology of hard work and personal independence—an ideology considered more in accord with the latter industry. In the wider view, the conclusion is held as establishing that the moral order can sometimes be instrumental to cultural change, and not merely follow it.

3703 Leonard, Arthur Glyn
Life and death in the Niger delta. *Blackwood's mag.*, Apr. 1898: 451–460.

3704 McCarthy, G. S.
The gentle art in Opobo, S. Nigeria. *W. Eq. Afr. dioc. mag.*, 12 (139) Jan. 1906: 100–102.

Notes on methods of fishing used in and around Opobo.

3705 Murray, Kenneth Crosthwaite
Opobo today. *Afr. affairs*, 43 (172) Jl. 1944: 134–137.

Notes on history, kingship, housing, occupation, shrines, plays and the general appearance of the town in the 1940's.

3706 Nigeria. Eastern. Commission of inquiry into outbreaks of violence at Okrika.
Summary of the report and recommendations . . . including Government announcement. [R. J. Graham, sole commissioner] Enugu, Government printer, 1963. [iii] 7p. (Official document, no. 23 of 1963).

3707 —Commission of inquiry into the Nembe chieftaincy dispute.
Report. [O. Ukelonu, sole commissioner] Enugu, Government printer, 1960. 38p. (Official document, no. 24 of 1960).

Includes notes on Nembe history, religion, judicial system and marriage and inheritance, with three appendices of tables of Nembe Kings—(1) according to popular legend; (2) according to Bassambiri party; and (3) according to Bassambiri improvement union.

3708 Nzekwu, Onuora
Iria ceremony. *Nig. mag.*, (63) 1959: 341–352, illus.

Traditional girl marriage ceremony in Okrika.

3709 Plotnicov, Leonard
'Nativism' in contemporary Nigeria. *Anthrop quart.*, 37 (3) Jl. 1964: 121–137.

On the persistence of Ijaw traditions and ceremonies in Opobo in spite of the growth of discouraging and inhibiting factors such as education, occupational commitments, labour migration, etc.

3710 *Pratt, J. A.
African town; or Village life in the Niger. *Western equatorial Africa diocesan*

magazine, 11 (129) 1905: 147–149; (130) 161–165.

3711 Uzoma, R. I.
Adult literacy work at Okrika in the delta of the Niger. *Oversea educ.*, 19 (4) Jl. 1948: 737–741.

3712 Williamson, Kay R. M.
Changes in the marriage system of the Okrika Ijo. *Africa*, 32 (1) Jan. 1962: 53–60.

Reviews marriage and family system in Okrika town and the response of this system to contemporary social changes in this area.

3. (ii) History

3713 Alagoa, Ebiegberi Joe
Ijo origins and migrations. 1. *Nig. mag.*, (91) Dec. 1966: 279–288, illus.

3714 —The small brave city state: a history of Nembe-Brass in the Niger. Ibadan, University press; Madison, Wis., University of Wisconsin press, 1964. 173p. illus. map.

3715 Amangala, G. I.
Short history of Ijaw, with appendix. [Oloibiri, the author, 1945] 31, 18p. Printed by Ikieso press, Port Harcourt.

Main work (author's introduction to which is dated December 1939) is a historical and ethnographic sketch of Ijaw people. The appendix (preface dated 1945) deals with the history of Ogbeyan (Ogbia) clan.

3716 Bonny. *Nig. mag.*, (59) 1958: 354–372, illus. (incl. facsim.)

History of Bonny town from its foundation in the 15th century to the late 19th century when it was engaged in war with King Jaja of Opobo.

3717 Brown-West, H. Wenike
A short genealogical history of Amachree 1 of Kalabari. (With appendix) Enugu [the author, 1956] [ix] 46p. illus.

Printed by Sankey printing press, Yaba.

3718 Cowan, Alex. A.
The story of Jaja. London, West African publishing co. 1928. 40p.

A re-examination of the circumstances leading to Jaja's deportation and the role played by Sir Harry H. Johnston who was then acting Consul for the area. Highly critical of Johnston, Originally appeared in *West Africa* Nov. 12, 1927. Appended (pp. 16–31) is a report of Sir William Geary's article "Jaja, an African merchant prince" which appeared in *West Africa* Jan. 14, 1922; as well as briefer notes by others on the same topic.

3719 Ekpelle, E. M. T.
The trial of Jaja. Enugu, Literary book co., 1959. 55p.

A historical play in four acts, about the capture, trial and deportation of King Jaja of Opobo. Depicts "in a dramatic form, the events immediately leading to the "Trial" and the 'Trial' itself."—Introd. p. 7. Useful bibliographical notes.

3720 —The Church in the Niger Delta. With an appendix on Archdeacon Crowther. [Aba] Niger Delta Diocese, 1955. 128p. illus. (ports.)

3721 Galway, Henry Lionel
The rising of the Brassmen. *J. Afr. soc.*, 34 (135) Apr. 1935: 144–162.
The causes, course and consequences of the Brassmen's attack on Akassa in 1895.

3722 Jones, Gwilym Iwan
European and African traditions on the Rio Real. *J. Afr. hist.*, 4 (3) 1963: 391–404.
The significance and limitations of European writings and African oral traditions in the study of West African history are illustrated by a brief review of both categories of historical sources for the Niger delta area.

3723 —Oral tradition and history. *Afr. notes*, 2 (2) Jan. 1965: 7–11.
Text of a lecture delivered at the Inst. of African studies, University of Ibadan. Discusses the dangers involved in the use of oral traditions as historical sources, illustrating specific points by drawing from the traditions of Ijaw villages and clans in the Eastern Delta.

3724 —Time and oral tradition with special reference to Eastern Nigeria. *J. Afr. hist.*, 6 (2) 1965: 153–160, bibliog.

3725 —The trading states of the oil rivers; a study of political development in Eastern Nigeria. London, Ibadan, O.U.P., for International African Institute, 1963. ix, 262p. tables, bibliog.
An ethnologico-historical study of the development and the political and economic structure of the Eastern Niger delta states in the 19th century. Emphasis on the two states of Kalabari and Bonny.

3726 Kaufmann, Herbert
The king's crocodile; translated by Stella Humphries. London, Methuen, 1962. 224p. illus.
A historical novel woven round King Jaja of Opopo and based substantially on actual events.

3727 King Ja-ja of Opobo. *Nig. mag.*, (62) 1959: 265–280, illus.

3728 Owonaro, S. K.
The history of Ijo (Ijaw) and her neighbouring tribes in Nigeria. Lagos [the author] 1949. [xii] 123, v p. illus.
Printed by Niger printing works, Lagos.

3729 Pratt, J. A.
A brief historical sketch of Opobo; with a journal account of a Mission expedition to Bende and Aro-Chuku, and a report of the building of St. Paul's Church. London, Missionary leaves association [1910] 70p. front., illus.

3730 Tepowa, Adebiyi
A short history of Brass and its people. *J. Afr. soc.*, 7 (25) Oct. 1907: 32–88, map. (fold.)
History of the Brass people, with a descriptive account of Brass life and culture. First published in sketchy form in *W. Afr. mail*. Includes an appendix of Brass vocabulary, grammatical notes and short sentences, which first appeared as "Notes on the (Nembe) Brass language" in *J. Afr. soc.* See [3763].

3. (iii) Religion

3731 Alagoa, Ebiegberi Joe
Idu: a creator festival at Okpoma (Brass) in the Niger delta. *Africa*, 34 (1) Jan. 1964: 1–8.
Introductory commentary on the *Idu* festival, followed by a day by day account of its celebration. French summary, p. 8.

3732 Cardi, Charles Napoleon, comte de.
Ju-ju laws and customs in the Niger delta. *J. Anthrop. inst. n.s.*, 2, 1899: 51–64, illus.
Niger delta and Old Calabar.

3733 Horton, Robin
Duminea: a festival for the water-spirits in the Niger Delta. *Nig. mag.*, (86) Sept. 1965: 187–193, illus.
Detailed account of the Duminea festival in Soku village. Duminea is a water spirit which controls the creeks and rivers and which during the fishing season, reduces the amount of water in them to facilitate fishing.

3734 —The gods as guests: an aspect of Kalabari religious life. Lagos, Nigeria Magazine, 1960. 71p. front. illus.
Discussion of Kalabari religion, and of the three modes of dramatization of the various gods worshipped—Mime, Masquerade and Possession.

3735 —Igbo; an ordeal for aristocrats. *Nig. mag.*, (90) Sept. 1966: 168–183, illus.
Describes Igbo, a water spirit masquerade dance of the Kalabari Ekine society, as performed in Buguma, and suggests an explanation for its high status among other masquerades of the Ekine society.

3736 —Kalabari diviners and oracles. *Odu*, 1 (1) Jl. 1964: 3–16.
The processes and techniques involved in the consultation of oracles and divination.

3737 —The Kalabari Ekine society: a borderland of religion and art. *Africa*, 33 (2) Apr. 1963: 94–114, illus.
French summary, pp. 113–114.

3738 —The Kalabari world-view: an outline and an interpretation. *Africa*, 32 (3) Jl. 1962: 197–219, bibliog.
An interpretative essay on Kalabari religio-philosophical conceptions and their explanation of the world around them.

3739   —New Year in the Delta. *Nig. mag.*, (67) Dec. 1960: 256–300, illus.
Describes both the traditional Kalabari year-changing rituals conducted within the framework of their indigenous calendar, and the celebrations associated with and carried out on the Christian new year's day.

3740   Leis, Philip E.
"Collective sentiments" as represented in Ijaw divination. *J. Folkl. inst.*, 1 (3) 1964: 167–179.

3741   MacJajah, N. O. M.
Trial of the wizard *Afr. affairs*, 50 (199) Apr. 1951: 147–153.
A play on the death of an African wizard. Based on Opobo beliefs.

3742   Nzekwu, Onuora
Carnival at Opobo. *Nig. mag.*, (63) 1959: 302–319, illus.

3743   Talbot, Percy Amaury
Some beliefs of today and yesterday (Niger delta tribes) *J.R.A.S.*, 15 (60) Jl. 1916: 305–319, illus.
Religious beliefs and sacred shrines of the people of Degema Division in the Niger Delta, and the influence of a new religious movement headed by a self styled Elijah II.

3744   —Some Nigerian fertility cults, London, O.U.P., 1927, repr. London, Frank Cass, 1967. xi, 140p. front., illus.
Describes shrines and religious rites connected with fertility in and around Degema Division of Eastern Nigeria.

3745   —Tribes of the Niger delta, their religions and customs. London, Sheldon press; New York, Macmillan, 1932, repr. London, Frank Cass, 1967. xi, 350p. front., illus., map.

3. (iv) Sculpture, Arts and Crafts

3746   Balfour, Henry
Ceremonial paddle of the Kalabari of Southern Nigeria. *Man*, 17, 1917: 57–58. (art. 44) illus.

3747   Horton, Robin
Kalabari sculpture. Lagos, Dept. of antiquities, 1965. [vii] 49p. + 72 plates.

3748   —A note on recent finds of brass-work in the Niger Delta. *Odu*, 1 (2) Jl. 1965: 76–91.

3749   Jeffreys, M. D. W.
Ogoni pottery: a note. *Man*, 47, Je. 1947: 81–83 (art. 84). illus.

4. LINGUISTIC STUDIES

3750   Agbegha, Matthew L.
Izǫn mǫ Beke mǫ ten-eye fun. Ijaw-English vocabulary. [Warri, the author] 1961. 80p. Printed by Kagbo industrial enterprises, Warri.

3751   Brosnahan, L. F.
Outlines of the phonology of the Gokana dialect of Ogoni. *J. W. Afr. lang.*, 1 (1) 1964: 43–48.

3751a   Carew, W. E. L., *tr.*
A portion of Simpson's primer . . . See [3761].

3752   —Primer in the Ubani dialect of the Idso language. London, C.M.S. house [1870] 27p.
A primer of the Bonny or Ibani dialect which according to K. Williamson is now spoken in only one ward of Bonny and in a few villages like Finnema. See her *A grammar of the Kolokuma dialect of Ijo, 1965*, p. 1. [3765].

3753   *Church of England. Liturgies.
Idzǫ common prayer (Brass dialect) Brass, 1886.

3754   *Johnson, F. E. G.
Primer in the Ijo language. London, 1911.

3755   *—Vocabulary of the Bonny language. Lagos, 1903.

3756   Kalio, Dinah D. S.
Kabo na gbun ekwein na kirikeni bipi bu. Port Harcourt, [the author] 1960. 48p.
Printed by C.M.S. (Nigeria) press, Port Harcourt. A collection of proverbs in Okrika dialect of Ijaw.

3756a   Köhler, H.
Einige Notizen über Bonny . . . Seine Sprache . . . mit einem Glossarium. See [3698].

3757   Onduku, T. Omette
Ezǫn bebę gę bra mę: How to write the Ijaw language. Warri [the author] 1960. [iv] 62p.
Printed by Unity press and stationery stores, Warri. Text in Ijaw and English.

3758   —2nd ed. Warri. 1961. [4] 66p.

3759   Rowlands, E. C.
Tone and intonation systems in Brass-Nembe Ijaw. *Afr. lang. stud.*, (1) 1960: 137–154.

3760   Sanki anunmo ma Nembe bebe. Selected Sankey songs in the Nembe language, Eastern Nigeria. Oshogbo, Printed by Kebo, 1962. 3 p. 1., 164p. front.

3761   Simpson
A portion of Simpson's primer translated by W. E. L. Carew. London [1870].
Simpson's primer translated into Ijaw.

3762   Taylor, John Christopher
Primer of the Ijo or Idsǫ language (with vocabulary) London, C.M.S., 1862. 40p.

3763   Tepowa, Adebiyi
Notes on the (Nembe) Brass language. *J. Afr. soc.*, (13) Oct. 1904: 117–133.

3764   Ward, Ida Caroline
A note on the Abua language. *Africa*, 8 (3) Jl. 1935: 377–378.
Brief note on a language spoken in Ahoada area in the Niger Delta, noting in particular the vowel and consonant characteristics.

3765   Williamson, Kay R. M.
A grammar of the Kolokuma dialect of Ijǫ. Cambridge, C.U.P., in association with the West African languages survey and Institute of African studies, Ibadan, 1965. vii, 127p. (W. African language monographs, 2).

A pioneering study, giving a descriptive analysis of the dialect of the Kolokuma-Opokuma clan especially as spoken in the town of Kaiama. Based on the author's Ph.D. thesis, Yale, 1963.

3766 —History through linguistics. *Ibadan*, (17) Nov. 1963: 10–11.

Explanation of the principles involved in building up an original vocabulary of a language for the purpose of linguistic comparison; with illustrations from the Okrika, Boma, Kolokuma, Kabo and Mein dialects of Ijaw language.

3767 —The syntax of verbs of motion in Ijọ. *J. Afr. lang.*, 2 (2) 1963: 150–154.

3768 —The units of an African tone language. *Phonetica*, 3 (2–3) 1959: 145–166.

Analysis of the tone system of the Kolokuma dialect of Ijaw.

3769 Wolff, Hans
Intelligibility and inter-ethnic attitudes. *Anthrop. ling.*, 1 (3) Mar. 1959: 34–41.

3770 —Niger Delta languages, I: Classification. *Anthrop. ling.*, 1 (8) Nov. 1959: 32–53.

3771 —Synopsis of the Ogoni languages. *J. W. Afr. lang.*, 3 (1) 1964: 38–51.

By Ogoni languages here are meant Kana, Gokana and Eleme languages spoken in Ogoni Division.

ITSEKIRI

(Awerri, Ishekiri, Itshekiri, Iwerri, Jakri, Jekri, Oere, Ouaire, Ouere, Oware, Warri)

1. BIBLIOGRAPHY

3772 Lloyd, Peter Cutt
Bibliography [of the Itsekiri] In *The Benin Kingdom, by R. E. Bradbury, 1957*: 203–205.

2. GENERAL AND ETHNOGRAPHIC STUDIES

3773 Allen, Henry A.
The Jekris: a tough race. *West African rev.*, 20 (262) Jl. 1949: 757–759.

3774 Atimomo, D. E.
Masquerade among the Itsekiri. *Nig. mag.*, (15) 1938: 238–239.

3775 Bowen, R. L.
The Olu of Itsekiris. *Nig. mag.*, (22) 1944: 62–63, illus.

3775a Burton, R. F.
My wanderings in West Africa: a visit to the renowned cities of Warri and Benin. See [1716].

3776 Ekwensi, Cyprian Odiatu Duaka
We are here—a photo feature on Itsekiri traditional dancing. *Nig. mag.*, (82) Sept. 1964: 164–172, illus.

Brief notes, with beautiful photographs depicting four Itsekiri traditional dances —*Ogbodun, Wuruye, Omoko* and *Yetsi*— staged in Lagos in 1964 by Itsekiri women from Origbo in the Warri area.

3777 Granville, Reginald K. and Roth, Felix N.
Notes on the Jekris, Sobos and Ijos of the Warri District of the Niger Coast Protectorate. *J. Anthrop. inst., n.s.*, 1 [old ser., 28] Aug.–Nov. 1899: 104–126, illus.

Also offprinted. London, Harrison, 1899.

3778 Ikime, Obaro
The coming of the C.M.S. into the Itsekiri, Urhobo and Isoko country. *Nig. mag.*, (86) Sept. 1965: 206–215.
See [4369] for full entry.

3779 —Nana Olumu: governor of the Benin River. *Tarikh*, 1 (2) 1966: 39–50, illus., map.

3780 Lloyd, Peter Cutt
Capitaine Landolphe and the Compagnie d'Owhere et de Benin. *Odù* (5) 1958: 14–21, bibliog.

3781 —The Itsekiri. In *The Benin kingdom, and the Edo-speaking peoples of Southwestern Nigeria, by R. E. Bradbury. 1957*: 172–205, map, bibliog.

3782 —The Itsekiri in the nineteenth century: an outline social history. *J. Afr. hist.*, 4 (2) 1963: 207–231, illus., maps.

3782a —The Portuguese in Warri. See [3783].

3783 Lloyd Peter Cutt and Ryder, Alvan Frederick Charles
Dom Domingos, Prince of Warri. *Odù*, (4) [1958] 27–39.

An introduction is followed by two articles: The Portuguese in Warri, by P. C. Lloyd, and The story of Dom Domingos, by A. F. C. Ryder.

3783a —Tribalism in Warri. See [4373].

3784 Moore, William A.
History of Itsekiri. London, Arthur H. Stockwell, [1930] 224p. front. (port.) repr. London, Frank Cass, 1970.

3785 Neville, George W.
Nanna Oloma of Benin *J. Afr. soc.*, 14 (54) Jan. 1914: 162–167, illus. (port.)

A biographical sketch of a powerful Itsekiri chief and trader who was exiled from his town, Brohimi, by the British in 1894. See also [3779].

3786 *Omoneukarin, C. O.
Itsekiri law and custom. Lagos, 1942.

3787 Palisot de Beauvois, Ambroise Marie François Joseph
Flore d'Oware et de Bénin en Afrique. Paris, Imprimerie deFain jeune, 1804–1807. 2v. plates.

3788 —Insectes recueillis en Afrique et en Amérique, dans les royaumes d'Oware et de Bénin, à Saint-Domingue et dans les États-Unis, pendant les années 1786–1797. Paris, Impr. de Fain, 1805. 2 p.l., xvi, 276p. illus. (plates).

3789   Roussier, P.
Documents sur les relations entre la France et le royaume de Ouaire à la côte d'Afrique, 1784–1787. *Bull. com. étud. hist. sci. A.O.F.*, 11, 1928: 352–385.

3790   Ryder, Alvan Frederick Charles
An early Portuguese trading voyage to the Forcados River. *J. Hist. soc. Nig.*, 1 (4) Dec. 1959: 294–321.

3791   —Missionary activity in the kingdom of Warri to the early 19th century. *J. Hist. Soc. Nig.*, 2 (1) Dec. 1960: 1–26.
The establishment and history of Roman Catholic Church in Warri from the 16th century to the end of the 18th century.

3791a   —The story of Dom Domingos. See [3783].

3792   Temietan, S. O.
Marriage amongst the Jekri tribes as contrasted with that amongst the Hausa tribes. *Nig. mag.*, (13) Mar. 1938: 75–78.

JEREWA

Including:

Afusara *(Fizere, Hill Jarawa)*
Amap *(Amo)*
Anaguta *(Naguta)*
Badawa
Bamberawa *(Bamboro)*
Bankalawa
Barawa *(Mbarawa)*
Buji *(Bujawa)*
Chara *(Fachara, Nfachara, Pakara, Teira)*
Chokobo

Das *(Dass)*
Gusuwa *(Gusum, Ibau)*
Janji *(Ijanyi)*
Jarawa *(Jar)*
Jengre
Jere
Limorro
Rebinawa *(Narabuna, Ribina)*
Rukuba
Sangawa
Taurawa

1. GENERAL AND ETHNOGRAPHIC STUDIES

3793   Ames, C. G.
The Jerewa group. In his *Gazetteer of Bauchi Province; recently abridged and revised, 1934*: 99–107.
Historical and ethnographic sketch.

3794   —The Rukuba tribe, In his *Gazetteer of Bauchi Province, recently abridged and revised, 1934*: 88–99.
Origin, history and ethnography.

3795   Anaguta. In *Notes on the tribes ... by O. Temple*, 2nd ed., 1922, repr. 1965: 8.

3796   Bristow, W. M.
Some notes on the Jarawa people near Jos, Plateau Province, Nigeria. *Afr. u. Übersee*, 37, 1953: 61–64.

3797   Chawai, Jengre, Rukuba group. In *Notes on the tribes ... by O. Temple*, 2nd ed, 1922, repr. 1965: 84–86.

3798   Conant, Francis P.
Contemporary communities and abandoned settlement sites. *Ann. N.Y. acd. sci.*, 96 (2) Jan. 1962: 539–573, illus., maps.
On the Barawa, Bankalawa and Jarawa.

3799   —Dodo of Dass: a study of a pagan religion of Northern Nigeria. 1960.
Ph.D. thesis, Columbia university.

3800   —Jarawa kin systems of reference and address: a componential comparison. *Anthrop. ling.*, 3 (2) Feb. 1961: 19–33.

3801   —The manipulation of rituals among Plateau Nigerians. *Africa*, 33 (3) Jl. 1963: 227–236, bibliog.
Rituals among the Barawa, Bankalawa and Jarawa. Summary in French, pp. 235–236.

3802   —Rocks that ring: their ritual setting in Northern Nigeria. *Trans. N.Y. Acad. sci.*, ser. 2, 23 (2) Dec. 1960: 155–162, bibliog.
On rock gongs in their ethnographic context among the Barawa and Bankalawa in Northern Nigeria.

3803   Dass. In *Notes on the tribes ... by O. Temple, 2nd ed., 1922, repr. 1965*: 422.

3804   Diamond, Stanley
Anaguta cosmography: the linguistic and behavioral implications. *Anthrop. ling.*, 2 (2) Feb. 1960: 31–38.
The Anaguta live in Jos Division of Plateau Province, Northern Nigeria.

3805   Gunn, Harold D.
The Afusare (Hill Jarawa) and related peoples of Bauchi Province. In his *Peoples of the Plateau area of Northern Nigeria, 1953*: 60–74.
On the Afusare and Anaguta groups.

3806   —The Jerawa group of Bauchi, Plateau and Zaria Provinces. In his *Peoples of the Plateau area of Northern Nigeria, 1953*: 11–52, bibliog.
Ethnographic and linguistic notes on the Chara, Gezewa, Rukuba, Amap,

Janji, Ribina, and other groups in the area.

3807   Jarawa. In *Notes on the tribes . . . by O. Temple, 2nd ed., 1922, repr. 1965*: 165–171.

3808   Limorro. In *Notes on the tribes . . . by O. Temple, 2nd ed., 1922, repr. 1965*: 258.

3809   Meek, Charles Kingsley
        The Janji. In his *Tribal studies in Northern Nigeria, v. 2, 1931*: 185–189, illus.

3809a   —Marriage by exchange in Nigeria. See [815].

2. LINGUISTIC STUDIES

3809b   Diamond, Stanley

Anaguta cosmography: the linguistic and behavioural implications. See [3804]

3810   Lukas, Johannes and Willms, A.
        Outline of the language of the Jarawa in Northern Nigeria (Plateau Province). *Afr. u. Übersee*, 45 (1–2) Oct. 1961: 1–66.

3811   Meek, Charles Kingsley
        [Janji vocabulary] In his *Tribal studies in Northern Nigeria, v. 2, 1931*: 186–189.

3812   Mukarovsky, Hans G.
        Some reflexions on a Nigerian class language. *Wiener Völkerkdl. Mitt., n.s.*, 6 (1–4) 1963: 65–83.
        On the classification of Jerawa and its relations with other Nigerian languages, as well as with Bantu.

JERRA

(Jara, Jera)

Including:

Hina
Kanakuru *(Dera)*
Maga

Nimalto
Terra *(Kemaltu, Terawa)*

1. GENERAL AND ETHNOGRAPHIC STUDIES

3813   Kanakuru, or Dera and Jera. In *Notes on the tribes . . . by O. Temple, 2nd ed., 1922, repr. 1965*: 214–215.

3814   Maga. In *Notes on the tribes . . . by O. Temple, 2nd ed. 1922, repr. 1965*: 263.
        Notes their historical connection with the Manga.

3815   Meek, Charles Kingsley
        The Kanakuru of Shellen. In his *Tribal studies in Northern Nigeria, v. 2, 1931*: 311–331, illus.
        Kanakuru or Dera in Adamawa Province.

3816   Nimalto. In *Notes on the tribes . . . by O. Temple, 2nd ed. 1922, repr. 1965*: 311–312.

3817   Tera. In *Notes on the tribes . . . by O. Temple, 2nd ed. 1922, repr. 1965*: 350–352.

2. LINGUISTIC STUDIES

3818   Meek, Charles Kingsley
        Hinna [vocabulary] In his *Tribal studies in Northern Nigeria, v. 2, 1931*: 422–427.
        With photograph of a Hinna.

3819   —Jerra (or Jera) vocabulary. In his *Tribal studies in Northern Nigeria, v. 2, 1931*: 416–422.
        With photograph of a Jera.

3820   —Kanukuru vocabulary. In his *Tribal studies in Northern Nigeria, v. 2, 1931*: 325–331.

3821   —Tera vocabulary. In his *Tribal studies in Northern Nigeria, v. 2. 1931*: 428–433.
        With photograph of a Tera.

3822   Newman, Paul
        A word list of Tera. *J.W. Afr. lang.*, 1 (2) 1964: 33–50, bibliog.

JUKUN

(Jukon, Kororofawa)

Including:

Bashar

Dampar
Garaga

Jibu *(Dschubu, Jibawa, Jubawa, Jubu)*
Kam
Kona

1. GENERAL AND ETHNOGRAPHIC STUDIES

3823   Bashar. In *Notes on the tribes . . . by O. Temple, 2nd ed., 1922, repr. 1965*: 39–40.

3824   Crowder, Michael
        The end of an empire. *Nig. mag.*, (64) Mar. 1960: 56–71, illus.
        Excursion into Jukun history from

the 17th century when it was at the
height of its power.

3825 Dampar. In *Notes on the tribes . . . by
O. Temple, 2nd ed., 1922, repr. 1965*:
94.

3826 Garaga. In *Notes on the tribes . . . by O.
Temple, 2nd ed., 1922, repr. 1965*: 115.

3827 Hogben, Sidney John
The Jukuns. In his *Mohammadan
emirates of Nigeria, 1960*: 196–199.
Origin, history, religion and magical
beliefs.

3828 Jukon or Kororofawa. In *Notes on the
tribes . . . by O. Temple, 2nd ed., 1922,
repr. 1965*: 172–178.

3829 Kirk-Greene, Anthony Hamilton Millard
Jukun. In his *Adamawa past and present,
1958*: 15–16.
Short historical notes on the Jukun
empire.

3830 Kona. In *Notes on the tribes . . . by
O. Temple, 2nd ed., 1922, repr. 1965*:
236–238.

3831 Lane, Michael G. M.
The Aku-Ahwa and Aku-Maga post-
burial rites of the Jukun peoples of
Northern Nigeria. *Afr. mus.*, (2) 1959:
29–32, illus.; *Nig. field*, 25 (3) Jl. 1960:
100–103.
Explains the two cults and describes
their celebration.

3832 Meek, Charles Kingsley
The Jibu. In his *Tribal studies in
Northern Nigeria, v. 2, 1931*: 499–519.
Ethnographic report on the Jibu
(Jibawa or Jubawa) a sub-tribe of the
Jukun.

3833 —The Kam. In his *Tribal studies in
Northern Nigeria, v. 2, 1931*: 538–550.

3834 —A Sudanese kingdom: an ethnographical study of the Jukun-speaking
peoples of Nigeria. With an introduction
by H. R. Palmer. London, K. Paul,
Trench, Trubner, 1931. xxxiii, 548p.
front., illus.

3835 Palmer, Herbert Richmond
Notes on the Korôrofawa and Jukun.
J. Afr. soc., 11 (44) Jl. 1912: 401–415.
Ethnographic sketch.

3836 Riad, Mohamed
The Jukun: an example of African
migrations in the sixteenth century.
Wiener Völkerkdl. Mitt., n.F., 2 (1–4)
1959: 37–44.
Traces origin of Jukun ruling class
and their migrations from Egypt to the
Lake Chad region and thence to their
present location.

3837 — Les Jukun: exemple de migrations
africaines au seizième siècle. *Bull.
IFAN*, 22 (3–4) 1960: 478–485.
French translation of [3836].

3837a Ruxton, U. F. H.
Notes on the tribes of the Muri Province.
See [2183].

3838 Tamuno, Tekena Nitonye
The Jukon. In *A thousand years of West
African history, ed. J. F. A. Ajayi and
I. Espie, 1965*: 201–204, map.

3840 Young, Michael W.
The divine kingship of the Jukun: a
re-evaluation of some theories. *Africa*,
36 (2) April 1966: 135–153.

2. LINGUISTIC STUDIES

3841 Fraser, W. K.
Vocabulary of the Jukon language
(English-Jukon & Jukon-English)
Zungeru, Government printing office,
1908. (i) 38p.
Author was Assistant Resident,
Bornu Province.

3842 Gba bi Karatu. [Zaria, NORLA, 1958]
36p.
Educational pamphlet in Jukon.

3843 Gba bi lasafi. [Zaria, NORLA, 1955]
31p.
Educational pamphlet in Jukon.

3844 Lukari, Abdu Garba
Aco bu karatu. [Zaria, NORLA, 1955]
27p.
Educational pamphlet in Jukon.

3845 Meek, Charles Kingsley
Kam vocabulary. In his *Tribal studies in
Northern Nigeria, v. 2, 1931*: 547–550.

3846 —Schedules of words and phrases in
the various Jukun dialects. In his *A
Sudanese kingdom, 1931*: 499–533.

KADARA

(Adara)

Including:

Kajuru (Ajure)

GENERAL AND ETHNOGRAPHIC
STUDIES

3847 Gunn, Harold D.
Kajuru (Ajure) Kadara (Adara) Kuturmi
(Ada). In his *Pagan peoples of the
central area of N. Nigeria, 1956*: 122–
137.

3848 Kadara. In *Notes on the tribes . . . by O.
Temple, 2nd ed., 1922, repr. 1965*: 179–
180.

Katurmi (Ada)

3849 Smith, Michael Garfield
Secondary marriage in Northern Nigeria.
Africa, 23 (4) Oct. 1953: 298–323.
Describes some of the customs of
the Kadara and Kagoro tribes in Zaria
Province, especially their marriage
customs. The institution of secondary
marriage is specially noted, and the
effect on it of recent legislation indicated.

KAGORO

(Agolok)

1. GENERAL AND ETHNOGRAPHIC STUDIES

3850 Gunn, Harold D.
Kagoro (Agolok) and Kafanchan. In his *Pagan peoples of the central area of N. Nigeria, 1956*: 88–103.
See also pp. 65–71.

3851 Kagoro. In *Notes on the tribes . . . by O. Temple, 2nd ed., 1922, repr. 1965*: 185–192.

3852 Meek, Charles Kingsley
The Kagoro. In his *Tribal studies in Northern Nigeria, v. 2, 1931*: 90–100, illus.

—The Katab and their neighbours. See [4056].

3853 Pageard, R.
Notes sur les Kagoro et la chefferie de Sora. *J. Soc. Afr.*, 29 (2) 1959: 261–272.

3854 Smith, Michael Garfield
Kagoro political development. *Human organization*, 19 (3) fall 1960: 137–149.
Sketch of the Kagoro, and of their political and administrative organization under the British.
—Secondary marriage in Northern Nigeria. See [3849].

3855 Tremearne, Arthur John Newman
Notes on the Kagoro and other Nigerian head-hunters. *J.R.A.I.*, 42, 1912: 136–199, illus. (plates & text figures)
Extensive ethnographic notes on the Kagoro, Moroa, Attakka, Katab and Kajji.

3856 —The tailed head-hunters of Nigeria; an account of an official's seven years' experience in the Northern Nigerian pagan belt, and a description of the manners, habits and customs of the native tribes. London, Seeley, Service, 1912. 341p. front., illus., map.

2. LINGUISTIC STUDIES

3857 Meek, Charles Kingsley
Kagoro [vocabulary] In his *Tribal studies in Northern Nigeria, v. 2, 1931*: 98–100.

KALERI

Including:

Mada
Mama

Numana
Nungu *(Lungu)*

GENERAL AND ETHNOGRAPHIC STUDIES

3858 Fiévet, Maurice and Fiévet, Jeannette M.
Les nègres rouges. [Les Kaléri de Jos] [Paris] B. Arthaud, 1955. 100 [8]p. illus., map.

3859 Kaleri. In *Notes on the tribes . . . by O. Temple, 2nd ed., 1922, repr. 1965*: 198.

3860 Mada. In *Notes on the tribes . . . by O. Temple, 2nd ed., 1922, repr. 1965*: 260–263.

3861 Mama. In *Notes on the tribes . . . by O. Temple, 2nd ed., 1922, repr. 1965*: 267–270.

3862 Matthews, H. F.
Duodecimal numeration in Northern Nigeria. *Nig. field*, 29 (4) Oct. 1964: 188–191.
Describes the duodecimal system of numeration among the Nungu, Mama, Mada, Numana, Mawa and other tribes around the southwestern edge of the Bauchi Plateau, and suggests the system might have been introduced to them by Germanic sailors and Norsemen who after the fall of the Roman empire could have reached this region via the Atlantic and the Niger in search of tin.

3863 Ogbe, G. A. E.
Some notes on land-use by the Mada tribes in Southern Division, Plateau Province. *Farm and forest*, 10, 1950: 64–66.

KAMBARI
(Kambali, Kamberi)
Including:

Abadi
Achifawa *(Achipawa, Atshefawa, Atsifawa)*
Agadi

Ashingini
Dukawa
Kimba
Mawuchi

1. GENERAL AND ETHNOGRAPHIC STUDIES

3864   Atsifawa or Achipawa. In *Notes on the tribes . . . by O. Temple, 2nd ed., 1922, repr. 1965*: 30–31.

3865   Clarke, J. C. O.
Dukawa. In *Gazetteer of the Kontagora Province, by E. C. Duff, 1920*: 62–65.
Ethnographic notes.

3866   —Kamberri. In *Gazetteer of the Kontagora Province, by E. C. Duff, 1920*: 65–67.
Ethnographic notes.

3867   Conant, Francis P.
Kambari (Abadi [Evadi] Agadi [Isanga] Ashinginni, Kimba, Mawuchi, et. al.) In *Peoples of the middle Niger region, Northern Nigeria, by H. D. Gunn and F. P. Conant, 1960*: 21–29.

3868   —Dukawa. In *Peoples of the middle Niger region, Northern Nigeria, by H. D. Gunn and F. P. Conant, 1960*: 49–54.
Ethnographic notes.

3869   Dukawa. In *Notes on the tribes . . . by O. Temple, 2nd ed., 1922, repr. 1965*: 96–100.

3870   Gunn, Harold D.
Achipawa (Achifawa, Atsifawa) In his *Peoples of the middle Niger region, Northern Nigeria, 1960*: 55–62.
Ethnographic notes.

3871   Hermon-Hodge, Henry Baldwin

Customs of the Kamberri. In his *Gazetteer of Ilorin Province, 1929*: 51–53.

3872   Kamberri. In *Notes on the tribes . . . by O. Temple, 2nd ed., 1922, repr. 1965*: 198–204.

3873   Meek, Charles Kingsley
Pot-burial in Nigeria. *Man*, 32 Je. 1932: 138 (art. 160).
Describes the custom of pot-burial among the Achifawa, Makangara, Kamuku, Ngwo; Kamberi in Niger and Sokoto Provinces, and among a number of communities in Dikwa district.

2. LINGUISTIC STUDIES

3874   Bertho, Jacques
Le groupe Kambéri. *Bull. IFAN.*, 14 (1) Jan. 1952: 264–266.
See also [1406].

3875   Hoffmann, Carl F.
The noun class system of central Kambari. *J. Afr. lang.*, 2 (2) 1963: 160–169.

3876   —A word list of central Kambari. *J. W. Afr. lang.*, 2 (2) 1965: 7–31.

3877   Krause, Gottlob Adolf
Beiträge zum Märchenschatz der Afrikaner. *Globus*, 72, 1899: 229–233; 254–258.
On Tši-šingini (Shingini) a language spoken by the Ashingini in Kontagoro Division, Northern Nigeria. Includes Tši-šingini texts.

KAMUKU
(Kamugu)
Including:

Baushi
Ngwoi *(Ngwo)*

Pongo *(Arringeu)*
Ura *(Uru)*

GENERAL AND ETHNOGRAPHIC STUDIES

3878   Fitzpatrick, Joseph F. J.
Customs of pagan tribes in the Kwongoma district of N. Nigeria. *J. Afr. soc.*, 11 (43) Apr. 1912: 332–338.
Customs of the Kamuku and Pongo tribes.

3879   Gunn, Harold D.
Peoples of the Kamugu group. In his *Peoples of the middle Niger region, N. Nigeria, 1960*: 62–67.

Ethnographic notes on the Kamugu, Baushi, Ngwoi (or Ngwo) Pongo, Ura, etc.

3880   Baushi. In *Notes on the tribes . . . by O. Temple, 2nd ed., 1922, repr. 1965*: 55–58.
Ethnographic notes on the Baushi and Arringeu.

3881   Kamuku. In *Notes on the tribes . . . by O. Temple, 2nd ed., 1922, repr. 1965*: 205–214.
Meek, Charles Kingsley
Pot burial in Nigeria. See [3873].

KANURI
(Kanoury)
Including:

Bede *(Bedde)*
Gamergu
Jetko
Kanembu *(Hamedj)*
Kotoko
Lerewa
Maguemi *(Magomi)*

Magumi
Mandara *(Ndara, Wandala, Wandara)*
Manga *(Mangawa)*
Mobber *(Mober)*
Nguzzur
Tubu

1. GENERAL

3882 Alexander, Boyd
Lake Chad. *J. Afr. soc.*, 7 (27) Apr.
1908: 225–238.
The Alexander-Gosling Expedition
(for a full account of which, see [102])
spent a considerable time in the Lake
Chad region. In this paper read before
the African Society on 17th Feb. 1908,
the author briefly reviews the work of
the Expedition on the Lake.

3883 Association for promoting the discovery
of the interior parts of Africa.
Proceedings, 1788–1810. vol. 1. 1810.
pp. 127–161.
Extensive account of life in Bornu.

3884 Barth, Heinrich
Travels and discoveries in North and
Central Africa. 1857. 5v. [125].
There are extensive accounts relating
to Bornu (and Kanem) of much historical and ethnographic interest, especially
in v. 2. pp. 197–350 and v. 3. pp. 1–185.

3885 Bernard, Augustin
La Nigéria, le Cameroun et la région
du Tchad. In *Géographie universelle.
vol. xi. Afrique septentrionale, par
Augustin Bernard, 1939*: 488–511, illus.,
maps.
A condensed geographical account
of the region.

3886 *Beurmann, von
Brief an Herrn Dr. H. Barth über einen
Ausflug um das Wadi Scherki und
seine Abreise nach Bornou. *Z. f.
allgemeine Erdkde.*, 1862: 321– ?

3887 *Blau, O.
Chronik der Sultane von Bornu. *Z.
deutschen morgem. Ges.*, 2, 1852: 305– ?

3888 Botting, Douglas
The knights of Bornu. London, Hodder
& Stoughton, 1961. 158p. illus., maps.

3889 Carrique, *Captain*
Notice sur la "Ville inconnue"
découverte à N'Galaka (Borkou) *J.S.
afr.*, 5 (1) 1935: 89–92, maps, illus.

3890 Decorse, Jules
Du Congo au lac Tchad: la brousse telle
qu'elle est, les gens tels qu'ils s'ont;
carnet de route. Paris, Asselin et
Houseau, 1906. vii, 347p. port.
At head of title: Mission Chari—Lac
Tchad, 1902–1904.

3891 Destenave,
Deux ans de commandement dans la
région du Tchad. *Rev. géog.*, 53, 1903:
4–13.

3892 —Le lac Tchad, le lac, ses affluents, les
archipels, les habitants, la faune, la
flore. *Rev. générale des sciences*, 14,
1903: 649–662; 717–727.

3893 D'Huart,
Le Tchad et ses habitants. Notes de
géographie physique et humaine. *La
géog.*, 9 (3) Mar. 1904: 161–176.

3894 Duisburg, Adolf von
Untersuchungen einiger Bornu-Namen.
Anthropos, 22, 1927: 563–568.

3895 —Untersuchungen über die Bedeutung
einiger Bornu-Namen. *Anthropos*, 26,
1931: 563–568.

3896 Dybowski, Jean
La route du Tchad; du Loango au
Chari. Paris, Librairie de Firmin-Didot,
1893. 3 p.l., 380p. illus., map.

3897 Ellison, R. E.
Three forgotten explorers of the later
half of the 19th century with special
reference to their journeys to Bornu.
J. Hist. soc. Nig., 1 (4) Dec. 1959: 322–
330.

3898 Gentil, Emile
La chute de l'empire de Rabah. Paris,
1902. [3] iv, 308p. illus., map.

3899 Guilleux, Charles
Journal de route d'un caporal de
tirailleurs de la Mission Saharienne
(Mission Foureau-Lamy) 1898–1900.
[Belfort, Impr. J. Spitzmuller] 1904.
398p.

3900 Gumprecht, Theo. E.
Barth und Overwegs Untersuchungs-
Reise nach dem Tschadsee und in das
innere Afrika. Berlin, Bei Simon
Schropp, 1852. 212p. maps.
Correspondence of Barth and
Overweg written in 1850–1851 during
their exploration to Lake Chad and
other parts of Central Africa.

3901 Hallam, W. K. R.
The Chad basin. *Nig. mag.*, (91) Dec.
1966: 255–264, illus.

3902 —Komadugu Yobe: the first and last river. *Nig. mag.*, (76) Mar. 1963: 4–15, illus., map.
Includes historical notes on the So, the Bulala and the Kanem-Bornu empire.

3903 —Rabeh: the tyrant of Bornu, *Nig. mag.*, (86) Sept. 1965: 164–175, illus.
A biography of Rabeh.

3904 Kirk-Greene, Anthony Hamilton Millard
The British consulate at Lake Chad: a forgotten treaty with the Sheikh of Bornu. *Afr. affairs*, 58 (233) Oct. 1959: 334–339.

3905 Konrad, W.
Die Wasserfahrzeuge der Tschadsee-Region. *Baessler-Archiv*, 5 (1) 1957: 121–143.

3906 Lebeuf, Jean-Paul
Les Kotoko, citadins et pêcheurs de la région Tchadienne. *Int. W. Afr. conf. proc., 3rd, 1949. 1956*: 297–302.

3907 Lippert, Julius
Rabah. *M.S.O.S.*, 2, 1899: 242–256.
Biographical notes. Includes Muhammed Beschir's account of Rabeh in Arabic, with German translation, pp. 251–256.

3908 Lukas, Johannes
Reise durch Bornu (Nigerien) und Nordkamerun. *Afr. u. Übersee*, 37, 1952: 5–6.

3909 Macleod, Olive
Journey to Lake Chad. *Trans. Liv. geog. soc.*, 1911: 8–20, illus.

3910 Mercier, *Le commandant.*
La mission de ravitaillement du Tchad par Kano, jan. 1912–déc. 1913. *Rens. col.*, 1914: 261–282.

3911 Migeod, Frederick William Hugh
Some notes on the Lake Chad region in British territory. *Geog. j.*, 60 (5) Nov. 1922: 347–359.

3912 —Through Nigeria to Lake Chad. London, Heath, Cranton, 1924. 330p. illus., maps.
Account of a tour of Nigeria. Gives ethnological and historical observations on Bornu, and geological notes on Lake Chad.

3913 *—Nachtigal, Gustav
Ankunft in Kuka. *Petermanns Mitt.*, 1871: 67– ?

3914 *—Das Becken des Tsade und seine Bewohner. *Z. Ges. f. Erkde. z. Berlin*, 1877: 30–88, map.

3915 *—Meine Reise von Murzuk nach Kuka, 1870. *Petermanns Mitt.*, 1871: 450– ?

3916 *—Nachrichten von Dr. Nachtigal in Kuka, bis Januar 1871. *Petermanns Mitt.*, 1871: 326– ?

3917 —Reise nach dem Barch-el-ghazal, Kanem, Egai, Bodele, und Borku. *Petermanns Mitt.*, 1873: 201–206.

3918 *—Reise von Kanem nach Borku. *Z. Ges. f. Erkde. z. Berlin*, 8, 1873: 61– ?; 141–158.

3919 *—Voyage au Bornou et au Bagirmi en 1872. *Tour du monde*, 1880. 2e sér.

3920 —Voyage dans l'Afrique centrale (1869–1874) *Bull. Soc. géog., 6e sér.*, 2, 1876: 129–277.

3921 Ness, Patrick (Mrs.)
Lake Chad picnic. *J.R.A.S.*, 40 (161) Oct. 1941: 316–326, illus.
Notes on her journey to Lake Chad in 1930.

3922 Nzekwu, Onuora
From Maiduguri to Lake Chad. *Nig. mag.*, (79) Dec. 1963: 234–247, illus., map.

3923 Palmer, Herbert Richmond
Gazetteer of Bornu Province. Revised by J. B. Welman. Lagos, Govt. printer, 1929. ii, 112p. map, bibliog.

3924 Petermann, A.
Dr. Eduard Vogels Reise nach Central-Afrika . . . Reise von Tripoli . . . bis zum Tsad-See, März 1853—Januar 1854.
Petermanns Mitt., 1855: 237–259.
Account of his journey from Tripoli to Kuka.

3925 —Dr. H. Barth's Reise von Kuka nach Timbuktu. *Petermanns Mitt.*, 1855: 3–14.

3926 Rohlfs, Gerhard
Quer durch Afrika. Reise vom Mittelmeer nach dem Tschadsee und zum Golf von Guinea. Leipzig, Brockhaus, 1874–1875. 2 vols.
v. 1. 352p. map.
v. 2. 248p. map.

3927 —Reise durch Nord-Afrika vom mittelländischen Meer bis zum Busen von Guinea, 1865 bis 1867. *Petermanns Geog. Mitt., Ergänzungsheft*, no. 25, 1867–68: 1–75, map; no. 34, 1871–72: 1–124, maps.
Account of his journey west of Lake Chad. Part I traces his journey from start to arrival at Kuka, including (from p. 46 onwards) description of Lake Chad area, Kuka town and market, his reception at Kuka, government and organisation of Bornu. Part II describes his trip to Vandela (Mandara) and back and traces his journey to Lagos which he did via the Benue to Gbebe, and then up the Niger to Rabbah, and finally southward through Ilorin to Lagos.

3928 *Sabatier, F.
Les territories du lac Tchad, *Bull. Soc. géog. de Marseille*, 29, 1905: 295– ?

3929 Schultze, Arnold
Das Sultanat Bornu, mit besonderer Berücksichtigung von Deutsch-Bornu, Essen, Baedeker, 1910. [iv] 136p. map, bibliog.
A useful work on the history, geography and people of the area by a member of the Anglo-German Commission for the Yola-Chad boundary.

3930 —The Sultanate of Bornu: translated from the German, with additions and appendices by P. Askell Benton. London, New York, etc., H. Milford, 1913, repr. London, Frank Cass, 1968. 401p. maps, bibliog.

3931 *Seetzen, de
Un récit recueilli au Caïre pres d'un bornouan. *Annales des voyages*, 19, 1812: 164– ?

3932 White, Stanhope
Descent from the hills. London, J. Murray, 1963. 231p.
A novel set among the Wakara, Buhe and other clans on the Mandara mountains.

2. PHYSICAL ANTHROPOLOGY

3933 Roberts, D. F. [and others]
Abnormal haemoglobins in Bornu (West Africa). *Amer. j. physical anthrop.*, 18 (1) Mar. 1960: 5–11.

3. SOCIAL AND CULTURAL ANTHROPOLOGY, ETHNOGRAPHY

(i) General

3934 Bedde. In *Notes on the tribes . . . by O. Temple, 2nd ed., 1922, repr. 1965*: 59–61.

3935 Carbou, Henri
La région du Tchad et du Ouadai. Paris, Leroux, 1912. 2v. in 1. map. (Faculté des lettres d'Alger. Bulletin de correspondance africaine, 47–48).
v. 1 Études ethnographiques, 378p.- is especially relevant, pp. 1–104 dealing with Kanem. v. 2. 272p.

3936 Denham, Dixon
Narrative of travels and discoveries in Northern and Central Africa . . . 1826. [192].
The first 335 pages are especially relevant to Bornu, with a supplementary chapter (pp. 314–335) devoted to a brief but comprehensive account of the general, economic and socio-cultural conditions.

3937 Devallée
Le Baghirmi. *Bull. Soc. rech. cong.*, (7) 1925: 3–76.
A comprehensive survey, including history and ethnography.

3938 Duisburg, Adolf von
Beiträge zur Volkskunde der Kanuri. *Kol. runds.*, 1932: 238–245; 1933: 15–22.

3939 —Gestalten des Mittelmeer-Sagenkreises in einem Bornu-Märchen? *Kol. runds.*, 1929: 322–327.

3940 —Im Lande des Cheghu von Bornu; Despoten und Völker südlich des Tschad. Berlin, D. Reimer, 1942. [xi] 162p. front., illus., map.

3941 *Fouqué
Le Kanem. *Rev. troupes col.*, 1900: 326–356.

3942 *—Le Kanem. *Mois col. mar.*, 1904: 535–544; 1905: 9–22.

3943 Gaillard, Raoul Clair and Poutrin, Léon
Étude anthropologique des populations des régions du Tchad et du Kanem. Paris, E. Larose, 1914. 111p. illus., map.

3944 Gamergu. In *Notes on the tribes . . . by O. Temple, 2nd ed., 1922, repr. 1965*: 113.

3945 Kanembu and their off-shoots the Jetkos, Magumi, Tubu and Mobber. In *Notes on the tribes . . . by O. Temple, 2nd ed., 1922, repr. 1965*: 215–217.

3946 Kanuri. In *Notes on the tribes . . . by O. Temple, 2nd ed., 1922, repr. 1965*: 217–222.

3947 Kirk-Greene, Anthony Hamilton Millard
A note on some spears from Bornu, Northern Nigeria. *Man*, 63, Nov. 1963: 174–176, illus., bibliog.

3948 Krause, Gottlob Adolf
Zur Völkerkunde Nordafrikas. 1. Die Teda und Kanuri. 2. Teda und die Garamanten. *Z. geog. Ges.*, 1876: 21–36.

3949 Lebeuf, Jean-Paul
Les bijoux parlants des femmes Kanouri. *La terre et la vie*, 9e année (4) Jl.–Aug. 1939: 124.

3950 Leo Africanus
Of the kingdome of Borno. In his *The history and description of Africa . . . 1896*: vol. 3, pp. 832–834.
See also explanatory notes to Leo's text on pp. 850–851.

3951 Lerewa. In *Notes on the tribes . . . by O. Temple, 2nd ed., 1922, repr. 1965*: 258.

3952 Lukas, Johannes
Mitteilungen über die Stämme und Sprache der östlichen Kanembu (Tschadseegebiet.) *Afr. u. Übersee*, 43, 1959: 106–115.

3953 Mandara. In *Notes on the tribes . . . by O. Temple, 2nd ed., 1922, repr. 1965*: 270.

3954 Manga. In *Notes on the tribes . . . by O. Temple, 2nd ed., 1922, repr. 1965*: 270–271.

3955 Mouchet, J.
Prospections ethnologiques sommaires de quelques massifs du Mandara. *Bull Soc. étud. cam.*, (17–18) 1947: 99–139; (19–20); 93–104; (21–22) 1948: 105–119.
Title varies slightly in 2nd and 3rd instalments.

3956 Nachtigal, Gustav
Sahara und Sudan. Ergebnisse sechsjähriger Reisen in Afrika. Berlin, Weidmann, 1879–1881. 2v. illus., maps, facsims.
Important for the history and description of Kahem, Bornu, Borku and Bagirmi.

3957 Nguzzur. In *Notes on the tribes . . by O. Temple, 2nd ed., 1922, repr. 1965*: 311.

3958 *Smith, Henry Frederick Charles
An early 18th century school textbook from Bornu. *Hist. soc. Nig. Bull. of news*, 4 (4) Mar. 1960.

3. (ii) History

3959 Ahmed ibn Fartua
History of the first twelve years of the

reign of Mai Idris Alooma of Bornu (1571–1583) by his Imam, Ahmed ibn Fartua. Together with the "Diwan of the Sultans of Bornu" and "Girgam" of the Magumi. Translated from the Arabic, with introduction and notes by H. R. Palmer. Lagos, Government printer, 1926, repr. London, Frank Cass, 1969. [iv] 121p. map.

Reign of Mai Idris Alooma, pp 8–55; notes pp. 56–83; Diwan of the Sultans of Bornu, pp. 84–91; Girgam of the Magumi mais, pp. 92–101; with two additional notes, one on the early Barbar cults of the Sahara and Sudan (Girgam no. 17) pp. 102–116; and the other on Yam (Girgam no. 18) pp. 117–121.

3960 *Barth, Heinrich
Tarik Mai Idris, being the typed transcript of Bornu Arabic manuscripts brought to Europe in 1855 from Bornu by Barth. Kaduna, Emir of Kano's press, 1932. ix, 137p.

3961 Benton, P. Askell
A Bornu almanac for the year A.D. 1916 (A.H. 1334 and Part of 1335) London, O.U.P., 1916. 119p. Reprinted in vol. II of *The languages and peoples of Bornu, being a collection of the writings of P. A. Benton.* With an introduction by A. H. M. Kirk-Greene. London, Frank Cass, 1968. 2v.

3962 Bivar, A. D. H. and Shinnie, P. L.
Old Kanuri capitals. *J. Afr. hist.*, 3 (1) 1962: 1–10, illus., map, plans.
Description of six sites in Nigeria, Niger Republic and Chad Republic believed to have been chief centres of Kanuri settlements at various periods in the past. Based on expedition to some of these sites by the authors in 1959.

3962a Cohen, Ronald
The just—so So? A spurious tribal grouping in Western Sudanic history. See [4238].

3963 Crocquevieille, J.
Histoire de l'islamisation du Tchad. *Tropiques,* [Paris] 55 (393) 1957– : 9–19.

3963a Fartua, Ahmed ibn. See Ahmed ibn Fartua.

3964 Gaden, Henri and Verneau, R.
Stations et sepultures néolithiques du territoire militaire, du Tchad. *L'Anthropologie,* 30, 1920: 513–543.

3965 Gana, A. J.
Notes on the history and origin of Bornu. Zaria, Gaskiya corporation, 1965. 54p. illus., map.

3966 Glenny, H. Q.
Notes on the history of Miga. *Afr. affairs,* 48 (193) Oct. 1949: 323–328.
History of Miga, a small town on the Hadejia River, as told by a Miga courtier. Covers the period 1170–1900, with a blank between 1208 and 1807.

3967 Hodgkin, Thomas
Kanem and Northern Nigeria; remarks on the history of Northern Nigeria. *W. Afr. rev.,* 30 (378) Mar. 1959: 169–171.
Brief historical sketch of Kanem-Bornu and other old empires of Northern Nigeria.

3968 Hogben, Sidney John
Kanem and the Bornu empire. In *Muhammadan emirates of Nigeria, by S. J. Hogben, 1930*: 35–40, map.

3968a Ibn Fartua, Ahmed. See Ahmed ibn Fartua.

3969 Ifemesia, C. Chieka
Bornu under the Shehus. In *A thousand years of West African history, ed. J. F. A. Ajayi and I. Espie, 1965*: 284–293.

3970 —States of the Central Sudan: I. Kanem-Bornu. In *A thousand years of West African history, ed. J. F. A. Ajayi and I. Espie, 1965*: 72–90.

3971 Joalland, Paul
De Zinder au Tchad, et conquête du Kanem. *La Géog.,* 3, 1901: 369–380.

3972 Kirk-Greene, Anthony Hamilton Millard
Capitals of Bornu. *W. Afr. rev.,* 33 (415) Jl. 1962: 37–45, illus.

3973 —Maiduguri and the capitals of Bornu. Zaria, NORLA, 1958.

3974 Landeroin, Moïse Augustin
Du Tchad au Niger—notice historique. In *Documents scientifiques de la Mission Tilho (1906–09) vol. 2, 1911*: 309–352, illus.

3975 Lanier, H.
L'ancien royaume du Baghirmi: histoire et coûtumes. *Rev. col.,* 35, 1925: 457–474.
Useful on the relationship between Bornu and Baghirmi.

3976 La Roncière, C. de
Une histoire du Bornou au XVIIe siècle, par un chirurgien français captif à Tripoli. *Rev. hist. col. franc.,* 1919: 73–88.

3977 Lebeuf, Jean-Paul
Le royaume du Kanem. In *Les populations du Tchad (Nord du 10e parallèle) 1959*: 33–60, map.
Ethnographic survey.

3978 —La civilisation du Tchad. *Int. W. Afr. conf. proc., 3rd, 1949. 1956*: 293–296.

3979 —Contribution à l'étude de l'histoire de la région tchadienne et considérations sur la méthode. In *The historian in tropical Africa, ed. by J. Vansina and others, 1964*: 239–253.
A review of archaeological investigations in the Chad-Cameroons region.

3980 —Prehistory, proto-history and history in Chad. *J. Hist. soc. Nig.,* 2 (4) Dec. 1963: 593–601.

3981 Lebeuf, Jean-Paul and Masson-Detourbet, Annie
La civilization du Tchad; suivi d'une étude sur les bronzes Sao par Raymond Lantier. Paris, Payot, 1950. 198p. illus., maps, bibliog. (Bibliothéque scientifique).

3982 Letchworth, Thomas Elwin and Patterson, John Robert
Bornu. In *Ency. Brit., 1960*: v. 3 pp. 914–916.
Brief general sketch of Bornu, including a summary of the history of the ancient empire.

3982a Malem, Malem Kaka.
Kitabu kanugumi. See [4042].

3983 Martin, B. G.
Five letters from the Tripoli archives. *J. Hist. soc. Nig.*, 2 (3) Dec. 1962: 350–372, illus.
Description, with commentaries, of five letters dating from 1842 to 1870, in the Tripoli archives and bearing on the relations between Tripoli and Bornu in the 19th century. The illustrations are photographs of the five letters.

3984 Migeod, Frederick William Hugh
Arab origins at Garun Gabbas. *Man*, 23, Je. 1923: 92–93 (art. 55).
Records the tradition that Garun Gabbas, a small town about 12 miles north of Hadeija and Daura, were founded by Arabs from Syria. Appends a Garun Gabbas kings list.

3985 Palmer, Herbert Richmond
The Bornu girgam. *J. Afr. soc.*, 12 (45) Oct. 1912: 71–83.
English translation of a Kanuri girgam or chronicle. Kanuri and English texts on opposite pages.

3986 —A Bornu mahram and the pre-Tunjur rulers of Wadai. *Sudan notes*, 5 (4) 1922: 197–199.

3987 —The Bornu Sahara and Sudan. London, John Murray, 1936. viii, 296p. illus., maps.

3988 —The central Sahara and Sudan in the twelfth century A.D. *J. Afr. soc.*, 28 (112) Jl. 1929: 368–378.

3989 —History of the first twelve years of the reign of Mai Idris Alooma of Bornu. See Ahmed Ibn Fartua.

3990 —Kanuri girgam of the Magumi Mais (Sultans) in possession of Mai Mufio. In *History of the first twelve years of the reign of Mai Idris Alooma of Bornu, by Ahmed ibn Fartua, 1926*, repr. 1969: 92–101.

3991 —The kingdom of Gaoga of Leo Africanus. *J. Afr. soc.*, 29 (115) Apr. 1930: 280–284; (116) Jl. 1930: 350–369, map.

3992 —A Muslim divine of the Sudan in the fifteenth century. *Africa*, 3 (2) Apr. 1930: 203–216.
Introductory commentary on, and a translation of an Arabic manuscript dealing with the time and reign of Ali Gaji Dunamami, a Sultan or Mai of Bornu who is believed to have ruled from A.D. 1472–1504.

3993 —Note on the early Barbar cults of the Sahara and Sudan. (Girgam No. 17) In *History of the first twelve years of the reign of Mai Idris Alooma of Bornu, by Ahmed ibn Fartua, 1926*, repr. 1969: 102–116. [3959].

3994 —Sudanese memoirs: being mainly translations of a number of Arabic manuscripts relating to the Central and Western Sudan. Lagos, Government printer, 1928, 3v., repr. 3v. in 1, London. Frank Cass, 1967. fronts., illus. (incl. ports.) maps.
Volume one is a translation of the account of Mai Idris Alooma's wars with Kanem as recorded by Imam Ahmed ibn Fartua, with a useful introduction dealing with the historical background of Kanem-Bornu. Volume two contains translations of the legends and traditions of Kanem-Bornu and other groups in the Chad region. Volume three continues with these translations and includes others concerned with the Hausa states to the west.

3995 Panikkar, K. Madhu
The empire of Bornu Kanem and the Haussa states. In his *The serpent and the crescent: a history of the negro empires of Western Africa, 1963*: 96–119.
A general account.

3996 Urvoy, Yves François Marie Aimé
Chronologie du Bornou. *J. Soc. afr.*, 11 (1–2) 1941: 21–32.

3997 —Histoire de l'empire du Bornou. Paris, Librairie Larose, 1949. 166p. maps (Mémoires de l'IFAN, no. 7).
Traces succinctly the course of Kanem-Bornu history from the 8th to the 19th century.

3998 Vossart, J.
Histoire du Sultanat du Mandara, province de l'empire du Bornou. *Etud. cam.*, 35–36, 1952: 19–52.

3999 Whitting, C. E. J.
Bornu. In *Encyclopaedia of Islam, ed. H. A. R. Gibb (and others) v. 1, 1960*: 1259–1261, bibliog.

3. (iii) Marriage, Family

4000 Bouillié, Robert
Les coutumes familiales au Kanem. Paris, Editions Domat. Montchrestien, 1937. 359p. illus., map. bibliog. (Institut de droit comparé. Etudes de sociologie et d'ethnologie juridiques, 24).

4001 Cohen, Ronald
Marriage instability among the Kanuri of Northern Nigeria. *Amer. anthrop.*, 63 (6) Dec. 1961: 1231–1249, bibliog.
Social and cultural implications of marriage among the Kanuri are analysed and factors that often lead to marriage instability discussed.

4002 Ellison, R. E.
Marriage and child-birth among the Kanuri. *Africa*, 9 (4) Oct. 1936: 524–535.

3. (iv) Government, Social Organization and Structure

4003 Büllow, von
Bericht über politsche Verhältnisse im

mittleren Sudan. *M.S.O.S.*, 7, 1904: 263–269.

4004 Cohen, Ronald
The analysis of conflict in hierarchical systems: an example from Kanuri political organisation. *Anthropologica, n.s.*, 4 (1) 1962: 87–120.

4005 —Conflict and change in a Northern Nigerian Emirate. In *Explorations in social change, ed. G. K. Zollscham and W. Hirsch, 1964*: 495–521, bibliog.
Conflict and change among the Kanuri. Revised version of [4004].

4006 —The structure of Kanuri society. 1960
Ph.D. thesis, University of Wisconsin.

4006a Duisburg, R. M.
Zur Geschichte der Sultanate Bornu und Wandala (Mandara) *Anthropos*, 22, 1927: 187–196.
Notes on social classes and stratification in the Dikwa region of Bornu emirate and on the origin of the Wandala.

4006b *Rebillet
État politique du Bornou et du Baghirmi. *C.r.Soc. geog. de Paris, 1894*: 265–266.

4006c Rosman, Abraham
Social structure and acculturation among the Kanuri of Bornu Province, Northern Nigeria. *Trans. N.Y. acad. sci., ser. 2*, 21 (7) May 1959: 620–630.

4006d —Social structure and acculturation among the Kanuri of Northern Nigeria. 1962.
Ph.D. thesis, Yale university.

3. (v) Economy, Agriculture, Trade

4006e Cohen, Ronald
Some aspects of institutionalized exchange: a Kanuri example. *Cah. etud. afr.*, 5 (3) 1965: 353–369, bibliog.

4006f —The success that failed: an experiment in cultural change in Africa. *Anthropologica*, 3 (1) 1961: 21–36.
Describes unsuccessful attempt to induce farmers in Magumeri to use superphosphate fertilizer. Suggests European orientation and youth of advisers as possible socio-cultural factors contributing to the rejection of the fertilizer.

4006g Orme-Smith, R.
Maiduguri market—Northern Nigeria. *J.R.A.S.*, 32 (148) Jl. 1938: 318–325.
A brief description of the wares and their sellers and buyers.

3. (vi) Recreation, Games, Music

4007 Alexander, D.
Dubbo-Dubbo; or Notes on Punch and Judy as seen in Bornu. *Man*, 10, 1910: 145–146 (art. 85) illus.
Notes on a play known in Bornu as Dubbo-dubbo.

4008 Ellison, R. E.
A Bornu puppet show. *Nig. field*, 40 (2) Apr. 1935: 89–91, illus.
Describes an age-old puppet show performed for entertainment in Bornu.

4009 Harris, Percy Graham
Chess in Bornu, Nigeria. *Man*, 39, 1939: 31–32 (art. 32).

4010 Meek, Charles Kingsley
Chess in Bornu, Nigeria. *Man*, 34, Mar. 1934: 33 (art. 48).
Describes a Bornu chess set, with a diagram showing arrangement and names of the pieces.

4011 Patterson, John Robert
Kanuri Songs; with a translation and introductory note by J. R. Patterson and a preface by H. R. Palmer [Lagos, Government printer, 1926] viii, 31p.

4012 Tremearne, Arthur John Newman
Nigerian strolling players. *Man*, 14, 1914: 193 (art. 95) illus.

3. (vii) Stories, Proverbs, Riddles

4013 *Bouillez
Deux légendes du Tchad. *Bull. du com, d'ét. hist. et sci. de l'A.O.F.*, 1916: 446– ?

4014 Cransac, Germaine J.
Légende de la tête qui parle, conte du pays bornouan. *Bull. Soc. rech. cong.*, (21) 1935: 111–116.

4014a Lukas, Johannes
Fabeln der Kanuri. See [4031].

4. LINGUISTIC STUDIES

4015 *Bailey,
Kanuri-English vocabulary. *J. Roy. Asiatic soc.*, 1911:

4016 Benton, P. Askell
Kanuri readings, including facsimiles of MSS., transliteration, interlinear translation and notes; also a complete English-Kanuri vocabulary and a partial Kanuri-English vocabulary. London, O.U.P., 1911. 110, [ii]p. Reprinted in vol. II of *The languages and peoples of Bornu, being a collection of the writings of P. A. Benton*. With an introduction by A. H. M. Kirk-Greene. London, Frank Cass, 1968. 2v.

4016a —Primer of Kanuri grammar. See [4022].

4017 Bible. N.T. Kanuri. John.
Bishara musko Yohannaben linjillan. [Edinburgh?] National Bible society of Scotland, 1965. 58p.
The Gospel of St. John in Kanuri.

4018 Bivar, A. D. H.
A dated Kuran from Bornu. *Nig. mag.*, (65) Je. 1960: 199–205, illus.
Notes on four copies of the Koran containing explanatory notes in Arabic script written between the lines in the Kanembu language. The illustrations show three pages of text from one of the copies.

4019 Denham, Dixon
Bornu vocabulary. In his *Narrative of travels and discoveries in Northern and Central Africa ... 1826*: 175–179.

4020 Drexel, Albert
Glenderung der afrikanischen Sprachen ... Die Bornu Sprachen. *Anthropos*, 20, 1925: 220–228.

4021 Duisburg, Adolf von
Grundriss der Kanuri-Sprache in Bornu,
zusammengestellt von A. Duisburg.
Berlin, G. Reimer, 1913. [vi] 185p.
(Archiv für das Studium deutscher
Kolonialsprachen . . . Band 15).

4022 —Primer of Kanuri grammar. (Transla-
ted and revised from the German of A.
von Duisburg) by P. A. Benton.
London, O.U.P., 1917. 130p. A transla-
tion of [4021] Reprinted in vol. II of
The languages and peoples of Bornu,
being a collection of the writings of P. A.
Benton. With an introduction by
A. H. M. Kirk-Greene. London, Frank
Cass, 1968. 2v.

4023 Ellison, R. E.
An English-Kanuri sentence book.
London, Crown agents for overseas
governments, 1937. [vii] 120p.

4024 Greenberg, Joseph Harold
Linguistic evidence for the influence of
the Kanuri on the Hausa. J. Afr. hist., 1
(2) 1960: 205–212.

4025 Homburger, Lilian
Les langues du Tchad et du Bornou. In
his Les langues négro-africaines et les
peuples qui les parlent, 1957: 39–42.

4026 Klaproth, Heinrich Julius
Essai sur la langue du Bournou, suivi
des vocabulaires du Begharmi, du
Mandara et de Timbouctou. Paris, 1826.
41p.

4027 Koelle, Sigismund Wilhelm
African native literature, or Proverbs,
tales, fables and historical fragments in
the Kanuri or Bornu language. To
which are added a translation of the
above and a Kanuri-English vocabulary.
London, Church Missionary House,
1854. xv, 434p.

4028 —Grammar of the Bornu or Kanuri
language. London, Church Missionary
House, 1854. [ix] 326p. front. (port.)

4029 Lukas, Johannes
Aus dem Leben der Kanuri ihre grossen
Tage, ihre Wohnung. Z.f.E.S., 29,
1938–39: 161–188.
Kanuri texts, with German transla-
tion.

4030 —Aus der Literatur der Badawi-
Kanuri in Borno. Z.f.E.S., 26, 1935–36:
35–57; 133–150.

4031 —Fabeln der Kanuri. Z.f.E.S., 30 (3)
1940: 161–181, 30 (4) 1940: 273–295.
Kanuri texts, with German translation. The second instalment carries a
Kanuri-German vocabulary (pp. 290–
295).

4032 —Genesis der Verbalformen im Kanuri
und Teda. Wiener Z. f. Kunde Morgen.,
34 (1 & 2) 1927: 87–104.

4033 —Kanuri-Texte. Übersetzt und bear-
beitet Johannes Lukas. M.S.O.S., 32,
1929: 41–92, i–xxvi, xxviii–xxxi.
Kanuri texts with German translation
in parallel columns, of stories written
by one Mallam Umr, a Kanuri and the
Kadi of Mobber District of Bornu.

4034 —Lautlehre des Badawi-Kanuri in
Borno. Z.f.E.S., 25 (1) 1934–5: 3–29.
On the phonetics of the Badawi
dialect of Kanuri.

4034a —Mitteilungen über die Stämme und
Sprache der östlichen Kanembu. See
[3952].

4035 —Die Sprache der Káidi-Kanembu in
Kanem. Berlin, D. Reimer, Hamburg,
Boysen, 1931. 116p. Beiheifte zur
Zeitschrift für Eingeborenen-Sprachen,
13).

4036 —Sprachenforschung in Nordnigeria
und Nordkamerun. Übersee-Rundschau,
1952: 467–468.

4037 —Sprachstudien im Tschadsee-Gebiet,
Nigerian. (Mitteilungen über die Ziele
und die vorlaufigen Ergebnisse der
linguistischen Expedition in das nord-
liche Nigerien.) Africa, 6 (4) Oct. 1933:
489–490. (Notes and news section).

4038 —Sprichwörter, Aussprüche und Rätsel
der Kanuri. Z.f.E.S., 28 (3) 1938: 161–
174.
Kanuri proverbs (Yerwa dialect) with
German translation.

4039 —A study of the Kanuri language:
grammar and vocabulary. London,
published for the International institute
of African languages and cultures by
O.U.P., 1937. xxvii, 253p.

4040 —Transition und Intransition in Kanuri.
Wien. Z.f. Kunde Morgen., 35 (3 & 4)
1928: 213–241.

4041 —Umrisse einer ostsaharanischen
Sprachgruppe. Afr. u. Übersee, 36 (1–2)
Mar. 1952: 3–8.
On the relationship between Kanuri,
Tuba and Zaghawa languages and the
need for including Zaghawa in the
Kanuri-Tubu group.

4042 Malem, Malem Kaka
Kitabu Kənugumi, Kitabu gargam
Kanəm-wa Borno-wabe Kasargata.
Kanuriro fasantəmanzə Malem Kaka
Malem. Zaria, Gaskiya corp., 1951. 80p.
(Kitabuwa Kanuribe, 5).
Summary history of Kanuri and
Bornu translated into Kanuri.

4042a *Müller, Friedrich
Die Kanuri-Sprache. In his Grundriss
der Sprachwissenschaft, 1–2, 1877: 192–
214.

4043 Noel, P.
Petit manuel français-Kanouri. Paris,
Librairie orientaliste Paul Geuthner,
1923. [iii] 130p.
In 3 parts. 1. Grammar; 2. Kanuri
texts; and 3. Kanuri-French vocabulary.

4044 Norris, Edwin
Grammar of the Bornu or Kanuri
language; with dialogue, translations,
and vocabulary. London, Printed by
Harrison & son, 1853. 1 p. 1., 101 [1] p.
—Contents:
"Dialogue [and translations] in Bornu
and English . . . transcribed from the
Bornu manuscripts sent from Africa by
the late Mr. Richardson pp. 1–46.

P

Grammatical sketch of the Bornu or Kanuri language", by Edwin Norris, pp. 47–74.
Vocabulary compiled from various sources.

4045   Prietze, Rudolf
       Bornu-Texte. *M.S.O.S.*, 33, 1930: 82–159, i–xxxii.

4046   —Bornulieder. *M.S.O.S.*, 17, 1914: 134–260.
       —Die spezifischen Verstärkungs-Adverbien im Hausa und Kanuri. See [2811].

4046a *Richardson, James
       Dialogues and a small portion of the New Testament, in the English, Arabic,

Hausa and Bornu languages. [Edited by Edwin Norris] London, printed by Harrison, 1853. 116p.

4046b —Grammar of the Bornu or Kanuri language. See [4044].

4047   *Strumpell, E.
       Worterverzeichnis der heidensprachen des Mandara-Gerbirges (Adamaua) *Z.f.E.S.*, Nov. 1922: 47–74; Jan. 1923: 109–149.

4048   Ward, Ida Caroline
       Some notes on the pronounciation of the Kanuri language of West Africa. *B.S.O.S.*, 4 (1) 1926: 139–146.
       Also offprinted. London, School of oriental studies, 1926.

KATAB

Including:

Ataka *(Attaka)*
Ikulu *(Ikolu)*
Jaba *(Ham)*
Kachichere *(Aticherak, Kachicheri)*
Kafanchan
Kagoma
Kaje *(Baju, Kache, Kaji)*

Kamantan
Kaninkon *(Tum)*
Kaura
Kentu *(Kyato, Kyeto)*
Morwa *(Asolio, Moroa)*
Yeskwa

1. GENERAL AND ETHNOGRAPHIC STUDIES

4049   Attaka. In *Notes on the tribes . . . by O. Temple, 2nd ed., 1922, repr. 1965*: 31–32.

4050   Gunn, Harold D.
       The Katab group of tribes. In his *Pagan peoples of the central area of Northern Nigeria, 1956*: 65–121, illus.
       Ethnographic notes on the Katab, Kaninkon (or Tum), Kachichere or Aticherak, Ikulu, Kamantan, Kagoro (Agolok or Agwolok), Moroa (Asolio), Ataka, Kaje (Baju) Jaba (Ham) Kagoma and Kafanchan.

4051   Jaba. In *Notes on the tribes . . . by O. Temple, 2nd ed., 1922, repr. 1965*: 162–164.

4052   Kagoma. In *Notes on the tribes . . . by O. Temple, 2nd ed., 1922, repr. 1965*: 180–185.

4053   Kaje. In *Notes on the tribes . . . by O. Temple, 2nd ed., 1922, repr. 1965*: 193–197.

4054   Katab. In *Notes on the tribes . . . by O. Temple, 2nd ed., 1922, repr. 1965*: 222.

4055   Kaura. In *Notes on the tribes . . . by O. Temple, 2nd ed., 1922, repr. 1965*: 223.

4056   Meek, Charles Kingsley
       The Katab and their neighbours. *J. Afr. soc.*, 27 (106) Jan. 1928: 104–126, (107) Apr. 1928: 269–280 (108) Jl. 1928: 364–379: 28 (109) Oct. 1928: 43–54, (111)

Apr. 1929: 265–273, (112) Jl. 1929: 385–393, illus, map.
       Ethnographic reports on the Katab, Kachichere, Moroa, Ataka, Kagoro, Kaje, Kamantan Jaba, Ikulu and Kagoma in Zaria and Plateau Provinces of Northern Nigeria. Includes short vocabularies and common phrases. Also reprinted in author's *Tribal studies in Northern Nigeria, vol. 2, 1931*: pp. 1–128.

4057   —The Kentu. In his *Tribal studies in Northern Nigeria, v. 2, 1931*: 605–623.

4058   Moroa. In *Notes on the tribes . . . by O. Temple, 2nd ed., 1922, repr. 1965*: 279–281.

4058a Tremearne, Aurthur John Newman
       Notes on the Kagoro and other Nigerian head hunters. See [3855].

4058b —The tailed head hunters of Nigeria. See [3856].

4059   Yeskwa. In *Notes on the tribes . . . by O. Temple, 2nd ed., 1922, repr. 1965*: 374–375.

2. LINGUISTIC STUDIES

4060   Meek, Charles Kingsley
       Jaba (Kwoi dialect) In his *Tribal studies in Northern Nigeria, v. 2, 1931*: 122–128.

4061   —Kachichere (a dialect of Katab) In his *Tribal studies in Northern Nigeria, v. 2, 1931*: 90.

4062 —Kaje [vocabulary] In his *Tribal studies in Northern Nigeria, v. 2, 1931*: 105–111.

4063 —Katab [vocabulary] In his *Tribal studies in Northern Nigeria, v. 2, 1931*: 81–86.

4064 —Kyâto or Kentu vocabulary. In his: *Tribal studies in Northern Nigeria, v. 2, 1931*: 616–623.

4065 —Morwa [vocabulary] In his *Tribal studies in Northern Nigeria, v. 2, 1931*: 117–119.

KOFYAR

(Kofia)

GENERAL AND ETHNOGRAPHIC STUDIES

4066 Ancient beverage center of cultural focus. *Sci. digest*, 53, Feb. 1963: 54–55.
Among the Kofyar.

4067 Netting, Robert McC.
Beer as a locus of value among the West African Kofyar. *Amer. anthrop.*, 66 (2) Apr. 1964: 375–384.

4068 —Kofyar agriculture: a study in the cultural ecology of a West African people. 1963. 227p.
Ph.D. thesis, University of Chicago. The Kofyar inhabit the Southern fringe of the Jos Plateau. Includes useful sections on family and lineage structure, land tenure, rationality and religion, and migratory farming.

KULU

Including:

Wurkum *(Urku, Wurkuru)*

GENERAL AND ETHNOGRAPHIC STUDIES

4069 Meek, Charles Kingsley
The Kulū in Northern Nigeria. *Africa*, 7 (3) Jl. 1934: 257–269.
Ethnographic notes on the people of Basak, Bambur, Jikono, Kirim,

Kwonshi, Darufwai and Bamingun, all in the Wurkum district of Adamawa Province.

4070 Wurkum. In *Notes on the tribes . . . by O. Temple, 2nd ed., 1922, repr. 1965*: 365–367.

KURAMA

Including:

Azura
Binawa *(Bogama)*
Dungi
Gurre *(Gurri)*
Kahugu *(Kahagu)*
Kaibi
Kibalo *(Kiballo)*
Kiniku *(Kimiku, Kinuka)*
Kitimi *(Kittimi)*

Kono
Piti *(Abisi, Bisi, Pitti)*
Ribam
Rishua *(Rishiwa)*
Rumaiya
Ruruma
Srubu

1. GENERAL AND ETHNOGRAPHIC STUDIES

4071 Binawa. In *Pagan peoples of the central area of Northern Nigeria, by H. D. Gunn, 1956*: 56.

4072 Dungi. In *Pagan peoples of the central area of Northern Nigeria, by H. D. Gunn, 1956*: 57.

4073 Gunn, Harold D.
Gure. In his *Pagan peoples of the central area of Northern Nigeria, 1956*: 49–52.

Short ethnographic notes on the Gure. See also pp. 36–40, and 48–49.

4074 —Kahugu. In his *Pagan peoples of the central area of Northern Nigeria, 1956*: 52–55.
See also pp. 36–40 and 48–49.

4075 —Kaibi. In his *Pagan peoples of the central area of Northern Nigeria, 1956*: 57–58.

4076 —Kiballo. In his *Pagan peoples of the central area of Northern Nigeria, 1956*: 58–59.

4077 —The Kurama and Azura. In his *Peoples of the Plateau area of Northern Nigeria, 1953*: 34–35.
Brief notes on the Kurama and Azura of Jere District.

4078 —The Kurama of Lere District. In his *Pagan peoples of the central area of Northern Nigeria, 1956*: 41–47.
See also pp. 36–40.

4079 —Kurama of Southern Kauru District. In his *Pagan peoples of the central area of Northern Nigeria, 1956*: 55.

4080 —Piti and Ribam. In his *Peoples of the Plateau area of Northern Nigeria, 1953*: 48–50.

4081 —Rumaiya. In his *Pagan people, of the central area of Northern Nigeria 1956*: 62.

4082 —Ruruma. In his *Pagan peoples of the central area of Northern Nigeria, 1956*: 62–63.

4083 —Srubu. In his *Pagan peoples of the central area of Northern Nigeria, 1956*: 63–64.

4084 Guri. In *Notes on the tribes . . . by O. Temple, 2nd ed., 1922, repr. 1965*: 118.
Mentions also the Kahagu, Shaini and Srubu.

4085 Kaibi. In *Notes on the tribes . . . by O. Temple, 2nd ed., 1922, repr. 1965*: 193.
Mentions also the Rishua, Ruruma and Rumaya.

4086 Kiballo, Kinuka, Kittimi. In *Notes on the tribes . . . by O. Temple, 2nd ed., 1922, repr. 1965*: 227–228.

4087 Kinuku. In *Pagan peoples of the central area of Northern Nigeria, by H. D. Gunn, 1956*: 59.

4088 Kitimi. In *Pagan peoples of the central*

area of Northern Nigeria, by H. D. Gunn, 1956: 59–60.

4089 Kono. In *Pagan Peoples of the central area of Northern Nigeria, by H. D. Gunn, 1956*: 60–61.

4090 Kurama. In *Notes on the tribes . . . by O. Temple, 2nd ed., 1922, repr. 1965*: 252–253.

4091 Meek, Charles Kingsley
The Gure. In his *Tribal studies in Northern Nigeria, v. 2, 1931*: 189–203, illus.

4092 —The Kahugu. In his *Tribal studies in Northern Nigeria, v. 2, 1931*: 203–219, illus.

4093 —The Kurama. In his *Tribal studies in Northern Nigeria, v. 2, 1931*: 164–184, illus.
Ethnographic notes.

4094 —The Piti. In his *Tribal studies in Northern Nigeria, v. 2, 1931*: 129–145, illus.

4095 Pitti. In *Notes on the tribes . . . by O. Temple, 2nd ed., 1922, repr. 1965*: 337.

4096 Rishuwa. In *Pagan peoples of the central area of Northern Nigeria, by H. D. Gunn, 1956*: 61.

2. LINGUISTIC STUDIES

4097 Meek, Charles Kingsley
Gure vocabulary. In his *Tribal studies in Northern Nigeria, v. 2, 1931*: 199–203.

4098 —Kahugu vocabulary. In his *Tribal studies in Northern Nigeria, v. 2, 1931*: 213–219.

4099 —Kurama [vocabulary] In his *Tribal studies in Northern Nigeria, v. 2, 1931*: 178–184.

4100 —Piti vocabulary. In his *Tribal studies in Northern Nigeria, v. 2, 1931*: 138–145.

MAMBILA

(Tobi)

Including:

Gelebda *(Gelevda)*   Kamkam
Hitkalanchi *(Hidkala)*   Magu

1. GENERAL AND ETHNOGRAPHIC STUDIES

4101 Crowder, Michael
Mambila Plateau. *Nig. mag.*, (65) Je. 1960: 154–176, illus.

4102 Meek, Charles Kingsley
[The Magu and Kamkam] In his *Tribal studies in Northern Nigeria, v. 1, 1931*: 563–566.
Brief notes on two groups of people inhabiting the two villages of Kamkam and Magu on the Mambila Plateau.

4103 —The Mambila. In his *Tribal studies in Northern Nigeria, vol. 1, 1931*: 532–582, illus.

4104 Meyer, E.
Mambila—Studie. *Z.f.E.S.*, 30, 1939–40: 1–52, 117–148, 210–232.

4105 Rehfisch, F. M.
The dynamics of multilineality on the Mambila plateau. *Africa*, 30 (3) Jl. 1960: 246–261, bibliog.
Summary in French, pp. 260–261.

4106 —Social structure of a Mambila village. 1956.
M.A. thesis, London University.

4107 Schneider, Rev. G.
Mambila album. *Nig. field.*, 20 (3) Jl. 1955: 112–132, illus.

A profusely illustrated account depicting the life of the Mambila.

2. LINGUISTIC STUDIES

4108 Büchner, H.
Vokabulare de Sprachen in und um Gava (Nordnigerien) *Afr. u. Übersee*, 48 (1) Dec. 1964: 36–45.
Short comparative vocabularies of six languages spoken in and around Gava in Sarduana Province. These are Glanda, Galavda, Yawotataxa, Saladwa, Truade, and an unidentified language spoken at Bokwa.

4109 Lukas, Johannes
Das Hitkalanci, eine Sprache um Gwoza (Nordostnigerien). *Afrika u. Ubersee*, 48 (2) Mar. 1965: 81–114.
Grammatical and descriptive notes on Hitkalanchi, a language spoken in and around Gwosa in Northeastern Nigeria, with an appendix of Hitkalanchi-German and German-Hitkalanchi vocabulary.

4110 Meek, Charles Kingsley
Kamkam vocabulary. In his *Tribal studies in Northern Nigeria, v. 1, 1931*: 578–581.
Vocabulary of the Bungnu or Kamkam.

4111 —[Mambila vocabulary] In his *Tribal studies in Northern Nigeria, v. 1, 1931*: 566–582.
Vocabularies of Kama, Warwar, Wa and Kila dialects.

4112 —Mvanip vocabulary, as spoken by the people of Magu and Ndunda. In his *Tribal studies in Northern Nigeria, v. 1, 1931*: 581–582.

MARGI

(Marghi)

Including:

Chibak *(Chibbuk, Chibuk, Cibak, Kibaku)*
Kilba

Sukur *(Sugur)*

Womdeo

1. GENERAL AND ETHNOGRAPHIC STUDIES

4113 Alexander, D.
Notes on ornaments of the Womdeo pagans, who are a section of the Marghi pagans (females only) *Man*, 11, 1911: 1 (art. 1) illus.

4114 Barth, Heinrich
The border-country of the Marghi. In his *Travels and discoveries in North and Central Africa, v. 2, 1857*: 374–403.

4115 Chibuk. In *Notes on the tribes . . . by O. Temple, 2nd ed., 1922, repr. 1965*: 86–87.

4116 Hoffmann, Carl F.
The Marghi. In his *A grammar of the Marghi language, 1963*: 1–4.

4117 Kilba. In *Notes on the tribes . . . by O. Temple, 2nd ed., 1922. repr. 1965*: 230–234.

4118 Kirk-Greene, Anthony Hamilton Millard
The kingdom of Sukur: a Northern Nigerian Ichabad. *Nig. field*, 25 (2) Apr. 1960: 67–96, illus.
Historical study of Sukur village (in Madagali District of Adamawa Province) and the traditional and ritual authority of the Llidi (the king) together with rites and ceremonies connected with his office.

4119 —Marghi. In his *Adamawa past and present, 1958*: 18.
Short historical notice.

4120 —The Mba ceremony of the Marghi. *Nig. field*, 24 (2) Apr. 1959: 80–87, illus.
Initiation ceremonies of the Marghi tribe in Southern Bornu and Northern Adamawa Provinces. Mba initiates the youth into manhood. Also reproduced in his *Adamawa past and present, 1958*: 214–217.

4121 Marghi. In *Notes on the tribes . . . by O. Temple, 2nd ed., 1922, repr. 1965*: 271–274.

4122 Meek, Charles Kingsley
The Kilba. In his *Tribal studies in Northern Nigeria, v. 1, 1931*: 181–213.

4123 —The Margi of Adamawa. In his *Tribal studies in Northern Nigeria, v. 1, 1931*: 213–251.

4124 —The Sukur group. In his *Tribal studies in Northern Nigeria, v. 1, 1931*: 312–320, illus.

4125 Neher, Gerald
Brass casting in North-east Nigeria. *Nig. field*, 29 (1) Jan. 1964: 16–27, illus.
Describes brass casting by craftsmen of the Marghi, Gude, Kilba, Higi, Chibuk, Bura, and other tribes and clans in the area.

4126 —Chibuk face marks. *Nig. field*, 28 (2) Apr. 1963: 72–78, illus.
Describes patterns of face marks among the Chibuk.

4127 Sasson, Hamo
Iron-smelting in the hill village of Sukur, north-eastern Nigeria. *Man*, 64, Nov.–Dec. 1964: 174–178 (art. 215) illus.
Detailed description. Sukkur is a

village about 30 miles south of Gwosa in Sardauna Province.

4128 Vaughan, James H.
Rock paintings and rock gongs among the Marghi of Nigeria. *Man*, 62, Apr. 1962: 49–52 (art. 83) illus., bibliog.
Describes rock gongs and rock paintings in the Marghi villages of Womdi and Uvu and shows both to be integral parts of the Marghi marriage ceremony known as *mba*. Gives a general account of *mba* and tries to interpret the painting-gong complex in terms of Marghi "pattern of initiation and marriage rites." The Marghi country borders on the Mandara Mountain in Sarduana Province.

2. LINGUISTIC STUDIES

4129 Church of brethren Mission, Jos.
Kakadur na aga sur gunggur sil au iju. Wu myar Margi. Jos, the mission, 1956. 161p.
Printed by S.I.M. Niger press, Jos.

4130 —Mdukur tsapu. Good manhood . . . Jos, the mission, 1952. 126p.
Printed by S.I.M. Niger press, Jos.

4131 Hoffmann, Carl F.
A grammar of the Margi language. London, O.U.P., for Int. Afr. inst., 1963. xix, 287p. bibliog.
A full-length descriptive grammar.

4132 Meek, Charles Kingsley
Kilba words and phrases. In his *Tribal studies in Northern Nigeria, v. 1, 1931*: 208–213.

4133 —Margi vocabulary and phrases. In his *Tribal studies in Northern Nigeria, v. 1, 1931*: 234–251.
Vocabularies of several Margi dialects, with a short note on Margi grammar, pp. 240–241.

4134 —Sukur vocabulary. In his *Tribal studies in Northern Nigeria, v. 1, 1931*: 317–320.

MUMUYE

Including:

Gengle
Gola *(Gomla, Gori)*
Kugama
Kumba
Teme

Waka
Yakoko
Yendang *(Yendan)*
Yundam
Zinna

1. GENERAL AND ETHNOGRAPHIC STUDIES

4135 Kirk-Greene, Anthony Hamilton Millard
Mumuye. In his *Adamawa past and present, 1958*: 20–21.

4136 Kugamma: In *Notes on the tribes . . . by O. Temple*, 2nd ed., 1922, repr. 1965: 244–246.

4137 Meek, Charles Kingsley
The Mumuye and neighbouring tribes. In his *Tribal studies in Northern Nigeria, v. 1, 1931*: 446–531, illus.
Ethnographic notes on the Mumuye, Gola, Yendang, Waka, Teme, Kumba, Gengle and Kugama.

4138 Mumuye. In *Notes on the tribes . . . by O. Temple*, 2nd ed., 1922, repr. 1965: 287–294.
Treats the Waka, Yakoko, Yundam and Zinna as off-shoots of the Mumuye.

2. LINGUISTIC STUDIES

4139 Meek, Charles Kingsley
Gengle and Kugama vocabulary. In his

Tribal studies in Northern Nigeria, v. 1, 1931: 529–531.

4140 —Gôla or Gomla vocabulary. In his *Tribal studies in Northern Nigeria, v. 1, 1931*: 517–519.

4141 —Kumba vocabulary. In his *Tribal studies in Northern Nigeria, v. 1, 1931*: 526–529.

4142 —[Mumuye vocabulary] In his *Tribal studies in Northern Nigeria, v. 1, 1931*: 505–516.
Vocabularies of Pugu, Ding-Ding and Yakoko dialects of Mumuye.

4143 —Teme vocabulary. In his *Tribal studies in Northern Nigeria, v. 1, 1931*: 524–526.

4144 —Waka vocabulary. In his *Tribal studies in Northern Nigeria, v. 1, 1931*: 522–524.

4145 —Yendang (of Bajama District) vocabulary. In his *Tribal studies in Northern Nigeria, v. 1, 1931*: 519–521.

NDORO

1. GENERAL AND ETHNOGRAPHIC STUDIES

4146   Meek, Charles Kingsley
        The Ndọro. In his *Tribal studies in Northern Nigeria, v. 2, 1931*: 589–605, illus.

2. LINGUISTIC STUDIES

4147   Meek, Charles Kingsley
        Ndọro vocabulary. In his *Tribal studies in Northern Nigeria, v. 2, 1931*: 599–605.

NGIZIM

(Ngezzim)

1. GENERAL AND ETHNOGRAPHIC STUDIES

4148   Meek, Charles Kingsley
        The Ngizim. In his *Tribal studies in Northern Nigeria, v. 2, 1931*: 247–269.

4149   Ngizim. In *Notes on the tribes . . . by*

O. Temple, 2nd ed., 1922, repr. 1965: 310–311.

2. LINGUISTIC STUDIES

4150   Meek, Charles Kingsley
        Ngizim [vocabulary] In his *Tribal studies in Northern Nigeria, v. 2, 1931*: 262–269.

NOK CULTURE

GENERAL, ARCHAEOLOGICAL AND ETHNOGRAPHIC STUDIES

4151   Fagg, Bernard E. B.
        An ancient site in Niger province. *Hist. soc. Nig. Bull. news*, 5 (4) Mar. 1961: 3.
        Advance report of author's excavations at Taruga some 40 miles southeast of Abuja. Notes Nok type figurine found in a dwelling site.

4152   —Carbon dates for Nigeria. *Man*, 65, 1965: 22–23.
        Advance report of results of radio carbon datings of 3 samples two from Nok, and one from Rop rock shelter (Jos Plateau) in Northern Nigeria.

4153   —Figures from Northern Nigeria. *Nig. digest*, 1 (5) May 1945: 5–6, illus.

4154   —A life size terra-cotta head from Nok. *Man*, 56, 1956: 89 (art. 95) illus.
        Describes and illustrates (plate) the terra-cotta head found at Nok in 1954.

4155   —Masterpieces of early Nigerian art; recently discovered figurines of a primitive culture in the Nok valley. *Illus. Lond. news*, (213) 1948: 586–587, illus.

4156   —Mining for history. *Nigeria, 1960*: 34–41, illus.
        On archaeological finds in the tin mines on the Plateau mine fields.

4157   —The Nok culture. *W. Afr. rev.*, 27 (351) Dec. 1956: 1083–1087, illus.

4158   —The Nok culture in pre-history. *J. Hist. soc. Nig.*, 1 (4) Dec. 1959: 228–293, illus.
        Brief account of the Nok culture in

Central Nigeria, based on evidence deduced from archaeological finds in the area. The author links Ife-Benin art with this culture which is said to have flourished from 500 B.C. to A.D. 200.

4159   —The Nok terra-cottas in West African art history. *Actes 4e congrès panafricain de préhistoire . . . ed. G. Mortelmans and J. Nenquin. Sect. 3, 1962*: 445–450.

4160   —Preliminary notes on a new series of pottery figures from Northern Nigeria. *Africa*, 15, 1945: 21–22, illus.
        Specimens, with descriptive notes, of pottery discovered in 1943 at Jemaa in Plateau Province and at Nok village.

4161   —Primitive art of problematic age: North Nigerian heads now at the British museum. *Illus. Lond. news*, (210) Apr. 26 1947: 442–443, illus.
        Describes and illustrates terra-cotta heads discovered in the Nok valley.

4162   Kennedy, Robert A.
        West Africa in prehistory. *History today*, 8 (9) Sept. 1958: 646–653, illus., map.

4163   Poole, H. E.
        The Jebba people of Nok, Nigeria. *Teacher educ.*, 4 (3) Feb. 1964: 218–221.

4164   Primitive Nigerian art: recently discovered traces of an early culture. *Tin and its uses*, (21) Oct. 1949: 10, illus.
        Comments on the terracotta and other finds in the Nok area.

4165   Radiocarbon dating of the Nok culture, Northern Nigeria. *Africa*, 35 (1) Jan. 1965: 102.
        Brief notice in the "notes and news" section.

NUPE

Including:

Basange *(Bassange, Nge)*   Kakanda *(Akanda, Yapa)*
Dibo *(Ganagana, Zitako)*   Kupa *(Gupa)*

1. GENERAL AND ETHNOGRAPHIC STUDIES

4166   Abdulkadir, *Makama*
       Ajo shani nya zamau. Zaria, Gaskiya
       corporation, 1952. 13p.
       On "ajo"—a modern marriage
       ceremony in Nupe.

4167   Baldwin, Kenneth D. S.
       Some social and economic enquiries at
       Mokwa. *WAISER conf. proc., 4th,
       Accra, 1955*: 92–97.

4168   Brooke, Graham Wilmot
       Outlines of the modern history of Nupe.
       Niger & Yoruba notes, 3 (32) Feb. 1897:
       58–62.

4169   Dupigny, E. G. M.
       Gazetteer of Nupe Province. London,
       Waterlow, 1920. 84p. tables, chart.

4170   Flint, J. E.
       The chequered history of Nupe. *W. Afr.
       rev.*, 30 (382) *1959*: 587–589.

4171   Forde, Cyril Daryll
       The Nupe. In his *Peoples of the Niger-
       Benue confluence, 1955*: 17–52, bibliog.

4172   Ganagana and Dibo. In *Notes on the
       tribes . . . by O. Temple, 2nd ed., 1922,
       repr. 1965*: 113–115.

4173   Gupa. In *Notes on the tribes . . . by O.
       Temple, 2nd ed., 1922, repr. 1965*: 117.

4174   Kakanda. In *Notes on the tribes . . . by
       O. Temple, 2nd ed., 1922, repr. 1965*:
       197–198.

4175   Kirk-Greene, Anthony Hamilton Millard
       The first battle of Bida. *W. Afr. rev.*, 28
       (363) Dec. 1957: 1207–1212, 1235; 29
       (364) Jan. 1958: 61–63.

4176   Large, W. H.
       The red walls of Bida. *Nig. mag.*, (30)
       1949: 271–315, illus.
       Description of Bida town.

4177   Macrow, Donald W.
       "Daura" and Nupe of Pategi. *Nig. mag.*,
       (50) 1956: 224–237; 260–279.

4178   May, D. J.
       Journey in the Yoruba and Nupe
       countries in 1858. *J. Roy. geog. soc.*, 30,
       1860: 212–233, map.

4178a Milum, John
       Notes on a journey from Lagos up the
       Niger to Bida. See [4464].

4179   Nadel, Siegfried Ferdinand
       A black Byzantium: the kingdom of
       Nupe in Nigeria. With a foreword by
       Lord Lugard. London, O.U.P., for Int.
       Afr. Inst., 1942. xv, 420p. front., illus.
       (ports.) 2 maps.
       Extensive ethnographic and socio-
       logical investigation of the Nupe. Em-

braces their history, economy, social
structure and political organisation.
See also [4187].

4180   —Experiments on culture psychology.
       Africa, 10 (4) Oct. 1937: 421–435.
       French summary, p. 435. Attempts to
       establish the relevance of psychology in
       anthropological and sociological in-
       vestigations. Based on his field experi-
       ments carried out among the Nupe and
       Yoruba in Nigeria. For a fuller account
       of the experiments, see [4181].

4181   —A field experiment in racial psychology.
       Brit. j. psychology, (General Section)
       28, (2) Oct. 1937: 195–211.
       A study to determine the "correlation
       between diversity of culture and psycho-
       logical differentiation," carried out in
       Northern Nigeria with school boys
       selected from two culture areas—
       Yoruba and Nupe.

4182   —The gani ritual of Nupe: a study in
       social symbiosis. *Africa*, 19 (3) Jl. 1949:
       177–186, illus.
       On the origin, non-indigenity and
       social significance of the gani ritual in
       Nupe. Describes its ceremonies.

4183   —Gunnu: a fertility cult of the Nupe
       in Northern Nigeria. *J.R.A.I.*, 67 (7)
       Ja.–Je. 1937: 91–130, illus.
       Describes the cult and its attendant
       ceremonies, with text of the relevant
       song at pp. 123–128. An appendix by
       Lisbeth Nadel (pp. 128–130) describes
       Nupe musical instruments.

4184   —The Kede: A riverain state in Northern
       Nigeria. In *African political systems, ed.
       M. Fortes and E. E. Evans-Pritchard,
       1940*: 164–195, map.
       Brief conspectus of Kede political and
       administrative systems, economic and
       social structure, tradition of origin,
       religious and state evolution.

4185   —The king's hangmen: a judicial
       organisation in Central Africa. *Man*,
       35, 1935: 129–132 (art. 143).
       Describes the organisation and opera-
       tion of criminal jurisdiction in Nupe
       kingdom, and its essential institution,
       the Ledu villages.

4186   —Morality and language among the
       Nupe. *Man*, 54 (77) Apr. 1954: 55–57.
       Nupe morality approached through a
       consideration of tabooed expressions in
       Nupe language usage.

4187   —Nupe religion. London, Routledge &
       K. Paul, 1954. x, 288p. plates, tables,
       diagrs.
       A study of religious beliefs and
       practices among the Nupe. Intended as

a sequel to the author's *A Black Byzantium* [4179].

4188 —Nupe state and community. *Africa*, 8 (3) Jl. 1935: 257–303, illus., map.

Investigation into the nature and method of social organisation and political control both in traditional Nupe communities and in the larger more artificial Nupe state or kingdom. The investigation proceeds from the smallest unit—the family and the village through the sub-tribe and the tribe onto the state. Summary in French, p. 303.

4189 —Social symbiosis and tribal organisation. *Man*, 38, Je. 1938: 85–90 (art. 85) illus.

The biologic concept of symbiosis is applicable to social groups. An ethnographic and socio-historical sketch of Kutigi, a Nupe town in Northern Nigeria, which developed out of the fusion of four originally distinct tribal groups, is given to illustrate this concept of "social symbiosis." First published in summary form: *Man*, 37, May 1937: 81 (art. 93).

4190 —Witchcraft and anti-witchcraft in Nupe society. *Africa*, 8 (4) Oct. 1935: 423–447, illus.

Based on account obtained in Bida and Jebba island. French summary, p. 447.

4191 —Witchcraft in four African societies: an essay in comparison. *Amer. anthrop.*, 54, 1952: 18–29, bibliog.

Comparative study of beliefs in witchcraft among the Nupe and Gwari of Northern Nigeria, and the Korongo and Mesakin of the Nuba Mountains in the Central region of Sudan Republic. Later reprinted in *Cultures and societies of Africa*, ed. Simon and Phoebe Ottenberg, 1960: 407–420 [720].

4192 New hopes for Nupe. *W. Africa*, (2354) 14 Jul. 1962: 773.

4192a Nge or Bassa-Nge. In *Notes on the tribes . . . by O. Temple*, 2nd ed, 1922, repr. 1965: 305–309.

4192b The Nupe of Pategi. *Nig. Mag.*, (50) 1956: 260–279, illus.

4193 Nupe. In *Notes on the tribes . . . by O. Temple*, 2nd ed., 1922, repr. 1965: 319–335.

4194 Pategi regatta. *Nig. mag.*, (54) 1957: 289–292, illus.

4195 The slave trade in Nupe. *Niger & Yoruba notes*, 2 (19) Jan. 1896: 52–53; 2 (20) Feb. 1896: 62–63; 2 (22) Apr. 1896: 75–76; 2 (23) May 1896: 84–85.

4196 Tamuno, Tekena Nitonye
The Nupe. In *A thousand years of West African history*, ed. J. F. A. Ajayi and I. Espie, 1965: 207–209.

4197 Vandeleur, C. F. S.
Nupe and Ilorin. *Geog. j.*, 10, 1897: 349–374, illus., map.

4198 Werder, Peter von
Staatsgefüge im Westafrika; eine ethno-

soziologische Untersuchung über Höchformen der sozialen und staatlichen Organisation im Westsudan. Stuttgart, F. Enke, 1938. 194p. (Beilageheft zur Z. für vergleichende Rechtswissenschaft, v. 52 no. 2).

On the family, social and political structure of the Yoruba (pp. 1–46) the Nupe (pp. 46–75) the Ashanti, the Mossi and the Mandingo. Includes age groups and secret societies.

2. SCULPTURE, ARTS AND CRAFTS

4199 *Aliyu
Bida glass workers: some more useful objects made from bottles. *Nig. teacher*, 2 (7) 1936: 17–19, illus.

Description of the making of beads, ear-rings, etc., from glass bottles by the Masaga guild of Bida.

4200 Brinkworth, Ian
Mystery on the Niger. *W. Afr. rev.*, 31 (389) 1960: 26–29, illus.

Description of nine Tsoede bronzes found at Jebba and Tada, in Northern Nigeria.

4201 Crafts of Bida. *Nig. mag.*, (49) 1956: 138–147, illus.

Notes on Bida smiths and smitheries.

4202 Daniel, F. de F.
Figures at Jebba and Tada. *Nig. mag.*, (20) 1940: 282–284, illus.

Describes two bronze figures from Jebba and four bronze, two copper and one brass-copper from Tada.

4203 Eccles, Polly
Nupe bronzes. *Nig. mag.*, (73) Je. 1962: 13–25, illus., map.

4204 Fagg, William Buller
The mysterious bronzes of Jebba and Tadda, Northern Nigeria. *Illus. Lond. news*, Feb. 20th 1960: 297–299, illus.

4205 Jeffries, W. F.
Mud building in Northern Nigeria. *Nig. mag.*, (14) 1938: 110.

4206 Lantz, S. P.
Jebba island embroidery. *Nig. mag.*, (14) 1938: 130–133, illus.

4207 Macrow, Donald W.
Crafts of Bida. *Nig. mag.*, (74) Sept. 1962: 55–60, illus.

4207a Meyerowitz, Eva L. R.
Ancient Nigerian bronzes. See [1214].

4208 Nadel, Siegfried Ferdinand
Glass making in Nupe [with a note by C. G. Seligman] *Man*, 40, 1940: 85–86 (art. 107).

4209 Nicholson, W. E.
Bida (Nupe) pottery. *Man*, 34, May 1934: 71–73 (art. 89) illus.

Step by step account of pot making in Bida.

4210 Palmer, Herbert Richmond
Ancient Nigerian bronzes. *Burl. mag.*, 81 (475) Oct. 1942: 252–254.

A rejoinder to an earlier article on the subject by Mrs. Eva L. Meyerowitz (*Burl. mag.*, Sept. Oct. 1941). Both discuss the Jebba and Tada bronzes, suggesting that the technique of working them originated in Nubia.

4211   —Gabi figures from Jebba island. *Man*, 31, 1931 : 261–262. (art. 261) illus.

4212   Vernon-Jackson, Hugh O. H.
Craft work in Bida. *Africa*, 30 (1) Jan. 1960 : 51–61.
Describes materials, method and products of metalwork, woodwork, spinning, weaving, dyeing, tailoring, embroidery, net-making, leatherwork, basket-making, hat-making, and other crafts. French summary, pp. 60–61.

4213   Walker, S. W.
Gabi figures and Edegi, first king of the Nupe. *Man*, 34, 1934 : 169–172 (art. 193) illus.
Description of bronze figures in Jebba island and Tada, a Nupe village about 25 miles east of Jebba, and an account of the legend associated with these figures. See [4211].

3. LINGUISTIC STUDIES

4214   Banfield, A. W.
Dictionary of the Nupe language. Shonga, Northern Nigeria, The Niger press, 1914. 2v.
v. 1. Nupe-English. xxi, 22–256p.
v. 2. English-Nupe. 257–514p.
Both vols. interleaved.

4215   Banfield, A. W. and Macintyre, J. L.
A grammar of the Nupe language, together with a vocabulary. London, S.P.C.K., 1915. viii, 186p.

4216   Bible. N.T. Nupe. John
Labári wángi nya Yohanu, nimi Nupé. London, British and foreign Bible society, 1887. 60p.
St. John's Gospel in Nupe, translated by Rev. Henry Johnson, and edited by Rev. J. F. Schon.

4217   Bible. N.T. Nupe. Luke
Labari wángi nya Luka, nimi Nupé.

London, British and foreign Bible society, 1887. 77p. Interleaved.
St. Luke's Gospel, translated into Nupe by Rev. Henry Johnson, and edited by Rev. J. F. Schon.

4218   Bible. N.T. Nupe. Mark.
Labári wangi nya Marku, nimi Nupe. London, British and foreign Bible society, 1886. 47p.
St. Mark's Gospel translated into Nupe by Rev. Henry Johnson, and edited by Rev. J. F. Schon.

4219   Bible. N.T. Nupe. Matthew.
The first seven chapters of the gospel according to St. Matthew in Nupe. Translated by the Rev. Samuel Crowther. London, British and foreign Bible society, 1860. 20p.

4220   Crowther, Samuel Ajai
Element of a grammar and vocabulary of the Nupe language. London, Church missionary house, 1864. 208p.

4220a   *—Nupe primer. London, C.M.S., 1860. 22p.

4221   Johnson, Henry
Nupe reading-book for the use of schools of the Niger Mission, etc. London, S.P.C.K., [1883] 48p.

4222   Laird, McGregor and Oldfield, R. A. N.
Vocabulary: English-Nufie or Nūpāysee. In their *Narrative of an expedition into the interior of Africa*, v. 2, 1837 : 442–443.

4222a   Lukas, J.
Der hamitische Gehalt der tschado-hamitischen Sprachen. See [1482].

4223   Smith, N. V.
A phonological and grammatical study of the verb in Nupe. 1964.
Ph.D. thesis, London.

4224   Westerman, Diedrich
Das Nupe in Nigerien: seine Stellung innerhalb der Kwa-Sprachen. *M.S.O.S.*, 30, 1927 : 173–207. (Westsudanische Studien, 4).

RESHE

(Barashe, Gungawa, Tsureshe)

Including:

Bakarawa

Larawa *(Laro, Laruawa)*

Lopawa *(Lupawa)*

Sorkowa *(Sorke, Sorko)*

Yaurawa *(Rasawa, Yauri, Yawuri)*

1. GENERAL AND ETHNOGRAPHIC STUDIES

4225   Gungawa. In *Notes on the tribes . . . by O. Temple*, 2nd ed., 1922, repr. 1965 : 117.

4226   Gunn, Harold D.
Riverain peoples of Yauri and Borgu. In his *Peoples of the Middle Niger region, N. Nigeria, 1960* : 11–20.

On the Reshe (Gungawa) Yaurawa, Lopawa, Larawa and Bakarawa.

4227   Hermon-Hodge, Henry Baldwin
Gungawa. In his *Gazetteer of Ilorin Province, 1929* : 57–60.
Brief ethnological notes on the Gungawa.

4228   Rouch, J.
The Sorkawa: nomad fishermen of the

middle Niger. [Translated by Denzil Griffiths] *Farm and forest*, 10, 1950: 36–53.
English translation of [4229] q.v.

4229 —Les Sorkawa: pêcheurs itinérants du Moyen Niger. *Africa*, 20 (1) Jan. 1950: 5–25, illus., maps.
A study of the Sorkawa, a fishing population on the middle Niger. Reviews their history and describes their fishing industry, including the rituals associated with that industry.

English summary, p. 25. For English translation, see [4228].

2. LINGUISTIC STUDIES

4230 Harris, Percy Graham
Notes on the Reshe language. *Afr. stud.*, 5 (4) Dec. 1946: 221–242.
Grammatical notes on Reshe or Tsureshe language. Includes a Reshe text with interlinear English translation and an English-Reshe vocabulary.

SHUWA ARABS

(Choua, Larabawa, Shiwa, Shoa)

1. GENERAL AND ETHNOGRAPHIC STUDIES

4231 Arabs (Larabawa) In *Notes on the tribes . . . by O. Temple, 2nd ed., 1922, repr. 1965*: 22–25.
Historical and ethnographic notes on the Shuwa Arabs of Bornu.

4232 Barth, Heinrich
The Shuwa Arabs. In his *Travels and discoveries in North and Central Africa, v. 2, 1857*: 355–357.

2. LINGUISTIC STUDIES

4233 Howard, C. G.
Shuwa Arabic stories, with an introduction and vocabulary. Oxford, University press, 1921. 116p.

4234 Lethem, Gordon James
Colloquial Arabic; Shuwa dialect of Bornu, Nigeria, and of the region of Lake Chad. Grammar and vocabulary, with some proverbs and songs. London, Crown agents for overseas governments, 1920. xv, 487p.

SO

1. BIBLIOGRAPHY

4235 Lebeuf, Jean Paul
Bibliographie Sao et Kotoko. *Étud. cam.*, 1 (21–22) Je.–Sept. 1948: 121–137.

2. GENERAL AND ETHNOGRAPHIC STUDIES

4236 Barth, Heinrich
[The Soy or Só] In his *Travels and discoveries in North and Central Africa, v. 2, 1857*: 277–278.
Short historical speculation about the So. See also op. cit. v. 3, pp. 278–279.

4237 *Bouillez,
Deux légendes du Tchad; réflexion sur les So, *Inst. franc. d'anthropologie, 1912*: 80–84.

4238 Cohen, Ronald
The just so So? A spurious tribal grouping in Western Sudanic history. *Man*, 62, Oct. 1962: 153–154 (art. 239).
Suggests that the word So was a generic term applied by the early

Kanuris to non-Muslim peoples South of their capital Birni Gazargamo and not the name of a specific tribe or a specific people as is often supposed.

4238a Fremantle, John M.
A history of the region comprising the Katagum Division of Kano Province. See [1625].

4239 Migeod, Frederick William Hugh
The ancient So people of Bornu. *J. Afr. soc.*, 23 (89) Oct. 1923: 19–29.
Historical notes on the So.

4240 Palmer, Herbert Richmond, *tr.*
The So. In his *Sudanese memoirs, v. 2, 1928, repr. London, 1967*: 64–65.

4241 —The So Dala N'gumami. In his *Sudanese memoirs, v. 2, 1928, repr. London, 1967*: 66–68.

4242 Sölken, Heinz
Untersuchungen über die sprachliche Stellung der einstigen So von Bornu. *Anthropos.*, 53 (5–6) 1958: 877–900.
On the linguistic position of the So of Bornu.

TIGONG

(Tigon, Tigum, Tikong, Tugong, Tugun, Tukum)

Including:

Ashiaku (Atsiku)   Nama

1. GENERAL AND ETHNOGRAPHIC STUDIES

4243   Meek, Charles Kingsley
       The Tikong. In his *Tribal studies in Northern Nigeria, v. 2, 1931*: 551–589, illus.
       In Sarduana Province.

2. LINGUISTIC STUDIES

4244   Meek, Charles Kingsley
       Tikong [vocabularies] In his *Tribal studies in Northern Nigeria, v. 2, 1931*: 569–589.
       Vocabularies of several Tikong dialects, including Ashiaku and Nana.

TIV

(Mitshi, Munshi, Tivi)

1. BIBLIOGRAPHY

4245   Bohannan, Paul J.
       Tiv bibliography. In : *Akiga's story . . . reprinted (with bibliography and new preface)* 1965: 419–425.

2. GENERAL

Bohannan, Paul J.
An alternate residence classification. See [2442].

4246   Bohannan, Paul J. and Bohannan Laura M. Three source notebooks in Tiv ethnography. New Haven, Conn., Human Relations Area Files, 1958. 2v. in 1 (480 l.) bibliog.

4247   Bowen, Elenore Smith [pseud.]
       Return to laughter. London, Gollancz, 1954. 255p.
       A novel by Laura Bohannan about a woman anthropologist's reactions to field work. Based on her experiences among the Tiv.

4248   —Le rire et les songes. [Transl. by Josette Hesse] Paris, Arthaud, 1957. 288p.
       French translation of *Return to laughter*. See [4247].

4249   Detzner, Hermann
       Im lande des Dju-dju. Reiseerlebnisse im östlichen Stromgebiet des Niger. Berlin, Scherl., 1923. 388p. illus., maps.
       Describes his travels and experiences in the Tiv country and other regions east of the Niger.

4250   Hardy, Donald
       Men from the bush. London, Muller, 1959. 191p.
       A novel set in the Tiv area of Northern Nigeria.

4251   Moseley, Lich H.
       Regions of the Benue. *J. & proc. Roy. geog. soc.*, 14, 1899: 630–637, map.

4252   Munshi. In *Notes on the tribes . . . by*
       O. Temple, 2nd ed., 1922, repr. 1965: 295–304.

4253   Nigeria. Northern. Premier's office
       A white paper on the government's policy for the rehabilitation of the Tiv native authority, Kaduna, Govt. Printer, 1965. 24p.
       Includes a summary of the report of the 1964 commission [Chairman, M. A. Coomassie] appointed to investigate the background of unrest in Tiv Division.

4254   *Sudan united mission
       The coming of the Gospel into Tivland. Mkar, 1961.

4255   White, Stanhope
       The Tiv. In his *Dan Bana . . . 1966*: 127–155, illus.

3. PHYSICAL ANTHROPOLOGY

4256   Malcolm, L. W. G.
       Notes on the physical anthropology of certain West African tribes.—(1) Munchi. *Man*, 20, 1920: 116–121 (art. 60) tables.

4. SOCIAL AND CULTURAL ANTHROPOLOGY, ETHNOGRAPHY

4. (i)   General

4257   Abraham, Roy Clive
       The Tiv people. 2nd ed. London, published on behalf of the Govt. of Nigeria by the Crown agents for the colonies, 1940. x, 177p. illus. 3 maps.
       An ethnographic study. Especially important in that it is the first major and original work on the Tiv. 1st ed. published 1933 by Govt. Printer, Lagos. [6] ii, 239, xvp. illus., map.

4258   Akiga [Benjamin Akighirga Sai]
       Akiga's story: the Tiv tribe as seen by one of its members. Translated and annotated by Rupert East. London, O.U.P., 1939. 466p.
       —Reprinted (with bibliography and

new preface) 1965. xiii [3] 444p. bibliography, pp. 419–425.

4259 Alexander, Boyd
[The Munchi] In his *From the Niger to the Nile, v. 1, 1907*: 31–37.
Short description of the Tiv.

4260 Bohannan, Laura M.
The frightened witch. In *In the company of man: twenty portraits by anthropologists. Ed. Joseph B. Casagrande, 1960*: 377–395, illus.
Portrait of Shingir, a Native Authority head of a large lineage segment in northern Tivland.

4261 *—Miching Mallecho. In *From the third program, ed. J. Morris, 1956*:

4262 Bohannan, Laura M. and Bohannan, Paul J.
The Tiv of central Nigeria. London, Int. Afr. Inst., 1953. 100p. map, bibliog. (Ethnographic survey of Africa. Western Africa, pt. 8).
Origin, family and kinship, economy, religion, social organization and political structure.

4263 Bohannan, Paul J.
Concepts of time among the Tiv of Nigeria. *S.–W. j. anthrop.*, 9 (3) Autumn 1953: 251–262.

4264 —The Tiv of Nigeria. In *Peoples of Africa, ed. J. L. Gibbs, 1965*: 514–546. illus., bibliog.
A compendious ethnographic summary of the Tiv people.

4265 Downes, R. M.
The Tiv tribe. Kaduna, Govt. printer, 1933. v, 99p. 2 maps, tables.

4266 Duggan, E. de C.
Notes on the Munshi ("Tivi") tribe of Northern Nigeria: some historical outlines. *J. Afr. soc.*, 31 (123) Apr. 1932: 173–182.

4266a East, Rupert, *trans.*
Akiga's story. See Akiga [Benjamin Akighirga Sai]

4267 Frobenius, Leo
Die Muntschi, ein Urwaldvolk in der Nachbarschaft der sudanischen Kulturvölker. In *Volksdichtungen aus Oberguinea, 1924*: Part. III.
Records over forty Tiv folk tales, with brief notes on Tiv culture.

4268 Judd, A. S.
Native education in the Northern provinces of Nigeria. *J. Afr. soc.*, 17 (65) Oct. 1917: 1–10.
Discusses education in relation to the traditions and customs of the Tiv, Nungu and allied tribes on the Benue.

4269 —Notes on the Munshi tribe and language. *J. Afr. soc.*, 16 (61) Oct. 1916: 52–61; (62) Jan. 1917: 143–148.
Brief ethnographic sketch of the Tiv, followed by grammatical notes.

4270 Price-Williams, Douglas Richard
Abstract and concrete modes of classification in a primitive society. *Brit. j. educ. psychology*, 32 (1) Feb. 1962: 50–61, bibliog.

4271 —Analysis of an intelligence test used in rural areas of central Nigeria. *Oversea educ.*, 33 (3) Oct. 1961: 124–133.
Intelligence test tried on Tiv school children of the Mbara clan.

4272 *—New attitudes emerge from old. In *International conference on health education: studies and research in health education, 1962, vol. 5*, pp. 554–557.

4273 —A study concerning concepts of conservation of quantities among primitive children. *Acta psychologica*, 18, 1961: 297–307.

4274 Sai, Benjamin Akiga See Akiga [Benjamin Akighirga Sai].

4274a The Tiv of Nigeria. In *Cultural patterns and technical change, ed. M. Mead, 1955*: 96–126.
Compendious ethnographic sketch, noting religion, social structure, birth and child rearing, status of women, food, organisation of work, death, etc.

4275 Washburne, Chandler
Primitive drinking: a study of the uses and functions of alcohol in pre-literate societies. New York, College and University press publishers, 1961. xxi, 282p.

4276 Westermann, Diedrich
Benjamin akiga aus Nordnigerien, der Verfasser der Geschichte seines Volkes. In *Afrikaner erzählen ihr leben, Elf Selbstdarstellungen afrikanischer Eingeborener aller Bildungsgrade und Berufe und aus allen Teilen Afrikas. 1938*: 316–336, illus.
Autobiography of Akiga written in Hausa, and now translated into German.

4. (ii) History

4277 Akiga [Benjamin Akighirga Sai].
The 'descent' of the Tiv from Ibenda hill. *Africa*, 24 (4) Oct. 1954: 295–310. map, table.
Extracts by Paul Bohannan from a hitherto untranslated chapter of *Akiga's story* describing the migration of the Tiv from Ibenda hill to their present location. Includes explanatory notes. French summary, p. 310.

4278 Bohannan, Paul J.
The migration and expansion of the Tiv. *Africa*, 24 (1) Jan. 1954: 2–16, illus., maps.
Notes the lineage structure and political organisation and examines different aspects of Tiv expansion and migration.

4279 Tamuno, Tekena Nitonye
The Tiv. In *A thousand years of West African history, ed. J. F. A. Ajayi and I. Espie, 1965*: 205–206.

4. (iii) Marriage, Family, Lineage Structure

4280 Bohannan, Laura M.
A genealogical charter. *Africa*, 22 (4) Oct. 1952: 301–315. tables, bibliog.
On genealogy among the Tiv.

4281 Crowder, Michael
Genealogy and the Tiv. *Nig. mag.*, (63)
1959: 282–301. illus., map, table.
Correlates the present administrative
arrangement of the Tiv to Tiv genealogical traditions.

4282 Sahlins, M. D.
Segmentary lineage: an organisation of
predatory expansion. *Amer. anthrop.*,
63, Apr. 1961: 322–345.
Comparative view of Tiv and Nuer
lineage structure.

**4. (iv) Government, Law, Social Organiz-
ation and Structure**

4283 Arnott, D. W.
Councils and courts among the Tiv:
traditional concepts and alien institutions in a non-Moslem tribe of Northern
Nigeria. *J. Afr. law*, 2 (1) Spring, 1958:
19–25.
A review of P. Bohannan's *Justice
and judgement among the Tiv.* [4228] q.v.

4284 Bohannan, Laura M.
A comparative study of social
differentiation in primitive society. 1952.
D.Phil. thesis, Oxford.

4285 ——Political aspects of Tiv social organisation. In *Tribes without rulers: studies
in African segmentary systems, ed. by
J. Middleton and D. Tait, 1958*: 33–66.

4286 Bohannan, Paul J.
Extra-processual events in Tiv political
institutions. *Amer. anthrop.*, 60, 1958:
1–12, bibliog.
Analysis of extrinsic or non-
institutional features of Tiv political
set up—features which are not part of
the constituted and accepted institutions
of their political control. Later reprinted
in *Cultures and societies of Africa. ed.
Simon and Phoebe Ottenberg, 1960*:
328–341. [720].

4287 ——Homicide among the Tiv of central
Nigeria. In *African homicide and
suicide, ed. P. Bohannan, 1960*: 30–64.

4288 ——Justice and judgement among the
Tiv. London, published for the Inter-
national African institute by O.U.P.,
1957. xiv, 221p.
Attempts to describe and define the
Tiv conceptions of "Law" and "Justice".
Based on proceedings in court cases in a
Grade D. Customary court in Tiv
Division, Northern Nigeria.

4289 ——'Land', 'tenure' and land-tenure. In
*African agrarian systems, ed. by D.
Biebuyck, 1963*: 101–115, bibliog.
Defines 'land', 'tenure' and 'land-
tenure' in the African context, as
distinguished from the Western context, basing his definition on Tiv concepts. Summary in French pp. 111–115.

4290 ——The political and economic aspects
of land tenure and settlement patterns
among the Tiv of Central Nigeria. 1952.
D.Phil. thesis, Oxford.

4291 Derwar, K.

Note on Tiv organisation, In *The Tiv
people, by R. C. Abraham, 2nd ed., 1940*:
154–158.
Note extracted from Northern
Provinces secretariat file no. 17048,
written in 1933. Comments on the
origins, status and significance of Tiv
political titles.

4292 Sautter, Gilles
Pression démographique et système
foncier Tiv. *Cah. étud. afr.*, 2 (2) 1961:
326–332.

4293 Wallace, J. G.
The Tiv system of election. *J. Afr. admin.*,
10 (2) Apr. 1958: 63–70.
An examination of the Tiv principle
of alternation in choosing representatives and the effect of the impact on it of
direct election introduced by the British.
Preceded by a brief sketch of Tiv
social structure.

4. (v) Economy, Agriculture, Trade

4294 *Betts, T. F.
The Tiv plantations, 1939–41. *Farm and
forest*, 2, 1941:

4295 Bohannan, Laura M. and Bohannan
Paul J.
Tiv markets. *Trans. N.Y. acad. sci.,
ser. II.*, 19 (7) May 1957: 613–621, maps.
Types and organisation of markets
among the Tiv.

4296 Bohannan, Paul J.
The impact of money on an African
subsistence economy. *J. econ. hist.*, 19
(4) Dec. 1959: 491–503.
The traditional exchange systems in
Tiv economy and the effects upon them
of the introduction of money, a general-
purpose medium of exchange.

4297 ——On the use of native language
categories in ethnology. *Amer. anthrop.*,
58 (3) 1956: 557.
A reply to Dr. Paula Brown's review
of author's *Tiv farm and settlement*,
criticising his "linguistic" approach.
For the review, see *Amer. anthrop.*, 57
(6) 1955: 1321–1322.

4298 ——Some principles of exchange and investment among the Tiv. *Amer. anthrop.*,
57 (1 pt. 1) Feb. 1955: 60–70, bibliog.
"(1) Tiv ideas of exchange as expressed
in their language; (2) Some traditional
modes of investment and exchange . . .
and (3) the impact of Western economy."

4299 ——Tiv farm and settlement. London,
H.M.S.O., 1954. iv, 87p. illus., maps,
(Colonial research studies, no. 15).

4300 Briggs, G. W. G.
Crop yields and food requirements in
Tiv Division, Benue Province, Nigeria.
Farm and forest, 5 (2) Je. 1944: 17–23.

4301 ——Soil deterioration in the southern
district of Tiv Division, Benue Province.
Farm and forest, 2 (1) 1941: 8–12.

4302 McIntosh, D.
The Tiv plantations: their history up to
1939. *Farm and forest*, 2 (1) Je. 1941:
26–30.

4303 Waterfield, O.
Tiv fishing party. *Nig. mag.*, (26) 1947: 408–411, illus.

4. (vi) Religion

4304 Bohannan, Paul J.
A Tiv political and religious idea. *S.–W. j. anthrop.*, 11 (2) Summer 1955: 137–149.

4305 Price-Williams, Douglass Richard
An analysis of reactions to illness among the Tiv of central Nigeria. 1964.
Ph.D. thesis, London university (S.O.A.S.).

4306 —A case study of ideas concerning disease among the Tiv. *Africa*, 32 (2) Apr. 1962: 123–131, illus.
A study of Tiv ideas concerning illness and its social aspects, as observed in Mbara clan in Tiv Division. French summary, p. 131.

4307 —Displacement and orality in Tiv witchcraft. *J. soc. psychology*, 65, 1965: 1–15.

4. (vii) Birth and Death Rituals, Miscellaneous Beliefs and Rites

4308 Bohannan, Paul J.
Circumcision among the Tiv. *Man*, 54, Jan. 1954: 2–6. (art. 2) illus.
General notes about circumcision among the Tiv, followed by a detailed, step by step account of the circumcision of 14 boys which he saw in Ukusu lineage of Raav in Iharev-Ityôshin in 1951.

4309 Malherbe, W. A.
Tiv beliefs and practices re death, burial and witchcraft. Mkar, Gboko, D.R.C.M., 1959. 43p.

4. (viii) Recreation, Games, Music

4310 Hornburg, Friedrich
Die Musik der Tiv. Ein Beitrag zur Erforschung der Musik Nigeriens. 1940. Phil.F. thesis, Berlin.

4311 —Phonographierte afrikanische Mehrstimmigkeit. *Die Musikforschung*, 3 (2) 1950: 120–142, 161–176.
Analysis of vocal and instrumental recorded Tiv music. Also offprinted, Kassel, Bärenreiter [1950].

4312 Lane, Michael G. M.
The music of the Tiv. *Afr. mus.*, 1 (1) 1954: 12–15, illus.; *Nig. field*, 20 (4) Oct. 1955: 177–182, illus.
Notes on traditional Tiv music, with musical notation.

4. (ix) Beauty Culture

4313 Bohannan, Paul J.
Beauty and scarification amongst the Tiv. *Man*, 56, 1956 (art. 129): 117–121, illus.; *World digest*, May 1957.
On Tiv scarification and tatooing. The illustrations include numerous text figures in addition to four photographs.

4314 Bohannan, Paul J. and Downes, R. M.
Tiv hair-dressing: a change in custom. *Man*, 56, 1956: 116 (art. 127) illus.
Brief correspondence indicating that women had taken over from men the dressing of women's hair within the 19th century.

4315 Rowe, Chas. F.
Abdominal cicatrisations of the Munshi tribe, Nigeria. *Man*, 28, Oct. 1928: 179–180. (art. 131) illus.

4. (x) Arts and Crafts

4316 Bohannan, Paul J.
Artist and critic in an African society. In *The artist in tribal society, ed. Marion W. Smith, 1961*: 85–94.

4317 Murray, Kenneth Crosthwaite
The decoration of calabashes by the Tiv. *Nig. mag.*, (36) 1951: 469–474, illus.

4318 —Tiv pattern dyeing. *Nig. mag.*, (32) 1949: 41–47, illus.

4319 —Tiv pottery: an account of the method of making pots, Gboko District, Benue Province. *Nig. field*, 11, Dec. 1943: 147–156.
Pot making in Ipav clan.

5. LINGUISTIC STUDIES

4320 Abraham, Roy Clive
Dictionary of the Tiv language. London, Crown agents, 1940. ix, 331p.

4321 —The grammar of Tiv. Kaduna, Govt. printer, 1933. 5 p. 1,. 213p.

4322 —The principles of Tiv. London, Crown agents, 1940. 102p.

4323 —A Tiv reader for European students. London, Crown agents, 1940. vii, 82p.

4324 Arnott, D. W.
The classification of verbs in Tiv. *B.S.O.A.S.*, 21 (1) Feb. 1958: 111–133.

4325 —Downstep in the Tiv verbal system. *Afr. lang. stud.*, (5) 1964: 34–51.

4326 Bible. Tiv.
Bibilo ka Kwaghôron u Aôndo je la Ikuryan i tse kua i he cii. London, British and foreign Bible society, 1964. 929, 295 [xvi]p. illus., maps.

4327 Bible. N.T. Tiv. Revelation
Kwaghpasen (Tiv) Prepared by the Dutch reformed Church mission, 1951. Zaria, Gaskiya corporation, 1951. [1] 28p.

4328 Bunyan, John
Dzande u Orkristu. Hi shin tar dzan dza ar sha tar u sha . . . "Pilgrim's Progress" in Tiv. London, 1933. 58p. illus.

4329 Catholic Church, Nigeria. Catechism. Tiv.
Catechism u dzwa u Tiv. Oturkpo, Catholic mission, 1951. 64p. Printed by Gaskiya corporation, Zaria.
Catechism in Tiv language.

4330 Chiniquy, Charles
Iwua i hemban cii. Markar, Dutch reformed Church mission, 1957. 32p.

4331 Dangel, R.
Grammatische Skizze der Yergum-Sprache. *Bibliotheca afr.*, 3 (2–3) 1929: 135–136.

Yergum language spoken in Northern Nigeria, classified in the Tiv group.

4332 Dutch reformed Church mission Anzaakaa. Prepared by the Dutch reformed Church mission. Zaria, Gaskiya corporation, 1951. i, 93p.
A collection of Tiv proverbs.

4333 Guthrie, F.
Simplified Tiv grammar. Markurdi, Roman catholic Church diocese, 1962.
Printed by Benue printing venture, Markurdi.

4334 Iyenga, Ali
Tiv grammar. Mkar, Printed by Gar's correspondence service [1961?].

4334a Judd, A. S.
Notes on the Munshi tribe and language. See [4269].

4335 Kwaghfan ngu yilan. Makar, D.R.C.M., 1957. 67p.

4336 Lukas, Johannes
Das Nomen im Tiv. *Anthropos*, 47 (1–2) 1952: 147–176.

On the noun class system in Tiv language.

4337 *Maher, H.
Scholar's vocabulary, English-Tiv. Zaria, Gaskiya corporation, 1961.

4338 Malherbe, W. A.
Tiv-English dictionary, with grammar, notes and index. Lagos, Govt. printer, 1932. xxxix, 207p.

4339 Ruamebera u Eseter. Makar, D.R.C.M., 1957. 32p.

4340 *Sudan united mission.
Tiv hymnal. Mkar, 1962.

4341 *—Atsam agen, no. 1. Mkar, 1963.

4342 *—Atsam agen, no. 2, Mkar, 1965.
Tiv hymns.

4343 Tepstra, Gerard
English-Tiv dictionary. Mkar, 1959. Mimeographed.

4344 Tepstra, Gerard and Ipema, Peter
Tiv grammar notes. Mkar, 1961. Mimeographed.

TULA

Including:

Awok
Billiri
Dadia
Jen
Kamu *(Kamo)*

Logunda *(Nunguda)*
Tangele
Waja

1. GENERAL AND ETHNOGRAPHIC STUDIES

4345 Awok. In *Notes on the tribes . . . by O. Temple, 2nd ed., 1922, repr. 1965*: 34.

4346 Dadia. In *Notes on the tribes . . . by O. Temple, 2nd ed., 1922, repr. 1965*: 88.

4347 Fagg, William Buller
Iron working with a stone hammer among the Tula of Northern Nigeria. *Man*, 52, Apr. 1952: 51–53 (art. 76) illus.

4348 Kamu. In *Notes on the tribes . . . by O. Temple, 2nd ed., 1922, repr. 1965*: 204–205.

4349 Longuda or Nunguda. In *Notes on the tribes . . . by O. Temple, 2nd ed., 1922, repr. 1965*: 259.

4350 Meek, Charles Kingsley
The Jen. In his *Tribal studies in Northern Nigeria, v. 2. 1931*: 519–538, illus.

4351 —The Longuda. In his *Tribal studies in Northern Nigeria, v. 2, 1931*: 331–368, illus.

4352 Mohr, Richard
Einige Notizen über die Tangale von Biliri. *Anthropos.*, 55 (5–6) 1960: 860–870, illus.
Describes housing, clothing, etc., social structure, monarchy, headhunting, cannibalism and religion, among the Tangale of Biliri, North of the Benue.

4353 Tangale. In *Notes on the tribes . . . by*

O. Temple, 2nd ed., 1922, repr. 1965: 347–350.

4354 Tula. In *Notes on the tribes . . . by O. Temple, 2nd ed., 1922, repr. 1965*: 354–355.

4355 Waja. In *Notes on the tribes . . . by O. Temple, 2nd ed., 1922, repr. 1965*: 361–362.

4356 Woodhouse, C. A.
Some account of the inhabitants of the Waja district of Bauchi Province, Nigeria. *J. Afr. soc.*, 23 (90) Jan. 1924: 110–121; (91) Apr. 1924: 194–207.
Ethnographic sketch.

2. LINGUISTIC STUDIES

4357 Grammar of the Tula language (Northern Provinces, Nigeria) by a missionary. *Afr. u. Übersee*, 39, 1955: 101–118.

4358 Jungraithmayr, Hermann
Vokalharmonie im Tangale. *Z. f. Phonetik*, 10 (2) 1957: 144–152.

4359 Meek, Charles Kingsley
Jen vocabulary. In his *Tribal studies in Northern Nigeria, v. 2, 1931*: 530–538.
Includes also vocabulary of the Munga dialect.

4360 —Longuda vocabulary. In his *Tribal studies in Northern Nigeria, v. 2, 1931*: 360–368.

URHOBO

(Osobo, Sobo, Usobo)

Including:

Isoko

1. GENERAL AND ETHNOGRAPHIC STUDIES

4361 Bradbury, R. E.
The Urhobo and Isoko of the Niger Delta. In his *The Benin kingdom . . . 1957*: 127–164.

4362 Clark, John Pepper
Poetry of the Urhobo dance Udje. *Nig. mag.*, (87) Dec. 1965: 282–287.

4363 Edoka, P. N.
Ojowu juju ceremony at Ugharefe. *Nig. mag.*, (15) 1938: 232–233, illus.

4364 Ewimoniya, Charles Y. E.
A short history of Okpolo clan. Warri, the author, 1962. 52p.
Printed by Kagho industrial enterprises, Warri.

4365 Granville, Reginald K. and Roth, Felix N.
Notes on the Jekris, Sobos and Ijos of the Warri District of the Niger Coast Protectorate. Prepared by H. Ling Roth. *J. Anthrop. inst.*, 28, 1899: 104–126, illus.

4366 Hubbard, John Waddington
The Isoko country, Southern Nigeria. *Geog. j.*, 77 (2) Feb. 1931: 110–122.

4367 —The Sobo of the Niger Delta: a work dealing with the history and language of the people inhabiting the Sobo (urhobo) Division, Warri Province, Southern Nigeria, and the geography of their land. Zaria, Gaskiya corporation, 1948. [7] xxvi, 369p. front., illus., maps.

4368 Ikime, Obaro
Chief Dogho: the Lugardian system in Warri, 1917–1932. *J. Hist. soc. Nig.*, 3 (2) Dec. 1965: 313–333.

4369 —The coming of the C.M.S. into the Itsekiri, Urhobo and Isoko country. *Nig. mag.*, (86) Sept. 1965: 206–215.
Outline history of the C.M.S. in the area, with mention of some social problems arising from the clash of the new faith with traditional institutions.

4371 —Consular authority in the Western Delta, 1850–1883. *Historia*, 2 (1) Apr. 1965: 85–99.

4372 —Traditional system of government and justice among the Urhobos and Isoko of Delta Province, Nigeria. *Nig. j. econ. soc. stud.*, 7 (3) Nov. 1965: 283–300.

4373 Lloyd, Peter Cutt
Tribalism in Warri. *WAISER conf. proc.*, 1956: 99–110.

4374 Numa, Frederick Yamu
Pride of Urhobo nation, by Yamu Numa. [Lagos, the author, 1950] [8] 56 [8]p. illus. (ports.) Printed by Ribway press, Lagos.

4375 Ogbodobri, A. A.
Mat-making industry in Warri. *Nig. mag.*, (23) 1946: 122–123, illus.

4376 *Okegberu, Uviri
A short history of Isoko people. Kano, [n.d.].

4377 Salubi, Thompson Edogbeji Aitkins
The establishment of British administration in the Urhobo country (1891–1913) *J. Hist. soc. Nig.*, 1 (3) Dec. 1958: 184–209, bibliog.
Traces the history of British penetration of the Urhobo country and its effective exploration from 1891 and gives a documented account of the subsequent establishment and consolidation of administrative machinery down to the early 20th century.

4378 —The origins of Sapele township. *J. Hist. soc. Nig.*, 2 (1) Dec. 1960: 115–131.

4379 —Revolutions of our time: a national day message by . . . [the] president-general, Urhobo progress union on the occasion of Urhobo national day held on Saturday 3rd November, 1962. Ibadan, Govt. printer, 1962. [iii] 24p.
Contains useful information about the Urhobo people and the achievements of the Urhobo progress union.

4380 Welch, James W.
An African tribe in transition. *Inter. rev. missions*, 20 (80) Oct. 1931: 556–574.
Historical notes on Isoko in the Delta Province of Mid-western Nigeria: the life and religion of the people before the introduction of Christianity and education, and the changes that have been taking place since then.

4381 —The Isoko tribe. *Africa*, 7 (2) Apr. 1934: 160–173.
Ethnographic account.

4382 —The Isoko clans of the Niger Delta. 1936.
Ph.D. thesis, Cambridge.

2. LINGUISTIC STUDIES

4383 Hubbard, John Waddington
The linguistic situation in the Western parts of the Niger delta. *Africa*, 6 (4) Oct. 1933: 490–492.

4384 Igbudu, W. I.
Obe oghere irueru ahwo Isoko. [Ibadan, Ministry of health and social welfare,

1959] 15p. (Social welfare pamphlet, SF).

4385   Onokpasa, B. E.
       Modern Urhobo readers. Book One. [Sapele, Augustinian publishers of Nigeria, 1961] 37p. (incl. front cover) illus.

4386   — —2nd ed. 1963. 33p. illus.

4387   —Urhobo poems. [Ibadan, Augustinian publishers of Nigeria, 1961] 24p. (incl. front cover) illus.

4388   Urhobo primer [Parts] I–II. Ibadan, Baptist press, 1954–55. [3] 2–27, 16p.

4389   Vese, F. M. E.
       Obe avesa Isoko. [Ughelli, the author, 1958] 59p. illus.
       Printed by the Kagho industrial enterprises, Warri.

4390   —Obe otuse Isoko. [P.H., C.M.S. (Nigeria) bookshops, 1954] 50p. illus.

4391   —Obe otuse Isoko no. [P.H. C.M.S. Nigeria bookshops, 1957] [81]p. illus.

4392   —One otuse Isoko: Obe avive Isoko. Port Harcourt, C.M.S. bookshop; London, Longmans, 1954. 48p.

VERRE

(Vere, Werre)

Including:

Bai
Boi
Gweri
Koma (Komawa)
Lima
Marki

Togi (Tuki)
Vomni
Zango

1. GENERAL AND ETHNOGRAPHIC STUDIES

4393   Komawa. In Notes on the tribes . . . by O. Temple, 2nd ed., 1922, repr. 1965: 235.

4394   Meek, Charles Kingsley
       The Verre. In his Tribal studies in Northern Nigeria, 1931, v. 1, pp. 413–445, illus.
       The Vere groups mentioned include Bai, Boi, Koma, Lima, Marki, Togi, Vomni, Zango and Gweri.

4395   Vere. In Notes on the tribes . . . by O. Temple, 2nd ed., 1922, repr. 1965: 357–360.

2. LINGUISTIC STUDIES

4396   Meek, Charles Kingsley
       Verre (of Sholi) vocabulary. In his Tribal studies in Northern Nigeria, 1931, v. 1, pp. 439–445.

WARJAWA

(Warji)

Including:

Afawa (Faawa, Paawa)
Ajawa
Denewa
Diryawa
Gamsawa
Gerewa
Germawa (Gerumawa)

Gezewa
Jimbinawa
Kirifawa
Lipkawa
Miyawa
Sirawa
Wudufawa

GENERAL AND ETHNOGRAPHIC STUDIES

4397   Afawa. In Notes on the tribes . . . by O. Temple, 2nd ed., 1922, repr. 1965: 3–4.

4398   Ajawa. In Notes on the tribes . . . by O. Temple, 2nd ed., 1922, repr. 1965: 7.

4399   Denewa, Germawa, Gamsawa Kirifawa.

In Notes on the tribes . . . by O. Temple, 2nd ed., 1922, repr. 1965: 95.

4400   Gerewa. In Notes on the tribes . . . by O. Temple, 2nd ed., 1922, repr. 1965: 116.

4401   Gezewa. In Notes on the tribes . . . by O. Temple, 2nd ed., 1922, repr. 1965: 116.

4402 Gunn, Harold D.
The Warjawa and linguistically related peoples of Ningi and environs. In his *Pagan peoples of central area of N. Nigeria, 1956*: 22–33.
Ethnographic notes on the Afawa, Ajawa, Diryawa, Lipkawa, Jimbinawa, Miyawa, Sirawa, Warjawa and Wudufawa. See also op. cit. pp. 11–16.

4403 Warjawa. In *Notes on the tribes . . . by O. Temple, 2nd ed. 1922, repr. 1965*: 362–364.

YORUBA

(Aku, Eyo, Nago, Yariba)

Including:

Akoko
Bunu
Ijumu

Ilorin
Kabba
Yagba

1. BIBLIOGRAPHY

4404 Forde, Cyril Daryll
The Yoruba speaking peoples of South-Western Nigeria. 1951.
Bibliography, pp. 84–102.
Includes linguistics, pp. 99–102. There is a supplement of 5 pages published 1963 and stuck in at the end.

2. GENERAL

4405 *Abeokuta: past and present. *Afr. world ann.*, 1917: 79–81.

4406 Adedeji, Adebayo, ed.
An introduction to Western Nigeria: its people, culture and system of government. Ife Institute of Administration, University of Ife [1966?] 121p.

4407 Ade-Odukoya, S.
Antiquities and places of interest round Ijebu Ode. *Nig. mag.*, (9) 1937: 56–59.

4408 Aderibigbe, A. A. B.
The expansion of the Lagos Protectorate, 1863–1900. 1959.
Ph.D. thesis, London University.

4409 Aiere, Ogidi, and Owe. In *Notes on the tribes . . . by O. Temple, 2nd ed., 1922, repr. 1965*: 6.

4410 Ajayi, E. S.
Ijebu-Ibadan boundary. [Ijebu Ode, the author] 1925. 26p. Printed by Ife Olu printing works, Lagos.

4411 Ajayi, W. O.
A history of the Yoruba Mission, 1843–1880. 1960.
M.A. thesis, Bristol.

4412 Akoko. In *Notes on the tribes . . . by O. Temple, 2nd ed., 1922, repr. 1965*: 7.

4413 Aluko, Timothy Mofolorunso
One man, one matchet. London, Heinemann, 1964. 197p.
A novel.

4414 —One man, one wife. Lagos, Nigerian printing and publishing co., 1959. 200p.
A novel.

4415 Anene, J. C.
The Nigeria-Dahomey boundary. *J. Hist. soc. Nig.*, 2 (4) Dec. 1963: 479–485.
A historical analysis of the factors—political, ethnic and commercial—which influenced the determination of the Nigeria-Dahomey boundary.

4416 Avril, A. d'.
La côte des esclaves: le Yoruba, le Dahomey. Paris, 1859.

4417 Aworo. In *Notes on the tribes . . . by O. Temple, 2nd ed., 1922, repr. 1965*: 34–36.

4418 Bascom, William Russell
Lander's routes through Yoruba country. *Nig. field*, 25 (1) Jan. 1960: 12–22, map.
Attempts to plot the possible routes followed by Clapperton and the Landers during their journeys through Yorubaland, and to identify the towns mentioned in their journals.

4419 Batty, R. Braithwaite
Notes on the Yoruba country. *J. Anthrop. inst.*, 19, 1890: 160–164, illus.
For details, see [4900].

4420 Bedingfield, *Capt.*
Narrative of a journey from Lagos to Odé, the capital of the Ijebu country. *J. Roy. geog. soc.*, 33, 1863: 214–217.

4421 Bowen, Thomas Jefferson
Central Africa: adventures and missionary labours in several countries in the interior of Africa from 1849–1856. Charleston, Southern Baptist publication society [c. 1857] xii, 359p. map (fold.).

4422 ——New impression, with an introduction, by E. A. Ayandele. London, Frank Cass, 1968. l. xii, 359p. map (fold.).

4423 Bulifant, Josephine
40 years in the African bush. Grand Rapids, Mich., Zondernan publishing house, 1950. 185p.

4424 Bunu. In *Notes on the tribes . . . by O. Temple, 2nd ed., 1922, repr. 1965*: 71–72.

4425 Burton, Richard Francis
Abeokuta and the Cameroons mountains; an exploration. London, Tinsley brothers, 1863. 2v. front. illus., map.
Volume one is about the author's journey to Abeokuta and volume two on his exploration of the Cameroons mountain.

4426   —Ascent of the Ogun or Abeokuta
River. *Proc. Roy. geog. soc.*, 6, 1861:
64–66.

4427   Campbell, Robert
A few facts relating to Lagos, Abeokuta
and other sections of Central Africa.
Philadelphia, King & Braid, 1860. 18p.

4428   —A pilgrimage to my motherland; an
account of a journey among the Egbas
and Yorubas of Central Africa, in 1859–
60. New York, Thomas Hamilton, 1861.
145p. front., map.

4429   — —Another issue, with an introduction
by Sir Culling E. Eardley. London,
W. J. Johnson, [1861].

4430   Carter, G. T. Gilbert
The colony of Lagos. *Proc. Roy. col.
inst.*, 28, 1896–97: 275–304.

4431   Clarke, John Digby
Omu; an African experiment in education. London, Longmans, Green, 1937.
xix, 167p. front., illus.
Account of the origins and development of a rural school in Omu village
in Ilorin Province, with notes on the
area and people.

4432   Cotton, E. P.
The kingdom of the Alake (Report on
the Egba boundary) [Lagos, Govt.
printer?] 1905. 21p.

4433   Dallimore, H.
The education of the West African
peoples, with especial reference to the
Yoruba tribes of Southern Nigeria. 1929.
B.Litt. thesis, Oxford.

4434   Delany, Martin, Robinson
Official report of the Niger valley
exploring party. New York, Thomas
Hamilton, 1861. 75p.

4435   Denton, George C.
Twenty-three years in Lagos and the
Gambia. *J. Afr. soc.*, 11 (42) Jan. 1912:
129–140, illus.
Author lived in Lagos for 12½ of the
23 years, from June 1888 to 1900. He
here describes Lagos colony as he saw
it, (pp. 129–133). The illus. refer to
Gambia.

4436   The Destruction of Lagos. 2nd ed.
London, James Ridgeway, 1852, 24p.

4437   Duckworth, E. H.
A journey through the creeks, Lagos to
Sapele. *Nig. mag.*, (10) Apr. 1937: 40–47.

4438   Duncan, John
Travels in Western Africa, in 1845 &
1846, comprising a journey from
Whydah, through the kingdom of
Dahomey to Adofoodia, in the interior.
London, R. Bentley, 1847, repr. London,
Frank Cass, 1968. 2v.

4439   Ekiti. In *Notes on the tribes . . . by O.
Temple, 2nd ed., 1922, repr. 1965*: 101–
107.

4440   Ekwensi, Cyprian Odiatu Duaka
The drummer boy. Cambridge, C.U.P.,
1960. 87p. illus.
A novel.

4441   Elphinstone, K. V. *ed.*
Gazetteer of Ilorin Province. London,
Waterlow, 1921. 67p. illus.

4442   Ewart, J. H.
Lagos; its hinterland, its products and
its people. *J. R. soc. arts.*, 50, 1903:
650–659.

4443   Freeman, Thomas Birch
Extracts from a journal of various
visits to the kingdoms of Ashanti,
Yariba and Dahomi in Western Africa
to promote the objects of the Wesleyan
Missionary Society. [London, Printed
by J. Nicholas, 1843] 24p.

4444   —Journal of various visits to the
Kingdoms of Ashanti, Aku and
Dahomi, in Western Africa. 2nd ed.
London, sold by J. Mason, 1844. x,
298p. illus., map.
Freeman, a Wesleyan missionary,
gives in his journal, useful account of
life and the state of affairs in the
Ashanti and Yoruba states, including
Abeokuta and Badagry (pp. 197–237)
which he visited in 1842.
Although described as 2nd edition,
there does not appear to have been any
1st edition, at least not in book form.

4444a   — —New Edition, with an introduction,
by Harrison M. Wright. London, Frank
Cass, 1968. xxxix, x, 298p. illus., maps
(fold.).

4445   Grant, James
A geography of Western Nigeria.
London; New York, O.U.P. 1960. 95p.
illus.
A useful introduction to the geography
of Western Nigeria (including Mid-
Western Nigeria) with good typo-
graphical design and many illustrations
to meet the secondary school level for
which the work is intended.

4446   —Okitipupa: a brief survey. *Nig. geog.
j.*, 1 (1) Apr. 1957: 7–13, map.
Descriptive sketch of Okitipupa
Division in Ondo Province, with
particular attention to Okitipupa and
Aiyetoro towns.

4447   Gwam, Lloyd Chike
The educational work of Christian
missions in the settlement of Lagos,
1842–1882. *Ibadan*, (12) Je. 1961: 18–21.
Educational activity of the Church
Missionary Society, the Wesleyan
Missionary Society, the Roman Catholic
Mission and the American Baptist
Mission in Lagos during the period.
These efforts consisted mainly in the
establishment of elementary, secondary
and teacher training schools.

4448   Halligey, J. T. F.
Yoruba country, Abeokuta, and Lagos.
J. Manch. geog. soc., 9, 1893: 28–44.

4449   Hawkesworth, E. G.
Ijebu Province. *Nig. mag.*, (15) Sept.
1938: 197–199.

4450   Hermon-Hodge, Henry Baldwin
Gazetteer of Ilorin Province. London,

G. Allen & Unwin, 1929. 301p. illus., maps (fold.) bibliog.

4451 Hinderer, Anna
Seventeen Years in the Yoruba country: memorials of Anna Hinderer. With an introduction by Richard B. Hone. New ed. London, Religious tract society [1877] x, 344p. illus. map.
Journal of the wife of Rev. David Hinderer, a C.M.S. missionary, kept during her stay with her husband in Ibadan.

4452 Holley, *missionary*
Lettre de M. Holley, supérieur de la mission d'Abéokuta, à M. Planque, Superieur général des Missions Africaines de Lyon. *Annals de la propagation de la foi*, 54 (320) Jan. 1882: 76–88, illus.

4453 Idanre. *Nig. mag.*, (46) 1955: 154–180. illus.
Notes describing the town of Idanre and the approaches to it.

4454 Igwe, E. Meyer
Thomas Birch Freeman: pioneer methodist mission to Nigeria. *Nig. mag.*, (77) Je. 1963: 79–89. illus.

4455 Jacoby, Jean Lorna
Abimbolu: a novel. London, L.U.P., 1955. 112p. illus., map.

4455a Jacolliot, Louis
Voyage aux pays mystérieux: Yebou, Borgu, Niger. See [1644].

4456 Johnson, A. W.
Abeokuta. *Nig. geog. j.*, 6 (2) Dec. 1963: 89–95, maps.
A brief geographical sketch of Abeokuta town.

4457 Johnson, Charles R.
Bryan Roe: a soldier of the cross. Missionary travels and adventure in West central Africa. London, 1896. 272p.

4458 Kirk-Greene, Anthony Hamilton Millard
America in the Niger valley: a colonization centenary. *Phylon*, (3) 1962: 225–239.
Account of Martin Robinson Delany's Niger Valley Exploring Party. See [4434].

4459 Lelard, L. C.
Lagos in Portugal and Lagos in Nigeria. *Nigeria mag.*, (39) 1952: 257–260, illus.

4460 Mann, Adolphus
Die Yoruba-Küste. Vortrag, gehalten von Missionar A. Mann am 18 December 1885. (Separat-Abdruck aus dem III. IV. Jahresbericht des Württembergischen Vereins fur Handelsgeographie.) Stuttgart, 1886. 8p.

4461 May, D. J.
Journey in the Yoruba and Nupe countries in 1858. *J. Roy. geog. soc.*, 30, 1860: 212–233, map.

4462 Millson, Alvan
Yoruba. *J. Manch. geog. soc.*, 7, 1891: 92–104.

4463 —The Yoruba country, West Africa. *Proc. Roy. geog. soc.*, ser. 2, 13 (10) Oct. 1891: 577–587, map. (p. 664).
Gives a description of the Yoruba country, its people and their agriculture and trade. Also printed separately.

4464 Milum, John
Notes of a journey from Lagos up the Niger to Bida, the capital of Nupe and Ilorin in the Yoruba country (1879–1880) *Proc. Roy. geogr. soc.*, n.s. 3 (1) Jan. 1881: 26–37,
Describes towns, fortifications, roads, law courts, etc., seen during the journey which took him from Lagos through Bonny, Warri, Onitsha, Lokoja, Bida and other towns. Also notes on local politics, especially in Ilorin.

4465 Moloney, C. Alfred
Notes on Yoruba and the Colony and Protectorate of Lagos. *Proc. Roy. geogr. soc.*, ser. 2, 12 (10) Oct. 1890: 596–614.
Estimated population of various towns, some useful plants, fishing and other industries, and the geology of the area. The Itsekiri, Ijaw and Bini also noted.

4466 —Exhibition of cross-bows, long-bows, quivers, etc., from the Yoruba country. *J. Anthrop. inst.*, 19, 1890: 213–215.

4467 Mondjannagni, A.
Quelques aspects historiques, économiques et politiques de la frontière Dahomey-Nigeria. *Étud. dahom. n.s.*, 1, 1963–64: 17–57, illus., maps.

4468 Onaeko, E. A.
Shagamu and its district: a short geographical account. *Nig. geog. j.*, 2 (1) Je. 1958: 14–25, illus., map.

4469 *Pinnock, James
Yoruba country: its people, customs, and missions. 1893. 90p.

4470 Southon, Arthur E.
The whispering bush; true tales of West Africa. London, Sheldon press, 1923. 160p.
A missionary's impressions of the Yoruba portrayed in nine short stories.

4471 Soyinka, Wole
A dance of the forests. London, Ibadan, O.U.P., 1963. [vi] 89p. (A three crowns book).
A play.

4472 —Five plays: A dance of the forests; the lion and the jewel; The swamp dwellers; The trials of Brother Jero; [and] The strong breed. London, Ibadan, O.U.P., 1964. [viii] 276p.

4473 Stone, Richard Henry
In Africa's forest and jungle; or Six years among the Yorubans. New York, Revell, [c. 1899] Edinburgh, Oliphant, Anderson and Ferrier, 1900. 282p. illus. (Stories of missions).

4474 Thompson, H. N. G.
Census of Lagos. London, published on behalf of the Govt. of Nigeria by the Crown agents for the colonies, 1932. 52p. (Census of Nigeria, 1931, vol. 4).

Full report of the 1931 census for Lagos. The statistical section gives data for nationality, sex, age, religion, etc. but excludes occupations, marital status and physical disabilities.

4475 Thörburn, J. W. A.
Some memories of Western Nigeria in the twenties and thirties. *Nig. field*, 23 (2) Apr. 1958: 85–89.
A former education officer recalls his days in Lagos, Ibadan, Akure and Benin.

4476 Tremearne, Arthur John Newman
The Yorubas . . . In his *The Niger and the West Sudan . . . 1910*: 64–70. [540].

4477 Tucker, Charlotte Maria
Abeokuta; or Sunrise within the tropics: an outline of the origin and progress of the Yoruba Mission. 5th ed. London, J. Nisbet, 1856. vii, 278p. illus., map.
A brief history of missionary efforts in Yoruba country. Contains many side lights to the general history and state of affairs of this region in the early part of the 19th century.

4478 Tutuola, Amos
Brave African huntress. London, Faber, 1958. 150p. illus.

4479 —Feather woman of the jungle. London, Faber, 1962. 132p.

4480 —My life in the bush of ghosts. London, Faber, 1954. 174p.

4481 —The palm-wine drinkard and his dead palm-wine tapster in the dead's town. London, Faber, 1952. 125p.

4482 —Simbi and the Satyr of the dark jungle. London, Faber, 1955. 136p.

4483 Upward, Allen
The Province of Kabba, Northern Nigeria. *J. Afr. soc.*, 2 (7) Apr. 1903: 235–260.
A general study by a former Resident. Embraces natural features, populations, industries, trade, indigenous governments, law, and religion.

4484 Vogt, H.
Die Bewohner von Lagos. *Globus*, 41, 1882: 236–238; 252–254.
The inhabitants of Lagos.

4485 W.
Native races of the Niger territories, the Yorubas. *Niger & Yoruba notes*, 2 (17) Nov. 1895: 37–38.

4486 Wann, J.
Travel in Ondo Province. *Nig. mag.*, (18) 1939: 118–119.

4487 Welldon, R. M. C.
The human geography of a Yoruba township in South-western Nigeria. 1958.
B.Litt. thesis, Oxford.

4488 Yagba. In *Notes on the tribes . . . by O. Temple, 2nd ed., 1922, repr. 1965*: 368.

4489 Yoruba. In *Notes on the tribes . . . by O. Temple, 2nd ed., 1922, repr. 1965*: 376–391.

Includes notes on the Igbona and Igbolo of Ilorin Province.

3. PHYSICAL ANTHROPOLOGY

4489a Allison, A. C. (and others)
Haptoglobin types in British, Spanish Basque and Nigerian African populations. *Nature*, 1958: 824–5.
The Nigerian African population refers to the Yoruba of Ilobi in Western Nigeria.

4490 Barnicot, N. A.
Albinism in South-West Nigeria. *Ann. eugenics*, 17, 1952–3: 37–74, illus.

4491 —Red hair in African negroes: a preliminary study. *Ann. eugenics*, 17, 1952–53: 211–232.
Studies carried out in Lagos and Benin.

4491a Blumberg, B. S.
The blood groups of the pastoral Fulani of Northern Nigeria and the Yoruba . . . See [2143].

4491b Charmers, J. N. M.
The ABO, MNS and Rh Blood groups of the Nigerians. See [572].

4492 Cockshott, W. Peter
Carpal anomalies amongst the Yorubas. *W. Afr. med. j.*, *n.s.*, 8 (5) Oct. 1959: 185–190, illus.
An examination of the wrists of 514 and 409 Yoruba men and women respectively by a standard radiographic technique revealed three types of carpal anomalies—lunate triquetral fusion, hamate capitate fusion, and hamate pisiform fusion.

4492a Edington, G. M.
The distribution of haemoglobin C in West Africa. See [573].

4493 Jelliffe, D. B. and Humphreys, John
The sickle-cell trait in Western Nigeria: a survey of 1,881 cases in the Yoruba. *Brit. med. j.*, 1, Feb. 23, 1952: 405.

4494 Watson-Williams, E. J. [and others].
A new haemoglobin, D Ibadan (B–87 threonine-lysine) producing no sickle-cell haemoglobin D disease with haemoglobin S. *Nature*, 205 (4978) 27 Mar. 1965: 1273–1276, illus.

4. SOCIAL AND CULTURAL ANTHROPOLOGY, ETHNOGRAPHY

4. (i) General

4495 Abiola, E. T.
The nature of intellectual development in Nigerian children. *Teacher educ.*, 6 (1) May 1965: 37–58.

4496 Adekanmbi, Sola
The Yoruba way: (a handbook of Yoruba customs) [Lagos, the author, 1955] 56p.
Printed by Remilekun press, 8 book depot, Mushin, Lagos.

4497 Aiyetoro. *Nig. mag.*, (55) 1957: 356–386, illus.

4498 Ajayi, Jacob F. Ade
Professional warriors in nineteenth-century Yoruba politics. *Tarikh*, 1 (1) Nov. 1965: 72–81, illus., map.

4499 Ajayi, Jacob F. Ade and Smith, Robert
Yoruba warfare in the nineteenth century. Cambridge, C.U.P., Ibadan, Inst. of African studies, 1964. x, 160p. illus., maps, bibliog.
A study of the nature of Yoruba warfare as seen in the protracted wars of 1820 to 1893–the armies and their organization, weapons, fortifications, strategies, & tactics, etc., with accounts of some specific campaigns, including a detailed study of the Ijaye wars, 1800–1805. Captain Jone's report on the Egba army in 1861, pp. 129–140.

4500 Akisola, J. A.
In an Ijebu forest. *Farm and forest*, 10, 1950: 8–10.

4501 Alade, S.
The awakening of Akure. [Akure, the author, 1950?] [viii] 31p. (Our affairs series, no. 1) Printed by Titilayo press, Oshogbo.

4502 Armstrong, Robert G.
Yoruba numerals. Ibadan, O.U.P., for NISER, 1962. 36p. (NISER studies, no. 1).

4503 Askari, E. V. A.
Concept of urban and rural in Yoruba land. 1964.
B. Litt. thesis, Oxford university.

4504 Asuni, T.
Maladjustment and delinquency: a comparison of two samples. *J. child psychol. psychiat.*, 4, 1963: 219–228.

4505 —Some aspects of children's problems in Western Nigeria. In *Pan-African psychiatric conference, 1st, Abeokuta, 1961.* [1962?]: 46–48.
Bedwetting, refusal of food, mental deficiency and delinquency.

4506 —Suicide in Western Nigeria. *Brit. med. j.*, 2, 1962: 1091–1097.

4507 —Suicide trends in Western Nigeria. In *Pan-African psychiatric conference, 1st, Abeokuta, 1961.* [1962?]: 164–173, bibliog.

4508 Avezac-Macaya, Armand d' (M.A.P. d'Avezac de Castera-Maya)
Notice sur le pays et le peuple des Yebeous en Afrique. *Mém. Soc. ethnol.*, 2 (2) 1845: 1–196, illus. Also published separately, Paris, Dondey-Dupré, 1845. [1] 271p. illus., map.
Account of Ijebu land and society in the early 19th century as described to author by one Osifekunde (Ochi-Fekoué) an Ijebu man who had been sold into slavery and whom he met in Paris in 1839. Gives a biographical account of Osifekunde himself, and a description of the political and social set up of his people. d'Avezac was archivist in the French Ministry of Marine and Vice President of the Societé Ethnologique de Paris. An extract from his story transla-

ted into English by Paul Hair appeared in *Nig. mag.* (68) Mar. 1961 [4540].

4509 Barber, Mary Ann Serrett.
Oshielle; or Village life in the Yoruba country; from the journals and letters of a catechist there, describing the rise of a Christian church in an African village. London J. Nisbet, 1857. xxiv, 222p. illus.

4510 Bascom, William Russell
The focus of Cuban Santeria. *S.–W. j. anthrop.*, 6 (1) Spring 1950: 64–68.

4511 Baumann, Margaret Irene Lee
Sons of sticks: sketches of everyday life in a Nigerian bush. With music of Yoruba songs and marches. London, Sheldon press, [1933] ix, 97, 12p. illus.
"Yoruba songs and marches" takes the extra 12 pages at end.

4512 Beier, Horst Ulrich
The Yoruba attitude to dogs. *Odù*, (7) Mar. 1959: 31–37.

4512a Bowen, T. J.
A grammar and dictionary of the Yoruba language, with an introductory description of the country and people of Yoruba. See [5323].

4513 Burton, Richard Francis
A mission to Gelele, king of Dahome. With notices of the so called "Amazons", the grand customs, the yearly customs, the human sacrifices, the present state of the slave trade, and the negro's place in nature. London, Tinsley, 1864. 2v. fronts.
— —New ed., with introduction and notes by C. W. Newbury. London, Routledge & K. Paul, 1966.

4514 Castillo-Fiel, Conde de
Manifestaciones culturales de los pueblos primitives: el teatro entre los Yoruba. *Africa* [Madrid] 7 (106) Oct. 1950: 452–453.

4515 Chatterji, Suniti Kumar
The culture and religion of the Yorubas of West Africa. Calcutta, Swami Pavitrananda, 1945. 12p.
Offprinted from *Prabuddha Bharata*, or "Awakened India", Oct. 1945. Also reprinted in his *Africanism; the African personality, 1960*: 76–105, illus.

4516 *Church Missionary Society
Yoruba names and salutations. Lagos, C.M.S., 1931.

4517 Collier, F. S.
Yoruba hunters' salutes. *Nig. field*, 18 (2) Apr. 1953: 52–67, illus.

4518 Collis, R. J. M.
The relationship between certain physical factors and psychiatric disorder among the Yoruba tribe of Nigeria: an evaluation of the cultural influences involved. 1962.
M.D. thesis, Trinity College, Dublin.

4519 Comhaire, Jean
A propos des "Brasiliens" de Lagos, *Grands-Lacs* [Namur, Belgium] Mar. 1949: 41–43.

4520 "Communism" in Aiyetoro. *W. Afr. rev.*, 30 (381) Je. 1959: 469–471, illus.
Account of a visit to Aiyetoro, with a brief historical sketch of the town.

4521 Cordwell, Justine Mayer
Some aesthetic aspects of Yoruba and Benin cultures. 1952.
Ph.D. thesis, Northwestern university.

4522 Crowther, Samuel Adjai
Account of Bishop Crowther's early life. Cape Town, Diocesan library [n.d.]

4522a D'Avezac, M. See Avezac-Macaya, Armand d' (M.A.P. d'Avezac de Castera-Maya).

4523 Delano, Isaac O.
Notes and comments from Nigeria. London and Redhill, United society for Christian literature, (Lutterworth press) [1944] 64p.
Describes the people, their customs and problems as seen during a tour of parts of Western and Northern Regions.

4524 —The soul of Nigeria. London, T. Werner Laurie, 1937. 252p. front. (port.) plates.
Religion, history, social life and customs of the Yoruba.

4525 Dennett, R. E.
How the Yoruba count; and the universal order in creation, etc. *J. Afr. soc.*, 16 (63) Apr. 1917: 242–250; 17 (65) Oct. 1917: 60–71.

4526 —My Yoruba alphabet. London, Macmillan, 1916. xi, 45p.

4527 —Yoruba salutations. *J. Afr. soc.*, 8 (30) Jan. 1909: 187–189.

4528 Duckworth, E. H.
A visit to the Apostles and the town of Aiyetoro; describing how a small group of Africans with vision and faith have created a new town and pioneered a new and improved way of life on the coast of Nigeria. *Nig. mag.*, (36) 1951: 387–440, map.

4529 Eaglesfield, Carrol Frederick
Listen to the drums: Nigeria and its peoples. Nashville, Tenn., Broadman press, 1950. [xii] 82p. illus.

4530 Ellis, Alfred Burdon
The Yoruba-speaking peoples of the slave coast of West Africa; their religion, manners, customs, laws, language, etc. With an appendix containing a comparison of the Tshi, Gã, Ewe, and Yoruba languages. London, Chapman and Hall, 1894. vii, 402p. map, bibliog.
A sister volume to author's *The Ewe-speaking peoples of the slave coast of West Afriva.*

4531 Fadipe, N. A.
The sociology of the Yoruba. 1940.
Ph.D. thesis, London.

4532 Fagg, William Buller and Willett, Frank
Ancient Ife: an ethnological summary. *Odù*, (8) Oct. 1960: 21–35. Also *Proc. 4th Pan-Afr. cong. pre-hist., Leopoldville, 1957:*
A bold attempt to reconstruct the ethnology of Ife during its classic period of art and culture, tentatively placed between the 14th and 18th centuries.

4533 Farrow, S.
A visit to Ilorin. *Nig. & Yoruba notes*, 1, 1895: 28–30; 37–39.

4534 Feilberg, C. G.
Ibadan. *Kultur-geografi*, 10 (59) Oct. 1958: 77–91.
English summary, pp. 90–91.

4535 Forde, Cyril Daryll
The Yoruba-speaking peoples of South-Western Nigeria. London, International African institute, 1951. [vi] 102p. 1 map (fold) bibliog. (Int. Afr. inst. Ethnographic survey of Africa, ed. Daryll Forde. Western Africa, part 4).

4536 Frobenius, Leo, 1873–1938. Leader of the German expedition which explored the antiquities of Yorubaland in 1910. Author of a number of works on Yoruba and African art and antiquities. For his works, see [662] to [673] especially [671].

4537 Gilles, H. M.
Akufo; an environmental study of a Nigerian village community. [Ibadan, Dept. of preventive and social medicine] University of Ibadan, 1964. 80p. illus.

4538 Gollmer, C. A.
African symbolic messages. *J.R.A.I.*, 14, 1885: 169–182.

4539 Gordon, Arnold
Crowther: a great African. *W. Afr. rev.*, 28 (360) Sept. 1957: 863–869.
Biography by a great-great-grandson.

4540 Hair, Paul
An Ijebu man in Paris, 1839. *Nig. mag.*, (68) Mar. 1961: 79–82, illus.
Extract from *Notice sur le pays et le peuple des Yebous en Afrique*, by M. A. P. d'Avezac de Castera-Maya. *Mem. Soc. ethnol.*, 2 (2) 1845: 1–196 [4508].

4541 Hennessy, M. N.
Owo: Nigeria's ideal 'village.' *New commonwealth*, 21 (1) Oct. 1950: 14.

4542 Hess, Jean
L'âme nègre. Paris, Calmann Lévy, 1898. 327p.

4543 Hoffmann-Burchardi, Helmut
Die Yoruba-Städte in Südwest-Nigeria. *Erdkunde*, 18 (3) 1964: 206–235.

4544 Holley, *missionary*
Étude sur les Egbas. *Miss. Cathol.*, 1881: 350–354.

4545 [Hughes, Charles C. and others]
Integrated and disintegrated Yoruba villages. In *Psychiatric disorder among the Yoruba, by Alexander H. Leighton [and others] 1963*: 203–240, illus.

4546 —Notes on the Egba Yoruba. In *Psychiatric disorder among the Yoruba, by Alexander H. Leighton [and others] 1963*: 289–293.

4547 Ibadan. [A brochure] Ibadan, published under the auspices of the University College, 1949. 53p. illus., 1 map (fold.)
A brochure containing brief articles on the history, geography, religion,

social life, etc., of Ibadan town, presented to the 3rd International West African conference held at the University College in Dec. 1949.

4548 Igun, A.
Demographic survey of Western Nigeria. *Nig. j. econ. soc. stud.*, 5 (1) Mar. 1963: 105–125.

4549 Izzett, Alison
The fears and anxieties of delinquent Yoruba children. *Odù*, (1) Jan. 1955: 26–34.

4550 —The Yoruba young delinquent in Lagos, Nigeria, 1955.
B.Litt. thesis, Oxford.

4551 Kaushik, S. C.
Patterns of neurological disease in Ibadan. In *Pan-African psychiatric conference, 1st, 1961.* [*1962?*]: 78–87.

4552 Kopytoff, Jean Herskovits
A preface to modern Nigeria: the "Sierra Leonians" in Yoruba, 1830–1890. Madison, London, University of Wisconsin press, 1965. xiii, 402p. maps, bibliog.
Evaluation of the roles—political, economic, religious and social—of liberated Africans of Yoruba descent who returned to Yorubaland from Sierra Leone in the 19th century.

4553 Lambo, T. Adeoyo
Observation on the role of cultural factors in paranoid psychosis among the Yoruba tribe. 1954.
M.D. thesis, Birmingham.

4554 —The role of cultural factors in paranoid psychosis among the Yoruba tribe. *J. mental sci.*, 101, Apr. 1955: 239–266.

4555 Laotan, A. B.
Brazilian influence on Lagos. *Nig. mag.*, (69) Aug. 1961: 157–165, illus.
Influence on Lagos of Brazilian repatriates of Yoruba origin who returned to West Africa in the middle of the 19th century. This influence was chiefly in architecture, painting, carpentry, dress-making, and other trades, and in social life.

4556 —The torch bearers; or Old Brazilian colony in Lagos. Lagos, Ife Olu printing works, [1943] 31p.

4557 Lasebikan, E. L.
The Yoruba in Brazil. *W. Afr.*, (2357) Aug. 4th 1962: 843, illus.

4558 Leighton, Alexander H. [and others]
Psychiatric disorder among the Yoruba: a report from the Cornell-Aro mental health research project in the Western Region, Nigeria. Ithaca, N.Y., Cornell university press; London, O.U.P., 1963. 432p.

4559 Leighton, A. H. and Hughes, Jane M.
Yoruba concepts of psychiatric disorder. In *Pan-African psychiatric conference, 1st, Abeokuta, 1961.* [*1962?*]: 138–141.

4560 Leighton, Dorothea C.
Psychiatric symptoms found in Yoruba respondents during the Cornell-Aro pilot study. In *Pan-African psychiatric conference, 1st, Abeokuta, 1961.* [*1962?*]: 141–143.

4561 Levine, Barbara B.
Yoruba students' memories of childhood, rewards and punishments. Ibadan, university press, 1962. 18p. (Ibadan. Univ. Institute of education. Occasional publication, no. 2).

4562 Life in a Yoruba fishing village: an adventure in friendship. *Nig. mag.*, (25) 1946: 243–282.

4563 Lloyd, Peter Cutt
Osifakorede of Ijebu. *Odù*, (8) Oct. 1960: 59–64.

4564 —Sallah at Ilorin. *Nig. mag.*, (70) Sept. 1961: 266–278, illus.

4565 —Sungbo's *eredo*. *Odù*, (7) Mar. 1959: 15–22.
Describes a series of embankments running to about 80 miles and traditionally believed to have been built round the ancient town of Oke Eri, in memory of a wealthy woman named Sungbo. The principal town within it today is Ijebu Ode.

4566 —The Yoruba of Nigeria. In *Peoples of Africa, ed. J. L. Gibbs, 1965*: 547–582. illus., map, bibliog.
A compendious ethnographic summary of the Yoruba.

4567 Mabogunje, Akin L.
The changing pattern of rural settlements and rural economy in Egba Division, South-western Nigeria. 1958.
M.A. thesis, London.

4568 —The evolution of rural settlement in Egba Division, Nigeria. *J. trop. geog.*, 13, Dec. 1959: 65–77, maps.
The unique, high density of rural settlement in Egba Division in contrast with the rest of Yoruba country is examined and its origins ascribed to outward movement of the Egbas in search of farm land soon after their settlement of Abeokuta.

4569 Mabogunje, Akin L. and Gleave, Michael B.
Changing agricultural landscape in Southern Nigeria: the example of Egba Division, 1850–1950. *Nig. geog. j.*, 7 (1) Je. 1964: 1–15, maps., bibliog.

4570 Macfie, John W. Scott
A Yoruba tattoer. *Man*, 13, 1913: 121–122. (art. 68) illus.

4571 MacGregor, William
Lagos, Abeokuta and the Alake. *J. Afr. soc.*, 3 (12) Jl. 1904: 464–481.
Social, political and commercial conditions in Lagos and Abeokuta, and the administration of Alake of Abeokuta.

4572 [Macrow, Donald W.]
Kabba. *Nig. mag.*, (61) 1959: 166–184, illus.
Macrow, Donald W. and Standfield, D.
Change in the hills. See [1774].

4573 McStallworth, Paul
Physical status of education in Western

Nigeria. *J. hum. rel.*, 10, autumn 1961: 59–66.

4573a Mann, Adolphus
Eine geschichtliche Sage aus der Zeit der ersten Niederlassungen der Egba. See [5368].

4574 —Notes on the numeral system of the Yoruba nation. *J. Anthrop. inst.*, 16, 1887: 59–64.

4575 Margetts, Edward L.
Traditional Yoruba healers in Nigeria. *Man*, 65, Jl.–Aug. 1965 (art. 102): 115–118, illus., bibliog.

4576 Mauny, Raymond
Rayonnement d'Ife: capitale artistique et religieuse ancienne du golfe de Guinée. *Présence afr., n.s.*, 4 Oct.–Nov. 1955: 80–82.

4577 Mercier, Paul
Notice sur le peuplement Yoruba au Dahomey-Togo. *Étud. dahom.*, (4) 1950: 29–40.

4578 Millson, Alvan
Indigenous plants of Yoruba land. *Kew bull.*, 1891: 206–219.
Gives vernacular names of the plants listed, with notes on their uses among the Yoruba.

4579 Monekosso, G. L.
Clinical survey of a Yoruba village. *W. Afr. med. j., n.s.*, 13 (2) Apr. 1964: 47–59, map.
Report of a survey of Igbile village in Ijebu Division, Western Nigeria. Factors investigated include demography, diet, heights and weights, social habits and general health.

4580 Morton-Williams, Peter
Varieties of sanctions among the Yoruba. *WAISER conf. proc., 1956*: 134.
Summary of a paper analysing the means of social control among the Yoruba on the basis of Radcliffe Brown's classification.

4581 —Yoruba responses to the fear of death. *Africa*, 30 (1) Jan. 1960: 34–40, illus., bibliog.
Considers "Some of the ways in which the Yoruba express their fear of death, and the response they make to it, especially through their traditional religion" French summary, p. 40.

4582 Murphy, Jane M. [and others].
The city of Abeokuta. In *Psychiatric disorders among the Yoruba, by Alexander H. Leighton [and others] 1963*: 294–305.

4583 [Murphy, Jane M. and Leighton, Alexander H.]
The Yoruba world. In *Psychiatric disorder among the Yoruba, by Alexander H. Leighton [and others] 1963*: 29–53.

4584 Newbury, C. W.
The Western slave coast and its rulers: European trade and administration among the Yoruba and Adja-speaking peoples of South-western Nigeria, Southern Dahomey and Togo. Oxford,

Clarendon press, 1961. xii, 234p. maps, bibliog.

4585 *Obasa, Denrele Adetimkan
Iwe kini ti awon Akewi (Yoruba philosophy) Ibadan, Egbe Agba-'O-Tan, 1927. 61p.

4586 *—Awon akewi (Yoruba philosophy) Ibadan, Ilare press, 1933. 120p.

4587 O'Connell, James
Government and politics in the Yoruba African churches: the claims of tradition and modernity. *Odu*, 1 (2) 1965: 92–108.

4588 Odukoya, S. Ade
Antiquities and places of interest around Ijebu-Ode. *Nig. mag.*, (9) 1937: 56–58, illus.

4589 Offonry, H. Kanu
The Yorubas. *W. Afr. rev.*, 18 (243) Dec. 1947: 1, 423–424.

4590 Ogunsheye, Felicia Adetowun
Société-traditionnelle et démocratie. *Présence afr.*, 23, Dec. 1958–Jan. 1959: 6–15.

4591 Ojo, G. J. Afolabi
Yoruba culture, a geographical analysis. London, University of London press, 1966. 303p. illus., maps, bibliog.
Based on his Ph.D. thesis, National University of Ireland, 1963.

4592 —Yoruba palaces; a study of afins of Yorubaland. London, University of London press, 1966. 110p. illus.

4593 *Ojo-Cole
The wisdom of my forefathers. Yoruba folk-wisdom. Conception of manhood. *WASU*, 1929.

4594 Okitipupa, Ondo Province; a pictorial survey of life and industry in a small Yoruba town. *Nig. mag.*, (32) 1949: 5–35.

4595 Parnis, R. O.
A visit to Aiyetoro. *Nig. field*, 30 (1) Jan. 1965: 37–40, illus.
Presents a short account of the town.

4596 Parrinder, Geoffrey
Yoruba-speaking peoples in Dahomey. *Africa*, 17 (2) Apr. 1947: 122–129, map.
French summary, pp. 128–129.

4597 Plummer, Gladys
Domestic subjects in an African town. [Lagos] *Oversea educ.*, 21 (4) 1950: 1102–1104.

4598 Prince, Raymond H.
Cultural mechanisms for the mastery of grief among the Yoruba. *N.I.S.E.R. conf. proc., 1958*: 232–233.
Summary of a paper on Yoruba institutions and beliefs embodying cultural mechanisms for overcoming grief arising from bereavement.

4599 Schwab, William B.
An experiment in methodology in a West African urban community. *Human organization*, 13 (1) Spring 1954: 13–19.
Techniques employed in conducting a social and economic survey of Oshogbo.

4600 —The political and social organization of an urban African community. 1952.
Ph.D. thesis, University of Pennsylvania, Philadelphia.
An extensive investigation of Oshogbo town, embracing politics, history, town organisation and residence units, seniority and status, lineage structure and functions, kinship terminology, family organisation, marriage, and inter-family relationships. Useful appendices, including a chronological list of important events in Oshogbo history, chiefs of Oshogbo town, and social, economic and religious structure guides.

4601 Sociological association, University of Nigeria, Nsukka.
A report on the holy city of Aiyetoro (Okitipupa Division, Western Nigeria) Nsukka, Sociological Association, University of Nigeria, 1962. [ii] 21p.
Report of a three day study visit to the town of Aiyetoro by students of the Sociology Dept. of the University.

4602 Solanke, Ladipo
Ogboni institution in Yoruba. W.A.S.U., (2) 1926: 28–34.

4603 *Southon, Arthur E.
Ilesha and beyond. London, Cargate press, [n.d.].

4604 Stone, R. H.
Yoruba lore and the universe. Ibadan, university press, 1965. 28p. (Ibadan. Univ. Institute of education. Occasional publication, no. 4).

4605 Tidjani, A. Serpos
Formes déférentes en Yorouba. Notes afr., (17) Jan. 1943: 4–5.

4606 —Le nom Yorouba (Dahomey) Notes afr., (26) Apr. 1945: 19–21.

4607 Turner, Lorenzo Dow
Some contacts of Brazilian ex-slaves with Nigeria, West Africa. J. Negro hist., 27 (1) Jan. 1942: 55–67.
Also offprinted. Washington, Association for the study of Negro life and history, 1942.

4608 Verger, Pierre
Nigeria, Brazil and Cuba. Nigeria, 1960: 113–123, illus.

4609 —Yoruba influences in Brazil. Odù, (1) Jan. 1955: 3–11, illus.

4610 —Rôle joué par le tabac de Bahia dans la traite des esclaves au Golfe du Bénin. Cah. étud. afr., 4 (3) 1964: 349–369.

4611 Wainwright, G. A.
The Egyptian origin of a ram-headed breast-plate from Lagos. Man, 51, 1951: 133–134 (art. 231), illus.

4612 Ward-Price, Henry Lewis
Dark subjects. London, Jarrolds, 1939. 287p. plates.
Memoirs of author's days as administrative officer in Nigeria.

4613 Webster, J. B.
The African churches. Nig. mag., (79) Dec. 1963: 254–266, illus.

4614 —The African churches among the Yoruba, 1888–1922. London, Clarendon press, 1964. xvii, 217p. map, illus. (Oxford studies in African affairs).

4615 —Agege plantations and the African Church, 1901–1920. NISER conf. proc. 8th, Ibadan, 1962: 124–130.
A history of the development of plantation farming in Agege and of the inter-dependence of evangelism and this farming in the early history of the African Church.

4616 Werder, Peter von
Staatsgefüge in Westafrika; eine ethnosociologische Untersuchung über Hochformen der sozialen und staatlichen Organisation im Westsudan. Stuttgart, 1938.
See full entry at [4198].

4617 "White ant" [pseud.]
Practical notes on the Yoruba country and its development. J. Afr. soc., 1 (3) Apr. 1902: 316–324.
Notes on various aspects of Yorubaland—chieftaincy, land tenure, farming, transport, labour supply, etc.

4618 Wyndham, John
A cure for sudden and serious illness. Man, 20, 1920: 41 (art. 23).

4. (ii) History

4619 Abimbola, 'Wande
The ruins of Oyo Division. Afr. notes, 2 (1) Oct. 1964: 16–19.

4620 Abiola, J. D. E. [and others].
Iwe itan Ijesa, by J. D. E. Abiola, J. A. Babafemi, Prince Same O. S. Ataiyero. Ilesha, [the authors] 1932. 151p.

4621 Adegbamigbe, A. A.
History, laws and customs of Ile-Oluji. [Ile-Oluji, the author, 1962.] 74p. illus. (port.) Printed by Eniola printing works, Ibadan.

4622 Adegunwa, E. A. and Ojo, Oluwafemi
Iwe itan Saki, nipa E. A. Adegunwa, oti Oluwafemi Ojo. Shaki [the authors, 1955?] [x] 33p.

4623 Ademakinwa, J. A.
Ife, cradle of the Yoruba; a handbook on the history of the origin of the Yorubas. Lagos [the author, 1958–1960].
Printed by Pacific printing works, Lagos. In three parts:
Part I. 1958. 92p.
Part II. 1958. 60p.
Part III. 1960. 71p.

4624 Aderemi, Adesoji, Oni of Ife.
Notes on the city of Ife. Nig. mag., (12) 1937: 3–7, illus.

4625 Aderibigbe, A. A. B.
Rivalry among Yoruba states in the 19th century. Historia, 2 (1) Apr. 1965: 103–112.

4626 —Yoruba origins [and] Old Oyo empire. In A thousand years of West African history, ed. J. F. A. Ajayi and I. Espie, 1965: 186–192.

4627 Adewale, T. J.
The Ijanna episode in Yoruba history.
Int. W. Afr. conf. proc., 3rd, 1949. 1956:
251–256.
Outline history of Ijanna village, a
once important centre in Egbado.

4628 Adeyemi, M. C.
Iwe itan Ọyọ-ile ati Ọyọ isisiyi abi Ago-
d'Ọyọ. Ibadan, "Egbe agba-o-tan",
[1914] 32p. illus.
History of Old & new Ọyọ.

4629 Ajisafe, Ajayi Kolawole
Abeokuta centenary and its celebra-
tions. [Lagos, the author, 1931] 40p.
Printed by Ife-Olu printing works,
Lagos.

4630 —History of Abeokuta, by E. Olympus
O. Moore (Ajisafe) Bungay, Printed for
the author by Richard Clay, 1916.
[iii] 150p.
— —Revised ed. Bungay, Printed for
author by Richard Clay, 1924. 255p.

4631 —Ogorun odun lori ilu Abeokuta ati
ere ajoyo re. [Lagos, the author, 1931]
42p. Printed by Ife-Olu printing works,
Lagos.
Yoruba edition of [4629].

4632 Akindele, A. and Aguessey, C.
Contribution à l'étude de l'histoire de
l'ancien royaume de Porto-Novo.
Dakar, IFAN, 1953. 168p. illus., maps.
(Mémoires IFAN, no. 25).

4633 Akindoju, S. A. and Olagundoye, M. O.
The history of Idanre. Idanre [the
authors] 1962. 28p. Printed by
Adebambo printing press, Ibadan.
Features the migration of Idanre
people from their original settlement at
Ile-Ife to Utaja, and thence to their
present location. The first named author
is the *Oludaiye* of Idanre.

4634 Akinjogbin, I. A.
Agaja and the conquest of the coastal
Aja states, 1724–1730. *J. Hist. soc. Nig.*,
2 (4) Dec. 1963: 545–556.

4635 —Dahomey and its neighbours, 1708–
1818. 1963.
Ph.D. thesis, London.

4636 —Dahomey and Yoruba in the nine-
teenth century. In *A thousand years of
West African history, ed. J. F. A.
Ajayi and I. Espie, 1965*: 309–326, map.

4637 —Enactment ceremonies as a source of
unwritten history. *N.S.E.R. conf. proc.,
1958*: 168–179.
Shows the importance of enactment
ceremonies in the reconstruction of
Yoruba history.

4638 —The prelude to the Yoruba civil wars
of the nineteenth century. *Odu*, 1 (2)
1965: 24–46.

4639 Akinyele, Isaac Babalola
Iwe itan Ibadan ati die ninu awon ilu
agbegbe rè bi Iwo, Oshogbo, ati
Ikirun. Edition kẹta. Ibadan, [the
author] 1950. 304p. illus.

4640 —Iwe itan Ibadan, ati Iwo Ikirun ati
Oshogbo. [Ibadan, the author, 1911].

4641 —The outlines of Ibadan history.
[Ibadan, the author] 1946. viii, 135p.
illus. Printed by Alebiosu printing press,
Lagos.

4642 Allison, Philip A.
The first travelling commissioners of
the Ekiti country. *Nig. field*, 17 (3) Jl.
1952: 100–115, illus.
Historical sketches of parts of
Yorubaland during 1899 to 1902, based
on two diaries kept by Travelling
Commissioners for Ilesha and Ekiti for
these years.

4643 —The last days of Old Oyo. *Odù*, (4)
[1958]: 16–27, map.
Commentaries on, and extracts from
Richard Lander's description of Old
Oyo and Yorubaland.

4644 Apena, Moses Botu Okubọte
Iwe Ikekuru ti itan Ijebu. Ibadan, F. O.
Botu, Ola-Olu stores, [1937] vii, 110p.
illus.

4645 Avoseh, T. Ola
A short history of Badagry. Lagos,
Ife-Olu printing works, 1938. 65p.

4646 Awe, B.
The Ajele system (a study of Ibadan
imperialism in the nineteenth century).
J. Hist. soc. Nig., 3 (1) Dec. 1964: 47–71.

4647 —The rise of Ibadan as a Yoruba power
in the nineteenth century. 1964.
D.Phil. thesis, Oxford.

4648 Beier, Horst Ulrich
Before Oduduwa. *Odù*, (3) 1956: 25–32.
Attempts to trace the original inhabitants of the Yoruba country before
the arrival of the Yoruba.

4648a —The historical and psychological
significance of Yoruba myths. See [4659].

4649 —Yoruba enclave. *Nig. mag.*, (58)
1958: 238–251, illus.
History of three Yoruba villages in
the heart of Western Ibo, far removed
from the rest of Yorubaland.

4650 Bertho, Jacques
La parenté des Yoruba aux peuplades
de Dahomey et Togo. *Africa*, 19 (2)
Apr. 1949: 121–132, map.
Traces the movement of the Adja,
Ewe and Quatchi peoples from the
Yoruba region of Nigeria into Dahomey
and Togo, and notes the mingling of
ethnic groups. Based on traditional and
archaeological evidence. English
summary, p. 132.

4651 Biobaku, Saburi O.
The Egba and their neighbours, 1842–
1872. Oxford, Clarendon press, 1957.
viii, 128p. maps, bibliog.
A lucid history of the Egbas from the
time of their arrival in Abeokuta up to
the period of Commander J. H. Glover's
Lieutenant Governorship at Lagos.
Based on his Ph.D. thesis: The Egba
state and its neighbours (1842–1872).
London, 1952.

4652 —An historical sketch of the peoples of
Western Nigeria. *Odù*, (6) Je. 1958: 24–
28.

A summary of the history of the Yoruba-, Edo-, Ijaw-, and Ibo-speaking peoples of Western Nigeria from the time of their immigrations into their present territories to the British occupation.

4652a —Myths and oral history. *Odù*, (1) Jan. 1955: 12–17. See [4659].

4653 —[Origins of the Yoruba] Lagos, Federal information service [1955] 23p. (Lugard lectures, 1955).
Reviews the principal theories concerning the origins of the Yoruba, and holds upper Egypt as their original home. This was the first of the Lugard lecture series and was given in 1955 in six separate talks.

4654 —The pattern of Yoruba history. *Afr. south.*, 2 (2) 1958: 63–67.
Yoruba history from their migration from the Near East in the 7th and 10th centuries to their occupation and settlement of their present territories.

4655 —The problem of traditional history with special reference to Yoruba traditions. *J. Hist. soc. Nig.*, 1 (1) Dec. 1956: 43–47.

4656 —The wells of West African history. *W. Afr. rev.*, 24 (304) Jan. 1953: 18–19.
Discusses the significance of oral traditions and folklore in historical research, illustrating them with a consideration of Yoruba history.

4657 —The Yoruba historical research scheme. *W. Afr. j. ed.* 2 (1) Feb. 1958: 9–10.

4658 —The Yoruba historical research scheme. *J. Hist. soc. Nig.*, 1 (1) Dec. 1956: 59–60.
Brief notes by the director of the scheme outlining its objectives and the methods to be adopted.

4659 Biobaku, Saburi O. and Beier, Horst Ulrich
The use and interpretation of myths. *Odù*, (1) Jan. 1955: 12–25.
Two articles: "Myths and oral history" by S. O. Biobaku, pp. 12–17; and "The historical and psychological significance of Yoruba myths" by H. U. Beier, pp. 17–25. Both illustrate (using Yoruba legends and traditions of origin) the significance of myths and traditions in historical reconstruction. The articles (translated into French) also appear in *Présence africaine, n.s. 7, 1956*: 125–132.

4659a Bradbury, R. E.
The historical uses of comparative ethnography with special reference to Benin and the Yoruba. See [1790].

4660 Brown, Spencer Hunter
A history of the people of Lagos, 1852–1886. 1964. 499p.
Ph.D. thesis, Northwestern university.

4661 Clarke, John Digby
A visit to Old Oyo. *Nig. field*, 7 (3) 1938: 139–142.

Account of a visit to the site of Old Oyo in Dec. 1937.

4662 Dalzel, Archibald
The History of Dahomey, an inland kingdom of Africa; compiled from authentic memoirs; with an introduction and notes. London, the author, 1793. xxxi, [1] xxvi, [4] 230p. illus. map (fold.)

4662a — —New Impression, with an introduction, by J. D. Fage. London, Frank Cass, 1967. 22, xxvi, xxxii, 230p. illus., map (fold.).

4663 Davidson, A. McL.
The origin and early history of Lagos, by A. McL. Davidson, with additional observations by the late Rev. J. A. J. Ogunbiyi and the late Sir Adeyemo Alakija; and with photographs by P. A. Bello. *Nig. field*, 19 (2) Apr. 1954: 52–69, illus.
History of Lagos from its first settlement by Ogunfunminire and his followers to its cession to the British Crown in August 1861. To this are subjoined the two briefer accounts given from memory by the Rev. Ogunbiyi and Sir Adeyemo.

4664 Delano, Isaac O.
Itan Eko. London, Evans brothers, 1962. 63p. illus., maps. (Iránti ànfani, book 1).
A history of Lagos (in Yoruba).

4665 —Itan Egba. London, Evans brothers, 1963. vi, 64p. illus., map (Iránti ànfani, book 2).
History of the Egbas.

4666 —Itan Oyo. London, Evans brothers, 1964. xii, 47p. illus., map (Iránti ànfani, book 3).
History of Oyo.

4667 Dittmer, Kunz
Zur Herkunft und Bedeutung der altyorubischen Kronen und des älthiopischen kalatscha. In *Festschrift für A. E. Jensen; hrsg. von Eike Haberland [et al.] Teil I. 1964*: 63–90.

4668 Dosumu, Gbadebo Adeoyo
"Oduduwa". The origin of mankind; the Yorubas, Binis, Dahomians, etc. [Ibadan, the author, 1951] 18p.
Printed by Church of Africa press, Ibadan.

4669 Duckworth, E. H.
Badagry—its place in the pages of history. *Nig. mag.*, (38) 1952: 145–173.

4670 [Dunglas, Edouard]
The first Dahomey war against Abeokuta, 1851. *Nig. mag.*, (69) Mar. 1960: 4–17, illus., maps.
Account of the 1851 attack on Abeokuta by Dahomeyan Amazons, reprinted in a shortened version and with introductory commentary, from the original published by the author in *Études Dahoméennes* in 1948. [4671] q.v.

4671 —La première attaque des Dahoméens contre Abéokuta (3 mars 1851). *Étud. dahom.*, 1, 1948: 7–19.

4671a — —La deuxième attaque des Dahoméens contre Abéokuta. *Etud. dahom.*, 2, 1949: 37–57.
Account of events leading up to the attack and of the attack itself. Based largely on Ajisafe, Burton and others.

4672 Elgee, C. H.
The evolution of Ibadan. Lagos, Govt. printer, 1914. [ii] 41p.
History of Ibadan from 1813–1913, with remarks on Ife and Illa.

4673 Epega, D. Onadele
Iwe itan Ijebu ati awon illu miran. 2nd ed. Lagos, 1934.

4674 Folarin, Adebesin
The demise of the independence of Egba-land. (The Ijemo trouble) Part I. **Lagos**, Tika-Tore printing works [1916] 67p.

4675 —Egba history: life review, 1829–1930. Abeokuta, E. N. A. press, 1931.

4676 —A short historical view of the Egbas from 1829 to 1930. [Abeokuta, the author, 1931] 180p.

4677 Gbolahan, Diya
Iwe itan Aha. [Ibadan, the author, 1951] 10p. Printed by Iranlowo printing works, Ibadan.
History of Aha.

4678 George, J. O.
Historical notes on the Yoruba country and its tribes. [Lagos, the author, 1895] 87p. Printed by E. K. Kaufmann, Lahr., Baden.
Yoruba text, pp. 67–87.

4679 George, S. Adeyemi
The fact of the history of Ilare, the first settler of Ijeshas. Oshogbo [the author, 1954] 12p. Printed by Evangelist press, Oshogbo.

4680 Gleave, Michael B.
Hill settlements and their abandonment in Western Yorubaland. *Africa*, 33 (4) Oct. 1963: 343–352, map.
"This paper outlines the reasons for the earlier choice of hill-top sites and for later movement of settlements in a small part of the derived savanna in Ibadan and Oyo Provinces." French summary, pp. 351–352.

4681 Herskovits, Jean F.
Liberated Africans and the history of Lagos Colony to 1886. 1960.
D.Phil. thesis, Oxford University.

4682 History [of the peoples of Western Nigeria] In *Annual report of the Western Region government, 1957. Ibadan, 1960*: 1–4, illus.
Brief summary of the known history of the major ethnic groups in the then Western Nigeria—Yoruba, Bini, Ishan, Urhobo, Itsekiri, Ijaw, etc.

4683 Hodder, Bramwell William
Badagri, I: slave port and mission centre. *Nig. geog. j.* 5 (2) Dec. 1962: 75–86.
A brief examination of aspects of Badagri history up to 1863. Illus. with sketch maps.

4684 —Badagri: II. One hundred years of change. *Nig. geog. j.*, 6 (1) Je. 1963: 17–30. maps, bibliog.
Brings the examination of Badagri history commenced in Pt. I up to 1963.

4685 Ilorin. *Nig. mag.*, (49) 1956: 148–167, illus.
History and description of Ilorin.

4686 Jeffreys, M. D. W.
Braima, alias Abraham—a study in diffusion. *Folklore*, 70, Mar. 1959: 323–333.
Discusses the several traditions of origin of the Yoruba and holds that Braima or Ibraima mentioned by the Yoruba in their own tradition of origin and said to have lived about A.D. 650 was none other than Abraham the Chaldees who flourished about 2,000 B.C.

4687 —When was Ile Ife founded? *Nig. field*, 23 (1) Jan. 1958: 21–23, bibliog.
Reviews previous authors who had touched on the question and suggests 1050 ± 30 A.D. as the probable date.

4688 *Johnson, O.
Lagos past. Lagos, 1901. 32p. (Proc. Lagos institute).

4689 Johnson, Samuel
The history of the Yorubas from the earliest times to the beginning of the British protectorate; edited by O. Johnson. Lagos, C.M.S. (Nigeria) bookshops, 1921. 1v, 684p. map.

4690 Kenyo, Elisha Alademomi
Awon ilu Oyo ati isedale won. Lagos, Yoruba historical research co. [1958?] 35p. illus.
Printed by Pacific printing & publishing works, Lagos.

4691 —Awon olori Yoruba ati isèdálè won . . . [Lagos, the author] 1952. 92p. illus.
Printed by Ife-Olu printing works, Lagos.

4692 —Flood light on the Yoruba region. Lagos, the Yoruba historical research co., 1954. 191p. illus.
Printed by the Twentieth century press, Ebute Metta, Lagos.

4693 —Isedele Yoruba. Lagos, Yoruba historical research co., 1953. 143p. illus.
Printed by Twentieth century press, Lagos.

4694 —Itan isedale Iwo. Ibadan. Yoruba historical research co., 1962. 57p. illus.

4695 —Iwe awon oba alade Yoruba. Lagos, Yoruba historical research co., 1955. 40p. illus.
Printed by Amalgamated press of Nigeria, Lagos.

4696 —Origin of the progenitor of the Yoruba race. Lagos, Yoruba historical research co. [1951] 84p. illus.
Printed by Pacific printing works, Lagos.

4697 Langton, Malcolm
The River Ogun: an historical journey. *Nig. mag.*, (72) Mar. 1962: 34–44, illus.

Describes a journey from Lagos to Abeokuta by the River Ogun, with useful historical notes on the Egbas.

4698 Losi, John B. Ogunjimi
History of Abeokuta. Lagos, Bosere press, 1924. 176p.

4699 —History of Lagos. Lagos, Tika-Tore printing works, 1914. iii, 112 [6]p.

4700 — —2nd ed. Lagos, C.M.S. bookshop, 1921. 75p.
Brief account by a headmaster of a Roman Catholic school. Originally published in Yoruba. See [4702].

4701 —Iwe itan Abeokuta. Exeter, J. Townsend, 1920. 135p.

4702 —Iwe itan Eko, [Lagos, author] 1913. iv, 29p.
Printed by Tika-Tore printing works, Lagos.

4703 — —3rd ed. Lagos, C.M.S. press, 1921, 60p.

4704 Lucas, Jonathan Olumide
Oduduwa. Lagos, Twentieth century press, 1949. [ii] 23p. illus.
Text of a lecture delivered under the auspices of the Egbe Omo Oduduwa during the 1949 anniversary of that organisation. Discusses origin and meaning of the name. Much of the argument is derived from his book: The Religion of the Yorubas [4949].

4705 Martin, B. G.
A new Arabic history of Ilorin. Research bull., 1 (2) Jan. 1965: 20–27.
Tentative account of three Arabic manuscripts found in Ilorin in April, 1964, all copies of Ibn Kūkūra's historical work on Ilorin entitled: Ta'lif akhbār alqurūn min '-umarā' bitād Ilurun. Photo-copies of all three are kept at the university of Ibadan library.

4706 Mercier, Paul
Histoire et légende: la bataille d'Ilorin. Notes afr., (47) Jl. 1950: 92–95, map.

4707 Morton-Williams, Peter
The Oyo Yoruba and the Atlantic trade, 1670–1830. J. Hist. soc. Nig., 3 (1) Dec. 1964: 25–45, bibliog.

4708 Nesham, E. W.
The Idanre hills. Nig. mag., (16) 1938: 267–270.

4709 Niven, Cecil Rex
A short history of the Yoruba peoples. London, Longmans, Green, 1958. [ii] 135p. maps.

4710 Odutola, Odubanjo
Iwe kini iḷọsiwaju Ẹkọ itan Ijebu ni Ede Yoruba fun Tagba-Tewe Ile-Ijebu. Ijebu-Ode, Eruobodo press, 1946. [2] 40p.

4711 Ogunkoya, T. O.
The early history of Ijebu. J. Hist. soc. Nig., 1 (1) Dec. 1956: 48–58.
History of Ijebu Yoruba from the earliest migrations, with notes on their governmental and judicial systems.

4712 Oguntuyi, A.

Itan Ado Ekiti. Apa keji [Akure, the author, 194. . ?] [viii] 171p. illus., map. Printed by Aduralere printing works, Akure.
Yoruba edition of [4713].

4713 —A short history of Ado-Ekiti. Pt. III. [Ado-Ekiti, the author, 1953] [1] x, 180p. illus., map.
Printed by Aduralere printing works, Akure.

4714 Ojo, Samuel Olaje
Iwe itan Yoruba (Apa kini) 1st ed. 205p. illus., map.
Printed by Abiodun printing works, Ibadan.

4715 —The origin of the Yorubas. Part I. Their tribes, language, and native laws and customs. 3rd ed. (revised) Ibadan, Abiodun printing works, 1953. 40p. illus.

4716 —The origin of the Yorubas: Part II. Oyo [the author, 1957].
Printed by Atoro printing works, Oyo. 70p. illus.
Part II based on fresh additional data collected by author.

4717 —Short history of Ilorin. [Oyo, the author, 1957] 41p.
Printed by Atoro printing works, Oyo.

4718 Ojo, William
Folk history of Imesi Ile. Nig. mag., (42) 1953: 98–117.

4719 Olafimihan, J. B.
Iwe itan Ọfa ati diẹ nimu awọn ilu agbegbe rẹ bi Igosun, Ijagbo, Ipẹẹ, Igboma ati Ira. [Ọfa, the author] 1950. v, 143p. illus. Printed by Abiodun printing works, Ibadan.
History of Ofa and neighbouring towns: Igbosun, Ijagbo, etc.

4720 Olugunna, Deji
Osogbo (the origin, growth & problems) [Oshogbo, the author] 1959. 45p. maps. Printed by Fad's printing works, Oshogbo.

4721 Olunlade, [E. A.] Otun serikiy Ede
Ede: a short history. Translated from the Yoruba [by] I. A. Akinjogbin. Edited and annotated by Ulli Beier. Ibadan, General publications section, Ministry of education, 1961. 56p. illus. (on cover) (Yoruba traditional histories, no. 1).

4722 Owade, Ayo and Ogunremi, Deji
Oke Badan. Afr. hist., 1 (1) Mar. 1963: 22–25.

4723 Oyebade, D. A.
Igbeti town, Oyo Province. Farm and forest, 9 (1) Jan.–Je. 1948: 20–21.
Origin of Igbeti town.

4724 Oyerinde, N. D.
Iwe itan Ogbomosho. Jos, Printed by Niger press, 1934. 210p.
History of Ogbomosho.

4725 Oyo progressive union
In truth and justice—a handbook of the Oyo progressive union, containing historical sketches of the relationship

between Oyo and Ibadan. Lagos, "Asaoku" printing press, 1938. 132p.

4726 Panikkar, K. Madhu
Oyo and the emergence of the coastal states. In his *The serpent and the crescent: a history of the negro empires of Western Africa, 1963*: 141–165.
Includes a general account of Yoruba history, pp. 141–146, and Benin history, pp. 146–151.

4727 Parrinder, Geoffrey
Some western Yoruba towns. *Odù*, (2) 29–34.
Discusses the traditions of origin of many Yoruba towns, both in Dahomey and in Nigeria.

4728 —The story of Ketu, an ancient Yoruba kingdom.
Ibadan, University press, 1956. vi, 92p. map, bibliog.
History of the Yoruba town of Ketu (in the Republic of Dahomey) from its foundation by king Ede to date.

4729 Payne, John Augustus Otonba
Table of principal events in Yoruba history, with certain other matters of general interest, compiled principally for use in courts within the British Colony of Lagos, West Africa. [Lagos, the author, 1893] [v] 113p. Printed by Andrew M. Thomas, Lagos,.

4729a Ryder, A. F. C.
A reconsideration of the Ife-Benin relationship. See [1810].

4730 St. Mary's Catholic Church, Oyo
A short history of Catholicism in Oyo. Oyo, 1965. 64p. illus.

4731 Sibthorpe, A. B. C.
Bible review of reviews, the discovery of the lost ten tribes, Yorubas or Akus, by A. B. C. Sibthorpe, alias Aucandu, Prince of Cucuruku, Niger, F.P.V.I., proof 1. Printed at Cline Town, Sierra Leone by S. R. Sibthorpe, January, 1909. 53p.
Seven reasons are listed to show that the Yorubas represent the ten lost tribes of Israel. But in this volume, only one of these reasons—the similarity between Yoruba and Jewish traditions— is discussed.

4732 Smith, Robert
The Alafin in exile: a study of the Igboho period in Oyo history. *J. Afr. hist.*, 6 (1) 1965: 57–77.

4733 —Erin and Iwawun, forgotten towns of the Ọkè Ọgùn. *Odu*, 1 (1) Jl. 1964: 17–32, 1 plan.
Account of two hill towns some ten and a half miles southwest of Iseyin. The two towns were captured during the Ijaye war of 1860-65 and finally abandoned and deserted.

4734 —Ijaiye, the Western palatinate of the Yoruba. *J. Hist. soc. Nig.*, 2 (3) Dec. 1962: 329–349.
History of Ijaiye from its capture in 1830 by Ikoyi chiefs to its destruction in 1862. Much documented.

4735 Verger, Pierre
Notes on some documents in which Lagos is referred to by the name 'Onim' and which mentions relations between Onim and Brazil. *J. Hist. soc. Nig.*, 1 (4) Dec. 1959: 343–350.

4736 Wescott, Roger W.
Did the Yoruba come from Egypt [sic] *Odù*, (4) 10–15.
A critical review of J. O. Lucas's "The religion of the Yorubas" [4949] q.v.

4737 *Wood, J. Buckley
Historical notices of Lagos, West Africa, and on the inhabitants of Lagos: their character, pursuits, and languages. 2nd ed. Lagos, Church missionary society, 1933.

4. (iii) Marriage, Family, Lineage Structure

4738 Aluko, Timothy Mofolorunso
Polygamy and the surplus women. *W. Afr. rev.*, 21 (270) 1950: 259–260.

4738a Baker, Tanya
[Women's role in] Nigeria. See [1595].

4738b Baker, Tanya and Bird, Mary
Urbanization and the position of women. See [5244].

4739 Bassir, Olumbe
Marriage rites among the Aku (Yoruba) of Freetown. *Africa*, 24 (3) Jl. 1954: 251–256.
French summary, pp. 255–256.

4740 Beier, Horst Ulrich
The position of Yoruba women. *Présence afr., n.s.*, (1–2) Apr.–Jl. 1955: 39–46.
Position of women in Ede in relation to religious and economic activities, marriage, divorce and family life.

4741 Bird, Mary E. C.
Social change in kinship and marriage among the Yoruba of Western Nigeria. 1959.
Ph.D. thesis, Edinburgh.

4742 —Urbanization, family and marriage in Western Nigeria. In *Urbanization in African social change, 1963*: 59–74.

4743 Coker, G. B. A.
Family property among the Yorubas. London, Sweet & Maxwell, 1958. xxiv, 314p. bibliog.

4744 — —2nd ed. 1965.

4745 Comhaire, Jean
Enseignement féminin et mariages à Lagos, Nigeria. *Zaire*, 9 (3) Mar. 1955: 261–277.

4746 Comhaire-Sylvain, S.
Le probléme du marriage à Lagos, Nigeria (étude ethnographique) *Revue de l'Inst. de sociol.*, (4) 1956: 499–521. See also [4840].

4747 —Le travail des femmes à Lagos, Nigeria. *Zaire*, 5 (2) 1951: 169–187; (5) May: 475–502.

4748 Delano, Isaac O.
The Yoruba family as the basis of Yoruba culture. *Odù*, (5) 21–28.

On the significance of the Yoruba family structure and of cultural training within it in the sustenance of Yoruba culture.

4749   Ijebu anti-high bride price league, Ibadan.
Memorandum on high and exorbitant cost of marriage in Ijebu land and associated social evils, submitted . . . to Ijebu native authority council. [Ibadan, the league, 1951] 8p. Printed by the African press, Ibadan.

4750   Izzet, Alison
Family life among the Yoruba, in Lagos, Nigeria. In *Social change in modern Africa, ed. A. Southal, 1961*: 305–315.
A brief general picture of the patterns of Yoruba family life in urban and cosmopolitan Lagos.

4751   Kasunmu, A. B.
Marriage and divorce among the Yorubas. 1962.
LL.M. dissertation, London.

4752   Lloyd, Peter Cutt
Agnatic and cognatic descent among the Yoruba. *Man*, 1 (4) Dec. 1966: 484–500.

4753   —Family property among the Yoruba. *J. Afr. law*, 3 (2) Summer 1959: 105–115.
A review article on G.B.A. Coker's book of the same title.

4754   —The status of the Yoruba wife. *Sudan soc.*, 2, 1963: 35–42.

4755   —The Yoruba lineage. *Africa*, 25 (3) Jl. 1955: 235–251. tables.
A detailed analysis of Yoruba lineage structure and the relation of the lineage to the clan and the town. French summary, p. 251.

4755a   Mabogunje, Akin L.
The market women. See [4863].

4756   —The Yoruba home. *Odù*, (5) 28–36.
A general description of the Yoruba family.

4756a   Marris, Peter
Family and social change in an African city. See [5266].

4756b   —Slum clearance and family life in Lagos. See [5267].

4757   Marshall, Gloria A.
Women, trade and the Yoruba family. 1964.
Ph.D. thesis, Columbia university.

4758   Okunniga, A. A. O.
The impact of common law on the customary law of marriage and property among the Yoruba of the Western Region of Nigeria. 1962.
LL.M. thesis, Belfast.

4759   Papafio, A. B. Quartey
Native law and custom in Egbaland. *J. Afr. soc.*, 10 (40) Jl. 1911: 422–433.
Egba marriage, family relationship, guardianship, and property rights. Written in Abeokuta in July 1906.

4760   Salacuse, Jeswald
Igbomina family law. In his *A selective survey of Nigerian family law, 1965*: 79–92.

4761   Schwab, William B.
Continuity and change in the Yoruba lineage system. *Ann. N.Y. acad. sci.*, 96 (2) Jan. 1962: 590–605.
A discussion of the continuous but gradual loosening of authority and changes in relationships within the traditional lineage structure of the Yoruba as observed in Oshogbo, and the overall effects of these social changes on the Yoruba lineage as a factor of family cohesion and a system of social and administrative authority.

4762   —Kinship and lineage among the Yoruba. *Africa*, 25 (4) Oct. 1955: 352–374, illus.
"An analytic description of the principles underlying the traditional kinship system of the Yoruba people of Western Nigeria in the community of Oshogbo." French summary, pp. 373–374.

4763   —The terminology of kinship and marriage among the Yoruba. *Africa*, 18 (4) Oct. 1958: 301–313.
On "Yoruba systems of terminology towards kin and affinal relations, as exemplified in the community of Oshogbo."

4764   Sofola, Johnson Adeyemi
Changes in the Yoruba family and kin. 1962. 81p.
M.A. thesis, Howard university, Washington, D.C.

4765   Sofoluwe, G. O.
A study of divorce cases in Igbo-Ora. *Nig. j. econ. soc. stud.*, 7 (1) Mar. 1965: 51–62. tables.
Includes a section: "Customary marriage in Igbo-ora" pp. 53–55. Igboora is a rural town in Western Nigeria.

4766   Ward, Edward
Marriage among the Yoruba. Washington, Catholic university of America, 1937. 55p. bibliog. (Catholic university of America. Anthropological series, no. 4).

4767   —The parent-child relationship among the Yoruba. *Primitive man*, 9, 1936: 56–63.

4768   —The Yoruba husband-wife code. Washington, Catholic university of America, 1938. ix, 178p. (Catholic university of America. Anthropological series. no. 6).
Ph.D. thesis, Catholic university of America. This and the above work [4766] study the relationship between husband and wife among the Yoruba in all its aspects, noting in particular their respective responsibilities and obligations.

4. (iv) Government, Kingship, Law

4769   Adegoriola, Alaiyeluwa. *Ogoga of Ikerre*.
A note on the administration of Ikerre

before the advent of the British. *Odù*, (3) 19–24.

4770 Ajisafe, Ajayi Kolawole
The laws and customs of the Yoruba people. London, G. Routledge; Lagos, C.M.S. bookshop, 1924. [ix] 97p. front. (port.).

4771 Asabia, S. O.
Foundation of Yoruba government. *Odù*, (7) Mar. 1959: 23–27, illus.

4772 Biobaku, Saburi O.
The Egba council, 1899–1918. *Odù*, 2, 1955: 14–20.

4773 —An historical sketch of Egba traditional authorities. *Africa*, 22 (1) Jan. 1952: 35–49, map.
A brief account of Egba political and administrative history, sketching the organisation and repositories of administrative offices and their hierarchical structure. Summary in French, p. 49.

4774 —The kingly titles of Western Nigeria. *W. Afr.*, (1836) 3rd May 1952: 391–392.

4775 —Ogboni, the Egba senate. *Int. W. Afr. conf., 3rd Lagos, 1949. 1956*: 257–263. illus., bibliog.
On the origin of the Ogboni society and on its organisation, political role and function, particularly among the Egbas.

4776 *Cameron, Donald
A note on land tenure in the Yoruba provinces. Lagos, 1933.

4776a Coker, G. B. A.
Family property among the Yorubas. See [4743].

4777 *Crohar, J.
Le roi de Yoruba. Fête de l'igname et fête du feu à Oyo. *L'Africain Almanach des Missions africaines de Lyon, 1924*: 46–48.

4778 *Deniga, Adeoye
Yoruba titles and their meanings. Lagos, 1921.

4779 Dennett, R. E.
Nigerian studies, or The religious and political system of the Yoruba. London, Macmillan, 1910, repr. London, Frank Cass, 1968. xvii, 235p. front., plates, map.

4780 —Notes on the land laws in the Western Province of Nigeria. *J. Afr. soc.*, 9 (34) Jan. 1910: 129–145.
Discusses both customary and statutory modes of land tenure in Yorubaland.

4781 —The Ogboni and other secret societies in Nigeria. *J. Afr. soc.*, 16 (61) Oct. 1916: 16–29.
A general study of the Ogboni society in Yorubaland.

4782 Dosumu, Gbadebo Adeoyo
Ogboni-Osugbo: the ancient government of Yorubaland. [Ibadan, the author] 1952. [7]p. Printed by the Church of Africa press, Ibadan.

4783 Elgee, C. H.
Ensigns of royalty in West Africa. *J. Afr.*

soc., 4 (16) Jl. 1905: 391–396.
On the regalia and sacred altars of Yoruba Obas.

4784 Elias, Taslim Olawale
The Yoruba rules of inheritance. In his *Nigerian land law and custom, 3rd ed., 1962*: 230–242.

4785 Folarin, Adetesin
The laws and customs of Egbaland. Part. I. Abeokuta, E.N.A. printing press, 1939. 133p.

4786 Garigue, Philip
Changing political leadership in West Africa. *Africa*, 24 (3) Jl. 1954: 220–232.
Discusses the changes that have taken place in the economic, religious, social and political life of the Yoruba, Ashanti and Dahomey peoples during the period of colonial rule, to show how "leadership", as the focus of political authority", has changed over this period. French summary, p. 232.

4787 Keith, A. Berriedale
Tribal ownership of land. *J. Afr. Soc.*, 1 (4) Jl. 1902: 455–461.
A letter to the editor in which attempt is made to interpret the concept of tribal ownership of land among the Yoruba. The letter is preceded by introductory note by the editor, and followed by a reprint of a judgement in a land case delivered in the Supreme Court of Lagos in July 1892.

4788 Keuning, J.
Some aspects of the administration of justice in Yorubaland. *NISER conf. proc., 1962*: 31–40, bibliog.
A rapid review of native law and customs in Yoruba land under the British, followed by a critical evaluation of the working of the new system introduced by the Western Nigeria Customary Courts Law of 1957.

4789 'Laoye, John Adetoyese, *Timi of Ede.*
The story of my installation. Ede, the author, 1956. [1] 21p. illus.

4790 Lloyd, Peter Cutt
The changing role of the Yoruba traditional ruler. *WAISER conf. proc., 1954*: 57–65.

4791 —A comparative study of the political institutions of some Yoruba kingdoms. 1953.
B.Sc. thesis, Oxford.

4792 —The development of political parties in Western Nigeria. *Amer. pol. sci. rev.*, 49 (3) Sept. 1955: 693–707.
See also R. L. Sklar's The contribution of tribalism to nationalism in Western Nigeria [4824].

4792a —Family property among the Yoruba. See [4753].

4793 —The impact of local government in the Yoruba towns of Western Nigeria: an analysis of the parts played today by the obas and chiefs and by the new groups of traders and literates. 1959.
D.Phil. thesis, Oxford.

4794 —Installing the Awujale. *Ibadan*, (12) Je. 1961: 7–10.

Describes the installation of Siriku Adetona as the Awujale of Ijebu in April 1960, giving some details of both the traditional ceremonies and the innovations.

4795 —The integration of the new economic classes into local government in Western Nigeria. *Afr. affairs*, 52 (209) Oct. 1953: 327–334.

The "new economic classes" are composed of "prosperous farmers, produce buyers, traders, lorry owners, craftsmen and literate clerks, teachers and lawyers."

4796 —Kings, chiefs and local government. *W. Afr.*, (1875) Jan. 31, 1953: 79; (1876) Feb. 7, 1953: 103.

4797 —Land settlement and tenure in Ibadan. *Int. W. Afr. conf. proc., 3rd, 1949. 1956*: 264–268.

". . . a description of the land settlement in Ibadan as illustrated by the site acquired for the permanent buildings of the University College."—author.

4798 —Sacred kingship and government among the Yoruba. *Africa*, 30 (3) Jl. 1960: 221–237.

An exhaustive analysis, with special reference to Ado in Ekiti. French summary, p. 237.

4799 —Some modern changes in the government of Yoruba towns. *WAISER conf. proc., (Sociology section) 1953*: 7–20.

On the changing aspects of the political administration of Yoruba towns, including those arising from British administration and those engendered by the present economic pattern.

4800 —Some modern developments in Yoruba customary land law. *J. Afr. admin.*, 12 (1) Jan. 1960: 11–20.

4801 —Some notes on Yoruba rules of succession and on "family property". *J. Afr. law*, 3 (1) Spring 1959: 7–32.

Analysis of Yoruba customary rules of succession as gleaned from cases heard in native courts in Abeokuta, Ijebu Ode, Ondo and Ado Ekiti.

4802 —Some problems of tenancy in Yoruba land tenure. *Afr. studies*, 12 (3) Sept. 1953: 93–103.

4803 —The traditional political system of the Yoruba. *S.–W. j. anthrop.*, 10 (4) Winter 1954: 366–384.

4804 —Yoruba inheritance and succession. In *Studies in the laws of succession in Nigeria, edited by J. D. M. Derrett, 1965*: 139–169.

4805 —Yoruba land law. London, published for the Nigerian inst. of soc. and econ. research, by O.U.P., 1962. xii, 378p. illus., maps, bibliog.

4806 Local government in the Western Provinces of Nigeria. Lagos, Govt. printer, 1950. 24p.

4807 Lucas, Jonathan Olumide

Traditional kingship in Lagos. *Nig. mag.*, (69) Aug. 1961: 122–127, illus.

Traditional rites and customs associated with the Eleko or king of Lagos.

4808 Mabogunje, Akin L.
Some comments on land tenure in Egba Division, Western Nigeria. *Africa*, 31 (3) Jl. 1961: 258–269, map.

A historical investigation into the nature of land tenure and the extent to which land sale was practised in Egbaland prior to, and in the early years of the 20th century. French summary, p. 269.

4809 Macrow, Donald W.
Natural ruler—a Yoruba conception of monarchy. *Nig. mag.*, (47) 1955: 222–245, illus.

A discussion of the Yoruba system of monarchy, illustrated with a survey of the position of the *Timi* of Ede. Includes historical sketch of the town.

4810 Morton-Williams, Peter
The Yoruba Ogboni cult in Oyo. *Africa*, 30 (4) Oct. 1960: 362–374, illus., bibliog.
French summary, p. 374.

4811 Native crowns. *J. Afr. soc* 2 (7) Apr., 1903: 312–315.

Summary account of a meeting of the "Native Council" (of Yoruba chiefs) in 1903, to which the Governor invited the Oni of Ife to advise on the dispute arising over the claim of the Elepe of Epe to wear a crown. From the proceedings may be gleaned useful information on the traditional role of the Oni in relation to other obas and their crowns. Full account to be found in Government Gazette, Lagos, Feb. 28th, 1903.

4812 "A Native of Yoruba"
Native system of government and land tenure in the Yoruba country. *J. Afr. soc.*, 1 (3) Apr. 1902: 312–315.

Notes on administrative structure and land tenure system in Yorubaland.

4813 Nigeria. Ministry of information
The Iga Idungaran palace of the Obas of Lagos. Lagos, Govt. printer [1960] [12]p. illus.

"The story of the palace . . . and a note about its occupants since 1630."

4814 Nigeria. Western. Commission of enquiry.
Report of the committee appointed to consider the registration of title to land in Western Nigeria. [P.C. Lloyd, Chairman] Ibadan, Govt. printer, 1962. vii, 26p. (Sessional paper, no. 2 of 1962).

4815 Odutola, Odubanjo
Eto iselu ti Obanta ati awon ijoye re; or Ijebu government constitution, by the Obanta & his chiefs (Yoruba & English) Ijebu Ode, the author, 1951 [ii] 27p.

4816 Ogunba, Oyin
Crowns and 'Okute' at Idowa. *Njg. mag.*, (83) Dec. 1964: 249–261, illus.
Idowa town is some five miles south of Ijebu Ode.

4816a Okunniga, A. A. O.
The impact of common law on the customary law of marriage and property among the Yoruba. See [4758].

4817 Oshodi chieftaincy family
Nigeria: the Epetedo lands—representations of the Oshodi chieftaincy family to the commissioner, Lagos land inquiry. Lagos, Hope rising press, 1939. 29p.

4818 Palau Marti, Montserrat
Ọba só, Ọba kò só (Le roi s'est pendu, le roi ne s'est pas pendu) In *Congrès international des sciences anthropologiques, 6th, Paris, 1960. Tome 2, Ethnologie (deuxième vol.) 1964*: 253–257.

4818a —Le roi-dieu au Benin . . . See [1834].

4819 Parrinder, Geoffrey
Divine kingship in West Africa. *Nuoen.*, 3 (2) 1956: 111–121.

4820 Partridge, Charles
Native law and custom in Egbaland. *J. Afr. soc.*, 10 (40) Jl. 1911: 422–433.

4821 Punch, Cyril
Land tenure and inheritance in Yoruba. In *Great Benin, its customs, arts and horrors, by H. L. Roth, 1903*: xxi-xxiv.

4822 Rowling, Cecil William
Land tenure in Ijebu province. Ibadan, Govt. printer, 1956. [4] 67p.

4823 —Report on land tenure in Ondo Province. Lagos, Govt. printer, 1952. 87p. (Sessional paper, no. 5 of 1952).

4824 Sklar, Richard Lawrence
The contribution of tribalism to nationalism in Western Nigeria. *J. human rel.*, 8 (3–4) 1960: 407–418. See also (4792).

4825 *Solanke, Ladipo
"The constitution of Oba houses" (Kingship and other political institutions among the Yoruba.) *Wasu*, (8).

4826 —The Egba-Yoruba constitutional law and its historical development. [Abeokuta, the author] 1931. [iii] 48p. Printed by "Asaoku printing press, Lagos.

4827 —A special lecture addressed to A. K. Ajisafe on "Egba-Yoruba constitutional law and its historical development." 82p.
"A supplement to Mr. Ladipo Solanke's pamphlet on "Egba-Yoruba constitutional law and its historical development," with a view to correcting the erroneous ideas and views of Mr. A. K. Ajisafe and his associates on the subject." –t.p.

4828 *—Yoruba (or Aku) constitutional law and its historical development. *Wasu*, (9) 1932:

4829 Sowole, M. S.
Local administration in Nigeria: the Egba Native administration at work. *W. Afr. rev.*, 17 (230) Nov. 1946: 1242–1244.

4830 Stopford, J. G. B.
Glimpses of native law in West Africa. *J. Afr. soc.*, 1 (1) Oct. 1901: 80–97.

Illustrations of Yoruba customary law relating to inheritance, the palm tree, breach of promise, slander and secret societies, all taken from the record of judgement of Sir Smalman Smith who was Chief Justice of Lagos in the 1880's and 1890's.

4831 Thomas, Isaac B., *comp.*
Full proceedings of an inquiry into the method of selection of a head to the House of Docemo, before H. L. Ward-Price, Commissioner, Lagos, Printed by Tika-Tore press, 1933. 131p. port.

4832 Ward-Price, Henry Lewis
Ekun Ibadan, iyipada ti o yiwọ inu àsà-lailai ni ekun Ibadan. Iwadi mimu ati nimi ilẹ ninu awọn ilu Yoruba. Ibadan, Lisabi press and bookshop, 1934. 41p.
On changes in traditional land tenure system in the Ibadan area.

4833 —Land tenure in the Yoruba provinces (1933). Lagos, Govt. printer, 1939. 146, xip.

4834 *—Notes of evidence regarding the House of Docemo, Lagos, 1933.

4835 *—Report on a commission of inquiry regarding the House of Docemo. Lagos, 1933.

4. (v) Social Organization and Structure, Social Relationships

4836 *Baker, Tanya
Women elite in Western Nigeria. 1957. [Ph.D. ?] thesis, Edinburgh.

4837 Bascom, William Russell
The principle of seniority in the social structure of the Yoruba. *Amer. anthrop.*, 44 (1) Jan.–Mar. 1942: 37–46.

4838 —"Secret societies", religious cult—groups and kinship units among the West African Yoruba. 1939.
Ph.D. thesis, Northwestern university. Subsequently published as The sociological role of the Yoruba cult group, *Amer. anthrop.*, 46 (1, pt. 2) Jan. 1944: 1–75. (American anthropological association. Memoir, no. 63).

4839 —Social status, wealth and individual differences among the Yoruba. *Amer. anthrop.*, 53 (4) Oct. 1951: 490–506.
Yoruba social structure and stratification are analysed and the various factors which determine the status of the individual in the social hierarchy listed.
—The sociological role of the Yoruba cult group. See [4838].

4840 Comhaire-Sylvain, S.
The status of women in Lagos, Nigeria. *Pi Lambda Theta j.*, 27 (3) Mar. 1949: 158–163. See also [4745].

4841 Lloyd, Barbara B.
Education and family life in the development of class identification among the Yoruba. In *The new elites of tropical Africa, edited by P. C. Lloyd, 1966*: 163–183.
French summary, pp. 182–183.

4842 Lloyd, Peter Cutt
Class consciousness among the Yoruba.
In *The new elites of tropical Africa*, ed.
by P. C. Lloyd, 1966: 328–341.
French summary, pp. 340–341.

4844 —Cocoa, politics and the Yoruba middle
class. *W. Afr.*, (1873) 17 Jan. 1953: 39.

4845 Morton-Williams, Peter
A discussion of the theory of élites in
West African (Yoruba) context.
WAISER conf. proc., 4th, Accra, 1955.
1956: 25–32.

4. (vi) Economy, Agriculture, Trade (Including Currency)

4846 Adejuwon, J. O.
Farming and farmlands in Ibadan
Division of Western Nigeria. 1963.
M.Sc. thesis, London.

4847 Aderemi, Adesoji, *Oni of Ife*
Iwofa. *Odù*, (3) 16–18.
Description of a Yoruba credit
system interpreted as pawning, but
which in its operation, may serve not
only as a money lending, but also as an
educational system. Culled from an
address delivered at the opening of a
course on Yoruba culture organized at
Ede by Ibadan University Extra-Mural
Dept. in April, 1955.

4848 *Baldwin, Kenneth D. S.
Group-farming in the West Region of
Nigeria. *Economic weekly*, Feb. 2, 1952:

4849 Bascom, William Russell
The Esusu: a credit institution of the
Yoruba. *J.R.A.I.*, 82 (1) 1952: 63–69.

4850 Carter, G. F.
Archaeological maize in West Africa:
a discussion of Stanton and Willett.
Man, 64, May–Je. 1964: 85–86. (art. 95)
bibliog.
A critical evaluation of Stanton and
Willett's article [4868] on changes in
maize type in West Africa and on the
possible route by which maize reached
this region.

4850a Cohen, Abner
Politics of the Kola trade . . . See [2563].

4851 —The social organisation of credit in a
West African cattle market. *Africa*, 35
(1) Jan. 1965: 8–20.
Describes organisation of the cattle
market in Ibadan, the operation of a
credit system which has evolved therein,
and the economic and other relationships existing between the various
groups involved in this market. French
summary, pp. 19–20.

4852 Forde, Cyril Daryll
The Yoruba and Boloki: hoe cultivators
in the African forests. In his *Habitat,
economy and society, 1934*: 148–172,
map.

4853 Galletti, R. [and others]
Nigerian cocoa farmers: an economic
survey of Yoruba cocoa farming
families, by R. Galletti, R. D. S.
Baldwin and I. O. Dina. London,

O.U.P., for Nigeria Cocoa Marketing
Board, 1956. xxxix, 744p. maps, bibliog.
An exhaustive survey of the economic
life of Yoruba cocoa farmers and of the
economics of cocoa production in the
Yoruba area of Nigeria.

4854 Goddard, S.
Town-farm relationship in Yorubaland:
a case study from Oyo. *Africa*, 35 (1)
Jan. 1965: 21–29, map, bibliog.
Based on a close study in one Oyo
compound—Abu compound. French
summary, p. 29.

4855 Gourou, Pierre
Les plantations de cacaoyers en pays
yoruba; un exemple d'expansion
économique spontanée. *Ann. econ. soc.
civilisations*, 15 (1) Jan.–Feb. 1960:
60–82, map.

4856 Hodder, Bramwell William
Markets in Yorubaland. 1964.
Ph.D. thesis, London University.

4857 —Rural periodic day markets in parts
of Yorubaland. *Tr. & papers inst. Brit.
geog.*, 29, 1961: 149–159.

4859 —The Yoruba rural market. In *Markets
in Africa*, ed. P. Bohannan and G. Dalton,
1962: 103–117.
Characteristics of the rural markets
in Yorubaland and the role of these
markets in the economic process in the
area.

4859 —The Yoruba rural market ring. *Res.
notes*, (12) Feb. 1959: 29–36, maps.

4860 Hopkins, Anthony Gerald
An economic history of Lagos, 1880–
1914. London, 1964.
Ph.D. thesis, London (S.O.A.S.).

4861 Jeffreys, M. D. W.
The history of maize in Africa. *S. Afr.
j. sci.*, 50 (8) Mar. 1954: 197–200,
bibliog.

4861a —Pre-Columbian maize in Africa.
See [925].

4862 Lloyd, Peter Cutt
Craft organisation in Yoruba towns.
Africa, 23 (1) Jan. 1953: 30–44.
Includes description of the structure,
organisation and functions of craft
guilds. Based on material collected from
Iwo, Shaki and Ado (in Ekiti). French
summary, p. 44.

4863 Magbogunje, Akin L.
The market-women. *Ibadan*, (11) Feb.
1961: 14–17.
A general study of the market women
in Nigeria including their trading
activity, family roles, and attitude to
politics.

4865 Marshall, Gloria A.
The marketing of farm produce: some
patterns of trade among women in
Western Nigeria. *N.I.S.E.R. conf. proc.,
8th, Ibadan, 1962*: 88–99.
"Investigation into social patterns
which are correlated with, affected by,
or have arisen out of the involvement of
women in trade."

4865a —Women, trade and the Yoruba family. See [4757].

4866 Ojo, G. J. Afolabi
The changing patterns of traditional group farming in Ekiti, north-eastern Yoruba country. *Nig. geog. j.*, 6 (1) Je. 1963: 31–38, maps, bibliog.

4867 Prothero, R. Mansell
Some results from an investigation of land use in the cocoa growing region near Ibadan. *Res. notes*, Je. 1952: 21–25.

4868 Stanton, W. R. and Willett, Frank
Archaeological evidence for changes in maize type in West Africa: an experiment in technique. *Man*, 63, Aug. 1963: 117–123 (art. 150) illus., map., bibliog.
An interesting investigation into maize markings on pottery recovered from Old Oyo and Ife, to shed light on the problem of dating the introduction of maize into West Africa.

4869 Takes, Charles A. P.
Socio-economic factors affecting agricultural productivity in some villages of Oshun Division (Western region) Ibadan, NISER, 1963, 67p.
A preliminary report. Mimeographed.

4870 Willett, Frank
The introduction of maize into West Africa: an assessment of recent evidence. *Africa*, 32 (1) Jan. 1962: 1–13, bibliog.
See also Jeffreys: *How ancient is West African maize?* [922] in which this assessment is rejected. French summary, p. 13.

4871 —Maize impressions on ancient Nigerian pottery. *Man*, 60, Jan. 1960: 10 (art. 8).
Believes maize was introduced into West Africa in 1500 A.D.

4. (vii) Food Preparation and Consumption, Standard of Living

4872 Ajibola, J. O. and Samade, B.
Ounje ile Yoruba. London, O.U.P., 1947. 31p.
Yoruba food.

4873 Bascom, William Russell
Yoruba cooking. *Africa*, 21 (2) Apr. 1951: 125–137, bibliog.
A continuation of his *Yoruba food* [4874] Here he considers methods of cooking among the Yoruba, listing and describing 56 recipes from Ife, with brief notes on 44 additional ones. French summary, p. 137.

4874 —Yoruba food. *Africa*, 21 (1) Jan. 1951: 41–53, bibliog.
A detailed analysis of traditional Yoruba diet, noting the methods of food preparation and patterns of consumption. Based largely on observations in Ife. French summary, p. 53. See also [4873].

4875 Collis, William Robert Fitz-Gerald [and others].
On the ecology of child health and nutrition in Nigerian villages. *Trop. geog. med.*, 14, 1962: 140–163; 201–299.

The first instalment considers environment, population and resources, while the second deals with dietaries and medical surveys.

4876 Hills, M. A. LeC.
Protein malnutrition in the Western Region of Nigeria. 1960.
M.D. thesis, Sheffield.

4877 Jelliffe, D. B.
Infant feeding among the Yoruba of Ibadan. *W. Afr. med. j., n.s.*, 2 (3) Sept. 1953: 114–122.
A four year investigation of breast feeding and its duration, weaning, artificial feeding, the various foods used and their nutritional values.

4878 Mars, J. A. and Tooley, E. M. *eds.*
The Kudeti book of Yoruba cookery. Rev. ed. Lagos, C.M.S. bookshop, 1943. 58p.

4879 Matthews, D. S.
A preliminary note on the ethnological and medical significance of breast-feeding among the Yoruba. *Int. W. Afr. conf. proc., 3rd, 1949. 1956*: 269–279, bibliog.
Discusses the practice of prolonged lactation among the Yoruba of Ibadan, noting the advantages and disadvantages and the factors responsible for successful lactation among the Yoruba.

4880 Millson, Alvan
Notes on the preparation of Lagos palm oil. *Kew bull.*, 1892: 203–208, illus.
Traditional method of extracting palm oil and palm kernels from the fruits by the Yoruba of Lagos.

4881 Nicol, Bruce M.
Calorie requirements of Nigerian peasant farmers. *Brit. j. nutrition*, 13, 1959: 293–306.

4882 —Protein requirements of Nigerian peasant farmers. *Brit. j. nutrition*, 13, 1959: 307–320.

4883 Nicol, D. S. H. W.
Nutrition in Western Nigeria. 1956.
M.D. thesis, Cambridge university.

4884 Nicol, Davidson
A pilot nutrition survey in Nigeria. *W. Afr. med. j., n.s.* 2 (3) Sept. 1953: 123–128.

4885 Poynter, H. G.
Production and consumption of native foodstuffs in Abeokuta Province. *Farm & forest*, 2, 1941: 68–71.

4886 Williams, R. Omosunlola
About your cookery. Illustrated by Mora Dickson. London, Longmans, 1960. [8] 114p. illus.
Abridged and simplified version of her "Miss Williams' cookery book" [4887].

4887 —Miss Williams' cookery book. London, Longmans, Green, 1957. xii, 260p. front. (col.) illus.
Useful discussions of, and recipes for traditional and modern Nigerian dishes, mostly Yoruba and Ibo.

4. (viii) Religion (Including Associated Festivals)

See also 4 (xv) *Sculpture; Carving.*

Much of Yoruba sculpture is rooted in the religious beliefs of the people, and explicable in terms of those beliefs. But for convenience of arrangement, all works on sculpture have been collected in sub-section xv, p. 235. For a comprehensive view of Yoruba religion therefore, that sub-section should also be consulted.

4888 Adedeji, G. O.
The Arę ceremony in Ilofa. *Nig. field,* 4 (1) Jan. 1935: 35–39, illus.
Account of the Arę festival as observed in 1934 in Ilofa, a village to the south-east of Ilorin Province.

4889 Adesanya, Adebayo
Yoruba metaphysical thinking. *Odù,* (5) [1958]: 36–41.

4890 The African explains witchcraft. *Africa,* 8 (4) Oct. 1935: 504–559.
A collection of information and views on witchcraft from different parts of Africa. The Yoruba account, by a school teacher in Abeokuta, is given at p. 548.

4891 Arriens, C.
Ein westafrikanischer Priesterstaat. *Kol. Runds.,* (4, 5, 6) Apr.–Je. 1930: 119–123.

4892 Bascom, William Russell
Ifa divination: comments on the paper by J. D. Clarke, *J.R.A.I.,* 69, 1939: 235–256. *Man,* 42, 1942: 41–43 (art. 21).

4893 —Odu Ifa: the names of the signs. *Africa,* 36 (4) Oct. 1966: 408–421.

4894 —Odu Ifa: the order of the figures of Ifa. *Bull. IFAN,* 23 (3–4) 1961: 676–682.

4895 —The relationship of Yoruba folklore to divining. *J. Amer. folkl.,* 56 (220) 1943: 127–131.

4896 —The sanctions of Ifa divination. *J.R.A.I.,* 71 (1–2) 1941: 43–54.

4897 —Yoruba concepts of the soul. In *Men and cultures: selected papers of the 5th International congress of anthropological and ethnological sciences, Philadelphia, Sept. 1–9, 1956, ed. A. F. C. Wallace, 1960:* 401–410.

4898 —Yoruba in Cuba. *Nig. mag.,* (37) 1951: 14–20.
An illustrated account of Yoruba religious rites in Cuba.

4899 Bastide, Roger
Les métamorphoses du sacré dans les sociétés en transition. *Civilisations,* 9 (4) 1959: 432–443.
English summary, pp. 441–443.

4900 Batty, R. Braithwaite
Notes on the Yoruba country. *J. Anthrop. inst.,* 19, 1890: 160–164, illus.
Abstract only of the original paper. Gives account of the worship of Oro, the god of terror and vengeance.

4901 Beier, Horst Ulrich
The *egungun* cult. *Nig. mag.,* (51) 1956: 380–392, illus.
Describes the worship of the cult in Ede.

4902 —The *egungun* cult among the Yoruba.

Pres. afr., n.s. (17–18) Feb.–May 1958: 33–36.

4903 —Festival of the images. *Nig. mag.,* (45) 1954: 14–20, illus.
Account of Ere festival, a Yoruba religious ceremony performed annually.

4904 —Gelede masks. *Odù,* (6) Je. 1958: 4–23, illus.
Describes the Gelede masks—one of the principal types of Yoruba mask—and comments on the dance and other religio-cultural customs associated with the masks.

4905 —The Oba's festival at Ondo. *Nig. mag.* (50), 1956: 238–259, illus.

4906 —Obatala festival, Ondo. *Nig. mag.,* (52) 1956: 10–28, illus.

4907 —Oloku festival. *Nig. mag.,* (49) 1956: 168–183, illus.
Day by day account of a seven day festival celebrated annually in Okuku, near the boundary with Northern Region, in honour of *Orisha Oloku,* one of the goddesses of the town.

4908 —Ori-Oke festival, Iragbiji. *Nig. mag.,* (56) 1958: 65–83, illus.
Annual festival of *Oke* in Iragbiji town.

4909 —Oshun festival. *Nig. mag.,* (53) 1957: 170–187, illus.

4910 —Three igbin drums from Igbomina. *Nig. mag.,* (78) Sept. 1963: 154–163, illus.
Origins of Igbin drums, a set of four drums used in the Obatala cult, and a description of four igbin drums three of which have carved surfaces.

4911 —A year of sacred festivals in one Yoruba town, edited by D. W. Macrow. Lagos, 'Nigeria magazine', 1959. 92p. front., 62 illus.
Annual cycle of Yoruba religious festivals in Ede. Copiously illustrated with photographs of scenes from celebrations observed by author.

4912 Beyioku, Akin Fagbenro
Ifa: basic principles of Ifa science. Lagos, Tika-Tore press, 1940. 36p.

4913 —Orumnlaism [sic] the basis of Jesuism. Lagos, Tika-Tore press, 1940. 36p.

4914 Brackmann, Richard W.
Der Umbanda-Kult in Brasilien. *Staden-Jahrbuch,* 7–8, 1959–60: 157–173.
On the Yoruba Shango cult in Brazil.

4915 Carneiro, Edison
The structure of African cults in Bahia. *J. Amer. folkl.,* 53 (210) Oct.–Dec. 1940: 271–278.

4916 Clarke, John Digby
Ifa divination. *J.R.A.I.,* 69 (2) 1939: 235–236. See also [4893].

4917 —Three Yoruba fertility ceremonies. *J.R.A.I.,* 74 (1–2) 1944: 91–96, illus.
Ceremonies observed in three villages in the south-eastern area of Ilorin Province.

4918 Comhaire, Jean
La vie religieuse á Lagos. *Zaire,* Mar. 1949: 549–556.

4919 Delange, Jacqueline
Sur un *oshe Shango. Objets et mondes*, 3
(3) autumn 1963: 205–210, illus.

4920 Dwyer, Pierce M.
On the thunder-stones of Nigeria. *Man*,
3, 1903: 183–184 (art. 103).
Account of the worship of Shango,
the Yoruba god of thunder, and of the
use of the axe-heads or "thunderbolt"
celts in the process. Extracted from a
report by the author, then Resident of
Ilorin Province.

4921 Epega, D. Onadele
The mystery of the Yoruba gods. Lagos,
Hope rising press, 1932. 2v. in 1.
Bk. 2. printed by Degosen printing
works, Ode-Remo.
English edition of his "Ifa-amọna
awọn baba-wa." Lagos, 1931.

4922 Epega, M. L.
Ifa—the light of my fathers. *Nig.
teacher*, (5) 1935: 11–14.

4923 *Esan, S. O.
The Delphic and Ifa oracles. *Nig. & the
classics*, 11.

4924 Faduma, Orishatukeh
Religious beliefs of the Yoruba people
in West Africa. In *Africa and the
American negro: addresses and proceedings of the Congress on Africa, held
under the auspices of the Stewart
Missionary foundation for Africa of
Gammon theological seminary, in connection with the Cotton states and
international exposition, Dec. 13–15,
1895. Ed. John Wesley Edward Bowen,
1896*: 31–36.
Includes portrait of the author, a
Yoruba educated in Sierra Leone,
London and at Yale University.

4925 Fagg, William Buller
Another Yoruba hunter's shrine. *Man*,
59, Dec. 1959: (art. 335): 216–217,
illus.
Describes a shrine in Egbe village near
Gbongan, erected in memory of a dead
hunter. See [5003] for account of similar
shrines.

4926 Farrow, Stephen Septimus
Faith, fancies and fetich; or Yoruba
paganism: being some account of the
religious beliefs of the West African
negroes, particularly of the Yoruba
tribes of Southern Nigeria. London,
S.P.C.K., New York, Macmillan, 1926.
xi, 180p. front., illus. (incl. music).
Earlier presented as Ph.D. thesis,
university of Edinburgh, 1924.

4927 The festival of Iya Mapo. *Nig. mag.*, (58)
1958: 212–224, illus.
On the annual festival celebrated in
honour of *Iya Mapo* (The Great
mother goddess) by the people of
Igbetti near Old Oyo.

4928 Garlanda, Ugo
Areopago di idoli in Nigeria. *Africa*
[Milano] 13 (1) Jan.–Feb. 1958: 27–31,
illus.
On Esie stone carvings.

4929 Gillilaud, William H.
Egungun Eshishe of the Yoruba-speaking
peoples. *Man*, 60, Aug. 1960 (art. 158):
122–123, illus.

4930 God of iron. *Nig. mag.* (49) 1956: 118–
137, illus.
Account of *Ogun*, the Yoruba "god
of iron".

4931 Gordon, Tin and Lancaster, Michael
Orisha houses in Ibadan. *Ibadan*, (11)
Feb. 1961: 22–23, illus.
Describes some Orishas (lesser gods)
and their functions in Yoruba religious
beliefs, and notes some of their shrines
and statues in Ibadan.

4932 Hall, Henry Usher
Some gods of the Yoruba. *Univ. Penn.
mus. j.*, 8 (1) 1917: 53–59, illus.

4933 Idowu, E. Bolaji
Olódùmarè: God in Yoruba belief.
London, Longmans, Green, 1962. viii,
222p. illus., map.
A study of Yoruba conception of the
deity, and of his position in their
religion.

4934 —Olodumare (the Yoruba supreme god)
and his relationship to the lesser
divinities. 1955.
Ph.D. thesis, London.

4935 Igogo festival. *Nig. mag.*, (77) Je. 1963:
91–104, illus.
Origins and day by day account of
the festival celebrated annually at Owo.

4936 *Johnson, James
Isin Orişa bibọ ni ilẹ Yoruba. Lagos,
1899.

4937 Jones, R. W. (Taffy)
Orisa oko—the Yoruba goddess of the
farm and agriculture. *Nig. mag.*, (23)
1946: 118–121, illus.
Traditions of origin and the worship
of the goddess Orisa Oko.

4938 Joyce, T. A.
Note on a carved door and three
fetish staves from Northern Nigeria.
Man, 3, 1903: 177–179, illus.
Description of a meticulously carved
wooden door said to have been used at
the gate of Akarre town in Northern
Nigeria, three staves from the Bunu
tribe in Kabba province and a chief's
axe apparently also from the area.

4939 *Keribo, O.
History of the Yoruba gods. Abeokuta,
1906.

4940 Khane, A.
Au pays des orishas et des vodruns:
Eshou Elegba, le messager des dieux.
Afr. en marche, (14) Mar.–Apr. 1958:
10–13.

4941 —Au pays des orishas et des vodruns:
Ifa, donneur d'oracles et porte-parole
des dieux. *Afr. en marche*, (15) Apr.–
May, 1958: 11–14.

4942 —Au pays des orishas et des vondruns:
les couvents. *Afr. en marche*, (16) May-
Je. 1958: 3–7.

4943 —Au pays des orishas et des vondruns:

l'initiation. *Afr. en marche*, (17) Je.–Jl. 1958: 11–15.

4944 —Au pays des orishas et des vonduns: Olodoumare et Obatala; ou "Le mythe de la création" *Afr. en marche*, (12–13) Jan.–Mar. 1958: 12–16.

4945 —Religions et traditions d'Afrique noire: au pays des orishas et des vonduns. *Afr. en marche*, (10–11) Nov. 1957/Jan. 1958: 4–5.

4946 Kiéner, L.
Notices sur les fetiches des populations Bassoundi (Yoruba) . . . de Pangala. *Bull. Soc. rech. congol.*, 1 (1) 1922: 21–27.

4946a King, Anthony
A report on the use of stone clappers for the accompaniment of sacred songs. See [5063].

4946b —Yoruba sacred music from Ekiti. See [5064].

4947 Lijadu, E. M.
Ifa: imole re ti ise ipile isin ni ile Yoruba. Exeter, J. Townsend, 1923. 72p.

4948 Lucas, Jonathan Olumide
The cult of the 'Adamu Orisha'. *Nig. field*, 11, Dec. 1943: 184–196, bibliog.
Extract from a lecture in which the author discussed Yoruba secret societies and their social significance and suggested Egyptian origin for one of them—the Adamu Orisha.

4949 —The religion of the Yorubas: being an account of the religious beliefs and practices of the Yoruba peoples of Southern Nigeria, especially in relation to the religion of ancient Egypt. Lagos, C.M.S. bookshop, 1948. xii, 420p. illus. map, bibliog.

4950 McClelland, E. M.
The significance of number in the Odu of Ifa. *Africa*, 36 (4) Oct. 1966: 421–431.
French summary, pp. 430–431. See also [4893] and [4961].

4951 Macfie, John W. Scott.
A Shango staffs [sic] *Man*, 13, 1931: 169–171 (art. 96) illus.

4952 Macrow, Donald W.
Oshogbo celebrates festival of Shango. *Nig. mag.*, (40) 1953: 298–313.
Detailed account of the celebration. Shango is the Yoruba god of thunder.

4953 Merriam, Alan P.
Songs of the *ketu* cult of Bahia, Brazil. *Afr. mus.*, 1 (3) 1956: 53–67; (4) 1957: 73–80.

4954 Messinger, Susan F.
Witchcraft in two West African societies. 1953. 146p.
M.A. thesis, University of Chicago. Presents a comparative study of witchcraft among the Yoruba and the Ibo.

4955 Meyerowitz, Eva Lewin Richter
Notes on the king-god Shango and his temple at Ibadan, Southern Nigeria. *Man*, 46, Mar.–Apr. 1946: 25–31. (art. 27). illus.
Discusses Shango's duality—as a

thunder-god and as an ancestral king of the Yoruba. Includes description of the temple.

4956 Milburn, S.
Magic and charms of Ijebu Province, southern Nigeria. *Man*, 32, Jl. 1932: 158–160. (art. 194).

4957 —A Yoruba household altar. *Nig. field*, 17 (1) Jan. 1952: 43–44, illus.
Describes a drawing seen on the walls of a house in Abeokuta in 1934 and identified as the figure of Obatala.

4958 Morton-Williams, Peter
The Atinga cult among the southwestern Yoruba: a sociological analysis of a witch-finding movement. *WAISER conf. proc., 1952*: 43–49; *Bull. IFAN*, 18 (3–4) Jl.–Oct. 1956: 315–334.
Summary only in *WAISER conf. proc.* The text in *Bull. IFAN* is a revised version of the original paper read at the WAISER conference.

4959 —The Egungun society in southwestern Yoruba kingdoms. *WAISER conf. proc., 1954*: 90–103.

4960 —An outline of the cosmology and cult organisation of the Oyo Yoruba. *Africa*, 34 (3) Jl. 1964: 243–261, illus., bibliog.
French summary, p. 261.

4961 —Two studies of Ifa divination. Introduction: The mode of divination. *Africa*, 36 (4) Oct. 1966: 406–408.
An introduction to William Bascom's Odu Ifa: the names of the signs [4893] and E. M. McClelland's The significance of number in the Odu of Ifa [4950].

4962 Mud shrines of Olokun. *Nig. mag.*, (50) 1956: 280–295, illus.

4963 Murray, Kenneth Crosthwaite
Oloku. *Nig. mag.*, (35) 1950: 364–365.
On the annual festival and worship of Oloku, a Yoruba god at the town of Okuku.

4964 —The stone images of Ęsie and their yearly festival. *Nig. mag.*, (37) 1951: 45–63, illus.
Brief historical notes on the images, followed by a detailed account of the annual festival.

4965 A New sanctuary at Oshogbo. *Nig. mag.*, (81) Je. 1964: 98–105, illus.
Notes on Alajire, a Yoruba deity, and its shrine in Oshogbo.

4966 Note on the Yoruba god, Shango. *Prés. afr.*, Eng. ed. 30 (58) 1966: 224–227.

4967 Obe, Peter
Igogo festival at Owo: dance of the Olowo. *W. Afr. rev.*, 29 (375) Dec. 1958: 1007–1013, illus.

4968 Odukoya, M. A.
Okosi festival at Epe town. *Odù*, (7) Mar. 1959: 28–30.

4969 Ogunba, Oyin
The Agemo cult in Ijebuland. *Nig. mag.*, (86) Sept. 1965: 176–186, illus.
Origin, status, and worship of Agemo, a Yoruba god which was once the most important deity among the Ijebu.

4970 Ogunbiyi, T. A. J.
Yoruba oracles and their modes of
divination. Lagos, C.M.S. bookshop,
1940.

4971 Ogundele, Joseph Ogunsina
Ibu-Olokun. London, U.L.P., 1956.
128p., illus.
Shrine of the sea goddess.

4972 Ogunkoya, Olatunji
Yoruba ancient religion and mythology.
Africana 1 (3) Summer 1949: 14–15, 30.

4973 Olaleye, Amos Mobolaj
A philosophy of the Yoruba religion.
1956. x, 54p.
M.A. thesis, Howard university,
Washington, D.C.

4974 Onadele Epega, D.
The mystery of Yoruba gods. [n.p.]
Oliewo institute, 1931. 30p.

4975 Parrinder, Geoffrey
Ibadan annual festival. *Africa*, 21 (1)
Jan. 1951: 54–58.
Gives the "character, origin and
purpose" of the annual festival of Oke
Ibadan (Oke'badan)—Hill of Ibadan.
French summary, p. 58.

4976 —Religion in an African city. London,
O.U.P., 1953. [viii] 211p., illus.
A comprehensive study of all religions
in Ibadan, including pagan and personal
religion as well as secret societies.

4977 Prince, Raymond H.
Curse, invocation and mental health
among the Yoruba. *J. Canadian psychiatric assoc.*, 5, Apr. 1960: 65–79.

4978 —Ifa: Yoruba divination and sacrifice.
[Ibadan, University press, 1964] 18p.

4979 —Indigenous Yoruba psychiatry. In
*Magic, faith and healing: studies in
primitive psychiatry today*, ed. Ari Kiev,
1964: 84–120.

4980 —Some notes on Yoruba native doctors
and their management of mental illness.
In *Pan-African psychiatric conference,
1st, Abeokuta, 1961.* [*1962*]: 279–288,
bibliog.

4981 —Western psychiatry and the Yoruba:
the problem of insight psychotherapy.
NISER conf. proc., 1962: 213–221.

4982 —The Yoruba image of the witch. *J.
mental sci.*, 107 (449) Jl. 1961: 795–805.

4983 *Ribeiro, Rene
Significado sócio cultural des ceremonias
de Ibeji. *Riv. de Antrop.* [São Paulo,
Brazil] 5 (2) Dec. 1957: 129–144.

4984 Schwab, William B.
The growth and conflicts of religion in a
modern Yoruba community. *Zaire*, 6
(8) Oct. 1952: 829–835.

4985 Simpson, George E.
The Shango cult in Nigeria and in
Trinidad. *Amer. anthrop.*, 64 (6) Dec.
1962: 1204–1219, bibliog.
Compares ceremonies associated with
the cult in the two places and indicates
both Trinidadian retention of many of
the Yoruba features of these ceremonies
as well as some syncretisms.

4986 Some Yoruba customs:
I. The festival of Obirinjuwu. *Nig.
field*, 13 (1) Jan. 1948: 24–27.
II. The Jigbo. *Nig. field*, 13 (2) Oct.
1948: 59–61.
III. Oluweri: a minor deity of Esure,
Ijebu Province. *Nig. field*, 15 (1) Jan.
1949: 33–37, illus.
IV. Belief in spirits. *Nig. field*, 15 (2)
Apr. 1949: 74–79, illus.

4987 Sowande, Fela
Ifa. Yaba, Foward press, 1964. 74p.
illus.

4788 Soyannwo, 'Biodun
Some aspects of traditional therapy in
Yorubaland. *Dokita*, (3) Oct. 1962: 21–
31, illus.
Traditional medical practice among
the Yoruba as seen by a study of some
traditional or "native doctors"—three
'general physicians' from Ijebu area, one
specialist in mental illness from
Abeokuta Province, and two families
engaged in circumcision and tatooing
from Ibadan.

4989 Stevens, Phillips
The festival of the images. *Nig. mag.*,
(87) Dec. 1965: 237–243, illus.
Step by step account of the annual
festival in honour of the Esie stone
figures.

4990 —Orisha-nla festival. *Nig. mag.*, (90)
Sept. 1966: 184–199, illus.

4991 Stillfried, Bernhard
Heilkundige bei einen westafrikanischen
Negervolk. *Wiener völkekdl. Mitt.*, 5
(2) 1957: 94–97.
Native medicine and native doctors
among the Yoruba.

4992 Verger, Pierre
Dieux d'Afrique. Culte des Orishas et
Vodouns à l'ancienne côte des esclaves
en Afrique et à Bahia . . . au Brésil.
Paris, Paul Hartmann, 1954. 193p.

4993 —Ejigbo festival. (Translated by Arthur
and Ghislaine Warren) *Nig. mag.*, (70)
Sept. 1961: 206–217.
Festival at Ejigbo in honour of the
deity Oshginyan, the orisha protector.

4994 —Grandeur et décadence du culte de
iyámi òsòròngà (ma mère la sorcière)
ches les Yoruba. *J. Soc. afr.*, 35 (1) 1965:
141–243.

4995 —Notes sur le culte des Orisa et vodun
à Bahia, la Baie de tous les Saints, au
Brésil et à l'ancienne côte des esclaves
en Afrique. Dakar, IFAN, 1957. 609p.
1 map + 144pp. of plates (IFAN.
Mémoires, no. 51).

4996 —Oral tradition in the cult of the
orishas and its connection with the
history of the Yoruba. *J. Hist. soc. Nig.*,
1 (1) Dec. 1956: 61–64.
On the significance to Yoruba
historical study of oral traditions
associated with the orisha cult.

4997 —Role joué par l'état d'hébétude au
cours de l'initiation de novices aux

cultes des Orisha et Vodun. *Bull. IFAN*, 16, 1954: 322–340.

4998 Walsh, Michael J.
The Edi festival at Ile Ife. *Afr. affairs.*, 47 (189) Oct. 1948: 231–238, illus.
Origin, significance and celebration of the festival.

4999 Webster, Douglas
A "spiritual church". *Pract. anthrop.*, 11 (5) Sep.–Oct. 1964: 229–232; 240.
Describes a Nigerian "nativist" or "spiritual" church in Lagos and one of their sunday worships in which he participated.

4999a Wescott, Joan A.
The sculpture and myths of Eshu-Elegba. See [5193].

5000 Wescott, Joan A. and Morton-Williams, Peter
The festival of Iya Mapo. *Nig. mag.*, (58) 1958: 212–224.
Describes the festival held annually at the Yoruba town of Igbetti in honour of the goddess Iya Mapo, patroness of Yoruba craftswomen.

5001 —The symbolism and ritual context of the Yoruba Laba Shango, *J.R.A.I.*, 92 (1) Jan.–Je. 1962: 23–37, illus., bibliog.
The symbol here discussed consists of four identical panel designs which decorate a flat red leather bag called the *laba*. An attempt is made "to discover by conceptual and aesthetic analysis what the panel design directly conveys to the Yoruba as a symbol".

5002 Willett, Frank
A further shrine for a Yoruba hunter. *Man*, 65, May–Je. 1965: 82–83 (art. 66) illus.
A shrine at Ife commemorating Aniwe who held the title of Ashipa of Ilode.

5003 —A hunter's shrine in Yorubaland, Western Nigeria. *Man*, 59, 1959: 215–216 (art. 334) illus.
Describes two shrines near Ifetedo erected by Yoruba hunters in memory of their dead colleagues.

5003a Wyndham, John
Ajija (the dust devil) *Man*, 20, 1920: 41–42 (art. 24).

5004 —The cult of Pĕrĕgún 'Gbo. *Man*, 19, 1919: 124–125 (art. 66).

5005 —The divination of Ifa (a fragment) *Man*, 19, 1919: 151–153 (art. 80) illus.

4. (ix) Stories, Proverbs, Riddles

5006 Adewa, E. A.
Qualities of African folklore. *Nig. mag.*, (15) 1938: 210–211.

5007 Ajibola, J. O.
Owe Yoruba . . . London, O.U.P. 1955. 83p.
Yoruba proverbs.

5008 Akinsemoyin, Kunle
Twilight and the tortoise. Illustrated by Stephen Erhabor. Lagos, A.U.P., 1963. 80p. (African readers library, no. 3).
Folktales.

5009 Arewa, E. Ojo and Dundes, Alan
Proverbs and the ethnography of speaking folklore. *Amer. anthrop.*, 66 (6) pt. 2, Dec. 1964: 70–85, bibliog.
A consideration of proverbs as an impersonal medium of communication. Illustrated with a discussion of twelve Yoruba proverbs bearing on child instruction. Yoruba texts of the proverbs supplied.

5009a Arikpo, Okoi
Legends and folklore. See [2481].

5010 Babalola, Adeboye
Folk-tales from Yorubaland. *W. Afr. rev.*, 23 (292) Jan. 1952: 14–15.
A continuation of his translations at [5036].

5011 —Yoruba folk-tales. *W. Afr. rev.*, 33 (415) Jl. 1962: 48–49.
Distinguishes three classes of Yoruba folk-tales and discusses their cultural functions and the narrator's styles and methods.

5012 Balogun, Kolawole
The crowning of the elephant and nine other stories: stories of African custom, both past and present, and folklores. Oshogbo, Tanimehin-Ola printing works [n.d.] 54p.

5013 Baumann, Margaret Irene Lee
Ajapa the tortoise: a book of Nigerian fairy tales. London, A. & C. Black, 1929. viii, 167p. illus.

5014 Bertho, Jacques
La légende de la reine qui sacrifie son fils unique: comparaison entre la version des Baoulé de la côte d'Ivoire et la version des Yoruba de la Nigéria. *Notes afr.*, (31) Jl. 1946: 19–20.

5015 Danford, John Alexander and Fuja, S. Aboyomi
Our folk lore and fables. Lagos, Public relations dept., [1952] [2] 14p. illus. (Crownbird ser., no. 14).
A selection of four Yoruba folk stories.

5016 Delano, Isaac O.
Òwe l'esin ọrọ; Yoruba proverbs—their meaning and usage. Ibadan, O.U.P., 1966. xi, 154p.

5017 Dundes, Alan
Some Yoruba Wellerisms, dialogue proverbs, and tongue-twisters. *Folklore*, 75, Summer 1964: 113–120.
17 Yoruba proverbs, etc., with English translations, and explanatory notes.

5018 Ellis, Alfred Burdon
[Yoruba] folklore tales. In his *The Yoruba-speaking peoples . . . 1894*: 243–274.

5019 —[Yoruba] proverbs. In his *The Yoruba speaking peoples . . . 1894*: 218–242.
Lists 250 Yoruba proverbs, with brief explanatory notes where necessary. These are followed by lists of aphorisms, riddles, etc.

5020 Fuja, S. Aboyomi
Fourteen hundred cowries: traditional stories of the Yoruba. London, O.U.P., 1962. vii, 164p. illus.

A collection of thirty-one Yoruba folk tales.

5021   Idewu, Olawale and Adu, Omotayo
Nigerian folk tales, told to and edited by Barbara K. and Warren S. Walker. New Brunswick, N. J. Rutgers university press, 1961. x, 113p. illus., bibliog.
A collection of Yoruba folk tales.

5022   Itayemi, Phebean and Gurrey, P.
Folk tales and fables. London, Penguin books, 1953. 123p.
Yoruba and Isoko folk tales, together with others from Ghana and Sierra Leone.

5023   Lloyd, Peter Cutt
Yoruba myths—a sociologist's interpretation. Odù, (2) 20–28.

5024   Lobagola, Bata Kindai Amgoza Ibn
The folk tales of a savage. London, A. A. Knopf, 1930. xvii, 200p. front., illus.
Folk tales from Ondo area in Western Nigeria.

5025   Ogumefu, M. I.
The staff of Oranyan and other Yoruba tales. London, Sheldon press, 1930. 32p.

5026   —Tales of tortoise: Yoruba tales. London, Sheldon press [n.d.] 32p.

5027   —Yoruba legends. London, Sheldon press, 1929. vi, 87p.
A collection of forty stories in Yoruba mythology.

5028   Parkinson, John
The legend of Oro. Man, 6, 1906: 103–105 (art. 66).

5029   —Yoruba folk-lore. J. Afr. soc., 8 (30) Jan. 1909: 165–186.
Thirteen stories from Oyo area, with explanatory notes. Two of the stories feature the god Shango, one, Ifa.

5030   Turner, Lorenzo Dow
The role of folklore in the life of the Yoruba of south-western Nigeria. In Report on the ninth annual round table meeting on linguistic and language studies: anthropology and African studies, edited by W. M. Austin, 1960: 45–56.

5031   Wyndham, John
Myths of Ifè. London, Erskine Macdonald, 1921. 72p.
Yoruba mythology in blank verse, by a former Assistant District Officer in the Yoruba area.

4. (x)   Literary Expression, Literature

5032   Babalola, Adeboye
The characteristic features of outer form of Yoruba Ijala chants. Odu, 1 (1) Jl. 1964: 33–44; 1 (2) 1965: 47–77.
"Ijala is the oral poetry of Yoruba hunters . . . a borderline type of spoken art in that it lies in an area of indeterminacy between what is quite clearly spoken art and what is the concern of the ethno-musicologist."—p. 33.

5033   —The content and form of Yoruba ijala. 1964.
Ph.D. thesis, London.

5034   —Village characters. Afr. affairs, 52 (207) Apr. 1953: 156–162.
Six more translations of the Yoruba Ijala. See [5035].

5035   —When I first heard of forest farms. Afr. affairs, 49 (197) Oct. 1950: 338–343.
Metrical versions of four Yoruba oral poems or Ijala. The titles translated are: "When I first heard of forest farms"; "On returning home from work"; "The son of Abuteni"; and "Kujọwu and the elephants".

5036   —Yoruba oral poetry. W. Afr. rev., 22 (281) Feb. 1951: 130–131.
Translation in blank verse of Yoruba traditional folk-stories. Continued at [5010].

5037   —Yoruba poetry. Prés. afr., 19 (47) 1963: 184–190.

5038   Bascom. William Russell
Literary style in Yoruba riddles. J. Amer. folklore, 62 (243) Jan.–Mar. 1949: 1–16.

5039   Beier, Horst Ulrich
The moon cannot fight: Yoruba children's poems collected and translated by Ulli Beier and Bakare Gbadamosi. Illustrated by Georgia Betts. [Ibadan] Mbari publications [1964] [44]p. illus.

5040   Gbadamosi, Bakare and Beier, Horst Ulrich
The poetry of masqueraders: four poems of egungun masqueraders (iwi) Odù, (7) Mar. 1959: 38–40.

5041   —Yoruba poetry; traditional poems collected and translated [into English] . . . With eight silkscreen prints and ten vignettes by Susanne Wenger. Ibadan, General publication section, Ministry of education, 1959. 68p. (A special publication of "Black Orpheus").

5042   Martinez Furé, Rogelio A. ed. & trans. Poesia Yoruba. [La Habana, Ediciones el Puente, 1963] 149p.

4. (xi)   Birth and Death Rituals, Miscellaneous Beliefs and Rites

5043   *Adesola,
Burial customs in the Yoruba country. Nig. chronicle, 1908–1910.

5044   Beier, Horst Ulrich
Spirit children among the Yoruba. Afr. affairs, 53 (213) Oct. 1954: 328–331.
Yoruba belief in reincarnation and their customs relevant thereto.

5045   Ellis, Alfred Burdon
[Yoruba] ceremonies at birth, marriage and death. In his The Yoruba-speaking peoples . . . 1894: 152–163.

5046   Nicol, Davidson
Twins in Yoruba-land. W. Afr. rev., 28 (360) Sept. 1957: 845–847.
On the Yoruba attitude to twins whom they believe are endowed by Orisa Ibeji the god of twins. The second-born is regarded as the elder, the first-born being merely its herald.

5047   Olumide, J. J.

Twin worship among the Egbas. *Niger & Yoruba notes*, 9 (97) Jl. 1902: 4–5.
Describes the rites and ceremonies associated with twin worship among the Egba.

5048 Simpson, George E.
Selected Yoruba rituals: 1964. *Nig. j. econ. soc. stud.*, 7 (3) 1965: 311–324.

5049 Smith, Robert
The Bara or royal mausoleum, at New Oyo. *J. Hist. soc. Nig.*, 3 (2) Dec. 1965: 415–420, illus.
Bara is the burial place of the Alafin of Oyo.

5050 Thomas, Northcote Whitridge
Twins in the Yoruba country. *Man*, 21, 1921: 140 (art. 85).

4. (xii) Recreation, Games, Music, Dance.

5051 Armattoe, R. E. G.
Nigerian impressions. *W. Afr. rev.*, 21 (275) 1950: 922–923, illus.
Dance of Yoruba and Ewe women.

5052 Bascom, William Russell
Drums of the Yoruba of Nigeria. New York, Ethnic folkways record and service corp., 1953. [7]p. illus.
Introduction and notes on the recordings of Yoruba drum music [Ethnic Folkways Library, album P. 441] The drums used were: *Igbin, Dundun* or *Gangan*, and *Bata*. The introduction and notes describe the drums and discuss their cultural significance.

5052a Baumann, Margaret Irene Lee
Music of Yoruba songs and marches. See [4511].

5053 Beier, Horst Ulrich
The Agbegijo masqueraders. *Nig. mag.*, (82) Sept. 1964: 188–199, illus.
Describes a category of the egungun masqueraders—the Agbegijo—whose function is to entertain. Based on a display he watched in Oshogbo.

5054 —The talking drums of Africa. *Afr. mus.*, 1 (1) 1954: 29–31, illus.
On Yoruba drums and Yoruba drum music.

5055 —Yoruba folk operas. *Afr. mus.*, 1 (1) 1954: 32–34, illus.

5056 —Yoruba vocal music. *Afr. mus.*, 1 (3) 1956: 23–28.
Discusses Yoruba folk songs for wedding, funeral, hunting and other occasions, and the works of Yoruba modern composers who compose church music and popular operas.

5056a Brewster, Paul G.
Some Nigerian games, with their parallels and analogues. See [2989].

5057 Carrol, K.
Yoruba religious music. *Afr. mus.*, 1 (3) 1956: 45–47.
Brief background account.

5058 Daji, T.
Talking drums. *Blackwood's mag.*, 281 (1695) Jan. 1957: 65–71.

5059 Dawodu, P. A.

Programme and words of a grand native air opera entitled "Alli Baba and the forty thieves". Ibadan, Native air research party [1937?] 24p.

5060 Fagg, William Buller
A Yoruba xylophone of unusual type. *Man*, 50, Nov. 1950 (art. 234): 145, illus.
Gives account of a brief visit to Ado town and Owo village, both at the extreme southwest corner of Western Nigeria, and describes two xylophones seen in the latter place, each constructed over a trench in front of the "House of Idejero"—an *orisha* cult.

5061 Kennett, B. L. A.
Afoshi dancers of Kabba Province, Northern Nigeria. *J.R.A.I.*, 61, 1931: 435–442.

5062 King, Anthony
Employment of the "standard pattern" in Yoruba music. *Afr. music*, 2 (3) 1960: 51–54.

5063 —A report on the use of stone clappers for the accompaniment of sacred songs. *Afr. mus.*, 2 (4) 1961: 64–71.
Sacred songs sung at Iwo, a Yoruba town, as part of the rites of some rock shrines.

5064 —Yoruba sacred music from Ekiti. Ibadan, University press, 1961. ix, 45, xlixp. illus., score.
Analysis of religious music from Ekiti. The author is lecturer in music at the University of Ibadan.

5065 Kingslake, Brian
The art of the Yoruba (and some Yoruba lyrics with tunes) *Afr. mus. soc. newsletter*, 1 (4) Je. 1951: 13–18. music scores.

5066 —Musical memories of Nigeria. *Afr. musc.*, 1 (4) 1957: 17–20.

5067 Ladipo, Duro
Three Yoruba plays: Qba koso; Qba moro; [and] Qba waja. English adaptations by Ulli Beier. Ibadan, Mbari publications, 1964. 75p.

5068 Laoye, John Adetoyose, *Timi of Ede*
Yoruba drums . . . *Nig. mag.*, (45) 1954: 4–13, illus.; *Odu*, (7) Mar. 1959: 5–14, illus.
Describes Yoruba drums and Yoruba drum music. The reprint in *Odu* has fewer illustrations.

5069 —Yoruba music and the Church. *W. Afr. rev.*, 29 (364) 1958: 77–78, illus.

5070 Lasebikan, E. L.
Brazilians adopt Yoruba games. *W. Afr.* (2391) 30 Mar. 1963: 352.

5071 Macrow, Donald W.
Folk opera. *Nig. mag.*, (44) 1954: 329–345, illus.

5072 Newberry, R. J.
Some games and pastimes of Southern Nigeria:
Pt. I. Yoruba games. *Nig. field*, 7 (2) Apr. 1938: 85–90, illus.
Pt. II. Okoto. *Nig. field*, 7 (3) Jl. 1938: 131–132, illus.

Pt. III. Ayo. *Nig. field*, 8 (2) Apr. 1939: 75–80, illus.

Pt. IV. Sundry Yoruba games. *Nig. field*, 9 (1) Mar. 1940: 40–43, illus.
Series of illustrated articles describing some indigenous Yoruba games.

5073　Nketia, Kwabena
Yoruba musicians in Accra. *Odù*, (6) Je. 1958: 35–44.
A general account of Yoruba musicians resident in Accra, noting their types of drum, their songs and the occasions at which they perform.

5074　Ogumefu, M. I.
Yoruba melodies. Adapted by Ebun Ogumefu. London, S.P.C.K., 1929. 16p.

5075　Ogunbọwale, P. O.
Àkójọpọ̀ orin ibilè Yoruba. London, Evans, 1961. 47p.
A selection of 48 Yoruba traditional songs, with musical notation for each.

5076　Phillips, Ekundayo
Yoruba music (African) fusion of speech and music. Johannesburg, African music society, 1953. 58p. mus.

5077　Schneider, Marius
Prolegomena zu einer Theorie des Rhythmus. In *Proc. 7th congress International musicological society, Cologne, 1958*: 264–278, illus.
Rhythm in Duala, Dogon and Yoruba music.

5078　Sowande, Fela
Three Yoruba songs. *Odù*, 3, 1956: 36–40.
With notation.

5079　Spielleute und Märchenerzähler Innerafrikas. *Westermanns Monatshefte,* [*Braunschweig*] (115) 1913: 373–385, illus.
Yoruba (Ilorin) and Hausa, musical instruments and players.

5080　Wright, R.
Safe safari to musical Africa. *Music j.*, 16 (8) Nov.–Dec. 1959: 28, 41.
Yoruba music.

5081　Yoruba music and the church: conference at Abeokuta. *W. Afr. rev.*, 29 (364) Jan. 1958: 77–78, illus.

4. (xiii) Beauty Culture

5082　Brinkworth, Ian
Hair styles with a difference. *W. Afr. rev.*, 29 (375) Dec. 1958: 1034–1035, illus.

5083　De Negri, Eve
Yoruba men's costume. *Nig. mag.*, (73) Je. 1962: 4–12, illus.

5084　—Yoruba women's costume. *Nig. mag.*, (72) Mar. 1962: 4–12, illus.

5085　Myers, Oliver
A note on some cosmetics used in Yorubaland. *Odu*, 1 (2) 1965: 92–103, illus.

5086　Yoruba hairdressing. *Nig. mag.*, (18) 1939: 163–165.

4. (xiv) Material Culture-General

5087　Beier, Horst Ulrich
Experimental art school. *Nig. mag.*, (86) Sept. 1966: 199–204, illus.

5088　Bertho, Jacques and Mauny, Raymond
Archéologie du pays Yoruba et du Bas Niger. *Notes afr.*, (56) Oct. 1952: 97–115, illus., map, bibliog.
A descriptive survey of archaeological finds in Ife, Esie, Jebba, Tada, and other centres, and a discussion of the origin of Yoruba art.

5089　Cordwell, Justine Mayer
Naturalism and stylization in Yoruba arts. *Mag. art.*, 46 (5) May 1953: 220–225, illus.
—The problem of process and form in W. African art. See [1190].

5090　Davidson, Basil
Yoruba achievement: art flourished when Old Oyo held sway (Empires of Old Africa, 3) *W. Afr. rev.*, 33 (414) Je. 1962: 17–21, 43, illus.

5091　De Huesch, Luc
Le rayonnement de l'Egypte antique dans l'art et la mythologie de l'Afrique occidentale. *J. Soc. afr.*, 28 (1–2) 1958: 91–109.
Compares religious beliefs in ancient Egypt and among the Yoruba and other West African peoples today, and infers that Ife art originated from Meroe.

5092　Duckworth, E. H.
Return of Ife antiquities from America. *Nig. mag.*, (35) 1950: 362–363, illus.

5093　Fagg, William Buller
De l'art des Yoruba. *Prés. afr.*, (10–11) 1951: 103–135, illus.

5094　—Ife and Benin; two pinnacles of African art. *Unesco courier*, 12 (10) Oct. 1959: 15–19, illus.

5094a　Goodwin, A. J. H.
Walls, paving, water paths and landmarks. See [608].

5095　Milburn, S.
Yoruba schools and Yoruba life: a plea for museums. *Nig. teacher*, 1 (1) 1933: 2–6.

5096　Wescott, Joan A.
Yoruba art in German and Swiss museums. Preface by S. O. Biobaku. Ibadan, [Yoruba historical research scheme] 1958. 38p. illus.
Twenty-seven plates (photographs) with descriptive notes, illustrating a selection of Yoruba art objects in German and Swiss collections.

5097　—Yoruba collections in Germany and Switzerland. *Man*, 57, 1957 (art. 161): 133–135.
A survey of Yoruba art objects in public and private collections in the two countries. Gives names of the collections, followed in each case by a summary of its holdings classified according to the cult to which the objects belong.

5098　Wescott, Roger W.
Tradition and the Yoruba artist. *Athen.* 2 (1) 1963: 9–16, illus.

5099 Willett, Frank
Investigation at Old Oyo, 1956–57; an interim report. *J. Hist. soc., Nig.*, 2 (1) Dec. 1960: 59–77, illus.
The main report of his 1956–57 archaeological mission to the site of Old Oyo. See [5198] and [5102] for additional account.

5100 *—The microlithic industry from Old Oyo, Western Nigeria. *Proc. W. Afr. congress pre-hist., 4th, Leopoldville, 1959*:

5101 —Recent archaeological discoveries at Ilesha. *Odù*, (8) Oct. 1960: 4–20, illus.
Account of author's excavation in Ilesha in 1958 and a description of some of the terra-cotta found.

5102 —Recent excavations at Old Oyo and Ife, Nigeria. *Man*, 59, Je. 1959: 99–100. (art. 135).
Summary of a lecture to the Royal Anthropological Institute describing his excavations in the two areas in 1956–1958.

4. (xv) Sculpture, Carving
See also 4 (viii) p. 227

5103 Akeredolu, J. D.
Ife bronzes. *Nig. mag.*, (59) 1958: 341–353, illus.
Describes bronzes discovered in Ife during the 1957–1958 excavations, and cleaned and restored by him.

5104 —Wood-carving at Owo government school. *Nig. teacher*, 1 (4) 1935: 53–54, illus.

5105 Allison, Philip A.
A carved stone figure of Eshu from Igbajo, Western Nigeria. *Man*, 64, Jl.–Aug. 1964: 104–105 (art. 131) illus.

5106 —Newly discovered stone figures from the Yoruba village of Ijara, Northern Nigeria. *Man*, 63, Je. 1963: 93–94 (art. 115) illus.

5107 —A terra-cotta head in the Ife style, from Ikirun, Western Nigeria. *Man*, 63, 1963: 156–157, illus.

5108 —A Yoruba wood-carver. *Nig. mag.*, (22) 1944: 49–50, illus.

5109 Arriens, C.
Die heiligen Steinfiguren von Ife. *Erdball* [Berlin] 4 (9) 1930: 333–341, illus.

5110 Barker, H.
Examination of the Ife bronze heads. *Man*, 65, Jan.–Feb. 1965: 23–24 (art. 10) illus.
Report on laboratory analysis of a number of Ife bronzes in the British museum.

5111 Bascom, William Russell
Brass portrait heads from Ile-Ife, Nigeria. *Man*, 38, Oct. 1938: 176 (art. 201).
Notes on seven brass heads found in Ife in January and February 1938, by labourers working on a building site.

5112 —The legacy of an unknown Nigerian "Donatello": the simple beauty of the mysterious bronze heads recently discovered at Ife. *Illus. London news*, Apr. 8, 1939: 592–594, illus., map.

5113 Beier, Horst Ulrich
The bochio, a little-known type of African carving. *Black Orpheus*, (3) May 1958: 28–31, illus.

5114 —Complicated carver: Lamidi Fakeye exhibition in Ibadan. *W. Afr. rev.*, 31 (391) Je. 1960: 30–31, illus.
Notes on Lamidi Fakeye's wood carving, with a brief auto-biographical account of him. The illustrations are photographs of some of his carvings exhibited by the British Council in Ibadan.

5115 —Shango shrine of the Timi of Ede. *Black Orpheus*, (4) Oct. 1958: 30–35, illus.
Contends that contrary to European critical opinion, individualism is present in African art, and illustrates this by a study of the works of four carvers in the Shango shrine in Ede.

5116 —Story of sacred wood-carvings from one small Yoruba town. Edited by D. W. Macrow. Lagos, 'Nigeria Magazine' [1957] [19]p. illus.

5117 —Yemi Bisiri: a Yoruba brass caster. Ibadan, Mbari publications, 1963. 20p. illus.

5118 —Yoruba cement sculpture. *Nig. mag.*, (46) 1955: 144–153, illus.

5119 Bertho, Jacques
Coiffures—masques à franges de perles chez les rois Yoruba de la Nigéria et du Dahomey, *Notes afr.*, (47) Jl. 1950: 71–74, illus.

5119a Boulton, Laura C.
Bronze artists of West Africa. See [1893].

5120 Braunholtz, H. J.
Bronze head from Ife, Nigeria. *Br. Mus. q.*, 14 (4) 1940: 75–77, illus.

5121 —The bronze heads of Ife, Nigeria. *Congr. int. sci. anthrop. et ethnol. 3e, Bruxelles, 1948. 1960*: 22–24.

5122 Brinkworth, Ian
Stone treasure of Esie. *W. Afr. rev.*, 29 (374) Nov. 1958: 910–913, illus.
Illustrations, with notes of the stone carvings found in Esie in 1934.

5123 Bronze head of Ife. *Nig. mag.*, (21) 1940: 341–343, illus.

5124 Bronze ornaments from Lagos. *Br. mus. q.*, (5) 1930: 30, illus.

5124a Burland, C. A.
Lost wax: metal casting on the Guinea Coast. See [1902].

5125 Carrol, K.
The carved door of the University Catholic chapel. *Ibadan*, (5) Feb. 1959: 18, illus.
Ten photographs showing the figures on the door of the Catholic chapel at the University of Ibadan, carved by Lamidi son of Fakeye, in 1954. All the photographs depict scenes in the Bible. Gives brief notes on Lamidi's carving career.

5126 —Ekiti Yoruba wood-carving. *Odù*, (4) [1958]: 3–10, illus.

5127 —Three generations of Yoruba carvers. *Ibadan*, (2) Je. 1961: 21–24, illus.
A study of three Yoruba carvers of three successive generations with a view to gauging and explaining deterioration in Yoruba wood-carving. The carvers were: Areogun, a pagan carver (c. 1880–1954); his son Bandele, a nominal Christian (c. 1915– ?); and Lamidi, Bandele's apprentice, a Moslem (1925– ?).

5128 —Yoruba masks: notes on the masks of the north-east Yoruba country. *Odù*, (3) 1956: 3–15, illus., bibliog.
Examination of Yoruba mask types, and their religio-cultural implications.

5129 Clarke, John Digby
Carved posts at Oyo. *Nig. mag.*, (15) Sept. 1938: 248–249, illus.

5130 —The stone figures of Esie. *Nig. mag.*, (14) Je. 1938: 106–109, illus.

5131 —Yoruba wood-carving. *Nig. mag.*, (14) 1938: 140–145, illus.

5132 Cornevin, R.
Masques de laiton de type Yoruba provenant du Nord-Togo. *Notes afr.*, (84) Oct. 1959: 101–102, illus.

5133 Crocker, H. E.
The bronzes of Ife. *J.R.A.S.*, 42 (166) Jan. 1943: 38–39.
Brief note on bronzes he saw in the Council chamber and in shrines in the surrounding bush.

5134 Crook, John
Ife portraits and Roman portraits. *Ibadan*, (17) Nov. 1963: 9–10, illus.
A striking resemblance to Roman portraits is seen in Ife bronzes, and a brief description of the social background of Roman portraiture given.

5135 Dalton, Ormonde Maddock
On carved doorposts from the West coast of Africa. *Man*, 1, 1901: 69 (art. 57) illus.

5136 Daniel, F.
The stone figures of Esie, Ilorin Province, Nigeria. *J.R.A.I.*, 67, 1937: 43–49, illus.

5137 Daniel, F. and Friend, Donald
Stone sculpture in Nigeria: stone figures at Ofaro. *Nig. mag.*, (18), 1939: 107–109, illus.
On the similarity and historical links between the Ofaro stone figures and those found at Esie 20 miles away.

5138 Discovery at Ife. *W. Afr. rev.*, 29 (365) 1958: 100–101, illus.
Short account of bronze finds dug out at a building site at Ita Yemeo in Ife, early in 1958.

5139 Donatellos of medieval Africa: the Ife bronze portrait heads. *Illus. Lond. news*, 1948: 213–214.

5140 Duckworth, E. H.
The bronze heads of Ife. *Nig. mag.*, (21) 1940: 341–342, illus.

5141 —Recent archaeological discoveries in the ancient city of Ife. *Nig. mag.*, (14) 1938: 101–105.
Description of 11 bronze heads found in Ife early in 1938.

5142 —Stone figures of Ife. *Illus. Lond. news.*, 103 (2678) 1938: 334–335, illus.

5143 Early African terra-cotta heads from Ife. *Illus. Lond. news*, 215, 1945: 27.

5144 Elgee, C. H.
The Ife stone carvings. *J. Afr. soc.*, 7 (28) Jl. 1908: 338–343, illus.
Brief notes.

5145 Excavations at Ife, Nigeria. *Man*, 58, 1958: (art. 17) 28–29.
Brief note on excavations which Mr. Frank Willett was then conducting at Ife, for an advanced notice of which see [5148].

5145a Fagg, Bernard E. B.
A fertility figure of unrecorded style from Northern Nigeria. See [1522].

5146 —New discoveries from Ife on exhibition at the Royal anthropological institute. *Man*, 49, Je. 1949: 61 (art. 79) illus.

5147 —Some archaeological problems at Ife. *Int. W. Afr. conf. proc., 5th, 1953 [1954]*: 125–126.
Abstract only.

5148 Fagg, Bernard E. B. and Fagg, William Buller
Remarkable new finds at Ife, Western Nigeria. *Man*, 58, Jan. 1958: Plate A. (opposite page viii).
Advanced notice of the bronzes discovered at Ita Yemeo near Ife, by a builder in November 1957. The illustrations (photographs) show five of the bronzes before they were cleaned.

5149 —The ritual stools of ancient Ife. *Man*, 60, Aug. 1960: 113–115, (art. 155) illus.
A survey of the clay, wooden and stone stools of Ife as art specimens. They are held to date from the Ife "classical" period (13th to 14th centuries).

5150 Fagg, William Buller
Antiquities of Ife. *Mag. art.*, 43 (4) 1950: 129–133, illus.

5151 —The antiquities of Ife, Southern Nigeria. *Image* (2) Autumn, 1949: 19–30, illus.

5152 —L'art Nigérien avant Jésus-Christ. *Présence afr.*, 10–11, 1951: 91–95, illus.

5153 —An Epa mask from North-East Yorubaland. *Brit. Mus. q.*, 15, 1941–50: 109–111, illus.

5154 —On a stone head of variant style at Esie, Nigeria. *Man*, 59, Mar. 1959: 41 (art. 60) illus.
Describes a carved stone head of peculiar style in the Esie collection, suggesting its derivation from Ife sometime between the Ife "classical" period and modern times.

5155 —Tribal sculpture and the Festival of

Britain. *Man*, 51, Je. 1951 (art. 124): 73–76, illus.

Largely a descriptive and interpretative account of Owo art (i.e. Owo wood and ivory sculpture) and the possible relations to it of Benin sculpture.

5156 Fagg, William Buller and Underwood, Leon
An examination of the so-called 'Olokun' head of Ife, Nigeria. *Man*, 49, Jan. 1949: 1–7. (art. 1).

Attempt to show, by a comparison with other Ife heads, that the present "Olokun" head in Ife is not the original one, but a modern replica.

5157 Filesi, Teobaldo
L'arte misteriosa e sorprendente di Ife. *Universo* [Firenze] (2) Apr. 1960: 315–328.

5158 Friend, Donald
Stone sculpture in Nigeria: carved stones at Effon. *Nig. mag.*, (18) 1939: 107–108, illus.

Carved stones at Effon Alaiye, a village in Ekiti Division, Western Nigeria.

5159 Frobenius, Leo
Terrakotten aus Ife. *Feuer* [Weimar] 3, 1921: 26, illus.

5160 Ife art comes home. *W. Afr. rev.*, 29 (368) 1958: 346–347, illus.

5161 Ife bronzes. *Nig. mag.*, (37) 1951: 20–24, illus.

5161a Ingham, K.
An introduction to the art of Ife. See [5183].

5162 Jensen, A.
De la technique à employer pour recueillir les poésies africaines. *Cah. d'art*, 5, 1930: 431–443.

5163 Krieger, Kurt
Terrakotten und Steinplastiken aus Ife, Nigeria. *Berliner Mus.*, N.F. 5 (3&4) 1955: 32–39, illus., bibliog.

5164 Lagos. National museum
An introduction to the art of Ife. Lagos, National museum, 1955. 28p.
Printed by Ditchling, Sussex, England.

5165 Leith-Ross, Sylvia
Une figurine à coupe. *Man*, 30, 1930: 16 (art. 4).

5166 Lombard, J.
À propos des pierres sculptées d'Ife. *Notes afr.*, (68) Oct. 1955: 97.

5167 Mauny, Raymond
A possible source of copper for the oldest brass heads of Ife. *J. hist. soc. Nig.*, 2 (3) 1962: 393–395.

5167a Meyerowitz, Eva L. R.
Ancient Nigerian bronzes. See [1214].

5168 —A bronze amulet from Old Oyo. *Man*, 41, 1941: 25–26 (art. 15) illus.

5169 —Bronzes and terra-cottas from Ile-Ife. *Burl. mag.*, 75 (439) Oct. 1939: 154–155, illus.

5170 —Ibeji statuettes from Yoruba, Nigeria. *Man*, 44, 1944: 105–107 (art. 94) illus.

5171 —Ogboni staves from Ife, Nigeria. *Antiquity*, 17 (65) Mar. 1943: 50–52, illus.

5172 —Stone figures of Esie in Nigeria. *Burl. mag.*, 82 (479) Feb. 1943: 31–36, illus.
Describes Esie stone figures, and tries to explain their origin.

5173 —Wood-carving in the Yoruba country today. *Africa*, 14 (2) Apr. 1943: 66–70, illus.
Reviews the then position of the wood-carving industry among the Yoruba. French summary, p. 70.

5174 Meyerowitz, E. H. and V. [sic].
Bronzes and terra-cottas from Ile-Ife. *Burl. mag.*, 75 (439) Oct. 1939: 150–155, illus.

5175 Milburn, S.
Stone sculptures at Esie, Ilorin Province. *Nig. teacher*, 1 (8) Sept. 1936: 2–7, illus.

5176 —These disgusting images. *Nig. teacher*, 1 (4) 1935: 14–17, illus.

5177 Murray, Kenneth Crosthwaite
The art of Ife. *Nig. digest*, 1 (4) Apr. 1945: 11–12, illus.
Brief account of Yoruba traditions of origin, and notes on Ife and the bronze discoveries there.

5178 —Frobenius and Ile Ife. *Nig. field*, 11, 1943: 200–203.

5179 —Nigerian bronzes: work from Ife. *Antiquity*, 15, 1941: 71–80, illus.

5180 —Wood-carving (Yoruba) *Nig. teacher*, 2 (7) 1936: 50–56, illus.

5180a Murray, Kenneth Crosthwaite and Fagg, Bernard E. B.
An introduction to the art of Ife. See [5183].

5181 Murray, Kenneth Crosthwaite and Willett, Frank
Ore grove at Ife, Western Nigeria. *Man*, 58, 1958: 131–141. (art. 187) illus., bibliog.
Detailed description of the Ore grove or *Igbo ore* at Ife and of the many carvings found therein.

5182 Newly found terra-cotta heads from Ife: early African classical masterpieces. *Illus. Lond. news*, 215, 1949: 27, illus.

5183 Nigeria. Antiquity service
Introduction to the art of Ife. Lagos, National Museum, 1955. 28p. illus.

5184 Nigeria. Western. Ministry of home affairs. Information division.
The sculpture of Western Nigeria. Introduction by Frank Willett. Ibadan [1964?] 7p. illus. (73 plates).

5185 Palau Marti, Montserrat
À propos de quelques monuments d'Ife. *Notes afr.*, (78) 1958: 35–36.
Notes on monoliths and stone statues he came across in Ife in July 1956.

5186 Peake, H. J. E. and Braunholtz, H. J.
Earthenware figure from Nigeria in Newbury museum. *Man*, 29, 1929: 117–118 (art. 87) illus.

S

5187 Richest find of Ife bronzes since 1938. *Illus. Lond. news*, 231, 1957: 1097, illus.

5187a Sachs, N. F., inc. New York. Art gallery African bronzes from Ife and Benin. See [2008].

5188 Segy, Ladislas Shango sculptures. *Acta tropica*, 12 (2) 1955: 136–173, illus., bibliog. Also offprinted.

5189 Shaw, C. Thurstan Archaeological excavations at Akure. *Afr. notes*, 3 (1) 1965: 5–8.

5190 Slye, Jonathan The strange stone figures of Ijara: a puzzling find in Northern Nigeria. *Illus. Lond. news*, 243 (6475) Sept. 7, 1963: 342–343, illus.
Brief description of stone sculptures discovered in Ijara village, some 45 miles from Ilorin. A comparison is drawn between them and the Esie stone figures to which they appear related.

5190a Sweeney, J. J. African bronzes from Ife and Benin. See [2008].

5191 Thorn figure carving. *Nig. mag.*, (14) 1938: 134–136, illus.
Notes on thorn figure carving by J. D. Akeredolu, an ex-craft-teacher at Owo, and G. A. Aghara, one of his former pupils.

5192 Wescott, Joan A. Eshure stone figures: a possible parallel. *Man*, 62, Je. 1962 (art. 148): 90, illus.
Notes the sculptured roof posts of the palace courtyard in Idanre and compares them to the Eshure stone sculptures described by Willett and Depstar [5202] A note by William Fagg on the same topic follows her article.

5193 —The sculpture and myths of Eshu-Elegba, the Yoruba trickster: definition and interpretation in Yoruba iconography. *Africa*, 32 (4) Oct. 1962: 336–354, illus.
Examines sculptures of Eshu-Elegba, a Yoruba god of mischief, and attempts an iconographic definition and interpretation by considering along with the sculptures the associated myths, praise songs and rituals. French summary, pp. 353–354.

5194 Willett, Frank L'art d'Ife; sa nature et son origine. *Congr. int. sci. anthrop. et ethnol., 6e, Paris, 1960. 1963*: 487–489, bibliog.

5195 —Bronze and terra-cotta sculptures from Ita Yemoo, Ife. *S. Afr. arch. bull.*, 14 (56) Dec. 1959: 135–137, illus.
Account of his 1957-58 excavations at Ita Yemoo. For a fuller description of the bronzes, See [5196]

5196 —Bronze figures from Ita Yemoo, Ife, Nigeria. *Man*, 59, Nov. 1959 (art. 308): 189–193, illus.
Description of the bronzes he found during his 1957-58 excavations.

5197 —The discovery of new brass figures at Ife. *Odu*, (6) Je. 1958: 29–34, illus.

First report of the terra-cottas and bronze figures found during author's excavations in Ife in November & Dec. 1957.

5198 —Excavations at Old Oyo and Ife. *W. Afr.*, 42 (2153) 19th July 1958: 675.
Brief report of his lecture to the Royal Anthropological Institute on his excavations in the two areas from 1956-1958.

5199 —Ife and its archaeology. *J. Afr. hist.*, 1 (2) 1960: 231–248, illus., map.

5200 —On the funeral effigies of Owo and Benin and the interpretation of the life-size bronze heads from Ife, Nigeria. *Man*, 1, Mar. 1966: 34–45 (art. 1) illus.

5201 —A terra-cotta head from Old Oyo, Western Nigeria. *Man*, 59 1959: 180–181 (art. 286) illus.
Notes on the only pottery found during his 1956–57 excavations at Old Oyo.

5202 Willett, Frank and Dempster, Alan Stone carvings in an Ife style from Eshure, Ekiti, Western Nigeria. *Man*, 62, Jan. 1962: 1–5 (art. 1) illus.
Describe with location maps seven carved stone figures discovered in and around Eshure in Ekiti Division in 1960.

5203 Williams, Denis The iconology of the Yoruba *edan Ogboni*. *Africa*, 34 (2) Apr. 1964: 139–166, illus. (incl. 26 plates).
French summary, p. 166.

4. (xvi) Other Arts and Crafts (Including Architecture)

5204 Afonja, S. A. Weaving and carving in St. Matthew's School, Ijebu Ijesha. *Nig. mag.*, (11) Jl. 1937: 63–64.

5205 Ancient pottery from Old Oyo. *Nig. mag.*, (18) 1939: 109, illus.
Two photographs of pottery remnants excavated at Old Oyo.

5206 Art on the drying field. *Nig. mag.*, (30) 1949: 325–329, illus.
On pattern dyeing by Yoruba women.

5207 Beier, Horst Ulrich The palace of the Ogogas in Ikerre. *Nig. mag.*, (44) 1954: 304–314, illus.

5208 —Sacred Yoruba architecture. *Nig. mag.*, (64) Mar. 1960: 93–104, illus.
Describes the salient features of Islamic architecture in Yorubaland.

5209 —Two Yoruba painters. *Black Orpheus*, (6) 1959: 29–32, illus.

5210 *—Wandmalereieu der Yoruba. *Das Kunstwerk*, 5, 1954-55.

5211 —Yoruba wall paintings. *Odù*, (8) Oct. 1960: 36–39, illus.
Describes interesting wall paintings seen by author in different parts of Yorubaland. Prefaced with general notes on Yoruba wall painting.

5212 *—Zeitgenössische Architektur der Yoruba-Neger. *Das Kunstwerk*, 3, 1954.

5213 Bellamy, C. V.
A West African smelting house. With an appendix containing analysis of the specimens described, by F. W. Harbord. *J. Iron & steel inst.*, (2) 1904: 99–126, illus. Also reprinted, London, Iron and steel inst., 1905. [28]p.
Account of iron smelting in the village of Ola-Igbi, near Oyo in Western Nigeria.

5214 Bertho, Jacques
Habitations à impluvium dans les régions de Porto-Novo et Kétou (Dahomey). *Notes afr.*, (47) 1950: 74–75.

5215 Brinkworth, Ian
Crown makers of Efon Alaye. *W. Afr. rev.*, 29 (32) Sept. 1958: 728–732, illus.
Notes on the beaded crowns of canvas especially as made in Efon Alaye, a village in Ekiti area.

5216 Carrol, K.
Yoruba craft work at Oye-Ekiti, Ondo Province. *Nig. mag.*, (35) 1950: 344–354, illus.

5217 Clarke, John Digby
Ilorin stone bead-making. *Nig. mag.*, (14) Je. 1938: 156–157, illus.

5218 —Ilorin weaving. *Nig. mag.*, (14) Je. 1938: 12–14; 121–124, illus.

5219 Daniel, F.
Bead workers of Ilorin, Nigeria. *Man*, 37, Jan. 1937 (art. 2) 7–8, illus.
Describes the process of bead making by the people of Ilorin. A further illustration (photograph of a beadworker and his tools) is given at p. 24 (art. 28).

5220 —Yoruba pattern dyeing. *Nig. mag.*, (14) Je. 1938: 125–129, illus.

5221 Dodwell, C. B.
Iseyin, the town of weavers. *Nig. mag.*, (46) 1955: 118–143, illus.
A profusely illustrated study of the cloth weaving and dyeing industry in the town of Iseyin in the South of Oyo Division, Western Nigeria.

5222 —The tim-tim makers of Oyo. *Nig. mag.*, (42) 1953: 126–131, illus.

5223 Fagg, William Buller
Grooved rocks at Apoje, near Ijebu-Igbo, Western Nigeria. *Man*, 59, Dec. 1959: 205 (art. 330) illus.
Describes grooves and basins in Apoje and Kute, some 50 miles apart, suggesting these to have been associated with the manufacture of beads or of net-sinkers.

5224 Indigo dyeing in Nigeria. *Progress*, 41 (230) 1951: 26–29.
Techniques of textile dyeing among Hausa and Yoruba dyers.

5225 Jack, W. Murray
Old houses of Lagos. *Nig. mag.*, (46) 1955: 96–117, illus., map.
In the main, the older buildings in Lagos exhibit strong Western European and Latin American (especially Brazilian) architectural styles. Nevertheless, they also reveal certain distinctive peculiarities indicating the evolution of a characteristic Lagos style.

5226 Jeffreys, M. D. W.
A pot from Oyo, Southern Nigeria. *Man*, 48 1948: 24 (art. 24) illus.

5227 Kennedy, Robert A.
Grooved rocks in Nigeria. *Man*, 60, Apr. 1960: 61 (art. 78).
Comments on W. Fagg's article, *Grooved rocks at Apoje* [5223], upholding the alternative suggestion that the grooves had been used in connection with net-sinker industry.

5228 *Macfie, John W. Scott
A jeweller in Northern Nigeria. *Revue d'ethnog. et de sociologie*, 3, 1912: 281–286.

5229 —The pottery industry of Ilorin. *Bull. Imp. inst.*, 11, 1913: 110–121, illus.

5230 *—Pottery of Ilorin, Northern Nigeria. *Memoir and proc. Manchester lit. & philosophical soc., 1913.*
Also offprinted, 11p.

5231 Mellor, W. F.
Bead embroiderers of Remo. *Nig. mag.*, (14) Je. 1938: 154–155, illus.

5232 Miller, N. S.
Aspects of the development of Lagos. *Nig. field*, 28 (4) Oct. 1963: 149–172, illus., maps, plans.
Brief historical account of Lagos from about 1669 to date; with 12 photographs, (mainly of houses) and sketch maps illustrating the growth of the town. This is an enlarged version of the author's "The beginnings of modern Lagos." [5233].

5233 —The beginnings of modern Lagos: progress over 100 years. *Nig. mag.*, (69) Aug. 1961: 107–121, illus., maps., plans.
Historical notes on the physical development of Lagos from the British occupation of 1861 to about the first quarter of this century. See also [5232].

5234 Morton-Williams, Peter
A cave painting, rock gong and rock slide in Yorubaland. *Man*, 57, Nov. 1957: 170–175. (art. 213) illus.
In Igbetti some 20 miles south-west of Old Oyo.

5235 Murray, Kenneth Crosthwaite
Women's weaving among the Yorubas at Omu-aran in Ilorin Province. *Nig. field*, 5 (4) Oct. 1936: 182–191, illus.

5235a Ojo, G. J. Afolabi
Yoruba palaces. See [4592].

5236 The painted court house of Inre. *Nig. mag.*, (16) 1938: 288–289.

5237 Parkinson, John
Yoruba string figures. *J. Anthrop. inst.*, 36, Jan.–Je. 1906: 132–141, illus.
Also offprinted. London, Anthropological inst. of G.B. & Ireland [1906].

5238 Roth, Henry Ling
Unglazed pottery from Abeokuta. *Man*, 31, 1931: 248–250 (art. 246) illus.

5239 Wenger, Susanne and Beier, Horst Ulrich

Adire, Yoruba pattern dyeing. *Nig. mag.*, (54) 1957: 208–225, illus.

5240 Yoruba architecture. *Nig. mag.*, (37) 1951: 39–44, illus.

5241 Yoruba brickmaking; an industry that could be much improved. *Nig. mag.*, (25) 1946: 297–298, illus.

4. (xvii) Acculturation and Social Change, Contact Situation, Urbanization

5242 Akinola, R. A.
Ibadan: a study in urban geography. 1963.
Ph.D. thesis, London.

5243 —The Ibadan region. *Nig. geog. j.*, 6 (2) Dec. 1963: 102–115, maps, bibliog.
A geographical survey of Ibadan and environs.

5244 Baker, Tanya and Bird, Mary E. C.
Urbanisation and the position of women. *Sociol. rev.*, 7 (1) Jl. 1959: 91–122.

5245 Barber, C. R.
Igbo-Ora, a town in transition: a sociological report on the Ibarapa project. Ibadan, O.U.P., for N.I.S.E.R., 1966. viii, 80p. illus., map.

5246 Bascom, William Russell
Les premiers fondements historiques de l'urbanisme Yoruba. *Prés. afr.*, n.s. (23) Dec. 1958–Jan. 1959: 22–40, bibliog.

5247 —Some aspects of Yoruba urbanism. *Amer. anthrop.*, 64 (4) Aug. 1962: 699–709, bibliog.
Analysis of Yoruba population data, involving the correlation of the degree of urbanism among the Yoruba to such factors as population density, ethnic diversity, sex ratio, occupational distribution, etc.

5248 —The urban African and his world. *Cah. étud. afr.*, 4 (2) 1964: 163–185, bibliog.
A general study illustrated largely with Yoruba urbanism.

5249 —Urbanism as a traditional African pattern. *Sociol. rev.*, 7 (1) Jl. 1959: 29–43.
West African cities before the European era. Emphasis on Yoruba cities.

5250 —Urbanization among the Yoruba. *Amer. j. sociol.*, 60, 1955: 446–454, bibliog.
Evaluation of Yoruba towns in terms of the sociological concepts of cities, urbanization and urban communities. Later reprinted in *Cultures and societies of Africa*, ed. Simon and Phoebe Ottenberg, 1960: 255–267. [720] q.v.

5251 —Yoruba acculturation in Cuba. In *Les Afro-Americains (Mémoires IFAN, no. 27) 1953*: 163–167.

5252 —Yoruba urbanism: a summary. *Man*, 58, Dec. 1958: 190–191. (art. 253) bibliog.

5253 Beier, Horst Ulrich
Changing face of a Yoruba town: *Nig. mag.*, (59) 1958: 373–382, illus.

"Changing face" of Erin, a town about six miles from Ede.

5254 —Oshogbo—portrait of a Yoruba town. *Nigeria, 1960*: 94–102, illus.

5254a Bird, Mary E. C.
Urbanization, family and marriage in Western Nigeria. See [4742].

5255 Blue, A. D.
West African boom town. *Afr. world*, Jl. 1957: 11–12.
Ibadan.

5256 Comhaire, Jean
Leopoldville, Lagos and Port au Prince: some points of comparison. *NISER conf. proc., 7th, Ibadan, 1960*: 73–83, bibliog.
Bibliography: pp. 79–83.

5257 Hughes, Charles C.
Socio-cultural disintegration and psychiatric disorder amongst the Egba. In *Pan-African psychiatric conference, 1st, Abeokuta, 1961*. [*1962?*]: 143–146.

5258 Lloyd, Peter Cutt
The Yoruba town today. *Sociol. rev.*, 7 (1) Jl. 1959: 45–63.
Examination of aspects of the Yoruba town as it is today and of the effects of political and economic developments on age and kinship groupings.

5259 —Yoruba towns. *Ibadan*, (9) Je. 1960: 26–29.

5260 Mabogunje, Akin L.
The growth of residential districts in Ibadan. *Geog. rev.*, 52 (1) Jan. 1962: 56–77.

5261 —Ibadan, black metropolis. *Nig. mag.*, (68) Mar. 1961: 12–26, illus.
A general account of the city of Ibadan—largest urban centre in Africa—giving its history, administrative structure, physical development, economic and commercial growth, educational facilities, health services, social and cultural aspects, religion, population and social stratification and segregation.

5262 —Lagos: a study in urban geography. 1962.
Ph.D. thesis, London.

5263 —Lagos—Nigeria's melting pot. *Nig. mag.*, (69) Aug. 1961: 128–155, illus., map.

5264 —Yoruba towns. Based on a lecture entitled 'Problems of a pre-industrial urbanization in the West' given before the Philosophical society on 12 April, 1961. Ibadan, University press, 1962. [iv] 22p. illus., maps, plans, bibliog.
A historical study of Yoruba towns from the pre-colonial era through the colonial to the post independence period, with attention on the effects of British administration and on the changing economic and social patterns.

5265 Mabogunje, Akin L. and Oyawoye, M. O.
The problems of the Northern Yoruba towns: the example of Shaki. *Nig. geog. j.*, 4 (2) Dec. 1961: 2–10, map.

5266 Marris, Peter
Family and social change in an African city: a study of rehousing in Lagos. Evanston, Ill., Northwestern university press, 1962. xv, 180p. illus., map, bibliog. (Northwestern university African studies, no. 8).

5267 —Slum clearance and family life in Lagos. *Human org.*, 19 (3) Fall 1960: 123–128.

5268 Mitchel, N. C.
Some comments on the growth and character of Ibadan's population. *Res. notes*, (4) Dec. 1953: 2–15, illus., maps. Population density, housing, ethnic composition, occupations, and markets.

5269 —Yoruba towns. In *Essays on African population, ed. K. M. Barbour and R. M. Prothero, 1961*: 279–301, maps. A general survey of Yoruba towns, noting their characteristics, origins, and morphology, with a more detailed study of Ibadan town.

5270 Morton-Williams, Peter
The social consequences of industrialism among the southwestern Yoruba; with comparisons from Hausa society. *WAISER conf. proc. (sociology section) 1953*: 21–30.

5271 —Some Yoruba kingdoms under modern conditions. *J. Afr. admin.*, 7, Oct. 1955: 174–179.

5272 —Yoruba kingdoms under modern conditions. *Int. W. Afr. conf. proc. 5th, 1953. [1954?]*: 139. Abstract only.

5273 Schwab, William B.
Oshogbo—an urban community? In *Urbanization and migration in West Africa, ed. Hilda Kuper, 1965*: 85–109.

5274 Tully, John
The biggest city-village in the world. *W. Afr. rev.*, 23 (294) Mar. 1952: 220–221, illus. Description of Ibadan.

4. (xviii) Social Problems; Applied Anthropology
See also 4 (xvii) p. 240

5275 Faulkner, Donald E.
A pilot scheme of village betterment in Lagos Colony, Nigeria. *Oversea educ.*, 22 (4) Jl. 1951: 152–159. Community development efforts in Isolo village a few miles from Lagos.

5276 Simpson, C. E. E. B.
An African village undertakes community development. *Mass educ. bull.*, 2, 1950: 7–9. On community development in Ilaje, Western Nigeria.

5277 Waide, C. L.
Slum clearance and town replanning in Lagos. *Nig. mag.*, (19) 1939: 199–205.

5. LINGUISTICS

5. (i) Bibliography

5278 Clark, Jeannine Smith
Some publications in English on the Yoruba language since 1831. 1962. 216p.
M.A. thesis, Howard University, Washington, D.C.

5279 Ogunsheye, Felicia Adetowun
A preliminary bibliography of the Yoruba language. Ibadan, [Institute of Librarianship] University of Ibadan, 1963. ii, 38p. Mimeographed.

5. (ii) Linguistic Studies

5280 Abraham, Roy Clive
Dictionary of modern Yoruba. London, Univ. of London press, 1958. [v] xli, 776p. illus.
An encyclopaedic dictionary which attempts to cover all aspects of Yoruba culture. Includes idioms, proverbs, riddles, and proper names from mythology and history. Numerous illustrations of the fauna, flora and Yoruba art objects appended at the end (pp. 715–776).

5281 *Adeyemi, M. C. and Latunde, S. V.
A companion to Yoruba language simplified. Ondo, [1932].

5282 *—Yoruba composition. Ondo, [1933].

5283 *—Yoruba conversation. Lagos, 1933.

5284 *—Yoruba language simplified. Ondo, 1932.

5285 Adeyi, E. Adeduntan
A Yoruba course for secondary schools and colleges, parts 1 & 2. Lagos, Adeduntan trading co. [1961] 124p. Printed by Kajola press, Ibadan.

5286 Ajayi, Jacob F. Ade
How Yoruba was reduced to writing. *Odù*, (8) Oct. 1960: 49–58, illus., bibliog.
Historical account of the efforts of Crowther and other missionaries to reduce Yoruba to writing and work out a standard orthography.

5287 Ajayi, Michael Thomas
A practical Yoruba grammar. Exeter, Thomas Townsend, 1896. 80p. Includes exercises and Yoruba dialogues.

5288 Akintan, E. A.
Dictionary of the Yoruba language. Parts 1 & 2. Lagos, C.M.S. bookshop, 1931.

5289 —English translation of Yoruba phrases and proverbs. Lagos, Alebiosu press, 1947. 50p.

5290 *—First steps in Yoruba composition. Lagos, Alebiosu press, 1941.

5291 —First steps in Yoruba composition. Lagos, Kash & Klare bookshop, 1947. 48p.

5292 —History and structure of Yoruba language. Lagos, Oluseyi press, 1950.

5293 —Lecture on the fundamental principles of the Yoruba language, and common errors in the writing of Yoruba words and sentences. Lagos [the author] 1947. 18p. Printed by B'aoku printing press, Lagos.

5294 —Lecture on Yoruba language, with special reference to its grammar. Lagos [the author] 1932. 16p. Printed by Ijaiye press, Lagos.

5295 *—Modern grammar of Yoruba language. Lagos [the author] 1945.

5296 —Second steps in Yoruba composition. Lagos, Alebiosu press, 1943. 50p.

5297 —Second steps in Yoruba composition. Lagos, Kash & Klare bookshop, 1947. 48p.

5298 —Training in English (Iwé akomo lede gesi) Lagos, C.M.S. bookshop, 1933. 142p.

5299 —Yoruba language as a syllabic and euphonic language. Lagos [the author] 1942. 10p. Printed by Alebiosu press, Lagos.
      Lecture delivered under the chairmanship of Herbert Macaulay on 14 May, 1942.

5300 Arington, E. A.
      Second steps in Yoruba composition. Lagos, Alebiosu press, 1943. 50p.

5301 Armstrong, Robert G.
      Comparative word lists of two dialects of Yoruba with Igala. *J. W. Afr. lang.*, 2 (2) 1966: 51–78.

5302 Atilade, Emmanuel Adekunle
      Akǫka Yoruba. Lagos [the author, 1947?—1961] 6v. illus.
      A series of graded readers in Yoruba. Printed by New Nigeria press, Mushin. Vol. 5 printed by Amalgamated press of Nigeria, Lagos.

5303 Atundaolu, H.
      Awon enia inu Bibeli. Lagos [n.p.] 1906. 208p.

5304 Avezac-Macaya, Armand d'(M.A.P. d'Avezac de Castera-Maya) Esquisse grammaticale de la langue Yéboue. In his *Notice sur le pays et le peuple des Yébous en Afrique. Paris, Donde-Dupré, 1845*: 106–196.

5305 B., C. and B., L.
      Guide pratique de conversation en français, anglais et yoruba ou nago, langue la plus répandue sur la côte occidentale d'Afrique, par C.B. & L. B. de la Société des missions africaines de Lyon. Strasbourg, F.X. Le Roux, 1908. 126p.

5306 Bamgbose, Ayo
      Assimilation and contraction in Yoruba. *J. W. Afr. lang.*, 2 (1) 1965: 21–27.

5307 —A grammar of Yoruba. Cambridge, C. U. P., in association with West African languages survey and Institute of African studies, Ibadan, 1966. xii, 175p. bibliog. (West African language monographs, 5).

5308 —Structure of Yoruba predicators. In *Actes du second colloque international de linguistique négro-africaine, 1962. 1963*: 119–126.

5309 —A study of structures and classes in the grammar of modern Yoruba. 1963. Ph.D. thesis, Edinburgh.

5310 —Verb-nominal collocations in Yoruba: a problem of syntatic analysis. *J. W. Afr. lang.*, 1 (2) 1964: 27–32.

5311 —Yoruba orthography: a linguistic appraisal with suggestions for reform. Ibadan, University press, 1965. 37p.

5312 Banjo, S. Ayodele
      The teaching of Yoruba in the secondary schools of Nigeria. *Nig. mag.*, (13) Mar. 1938: 58–69.

5313 *Bastian, P.
      Missel en langue Yoruba. Lyon, Société des missions africaines, 1893.

5314 Baudin, N.
      Essai de grammaire de langue Yoruba. Lyon, Société des missions africaines, 1884.

5315 Beecroft, W. S.
      Yoruba grammar and composition. [Lagos, the author?] 1914.

5316 Berlin. Preussische Staatsbibliothek
      Lautbibliothek; phonetische Platten und Umschriften. Nr. 44, Afrikanische Sprachen. Yoruba-Texte. Bearbeitet von D. Westermann. Herausgegeben von der Lautabteilung der Preussischen Staatsbibliothek. Berlin, 1931.
      Yoruba on gramophone record.

5317 Bertho, Jacques
      Parenté de la langue Yoruba de la Nigéria du sud et de la langue Adja de la region cotière du Dahomey et du Togo. *Notes afr.*, (35) Jl. 1947: 10–11.

5317a —La parenté des Yoruba aux peuplades de Dahomey et Togo. See [4650].

5318 Bible. Yoruba. Selections
      Iṣiẹṣẹ si otitọ. Fun ile-ẹko ojọisimi. Ti Eugene Stock ati Sara Geraldina Stock kọ ti a si yi si ede Yoruba. Exeter, J. Townsend, [190. .] 80p.

5319 Bolaji, Alfa Abdu Salami Bello
      Yẹ ẹsin rẹ wo fun imọlẹ ododo. [Lagos, the author] 1957. 306p. Printed by Tika-Tore press, Lagos.
      Religious text.

5320 Bolling, Sonja Mae
      A contrastive phonological analysis of Yoruba and English. 1963. 52p.
      M.A. thesis, Howard university, Washington, D. C.

5321 Bouché, Pierre Bertrand (Abbé)
      Étude sur la langue Nago. Bar-le-Duc, Libraire de l'Oeuvre de St. Paul, 1880. 54p. (Archives des pères missionaires, 1).

5322 —Les noirs peints par eux-mêmes. Paris, Librairie Poussielge frères, 1883. 144p. (Oeuvre de Saint-Jérome pour la publication des travaux philologiques des missionnaires, 1 fasc.).
      Yoruba proverbs, with French translation.

5323 Bowen, Thomas Jefferson
      A grammar and dictionary of the Yoruba language; with an introductory description of the country and people of Yoruba. Washington, Smithsonian institution, 1858. 21, 71, 136p. map

(Smithsonian contribution to knowledge, v. 10).

5324 Bunyan, John
Ilọ-siwaju Èro-mimọ lati aiye yi si eyi ti mbọ ni ifiwe alá. London, Exeter, printed 1911.
"The Pilgrim's progress" in Yoruba.

5325 —Ilo-siwaju éro-mimọ lati aiye yi si eyi ti mbọ, ni ifiwe àlá. Apa ekini ati ekeji [3rd ed.] Lagos, C.M.S. bookshop, 1951 [3] 369p. illus.

5326 Cabrera, Lydia
Anago vocabulario lucumi (el Yoruba que se habla en Cuba) Habana, Ediciones C.R., 1957. 326p.
A Yoruba-Spanish dictionary, based on a Yoruba dialect spoken in Cuba.

5327 Carnochan, J.
Pitch, tone and intonation in Yoruba. In *In honour of Daniel Jones: papers contributed on the occasion of his eightieth birthday, ed. D. Abercrombie [and others] 1964.*

5328 Catholic Church, Nigeria
Itan inu Iwe mimo. New ed., published with approbation of the R.R. Ferd. Terrien, Vic. ap. of the Bight of Benin. Ibadan, Claverianum press, 1961. 318p. illus.

5329 Church of England, Nigeria. Book of common prayer. Yoruba.
Iwe adua Yoruba. A selection from the Book of common prayer, according to the use of the United Church of England and Ireland. Translated into Yoruba for the use of the native Christians of that nation, by the Rev. Samuel Crowther. 3rd ed. London, C.M.S., 1862. 689 [1]p.

5330 Crowther, Samuel Adjai
Grammar and vocabulary of the Yoruba language; together with introductory remarks by O. E. Vidal. London, Seeleys, 1852. v, 38, vii, 52, 291p.

5331 —Grammar of the Yoruba language. London, Seeleys, 1852. vii, 52p.

5332 —Vocabulary and dictionary of the Yoruba language. London, W. M. Watts, [1865?] 254p.

5333 —Vocabulary of the Yoruba language. Pt. 1. English and Yoruba. Pt. 2. Yoruba and English. To which are prefixed the grammatical elements of the Yoruba language. London, C.M.S., 1843. vii, 48, 195p.

5334 De Gaye, J. A. and Beecroft, W. S.
Yoruba composition. London, Routledge and K. Paul, 1923. 96p.
Best used in conjunction with authors' Yoruba grammar [5335].

5335 —Yoruba grammar. London, K. Paul, Lagos, C.M.S. bookshop, 1914. 96p.

5336 —Yoruba grammar. 2nd ed. London, Routledge & K. Paul, 1923. 96p.

5337 Delano, Isaac O.
Agbékà ọrọ Yoruba. Appropriate words and expressions in Yoruba. London, O.U.P., 1960. xiv, 160p.
Pp. 1–61. Yoruba idioms; pp. 62–78, Yoruba proverbs. The latter with English equivalents.

5338 —Atúmọ ede Yoruba. London, Oxford university press, 1958. lxviii, 209p. map, tables.
Yoruba grammar and vocabulary, written entirely in Yoruba.
Grammar: pp. ix–lxviii.
Vocabulary pp. 1–206.

5339 —Conversation in Yoruba and English. New York, Praeger, 1963. 95p.

5340 —A modern Yoruba grammar. London, Lagos, Nelson, 1965. xiv, 185p.

5341 Dennett, R. E.
West African categories and the Yoruba language. *J. Afr. soc.*, 14 (53) Oct. 1914: 75–80.

5342 A dictionary of the Yoruba language. 2nd ed. London, O.U.P., 1937, repr. 1950. [vii] 218; [1] 243p.
In two sections: Pt. 1. English-Yoruba
Pt. 2. Yoruba-English
1st ed. publ. Lagos, C.M.S. bookshop, 1913.

5342a Ellis, Alfred Burdon
The Yoruba-speaking peoples of the slave coast of West Africa: their religion . . . language, etc. See [4530].

5343 Fabelo, Teodoro Diaz
Lengua de santeros, Guine gongori. Habana, Las Ydeas, 1956. 232p.
A Yoruba dialect in Cuba.

5344 Fagunwa, D. O.
Adiitú Olodùmare. Edinburgh, T. Nelson, 1961. xi, 148p. front., illus.

5345 Fagunwa, D. O. [and others]
Asàyàn itan. London, T. Nelson, 1959. v [3] 56p. illus.
Selected stories in Yoruba.

5345a Gaye, J. A. de, see De Gaye, J. A.

5346 Giwa, Salawu Cashious Osoyemi
English-Yoruba vocabulary. Books 1–IV. Ibadan [the author, 1950.] [2] 74p. illus. (port.) Printed by the Nubi printing press, Ibadan.

5347 Gouzien, Paul
Manuel Franco-Yoruba de conversation spècialement à l'usage du mèdicin. Paris, Augustin Challamel, 1899. viii, 62p.
At head of title: Contribution à l'étude des dialectes du Dahomey.

5348 Hair, P. E. H.
Notes on the early study of some West African languages. *Bull. IFAN*, 23 (3–4), Jl.–Oct. 1961: 683–695.
On Susu, Bullom-Sherbro, Temne, Mende, Vai and Yoruba.

5349 Heidt, K. M.
Laut und Ton im Yoruba. 1954.
Phil. F. thesis, Hamburg.

5350 Iwe ekini ti ède yoruba. Iranlowo fu kiko éde na ti a npè ni primeri. London, C.M.S., 1868. 20p.

5351 Iwe orin. London, C.M.S., 1865. vii, 112 [1]p.
Christian religious text.

5352   Iwe orin mimo. London, C.M.S., 1865.
       vii, 108p.
       A collection of hymns.

5353   *Jacquot
       Étude sur la langue nago ou Yoruba.
       Lyon, 1880.

5354   James, A. Lloyd
       The tones of Yoruba. B.S.O.S., 3,
       1923–25: 119–128.
       Includes musical notation.

5355   Lafinhan, E. O.
       Iwe komonwe keta fun Itesiwaju ni
       kika ede Yoruba. London, Macmillan,
       1955. 196p. illus.
       Yoruba reader.

5356   Language studies in Yoruba. Lagos,
       C.M.S. bookshop, 1914. 105p.
       "The aim of this book is to supply
       the need of a book between a full
       grammatical treatise and a phrase book"
       —Introduction.

5357   Laniyan, S. Oladele
       Àsiri aiye. London, Longmans, Green,
       1961. vi, 186p.

5358   Lapite, M. B.
       Yoruba for G.C.E. and similar examina-
       tions. [Oshogbo, the author, 1956] 46p.
       Printed by Kebo and sons, Oshogbo.

5359   — —2nd ed. 1961. [6] 103p.

5360   Lasebikan, E. L.
       Learning Yoruba. London, O.U.P.,
       1958. 87p.

5361   —Ojulowo Yoruba. Iwe keji. Asa ile
       Yoruba. London, O.U.P., 1955. 112p.
       illus.
       Yoruba customs.

5362   —Ojulowo Yoruba. Iwe keta. London,
       O.U.P., 1958. 94p. illus.

5363   —The tonal structure of Yoruba poetry.
       Prés. afr., n.s., 8–10, Je.–Nov. 1956:
       43–50.

5364   —Tone in Yoruba poetry. Odù, (2)
       1955: 35–36.

5365   Lasebikan, E. L. and Lewis, L. J.
       A Yoruba revision course. London,
       O.U.P., 1949. vi, 84p.
       Intended for use in secondary schools
       and training colleges.

5366   Layemi, Olasiji
       Yoruba course for secondary schools.
       Book one. [Yaba, Pacific printers,
       1963?] viii, 131p.

5367   Lucas, Jonathan Olumide
       Yoruba language: its structure and
       relationship to other languages. [Lagos,
       the author, 1965] [6] 168p. illus. Printed
       by Ore-ki-gbe press, Lagos.

5368   Mann, Adolphus
       Eine geschichtliche Sage aus der Zeit
       der ersten Niederlassungen der Egba,
       eines Stammes der Yoruba-Nation,
       Westafrika. Z. f. Afr. S., 2, Oct. 1888—
       Jl. 1889: 209–219.
       An Egba legend, reproduced with
       German translation and explanatory
       notes.

5369   Melzian, H. J.
       Beobachtungen über die Verwendung

der Töne in der Yoruba-Sprache.
M.S.O.S., 37, 1934: 197–234.
       Includes two Yoruba texts with
German interlinear translation and
Yoruba-German vocabulary with tone
markings.

5369a Millson, Alvan
       Indigenous plants of Yoruba land.
       See [4578].

5370   Nigeria. Western. Dept. of education.
       Grammatical terminology committee.
       Notes on grammatical and scientific
       terminology in the Yoruba language.
       Ibadan, Govt. printer, 1956.

5371   Nigerian Baptist convention
       Iwe orin ti ijo Baptist ni Nigeria
       [Lagos] Nigerian Baptist convention,
       1961. 521p.
       Hymn book.

5372   Nwafor, John O.
       Yoruba, English, Ibo made easy. Aba,
       the author, 1954. 28p. illus.
       Printed by Clergyman printing press,
       Aba.

5373   Olmstead, David L.
       Comparative notes on Yoruba and
       Lucumi. Language, 29 (2) Apr.–Je. 1953:
       157–164.
       Lucumi is spoken in Cuba. Examines
       the two languages and confirms the
       view that they are genetically related.

5374   —The phonemes of Yoruba. Word, 7
       (3) Dec. 1951: 245–249.
       Analysis of Yoruba phonemic
       structure as observed in a Yoruba
       speaker from Ogbomosho.

5375   Olusola, J. A.
       Amona si awon iwe Majemu Titun
       (Introduction to N.T.) Shagamu [the
       author, 1963] 78p. front. Printed by
       Ojokobiri-kale press, Shagamu.

5375a *Rabam, John
       A vocabulary of the Eyo, or Aku, a
       dialect of Western Africa. London,
       C.M.S., 1830–1832. 3v.
       Volume 3 has title 'The Eyo
       vocabulary'.

5376   *Rambaud, J. R.
       Des rapports de la langue Yoruba avec
       les langues de la famille Mandé.
       B.S.L.P., 44, 1897.

5377   Rowlands, E. C.
       Types of word junction in Yoruba.
       B.S.O.A.S., 16 (2) 1954: 376–388.

5378   —Yoruba and English: a problem of
       co-existence. Afr. lang. stud., (4) 1963:
       208–214.

5379   Siertsema, B.
       Problems of phonemic interpretation: 1.
       Nasalized sounds in Yoruba. Lingua,
       7 (4) 1957–8: 356–366.

5380   —Problems of phonemic interpretation.
       2. Long vowels in a tone language.
       Lingua, 8 (1) 1959: 42–64.
       Long vowels in Yoruba.

5381   —Some notes on Yoruba phonetics and
       spelling. Bull. IFAN, 20 (3–4) Jl.–Oct.
       1958: 576–595.

5382   —Stress and tone in Yoruba word composition. *Lingua*, 8, 1959: 385–402.

5383   —Three Yoruba dictionaries. *Bull. IFAN*, 21 (3–4) 1959: 572–578.

5384   Sowande, E. J. [and others]
A dictionary of the Yoruba language. London, O.U.P., 1913.

5385   Stevick, Earl W.
Pitch and duration in two Yoruba idiolects. *J. Afr. lang.*, 4 (2) 1965: 85–101.

5386   Stevick, Earl W. and Aremu, Olaleye
Yoruba basic course. Washington, Foreign service institute 1963. xxxviii, 343p.

5386a *Toy, C. H.
On the Yoruban language. *Trans. Amer. phil. assoc.*, 1878: 19–38.

5387   Wakeman, C. W.
A dictionary of the Yoruba language. 2nd ed. London, O.U.P., 1950. 243p.

5388   Ward, Ida Caroline
An introduction to the Yoruba language. Cambridge, W. Heffer, 1952. viii, 255p.

5389   Ward-Price, Henry Lewis

Yoruba phrase book, with phonetic spelling. With forewords by Sir Hugh Clifford and W. A. Ross. Lagos, C.M.S. bookshops, 1925. xiii, 101p.

5389a Westermann, D. *ed.*
Yoruba-Texte. See [5316].

5390   Winfunke, B. A.
Awon Owe Yoruba. Lagos, Tika-Tore press, [n.d.] 66p.

5391   Wolff, Hans
Rárà; a Yoruba chant. *J. Afr. lang.*, 1 (1) 1962: 45–56.

5392   Wood, J. Buckley
Notes on the construction of the Yoruba language. Exeter, Townsend, 1879. 47p.

5393   Yakovlyeva, V. K.
Yazyk Ioruba. Moskva, Izdatelstvo Vostochnoi Literatury, 1963. 152p. map.

5394   Yemitan, Oladipọ
Ijala are ọde. Ibadan, Lagos, O.U.P., 1963. [8] 85p. illus.

5395   The Yoruba primer. Iwe kini on ni fu awon ara egba ati awon ará Yoruba. London, C.M.S., 1863. 20p.

YUNGUR

(Bina, Yunguri)

Including:

Banga
Ga-Anda
Handa

Lala
Libo
Mboi *(Mboyi)*

1. GENERAL AND ETHNOGRAPHIC STUDIES

5396   Boyle, C. Vicars
The Lala people and their customs. *J. Afr. soc.*, 15 (57) Oct. 1915: 54–69, illus.
The Lala in Ga-Anda.

5397   —The marking of girls at Ga-Anda. *J. Afr. soc.*, 15 (60) Jl. 1916: 361–366, illus.
On La-La marriage customs and body scarification of girls.

5398   —The ordeal of manhood. *J. Afr. soc.*, 15 (59) Apr. 1916: 244–255.
Account of a septennial religious rite, the manhood initiation ceremony of the Lala as performed at Ga-Anda and seen by author.

5399   Kirk-Greene, Anthony Hamilton Millard
A Lala initiation ceremony. *Man*, 57, Jan. 1957: 9–11 (art. 5) illus.
Describes the *wasa nika* ceremony performed annually by the Lala.

5400   Lala. In *Notes on the tribes . . . by O. Temple*, 2nd ed., 1922, repr. 1965: 255–258.

5401   Meek, Charles Kingsley
Note on the Handa. In his *Tribal studies in Northern Nigeria, v. 2, 1931*: 483–484.

5402   —Note on the Libo. In his *Tribal studies in Northern Nigeria, v. 2, 1931*: 486–489.

5403   —Note on the Mboi. In his *Tribal studies in Northern Nigeria, v. 2, 1931*: 480.

5404   —Note on the people of Banga. In his *Tribal studies in Northern Nigeria, v. 2, 1931*: 484–486.

5405   —The Yungur-speaking peoples. In his *Tribal studies in Northern Nigeria, v. 2, 1931*: 434–489, illus.

5406   Yungur, or Yunguru. In *Notes on the tribes . . . by O. Temple*, 2nd ed., 1922, repr. 1965: 391–392.

2. LINGUISTIC STUDIES

5407   Meek, Charles Kingsley
Banga language. In his *Tribal studies in Northern Nigeria, v. 2, 1931*: 486.
Short vocabulary of the Banga dialect of Yungur language.

5408   —Handa dialect. In his *Tribal studies in Northern Nigeria, v. 2, 1931*: 483–484.
A dialect of Yungur.

5409   —The Libo language. In his *Tribal studies in Northern Nigeria, v. 2, 1931*: 487–489.
Vocabulary of a dialect of Yungur.

5410   —Mboi vocabulary. In his *Tribal studies in Northern Nigeria, v. 2, 1931*: 480–482.

5411   —Yungur [vocabulary] In his *Tribal studies in Northern Nigeria, v. 2, 1931*: 471–480.
Includes vocabulary of the Roba dialect, pp. 477–480.

AUTHOR INDEX

All numbers in the index refer to entries, not to pages.

Hofmann, I., 2728
Hoffmann-Burchardi, H., 4543
Hogben, S. J., 280–1, 3827, 3968
Hogg, J. F., 2888
Holden, M. J., 2567
Holland, J. H., 282
Holles, R. O., 283
Holley, *missionary*, 4452, 4544
Hollis, R., 1706, 2137
Holman, J., 2889–2890
Homburger, L., 1464–7, 2138, 2167, 2305–10, 4025
Homfray, J. M. B., 3695
Hooton, E. A., 1947
Hope, R. E., 284
Hopen, C. E., 2238–9
Hopkins, A. G., 285
Hoppe, E. O., 2411
Hornburg, F., 4310–1
Horton, J. A. B., 286, 3114
Horton, R., 985–6, 3696, 3733–9, 3747–8
Horton, W. R. G., 3314, 3378
Houdas, O. V., 287
Houis, M., 1468, 2311
Hovelacque, A., 686
Howard, A. C., 1384
Howard, C., 289
Howard, C. G., 4233
Howard University. Library. Moorland foundation, 22
Howeidy, A., 2729
Hubbard, J. W., 4366–7, 4383
Huber, H., 987
Hughes, C. C., 4545–6, 5257
Hughes, J. M., 4559
Hugot, P., 2730
Hulbert, C., 290, 1126
Humphreys, J., 4493
Hunt, E. E., 581
Hunwick, J. O., 23, 291, 778, 2502
Hutchinson, E., 292
Hutchinson, T. J., 293–5
Huxley, E. J., 296

Ibadan. University, 297
Ibadan. University. Dept. of geography, 68
Ibadan. University. Inst. of African studies, 69, 298–9
Ibadan. University. Library, 24
Ibadan. University press, 25–6
Ibesikpo convention, 2924
Ibeziako, M. O., 3245
Ibibio state union, 2925, 2959
Ibn Batuta, 300
Ibn Fartua, Ahmed, see Ahmed ibn Fartua.
Ibo state union, 3175–6
Ibrahim, M. B., 2168
Idewu, O., 5021
Idigo, M. C. M., 3246
Idowu, E. B., 988, 4933–4
Ifemesia, C. C., 779–80, 2206, 2503, 3969–70
Igbirra progressive union, 3661
Igboko, P. M., 1385
Igbudu, W. I., 4384
Igodan, E. O., 2043
Igun, A., 1299, 4548
Igwe, D. C., 301
Igwe, E. M., 4454
Igwe, G. E., 3566–7
Igwegbe, R. O., 3247
Igwi, A. O., 3248

Ije, M. C., 3115
Ijebu anti-high bride price league, 4749
Ijere, M. O., 3177–8, 3379
Ika Bible school, 3655
Ike, A., 3179, 3249
Ikime, O., 3778–9, 4368–72
Ilogu, E. C. O., 1300–5, 3380–1
Imegwu, C., 3382
Imohiosen, A. E., 1306
Institut francais d'Afrique noire, 687
International African Institute, 27–8, 1469
Inuwa Hassan, C., 2731–3
Inyang, P. E. B., 3068–9
Ipema, P., 4344
Irons, A. H., 850
Ishan divisional education committee, 2044
Isong, C. N., 915
Ita, E., 688
Itayemi, P., 5022
Iwuchuka, B., 3555
Iyawe, J. I. O., 2045
Iyenga, A., 4334
Izzet, A., 4549–50, 4750

Jack, W. M., 5225
Jackson, I. C., 3524–5
Jackson, J. G., 2412
Jackson, R. M., 3684
Jacob, S. M., 302
Jacoby, J. L., 4455
Jacolliot, L., 303, 1644
Jacquot, 5353
Jahn, J., 29, 3383
James, A. L., 2734, 5354
James, R. W., 810, 851
Jean-Léon de l'Africain, see Leo Africanus.
Jeekel, C. A., 304
Jeffreys, M. D. W., 305, 611, 781–2, 852, 916–26, 989–91, 1471, 1948–9, 2110, 2125, 2207–9, 2312, 2452, 2595, 2891–2, 2913, 2927–30, 2949, 2960, 2969, 2974, 2980, 2992, 2999–3001, 3014–5, 3070, 3117, 3181, 3250–1, 3287–91, 3343, 3384–90, 3445–7, 3458–61, 3483–91, 3500, 3508, 3697, 3749, 4686–7, 4861, 5226
Jeffries, W. F., 1180, 1273, 1386, 2622, 2638, 4205
Jelliffe, D. B., 4493, 4877
Jennings, J. H., 3118
Jensen, A., 5162
Jest, C., 2257
Joalland, P., 3971
Johnson, A. W., 4456
Johnson, C. R., 4457
Johnson, F. E. G., 3754–5
Johnson, H., 306, 1472, 4221
Johnson, J., 3391, 4936
Johnson, O., 4688
Johnson, S., 4689
Johnston, H. H., 307–9, 1473–4, 2126, 2313, 2893, 3685
Johnston, K., 310–1
Jones, A. M., 1049
Jones, F. M., 811
Jones, G. H., 927
Jones, G. I., 859a, 928, 1206–7, 2872, 2961, 3086, 3147, 3252, 3292, 3315–7, 3392–5, 3425–6, 3492–3, 3722–5
Jones, R. W., 4937
Jones, W. O., 929
Jordan, J. P., 3119, 3318

U

ETHNIC INDEX

Unless otherwise indicated, numbers refer not to pages but to entries.

Abadi, 3867
Abaiyonga, see Abayong
Abani, see Abine
Abayong, p. 103
Abine, p. 103
Abisi, see Piti
Achifawa, 3864, 3870
Achipawa, see Achifawa
Ada, 2947, 3197, 3493
Adara, see Kadara
Adun, 2108
Afao, see Afu
Afawa, 4397, 4402
Afo, see Afu
Afu, 815, 1520–1527
Afudu, 1485
Afusare, 3805
Agadi, 3867
Agala, 3601
Agalawa, see Agala
Agatara, see Igala
Agatu, 3601a, 3619
Agbisherea, see Ibibio
Agoi, p. 103
Agolok, see Kagoro
Agwolok, see Kagoro
Ahaju, see Akaju
Aike, 1589
Ajawa, 4398, 4402
Ajure, see Kajuru
Akaju, 2119
Akanda, see Kakanda
Akoko, 4412
Akpoto, see Okpoto
Aku see Yoruba
Akweya, 2058
Alago, see Arago
Amap, 3806
Amo, see Amap
Anaguta, 815, 3795, 3804–5
Anang, 2915, 2932–4, 2943, 2962, 2976, 2981–2,
    2993, 3002–3, 3014, 3027–8, 3030
Andoni, 2988, 3016
Angas, 325, 1528, 1536–7, 1541, 1543, 1546,
    1550, 1552–3
Angassawa, see Angas
Anjang, see Anyang
Ankwe, 1529, 1531, 1545, 2183
Anyang, 2128
Arago, 1554–7
Aran, see Adun
Aregwe, see Irigwe
Aro, 3135, 3140, 3180, 3195–6, 3222, 3240–1,
    3247, 3252, 3260, 3379, 3382, 3397, 3406,
    3456–7, 3466, 3729
Arringeu, 3880
Ashingini, 3867, 3877
Asiga, p. 103
Asolio, see Morwa

Ataka, 3855, 4049–50, 4056
Atam, p. 103
Aten, 1592, 1598, 1600, 1606, 1618
Aticherak, see Kachichere
Atsam, see Chawai
Atshefawa, see Achifawa
Atsifawa, see Achifawa
Attaka, see Ataka
Auyokawa, see Auyukawa
Auyukawa, 1622, 1625
Awerri, see Itsekiri
Awok, 4345
Aworo, 4417
Ayob, see Ayu
Ayokawa, see Auyukawa
Ayu, 815, 1590
Ayub, see Ayu
Azura 4077

Babir, see Pabir
Babira, see Pabir
Babur, see Pabir
Baburr, see Pabir
Bachama, 1558–61, 1563–4, 1566, 2865–6
Badagri, 4443–4a, 4645, 4669, 4683–4
Badawa, p. 178
Baghirmi, 1484, 3919, 3937, 3975, 4006b, 4026
Bagirmi, see Baghirmi
Bai, 4394
Baju, see Kaje
Bakarawa, 4226
Bamberawa, p. 178
Bamboro p. 178
Banga, 5404, 5407
Bangawa, 1700
Banjang, see Banyang
Bankalawa, 3798, 3801–2
Banyang, p. 103
Banyangi, 2113
Baram, see Ron
Barashe, see Reshe
Barawa, 3798, 3801–2
Barba, see Bariba
Barbar, see Bariba
Bargu, see Borgawa
Bariba, 1655
Baron, see Ron
Basa, see Bassa
Basange, see Bassa Nge
Bascho, see Anyang
Bashama, see Bachama
Bashamma, see Bachama
Bashar, 3823
Bassa, 815, 1567, 1570–1, 1574, 1576–7
Bassa Kaduna, 1570
Bassa Komo, 1568–70, 1572, 1575
Bassa-Nge, 4192a
Bata, 1561, 1578–9, 1581, 1583

265

INDEX OF ISLAMIC STUDIES

The following will provide a guide to the most useful studies and articles concerned with every aspect of the history and culture of Islam. Part II has not been indexed, but as Islam is the predominant religion among the peoples of Northern Nigeria, readers are advised to consult the separate ethnic divisions within this region for the relevant works. Especially to be consulted are the sections on Fulani, Hausa, and Kanuri.